A Modern Introduction to

PHILOSOPHY

THE FREE PRESS TEXTBOOKS
IN PHILOSOPHY

GENERAL EDITOR: *Paul Edwards*

A Modern Introduction to

PHILOSOPHY

READINGS FROM CLASSICAL AND CONTEMPORARY SOURCES

EDITED BY

PAUL EDWARDS
New York University

AND

ARTHUR PAP
Yale University

THE FREE PRESS
Glencoe, Illinois

SECOND PRINTING JANUARY 1958

© Copyright 1957 by The Free Press, a corporation

Printed in the United States of America

Designed by Sidney Solomon

CONTENTS

VIII.   MEANING, VERIFICATION AND METAPHYSICS

ACKNOWLEDGMENTS

IN MAKING our selections for this volume we have been fortunate to receive the advice of a number of friends and colleagues. In this connection we should like to thank Professors Brand Blanshard and John Smith of Yale University, Ernest Nagel of Columbia University, John Hospers and Martin Lean of Brooklyn College, Milton Munitz of New York University, Reuben Abel of the New School for Social Research, Joseph Katz, Philip Nochlin, and Frederick A. Olafson of Vassar College, Charles A. Fritz Jr. of the University of Connecticut, Monroe C. Beardsley and Richard Brandt of Swarthmore College, Adolf Grünbaum of Lehigh University, Morris Lazerowitz of Smith College, Roderick M. Chisholm, C. J. Ducasse, John Ladd, and Richard Taylor of Brown University, Frederick Will of the University of Illinois, Morris Weitz of Ohio State University, Herbert Feigl and Wilfrid Sellars of the University of Minnesota, Abraham Kaplan and Paul Wienpahl of the University of California, Antony Flew of the University College of North Staffordshire, D. J. O'Connor of the University of Liverpool, and Mr. James Bayley of Rutgers University. As a result of their kind help we believe that we have produced a much better book than would otherwise have been possible.

We should also like to express our gratitude to the following friends and students who aided us in seeing the manuscript through the press: Joelle Adlerblum, Hilda Barry, David Begelman, Rochelle Brozky, Barbara Cooper, Diana Datlow, Curtis Dewees, Barbara Doctor, Larry Doyle, Elizabeth Duda, Virginia Dunbar, Ludlow Fowler, Marvin Garelick, Sidney Gendin, Barry Gross, William Jefferson, Selma Kaplan, Robert Kestenbaum, Barbara Leavit, Burt Leiser, Norbert Lipper, Barry Luby, Bernard Maskit, Sheila Meyer, Susan Mok, George Munjo, Harry Nance, Mary-Jane Nides, Despina Pantazzi, Patsy Patterson, Lottie Rausa, Rena Regelson, Edmund Rosner, Ruth Salomon, Vera Scharman, Jean Stallmeister, Gideon Trokan, Marisel Usano, Herbert Vogel, Paul Voynow, Kenneth Winter, and Robert Zimmerman. We are particularly obliged to Mr. David Thomas of New York University who, in addition to helping us in many other ways, undertook the ungrateful task of compiling the index.

P. E.
A. P.

GENERAL INTRODUCTION

A s EVERY TEACHER of introductory courses in philosophy knows from painful experience in the class room, it is exceedingly difficult to begin such a course. The word "philosophy" has no clear and unique meaning at all in its everyday usage. The layman takes it perhaps to refer to a very "deep" subject dealing with highly "abstract" (or abstruse) matters, but obviously this won't do as a definition. The wisest procedure may well be to plunge into *medias res,* discuss specific philosophical problems and then leave it to the student to define philosophy at the end of the course as the sort of thinking he has been induced to do. But some people do not want to take the risk of spending mental energy on the study of a subject before making sure that such exertion is worth while. They, accordingly, will demand a preliminary definition of philosophy, a demand which we shall try to satisfy.

To begin with, it must be pointed out that "philosophy" is a highly ambiguous and vague word. Any definition of it, therefore, will be arbitrary in two respects: first, it will sharply demarcate philosophy from both science and "literature" whereas much of what philosophers have been writing is not so clearly distinguishable from science (at least theoretical science) or from literature (at least "philosophical" literature). Secondly, it will usurp the title "philosophy" for only one of various things that are commonly called by that name. Further, since this word usually has a laudatory flavor, i.e., connotes a respectable and important kind of intellectual activity, the definition will also be *persuasive,* that is, it will express the value judgment that such and such pursuits are indeed important and worthy of respect, and that people who do this sort of thing well ought to be commended for it. It is for this reason that no definition of philosophy can claim to be wholly descriptive and unbiased, no more than this could be claimed for a definition of such a laudatory term as "democracy."

However, the following definition may well be as unbiased as a definition of philosophy can be expected to be: critical reflection on the justification of basic human beliefs and analysis of basic concepts in terms of which such beliefs are expressed. Insofar as this definition is claimed to be descriptive, the test of its adequacy is, of course, whether the majority of problems that are commonly called "philosophical" conform to it. Since the editors believe that the problems discussed in the following eight sections by classical and contemporary philosophers of reputation constitute a fair sample of problems ordinarily called "philosophical," the definition can be tested quite easily by any student of this book. The question running through the first

3

section is how we can justify the belief in the absolute necessity of universal principles like the principles of mathematics or the principles of logic. Is our supposed knowledge of such principles based on experience or is it independent of experience, *"a priori"*? And this question evidently cannot be fruitfully tackled without attempting to clarify the meaning of the word "necessity." The following section is concerned with the logical foundations of empirical knowledge: in particular, how can we justify the belief which according to Hume and many other philosophers underlies all predictions made in everyday life and in science, the belief that the future will, or at least probably will resemble the past? In fact, how do we know whether there exists a physical world that is independent of human consciousness, whether the things we perceive exist also when they are not perceived? If a man were to raise such a question in the midst of the practical business of everyday life, he would be likely to be laughed at as a lunatic, but this simply means that ordinary mortals take it for granted that there are physical objects whether anyone perceives them or not; it does not mean that they can justify that belief. The third section is especially devoted to this time-honored dispute between "realists" who hold that the common sense belief in the existence outside of consciousness of a physical world is justifiable in some way or other and "idealists" who think that realism cannot survive philosophical scrutiny. Another common sense belief is that every human being has both a mind and a body which interact in various ways. But here the critical philosopher steps in and asks: can we consistently believe that the mind acts on the body and indirectly on the physical environment and also that physical science teaches the truth, especially in teaching the doctrine of the conservation of energy and that physical effects must have physical causes? Besides, what is meant by "mind" anyway? Is there such a thing? If there is, does it entirely depend on the functioning of the organism, especially the brain, or may it survive the disintegration of the organism? In other words, is there any rational justification for the belief in immortality? Such are the problems of Section IV. Again, can any of the proofs for the existence of a personal God that have been offered by theologians and philosophers survive logical criticism? This is the problem of Section VII. But philosophers have not only asked whether the teachings of religion can be reconciled with the teachings of science, they have also asked whether the latter are compatible with our moral beliefs. In particular, if all events whatever, including conscious actions, have causes, can man be said to have freedom of action in any respect? And if not, can we ever hold human beings responsible for their conduct? This is the problem of Section V, which is hardly separable from the general problem of Section VI: how, if at all, moral judgments are rationally justifiable—a question which invites analysis of the meanings of moral terms.

Some of the selections in Sections I-VII of this book are samples of what would generally be considered "metaphysical" speculations. They are attempts to discover truths about the universe by pure thinking rather than by the scientific method of testing theories by observation and controlled experiment. The Platonic theory that over and above the world of visible things there exists a realm of "intelligible" forms, the theory that there is a God who created the universe, the view that human beings possess an indestructible soul, or that consciousness is not restricted to the higher organisms but is present in all matter, are examples of metaphysical speculations. Until fairly recently (say, three or four decades ago) it was the opinion of the majority of philosophers that this sort of theorizing was one of the most important tasks of philosophy. Many contemporary philosophers, however, are in varying degrees sceptical about the fertility of such an enterprise. The most radical attack on metaphysical theorizing is that of the logical positivists who maintain that all metaphysical statements are really devoid of cognitive meaning, that metaphysics is a kind of conceptual poetry (sometimes written in forbidding prose) that does not convey solid knowledge or even testable conjecture, whatever its literary merits and psychological benefits may be. Whether this critique of metaphysics is justified is one of the most heatedly debated questions at the present time and it forms the subject-matter of the last section of our book.

A number of philosophers, who do not go so far as to condemn metaphysics as cognitively meaningless, nevertheless agree with the logical positivists that the proper, or at any rate the most rewarding task of philosophy is the clarification of certain basic concepts and propositions which are employed in everyday life and in the various sciences. This conception of philosophy as "analysis" is widespread at the present time, particularly in Great Britain and in the United States. Our book may be regarded as a "modern" introduction to philosophy because analytic philosophy is much more fully represented in it than in most introductory texts. Furthermore, while selections from several of the great classical philosophers are included (Plato, Aquinas, Descartes, Kant, Locke, Berkeley, Hume, Mill), the majority of our authors are figures on the contemporary philosophical scene. It should be noted, however, that not all contemporary philosophers represented in our book are analytic philosophers. Our only consideration in making selections from contemporary philosophical writing has been the clarity and intelligibility of the writer's language, the importance of his ideas and their relevance to the problems under discussion. In all eight sections we have tried to illustrate conflicting philosophical views and in several instances one selection directly criticizes another selection dealing with the same problem.

We hope that our book will be found useful in college courses introducing students to philosophy by a discussion of sample problems rather than by a purely historical approach (though some essential historical information is also supplied by the introductions to the various sections). Wherever possible, we have chosen fresh, unhackneyed material. Two of our selections are here published for the first time: the Ayer-Copleston debate on logical positivism and Herbert Feigl's dialogue "Empiricism versus Theology." Some of the others, although of unquestionable merit, are not widely known and are not easily accessible to most students.

We also believe that this book can be used with profit by the general reader who wishes to find out what philosophy is all about and especially what philosophers are doing today. As already indicated, we have done our best to confine the selections to writings which are free from obscurity and bombast; and for the reader's guidance we have provided each section with an introduction in which the problems and the main rival answers are briefly explained. At the end of each section there is a bibliography for the benefit of those who wish to pursue the subject beyond the elementary level, and biographical information about the authors may be found at the end of the book.

The order in which the sections are arranged is not, of course, binding on either teachers or general readers. We feel that it is a "logical" order in the sense that the problems in one section lead naturally, without abrupt change of topic, to those in the following section. On the other hand, the problems discussed in the earlier sections are not by any means easier or less technical than the problems discussed in the later sections. For example, Section I contains what many will undoubtedly regard as the most difficult selection in the whole book: Kant's introduction to his extremely difficult *Critique of Pure Reason* (though the introduction is child's play by comparison with that to which it introduces the reader). The problems which probably lie closest to the layman's "philosophical" thinking are those of Sections IV-VII, and accordingly it might not be a bad idea from the point of view of motivating the study of more technical philosophical problems to use them as the core of an introductory course. But it is impossible to lay down a rule as to what sequence of topics is pedagogically best. As every philosopher ought to know, all philosophical problems are organically related though it is advisable to tackle one at a time. One can begin with any problem and be logically led to any problem in philosophy.

P. E.
A. P.

I

A Priori Knowledge

INTRODUCTION

Ever since Plato philosophers have been impressed by the fact that there are universal propositions which we can apparently know to be true with absolute certainty, though we could not possibly observe all, or even a large proportion of the instances to which they apply. Such propositions, called "necessary propositions" by philosophers, are especially to be found in mathematics, the science which establishes its theorems with such infallible certainty that the expression "mathematical certainty" has become part of the everyday idiom. In Plato's dialogue *Meno* (Selection 1), a slave boy is led by Socrates to "see" that a square whose side is a diagonal of a given square has exactly twice the area of the latter (the proposition in question is a special case of the "Pythagorean theorem"). How can we know that it is so in every possible case of a square with inscribed diagonals? How can we know that not only the triangles we have drawn on the blackboard in order to "verify" by measurement that the internal angles add up to 180° have an angle sum of 180° but that all conceivable triangles have it? Philosophers who hold that experience is the only source of human knowledge ("empiricism") may, like John Stuart Mill, say that our conviction is nothing but a habit of association, built up by repeated observation that one property is conjoined with another, but a philosopher who holds such geometrical knowledge to be independent of experience, *a priori* ("rationalism"), retorts: If such were the case, why are we not convinced to an equal degree that all crows are black, or that all bodies have weight, or that the ground gets wet whenever it rains? It seems that we can conceive of exceptions to the latter propositions (even if we find it hard to believe that there ever will be any), in a way in which we cannot conceive of exceptions to the former propositions. If we found a square whose side is the diagonal of another foursided figure, yet whose area was not double that of the latter, we would conclude that the latter figure is not exactly square; indeed, we would abandon any previously entertained beliefs that were relevant *except* the belief in the absolute validity of the theorem.

At any rate, this is the way Plato, Kant, Leibniz, Locke and many other philosophers felt and feel about mathematical knowledge. In describing it as *a priori* knowledge (following Kant's terminology), philosophers refer to its apparent independence of experience: we claim to know that two pebbles and two pebbles make four pebbles even on Mars, before having verified this by actual counting after a strenuous trip in a rocketship. Perhaps we also believe that if there are crows on Mars they are black, yet we would admit that this is only *probable* on the basis of past experience; it is conceivable that on Mars or on some other planet there should be animals which are exactly like the

8

animals we usually call "crows" except that their feathers are, say, red. In this sense our knowledge of the proposition that all crows are black is said to be *empirical,* and traditionally empirical knowledge has been said to lack that *certainty* which attaches to *a priori* knowledge.

It is important to understand in exactly what sense *a priori* knowledge is "independent of experience." No philosopher has ever denied that a child has to learn that two and two make four by learning to count, and that the latter process involves contact with concrete objects. But this only means that without sense-experience one cannot acquire the *concepts* of number, in this case the concepts "two" and "four," that is, a child who has never learned to count, to associate different numerals with distinguishable objects, will not even understand what "two and two makes four" *means.* What the philosophers who believe in *a priori* knowledge assert is only that once the concepts have been acquired, the proposition can be "seen" to be true by just thinking about it (by "the mere operation of thought," in Hume's phrase). Consider the statement "for any objects A, B, C: if A is bigger than B and B is bigger than C, then A is bigger than C." Obviously, a being without sense of sight and sense of touch would have no concept of the relation designated by the word "bigger," hence such a being would not even understand that statement. But in saying that its truth is independent of experience, philosophers only mean that anyone who *understands* it will see that it is necessarily true, that it could not possibly be refuted by any observations at any time or place.

Therefore a philosopher who believes in *a priori* knowledge is not thereby committed to a belief in "innate ideas." It is true that some philosophers have maintained that there are concepts which in some sense are "in" our minds before all sense-experience. Thus Descartes believed that the concept of "substance," i.e., of a *thing* which is said to *have* various sensible qualities, was innate: we only perceive qualities, changing and stable, like colors, shapes, sizes, degrees of hardness and temperature, but not the identical thing which undergoes such observable changes; how, then, could we have acquired the idea of substance through sense-experience? And Kant added a famous battery of "categories," among them the concept of causal connection: experience tells us that one kind of event is regularly followed by another kind of event but it does not reveal necessary connections between events. We observe, said Kant (like Hume before him), that a stone gets warmer when the sun shines on it, but not that it *must* get warmer when exposed to sunshine; hence the concept of such necessary connections, said Kant, must have been in the mind before sense-experience. Nevertheless, the question of the origin of concepts is logically independent of the question of *a priori* knowledge of propositions. This is even historically indicated by the fact that both Locke and Hume, who insisted on the origin in experience of all ideas (concepts) whatsoever (see Selection 42, pp. 551 ff.), at the same time wrote at length about the shortcomings of empirical knowledge by comparison with the certainty of *a priori* knowledge. That nothing can be both red and blue all over at the same time, we know *a priori,* but unless our eyes had been appropriately stimulated we would have no ideas of these qualities.

The philosopher not only makes the distinction between *a priori* knowledge and empirical knowledge by reflecting on the appropriate methods of justifying our beliefs; he goes on to ask how *a priori* knowledge is possible. Plato apparently was so perplexed by the fact that we can know universal propositions independently of experience that he had to invent a myth in order to account for it: the soul remembers visions it has enjoyed in a former disembodied life. Other philosophers, less poetical than Plato, tried to account for it in terms of a distinction between two kinds of entities, a distinction that played a vital role in Plato's philosophy: universals (Plato called them "forms," Locke "ideas"), and particulars. When we look at the blackboard, we see particular triangles, but when we prove the Euclidean theorem about triangles we think of the universal *triangularity,* i.e., that which all the particular triangles have in common and by virtue of which they are all triangles. Every particular triangle has a particular size, for example, but when we classify it as a triangle we abstract from this particular feature and focus attention on a property which it shares with similar figures; it is this *common* property which philosophers call a *universal.* Again, we can see particular cubical objects at different places at the same time, or at the same place at different times, but when we think about the nature of a cube (as when we say to ourselves "every cube *must* have twelve edges") we think, in the terminology of those philosophers, about a universal that is identically present in all visible and tangible cubes. Whenever we classify a particular thing or event—in short, a "particular"—as being of such and such a kind, we consider it as an instance of some universal, or set of universals tied together by a single name, like "cow," "man," "table," "rain," "thunder." According to Locke's doctrine in the *Essay Concerning Human Understanding* and Russell's in *The Problems of Philosophy,* we can be certain that every particular which is an instance of universal A is also an instance of universal B, though we can never survey all past, present and future instances of these universals, if we "see" with our intellectual eye a certain relation between A and B, a relation which is sometimes called "necessary connection," sometimes "entailment." If we can see that squareness entails equilateralness, and that being a cube entails having twelve edges, then we can be sure in advance of sense-experience (think of the original meaning of *"a priori"* in Latin: before!) that there are no squares that are not equilateral, nor cubes that do not have twelve edges.

Kant complicated the question of how *a priori* knowledge is possible. He noticed, like Locke before him, that it is not in the least surprising that we should be absolutely certain that all squares are equilateral and that all bachelors are unmarried; after all, the predicates here are contained in the subjects, i.e. part of what we mean by "square" is an equilateral figure, and part of what we mean by "bachelor" is an unmarried individual; hence we are merely certain that nothing is both equilateral and not equilateral, and that nothing is both unmarried and married (at the same time, of course!). In Kant's terminology: these propositions are *analytic;* they can be proved by sole appeal to the "law of contradiction" according to which no proposition can be both true and false, nothing can both have and not have the same property at the same time. [Kant's distinction between analytic and synthetic propositions was anticipated by Locke, though Locke did not use these terms.] Yet, Kant was left with a difficult problem because he was convinced that *a priori* knowledge is not restricted to analytic propositions which, as he said, "do not really enlarge our knowledge." He believed that all arithmetical and geometrical propositions are *synthetic,* i.e., such that, unlike analytic propositions, they can be denied without self-contradiction, and at the same time are known *a priori;* hence his famous question "how are synthetic judgments *a priori* possible?" For example, we are absolutely certain that the shortest distance between any two points, anywhere in space, is the straight line; yet the subject "straight line" does not seem to contain the predicate "shortest distance between two points" as a part or the whole of its very meaning, the way this must be said of the relation between "square" and "equilateral." Therefore the denial of this axiom, viz. "there is a line connecting two points which is shorter than the straight line connecting them," is not self-contradictory though it is intuitively inconceivable. Kant's problem was this: if the property B is not part or all of what we mean by "A," how can we be certain that absolutely everything to which "A" applies has B? Experience cannot be the basis of our certainty, for experience only tells us that all instances of A that have so far been observed are also instances of B. Kant's answer is best elucidated by means of an analogy. Consider the proposition "every visible object is blue." It is undoubtedly synthetic, and experience even refutes it. But suppose that our eyes were so constituted that only blue light affecting the retinae gave rise to color sensations, so that objects emitting or reflecting light of different wave lengths remained invisible. In that case our universal synthetic proposition would be constantly confirmed by experience, and if we knew that our eyes were so constituted, we could even be certain that no object of different color would ever be seen. In somewhat the same sense, the space we experience must necessarily conform to the propositions of Euclidean geometry, according to Kant, because these propositions express the mind's ways of ordering what is "given" in sense-experience. In other words, they describe the mind's "forms of spatial intuition" which must be imposed on the material affecting our senses before it can become an object of scientific knowledge.

Whatever one may think of this rather obscure answer to the question "How are synthetic *a priori* judgments about space possible?" it must be admitted that Kant formulated distinctions and by means of them a problem that played a great role in subsequent inquiries into the nature of human knowledge. One who is not familiar with the distinctions between analytic propositions, self-contradictory propositions (i.e., propositions which violate the law of contradiction, like "some unmarried men are married," "some equilateral figures are not equilateral"), synthetic propositions that can be known by experience only and synthetic propositions that can be known *a priori,* will be unable to understand much of the technical discussions in modern philosophy. Furthermore, Kant for the first time raised the critical question of central concern to contemporary logical positivism, whether *metaphysical* knowledge, i.e., *a priori* knowledge of synthetic propositions about the world that are outside the province of mathematics, is at all possible. Metaphysicians and theologians before Kant were busy offering *a priori* proofs for such dogmas of Christianity as the existence of a personal God, the immortality of the soul, and the freedom of man. But Kant, noting that these propositions are synthetic and that the methods of mathematics were unavailable for their proof, urged philosophers to suspend controversy pro or con such propositions until they had investigated the "critical" problem whether a science of metaphysics in this sense is at all possible. To be sure, Kant's way of defining the distinction between analytic and synthetic in terms of the relation between "subject" and "predicate" is not satisfactory in the light of modern logic. A great many propositions do not have subject-predicate form at all; still we may ask whether they are analytic in the sense that the attempt to deny them would end in such plain self-contradiction as the attempt to deny that all white swans are white. For example, consider the two formally similar propositions: a) for any tennis players A, B, C: if A can beat B and B can beat C, then A can beat C (in tennis, of course!); b) for any events A, B, C: if A precedes B, and B precedes C, then A precedes C. Clearly a) is empirical; even if it were true, this could be known only by watching tennis matches, and at any rate we can *conceive* of an exception to this generalization. Just as clearly b) is known to be true *a priori*. In the above sense of "analytic," which is not restricted to propositions of the form "all A are B," we can then go on to ask whether b) is analytic or synthetic. If it were analytic, then a statement of the form "A precedes B and B precedes C but A does not precede C" should be reducible to a self-contradiction of the same kind as "A both precedes and does not precede B," "there are white swans that are not white," etc. That is the question.

According to Kant, such propositions of Euclidean geometry as "two straight lines cannot enclose a space (i.e., are either parallel or else intersect just once)" are not only self-evident, such that no mind can conceive of exceptions to them; they also hold necessarily for any part of physical space that might ever be experienced. This influential doctrine came to be challenged in the 19th century in two quite different ways. John Stuart Mill cited precedents in the history of science where propositions that seemed absolutely self-evident were later shown to be false. He argued that self-evidence is nothing more sacred than a habit of associating qualities which have always gone together in experience. Mill even maintained that the laws of arithmetic, like "2 + 2 = 4," are generalizations from experience, not *a priori* truths, a view which most philosophers of science find unacceptable. (See Blanshard, Selection 4 and Ayer, Selection 5, pp. 63-64.) The other challenge originated from the mathematicians. Since no mathematician had ever succeeded in deducing Euclid's "parallel axiom" (given a point outside a straight line S, there is exactly one straight line containing that point and parallel to S) from the other axioms of Euclidean geometry, it was suspected that it could be denied without resulting inconsistency in the geometrical system. Indeed, such "non-Euclidean" systems were constructed and found to be internally just as consistent as Euclidean geometry (if the latter *is* consistent). So far Kant's theory of geometry had not been dealt a fatal blow: for Kant might have replied that non-Euclidean geometry merely proves that the parallel axiom is not a necessary *consequence* of the other axioms of Euclidean geometry, which is perfectly compatible with their all being necessarily true. Yet, the situation became truly ticklish for the Kantians (who were academically so strong in Germany at that time that the great mathematician Gauss was afraid to publish his researches in non-Euclidean geometry!), when Riemannian geometry, which is a brand of non-Euclidean geometry, even proved to be applicable to physical space in the context of the general theory of relativity. For had not Kant maintained that physicists could rest assured—on the authority of his theory of knowledge—that no measurements would ever disconfirm the Euclidean axioms and theorems?

There remains to be mentioned still a third attack on Kant, launched by the modern logicians, and the historical stage will be set for a new, much more sophisticated kind of "empiricism," as philosophers call the doctrine that experience is the only source of knowledge about the universe we live in: *logical empiricism,* or *logical positivism.* Kant had maintained that some kind of "temporal intuition" is required to see the truth of an arithmetical equation, not just analysis of the meanings of symbols. The equation "7 + 5 = 12," he argued, does not just explicate the meaning of "the sum of five and seven," the way "all triangles have three interior angles" just explicates the meaning of "triangle." Indeed, it could not be maintained that "7 + 5" is synonymous with "12" the way "triangle" is synonymous with "closed rectilinear figure with three angles"; nor would it be plausible to hold that anybody who understands the expression "the sum of seven and five" as well as the meaning of "12" thereby already knows the equation to be true, for undoubtedly we first had to learn by counting that 7 and 5 add up to twelve. On this ground, roughly speaking, Kant held that such propositions are synthetic, though our knowledge of them is *a priori.* But Bertrand Russell pointed out that the psychological process of counting, of learning numbers, had nothing to do with the logical analysis of arithmetical concepts and propositions. Using the techniques of symbolic logic, a discipline of which he is a founding father, he undertook to define the concepts of mathematics, from such simple ones as "one" to such complicated ones as "integral," on the sole basis of logical concepts: "not," "all," "there is," "or," "and" etc. [He was anticipated by the German logician Gottlob Frege, who had been thinking about the logical foundations of arithmetic along surprisingly similar lines. But Frege was ignored by his countrymen.] As a result, it was shown in *Principia Mathematica,* a monumental work which is for modern logic what Newton's *Principia mathematica philosophiae naturalis* was for modern physics, that mathematics (geometry excepted) is really a branch of logic. If so, argued the logicians, then Kant was wrong in supposing that mathematical knowledge involved a faculty of "intuition" which is not involved in logical reasoning. In order to deduce, for example, from the premise that two collections A and B which have no elements in common each contain two elements, the conclusion that the sum of A and B contains four elements, only an appeal to laws of logic is required, such laws as "if every A is B and some A are C, then some B are C" or "if something is either A or B but is not A, then it is B."

Partly under the influence of Russell's work in logic and philosophy of mathematics, a group of Viennese thinkers (the "Vienna Circle") who were in close touch with developments in mathematics and physics and who were disgusted with the vague kind of speculative metaphysics that dominated the German universities, went further and inquired into the source of the infallibility of logic. If mathematics is not different from logic, then an understanding of the origin of logical necessity ought to lift the mystery with which the traditional philosophers, especially Kant, surrounded *a priori* knowledge.

Stimulated by the ideas of Wittgenstein (1889-1951), they declared that all logically necessary propositions, indeed all propositions that can be known *a priori,* are *tautologies.* The concept of tautology is similar to Kant's concept of analytic judgment, but more exactly a tautology is the following sort of statement: it is composed of simpler statements in such a way that it is true no matter whether the statements of which it is composed are true or false. The simplest example of tautology is a statement of the form "p or not p," e.g., "either it will rain tomorrow, or—it will not rain tomorrow." Clearly we do not need to wait and see in order to assent to this "prediction"; for that very reason it is not really a prediction at all, it tells us precisely nothing. A tautology is, in positivist terminology, devoid of factual content, it says nothing about the world. Most tautologies are far more complicated, and it may require subtle techniques of logical analysis to size them up as tautologies, but the principle remains the same: since a tautology is true no matter what may be the case, in other words, excludes no possibilities, it tells us nothing about the world. Such was the logical positivists' deflation of *a priori* knowledge: if we can be certain *a priori* of the truth of a proposition, then that proposition really says no more than "either it will rain or it won't." It should be noted that an attempted denial of a tautology would result in self-contradiction: I deny that it will rain, and I also deny that it will not rain; but if I deny that it will not rain, then I affirm that it will rain, which I have already denied. Therefore the positivist thesis that we can have *a priori* knowledge of tautologies only, is equivalent to a flat rejection of Kant's doctrine that some synthetic propositions can be known *a priori.*

What is the nature of geometrical propositions according to logical positivism? Is it not plain that the proposition "two nonparallel straight lines have only one point in common" is not a tautology like "a straight line is a straight line"? And is it not undeniable that exceptions to it are inconceivable, so that our knowledge of it is *a priori?* The logical positivist replies: what do you mean by "straight"? Would you call two lines straight if after diverging from a point of intersection they were found to meet again? If not, then you are implicitly *defining* straight lines as lines that satisfy the axiom in question, and the latter accordingly is analytic. If, on the other hand, you have an independent criterion of straightness, then the axiom is synthetic. But such an independent criterion must be formulated in physical terms, e.g., a straight line is the path of a light ray. In that case the axiom becomes a physical hypothesis subject to test but thereby loses its *a priori* certainty. As Einstein once put it: insofar as the propositions of geometry are certain, they say nothing about reality, and insofar as they say something about reality they are not certain.

What is the purpose of arithmetic and algebra if these models of exact science consist exclusively of tautologies, as asserted by logical positivism? In connection with this question it is important to understand that a tautology, as logical positivists use the term, is not necessarily a trivial, self-evident statement like "a house is a house" or "it will either rain or it won't." It may not at all be self-evident that a given proposition is a tautology but this may have to be revealed by a lengthy process of symbolic transformation. In particular, the equations of higher algebra and the calculus are transformable, step by step, into identities, but it may require great mathematical skill to perform the transformation, which is what their "proof" consists in. Once their tauto-logical validity has been established, they are used as tools of deduction in empirical inquiries. Suppose, for example, you want to know how many cubic inches are contained in a certain cubical box. If you have ascertained by measurement that its side has a length of 12 inches, you will use your arith-metical knowledge that $12 \times 12 \times 12 = 1728$, thereby saving yourself the trouble of trying to determine by a lengthy process of counting how many cubic inches can be fitted into the box. This shows that tautologies perform a useful function in empirical science as instruments of deduction.

The positivistic theory of *a priori* knowledge, however, provokes two ques-tions: 1) if *a priori* knowledge is not knowledge about the world, what sort of knowledge is it then? Is it knowledge at all? 2) We know that such and such propositions are tautologies, like the weatherman's foolproof "prediction"; and this means that we know that such propositions are true *in all possible cases*. Right. But how do we know that? It is not easy to get a clear-cut answer to these questions, but roughly speaking the answer to both of them that is offered is: it all amounts to knowing *how* to use words, how to stick to linguistic conventions consistently. Thus, consider again "all squares are equi-lateral." We are absolutely certain of this because we are determined to apply the word "square" only to equilateral figures. We can be sure that we shall never discover a square that is not equilateral, simply because we have decided, or rather have been conditioned, not to *call* a figure "square" unless we be-lieve it to have equal sides. Now consider a law of logic like the following: whatever proposition is implied by true propositions is itself true. How can we be absolutely sure of this? It would surely be naive to say that we believe it because we have just never come across a false proposition that was implied by true propositions. For what would it be like to encounter such an excep-tional case? Suppose you met a man who agreed with your prediction that if X were the Democratic candidate for the presidency, X would be elected president, and who like yourself is subsequently informed by the newspapers that X indeed was nominated by the Democratic Party. You then wait till the election comes around, and discover that the Democratic candidate is defeated in the election. You turn to your friend and say "our prediction has not come true." What would you say if he replied "well, it is true that X has not been elected although he was the selected candidate, but this does not refute my prediction that he would be elected if he were the chosen candidate; it rather refutes the principle that whatever proposition is implied by a true proposition must itself be true"? If you were properly trained in logic, you would retort as follows: If we have a true proposition p and another proposition q which is implied by p, then if somebody maintains that nevertheless q may be false, he is simply not using "imply" in its ordinary sense. In saying that p implies q one has already denied that p could be true if q were false. In saying "if p, then q" one has already denied that p could be true if q is false, hence "if p, then q; but p and not q" adds up to a flat contradiction.

Logical positivists conclude from this sort of consideration that a law of logic, like "if p implies q, and p is true, then q is true," is an implicit definition, in this instance of "implies" or "if, then." If one were to deny it, one would either change the conventional meanings of these expressions or else one would contradict oneself. The necessity of the laws of logic consists in the fact that, given the conventional definitions, or rules of usage of the relevant expressions, they cannot be denied without self-contradiction. Does this theory, however, lend support to the view that the logical necessity of a proposition results from arbitrary linguistic conventions? If this view were correct, then it should be possible to destroy the logical necessity of a proposition by a mere change of definition. It may seem that this is indeed possible. Decide, for example, to mean by "father" what is ordinarily meant by "man" and it will be quite easy to find exceptions to the allegedly necessary proposition that all fathers are parents. Yet, a moment's reflection should reveal the confusion underlying this argument: of course, whether the *sentence* "all fathers are parents" expresses a necessary truth depends on the meanings of the words "father" and "parent," and that these words are used the way they are at present used in English is a matter of convention; we could, if we so desired, use them otherwise. But this does not mean that the necessary truth of the *proposition* expressed by this sentence could be destroyed by altering linguistic conventions, for if the meanings of the words are changed then the same sentence will express a different proposition. Similarly, if we decided to mean by "12" what is now meant by "11" then we would no longer be asserting something true by the sentence "$7 + 5 = 12$." This, however, would in no way affect the necessary truth of what we are *now* asserting by means of this sentence. A proposition is something one intends to affirm by means of a given sentence, not the sentence itself. *That which* a Frenchman asserts by means of the sentence "le chat est dans la cuisine" is the same as *that which* an American would assert by means of the different sentence "the cat is in the kitchen." It is what is here technically called "proposition" (though it is but fair to warn the reader that some philosophers—e.g., Ayer in Selection 43, pp. 555 ff., use the word "proposition" to refer to declarative *sentences*). And obviously the truth of what a man intends to say, of the proposition he asserts, cannot be destroyed by putting a different interpretation on the words he uses.

It is not easy to say in what precise sense the necessity of a proposition is, according to logical positivists like Ayer, "based" on linguistic rules. As we have seen, it would be completely indefensible to say it is based on linguistic rules in the sense that the *same proposition* which is necessarily true might not have been necessarily true if words had been used differently and would cease to be necessarily true if words should be used differently in the future. And most logical positivists would probably concede this point. But the reader will have to decide for himself whether there remains, after this concession has been made, a significant issue between logical positivists and their critics in regard to the nature of *a priori* knowledge. A close comparative study of Ayer's "The *A Priori*" (Selection 5) and Blanshard's "Logical Positivism and Necessity" (Selection 6) is recommended for that purpose.

A. P.

1

KNOWLEDGE AS RECOLLECTION

Plato

. . . MEN. And how will you inquire, Socrates, into that which you do not know? What will you put forth as the subject of inquiry? And if you find what you want, how will you ever know that this is the thing which you did not know?

SOC. I know, Meno, what you mean; but just see what a tiresome dispute you are introducing. You argue that a man cannot inquire either about that which he knows, or about that which he does not know; for if he knows, he has no need to inquire; and if not, he cannot; for he does not know the very subject about which he is to inquire.

MEN. Well, Socrates, and is not the argument sound?

SOC. I think not.

MEN. Why not?

SOC. I will tell you why: I have heard from certain wise men and women who spoke of things divine that—

MEN. What did they say?

SOC. They spoke of a glorious truth, as I conceive.

MEN. What was it and who were they?

SOC. Some of them were priests and priestesses who had studied how they might be able to give a reason of their profession; there have been poets also who spoke of these things by inspiration, like Pindar and many others who were inspired. And they say—mark now and see whether their words are true—they say that the soul of man is immortal, and at one time has an end, which is termed dying, and at another time is born again, but is never destroyed. And the moral is that a man ought to live always in perfect holiness. *"For in the ninth year*

[This extract is taken from Plato's dialogue *Meno,* and is reproduced in Benjamin Jowett's translation. Whenever in this dialogue the word "feet" is used in connection with areas, it means "square feet." (Eds.)]

Persephone sends the souls of those from whom she has received the penalty of ancient crime back again from beneath into the light of the sun above, and these are they who become noble kings and mighty men and great in wisdom and are called saintly heroes in after ages." The soul, then, as being immortal, and having been born again many times, and having seen all things that exist, whether in this world or in the world below, has knowledge of them all; and it is no wonder that she should be able to call to remembrance all that she ever knew about virtue and about everything; for as all nature is akin, and the soul has learned all things, there is no difficulty in her eliciting, or as men say learning, out of a single recollection, all the rest, if a man is strenuous and does not faint; for all inquiry and all learning is but recollection. And therefore we ought not to listen to this sophistical argument about the impossibility of inquiry; for it will make us idle, and is sweet only to the sluggard; but the other saying will make us active and inquisitive. In that confiding, I will gladly inquire with you into the nature of virtue.

MEN. Yes, Socrates; but what do you mean by saying that we do not learn, and that what we call learning is only a process of recollection? Can you teach me how this is?

Soc. I told you, Meno, just now that you were a rogue, and now you ask whether I can teach you, when I am saying that there is no teaching, but only recollection; and thus you imagine that you will involve me in a contradiction.

MEN. Indeed, Socrates, I protest that I had no such intention. I only asked the question from habit; but if you can prove to me that what you say is true, I wish that you would.

Soc. It will be no easy matter, but I will try to please you to the utmost of my power. Suppose that you call one of your numerous attendants, that I may demonstrate on him.

MEN. Certainly. Come hither, boy.

Soc. He is Greek, and speaks Greek, does he not?

MEN. Yes, indeed; he was born in the house.

Soc. Attend now to the questions which I ask him, and observe whether he learns of me or only remembers.

MEN. I will.

Soc. Tell me, boy, do you know that a figure like this is a square?

BOY. I do.

Soc. And you know that a square figure has these four lines equal?

BOY. Certainly.

Soc. And these lines which I have drawn through the middle of the square are also equal?

BOY. Yes.

Soc. A square may be of any size?

BOY. Certainly.

Soc. And if one side of the figure be of two feet, and the other side be of two feet, how much will the whole be? Let me explain: if in one direction the space was of two feet, and in the other direction of one foot, the whole would be of two feet taken once?

Boy. Yes.

Soc. But since this side is also of two feet, there are twice two feet?

Boy. There are.

Soc. Then the square is of twice two feet?

Boy. Yes.

Soc. And how many are twice two feet? Count and tell me.

Boy. Four, Socrates.

Soc. And might there not be another square twice as large as this, and having like this the lines equal?

Boy. Yes.

Soc. And of how many feet will that be?

Boy. Of eight feet.

Soc. And now try and tell the length of the line which forms the side of that double square: this is two feet—what will that be?

Boy. Clearly, Socrates, it will be double.

Soc. Do you observe, Meno, that I am not teaching the boy anything, but only asking him questions; and now he fancies that he knows how long a line is necessary in order to produce a figure of eight square feet; does he not?

Men. Yes.

Soc. And does he really know?

Men. Certainly not.

Soc. He only guesses that because the square is double, the line is double.

Men. True.

Soc. Observe him when he recalls the steps in regular order. (*To the Boy.*) Tell me, boy, do you assert that a double space comes from a double line? Remember that I am not speaking of an oblong, but of a figure equal every way, and twice the size of this—that is to say of eight feet; and I want to know whether you still say that a double square comes from a double line?

Boy. Yes.

Soc. But does not this line become doubled if we add another such line here?

Boy. Certainly.

Soc. And four such lines will make a space containing eight feet?

Boy. Yes.

Soc. Let us describe such a figure: Would you not say that this is the figure of eight feet?

Boy. Yes.

Soc. And are there not these four divisions in the figure, each of which is equal to the figure of four feet?

Boy. True.

Soc. And is not that four times four?

Boy. Certainly.

Soc. And four times is not double?

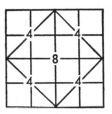

Boy. No, indeed.

Soc. But how much?

Boy. Four times as much.

Soc. Therefore the double line, boy, has given a space, not twice, but four times as much.

Boy. True.

Soc. Four times four are sixteen—are they not?

Boy. Yes.

Soc. What line would give you a space of eight feet, as this gives one of sixteen feet—do you see?

Boy. Yes.

Soc. And the space of four feet is made from this half line?

Boy. Yes.

Soc. Good; and is not a space of eight feet twice the size of this, and half the size of the other?

Boy. Certainly.

Soc. Such a space, then, will be made out of a line greater than this one, and less than that one?

Boy. Yes, I think so.

Soc. Very good; I like to hear you say what you think. And now tell me, is not this a line of two feet and that of four?

Boy. Yes.

Soc. Then the line which forms the side of eight feet ought to be more than this line of two feet, and less than the other of four feet?

Boy. It ought.

Soc. Try and see if you can tell me how much it will be.

Boy. Three feet.

Soc. Then if we add a half to this line of two, that will be the line of three. Here are two and there is one; and on the other side, here are two also and there is one: and that makes the figure of which you speak?

BOY. Yes.

SOC. But if there are three feet this way and three feet that way, the whole space will be three times three feet?

BOY. That is evident.

SOC. And how much are three times three feet?

BOY. Nine.

SOC. And how much is the double of four?

BOY. Eight.

SOC. Then the figure of eight is not made out of a line of three?

BOY. No.

SOC. But from what line?—tell me exactly; and if you would rather not reckon, try and show me the line.

BOY. Indeed, Socrates, I do not know.

SOC. Do you see, Meno, what advances he has made in his power of recollection? He did not know at first, and he does not know now, what is the side of a figure of eight feet; but then he thought that he knew, and answered confidently as if he knew, and had no difficulty; now he has a difficulty, and neither knows nor fancies that he knows.

MEN. True.

SOC. Is he not better off in knowing his ignorance?

MEN. I think that he is.

SOC. If we have made him doubt, and given him the "torpedo's shock," have we done him any harm?

MEN. I think not.

SOC. We have certainly, as would seem, assisted him in some degree to the discovery of the truth; and now he will wish to remedy his ignorance, but then he would have been ready to tell all the world again and again that the double space should have a double side.

MEN. True.

SOC. But do you suppose that he would ever have inquired into or learned what he fancied that he knew, though he was really ignorant of it, until he had fallen into perplexity under the idea that he did not know, and had desired to know?

MEN. I think not, Socrates.

SOC. Then he was the better for the torpedo's touch?

MEN. I think so.

SOC. Mark now the further development. I shall only ask him, and not teach him, and he shall share the inquiry with me; and do you watch and see if you find me telling or explaining anything to him, instead of eliciting his opinion. Tell me, boy, is not this a square of four feet which I have drawn?

BOY. Yes.

Soc. And now I add another square equal to the former one?

Boy. Yes.

Soc. And a third, which is equal to either of them?

Boy. Yes.

Soc. Suppose that we fill up the vacant corner?

Boy. Very good.

Soc. Here, then, there are four equal spaces?

Boy. Yes.

Soc. And how many times larger is this space than this other?

Boy. Four times.

Soc. But it ought to have been twice only, as you will remember.

Boy. True.

Soc. And does not this line, reaching from corner to corner, bisect each of these spaces?

Boy. Yes.

Soc. And are there not here four equal lines which contain this space?

Boy. There are.

Soc. Look and see how much this space is.

Boy. I do not understand.

Soc. Has not each interior line cut off half of the four spaces?

Boy. Yes.

Soc. And how many spaces are there in this section?

Boy. Four.

Soc. And how many in this?

Boy. Two.

Soc. And four is how many times two?

Boy. Twice.

Soc. And this space is of how many feet?

Boy. Of eight feet.

Soc. And from what line do you get this figure?

Boy. From this.

Soc. That is, from the line which extends from corner to corner of the figure of four feet?

Boy. Yes.

Soc. And that is the line which the learned call the diagonal. And if this is the proper name, then you, Meno's slave, are prepared to affirm that the double space is the square of the diagonal?

Boy. Certainly, Socrates.

Soc. What do you say of him, Meno? Were not all these answers given out of his own head?

Men. Yes, they were all his own.

Soc. And yet, as we were just now saying, he did not know?

Men. True.

SOC. But still he had in him those notions of his—had he not?

MEN. Yes.

SOC. Then he who does not know may still have true notions of that which he does not know?

MEN. He has.

SOC. And at present these notions have just been stirred up in him, as in a dream; but if he were frequently asked the same questions, in different forms, he would know as well as any one at last?

MEN. I dare say.

SOC. Without any one teaching him he will recover his knowledge for himself, if he is only asked questions?

MEN. Yes.

SOC. And this spontaneous recovery of knowledge in him is recollection?

MEN. True.

SOC. And this knowledge which he now has must he not either have acquired or always possessed?

MEN. Yes.

SOC. But if he always possessed this knowledge he would always have known; or if he has acquired the knowledge he could not have acquired it in this life unless he has been taught geometry; for he may be made to do the same with all geometry and every other branch of knowledge. Now, has any one ever taught him all this? You must know about him if, as you say, he was born and bred in your house.

MEN. And I am certain that no one ever did teach him.

SOC. And yet he has the knowledge?

MEN. The fact, Socrates, is undeniable.

SOC. But if he did not acquire the knowledge in this life, then he must have had and learned it at some other time?

MEN. Clearly he must.

SOC. Which must have been the time when he was not a man?

MEN. Yes.

SOC. And if there have been always true thoughts in him, both at the time when he was and was not a man, which only need to be awakened into knowledge by putting questions to him, his soul must have always possessed this knowledge, for he always either was or was not a man?

MEN. Obviously.

SOC. And if the truth of all things always existed in the soul, then the soul is immortal. Wherefore be of good cheer and try to recollect what you do not know, or rather what you do not remember.

MEN. I feel, somehow, that I like what you are saying.

SOC. And I, Meno, like what I am saying. Some things I have said of which I am not altogether confident. But that we shall be better and braver and less helpless if we think that we ought to inquire, than we should have been if we indulged in the idle fancy that there was no knowing and no use in seeking to know what we do not know—that is a theme upon which I am ready to fight, in word and deed, to the utmost of my power. . . .

2

INTRODUCTION TO THE
"CRITIQUE OF PURE REASON"

Immanuel Kant

I. The Distinction between Pure
and Empirical Knowledge

THERE CAN BE NO DOUBT that all our knowledge begins with experience. For how should our faculty of knowledge be awakened into action did not objects affecting our senses partly of themselves produce representations, partly arouse the activity of our understanding to compare these representations, and, by combining or separating them, work up the raw material of the sensible impressions into that knowledge of objects which is entitled experience? In the order of time, therefore, we have no knowledge antecedent to experience, and with experience all our knowledge begins.

But though all our knowledge begins with experience, it does not follow that it all arises out of experience. For it may well be that even our empirical knowledge is made up of what we receive through impressions and of what our own faculty of knowledge (sensible impressions serving merely as the occasion) supplies from itself. If our faculty of knowledge makes any such addition, it may be that we are not in a position to distinguish it from the raw material, until with long practice of attention we have become skilled in separating it.

This, then, is a question which at least calls for closer examination, and does not allow of any off-hand answer:—whether there is any knowl-

[This selection consists of the first six sections of the introduction to the second edition of Kant's *Critique of Pure Reason*. The first edition of this work was published in 1781, the second in 1787. The translation here used is that of Norman Kemp Smith and is reprinted with the kind permission of the translator, of Macmillan and Company, Ltd., London, and St. Martin's Press, New York.]

edge that is thus independent of experience and even of all impressions of the senses. Such knowledge is entitled *a priori,* and distinguishd from the *empirical,* which has its sources *a posteriori,* that is, in experience.

The expression *"a priori"* does not, however, indicate with sufficient precision the full meaning of our question. For it has been customary to say, even of much knowledge that is derived from empirical sources, that we have it or are capable of having it *a priori,* meaning thereby that we do not derive it immediately from experience, but from a universal rule—a rule which is itself, however, borrowed by us from experience. Thus we would say of a man who undermined the foundations of his house, that he might have known *a priori* that it would fall, that is, that he need not have waited for the experience of its actual falling. But still he could not know this completely *a priori.* For he had first to learn through experience that bodies are heavy, and therefore fall when their supports are withdrawn.

In what follows, therefore, we shall understand by *a priori* knowledge, not knowledge independent of this or that experience, but knowledge absolutely independent of all experience. Opposd to it is empirical knowledge, which is knowledge possible only *a posteriori,* that is, through experience. *A priori* modes of knowledge are entitled pure when there is no admixture of anything empirical. Thus, for instance, the proposition, "every alteration has its cause," while an *a prior* proposition, is not a pure proposition, because alteration is a concept which can be derived only from experience.

II. We Are in Possession of Certain Modes
of A Priori *Knowledge, and Even the Common*
Understanding Is Never Without Them

What we here require is a criterion by which to distinguish with certainty between pure and empirical knowledge. Experience teaches us that a thing is so and so, but not that it cannot be otherwise. First, then, if we have a proposition which in being thought is thought as *necessary,* it is an *a priori* judgment; and if, besides, it is not derived from any proposition except one which also has the validity of a necessary judgment, it is an absolutely *a priori* judgment. Secondly, experience never confers on its judgments true or strict, but only assumed and comparative *universality,* through induction. We can properly only say, therefore, that, so far as we have hitherto observed, there is no exception to this or that rule. If, then, a judgment is thought with strict universality, that is, in such manner that no exception is allowed as possible, it is not derived from experience, but is valid absolutely *a priori*. Empirical universality is only an arbitrary extension of a validity holding in most cases to one which holds in all, for instance, in the proposition, "all bodies are heavy." When, on the other hand, strict universality is essential to a judgment, this indicates a special source of knowledge, namely, a faculty of *a priori* knowledge. Necessity and strict universality are thus sure criteria of *a priori* knowledge, and are inseparable from one another. But since in the employment of these criteria the contingency of judgments is sometimes more easily shown than their empirical limitation, or, as sometimes also happens, their unlimited universality can be more convincingly proved than their necessity, it is advisable to use the two criteria separately, each by itself being infallible.

Now it is easy to show that there actually are in human knowledge judgments which are necessary and in the strictest sense universal, and which are therefore pure *a priori* judgments. If an example from the sciences be desired, we have only to look to any of the propositions of mathematics; if we seek an example from the understanding in its quite ordinary employment, the proposition, "every alteration must have a cause," will serve our purpose. In the latter case, indeed, the very concept of a cause so manifestly contains the concept of a necessity of connection with an effect and of the strict universality of the rule, that the concept would be altogether lost if we attempted to derive it, as Hume* has done, from a repeated association of that which happens with that which precedes, and from a custom of connecting representations, a custom originating in this repeated association, and constituting therefore a merely subjective necessity. Even without appealing to such examples, it is possible to show that pure *a priori* principles are indispensable for the possibility of experience, and so to prove their existence *a priori*. For whence could experience derive its certainty, if all the rules, according to which it proceeds, were always themselves empirical, and therefore contingent? Such rules could hardly be regarded as first principles. At present, however, we may be content to have established the fact that our faculty of knowledge does have a pure employment, and to have shown what are the criteria of such an employment.

Such *a priori* origin is manifest in certain concepts, no less than in judgments. If we remove our empirical concept of a body, one by one, every feature in it which is [merely] empirical, the color, the hardness or softness, the weight, even the impenetrability, there still remains the space which the body (now entirely vanished) occupied, and this cannot be removed. Again, if we remove from our empirical concept of any

---

* Kant here disputes Hume's denial of "necessary connections" between causes and their effects; see Selection 8 in Section II. Hume's analysis of causation as "constant conjunction" between events whose conjunction is not logically necessary, is also discussed in Selection 16, Section III. (Eds.)

object, corporeal or incorporeal, all properties which experience has taught us, we yet cannot take away that property through which the object is thought as substance or as inhering in a substance (although this concept of substance is more determinate than that of an object in general). Owing, therefore, to the necessity with which this concept of substance forces itself upon us, we have no option save to admit that it has its seat in our faculty of *a priori* knowledge.

III. Philosophy Stands in Need of a Science Which Shall Determine the Possibility, the Principles, and the Extent of all A Priori *Knowledge*

But what is still more extraordinary than all the preceding is this, that certain modes of knowledge leave the field of all possible experiences and have the appearance of extending the scope of our judgments beyond all limits of experience, and this by means of concepts to which no corresponding object can ever be given in experience.

It is precisely by means of the latter modes of knowledge, in a realm beyond the world of the senses, where experience can yield neither guidance nor correction, that our reason carries on those enquiries which owing to their importance we consider to be far more excellent, and in their purpose far more lofty, than all the understanding can learn in the field of appearances. Indeed we prefer to run every risk of error rather than desist from such urgent enquiries, on the ground of their dubious character, or from disdain and indifference. These unavoidable problems set by pure reason itself are *God, freedom,* and *immortality.* The science which, with all its preparations, is in its final intention directed solely to their solution is metaphysics; and its procedure is at first dogmatic, that is, it confidently sets itself to this task without any previous examination of the capacity or incapacity of reason for so great an undertaking.

Now it does indeed seem natural that, as soon as we have left the ground of experience, we should, through careful enquiries, assure ourselves as to the foundations of any building that we propose to erect, not making use of any knowledge that we possess without first determining whence it has come, and not trusting to principles without knowing their origin. It is natural, that is to say, that the question should first be considered, how the understanding can arrive at all this knowledge *a priori,* and what extent, validity, and worth it may have. Nothing, indeed, could be more natural, if by the term "natural" we signify what fittingly and reasonably ought to happen. But if we mean by "natural" what ordinarily happens, then on the contrary nothing is more natural and more intelligible than the fact that this enquiry has been so long neglected. For one part of this knowledge, the mathematical, has long been of established reliability, and so gives rise to a favourable presumption as regards the other part, which may yet be of quite different nature. Besides, once we are outside the circle of experience, we can be sure of not being *contradicted* by experience. The charm of extending our knowledge is so great that nothing short of encountering a direct contradiction can suffice to arrest us in our course; and this can be avoided, if we are careful in our fabrications—which none the less will still remain fabrications. Mathematics gives us a shining example of how far, independently of experience, we can progress in *a priori* knowledge. It does, indeed, occupy itself with objects and with knowledge solely in so far as they allow of being exhibited in intuition.* But this circumstance is easily overlooked, since this intuition can itself be given *a priori,* and is therefore hardly to be distinguished from a bare and pure concept. Misled by such a proof of the power of reason, the demand for the extension of knowledge recognises no limits. The light dove, cleaving the air in her free flight, and feeling its resistance, might imagine that its flight would be still easier in empty space. It was thus that Plato left the world of the senses, as setting too narrow limits to the understanding, and ventured out beyond it on the wings of the ideas, in the empty space of the pure understanding. He did not observe that with all his efforts he made no advance—meeting no resistance that might, as it were, serve as a support upon which he could take a stand, to which he could apply his powers, and so set his understanding in motion. It is, indeed, the common fate of human reason to complete its speculative structures as speedily as may be, and only afterwards to enquire whether the foundations are reliable. All sorts of excuses will then be appealed to, in order to reassure us of their solidity, or rather indeed to enable us to dispense altogether with so late and so dangerous an enquiry. But what keeps us, during the actual building, free from all apprehension and suspicion, and flatters us with a seeming thoroughness, is this other circumstance, namely, that a great, perhaps the greatest, part of the business of our reason consists in analysis of the concepts which we already have of objects. This analysis supplies us with a considerable body of knowledge, which, while nothing but explanation or elucidation of what has already been thought in our concepts, though in a confused manner, is yet prized as being, at least as regards

---

* Kant means that geometrical concepts can be represented by diagrams. In proving, e. g., the Euclidean theorem that the sum of the interior angles of a triangle equals 180° one usually draws a triangle and then draws a straight line through one vertex parallel to the opposite side. He also refers to the possibility of representing numbers by points. (Eds.)

its form, new insight. But so far as the matter or content is concerned, there has been no extension of our previously possessed concepts, but only an analysis of them. Since this procedure yields real knowledge *a priori,* which progresses in an assured and useful fashion, reason is so far misled as surreptitiously to introduce, without itself being aware of so doing, assertions of an entirely different order, in which it attaches to given concepts others completely foreign to them, and moreover attaches them *a priori.* And yet it is not known how reason can be in position to do this. Such a question is never so much as thought of. I shall therefore at once proceed to deal with the difference between these two kinds of knowledge.

IV. The Distinction between Analytic and Synthetic Judgments

In all judgments in which the relation of a subject to the predicate is thought (I take into consideration affirmative judgments only, the subsequent application to negative judgments being easily made), this relation is possible in two different ways. Either the predicate B belongs to the subject A, as something which is (covertly) contained in this concept A; or B lies outside the concept A, although it does indeed stand in connection with it. In the one case I entitle the judgment analytic, in the other synthetic. Analytic judgments (affirmative) are therefore those in which the connection of the predicate with the subject is thought through identity; those in which this connection is thought without identity should be entitled synthetic. The former, as adding nothing through the predicate to the concept of the subject, but merely breaking it up into those constituent concepts that have all along been thought in it, although confusedly, can also be entitled explicative. The latter, on the other hand, add to the concept of the subject a predicate which has not been in any wise thought in it, and which no analysis could possibly extract from it; and they may therefore be entitled ampliative. If I say, for instance, "All bodies are extended," this is an analytic judgment. For I do not require to go beyond the concept which I connect with "body" in order to find extension as bound up with it. To meet with this predicate, I have merely to analyse the concept, that is, to become conscious to myself of the manifold which I always think in that concept. The judgment is therefore analytic. But when I say, "All bodies are heavy," the predicate is something quite different from anything that I think in the mere concept of body in general; and the addition of such a predicate therefore yields a synthetic judgment.

Judgments of experience, as such, are one and all synthetic. For it would be absurd to found an analytic judgment on experience. Since, in framing the judgment, I must not go outside my concept, there is no need to appeal to the testimony of experience in its support. That a body is extended is a proposition that holds *a priori* and is not empirical. For, before appealing to experience, I have already in the concept of body all the conditions required for my judgment. I have only to extract from it, in accordance with the principle of contradiction, the required predicate, and in so doing can at the same time become conscious of the necessity of the judgment—and that is what experience could never have taught me. On the other hand, though I do not include in the concept of a body in general the predicate "weight," none the less this concept indicates an object of experience through one of its parts, and I can add to that part other parts of this same experience, as in this way belonging together with the concept. From the start I can apprehend the concept of body and analytically through the characters of extension, impenetrability, figure, etc., all of which are thought in the concept. Now, however, looking back on the experience from which I have derived this concept of body, and finding weight to be invariably connected with the above characters, I attach it as a predicate to the concept; and in doing so I attach it synthetically, and am therefore extending my knowledge. The possibility of the synthesis of the predicate "weight" with the concept of "body" thus rests upon experience. While the one concept is not contained in the other, they yet belong to one another, though only contingently, as parts of a whole, namely, of an experience which is itself a synthetic combination of intuitions.

But in *a priori* synthetic judgments this help is entirely lacking. [I do not here have the advantage of looking around in the field of experience.] Upon what, then, am I to rely, when I seek to go beyond the concept A, and to know that another concept B is connected with it? Through what is the synthesis made possible? Let us take the proposition, "Everything which happens has its cause." In the concept of "something which happens," I do indeed think an existence which is preceded by a time, etc., and from this concept analytic judgments may be obtained. But the concept of a "cause" lies entirely outside the other concept, and signifies something different from "that which happens," and is not therefore in any way contained in this latter representation. How come I then to predicate of that which happens something quite different, and to apprehend that the concept of cause, though not contained in it, yet belongs, and indeed necessarily belongs, to it? What is here the unknown =X which gives support to the understanding when it believes that it can discover outside the concept A a predicate B foreign to this concept, which it yet at the same time considers to be connected with it? It cannot be experience, because the suggested principle has connected the second representation with the first, not only with greater universality, but also with the character of necessity, and therefore completely *a priori* and on the basis of mere concepts. Upon such synthetic, that is, ampliative principles, all our *a priori* speculative knowledge must ultimately rest; analytic judgments are very important, and indeed necessary, but only for obtaining that clearness in the concepts which is requisite for such a sure and wide synthesis as will lead to a genuinely new addition to all previous knowledge.

V. In All Theoretical Sciences of Reason Synthetic
A Priori *Judgments Are Contained as Principles*

1. *All mathematical judgments, without exception, are synthetic.* This fact, though incontestably certain and in its consequences very important, has hitherto escaped the notice of those who are engaged in the analysis of human reason, and is, indeed, directly opposed to all their conjectures. For as it was found that all mathematical inferences proceed in accordance with the principle of contradiction (which the nature of all apodeictic certainty requires), it was supposed that the fundamental propositions of the science can themselves be known to be true through that principle. This is an erroneous view. For though a synthetic proposition can indeed be discerned in accordance with the principle of contradiction, this can only be if another synthetic proposition is presupposed, and if it can then be apprehended as following from this other proposition; it can never be so discerned in and by itself.

First of all, it has to be noted that mathematical propositions, strictly so called, are always judgments *a priori,* not empirical; because they carry with them necessity, which cannot be derived from experience. If this be demurred to, I am willing to limit my statement to *pure* mathematics, the very concept of which implies that it does not contain empirical, but only pure *a priori* knowledge.

We might, indeed, at first suppose that the proposition $7 + 5 = 12$ is a merely analytic proposition, and follows by the principle of contradiction from the concept of a sum of 7 and 5. But if we look more closely we find that the concept of the sum of 7 and 5 contains nothing save the union of the two numbers into one, and in this no thought is being taken as to what that single number may be which combines both. The concept of 12 is by no means already thought in merely thinking this union of 7 and 5; and I may analyse my concept of such a possible sum as long as I please, still I shall never find the 12 in it. We have to go outside these concepts, and call in the aid of the intuition which corresponds to one of them, our five fingers, for instance, or, as Segner does in his *Arithmetic,* five points, adding to the concept of 7, unit by unit, the five given in intuition. For starting with the number 7, and for the concept of 5 calling in the aid of the fingers of my hand as intuition, I now add one by one to the number 7 the units which I previously took together to form the number 5, and with the aid of that figure [the hand] see the number 12 coming into being. That 5 should be added to 7, I have indeed already thought in the concept of a sum $= 7 + 5$, but not that this sum is equivalent to the number 12. Arithmetical propositions are therefore always synthetic. This is still more evident if we take larger numbers. For it is then obvious that, however we might turn and twist our concepts, we could never, by the mere analysis of them, and without the aid of intuition, discover what [the number is that] is the sum.

Just as little is any fundamental proposition of pure geometry analytic. That the straight line between two points is the shortest, is a synthetic proposition. For my concept of *straight* contains nothing of quantity, but only of quality. The concept of the shortest is wholly an addition, and cannot be derived, through any process of analysis, from the concept of the straight line. Intuition, therefore, must here be called in; only by its aid is the synthesis possible. What here causes us commonly to believe that the predicate of such apodeictic judgments is already contained in our concept, and that the judgment is therefore analytic, is merely the ambiguous character of the terms used. We are required to join in thought a certain predicate to a given concept, and this necessity is inherent in the concepts themselves. But the question is not what we *ought* to join in thought to the given concept, but what we *actually* think in it, even if only obscurely; and it is then manifest that, while the predicate is indeed attached necessarily to the concept, it is so in virtue of an intuition which must be added to the concept, not as thought in the concept itself.

Some few fundamental propositions, presupposed by the geometrician, are, indeed, really analytic, and rest on the principle of contradiction. But, as identical propositions, they serve only as links in the chain of method and not as principles; for instance, $a = a$; the whole is equal to itself; or $(a + b) > a,$ that is, the whole is greater than its part. And even these propositions, though they are valid according to pure concepts, are only admitted in mathematics because they can be exhibited in intuition.

2. *Natural science (physics) contains* a priori *synthetic judgments as principles.* I need cite only two such judgments: that in all changes of the material world the quantity of matter remains unchanged; and that in all communication of motion, action and reaction must always be equal. Both propositions, it is evident, are not only necessary, and therefore in their origin *a priori,* but also synthetic. For in the concept of

matter I do not think its permanence, but only its presence in the space which it occupies. I go outside and beyond the concept of matter, joining to it *a priori* in thought something which I have not thought *in* it. The proposition is not, therefore, analytic, but synthetic, and yet is thought *a priori;* and so likewise are the other propositions of the pure part of natural science.

3. *Metaphysics,* even if we look upon it as having hitherto failed in all its endeavours, is yet, owing to the nature of human reason, a quite indispensable science, and *ought to contain* a priori *synthetic knowledge.* For its business is not merely to analyse concepts which we make for ourselves *a priori* of things, and thereby to clarify them analytically, but to extend our *a priori* knowledge. And for this purpose we must employ principles which add to the given concept something that was not contained in it, and through *a priori* synthetic judgments venture out so far that experience is quite unable to follow us, as, for instance, in the proposition, that the world must have a first beginning, and such like. Thus metaphysics consists, at least *in intention,* entirely of *a priori* synthetic propositions.

VI. The General Problem of Pure Reason

Much is already gained if we can bring a number of investigations under the formula of a single problem. For we not only lighten our own task, by defining it accurately, but make it easier for others, who would test our results, to judge whether or not we have succeeded in what we set out to do. Now the proper problem of pure reason is contained in the question: How are *a priori* synthetic judgments possible?

That metaphysics has hitherto remained in so vacillating a state of uncertainty and contradiction, is entirely due to the fact that this problem, and perhaps even the distinction between analytic and synthetic judgments, has never previously been considered. Upon the solution of this problem, or upon a sufficient proof that the possibility which it desires to have explained does in fact not exist at all, depends the success or failure of metaphysics. Among philosophers, David Hume* came nearest to envisaging this problem, but still was very far from conceiving it with sufficient definiteness and universality. He occupied himself exclusively with the synthetic proposition regarding the connection of an effect with its cause (*principium causalitatis*), and he believed himself to have shown that such an *a priori* proposition is entirely impossible. If we accept his conclusions, then all that we call metaphysics is a mere

---

* See Selection 8, Section II. (Eds.)

delusion whereby we fancy ourselves to have rational insight into what, in actual fact, is borrowed solely from experience, and under the influence of custom has taken the illusory semblance of necessity. If he had envisaged our problem in all its universality, he would never have been guilty of this statement, so destructive of all pure philosophy. For he would then have recognised that, according to his own argument, pure mathematics, as certainly containing *a priori* synthetic propositions, would also not be possible; and from such an assertion his good sense would have saved him.

In the solution of the above problem, we are at the same time deciding as to the possibility of the employment of pure reason in establishing and developing all those sciences which contain a theoretical *a priori* knowledge of objects, and have therefore to answer the questions:

How is pure mathematics possible?
How is pure science of nature possible?

Since these sciences actually exist, it is quite proper to ask *how* they are possible; for that they must be possible is proved by the fact that they exist.[1] But the poor progress which has hitherto been made in metaphysics, and the fact that no system yet propounded can, in view of the essential purpose of metaphysics, be said really to exist, leaves everyone sufficient ground for doubting as to its possibility.

Yet, in a certain sense, this *kind of knowledge* is to be looked upon as given; that is to say, metaphysics actually exists, if not as a science, yet still as natural disposition (*metaphysica naturalis*). For human reason, without being moved merely by the idle desire for extent and variety of knowledge, proceeds impetuously, driven on by an inward need, to questions such as cannot be answered by any empirical employment of reason, or by principles thence derived. Thus in all men, as soon as their reason has become ripe for speculation, there has always existed and will always continue to exist some kind of metaphysics. And so we have the question:

How is metaphysics, as natural disposition, possible?

that is, how from the nature of universal human reason do those questions arise which pure reason propounds to itself, and which it is impelled by its own need to answer as best it can?

But since all attempts which have hitherto been made to answer these natural questions—for instance, whether the world has a beginning or is from eternity—have always met with unavoidable contradictions, we

---

1. Many may still have doubts as regards pure natural science. We have only, however, to consider the various propositions that are to be found at the beginning of (empirical) physics, properly so called, those, for instance, relating to the permanence in the quantity of matter, to inertia, to the equality of action and reaction, etc., in order to be soon convinced that they constitute a *physica pura*, or *rationalis*, which well deserves, as an independent science, to be separately dealt with in its whole extent, be that narrow or wide.

cannot rest satisfied with the mere natural disposition to metaphysics, that is, with the pure faculty of reason itself, from which, indeed, some sort of metaphysics (be it what it may) always arises. It must be possible for reason to attain to certainty whether we know or do not know the objects of metaphysics, that is, to come to a decision either in regard to the objects of its enquiries or in regard to the capacity or incapacity of reason to pass any judgment upon them, so that we may either with confidence extend our pure reason or set to it sure and determiniate limits. This last question, which arises out of the previous general problem, may, rightly stated, take the form:

How is metaphysics, as science, possible?

Thus the critique of reason, in the end, necessarily leads to scientific knowledge; while its dogmatic employment, on the other hand, lands us in dogmatic assertions to which other assertions, equally specious, can always be opposed—that is, in *scepticism*.

This science cannot be of any very formidable prolixity, since it has to deal not with the objects of reason, the variety of which is inexhaustible, but only with itself and the problems which arise entirely from within itself, and which are imposed upon it by its own nature, not by the nature of things which are distinct from it. When once reason has learnt completely to understand its own power in respect of objects which can be presented to it in experience, it should easily be able to determine, with completeness and certainty, the extent and the limits of its attempted employment beyond the bounds of all experience.

We may, then, and indeed we must, regard as abortive all attempts, hitherto made, to establish a metaphysic *dogmatically*. For the analytic part in any such attempted system, namely, the mere analysis of the concepts that inhere in our reason *a priori,* is by no means the aim of, but only a preparation for, metaphysics proper, that is, the extension of its *a priori* synthetic knowledge. For such a purpose, the analysis of concepts is useless, since it merely shows what is contained in these concepts, not how we arrive at them *a priori*. A solution of this latter problem is required, that we may be able to determine the valid employment of such concepts in regard to the objects of all knowledge in general. Nor is much self-denial needed to give up these claims, seeing that the undeniable, and in the dogmatic procedure of reason also unavoidable, contradictions of reason with itself have long since undermined the authority of every metaphysical system yet propounded. Greater firmness will be required if we are not to be deterred by inward difficulties and outward opposition from endeavouring, through application of a method entirely different from any hitherto employed, at last to bring to a prosperous and fruitful growth a science indispensable to human reason—a science whose every branch may be cut away but whose root cannot be destroyed.

3

MATHEMATICS AND EXPERIENCE

John Stuart Mill

IF, AS LAID DOWN in the two preceding chapters, the foundation of all sciences, even deductive or demonstrative sciences, is induction, if every step in the ratiocinations even of geometry is an act of induction, and if a train of reasoning is but bringing many inductions to bear upon the same subject of inquiry and drawing a case within one induction by means of another, wherein lies the peculiar certainty always ascribed to the sciences which are entirely, or almost entirely, deductive? Why are they called the exact sciences? Why are mathematical certainty and the evidence of demonstration common phrases to express the very highest degree of assurance attainable by reason? Why are mathematics by almost all philosophers, and (by some) even those branches of natural philosophy which, through the medium of mathematics, have been converted into deductive sciences, considered to be independent of the evidence of experience and observation and characterized as systems of necessary truth?

The Alleged Necessity of the Propositions of
Geometry is Illusory

The answer I conceive to be that this character of necessity ascribed to the truths of mathematics and (even with some reservations to be hereafter made) the peculiar certainty attributed to them is an illusion, in order to sustain which, it is necessary to suppose that those truths relate to, and express the properties of, purely imaginary objects. It is acknowledged that the conclusions of geometry are deduced, partly at

[This selection is taken from Chapters V and VI of Book II of *A System of Logic*, a book first published in 1843.]

least, from the so-called definitions, and that those definitions are assumed to be correct representations, as far as they go, of the objects with which geometry is conversant. Now we have pointed out that from a definition as such no proposition, unless it be one concerning the meaning of a word, can ever follow, and that what apparently follows from a definition follows in reality from an implied assumption that there exists a real thing conformable thereto. This assumption, in the case of the definitions of geometry, is not strictly true; there exist no real things exactly conformable to the definitions. There exist no points without magnitude; no lines without breadth, nor perfectly straight; no circles with all their radii exactly equal, nor squares with all their angles perfectly right. It will perhaps be said that the assumption does not extend to the actual, but only to the possible, existence of such things. I answer that, according to any test we have of possibility, they are not even possible. Their existence, so far as we can form any judgment, would seem to be inconsistent with the physical constitution of our planet at least, if not of the universe. To get rid of this difficulty and at the same time to save the credit of the supposed system of necessary truth, it is customary to say that the points, lines, circles, and squares which are the subject of geometry exist in our conceptions merely and are part of our minds, which minds, by working on their own materials, construct an *a priori* science, the evidence of which is purely mental and has nothing whatever to do with outward experience. By howsoever high authorities this doctrine may have been sanctioned, it appears to me psychologically incorrect. The points, lines, circles, and squares which anyone has in his mind are (I apprehend) simply copies of the points, lines, circles, and squares which he has known in his experience. Our idea of a point I apprehended to be simply our idea of the *minimum visibile,* the smallest portion of surface which we can see. A line, as defined by geometers, is wholly inconceivable. We can reason about a line as if it had no breadth, because we have a power, which is the foundation of all the control we can exercise over the operations of our minds, the power, when a perception is present to our senses or a conception to our intellects, of *attending* to a part only of that perception or conception instead of the whole. But we cannot *conceive* a line without breadth; we can form no mental picture of such a line; all the lines which we have in our minds are lines possessing breadth. If anyone doubts this, we may refer him to his own experience. I much question if anyone who fancies that he can conceive what is called a mathematical line thinks so from the evidence of his consciousness; I suspect it is rather because he supposes that, unless such a conception were possible, mathematics could not exist as a science, a supposition which there will be no difficulty in showing to be entirely groundless.

Since, then, neither in nature nor in the human mind do there exist any objects exactly corresponding to the definitions of geometry, while yet that science cannot be supposed to be conversant about nonentities, nothing remains but to consider geometry as conversant with such lines, angles, and figures as really exist, and the definitions, as they are called, must be regarded as some of our first and most obvious generalizations concerning those natural objects. The correctness of those generalizations, *as* generalizations, is without a flaw; the equality of all the radii of a circle is true of all circles, so far as it is true of any one, but it is not exactly true of any circle; it is only nearly true, so nearly that no error of any importance in practice will be incurred by feigning it to be exactly true. When we have occasion to extend these inductions or their consequences to cases in which the error would be appreciable—to lines of perceptible breadth or thickness, parallels which deviate sensibly from equidistance, and the like—we correct our conclusions by combining with them a fresh set of propositions relating to the aberration, just as we also take in propositions relating to the physical or chemical properties of the material if those properties happen to introduce any modification into the result, which they easily may, even with respect to figure and magnitude, as in the case, for instance, of expansion by heat. So long, however, as there exists no practical necessity for attending to any of the properties of the object except its geometrical properties or to any of the natural irregularities in those, it is convenient to neglect the consideration of the other properties and of the irregularities and to reason as if these did not exist; accordingly, we formally announce in the definitions that we intend to proceed on this plan. But it is an error to suppose, because we resolve to confine our attention to a certain number of the properties of an object, that we therefore conceive, or have an idea of, the object denuded of its other properties. We are thinking, all the time, of precisely such objects as we have seen and touched and with all the properties which naturally belong to them, but, for scientific convenience, we feign them to be divested of all properties except those which are material to our purpose and in regard to which we deign to consider them.

The peculiar accuracy supposed to be characteristic of the first principles of geometry thus appears to be fictitious. The assertions on which the reasonings of the science are founded do not, any more than in other sciences, exactly correspond with the fact, but we suppose that they do so, for the sake of tracing the consequences which follow from the supposition. The opinion of Dugald Stewart respecting the foundations of geometry is, I conceive, substantially correct: that it is built on hypotheses; that it owes to this alone the peculiar certainty supposed to distinguish it; and that in any science whatever, by reasoning from a set of hypotheses, we may obtain a body of conclusions as certain as those of geometry, that is, as strictly in accordance with the hypotheses and as irresistibly compelling assent, *on condition* that those hypotheses are true.

When, therefore, it is affirmed that the conclusions of geometry are necessary truths, the necessity consists in reality only in this, that they correctly follow from the suppositions from which they are deduced. Those suppositions are so far from being necessary that they are not even true; they purposely depart, more or less widely, from the truth. The only sense in which necessity can be ascribed to the conclusions of any scientific investigation is that of legitimately following from some assumption which, by the conditions of the inquiry, is not to be questioned. In this relation, of course, the derivative truths of every deductive science must stand to the inductions or assumptions on which the science is founded, and which, whether true or untrue, certain or doubtful in themselves, are always supposed certain for the purposes of the particular science. . . .

The Axioms Are Experimental Truths

. . . What is the ground of our belief in axioms—what is the evidence on which they rest? I answer, they are experimental truths, generalizations from observation. The proposition, "Two straight lines cannot inclose a space"—or, in other words, "Two straight lines which have once met, do not meet again, but continue to diverge"—is an induction from the evidence of our senses.

This opinion runs counter to a scientific prejudice of long standing and great strength, and there is probably no proposition enunciated in this work for which a more unfavorable reception is to be expected. It is, however, no new opinion, and, even if it were so, would be entitled to be judged not by its novelty, but by the strength of the arguments by which it can be supported. I consider it very fortunate that so eminent a champion of the contrary opinion as Dr. Whewell has found occasion for a most elaborate treatment of the whole theory of axioms in attempting to construct the philosophy of the mathematical and physical sciences on the basis of the doctrine against which I now contend. Whoever is anxious that a discussion should go to the bottom of the subject must rejoice to see the opposite side of the question worthily represented. If what is said by Dr. Whewell, in support of an opinion which he has made the foundation of a systematic work, can be shown not to be conclusive, enough will have been done, without going elsewhere in quest of stronger arguments and a more powerful adversary.

It is not necessary to show that the truths which we call axioms are originally *suggested* by observation and that we should never have known that two straight lines cannot inclose a space if we had never seen a straight line, thus much being admitted by Dr. Whewell and by all, in recent times, who have taken his view of the subject. But they contend that it is not experience which *proves* the axiom, but that its truth is perceived *a priori,* by the constitution of the mind itself, from the first moment when the meaning of the proposition is apprehended, and without any necessity for verifying it by repeated trials, as is requisite in the case of truths really ascertained by observation.

They cannot, however, but allow that the truth of the axiom, "Two straight lines cannot inclose a space," even if evident independently of experience, is also evident from experience. Whether the axiom needs confirmation or not, it receives confirmation in almost every instant of our lives, since we cannot look at any two straight lines which intersect one another without seeing that from that point they continue to diverge more and more. Experimental proof crowds in upon us in such endless profusion, and without one instance in which there can be even a suspicion of an exception to the rule, that we should soon have stronger ground for believing the axiom, even as an experimental truth, than we have for almost any of the general truths which we confessedly learn from the evidence of our senses. Independently of *a priori* evidence, we should certainly believe it with an intensity of conviction far greater than we accord to any ordinary physical truth, and this, too, at a time of life much earlier than that from which we date almost any part of our acquired knowledge, and much too early to admit of our retaining any recollection of the history of our intellectual operations of that period. Where, then, is the necessity for assuming that our recognition of these truths has a different origin from the rest of our knowledge when its existence is perfectly accounted for by supposing its origin to be the same? when the causes which produce belief in all other instances exist in this instance, and in a degree of strength as much superior to what exists in other cases as the intensity of the belief itself is superior? The burden of proof lies on the advocates of the contrary opinion; it is for them to point out some fact inconsistent with the supposition that this part of our knowledge of nature is derived from the same sources as every other part.

This, for instance, they would be able to do, if they could prove chronologically that we had the conviction (at least practically) so early in infancy as to be anterior to those impressions on the senses upon which, on the other theory, the conviction is founded. This, however, cannot be proved, the point being too far back to be within the reach of memory and too obscure for external observation. The advocates of the *a priori* theory are obliged to have recourse to other arguments. These are reducible to two, which I shall endeavor to state as clearly and as forcibly as possible.

In the first place it is said that if our assent to the proposition that two straight lines cannot inclose a space were derived from the senses, we could only be convinced of its truth by actual trial, that is, by seeing or feeling the straight lines, whereas, in fact, it is seen to be true by merely thinking of them. That a stone thrown into water goes to the bottom may be perceived by our senses, but mere thinking of a stone thrown into the water would never have led us to that conclusion; not so, however, with the axioms relating to straight lines: if I could be made to conceive what a straight line is, without having seen one, I should at once recognize that two such lines cannot inclose a space. Intuition is "imaginary looking,"[1] but experience must be real looking; if we see a property of straight lines to be true by merely fancying ourselves to be looking at them, the ground of our belief cannot be the senses, or experience; it must be something mental.

To this argument it might be added in the case of this particular axiom (for the assertion would not be true of all axioms) that the evidence of it from actual ocular inspection is not only unnecessary but unattainable. What says the axiom? That two straight lines *cannot* inclose a space; that, after having once intersected, if they are prolonged to infinity they do not meet, but continue to diverge from one another. How can this, in any single case, be proved by actual observation? We may follow the lines to any distance we please, but we cannot follow them to infinity; for aught our senses can testify, they may, immediately beyond the farthest point to which we have traced them, begin to approach, and at last meet. Unless, therefore, we had some other proof of the impossibility than observation affords us, we should have no ground for believing the axiom at all.

To these arguments, which I trust I cannot be accused of understating, a satisfactory answer will, I conceive, be found, if we advert to one of the characteristic properties of geometrical forms—their capacity of being painted in the imagination with a distinctness equal to reality; in other words, the exact resemblance of our ideas of form to the sensations which suggest them. This, in the first place, enables us to make (at least with a little practice) mental pictures of all possible combinations of lines and angles which resemble the realities quite as well as any which we could make on paper; and, in the next place, make those pictures just as fit subjects of geometrical experimentation as the realities themselves, inasmuch as pictures, if sufficiently accurate, exhibit, of course, all the properties which would be manifested by the realities at one given instant and on simple inspection; and in geometry we are concerned only with such properties, and not with that which pictures could not exhibit, the mutual action of bodies one upon another. The foundations of geometry would, therefore, be laid in direct experience, even if the experiments (which in this case consist merely in attentive contem-

---

1. Whewell's *History of Scientific Ideas*, I, 140.

plation) were practiced solely upon what we call our ideas, that is, upon the diagrams in our minds, and not upon outward objects. For in all systems of experimentation we take some objects to serve as representatives of all which resemble them, and in the present case the conditions which qualify a real object to be the representative of its class are completely fulfilled by an object existing only in our fancy. Without denying, therefore, the possibility of satisfying ourselves that two straight lines cannot inclose a space by merely thinking of straight lines without actually looking at them, I contend that we do not believe this truth on the ground of the imaginary intuition simply, but because we know that the imaginary lines exactly resemble real ones and that we may conclude from them to real ones with quite as much certainty as we could conclude from one real line to another. The conclusion, therefore, is still an induction from observation. And we should not be authorized to substitute observation of the image in our mind for observation of the reality, if we had not learned by long continued experience that the properties of the reality are faithfully represented in the image, just as we should be scientifically warranted in describing an animal which we have never seen from a picture made of it with a daguerreotype, but not until we had learned by ample experience that observation of such a picture is precisely equivalent to observation of the original. . . .

What We Cannot Conceive
Is Not Therefore Impossible

. . . The first of the two arguments in support of the theory that axioms are *a priori* truths having, I think, been sufficiently answered, I proceed to the second, which is usually the most relied on. Axioms (it is asserted) are conceived by us not only as true, but as universally and necessarily true. Now, experience cannot possibly give to any proposition this character. I may have seen snow a hundred times and may have seen that it was white, but this cannot give me entire assurance even that all snow is white, much less that snow *must* be white. "However many instances we may have observed of the truth of a proposition, there is nothing to assure us that the next case shall not be an exception to the rule. If it be strictly true that every ruminant animal yet known has cloven hoofs, we still cannot be sure that some creature will not hereafter be discovered which has the first of these attributes, without having the other. . . . Experience must always consist of a limited number of observations; and, however numerous these may be, they can show nothing with regard to the infinite number of cases in which the experiment has not been made." Besides, axioms are not only universal, they are also necessary. Now "experience cannot offer the smallest ground for the necessity of a proposition. She can observe and record what has happened; but she cannot find, in any case, or in any accumulation of cases, any reason for what *must* happen. She may see objects side by side; but she cannot see a reason why they must ever be side by side. She finds certain events to occur in succession; but the succession supplies, in its occurrence, no reason for its recurrence. She contemplates external objects; but she cannot detect any internal bond, which indissolubly connects the future with the past, the possible with the real. To learn a proposition by experience, and to see it to be necessarily true, are two altogether different processes of thought."[2] And Dr. Whewell adds, "If anyone does not clearly comprehend this distinction of necessary and contingent truths, he will not be able to go along with us in our researches into the foundations of human knowledge; nor, indeed, to pursue with success any speculation on the subject."[3] . . .

Although Dr. Whewell has naturally and properly employed a variety of phrases to bring his meaning more forcibly home, he would, I presume, allow that they are all equivalent, and that what he means by a necessary truth would be sufficiently defined, a proposition the negation of which is not only false but inconceivable. I am unable to find in any of his expressions, turn them what way you will, a meaning beyond this, and I do not believe he would contend that they mean anything more.

This, therefore, is the principle asserted: that propositions, the negation of which is inconceivable, or, in other words, which we cannot figure to ourselves as being false, must rest on evidence of a higher and more cogent description than any which experience can afford.

Now I cannot but wonder that so much stress should be laid on the circumstance of inconceivableness when there is such ample experience to show that our capacity or incapacity of conceiving a thing has very little to do with the possibility of the thing in itself, but is, in truth, very much an affair of accident, and depends on the past history and habits of our own minds. There is no more generally acknowledged fact in human nature than the extreme difficulty at first felt in conceiving anything as possible, which is in contradiction to long established and familiar experience, or even to old familiar habits of thought. And this difficulty is a necessary result of the fundamental laws of the human mind. When we have often seen and thought of two things together and have never in any one instance either seen or thought of them separately, there is by the primary law of association an increasing difficulty, which may in the end become insuperable, of conceiving the two things apart. This is most of all conspicuous in uneducated persons who are, in general, utterly

---

2. *History of Scientific Ideas*, I, 65-67.
3. *Ibid.*, I, 60.

unable to separate any two ideas which have once become firmly associated in their minds; and if persons of cultivated intellect have any advantage on the point, it is only because, having seen and heard and read
more, and being more accustomed to exercise their imagination, they
have experienced their sensations and thoughts in more varied combinations and have been prevented from forming many of these inseparable
associations. But this advantage has necessarily its limits. The most practiced intellect is not exempt from the universal laws of our conceptive
faculty. If daily habit presents to anyone for a long period two facts in
combination, and if he is not led during that period either by accident
or by his voluntary mental operations to think of them apart, he will
probably in time become incapable of doing so even by the strongest
effort, and the supposition that the two facts can be separated in nature
will at last present itself to his mind with all the characters of an inconceivable phenomenon. There are remarkable instances of this in the
history of science, instances in which the most instructed men rejected
as impossible, because inconceivable, things which their posterity, by
earlier practice and longer perseverance in the attempt, found it quite
easy to conceive, and which everybody now knows to be true. There
was a time when men of the most cultivated intellects and the most
emancipated from the dominion of early prejudice could not credit the
existence of antipodes, were unable to conceive, in opposition to old
association, the force of gravity acting upward instead of downward. The
Cartesians long rejected the Newtonian doctrine of the gravitation of all
bodies toward one another, on the faith of a general proposition, the
reverse of which seemed to them to be inconceivable—the proposition
that a body cannot act where it is not. All the cumbrous machinery of
imaginary vortices, assumed without the smallest particle of evidence,
appeared to these philosophers a more rational mode of explaining the
heavenly motions than one which involved what seemed to them so
great an absurdity. And they no doubt found it as impossible to conceive
that a body should act upon the earth from the distance of the sun or
moon as we find it to conceive an end to space or time, or two straight
lines inclosing a space. Newton himself had not been able to realize the
conception or we should not have had his hypothesis of a subtle ether,
the occult cause of gravitation, and his writings prove that though he
deemed the particular nature of the intermediate agency a matter of conjecture, the necessity of *some* such agency appeared to him indubitable.

If, then, it be so natural to the human mind, even in a high state of
culture, to be incapable of conceiving and on that ground to believe
impossible what is afterward not only found to be conceivable but proved
to be true, what wonder if in cases where the association is still older,
more confirmed, and more familiar, and in which nothing ever occurs
to shake our conviction or even suggest to us any conception at vari-

ance with the association, the acquired incapacity should continue and be mistaken for a natural incapacity? It is true, our experience of the varieties in nature enables us, within certain limits, to conceive other varieties analogous to them. We can conceive the sun or moon falling, for though we never saw them fall, nor ever, perhaps, imagined them falling, we have seen so many other things fall, that we have innumerable familiar analogies to assist the conception, which, after all, we should probably have some difficulty in framing, were we not well accustomed to see the sun and moon move (or appear to move) so that we are only called upon to conceive a slight change in the direction of motion, a circumstance familiar to our experience. But when experience affords no model on which to shape the new conception, how is it possible for us to form it? How, for example, can we imagine an end to space or time? We never saw any object without something beyond it, nor experienced any feeling without something following it. When, therefore, we attempt to conceive the last point of space, we have the idea irresistibly raised of other points beyond it. When we try to imagine the last instant of time, we cannot help conceiving another instant after it. Nor is there any necessity to assume, as is done by a modern school of metaphysicians, a peculiar fundamental law of the mind to account for the feeling of infinity inherent in our conceptions of space and time; that apparent infinity is sufficiently accounted for by simpler and universally acknowledged laws.

Now, in the case of a geometrical axiom, such, for example, as that two straight lines cannot inclose a space—a truth which is testified to us by our very earliest impressions of the external world—how is it possible (whether those external impressions be or be not the ground of our belief) that the reverse of the proposition *could* be otherwise than inconceivable to us? What analogy have we, what similar order of facts in any other branch of our experience, to facilitate to us the conception of two straight lines inclosing a space? Nor is even this all. I have already called attention to the peculiar property of our impressions of form, that the ideas or mental images exactly resemble their prototypes and adequately represent them for the purposes of scientific observation. From this and from the intuitive character of the observation, which in this case reduces itself to simple inspection, we cannot so much as call up in our imagination two straight lines, in order to attempt to conceive them inclosing a space, without by that very act repeating the scientific experiment which establishes the contrary. Will it really be contended that the inconceivableness of the thing, in such circumstances, proves anything against the experimental origin of the conviction? Is it not clear that in whichever mode our belief in the proposition may have originated, the impossibility of our conceiving the negative of it must, on either hypothesis, be the same? As, then, Dr. Whewell exhorts those who have any difficulty in recognizing the distinction held by him between necessary and contingent truths to study geometry—a condition which I can assure him I have conscientiously fulfilled—I, in return, with equal confidence, exhort those who agree with him to study the general laws of association, being convinced that nothing more is requisite than a moderate familiarity with those laws to dispel the illusion which ascribes a peculiar necessity to our earliest inductions from experience and measures the possibility of things in themselves by the human capacity of conceiving them. . . .

The Science of Numbers Is Inductive

. . . What we have now asserted, however, cannot be received as universally true of deductive or demonstrative sciences until verified by being applied to the most remarkable of all those sciences, that of Numbers, the theory of the Calculus, Arithmetic and Algebra. It is harder to believe of the doctrines of this science than of any other, either that they are not truths *a priori* but experimental truths, or that their peculiar certainty is owing to their being not absolute but only conditional truths. This, therefore, is a case which merits examination apart, and the more so because on this subject we have a double set of doctrines to contend with: that of the *a priori* philosophers on one side; and, on the other, a theory the most opposite to theirs which was at one time very generally received and is still far from being altogether exploded among metaphysicians.

This theory attempts to solve the difficulty apparently inherent in the case by representing the propositions of the science of numbers as merely verbal and its processes as simple transformations of language, substitutions of one expression for another. The proposition, "Two and one is equal to three," according to these writers, is not a truth, is not the assertion of a really existing fact, but a definition of the word three, a statement that mankind have agreed to use the name three as a sign exactly equivalent to two and one, to call by the former name whatever is called by the other more clumsy phrase. According to this doctrine, the longest process in algebra is but a succession of changes in terminology by which equivalent expressions are substituted one for another, a series of translations of the same fact from one into another language; though how, after such a series of translations, the fact itself comes out changed (as when we demonstrate a new geometrical theorem by algebra) they have not explained, and it is a difficulty which is fatal to their theory.

It must be acknowledged that there are peculiarities in the processes of arithmetic and algebra which render the theory in question very plausible, and have not unnaturally made those sciences the stronghold of Nominalism. The doctrine that we can discover facts, detect the hidden processes of nature, by an artful manipulation of language is so contrary to common sense that a person must have made some advances in philosophy to believe it: men fly to so paradoxical a belief to avoid, as they think, some even greater difficulty which the vulgar do not see. What has led many to believe that reasoning is a mere verbal process is that no other theory seemed reconcilable with the nature of the science of numbers. For we do not carry any ideas along with us when we use the symbols of arithmetic or of algebra. In a geometrical demonstration we have a mental diagram, if not one on paper; AB, AC, are present to our imagination as lines, intersecting other lines, forming an angle with one another, and the like; but not so *a* and *b*. These may represent lines or any other magnitudes, but those magnitudes are never thought of; nothing is realized in our imagination but *a* and *b*. The ideas which, on the particular occasion, they happen to represent are banished from the mind during every intermediate part of the process between the beginning, when the premises are translated from things into signs, and the end, when the conclusion is translated back from signs into things. Nothing, then, being in the reasoner's mind but the symbols, what can seem more inadmissible than to contend that the reasoning process has to do with anything more? We seem to have come to one of Bacon's prerogative instances, an *experimentum crucis* on the nature of reasoning itself.

Nevertheless, it will appear on consideration that this apparently so decisive instance is no instance at all; that there is in every step of an arithmetical or algebraical calculation a real induction, a real inference of facts from facts; and that what disguises the induction is simply its comprehensive nature and the consequent extreme generality of the language. All numbers must be numbers of something; there are no such things as numbers in the abstract. *Ten* must mean ten bodies, or ten sounds, or ten beatings of the pulse. But though numbers must be numbers of something, they may be numbers of anything. Propositions, therefore, concerning numbers have the remarkable peculiarity that they are propositions concerning all things whatever, all objects, all existences of every kind known to our experience. All things possess quantity, consist of parts which can be numbered, and in that character possess all the properties which are called properties of numbers. That half of four is two must be true whatever the word four represents, whether four hours, four miles, or four pounds weight. We need only conceive a thing divided into four equal parts (and all things may be conceived as so divided) to be able to predicate of it every property of the number four, that is, every arithmetical proposition in which the number four stands on one side of the equation. Algebra extends the generalization still farther; every number represents that particular number of all things without distinction, but every algebraical symbol does more; it represents all numbers without distinction. As soon as we conceive a thing divided into equal parts, without knowing into what number of parts, we may call it a or x, and apply to it, without danger of error, every algebraical formula in the books. The proposition, $2(a + b) = 2a + 2b$, is a truth coextensive with all nature. Since, then, algebraical truths are true of all things whatever, and not, like those of geometry, true of lines only or of angles only, it is no wonder that the symbols should not excite in our minds ideas of any things in particular. When we demonstrate the forty-seventh proposition of Euclid, it is not necessary that the words should raise in us an image of all right-angled triangles, but only of some one right-angled triangle; so in algebra we need not, under the symbol a, picture to ourselves all things whatever, but only some one thing; why not, then, the letter itself? The mere written characters, a, b, x, y, z, serve as well for representatives of things in general as any more complex and apparently more concrete conception. That we are conscious of them, however, in their character of things and not of mere signs is evident from the fact that our whole process of reasoning is carried on by predicating of them the properties of things. In resolving an algebraic equation, by what rules do we proceed? By applying at each step to a, b, and x the proposition that equals added to equals make equals, that equals taken from equals leave equals, and other propositions founded on these two. These are not properties of language or of signs as such, but of magnitudes, which is as much as to say of all things. The inferences, therefore, which are successively drawn are inferences concerning things, not symbols; though as any things whatever will serve the turn, there is no necessity for keeping the idea of the thing at all distinct, and consequently the process of thought may, in this case, be allowed without danger to do what all processes of thought, when they have been performed often, will do if permitted, namely, to become entirely mechanical. Hence the general language of algebra comes to be used familiarly without exciting ideas, as all other general language is prone to do from mere habit, though in no other case than this can it be done with complete safety. But when we look back to see from whence the probative force of the process is derived, we find that at every single step, unless we suppose ourselves to be thinking and talking of the things and not the mere symbols, the evidence fails.

There is another circumstance which, still more than that which we have now mentioned, gives plausibility to the notion that the propositions of arithmetic and algebra are merely verbal. That is that when considered as propositions respecting things, they all have the appearance of being identical propositions. The assertion, "two and one is equal to three," considered as an assertion respecting objects, as for instance, "two pebbles and one pebble are equal to three pebbles," does not affirm equality between two collections of pebbles, but absolute identity. It affirms that if we put one pebble to two pebbles, those very pebbles are three. The objects, therefore, being the very same, and the mere assertion that "objects are themselves" being insignificant, it seems but natural to consider the proposition, "two and one is equal to three," as asserting mere identity of signification between the two names.

This, however, though it looks so plausible, will not bear examination. The expression "two pebbles and one pebble" and the expression "three pebbles" stand, indeed, for the same aggregation of objects, but they by no means stand for the same physical fact. They are names of the same objects, but of those objects in two different states; though they *de*note the same things, their *con*notation is different. Three pebbles in two separate parcels, and three pebbles in one parcel, do not make the same impression on our senses; and the assertion that the very same pebbles may by an alteration of place and arrangement be made to produce either the one set of sensations or the other, though a very familiar proposition, is not an identical one. It is a truth known to us by early and constant experience, an inductive truth, and such truths are the foundation of the science of number. The fundamental truths of that science all rest on the evidence of sense; they are proved by showing to our eyes and our fingers that any given number of objects—ten balls, for example—may by separation and rearrangement exhibit to our senses all the different sets of numbers the sums of which is equal to ten. All the improved methods of teaching arithmetic to children proceed on a knowledge of this fact. All who wish to carry the child's *mind* along with them in learning arithmetic, all who wish to teach numbers, and not mere ciphers—now teach it through the evidence of the senses, in the manner we have described. . . .

. . . The inductions of arithmetic are of two sorts: first, those which we have just expounded, such as "one and one are two," "two and one are three," etc., which may be called the definitions of the various numbers, in the improper or geometrical sense of the word *definition;* and secondly, the two following axioms: "The sums of equals are equal," "The differences of equals are equal." These two are sufficient, for the corresponding propositions respecting unequals may be proved from these by a *reductio ad absurdum.*

These axioms, and likewise the so-called definitions, are, as has already been said, results of induction, true of all objects whatever and, as it may seem, exactly true without the hypothetical assumption of unqualified truth where an approximation to it is all that exists. The conclusions, therefore, it will naturally be inferred, are exactly true, and the science of number is an exception to other demonstrative sciences in this, that the categorical certainty which is predicable of its demonstrations is independent of all hypothesis.

On more accurate investigation, however, it will be found that, even in this case, there is one hypothetical element in the ratiocination. In all propositions concerning numbers, a condition is implied without which none of them would be true, and that condition is an assumption which may be false. The condition is that $1 = 1$, that all the numbers are numbers of the same or of equal units. Let this be doubtful, and not one of the propositions of arithmetic will hold true. How can we know that one pound and one pound make two pounds, if one of the pounds may be troy and the other avoirdupois? They may not make two pounds of either, or of any weight. How can we know that a forty horse power is always equal to itself, unless we assume that all horses are of equal strength? It is certain that 1 is always equal in *number* to 1, and, where the mere number of objects, or of the parts of an object, without supposing them to be equivalent in any other respect, is all that is material, the conclusions of arithmetic, so far as they go to that alone, are true without mixture of hypothesis. There are such cases in statistics, as, for instance, an inquiry into the amount of the population of any country. It is indifferent to that inquiry whether they are grown people or children, strong or weak, tall or short; the only thing we want to ascertain is their number. But whenever, from equality or inequality of number, equality or inequality in any other respect is to be inferred, arithmetic carried into such inquiries becomes as hypothetical a science as geometry. All units must be assumed to be equal in that other respect, and this is never accurately true, for one actual pound weight is not exactly equal to another, nor one measured mile's length to another; a nicer balance or more accurate measuring instruments would always detect some difference.

What is commonly called mathematical certainty, therefore, which comprises the twofold conception of unconditional truth and perfect accuracy, is not an attribute of all mathematical truths, but of those only which relate to pure number, as distinguished from quantity in the more enlarged sense, and only so long as we abstain from supposing that the numbers are a precise index to actual quantities. The certainty usually ascribed to the conclusions of geometry and even to those of mechanics is nothing whatever but certainty of inference. We can have full assurance of particular results under particular suppositions, but we cannot have the same assurance that these suppositions are accurately true, nor that they include all the data which may exercise an influence over the result in any given instance. . . .

4

EMPIRICISM AND NECESSITY

Brand Blanshard

. . . ON THE FACE OF THINGS, necessity as clearly links some characters of experience as it is clearly absent between others. No one perhaps would claim to see not only that snow is white and leaves are green, but also that they *had* to have just these colors, and that their having any other is inconceivable. Yet such necessity does often seem to be present. If we start with two straight lines, arranged in any way we please, we can see that they not only do not, but cannot, enclose a space. If we start with a semi-circle and, using the diameter as a base, inscribe a triangle in it, we can see, if we attend carefully to the conditions, that the triangle *must* be right-angled. Between these two extremes, in one of which necessity seems clearly absent and in the other as clearly present, there are many intermediate cases. "Matter gravitates," "while there is life there is hope"; if it is difficult to say that either of these is self-evident, one also hesitates to say that they express nothing but bare conjunction; they fall somewhere between.

The empiricist agrees that we must start with such data as these, and he offers a theory which at first sight explains them with a persuasive neatness and completeness. Necessity, he says, is nothing whatever but habituation; and he shows this by pointing to a correlation between degree of certainty and degree of fixity in habit. Are leaves necessarily green? Of course not. How can we be so sure they are not? Because we have not uniformly seen them so: we have often seen them brown or red. Is snow necessarily white? We have never seen it any other color, to be sure; but we have often seen things otherwise like it—powdery substances of various kinds—that were red or blue or yellow, and it is perfectly easy

---

[This selection consists of Sections 2-8 of Chapter XXVIII of Blanshard's *The Nature of Thought*, published by George Allen and Unwin, Ltd., in 1939. It is here reprinted with the kind permission of the author and the publisher.]

to imagine these colors as belonging to snow also. In neither of these propositions, then, is there any necessity. But it begins to awake as we approximate universality. Is hopefulness an attribute of human life? It usually is—so usually that we feel there is point in the proverb; yet we may have known in ourselves, or observed in others, some total eclipse of hope which left the saying forever less than certain. Does all matter gravitate? We may be pretty confident that it does; we have never, as in the previous case, known an exception; yet our notion of matter is somewhat foggy, and its kinds sharply limited in our experience; so it seems not inconceivable that somewhere and somehow the rule should be violated. Can two straight lines enclose a space? No, we say; the thing is impossible. We seem to reach here the ultimate in the way of certainty. But the empiricist points out that at the same time we reach the ultimate firmness in habitual connection. This statement about the lines "receives confirmation in almost every instant of our lives, since we cannot look at any two straight lines which intersect one another without seeing that from that point they continue to diverge more and more. Experimental proof crowds in upon us in . . . endless profusion, without one instance in which there can be even a suspicion of an exception. . . ." Thus, if we follow the varying degrees of apparent necessity, we find another variant that dogs them like a shadow. When A and B sometimes appear together and sometimes not, we say there is no necessity. When they appear together so constantly that exceptions are rare and doubtful, there is a proverbial or virtual necessity. When they are connected so uniformly that every waking moment exemplifies them anew without a single reported exception, their necessity is complete; we call the proposition certain or self-evident. But is it not plain to the reflective mind that this necessity is no iron linkage in the facts but simply a fixed association in us? A and B have come to us so regularly together that we can no longer think of them as separated; and because we cannot think them so, we say they cannot *be* so.

To this, the central position of empiricism, an addition was made by Spencer that for many increased its plausibility. The experience that gave rise to certainty was not, he said, our own personal experience only, but the experience of the entire race. This immense extension of the learning period gives room for a far deeper and firmer fixity in habit. Behind those laws of logic that are the most transparent certainties we possess, there is now seen to be the unvarying experience of thousands of generations.

> The universal law that, other things equal, the cohesion of psychical states is proportionate to the frequency with which they have followed one another in experience, supplies an explanation for the so-called "forms of thought," as soon as it is supplemented by the law that habitual psychical successions entail some hereditary tendency to such successions, which,

under persistent conditions, will become cumulative in generation after generation . . . if there exist certain external relations which are experienced by all organisms at all instants of their waking lives—relations which are absolutely constant, absolutely universal—there will be established answering internal relations that are absolutely constant, absolutely universal.

The attempt of empiricism to do away with necessity has often been criticized, and I think decisively. Nevertheless it is a ghost that will not down. It is accepted, and will no doubt continue to be accepted, by many who, without formulating or examining it explicitly, feel that some such position is a plain dictate of common sense. It is well, therefore, to look into it again.

(1) The first remark that suggests itself is that the pretty parallel between habituation and apparent necessity will not stand. There are some connections that are common and unvarying, to which exceptions are conceived easily; on the other hand, certain connections that we have experienced seldom, or perhaps only once, present themselves as completely necessary. Whenever we have put our hand in water or any other fluid, we may have experienced it as wet. Our ancestors for untold generations may similarly have experienced it as wet. Is it therefore inconceivable that when we put our hand in water, we should experience, not wetting, but a dry burn? The question is not, of course, one of probability, or even of practical possibility, but of conceivability. And the answer is that such a novelty is not even difficult to conceive. I can quite easily conceive that on some occasion burning rather than wetting should be conjoined with the other properties of water. On the other hand, a clever boy who is studying geometry for the first time and who comes to the proposition about the triangle inscribed in the semi-circle may see at his very first reading, that, given these conditions, just this proposition *must* follow. All this is the opposite of what it should be if certainty rests on frequency.

It may be replied that although the demonstration as a whole is new to the schoolboy, the individual steps are not, and that each step is the sort of insight that, according to Mill and Spencer, is impressed upon our minds by almost every waking experience. But this defence is doubly inadequate. In the first place, even if the individual steps are familiar, the particular combination of them that now produces the certainty is new, and hence if certainty is a function of frequency, it is in this case unaccountable. Secondly, the individual steps are by no means all of the kind that are impressed at every glance. It is easy to draw figures which ordinary experience never presents, but which have relations among their parts—for example, equality in length or area—that are obvious at the first careful scrutiny. Draw a square with intersecting diagonals, and even the uninstructed can reel off propositions about it with a singularly complete confidence: the halves of the diagonals are equal; the central angles are equal; the triangles are equal; and so on. Is this confidence to be accounted for by the number of times oneself or one's ancestors— savages for the most part—have encountered such figures in the past, and, examining them, have seen these things to hold? That seems incredible.

(2) Again, when an unbroken experience is claimed for the connections of greatest necessity, the claim runs far beyond verifiable fact. What ground have I, on empiricist principles, for supposing that, in respect to a geometrical figure, the experience of all my ancestors *has* been precisely like mine? I cannot enter into their experience; I cannot learn it by word of mouth; the vast majority of them have left no record of any kind. The answer, of course, is that I am assuming nature to be uniform; I am assuming that what happens to me under certain conditions is a safe guide to what happened to others under similar conditions. The question becomes, what is the ground of this assumption? What right have I to believe that what happens at one time is a guide to what happens at other times, that like conditions will give like results? To this the empiricist must answer that the belief in uniformity is itself a result of association. A has so constantly come along with B, C has so constantly come with D, E with F, and so on, that I am forced to believe that for everything there is a similar condition from which it invariably follows. It is evident that if the empiricist is to establish the long runs of experience required to show how any proposition came to be regarded as necessary, he must establish them, not directly, but through appeal to this law of uniformity. Has he a right to appeal to this law? Notoriously he has not.

It is an interesting exercise in logic to recount the ways in which the empiricist begs the question in his argument here. The point at issue is whether nature is uniform in the sense that would give one a right to hold that what is happening now would hold, under like conditions, everywhere and always. What precisely is under dispute is thus the right to use a limited experience as a guide to what holds generally. And the empiricist proposes to prove this right by arguing that since in his own limited experience, nature has proved uniform, therefore it must be so generally. But it is obvious that his argument holds only if the principle he is supposed to prove is used to prove itself. That principle must be somehow established, but consider his difficulties in establishing it.

(i) He is in a dilemma. If he claims that he has an inside track to the truth of the principle, then he is admitting that the empirical method is not the only means to certainty, and with this the empiricist view of necessity is abandoned. On the other hand, if he sticks to his guns and insists on an empirical proof of the principle, he can never prove it at all, for since it is itself the principle on which proof must proceed, whatever doubt attaches to it will attach equally to its proof. Thus in either case the attempt at proof fails.

(ii) It fails in another way. The argument starts by saying that uniformity has been found in one's own limited experience. But is this strictly true? "There can be no doubt whatsoever that, while much in our experience suggests regularity of sequence, much suggests irregularity also. Unsupported apples fall regularly to the ground; but some sparks fly upwards. The seasons come and go in a stately, inevitable succession, but the wind (even now) appears to blow where it lists. The *prima facie* evidence is therefore conflicting." Of course we believe that when the sparks fly upward they are secretly obeying, not violating, the law of gravitation, and that even in the blowing of the winds there is order. But this is not what we ought to believe if our beliefs are compound photographs of what nature actually presents to us, for what it does present is something far more chaotic. Once the conviction of uniformity is present to guide our search and arouse suspicion of the outward show, we overlook these non-uniformities, or look beneath the surface till uniformity comes to light. But if, to get the conviction, we had to wait till nature forced it on us, we should never reach it at all.

(iii) And it is not only that we override non-uniformities in what, for the empiricist, is an unaccountably high-handed way; we also stretch absurdly the runs of uniformity. In arguing that nature is generally uniform we point to many particular sequences: when the heart stops beating, life invariably ceases; smallpox is invariably produced by a bacillus; the stars move day by day invariably in their orbits. On particular sequences of this sort, we found our general law. But how do we know that these sequences are uniform? What proportion of the cases in which the stars have moved, or smallpox has broken out, or hearts have stopped, have we actually observed? Only a proportion microscopically small; yet we are confident that the sequence is regular. Why? Clearly because we have fallen back on the general law to help us establish the particular sequence. Our real argument is in two stages, and runs as follows: Since under the same conditions the same thing happens always, it is safe to say that all cases of smallpox follow the law of the relatively few cases actually observed; that is the first stage, which establishes the particular sequence. The second is: since smallpox shows a regular behavior, and so also do stopping hearts and moving stars and all the rest, we must suppose that everything shows similarly regular behavior. But what logic! We have established the general law by appealing to the particular sequences; but then to establish the particular sequences we have had to use the general law. The argument sums up to zero.

(iv) The vicious circularity of the argument may be brought out in yet another way. When the empiricist offers his argument for the law of uniformity, he commonly supposes that he is offering the same kind of argument that is offered for a law of science. He sees that scientists are continually establishing laws by citing particular cases, and to himself he seems to be doing the same thing when he uses these laws as a springboard for a further leap and, in the second stage of the argument, contends that since some events are governed by law, all are so governed. But the two arguments are not parallel. The arguments of the scientist is: *assuming that there is some law governing the phenomenon I am studying,* the connection I have now uncovered must be it. The parallel argument in the second stage would be: assuming that all events occur lawfully, then from the lawful events I have observed I may infer that all events occur lawfully. That is nonsense, because the assumption one has to make is the conclusion one has to prove. The scientist, who is not raising ultimate questions, begins with the frank, unargued assumption of uniformity, and makes out his laws with the help of it. But the empiricist, who is not entitled to this same assumption, since it is the point he has to establish, finds himself checkmated from the start.

(3) But apart from these circularities, the empiricist's case is fatally weak. He holds that in the widest generalizations, such as the law of uniformity and the laws of logic, we should have the highest degree of certainty; but if his account of how we reach such certainty is sound, these generalizations must possess, not more certainty than those they rest on, but less.

Consider the way in which we are supposed to arrive at them. We have found A accompanied by B a certain number of times, C by D, E by F, and so on. Now when we make the leap of thought from a few cases of A-B to the rule A-B, we are making a leap from something we are sure of to something we are by no means sure of; for it must be remembered that in making the leap we cannot rely on the rule that what happens once will, in like conditions, happen always; that rule is still ahead. The only way in which the general rule A-B can really be established is by complete enumeration, and to leap to it from an enumeration less than complete is to pass into the realm of conjecture. Now in reaching laws of wider generality, such as the uniformity of nature, which is really a law to the effect that everything is governed by law, we are making another leap, as we have seen; only this time it is not from particular events but from special laws. And just as the first leap was a leap into comparative uncertainty, so also is the second; but whereas the first was a leap from the certain to the uncertain, the second is a leap from a set of uncertainties to a still greater uncertainty. If the particular laws established by simple enumeration hold only doubtfully, is it not obvious that the more general law which says that *all* these laws hold without exception must be far more doubtful still? Yet it is precisely these laws of greatest generality, such as the law of uniformity and the laws of logic, which the empiricist says are the most certain of all. His scale of certainties is thus the opposite of what his method will justify.

The curious conclusion is thus forced upon us that every argument the empiricist uses is bound to be invalid. Mill saw that merely to assert what one has observed is not argument; argument must go beyond the premises to something new. But this something new can never be certain, since it has neither been given in experience already, nor is there any certain law which would enable us to go beyond experience. Thus in admitting inference at all, Mill is exceeding the bounds of empiricism, since this process

> involves a presupposition that he has not reflected upon; it implies that the new knowledge is not the result of experience, and must therefore be due to the inferring process itself. Thus the conclusion is unavoidable that in some important sense a mental process which is not experience can originate knowledge. It is futile to object that the mind merely works on the material which is given in experience, for this implies that we are able in the process to get on to new knowledge not in the material. This, then, must be due to the mental process which brings the new result. Such origination contradicts the very foundation of an empirical philosophy like that of Locke and Mill.[1]

(4) We have already pointed out that what experience presses upon us is far from being the mass of orderly sequences which the empiricist nevertheless believes in. The half-conscious process by which he turns this raw material into grist for his mill illustrates again how impossible it is to square his theory with the actual procedure of thought.

According to the empiricist, when we find something holding of certain cases we normally reason that the same will hold in other cases resembling them in relevant respects. When he comes to examine the syllogistic classic—All men are mortal; Socrates is a man; therefore Socrates is mortal—he holds that the real argument is this: we have known many particular cases of men's dying; Socrates resembles these men in all essential respects; hence he resembles them in the liability to death. "From instances which we have observed, we feel warranted in concluding that what we have found true in those instances holds *in all similar ones,* past, present, and future." If such similarity is to be of use, it must mean, not any similarity, but relevant similarity. Has the empiricist an adequate criterion for this? Unfortunately, no.

Suppose that a boy is learning to demonstrate some property of a circle. This property depends, of course, on the form of the figure, its circularity; and whether the circles he has observed are big or little, whether they are red or green, whether they are embodied in chalk or ink or barrel-hoops—such things he takes as making no difference. How,

---

1. Cook Wilson, *Statement and Inference,* Vol. II, p. 417, see also pp. 609-610.

according to the empiricist, does he *know* that they make no difference, and that the property follows from the circularity alone? The only way is by a long-continued eliminatory experience of individual cases. If the circles he has worked with happen to be red circles, he will have no means of knowing that the redness is not essential to the property in question; indeed he will hold that it *is* essential until he finds that circles of other colors have this property too. If he has found a property to hold of a circle of a certain size, he has no reason to suppose it will hold of a circle of a larger size until he has found in particular cases that it does. Nothing that is presented along with the property is irrelevant to it until he or nature has contrived cases in which the two can be dissociated.

Now we are not nearly so stupid as this. A mind of normal intelligence does not have to wait for experience of circles of various sizes and colors in order to see that these things are irrelevant; it penetrates straight through to the connection between circularity and the property entailed. Grasping the self-evident link between form and property, it is able to lop off at a stroke the whole mass of attendant irrelevancies, actual or possible. It does not have to try its conclusion with circles of different sizes, because it sees that circularity is in the nature of the case independent of change in size; it does not have to exhaust the series of colors, because it can see that color as such has nothing to do with the figure. In short, it does not have to stand and wait humbly for experiences to supply it with standards, for it has standards of its own to which it demands, and confidently expects, that nature will conform. "Only in the light of ideals can we distinguish between what is relevant and irrelevant to any natural transformation,"[2] and it is clear that the ideals of relevance we use are not mere habits.

Is the experience of conjunction, then, of no value in revealing necessary connections? To say this would be going much too far. The empiricist is right when he holds that without the experience of particular cases we should have no knowledge at all. If one were to take the keenest of mathematical minds, and by some unheard-of process imprison it at the beginning within its own intelligence, cutting off all access to the world of sensible things, it would never arrive even at $2 + 2 = 4$. So much we may concede to the empiricist. We may concede more. Not only perceptual experience, but a repetition of experiences, is often required to bring a necessary connection to light. Frequently it is only after a long course of finding characters in conjunction that we come to see in their togetherness something more than conjunction; and similarly it may only be through finding that certain things never come together that we begin to realize that they *cannot* come together, because they

---

2. Morris Cohen, *Reason and Nature,* p. 205.

are incompatible. And to the empiricist it has sometimes seemed perverse that one should admit so much, and yet refuse to go with him the whole way. But between the admissions we have made to him and the conclusion that we draw there is an immense interval that he is inclined to bridge by a confusion. He mistakes acquiring knowledge *through* experience for acquiring it *from* experience. The two are radically different. The child who learns that his puppy is pleased when its tail wags is learning something *from* experience. So far as we can see, there is no intrinsic necessity in a puppy's expressing his pleasure in this particular way, and if the child connects the two, it is simply and solely because the two happen to occur together. There is nothing in the conjunction to make him certain that it would repeat itself in another case; and of course when he comes to the cat, it conspicuously fails to repeat itself. All this is otherwise in learning *through* experience. When the child, in pushing the balls about on the rods of his counting frame, first finds that two groups of three count up to six, the result may be as much a matter of mere conjunction as the pleasure and the wagging tail. He may need to see the truth illustrated in various other materials—apples, clothespins, and blocks—before he really seizes it. But could anyone say that when he does seize it, he finds it, like the other, a mere conjunction, and liable, like it, to breakage in the next case he comes to? Surely this is wide of the mark. In both, experience is admittedly equally necessary; but in the one, it furnishes the whole ground for the insight, in the other, the occasion only; in the one, sense experience is the source of the rule, in the other merely its vehicle; in the one, the number of cases observed is an essential point, in the other, it is unimportant; in the one, knowledge comes *from* experience; in the other, *through* it. . . .

5

THE A PRIORI

A. J. Ayer

Empiricism and Rationalism

. . . HAVING ADMITTED that we are empiricists, we must now deal with
the objection that is commonly brought against all forms of empiricism;
the objection, namely, that it is impossible on empiricist principles to
account for our knowledge of necessary truths. For, as Hume conclusively showed, no general proposition whose validity is subject to the
test of actual experience can ever be logically certain. No matter how
often it is verified in practice, there still remains the possibility that it
will be confuted on some future occasion. The fact that a law has been
substantiated in $n - 1$ cases affords no logical guarantee that it will be
substantiated in the nth case also, no matter how large we take n to be.
And this means that no general proposition referring to a matter of fact
can ever be shown to be necessarily and universally true. It can at best
be a probable hypothesis. And this, we shall find, applies not only to
general propositions, but to all propositions which have a factual content. They can none of them ever become logically certain. This conclusion, which we shall elaborate later on, is one which must be accepted
by every consistent empiricist. It is often thought to involve him in complete scepticism; but this is not the case. For the fact that the validity of
a proposition cannot be logically guaranteed in no way entails that it is
irrational for us to believe it. On the contrary, what is irrational is to
look for a guarantee where none can be forthcoming; to demand certainty where probability is all that is obtainable. We have already remarked upon this, in referring to the work of Hume. And we shall make

[This selection is Chapter IV, except for small omissions, of Ayer's *Language,
Truth and Logic,* published in Great Britain by Victor Gollancz, Ltd., and in the
United States by Dover Publications, Inc. It is here reprinted with the kind permission of
Professor Ayer and the publishers.]

the point clearer when we come to treat of probability, in explaining the use which we make of empirical propositions. We shall discover that there is nothing perverse or paradoxical about the view that all the "truths" of science and common sense are hypotheses; and consequently that the fact that it involves this view constitutes no objection to the empiricist thesis.

Where the empiricist does encounter difficulty is in connection with the truths of formal logic and mathematics. For whereas a scientific generalization is readily admitted to be fallible, the truths of mathematics and logic appear to everyone to be necessary and certain. But if empiricism is correct no proposition which has a factual content can be necessary or certain. Accordingly the empiricist must deal with the truths of logic and mathematics in one of the two following ways: he must say either that they are not necessary truths, in which case he must account for the universal conviction that they are; or he must say that they have no factual content, and then he must explain how a proposition which is empty of all factual content can be true and useful and surprising.

If neither of these courses proves satisfactory, we shall be obliged to give way to rationalism. We shall be obliged to admit that there are some truths about the world which we can know independently of experience; that there are some properties which we can ascribe to all objects, even though we cannot conceivably observe that all objects have them. And we shall have to accept it as a mysterious inexplicable fact that our thought has this power to reveal to us authoritatively the nature of objects which we have never observed. Or else we must accept the Kantian explanation which, apart from the epistemological difficulties which we have already touched on, only pushes the mystery a stage further back.

It is clear that any such concession to rationalism would upset the main argument of this book. For the admission that there were some facts about the world which could be known independently of experience would be incompatible with our fundamental contention that a sentence says nothing unless it is empirically verifiable. And thus the whole force of our attack on metaphysics would be destroyed. It is vital, therefore, for us to be able to show that one or other of the empiricist accounts of the propositions of logic and mathematics is correct. If we are successful in this, we shall have destroyed the foundations of rationalism. For the fundamental tenet of rationalism is that thought is an independent source of knowledge, and is moreover a more trustworthy source of knowledge than experience; indeed some rationalists have gone so far as to say that thought is the only source of knowledge. And the ground for this view is simply that the only necessary truths about the world which are known to us are known through thought and not through experience. So that if we can show either that the truths in question are not necessary or that they are not "truths about the world," we shall be taking away the support on which rationalism rests. We shall be making good the empiricist contention that there are no "truths of reason" which refer to matters of fact.

The course of maintaining that the truths of logic and mathematics are not necessary or certain was adopted by Mill. He maintained that these propositions were inductive generalizations based on an extremely large number of instances. The fact that the number of supporting instances was so very large accounted, in his view, for our believing these generalizations to be necessarily and universally true. The evidence in their favor was so strong that it seemed incredible to us that a contrary instance should ever arise. Nevertheless it was in principle possible for such generalizations to be confuted. They were highly probable, but, being inductive generalizations, they were not certain. The difference between them and the hypotheses of natural science was a difference in degree and not in kind. Experience gave us very good reason to suppose that a "truth" of mathematics or logic was true universally; but we were not possessed of a guarantee. For these "truths" were only empirical hypotheses which had worked particularly well in the past; and, like all empirical hypotheses, they were theoretically fallible.

I do not think that this solution of the empiricist's difficulty with regard to the propositions of logic and mathematics is acceptable. In discussing it, it is necessary to make a distinction which is perhaps already enshrined in Kant's famous dictum that, although there can be no doubt that all our knowledge begins with experience, it does not follow that it all arises out of experience.[1] When we say that the truths of logic are known independently of experience, we are not of course saying that they are innate, in the sense that we are born knowing them. It is obvious that mathematics and logic have to be learned in the same way as chemistry and history have to be learned. Nor are we denying that the first person to discover a given logical or mathematical truth was led to it by an inductive procedure. It is very probable, for example, that the principle of the syllogism was formulated not before but after the validity of syllogistic reasoning had been observed in a number of particular cases. What we are discussing, however, when we say that the logical and mathematical truths are known independently of experience, is not a historical question concerning the way in which these truths were originally discovered, nor a psychological question concerning the way in which each of us comes to learn them, but an epistemological question. The contention of Mill's which we reject is that the propositions of logic and mathematics have the same status as empirical hypotheses; that their validity is determined in the same way. We maintain that they are independent of experience in the sense that they do not owe their validity to empirical verification. We may come to discover

---

1. *Critique of Pure Reason,* 2nd ed., Introduction, section i. (See p. 25, above.)

them through an inductive process; but once we have apprehended them we see that they are necessarily true, that they hold good for every conceivable instance. And this serves to distinguish them from empirical generalizations. For we know that a proposition whose validity depends upon experience cannot be seen to be necessarily and universally true.

In rejecting Mill's theory, we are obliged to be somewhat dogmatic. We can do no more than state the issue clearly and then trust that his contention will be seen to be discrepant with the relevant logical facts. The following considerations may serve to show that of the two ways of dealing with logic and mathematics which are open to the empiricist, the one which Mill adopted is not the one which is correct.

The Irrefutability of the Proposition of Mathematics and Logic

The best way to substantiate our assertion that the truths of formal logic and pure mathematics are necessarily true is to examine cases in which they might seem to be confuted. It might easily happen, for example, that when I came to count what I had taken to be five pairs of objects, I found that they amounted only to nine. And if I wished to mislead people I might say that on this occasion twice five was not ten. But in that case I should not be using the complex sign "$2 \times 5 = 10$" in the way in which it is ordinarily used. I should be taking it not as the expression of a purely mathematical proposition, but as the expression of an empirical generalization, to the effect that whenever I counted what appeared to me to be five pairs of objects I discovered that they were ten in number. This generalization may very well be false. But if it proved false in a given case, one would not say that the mathematical proposition "$2 \times 5 = 10$" had been confuted. One would say that I was wrong in supposing that there were five pairs of objects to start with, or that one of the objects had been taken away while I was counting, or that two of them had coalesced, or that I had counted wrongly. One would adopt as an explanation whatever empirical hypothesis fitted in best with the accredited facts. The one explanation which would in no circumstances be adopted is that ten is not always the product of two and five.

To take another example: if what appears to be a Euclidean triangle is found by measurement not to have angles totalling 180 degrees, we do not say that we have met with an instance which invalidates the mathematical proposition that the sum of the three angles of a Euclidean triangle is 180 degrees. We say that we have measured wrongly, or, more probably, that the triangle we have been measuring is not Euclidean. And this is our procedure in every case in which a mathematical truth might appear to be confuted. We always preserve its validity by adopting some other explanation of the occurrence.

The same thing applies to the principles of formal logic. We may take an example relating to the so-called law of excluded middle, which states that a proposition must be either true or false, or, in other words, that it is impossible that a proposition and its contradictory should neither of them be true. One might suppose that a proposition of the form "*x* has stopped doing *y*" would in certain cases constitute an exception to this law. For instance, if my friend has never yet written to me, it seems fair to say that it is neither true nor false that he has stopped writing to me. But in fact one would refuse to accept such an instance as an invalidation of the law of excluded middle. One would point out that the proposition "My friend has stopped writing to me" is not a simple proposition, but the conjunction of the two propositions "My friend wrote to me in the past" and "My friend does not write to me now": and, furthermore, that the proposition "My friend has not stopped writing to me" is not, as it appears to be, contradictory to "My friend has stopped writing to me," but only contrary to it. For it means "My friend wrote to me in the past, and he still writes to me." When, therefore, we say that such a proposition as "My friend has stopped writing to me" is sometimes neither true nor false, we are speaking inaccurately. For we seem to be saying that neither it nor its contradictory is true. Whereas what we mean, or anyhow should mean, is that neither it nor its apparent contradictory is true. And its apparent contradictory is really only its contrary. Thus we preserve the law of excluded middle by showing that the negating of a sentence does not always yield the contradictory of the proposition originally expressed.

There is no need to give further examples. Whatever instance we care to take, we shall always find that the situations in which a logical or mathematical principle might appear to be confuted are accounted for in such a way as to leave the principle unassailed. And this indicates that Mill was wrong in supposing that a situation could arise which would overthrow a mathematical truth. The principles of logic and mathematics are true universally simply because we never allow them to be anything else. And the reason for this is that we cannot abandon them without contradicting ourselves, without sinning against the rules which govern the use of language, and so making our utterances self-stultifying. In other words, the truths of logic and mathematics are analytic propositions or tautologies. In saying this we are making what will be held to be an extremely controversial statement, and we must now proceed to make its implications clear.

The Nature of Analytic Propositions

The most familiar definition of an analytic proposition, or judgement, as he called it, is that given by Kant. He said[2] that an analytic judgement was one in which the predicate B belonged to the subject A as something which was covertly contained in the concept of A. He contrasted analytic with synthetic judgements, in which the predicate B lay outside the subject A, although it did stand in connection with it. Analytic judgements, he explains, "add nothing through the predicate to the concept of the subject, but merely break it up into those constituent concepts that have all along been thought in it, although confusedly." Synthetic judgements, on the other hand, "add to the concept of the subject a predicate which has not been in any wise thought in it, and which no analysis could possibly extract from it." Kant gives "all bodies are extended" as an example of an analytic judgement, on the ground that the required predicate can be extracted from the concept of "body," "in accordance with the principle of contradiction"; as an example of a synthetic judgement, he gives "all bodies are heavy." He refers also to "7 + 5 = 12" as a synthetic judgement, on the ground that the concept of twelve is by no means already thought in merely thinking the union of seven and five. And he appears to regard this as tantamount to saying that the judgement does not rest on the principle of contradiction alone. He holds, also, that through analytic judgements our knowledge is not extended as it is through synthetic judgements. For in analytic judgements "the concept which I already have is merely set forth and made intelligible to me."

I think that this is a fair summary of Kant's account of the distinction between analytic and synthetic propositions, but I do not think that it succeeds in making the distinction clear. For even if we pass over the difficulties which arise out of the use of the vague term "concept," and the unwarranted assumption that every judgement, as well as every German or English sentence, can be said to have a subject and a predicate, there remains still this crucial defect. Kant does not give one straightforward criterion for distinguishing between analytic and synthetic propositions; he gives two distinct criteria, which are by no means equivalent. Thus his ground for holding that the proposition "7 + 5 = 12" is synthetic is, as we have seen, that the subjective intension of "7 + 5" does not comprise the subjective intension of "12"; whereas his ground for holding that "all bodies are extended" is an analytic proposition is that it rests on the principle of contradiction alone. That is, he employs

2. *Critique of Pure Reason*, 2nd ed., Introduction, sections iv and v. (See pp. 30 ff., above.)

a psychological criterion in the first of these examples, and a logical criterion in the second, and takes their equivalence for granted. But, in fact, a proposition which is synthetic according to the former criterion may very well be analytic according to the latter. For, as we have already pointed out, it is possible for symbols to be synonymous without having the same intensional meaning for anyone: and accordingly from the fact that one can think of the sum of seven and five without necessarily thinking of twelve, it by no means follows that the proposition "7 + 5 = 12" can be denied without self-contradiction. From the rest of his argument, it is clear that it is this logical proposition, and not any psychological proposition, that Kant is really anxious to establish. His use of the psychological criterion leads him to think that he has established it, when he has not.

I think that we can preserve the logical import of Kant's distinction between analytic and synthetic propositions, while avoiding the confusions which mar his actual account of it, if we say that a proposition is analytic when its validity depends solely on the definitions of the symbols it contains, and synthetic when its validity is determined by the facts of experience. Thus, the proposition "There are ants which have established a system of slavery" is a synthetic proposition. For we cannot tell whether it is true or false merely by considering the definitions of the symbols which constitute it. We have to resort to actual observation of the behavior of ants. On the other hand, the proposition "Either some ants are parasitic or none are" is an analytic proposition. For one need not resort to observation to discover that there either are or are not ants which are parasitic. If one knows what is the function of the words "either," "or," and "not," then one can see that any proposition of the form "Either p is true or p is not true" is valid, independently of experience. Accordingly, all such propositions are analytic.

It is to be noticed that the proposition "Either some ants are parasitic or none are" provides no information whatsoever about the behavior of ants, or, indeed, about any matter of fact. And this applies to all analytic propositions. They none of them provide any information about any matter of fact. In other words, they are entirely devoid of factual content. And it is for this reason that no experience can confute them.

When we say that analytic propositions are devoid of factual content, and consequently that they say nothing, we are not suggesting that they are senseless in the way that metaphysical utterances are senseless. For, although they give us no information about any empirical situation, they do enlighten us by illustrating the way in which we use certain symbols. Thus if I say, "Nothing can be colored in different ways at the same time with respect to the same part of itself," I am not saying anything about the properties of any actual thing; but I am not talking nonsense. I am expressing an analytic proposition, which records our determination to call a color expanse which differs in quality from a neighboring color expanse a different part of a given thing. In other words, I am simply calling attention to the implications of a certain linguistic usage. Similarly, in saying that if all Bretons are Frenchmen, and all Frenchmen Europeans, then all Bretons are Europeans, I am not describing any matter of fact. But I am showing that in the statement that all Bretons are Frenchmen, and all Frenchmen Europeans, the further statement that all Bretons are Europeans is implicitly contained. And I am thereby indicating the convention which governs our usage of the words "if" and "all."

We see, then, that there is a sense in which analytic propositions do give us new knowledge. They call attention to linguistic usages, of which we might otherwise not be conscious, and they reveal unsuspected implications in our assertions and beliefs. But we can see also that there is a sense in which they may be said to add nothing to our knowledge. For they tell us only what we may be said to know already. Thus, if I know that the existence of May Queens is a relic of tree-worship, and I discover that May Queens still exist in England, I can employ the tautology "If p implies q, and p is true, q is true" to show that there still exists a relic of tree-worship in England. But in saying that there are still May Queens in England, and that the existence of May Queens is a relic of tree-worship, I have already asserted the existence in England of a relic of tree-worship. The use of the tautology does, indeed, enable me to make this concealed assertion explicit. But it does not provide me with any new knowledge, in the sense in which empirical evidence that the election of May Queens had been forbidden by law would provide me with new knowledge. If one had to set forth all the information one possessed, with regard to matters of fact, one would not write down any analytic propositions. But one would make use of analytic propositions in compiling one's encyclopedia, and would thus come to include propositions which one would otherwise have overlooked. And, besides enabling one to make one's list of information complete, the formulation of analytic propositions would enable one to make sure that the synthetic propositions of which the list was composed formed a self-consistent system. By showing which ways of combining propositions resulted in contradictions, they would prevent one from including incompatible propositions and so making the list self-stultifying. But in so far as we had actually used such words as "all" and "or" and "not" without falling into self-contradiction, we might be said already to know what was revealed in the formulation of analytic propositions illustrating the rules which govern our usage of these logical particles. So that here again we are justified in saying that analytic propositions do not increase our knowledge. . . .

The Propositions of Geometry

The mathematical propositions which one might most pardonably suppose to be synthetic are the propositions of geometry. For it is natural for us to think, as Kant thought, that geometry is the study of the properties of physical space, and consequently that its propositions have factual content. And if we believe this, and also recognize that the truths of geometry are necessary and certain, then we may be inclined to accept Kant's hypothesis that space is the form of intuition of our outer sense, a form imposed by us on the matter of sensation, as the only possible explanation of our *a priori* knowledge of these synthetic propositions. But while the view that pure geometry is concerned with physical space was plausible enough in Kant's day, when the geometry of Euclid was the only geometry known, the subsequent invention of non-Euclidean geometries has shown it to be mistaken. We see now that the axioms of a geometry are simply definitions, and that the theorems of a geometry are simply the logical consequences of these definitions.[3] A geometry is not in itself about physical space; in itself it cannot be said to be "about" anything. But we can use a geometry to reason about physical space. That is to say, once we have given the axioms a physical interpretation, we can proceed to apply the theorems to the objects which satisfy the axioms. Whether a geometry can be applied to the actual physical world or not, is an empirical question which falls outside the scope of the geometry itself. There is no sense, therefore, in asking which of the various geometries known to us are false and which are true. In so far as they are all free from contradiction, they are all true. What one can ask is which of them is the most useful on any given occasion, which of them can be applied most easily and most fruitfully to an actual empirical situation. But the proposition which states that a certain application of a geometry is possible is not itself a proposition of that geometry. All that the geometry itself tells us is that if anything can be brought under the definitions, it will also satisfy the theorems. It is therefore a purely logical system, and its propositions are purely analytic propositions.

It might be objected that the use made of diagrams in geometrical treatises shows that geometrical reasoning is not purely abstract and logical, but depends on our intuition of the properties of figures. In fact, however, the use of diagrams is not essential to completely rigorous geometry. The diagrams are introduced as an aid to our reason. They provide us with a particular application of the geometry, and so assist us to perceive the more general truth that the axioms of the geometry

3. Cf. H. Poincaré, *La Science et l'Hypothèse*, Part II, Chapter iii.

involve certain consequences. But the fact that most of us need the help of an example to make us aware of those consequences does not show that the relation between them and the axioms is not a purely logical relation. It shows merely that our intellects are unequal to the task of carrying out very abstract processes of reasoning without the assistance of intuition. In other words, it has no bearing on the nature of geometrical propositions, but is simply an empirical fact about ourselves. Moreover, the appeal to intuition, though generally of psychological value, is also a source of danger to the geometer. He is tempted to make assumptions which are accidentally true of the particular figure he is taking as an illustration, but do not follow from his axioms. It has, indeed, been shown that Euclid himself was guilty of this, and consequently that the presence of the figure is essential to some of his proofs.[4] This shows that his system is not, as he presents it, completely rigorous, although of course it can be made so. It does not show that the presence of the figure is essential to a truly rigorous geometrical proof. To suppose that it did would be to take as a necessary feature of all geometries what is really only an incidental defect in one particular geometrical system.

We conclude, then, that the propositions of pure geometry are analytic. And this leads us to reject Kant's hypothesis that geometry deals with the form of intuition of our outer sense. For the ground for this hypothesis was that it alone explained how the propositions of geometry could be both true *a priori* and synthetic: and we have seen that they are not synthetic. Similarly our view that the propositions of arithmetic are not synthetic but analytic leads us to reject the Kantian hypothesis[5] that arithmetic is concerned with our pure intuition of time, the form of our inner sense. And thus we are able to dismiss Kant's transcendental æsthetic without having to bring forward the epistemological difficulties which it is commonly said to involve. For the only argument which can be brought in favor of Kant's theory is that it alone explains certain "facts." And now we have found that the "facts" which it purports to explain are not facts at all. For while it is true that we have *a priori* knowledge of necessary propositions, it is not true, as Kant supposed, that any of these necessary propositions are synthetic. They are without exception analytic propositions, or, in other words, tautologies.

We have already explained how it is that these analytic propositions are necessary and certain. We saw that the reason why they cannot be confuted in experience is that they do not make any assertion about the empirical world. They simply record our determination to use words in a certain fashion. We cannot deny them without infringing the conventions which are presupposed by our very denial, and so falling into

---

4. Cf. M. Black, *The Nature of Mathematics*, p. 154.
5. This hypothesis is not mentioned in the *Critique of Pure Reason*, but was maintained by Kant at an earlier date.

self-contradiction. And this is the sole ground of their necessity. As Wittgenstein puts it, our justification for holding that the world could not conceivably disobey the laws of logic is simply that we could not say of an unlogical world how it would look.[6] And just as the validity of an analytic proposition is independent of the nature of the external world, so is it independent of the nature of our minds. It is perfectly conceivable that we should have employed different linguistic conventions from those which we actually do employ. But whatever these conventions might be, the tautologies in which we recorded them would always be necessary. For any denial of them would be self-stultifying.

We see, then, that there is nothing mysterious about the apodeictic certainty of logic and mathematics. Our knowledge that no observation can ever confute the proposition "7 + 5 = 12" depends simply on the fact that the symbolic expression "7 + 5" is synonymous with "12," just as our knowledge that every oculist is an eye-doctor depends on the fact that the symbol "eye-doctor" is synonymous with "oculist." And the same explanation holds good for every other *a priori* truth.

How Can Tautologies Be Surprising?

What is mysterious at first sight is that these tautologies should on occasion be so surprising, that there should be in mathematics and logic the possibility of invention and discovery. As Poincaré says: "If all the assertions which mathematics puts forward can be derived from one another by formal logic, mathematics cannot amount to anything more than an immense tautology. Logical inference can teach us nothing essentially new, and if everything is to proceed from the principle of identity, everything must be reducible to it. But can we really allow that these theorems which fill so many books serve no other purpose than to say in a round-about fashion 'A = A'?"[7] Poincaré finds this incredible. His own theory is that the sense of invention and discovery in mathematics belongs to it in virtue of mathematical induction, the principle that what is true for the number 1, and true for $n + 1$ when it is true for n,[8] is true for all numbers. And he claims that this is a synthetic *a priori* principle. It is, in fact, *a priori*, but it is not synthetic. It is a defining principle of the natural numbers, serving to distinguish them from such numbers as the infinite cardinal numbers, to which it cannot be applied.[9] Moreover, we must remember that discoveries can be made, not only

---

6. *Tractatus Logico-Philosophicus*, 3.031.
7. *La Science et l'Hypothèse*, Part I, Chapter i.
8. This was wrongly stated in previous editions as "true for n when it is true for $n + 1$."
9. Cf. B. Russell's *Introduction to Mathematical Philosophy*, Chapter iii, p. 27.

in arithmetic, but also in geometry and formal logic, where no use is made of mathematical induction. So that even if Poincaré were right about mathematical induction, he would not have provided a satisfactory explanation of the paradox that a mere body of tautologies can be so interesting and so surprising.

The true explanation is very simple. The power of logic and mathematics to surprise us depends, like their usefulness, on the limitations of our reason. A being whose intellect was infinitely powerful would take no interest in logic and mathematics.[10] For he would be able to see at a glance everything that his definitions implied, and, accordingly, could never learn anything from logical inference which he was not fully conscious of already. But our intellects are not of this order. It is only a minute proportion of the consequences of our definitions that we are able to detect at a glance. Even so simple a tautology as "$91 \times 79 = 7189$" is beyond the scope of our immediate apprehension. To assure ourselves that "7189" is synonymous with "91×79" we have to resort to calculation, which is simply a process of tautological transformation —that is, a process by which we change the form of expressions without altering their significance. The multiplication tables are rules for carrying out this process in arithmetic, just as the laws of logic are rules for the tautological transformation of sentences expressed in logical symbolism or in ordinary language. As the process of calculation is carried out more or less mechanically, it is easy for us to make a slip and so unwittingly contradict ourselves. And this accounts for the existence of logical and mathematical "falsehoods," which otherwise might appear paradoxical. Clearly the risk of error in logical reasoning is proportionate to the length and the complexity of the process of calculation. And in the same way, the more complex an analytic proposition is, the more chance it has of interesting and surprising us.

It is easy to see that the danger of error in logical reasoning can be minimized by the introduction of symbolic devices, which enable us to express highly complex tautologies in a conveniently simple form. And this gives us an opportunity for the exercise of invention in the pursuit of logical enquiries. For a well-chosen definition will call our attention to analytic truths, which would otherwise have escaped us. And the framing of definitions which are useful and fruitful may well be regarded as a creative act.

Having thus shown that there is no inexplicable paradox involved in the view that the truths of logic and mathematics are all of them analytic, we may safely adopt it as the only satisfactory explanation of

---

10. Cf. Hans Hahn, "Logik, Mathematik und Naturerkennen," *Einheitswissenschaft*, Heft II, p. 18. "Ein allwissendes Wesen braucht Logik und keine Mathematik." (An English translation of this pamphlet will shortly be available in the book, *Logical Positivism*, edited by Professor Ayer and published by the Free Press—Eds.)

their *a priori* necessity. And in adopting it we vindicate the empiricist claim that there can be no *a priori* knowledge of reality. For we show that the truths of pure reason, the propositions which we know to be valid independently of all experience, are so only in virtue of their lack of factual content. To say that a proposition is true *a priori* is to say that it is a tautology. And tautologies, though they may serve to guide us in our empirical search for knowledge, do not in themselves contain any information about any matter of fact.

6

LOGICAL POSITIVISM
AND NECESSITY

Brand Blanshard

LOGICAL POSITIVISM is a blend of the older empiricism with the newer
formal logic. It holds that all propositions can be divided into two
classes, the necessary and the factual. Its theory of necessary propositions derives from the symbolic logic with which we were concerned
in the last chapter;* as for factual propositions, it sides, roughly speaking,
with the empiricism discussed in the last chapter but one.† We must
try to understand these two positions; and in doing so we shall follow
a text which, if not the most authoritative, is I think the most intelligible,
exposition of the theory, that of Mr. A. J. Ayer.

According to Mr. Ayer, no necessary proposition says anything
about the world of fact at all. The only propositions that do so are
empirical ones, and many, even of those that seem empirical, turn out
on examination to have no "factual content," and therefore, strictly, no
meaning. The test whether a proposition does have meaning is to ask
whether it could conceivably be verified, and the only terms in which it
can be verified are those of sense experience. This does not mean that
all statements are meaningless that cannot in fact be so verified; a
statement about the mountains on the other side of the moon is a case
in point; but here I know the sort of sense impressions that would verify
it if I could get them; "therefore I say that the proposition is verifiable
in principle if not in practice, and is accordingly significant." But if one

---

[This selection consists of Sections 1-8 and 11-13 of Chapter XXX of Blanshard's *The
Nature of Thought*. It is here reprinted with the kind permission of the author and the
publisher.]

* Blanshard here refers to Ch. XXIX of *The Nature of Thought*, entitled "Formalism
and Necessity."
† See Selection 4, above.

cannot imagine *any* sense experience that would refute it or bear it out, then the statement is meaningless and not really a statement at all. Furthermore even when such statements are meaningful, they are never certain. Sense contents themselves are never connected necessarily. If statements about them are not expressions of the meaning of words, like "red is a color," they report mere empirical conjunctions; such propositions as "man is mortal" are no more necessary than "crows are black," and since if the latter is to be a certainty we must exhaust the whole tribe of crows in our observations, it is and must remain merely probable.

So much for empirical propositions; now for the other, and in the present context more important, class of necessary propositions. These it is, and particularly the logico-mathematical type of them, that have been the perpetual thorn in the empiricist side. And "the empiricist," says Mr. Ayer, "must deal with the truths of logic and mathematics in one of the two following ways: he must say either that they are not necessary truths, in which case he must account for the universal conviction that they are; or he must say that they have no factual content, and then he must explain how a proposition which is empty of all factual content can be true and useful and surprising." Traditional empiricism has taken the former of these two lines and tried to explain necessity away as nothing but high probability; it failed, and in a recent chapter we saw why. The novelty of logical positivism is that, with the aid of the new techniques of symbolic logic, it resolutely takes the second line. It seeks, like the older empiricism, to explain necessary knowledge away; but instead of reducing the necessary to the empirical, it reduces it to empty form. This it does in two distinguishable ways, which amount in its estimation to the same thing, but are outwardly different enough to merit separate statement. Necessary propositions are explained sometimes as (1) tautologies, sometimes as (2) conventions of language.

(1) Logical propositions "tell us only what we may be said to know already." According to the material logic that the positivists generally follow, the statement "*p* implies *q*" is simply a reminder that *p* does not in fact occur in the absence of *q,* that one or other of the three remaining combinations is the case, i.e., either both present, both absent, or the first absent and the second present. Such a statement is not properly a logical statement at all, but a disjunctive report of empirical facts. Suppose, however, that we wish to proceed from one proposition to another by means of logical deduction. We know, for example, that *p* is true; then if we know also that *p* implies *q,* we can perform an act of inference and say that *q* is true. It looks at first glance as if, in saying this, we had arrived at something new. But the positivists insist that this is an illusion. In stating our conclusion we

are only putting in a different form what has already been stated in our premises. This will be clearer, perhaps, from a simple use of what symbolic logicians call "the matrix method." Consider this table:

	p	q	$p \supset q$	$p.p \supset q$	$p.p \supset q. \supset q$
(1)	1	1	1	1	1
(2)	1	0	0	0	1
(3)	0	1	1	0	1
(4)	0	0	1	0	1

Here "1" means true, and "0" means false. In the first two columns are given all the possible combinations of truth and falsity for p and q. In column 3 is given, on each line, a statement of whether $p \supset q$ holds in the light of the values for p and q just given on that line. This column is thus a definition of what we mean by $p \supset q$; it tells us that we mean one or other of the pairs of truth-values given on lines (1), (3), and (4). Let us now inspect the statement $p.p \supset q. \supset q$, i.e., "if p is true, and p implies q, then q is true." When, to begin with, we say "p is true," we rule out the combinations given on lines (3) and (4), for in both of these p is false. When we go on to say that p implies q, we rule out line (2), since that particular combination is no part, as we have just seen, of what we mean by "p implies q." There remains only line (1), and on inspecting it we find that q is actually given along with "p" and "p implies q." This conjunction is recorded in the 1 of column 4. But that column adds nothing new; it summarizes statements already made. A little reflection, without the matrix, will show us in column 5 that if we define "$p \supset q$" in material terms, then the assertion of p together with "p implies q" *includes* the assertion of q. The final statement only unfolds explicitly what we have said before. And that is all there is to our deduction. That is all there ever is to any statement of necessity. "To find that a proposition is necessarily to be asserted only means to find that it has already been asserted."

(2) Since all necessary propositions are tautologies, i.e., explicit statements of what is already contained in the meaning of our terms, they are not assertions about the world of fact but illustrations of our use of language. "The principles of logic and mathematics are true universally simply because we never allow them to be anything else. And the reason for this is that we cannot abandon them without contradicting ourselves, without sinning against the rules which govern our use of language, and so making our utterances self-stultifying." In the absurdity of this alternative, indeed, we find "the sole ground of their necessity." When we say that p is true and that it implies q, the assertion of q is contained, as has been said, in the meaning of our words; to assert it explicitly is merely to illustrate or confirm that we are using words in one sense rather than another. Of course we could adopt different conventions if we wished; "modern" logic has thrown open to us innumer-

able definitions of "implication." "But whatever these conventions might be, the tautologies in which we recorded them would always be necessary. For any denial of them would be self-stultifying."

If one puts together the two main doctrines of the positivists, that all necessary propositions are tautologies, and that other propositions have meaning only if they are sensibly verifiable, it is clear that what is proposed is a philosophical revolution. The "high priori road" travelled by so many classic philosophers is now seen to lead nowhere. The very statements in which they offered their views about God, the Absolute, the soul, freedom, good and evil, an independent material world, are meaningless because incapable of sensory verification. Metaphysics in its old ambitious sense goes overboard. Indeed philosophy generally goes overboard as a discipline engaged in the search for truth. "Philosophy is a department of logic," and its business henceforth is that of logical lexicographer and grammarian. It lays down the conditions under which propositions have meaning, lists the more useful of the arbitrary definitions that people employ in their thinking, and exhibits, through the newer techniques, what these definitions formally imply.

While it is naturally the wholesale destructiveness of this philosophic bombshell that has aroused most interest in it, this is not the point of our direct concern. The one question we can ask about the doctrine is whether it is right about necessity. And if we review the account just given, we shall find that three points of vital importance emerge from it. All necessary propositions are said (1) to be tautologies, hence (2) to express only linguistic conventions, and therefore (3) to say nothing of fact. These views call for comment.

(1) The positivist view on tautologies is admitted to rest on the analysis of necessity made by symbolic logic. And within this logic it takes its guidance, not from any intensional theory, or from any partly intensional theory like that of Professor Lewis, but from the thorough-going logical atomism of Messrs. Russell and Wittgenstein. This theory would make logic purely extensional. According to it, a statement of material implication is, as we have seen, a disjunctive statement of fact; a formal implication is the same statement generalized. " 'Socrates is a man' implies 'Socrates is mortal' " is a material implication; "if *any-thing* is a man, that thing is mortal" is a formal implication. Now it is of the first importance to remember that this statement is purely extensional; it does not mean "the attribute 'being human' necessitates the attribute 'being mortal' "; it means that the attribute of being a man and that of not being mortal are never in fact conjoined; this is the sense of "for all values of x, x is a man implies x is mortal." When, with this major, I say "Socrates is a man and therefore mortal," I am clearly tautologizing, since Socrates is one of the values I must have considered in laying down my major. We thus go back to the *dictum de omni* as the

true principle of the syllogism and indeed of reasoning generally. And not only is every syllogism a tautology; the principle of syllogism is itself a tautology. If we put it in its usual form, $p \supset q.q \supset r: \supset .p \supset r$, we could easily show by the matrix method that this merely illustrates in a new form what we take implication to mean.

Is this sound? I am convinced that it is not. Indeed the answer to it is as old as Aristotle, namely that when we think about implications, or about one thing's implying another, we are not thinking in extensional terms. When we say that being human implies being mortal, we do not have in mind an enormous class of rational bipeds past, present, and future, with each and every one of whom death, by the purest accident, is conjoined. We mean, foggily without doubt, and if you will, unjustifiably, but still beyond all question, that the *character* of being human has some special and intimate connection with liability to die. And when we say that if p implies q, and q, r, then p implies r, what are we trying to say? The extensional logicians tell us that what we really mean is this (I expand the above formula to give its exact import): no case in which it is conjointly the case that p is not the case conjointly with a case of the falsity of q, and also that q is not the case conjointly with a case of the falsity of r, is the case conjointly with a case which conjoins p's truth with q's falsity. Now if anyone charges me with meaning this when I state the principle of syllogism, I can only plead not guilty. I do not deny that I am asserting the kind of connection between three terms which would carry with them all the conjunctions of truth and falsity here set down. But if the conjunctions held, it would be in virtue of something else, a connection of content. It is this connection of content that I directly mean. And it is just this that extensional logic disregards.

Thus the view that necessary propositions are tautologies is achieved by squeezing out of them what they primarily mean. It may be replied, however, that one cannot escape tautology simply by abandoning the extensional reading, for tautology may belong to intensional readings too. Kant's analytic propositions, for example, were all intensional tautologies; they were propositions in which the subject concept contained the predicate concept; "body is extended," he said, only makes explicit in the predicate an element that is contained in the thought of body and is a part of its definition. And it may be held that necessary propositions, if not tautologous extensionally, are at least tautologous intensionally.

But that will not do either. For in the first place, a proposition that is tautologous in this sense is not a proposition at all. A proposition must make an assertion; but if by "body" you *mean* an extended something, then your proposition is "something that is extended is extended"; and just what does this assert? Nothing, if only for the reason that it offers nothing that could intelligibly be denied.

Positivists like Mr. Ayer, however, would not only accept this, but would turn it instantly against us. "Abandon if you will," they would say, "the extensional interpretation, and fall back on necessity as a nexus of meanings; you will find it a worthless refuge. Take any proposition you now regard as necessary, examine it, and you will see that it owes its necessity to its being analytic, that is, to the predicate's being contained in the subject in such a way that to deny it would be self-contradictory. We should agree with you that such a statement is not a meaningful assertion at all. Indeed that is just what we are saying when we call it a tautology. Tautology is equally tautology, whether the predicate states part of the extensional range or part of the intensional content of the subject."

Where, then, do we part from the positivist? It is here: we hold that there are necessary propositions that are *not* analytic, even in this intensional sense. Indeed we should hold that many of the propositions Kant would have described as analytic express, in actual use, a non-analytic necessity. Take the proposition "red is a color." If by "red" I mean a conjunction of certain elements of which color is one, then to say that red is a color would, no doubt, be as truly tautology, and its denial as truly self-stultifying, as if I had said "red is red." But if I mean that within what I call "red" there are distinguishable aspects, such that one involves the other in the peculiarly intimate relation of genus and species, then my assertion does say something. It may be replied that red could not be red without being of the genus color, that being a color is part of what I mean by red, and that I could not withhold it without absurdity. Granted. But it does not follow that my subject is a conjunction of attributes, externally related, of which in my predicate I restate one; and if a so-called logical analysis forces me to say this, then there is something wrong with the analysis. I certainly may, and I often do, mean by statements of this kind, not that SP is P, but that within the whole SP, S is related to P in that manner which we call necessary. And the relation of species to genus is an example of such necessity.

But we are understating our case. To show that there are intensional necessities that are non-analytic in Kant's sense, we have taken an example that he himself would have called analytic. But he recognized also a class of *synthetic* necessary judgments; indeed it was they that set the problem of the *Critique*; and though he said much that was questionable about them, we hold that at least he was right that there are such things. Nor do we think there is any difficulty in finding examples; there follows a considerable list of them. Of each of the propositions below we should hold (*a*) that at least two characters or contents are involved which are qualitatively distinct; (*b*) that neither is contained in the other, nor asserted to be so contained; (*c*) that therefore the proposition is not, or at least need not be, tautologous; (*d*) that the primary meaning asserted is a connection of content; (*e*) that the connection is not simply conjunction, but a far more intimate one for which, in logical positivism, there is no place.

> Whatever is colored must be extended.
> Whatever has shape has size.
> Whatever is an integer is odd or even.
> Pleasure is good.
> The infliction of needless pain is evil.
> If I ought to do something I can do it.
> Of all plane figures whose perimeters are of a given length, the circle encloses the largest area.
> Any quantity is divisible without limit.
> In Euclidean space a straight line is the shortest line between two points.
> If A is hotter than B, and B than C, then A is hotter than C.
> If A precedes B in time, and B, C, then A precedes C.
> If A is north of B in a plane, and B west of C, C is southeast of A.

Everyone of these, we should hold, is at once synthetic and necessary. "Yes," it may be said, "synthetic in the psychological sense, in the sense that the subject, or antecedent, can in fact be thought of without referring to the predicate or consequent. But still analytic and tautologous by the only sound criterion, namely, whether the predicate or the consequent could be denied without contradiction." No, we reply, but synthetic even by that test.

The positivist is here confusing contradiction with self-contradiction. Fairly interpreted the test says, " a proposition is analytic when to deny the predicate would contradict the subject." Now when you deny that what is red is extended, you are not saying "what is red is not red"; extension is not one element in the quality red, which you first accept and then deny. What you are rejecting is a web or scheme which embraces both red and extension in one small system and which is so articulated that if one of these is replaced by its negative the scheme falls into incoherence. And there is an immense difference between saying "This proposition is true on pain of S's not being S," and "This proposition is true on pain of S-P's incoherence." For the first guarantee is based simply on the law of contradiction, that the same cannot be different; the second is based on the insight that where diverse elements are linked by necessity, to deny either disrupts the system. The first ignores the possibility that elements really different may be intelligibly connected: the second allows for it and uses it. And for every one of the propositions just listed it is the second that is the actual warrant. Consider the final example: "If A is north of B in a plane, and B west of C, then C is southeast of A." No doubt with a little manipulating we could get this into the form of an analytic proposition in which the subject could not meaningfully be denied. But it is clear that what really guarantees the statement is the construction of a system within which we see that if one set of relations holds, another must hold.

(2) Positivists like Mr. Ayer, however, would say that all these propositions, unless indeed they state empirical probabilities, are statements of convention in language. They "enlighten us by illustrating the way in which we use certain symbols. Thus if I say, 'Nothing can be colored in different ways at the same time with respect to the same part of itself,' I am not saying anything about the properties of any actual thing; but I am not talking nonsense. I am expressing an analytic proposition, which records our determination to call a color expanse which differs in quality from a neighboring color expanse a different part of a given thing. In other words, I am simply calling attention to the implications of a certain linguistic usage."

The first thing to notice about this theory is that if it is taken at its face value, it contradicts itself. No analytic propositions, we are told, say anything about empirical fact. What they really do is to "record our determination" to use words in a certain way; or, as is said on the next page, their work is that of "indicating the convention which governs our usage" of words. But if to "record our determination" means to state that we are so determined, if to indicate conventions of usage means, as one would naturally take it to mean, that such conventions are actually in use, then analytic propositions do report empirical facts; the very propositions that were said never to report such facts are defined in such a way that they must. But it would be unfair to make much of this. In spite of such statements as these, other expressions of Mr. Ayer's and the general tenor of the positivists' writing make it sufficiently clear that they do not mean by "conventions of usage" the sort of facts that are reported in dictionaries.

What, then, do they mean? It is brought out in another statement of Mr. Ayer's, that "a proposition is analytic when its validity depends solely on the definitions of the symbols it contains." Now definitions, we are told, are arbitrary. You may define implication, for example, in an endless variety of ways, but in whatever way you define it, your assertion that p implies q will merely illustrate that definition; to say that it does anything more is to forget that your definition is optional, that you might have chosen any one among countless others and your statement might still have been valid. This, then, is what the positivists apparently mean. When they say that "necessary" propositions express conventions of language, they mean that the logical constants involved (for example, "if," "not," "or," "implies") have all of them arbitrary meanings which, so far as validity is concerned, might equally well have been otherwise, just as the words in our language might all have had different meanings from those that are actually attached to them.

We may well attend to this with some care, for it is the sort of reasoning by which metaphysics generally is to be ruled out of court. Once we understand this matter of conventions, we are expected to see that what Plato and Plotinus, Spinoza and Hegel, Bradley and Royce, considered the most important part of their thought is literally non-sense, and that traditional ethics, aesthetics and theology have all been following will-o'-the-wisps. I have no doubt there is more in the argument than I have succeeded in seeing, but I can only record that all I do see is a quibble, a bad analogy or two, and an implicit self-contradiction.

(i) The quibble is about definition. "Definitions, of course, are arbitrary." How many an argument of pith and moment has had its current turned awry by that tiresome remark! There is an air of sophistication about it, as though one had seen how idle it is to ask *the* truth about anything; "it's all a matter of definition, you see; start with a different set of definitions and you can prove anything." I say the remark is tiresome because in spite of its many repetitions there is far more falsity than truth in it. That there is *some* truth in it is obvious. There is no word in our language that might not have meant something else if its users had so chosen. And at the present time I can agree with myself or others that whenever I make a certain noise, say "Popocatepetl," I shall be referring to a certain mountain, and not, as I might, to justice or the north star. This free choice is always open to us, and in technical discussions it is sometimes of advantage to use it, though in ninety-nine cases out of a hundred of ordinary speech, to do so would be foolish. But in the commoner and more important cases of definition to call the process arbitrary is plainly false. When someone asks me the meaning of "right" or "the equator" or "necessary," am I free to offer anything I please? By no means. It is assumed that in my answer I will not tie meanings to words at random, but that I will carefully suit words to what is antecedently meant, that my interest is not in how a word is used but in what an object is. Now when I am called on to define such constants of logic as "and," "not," and "implies," which kind of definition is in order? Both are open to me. But if I adopt the first kind of definition, there would be no conceivable interest in what I might say, except to someone silly enough to want to study my whims. If I adopt the second, I may bring to explicit awareness a relation constantly used but dimly apprehended. Surely in logical matters this second kind alone has any importance or interest; and there is nothing arbitrary about it. It is hard to resist the conclusion that some persons have confused the two senses of definition. Realizing that definition in the first sense is arbitrary, and being called on to define certain logical terms, they have supposed that definition there too is arbitrary. Unknowingly they are quibbling. . . .

. . . (iii) We have owned to the suspicion that in his doctrine of conventions the positivist is not consistent with himself. What we mean is this: in spite of holding that logical laws are conventions and arbitrary, he seems careful in his own practice to follow one kind of logic rather than others, a course which needs a justification it does not get. In defining implication, for example, he starts with a simple matrix consisting of the four combinations of truth and falsity in p and q. These four he declares to be the only ones possible. But how does he know that they are the only ones possible? He may say we arrive at it by experience, by finding of every experienced character that it is either present or absent, with no co-ordinate third state occurring. But it is not clear how an impossibility can be established by experience, however protracted. If not based on experience, the assertion that the matrix gives the only possibilities must be a convention, and therefore arbitrary, and therefore not, on simply logical grounds, preferable to another. But when it is said that the statement "these are the only possibilities" is arbitrary, that can only mean that one is free, if one wishes, to replace it by an alternative, such as that there *are* other possibilities. Why, in the light of this alternative, positivist logicians should lay so much stress on the matrix method, should cling so pertinaciously to a view of implication based on it, and should pride themselves as they do on their logical rigor, is somewhat puzzling. It would almost seem as if they thought their logic *the* right one.

Necessary propositions, says Mr. Ayer, "simply record our determination to use words in a certain fashion. We cannot deny them without infringing the conventions that are presupposed by our very denial, and so falling into self-contradiction. And this is the sole ground of their necessity . . . any denial of them would be self-stultifying." But why should we not stultify ourselves? To be sure, the denial of a necessary proposition would mean "infringing conventions," but if they really are only conventions, why may we not adopt the infringing of conventions as our particular pet convention? If you say that is the one thing that is *streng verboten,* it is idle to say also that you are putting conventions on the same level, for you are elevating one to a position of primacy; you are not only taking it for your own, but are saying that anyone who fails to follow it is ruled out of court. Now we have not the least objection to anyone's saying this, for to us it seems perfectly sound. What does seem unacceptable, because inconsistent, is to say, first, that all necessary propositions are conventions with alternatives, and then, in the case of one of these, to accuse anyone of talking nonsense who tries to avail himself of an alternative. Is not that equivalent to the admission that here there *is* no alternative and hence that the rule is *not* mere convention?

And what of the proposition itself that all necessary propositions are conventions? Which of the two classes does it fall in, the class of empirical probabilities or the class of tautologies? If in the former, then at any moment a necessary proposition may turn up that is not tautology, and hence the sweeping statement above is illegitimate. If in the latter, the theory is self-contradictory again, for having laid it down that no necessary proposition says anything about facts, it lays down a necessary proposition about propositions; and since a proposition is described as "a class of sentences," and sentences are facts, we have a necessary statement about facts after all And apart from that, it is hard to believe that this theory about conventions figures in the minds of its advocates as just another convention which "records our determination to use words in a certain fashion." It does not seem, in their discussion of it, to be that kind of proposition, yet it will fit nowhere else in their system.

(3) Of the three positivist contentions about necessity, we have now commented on two, namely, that assertions of it are tautologies and that they are linguistic conventions. There remains the third, that they say nothing about fact. "They none of them provide any information about any matter of fact. In other words they are entirely devoid of factual content."

Now by "factual content" the logical positivist means something extremely narrow. According to his principle of verifiability, the meaning of a statement is yielded by the method of its verification; a statement *means* the set of observations that would verify it. And by "observations" he means sensations; an empirical proposition is really "a forecast of our sensation." It follows that only those propositions that refer to our own future sensations have any factual content. From this it follows again that many statements that are constantly made without a doubt of their being significant must be set down as unmeaning. Most persons, perhaps, would contemplate serenely enough that elimination of metaphysics which is a main article in the positivist creed. But even they must grow uneasy as they consider the following developments: All statements about the consciousness of other people are meaningless, since none of our own sensations can verify its existence; the best we can do is to observe their bodily behavior; and hence when we speak of their experience, it is their behavior that we mean. As regards everyone but himself, the positivist is therefore a behaviorist. Every statement about the past must be unmeaning, or at least if it does have a meaning, that is utterly different from anything we had supposed we meant; if we judge that the Greeks won at Marathon, we are really laying down "a rule for the anticipation of future experience." As for ethical judgments, "they have no objective validity whatsoever." If they are not "pure expressions of feeling" they are statements of how I or other people feel. Now when we are called upon to say whether necessary propositions are factual, is it this sense of "factual" that we shall find most useful? No doubt it is, if our interest is solely in contriving a polemic against positivism. But our interest goes beyond that; we are trying to find whether necessary judgments in any important sense say something about the real world. And we must confess that the positivist interpretation of "factual" seems so implausible, so evidently at variance with the plain meaning with which people commonly use words, that we should prefer not to forfeit a wider interest in our discussion by conducting it in these terms. The question whether necessary propositions are factual or not in the restricted positivist sense is not the question of first importance. That question is whether or not they can be *true,* in the sense, whatever that is, in which other propositions are true. And since the positivist claim that they are not factual statements, but merely linguistic conventions, carries with it the further claim that they are neither true nor false, we have here a real issue. It seems to us clear that some necessary propositions are meant to state what holds of the real world, and are true or false in the same sense as other propositions.

An example already given by Mr. Ayer is worth meditating on. "If I say, 'Nothing can be colored in different ways at the same time with respect to the same part of itself,' I am not saying anything about the properties of any actual thing; but I am not talking nonsense. I am expressing an analytic proposition, which records our determination to call a color expanse which differs in quality from a neighboring color expanse a different part of a given thing." If the reader is like the present writer, he will have, on reading this, a curious sense that the cart has got before the horse and is pulling it energetically around. It is very much like saying that when, with Smith and Jones before me, I remark that they cannot be the same, what I really mean to say is that I am determined to call Smith Smith and not Jones, and Jones Jones and not Smith. Surely if my statement does record such a determination, it is in virtue of my seeing in the facts something that calls for this difference of names, to wit that Smith and Jones are exclusive of each other. And if I assign to differently colored parts of the same thing the *names* of different parts, my naming is surely based on the insight that, *being* qualitatively different, they *are* not the same. Again, why should I "determine" not to describe the same spot, seen under the same conditions, by the names of different colors? To do so would of course be easy enough. Is it replied that it would also be extremely inconvenient? Yes, it would, but why? Because the plurality of my words would be in constant conflict with the singleness of fact; I should be using two names when I could see from the nature of the case that one of them would always be impertinent. Thus our determination or convention is anything but arbitrary; it is an attempt to conform our speech to the apprehended character of fact. And even if we were entirely mistaken about this character of fact, the positivist theory would still be wrong. For it says we do not *mean* to assert a character of fact. And whether the character is there or not, it is clear that we do mean to assert it. We mean that nature itself, at this particular point, and under these conditions, will not admit two colors at once. We are asserting a necessity understood to be imposed on us by the real world. . . .

SELECTED BIBLIOGRAPHY

(ITEMS PROVIDED WITH ASTERISK ARE MORE ADVANCED)

Locke's *Essay Concerning Human Understanding* is a classic on the problem of *a priori* knowledge. Book I criticizes the Cartesian theory of innate ideas. Book IV deals with the extent and certainty of knowledge. It contains the theory that universal propositions which are not merely verbal ("trifling") can be known with certainty only if one sees, intuitively or with the help of deduction, a necessary connection between distinct ideas. This is the first comprehensive treatise on the nature and origin of human knowledge in the history of philosophy. Leibniz' *New Essays Concerning Human Understanding* is a critical commentary, from the point of view of rationalism, on Locke's *Essay*. Book I, containing a defense of "innate ideas" against Locke's attack, is especially recommended. A theory of *a priori* knowledge resembling Locke's may be found in Bertrand Russell's lucid and elementary book, *The Problems of Philosophy* (London: Oxford University Press, 1912), Chapters 7-11. It also contains a simplified exposition and critique of Kant's theory. A critical treatment of Kant from the point of view of American pragmatism may be found in C. I. Lewis, *Mind and the World Order* (New York: Charles Scribner's Sons, 1929). Lewis emphasizes, against Kant, the analytic nature of all *a priori* truth and discusses the function of *a priori* propositions in empirical inquiry. A more sophisticated and technical elaboration of his theory is contained in his later book, *An Analysis of Knowledge and Valuation** (LaSalle, Illinois: Open Court, 1947), especially Chapters 3-6. Hans Reichenbach, *The Rise of Scientific Philosophy* (Berkeley and Los Angeles: University of California Press, 1951), contains a critique of Kantian rationalism by a leading logical empiricist. Chapter 8, dealing with geometry, is especially recommended. Elementary introductions to the problem of *a priori* knowledge may be found in A. Pap, *Elements of Analytic Philosophy* (New York: Macmillan, 1949), Chapter 6, and Sections b and c in Chapter 16, and in J. Hospers, *An Introduction to Philosophical Analysis* (New York: Prentice-Hall, 1953), Chapter 2.

The theory that mathematical propositions are empirical generalizations is developed more fully by John Stuart Mill in his *An Examination of Sir William Hamilton's Philosophy* (London: Longmans, Green and Co., 1872), and in Alexander Bain, *Deductive Logic* (London: Longmans, Green and Co., 1879). Mill's theory was criticized at length by James McCosh in *An Examination of Mr. J. S. Mill's Philosophy* (New York: R. Carter, 1880). A recent statement of a theory in some ways similar to Mill's is found in Sidney Hook's article, "Experimental Logic," *Mind*, 1931. An interesting contemporary criticism of the theory is contained in Max Wertheimer, *Productive Thinking* (New York and London: Harper and Brothers, 1945).

A much debated thesis in contemporary philosophy is that mathematics is reducible to logic. Recommended to laymen as an introduction to this point of view is Bertrand Russell, *Introduction to Mathematical Philosophy* (London: Allen and Unwin, 1919), especially Chapters 1, 2, 13, 14, and 18. The nature of mathematics and logic is discussed also in R. Carnap's "The Old and the New Logic," translated from the German, in A. J. Ayer (ed.), *Logical Positivism* (Glencoe, Illinois: Free Press, 1957); in the same author's "Formal and Factual Science,"* in Feigl and Brodbeck (eds.), *Readings in the Philosophy of Science,* (New York: Appleton-Century-Crofts, 1953); in C. G. Hempel's "The Nature of Mathematical Truth" and "Geometry and Empirical Science," both reprinted in H. Feigl and W. Sellars, *Readings in Philosophical Analysis* (New York: Appleton-Century-Crofts, 1949); in G. Ryle, K. Popper, C. Lewy, "Why are the Calculuses of Logic and Mathematics Applicable to Reality?," a symposium in the *Proceedings of the Aristotelian Society,* 1946*; in D. Gasking's "Mathematics and the World," in A. Flew (ed.), *Logic and Language,* Second Series (Oxford: Basil Blackwell, 1953); in R. von Mises, "Mathematical Postulates and Human Understanding," reprinted in J. Newman (ed.), *The World of Mathematics,* Vol. 3 (New York: Simon and Schuster, 1956); in K. Menger's "The New Logic," *Philosophy of Science,* 1937; and in W. Kneale's "Truths of Logic," in *Proc. of the Arist. Soc.,* 1946.

The theory that all necessary propositions are tautologies was clearly worked out for the first time by Ludwig Wittgenstein in his *Tractatus Logico-Philosophicus* (London: Kegan Paul, New York: Harcourt, Brace and Co., 1922). An account of Wittgenstein's views on mathematics over the years is given in Alice Ambrose's "Wittgenstein on Some Questions in the Foundations of Mathematics," *Journal of Philosophy,* 1955. A simple and unsophisticated exposition of the linguistic or conventionalistic theory of *a priori* propositions, one of the first formulations of such a theory, is given by a member of the "Vienna Circle," H. Hahn, in "Logic, Mathematics and Knowledge of Nature," English translation in A. J. Ayer (ed.), *Logical Positivism, op. cit.* The following articles are sympathetic or critical discussions of this approach: D. Williams, "The Nature and Variety of the A Priori," *Analysis,* 1938 (critical); D. Gasking, "Mr. Williams on the A Priori," *Analysis,* 1939 (sympathetic); M. Black, "Conventionalism in Geometry," *Philosophy of Science,* 1942; W. V. Quine, "Truth by Convention,"* reprinted in Feigl and Sellars, *op. cit.*; K. Britton, "Are Necessary Truths True by Convention?" *Proc. of the Arist. Soc.,* Suppl. Vol. 21, 1947 (sympathetic); W. Kneale, "Are Necessary Truths True by Convention?" *ibid.* (critical); A. Pap, "Necessary Propositions and Linguistic Rules,"* in *Semantica* (issued by *Archivio di Filosofia*), Rome 1955 (critical); P. Edwards, "Do Necessary Propositions 'Mean Nothing'?" *Journal of Philosophy,* 1949 (sympathetic); C. H. Whiteley, "Truths by Convention," *Analysis,* 1937 (critical); A. C. Ewing "The Linguistic Theory of A Priori Propositions,"* *Proc. of the Arist. Soc.,* 1940 (critical); N. Malcolm, "Are Necessary Propositions Really Verbal?" *Mind* 1940 (sympathetic); and "The Nature of Entailment," *Mind,* 1940 (sympathetic). For a view that combines the linguistic approach with the contextualistic logic of John Dewey see E. Nagel's much discussed article "Logic Without Ontology," reprinted in Feigl and Sellars, *op. cit.,* also in E. Nagel, *Logic Without Metaphysics* (Glencoe, Illinois: Free Press, 1957).

The question of synthetic *a priori* propositions has been much discussed by philosophers since the time Kant first raised it. The analytic-synthetic distinction was for a long time accepted without much dispute. Within the last decade, however, doubts have been voiced about the validity of, or necessity for, this distinction. The following articles deal especially with the synthetic *a priori* and the controversy over the distinction between synthetic and analytic propositions: One of the first critiques of the analytic-synthetic dichotomy is M. G. White's "Analytic-Synthetic: an Untenable Dualism," reprinted in L. Linsky (ed.), *Semantics and the Philosophy of Language* (Urbana: University of Illinois Press, 1952). A similar critique is contained in W. V. Quine's important paper, "Two Dogmas of Empiricism,"* reprinted in W. V. Quine, *From a Logical Point of View* (Cambridge: Harvard University Press, 1953). There are replies to Quine in A. Hofstadter's "The Myth of the Whole," *Journal of Philosophy*, 1954, in M. Weitz' "Analytic Statements," *Mind*, 1954, and in an article by H. P. Grice and P. F. Strawson, entitled "In Defense of a Dogma," *Philosophical Review*, 1956. F. Waismann has a series of articles entitled "Analytic-Synthetic" in *Analysis*, 1949-1952.

A defense of the linguistic theory by one of the founders of logical positivism against Kantians and phenomenologists is M. Schlick's "Is there a Material A Priori?" in Feigl and Sellars, *op. cit.* An article sympathetic to the synthetic *a priori* is S. Toulmin, "A Defense of Synthetic Necessary Truth," *Mind*, 1949, which is criticized in D. Pears, "Synthetic Necessary Truth,"* *Mind*, 1950. Pears' views are also expressed in "Color Incompatibilities,"* in A. Flew (ed.), *Logic and Language*, Second Series (Oxford: Basil Blackwell, 1953). The following also present statements of opposing viewpoints on this question: W. Sellars, "Is there a Synthetic A Priori?"* *Philosophy of Science*, 1953; A. Pap, "Are All Necessary Propositions Analytic?" *Philosophical Review*, 1949; the same author's "Logic and the Synthetic A Priori,"* *Philosophy and Phenomenological Research*, 1950; H. Langford, "A Proof that Synthetic A Priori Propositions Exist," *Journal of Philosophy*, 1949; C. D. Broad, "Are there Synthetic A Priori Truths?" *Proc. of the Arist. Soc.*, 1936; H. Putnam, "Reds, Greens and Logical Analysis,"* *Phiolsophical Review*, 1956; A. Pap, "Once More: Colors and the Synthetic A Priori,"* *Philosophical Review*, 1957 (reply to Putnam); and H. Putnam, "Reds and Greens Again: a Rejoinder to Arthur Pap,"* *ibid.*

II

Scepticism and the Problem of Induction

INTRODUCTION

W HETHER OR NOT the logical positivists are right in deny-
ing that anything at all can be known *a priori* about the universe we live in,
most philosophers are agreed that we must rely on *induction* in order to arrive
at interesting general conclusions in empirical science—that is, in all sciences
except logic and mathematics. For example, every educated boy or girl "knows"
that water is H_2O. This means that water is composed of molecules which are
themselves composed of two atoms of hydrogen and one atom of oxygen. Obviously, the chemist did not arrive at this conclusion by examining water
molecules through a microscope. He arrived at it by interpreting by means of
the atomic theory of matter the experimentally established law that in order
to produce water by synthetic chemistry one must mix oxygen and hydrogen
in the volume proportion 1:2. How is this law "established"? Well, you just
experiment and see! But experiment can only tell you that such and such a
result followed such and such conditions at a definite place and time; when
you conclude that the same result will follow the same conditions at *any*
time and place, you perform an induction, you *generalize* from the observed
facts; you argue from what has actually been observed to cases which have
not been observed. On a less technical level: whenever you bite into an apple,
you generalize from past experience, for you expect that this things tastes like
an apple on the ground that similar things have always produced that unique
taste sensation in your experience.

Now, Hume, the classical "sceptic" with respect to the foundations of
empirical knowledge, asked the following question: since obviously you can
conceive (imagine) that a thing which looks and feels like an apple should
not taste like an apple, the proposition that all things which look and feel like
apples taste like apples is not *necessary;* no *a priori* proof of it is possible. If
so, do you have any *reason* for believing that the thing which you now hold
in your hand will taste like an apple? "Of course I have a reason," you reply;
"the reason is that similar things have always been found to taste like that."
But then Hume would have pressed you as follows: you presuppose that if
qualities A and B have always been accompanied by quality C in the instances
you have observed, then they will also be accompanied by C in future instances. You presuppose, in other words, that *nature is uniform.* Clearly, unless you have a reason for believing this general presupposition, you have no
reason for believing any specific proposition that is, as it were, supported by it.
But this general presupposition is not a necessary proposition either; if it were,
then a chaotic world—a world in which what looks like fire sometimes feels

hot and sometimes feels cold, in which what looks like milk sometimes tastes like milk, sometimes like orange juice, and sometimes evaporates the moment it is touched by lips, etc.—would be inconceivable, which it is not by any means. What then is our reason for believing that *it* is true? Is is that we infer that nature *will be* uniform from the fact that it *has been* uniform? But to justify this inference and to prove the alleged presupposition of the uniformity of nature is one and the same thing; hence we beg the question if we attempt to prove that nature must be uniform by relying on the inference from what has happened to what will happen (See Hume: Selection 8, p. 114, and Russell: Selection 10, pp. 127 ff.). Conclusion: induction cannot be logically justified at all; it is not even a process of reasoning, but a *habit* of expecting what has happened in such and such circumstances to happen again in simliar circumstances. It should be noted that neither Hume nor other sceptics deny the *psychological* fact that we are strongly inclined to believe that the future will be like the past. They and other philosophers discussing this subject are not concerned with questions of psychology but with *logical* problems—with the question of the justification or validity of inductive inferences.

Some modern philosophers have attempted to get around Hume's pessimistic assessment of the power of reason by accusing him of having asked for too much: of course, they say, you can never be *certain* that a prediction will be fulfilled; to that extent Hume was right. But in order to justify an inductive inference—i.e., an inference whose conclusion does not follow with logical necessity from the premises, though the latter are offered as reasons justifying one's acceptance of the conclusion—it is sufficient to show that the conclusion is *probable* relative to the known facts. Hume, however, cannot be accused of having overlooked this answer to his scepticism. What is your basis for saying, he inquired, that given A and B, C is probable? Just that C has been observed to be frequently, though not invariably, present when A and B were present. We predict that probably, though not certainly, this man will get angry if we insult him, because men, or men which in certain relevant respects resemble this man, have in the past been observed to react that way to an insult *in most cases*. Therefore probable reasoning, said Hume, likewise presupposes the uniformity of the course of nature, though a smaller degree of uniformity ("statistical" uniformity, as it is called nowadays), and the problem of justifying predictions remains essentially the same.

John Stuart Mill set himself the task of liberating inductive science from Hume's scepticism without relying, like the Kantians, on *a priori* knowledge of universal propositions about nature. He regarded the experimental methods used by scientists as methods for discovering the true hypothesis by elimination of all but one of the initially possible hypotheses. You wonder whether A is the cause of B (where A and B are repeatable *kinds* of events). You cannot prove that every instance of A will be followed by an instance of B, or every instance of B preceded by an instance of A, by observing all possible instances of these kinds of events. But Mill believed that true generalizations could be discovered *negatively*: a generalization can be *disproved* by a single instance. Nobody could prove that aspirin is an infallible remedy against headache by observing all possible cases of consumption of aspirin, but it is easy to disprove this claim by finding just once that the headache remains after aspirin has been swallowed. Now, suppose you knew that a given kind of effect E must have been caused by either A or B or C, which are circumstances that were present when, or immediately before, an observed instance of E occurred. By applying Mill's experimental methods (which are discussed in most elementary textbooks of logic and scientific method) you might quickly find that neither A nor B is the cause. And then you would have established with certainty that C is the cause, though a conclusive verification of the generalization "every instance of C is followed by an instance of E" or "every instance of E is preceded by an instance of C" by the *direct* method would be impossible.

Mill was acutely aware of a big assumption involved in the use of this indirect method of getting at the true explanation of an effect by elimination of all initially possible alternative explanations: that every event has a cause, called by him "the law of universal causation." If it is indeed presupposed by indirect induction, it would be circular to try to prove it by indirect induction. But can we trust direct induction ("induction by simple enumeration" is the usual name, given to this method by Francis Bacon, the first philosopher of inductive science) in this one instance, though it cannot be trusted in any other instance? Mill tried hard to convince himself and his readers of an affirmative answer to this crucial question. He argued that direct induction is reliable if the sample of instances from which we generalize is very large and diversified, and maintained that this condition of reliability is fulfilled by the generalization that every event has a cause. It may be countered, however, that Mill overlooked that the *instances* which confirm the law of universal causation are themselves specific causal laws, which on his own theory cannot be established by direct induction. And if they are established by indirect induction, which presupposes the law of universal causation, then Mill's attempted empirical proof of the latter is circular after all. But be this as it may, the majority of contemporary philosophers would say that Mill did not succeed in solving Hume's doubt.

As regards their attitude towards this "problem of induction," contemporary philosophers fall roughly into three groups: 1) the enemies of empiricism who commend Hume for having shown brilliantly that a consistent empiricism must shovel its own grave. For, so they argue, according to empiricism synthetic universal propositions, like the propositions we believe to express laws of nature, can be established only by induction from observed instances, not *a priori*. And induction is not a valid method of inference unless we have reason to believe in the validity of some synthetic universal proposition, like Mill's law of universal causation, or some version of a principle of the uniformity of nature. But if so, then we cannot justify our acceptance of any synthetic universal propositions. A consistent empiricism, they maintain, cannot provide a man with reasons for believing any synthetic propositions except those that just describe his present sense-experience, because a belief in what is not perceived here and now is based on inductive inference—as shown by Hume—and inductive inference is not justifiable on empiricist principles. To illustrate: at this moment I believe that there is a bookcase behind the chair in which I am sitting. As I am not perceiving the bookcase now, this belief must rest on inference. I seem to remember to have seen a bookcase at the described place on a number of occasions, and hence infer that I actually did see one there. But it is logically possible, even if this inference from memory be granted, that the bookcase should have been removed, or even should just have vanished, in the meantime. If I exclude this logical possibility without hesitation, it is because I cannot think of any *cause* of the bookcase's disappearance since I last saw it, and refuse to believe that anything happens without cause. Thus belief in a general synthetic proposition emerges once we analyze our grounds for believing the simplest proposition about what is not present to our senses. At this point the paths followed by the critics of empiricism divide: some are content to have pointed up the alternative "either abandon empiricism or remain a Humean sceptic!" without offering a constructive alternative to empiricism; others more or less openly revive Kantianism by claiming *a priori* knowledge of some suitable "principle of induction," i.e., synthetic proposition about nature which must be true if any empirical evidence is to make any inductive conclusion probable. Members of the latter subgroup, though, do not always seem to be clear about what they are doing. They assign to philosophy the task of "justifying" inductive inference and therewith scientific method by making explicit the "presuppositions" on which it rests—as though by showing that p can be true only if q is true one had shown that p *is* true. Group (1) is represented by our selection from Russell's early little book *The Problems of Philosophy*. Students of Russell's later writings are, however, of divided opinion as to whether Russell falls into the first or the second subgroup.

2) Those who seek a solution of Hume's problem within the logic or theory of probability. Nothing less than a painstaking study of the logic of probability is needed for a full understanding of the issues raised by these thinkers from Laplace to Carnap. Expositions of this approach tend to be very technical and for this reason it is not represented in our selections. Very roughly, the problem is this. From the information that all ten marbles in a specified urn are white (and that marbles do not change their color in the process of being drawn) we can deduce the conclusion that, say, the first seven marbles we shall draw are white. The conclusion follows necessarily in the sense that it would be self-contradictory to affirm the premise and at the same time deny the conclusion. Now, the converse inference is not by any means necessary: it does not follow from the fact that the first seven marbles turned out to be white that all the marbles are white. On the other hand, the supposed uniformity of the outcomes of more than half of the possible drawings makes the conclusion that all the marbles are white fairly probable. If the conclusion were false, i.e., if at least one marble in the urn were not white, then it would be fairly improbable that a run of seven white marbles should have occurred. For suppose you compute the number of possible sets of seven marbles that can be formed out of a set of ten marbles, and suppose that all but one of the ten marbles are white, then you would find that the proportion of sets of that size that contain that lone nonwhite marble is much larger than the proportion of those that do not contain it. If we suppose each marble to be as likely to be drawn as any other, and further that the drawn marbles are not replaced before the next drawing, the probability of a run of seven white marbles on the assumption that initially there are nine white and one nonwhite marble, equals 3/10. Or, suppose that in fact only 800 of 1000 beans

in a large bag of beans were good. What would be the probability then that all the beans in a large sample from the bag are good? It would be small, in the sense that among all the possible large samples (say, samples of fifty) only a small proportion would be entirely devoid of bad beans. Therefore, given that nothing but good specimens are found in a large random sample, it is probable that almost all the beans in the bag are good. The idea behind this approach to the problem of induction is that judgments of probability may themselves be *logically certain,* in the same sense in which it is logically certain that if all A are B, then all the members of any given sample of the class A are B. The judgments of probability which are needed to justify our predictions can be established, according to this school of thought, by logic alone; contrary to Hume's claim, no inductive inference is required to establish *them.* It can be proved in the theory of probability, a subject whose theorems are as infallibly certain as any mathematical theorem, that the probability that a sample approximately matches in composition the class from which it is drawn increases as the sample increases. This theorem does not guarantee that the method of induction *will* lead us to the truth. Even if a generalization has been confirmed a million times and not a single exception to it has been found it does not follow that it is exceptionless. But relative to such extensive confirming evidence it is, according to the mentioned theorem, highly probable that the generalization is true or has very few exceptions. And the validity of this judgment of probability does not depend on any assumptions about the constitution of nature.

3) Those who maintain that the time-honored "problem of induction," whose apparent insolubility has been called by some "the scandal of modern philosophy," is not a genuine problem at all. The paper by Frederick Will in our readings represents this point of view. (See Selection 11, pp. 131 ff.) If a man admits, they say, that things which look and feel like eggs have always (or nearly always) tasted like eggs in past experiences, yet denies that this is a *reason* for believing that the next egg will have the same familiar taste, in other words, that this evidence makes it probable that the next egg will taste similarly, then he just cannot mean by the words "reason" and "probable" what is ordinarily meant by them. He may be using "reason" in the strong sense of "logically conclusive reason," the sense in which the premises of a valid syllogism are a reason for its conclusion. In this sense of "reason" it would be self-contradictory to accept the propositions proferred as reasons and at the same time to question a proposition inferred from them. But then, what more is he denying than that the conclusion of an inductive argument follows *necessarily* from its premises? And isn't this trivial, since the very definition of "induction" implies that the conclusion is not a necessary consequence of the premises that describe the observed facts? The sceptic on this view is simply bemoaning that induction is not deduction. But this seems a senseless complaint. One might as well complain that deduction is not induction.

Furthermore, is it really true that we have to fall back on a principle of the uniformity of nature in order to justify our belief that the fact that dry leaves always burned when lit in the past makes it probable that such matter will burn again if set afire now? What exactly does this alleged principle assert? "Same cause, same effect" is one familiar answer, but it is not clear what this means. If it means "whenever and wherever *exactly* the same conditions are repeated which in the past were attended by effect E, there and then E will occur again," then it is inapplicable for the purpose of justifying a particular inductive inference; for there are always some variations in the conditions. If it means "if the same *relevant* conditions are repeated, then the effect is repeated," the question arises how one is to distinguish relevant from irrelevant conditions. Presumably the recurrence of E is our very criterion for determining whether all relevant conditions were present; that is, if C′ is not followed by E whereas C was followed by E, we conclude that some relevant condition must have failed to accompany C′; we do not conclude that in this instance the "same" cause failed to give rise to the "same" effect. But if the principle is thus irrefutable by experience, say the logical positivists, then it is a mere tautology and says nothing about the world at all. And if specific empirical evidence cannot by itself make a specific prediction probable, a tautology will not help either.

Hume raised the problem whether we can ever be justified in accepting the conclusion of an inductive argument. As already pointed out, he questioned not only whether inductive conclusions can ever be certain but even whether they can ever be so much as probable. A position which is less critical of common sense beliefs about matters of fact is that of the philosophers who maintain that no empirical proposition can ever be absolutely certain. The most we can ever obtain is a high degree of probability. Common sense readily admits that generalizations about nature, like "the planets always revolve around the sun in elliptical orbits," "cats who mate with cats always give birth to cats and never to dogs," "a tooth extraction which is not preceded by some anesthetic always causes pain," cannot be known with absolute certainty. But people who have not been enlightened, or corrupted by philosophical analysis will say that just the same there remain millions of empirical propositions (i.e., propositions whose truth or falsehood must be discovered by experience) of whose truth we can be absolutely certain. To take an extreme example: if I feel and see a table, and my friends assure me that they see and feel the same thing, if further, just to make sure, I sit on what looks and feels like a table and find myself supported, have I not made absolutely certain, then, that there *is* a solid table in the room? Yet, ever since Descartes claimed—at least as critical philosopher, if not as devout Christian—that the only thing which indubitably exists is his own doubt of the existence of anything else, and therewith his own mind ("I think, therefore I exist"), many philosophers have denied that any propositions about the physical world (including the proposition that there is one) are ever certain. Briefly the argument is this: suppose I see what looks like a table but, having recently read Descartes, am in doubt whether what I see is a physical table: perhaps my sense of sight deceives me, perhaps I am dreaming. The natural way to resolve my doubt is to touch the apparent table, put heavy objects on it in order to see whether they are supported, etc. If I still remain in doubt, I may ask other people to come into the room and report whether their sensory experience is the same. But no matter how much corroborating testimony is obtained, a determined sceptic need not concede. For he can always describe possible evidence which, if it became actual, might make one doubtful of the truth of the physical proposition. Thus, what would you say if, after ten carefully selected observers confirmed the verdict of your senses, the next ten observers who had equally proven their visual normality reported that they see nothing at all at the place allegedly occupied by a table, while you and the first group of observers continued to see a table? Perhaps you would then be inclined to doubt their honesty instead of doubting the proposition in question. But what if you then saw them walk through the space seemingly occupied by a solid table? No doubt you would begin to doubt your own perceptual normality: "I must be suffering from an hallucination!" But what if the first group of observers reported that they saw the miraculous event too? You might conclude that there was a table which suddenly vanished without assignable cause, or that you are in the presence here of a kind of table that exists but intermittently, going in and out of existence at intervals for no known reason. But since continuous existence and public observability seem to be part of what one means by a "physical object," it is more likely that in such an event one would doubt the initially confirmed proposition that there was a table in the room.

At any rate, this is the sort of thing philosophers mean when they deny that any physical propositions are verifiable with absolute conclusiveness. They deny it on the ground that any such proposition has an "infinite number of consequences"—such as that the just imagined kinds of events will not occur. Some well known contemporary representatives of this view are John Dewey, Bertrand Russell, Hans Reichenbach, C. I. Lewis, Rudolf Carnap, and A. J. Ayer. Some go to the extreme of denying that any empirical propositions can be known with complete certainty, others claim that at least propositions which assert nothing beyond what is immediately sensed can be so known: I may be mistaken in saying that there is a white sheet of paper before me, but how could I be mistaken in the cautious assertion that there *seems* to be such a thing before me? (See the selection from Descartes, p. 105.) However, some modern philosophers, who feel that most of the traditional disputes among philosophers are verbal, maintain that the philosophical theory which asserts that no physical proposition can ever be known beyond the shadow of a (theoretical) doubt is nothing but a pointless departure from the ordinary usage of the word "certain." When we say "we have made absolutely certain that there is a table here," we do not mean that we cannot conceive of any future experience that might *then* make us doubtful of the truth of the proposition. Therefore the sceptic is not really refuting a view that is held by common sense. It only looks as though he were refuting the proposition "some physical propositions can be verified with absolute certainty," they say, because in denying this sentence he is using the same *word* "certainty." But since he assigns a new, unusually strong meaning to this word, his disagreement with the common sense view is merely *verbal*. It is like "refuting" the apparently well confirmed belief that we frequently see the *same* thing at different times by the argument that nothing has exactly the same properties at two different times, that every thing constantly changes in some respect. The proper way of countering this refutation is to point out that in saying, for example, "I have seen the same house before," one just does not *mean* that the house in question has undergone no changes whatever.

Whether nevertheless such a philosophical definition of "certainty" has some point—unlike the definition of a "man" as a biped which is omniscient and 20 feet tall, which entails the surprising consequence that contrary to your previous beliefs there are no men on earth (or does it?)—is a question beyond the scope of an introductory book.

A. P.

7

THE SPHERE OF THE DOUBTFUL

Rene Descartes

Meditation I

IT IS NOW some years since I detected how many were the false beliefs
that I had from my earliest youth admitted as true, and how doubtful
was everything I had since constructed on this basis; and from that time
I was convinced that I must once for all seriously undertake to rid
myself of all the opinions which I had formerly accepted, and commence to build anew from the foundation, if I wanted to establish any
firm and permanent structure in the sciences. But as this enterprise appeared to be a very great one, I waited until I had attained an age so
mature that I could not hope that at any later date I should be better
fitted to execute my design. This reason caused me to delay so long
that I should feel that I was doing wrong were I to occupy in deliberation
the time that yet remains to me for action. To-day, then, very oppor-
tunely for the plan I have in view I have delivered my mind from every
care [and am happily agitated by no passions] and since I have procured for myself an assured leisure in a peaceable retirement, I shall at
last seriously and freely address myself to the general upheaval of all
my former opinions.

Now for this object it is not necessary that I should show that all
of these are false—I shall perhaps never arrive at this end. But inasmuch
as reason already persuades me that I ought no less carefully to withhold my assent from matters which are not entirely certain and indubitable than from those which appear to me manifestly to be false, if I
am able to find in each one some reason to doubt, this will suffice to justify

[This selection is taken from the first and the second of Descartes' *Meditations,* a work
first published in 1641. The translation is by Elizabeth S. Haldane and G. R. T. Ross and
is reproduced here with the kind permission of the Cambridge University Press.]

my rejecting the whole. And for that end it will not be requisite that I should examine each in particular, which would be an endless undertaking; for owing to the fact that the destruction of the foundations of necessity brings with it the downfall of the rest of the edifice, I shall only in the first place attack those principles upon which all my former opinions rested.

All that up to the present time I have accepted as most true and certain I have learned either from the senses or through the senses; but it is sometimes proved to me that these senses are deceptive, and it is wiser not to trust entirely to any thing by which we have once been deceived.

But it may be that although the senses sometimes deceive us concerning things which are hardly perceptible, or very far away, there are yet many others to be met with as to which we cannot reasonably have any doubt, although we recognise them by their means. For example, there is the fact that I am here, seated by the fire, attired in a dressing gown, having this paper in my hands and other similar matters. And how could I deny that these hands and this body are mine, were it not perhaps that I compare myself to certain persons, devoid of sense, whose cerebella are so troubled and clouded by the violent vapors of black bile, that they constantly assure us that they think they are kings when they are really quite poor, or that they are clothed in purple when they are really without covering, or who imagine that they have an earthenware head or are nothing but pumpkins or are made of glass. But they are mad, and I should not be any the less insane were I to follow examples so extravagant.

At the same time I must remember that I am a man, and that consequently I am in the habit of sleeping, and in my dreams representing to myself the same things or sometimes even less probable things, than do those who are insane in their waking moments. How often has it happened to me that in the night I dreamt that I found myself in this particular place, that I was dressed and seated near the fire, whilst in reality I was lying undressed in bed! At this moment it does indeed seem to me that it is with eyes awake that I am looking at this paper; that this head which I move is not asleep, that it is deliberately and of set purpose that I extend my hand and perceive it; what happens in sleep does not appear so clear nor so distinct as does all this. But in thinking over this I remind myself that on many occasions I have in sleep been deceived by similar illusions, and in dwelling carefully on this reflection I see so manifestly that there are no certain indications by which we may clearly distinguish wakefulness from sleep that I am lost in astonishment. And my astonishment is such that it is almost incapable of persuading me that I now dream.

Now let us assume that we are asleep and that all these particulars, e.g. that we open our eyes, shake our head, extend our hands, and so on, are but false delusions; and let us reflect that possibly neither our hands nor our whole body are such as they appear to us to be. At the same time we must at least confess that the things which are represented to us in sleep are like painted representations which can only have been formed as the counterparts of something real and true, and that in this way those general things at least, i.e. eyes, a head, hands, and a whole body, are not imaginary things, but things really existent. For, as a matter of fact, painters, even when they study with the greatest skill to represent sirens and satyrs by forms the most strange and extraordinary, cannot give them natures which are entirely new, but merely make a certain medley of the members of different animals; or if their imagination is extravagant enough to invent something so novel that nothing similar has ever before been seen, and that then their work represents a thing purely fictitious and absolutely false, it is certain all the same that the colors of which this is composed are necessarily real. And for the same reason, although these general things, to wit, [a body], eyes, a head, and such like, may be imaginary, we are bound at the same time to confess that there are at least some other objects yet more simple and more universal, which are real and true; and of these just in the same way as with certain real colours, all these images of things which dwell in our thoughts, whether true and real or false and fantastic, are formed.

To such a class of things pertains corporeal nature in general, and its extension, the figure of extended things, their quantity or magnitude and number, as also the place in which they are, the time which measures their duration, and so on.

That is possibly why our reasoning is not unjust when we conclude from this that Physics, Astronomy, Medicine and all other sciences which have as their end the consideration of composite things, are very dubious and uncertain; but that Arithmetic, Geometry and other sciences of that kind which only treat of things that are very simple and very general, without taking great trouble to ascertain whether they are actually existent or not, contain some measure of certainty and an element of the indubitable. For whether I am awake or asleep, two and three together always form five, and the square can never have more than four sides, and it does not seem possible that truths so clear and apparent can be suspected of any falsity [or uncertainty].

Nevertheless I have long had fixed in my mind the belief that an all-powerful God existed by whom I have been created such as I am. But how do I know that He has not brought it to pass that there is no earth, no heaven, no extended body, no magnitude, no place, and that nevertheless [I possess the perceptions of all these things and that] they seem to me to exist just exactly as I now see them? And, besides, as I sometimes imagine that others deceive themselves in the things which they think they know best, how do I know that I am not deceived every time that I add two and three, or count the sides of a square, or judge of things yet simpler, if anything simpler can be imagined? But possibly God has not desired that I should be thus deceived, for He is said to be supremely good. If, however, it is contrary to His goodness to have made me such that I constantly deceive myself, it would also appear to be contrary to His goodness to permit me to be sometimes deceived, and nevertheless I cannot doubt that He does permit this.

There may indeed be those who would prefer to deny the existence of a God so powerful, rather than believe that all other things are uncertain. But let us not oppose them for the present, and grant that all that is said of a God is a fable; nevertheless in whatever way they suppose that I have arrived at the state of being that I have reached—whether they attribute it to fate or to accident, or make out that it is by a continual succession of antecedents, or by some other method—since to err and deceive oneself is a defect, it is clear that the greater will be the probability of my being so imperfect as to deceive myself ever, as is the Author to whom they assign my origin the less powerful. To these reasons I have certainly nothing to reply, but at the end I feel constrained to confess that there is nothing in all that I formerly believed to be true, of which I cannot in some measure doubt, and that not merely through want of thought or through levity, but for reasons which are very powerful and maturely considered; so that henceforth I ought not the less carefully to refrain from giving credence to these opinions than to that which is manifestly false, if I desire to arrive at any certainty [in the sciences]. . . .

. . . I shall then suppose, not that God who is supremely good and the fountain of truth, but some evil genius not less powerful than deceitful, has employed his whole energies in deceiving me; I shall consider that the heavens, the earth, colors, figures, sound, and all other external things are nought but the illusions and dreams of which this genius has availed himself in order to lay traps for my credulity; I shall consider myself as having no hands, no eyes, no flesh, no blood, nor any senses, yet falsely believing myself to possess all these things; I shall remain obstinately attached to this idea, and if by this means it is not in my power to arrive at the knowledge of any truth, I may at least do what is in my power [i.e. suspend my judgment], and with firm purpose avoid giving credence to any false thing, or being imposed upon by this arch deceiver, however powerful and deceptive he may be. But this task is a laborious one, and insensibly a certain lassitude leads me into the course of my ordinary life. And just as a captive who in sleep enjoys imaginary liberty, when he begins to suspect that his liberty is but a dream, fears to awaken, and conspires with these agreeable illusions that the deception may be prolonged, so insensibly of my own accord I fall back into my former opinions, and I dread awakening from this slumber, lest the laborious wakefulness which would follow the tranquillity of this repose should have to be spent not in daylight, but in the excessive darkness of the difficulties which have just been discussed.

Meditation II

The Meditation of yesterday filled my mind with so many doubts that it is no longer in my power to forget them. And yet I do not see in what manner I can resolve them; and, just as if I had all of a sudden fallen into very deep water, I am so disconcerted that I can neither make certain of setting my feet on the bottom, nor can I swim and so support myself on the surface. I shall nevertheless make an effort and follow anew the same path as that on which I yesterday entered, i.e. I shall proceed by setting aside all that in which the least doubt could be supposed to exist, just as if I had discovered that it was absolutely false; and I shall ever follow in this road until I have met with something which is certain, or at least, if I can do nothing else, until I have learned for certain that there is nothing in the world that is certain. Archimedes, in order that he might draw the terrestrial globe out of its place, and transport it elsewhere, demanded only that one point should be fixed and immoveable; in the same way I shall have the right to conceive high hopes if I am happy enough to discover one thing only which is certain and indubitable.

I suppose, then, that all the things that I see are false; I persuade myself that nothing has ever existed of all that my fallacious memory represents to me. I consider that I possess no senses; I imagine that body, figure, extension, movement and place are but the fictions of my mind. What, then, can be esteemed as true? Perhaps nothing at all, unless that there is nothing in the world that is certain.

But how can I know there is not something different from those things that I have just considered, of which one cannot have the slightest doubt? Is there not some God, or some other being by whatever name we call it, who puts these reflections into my mind? That is not necessary, for is it not possible that I am capable of producing them myself? I myself, am I not at least something? But I have already denied that I had senses and body. Yet I hesitate, for what follows from that? Am I so independent on body and senses that I cannot exist without these? But I was persuaded that there was nothing in all the world, that there was no heaven, no earth, that there were no minds, nor any bodies: was I not then likewise persuaded that I did not exist? Not at all; of a surety I myself did exist since I persuaded myself of something [or merely because I thought of something]. But there is some deceiver or other, very powerful and very cunning, who ever employs his ingenuity in deceiving me. Then without doubt I exist also if he deceives me, and let him deceive me as much as he will, he can never cause me to be nothing so long as I think that I am something. So that after having reflected well and carefully examined all things, we must come to the definite conclusion that this proposition: I am, I exist, is necessarily true each time that I pronounce it, or that I mentally conceive it.

But I do not yet know clearly enough what I am, I who am certain that I am; and hence I must be careful to see that I do not imprudently take some other object in place of myself, and thus that I do not go astray in respect of this knowledge that I hold to be the most certain and most evident of all that I have formerly learned. That is why I shall now consider anew what I believed myself to be before I embarked upon these last reflections; and of my former opinions I shall withdraw all that might even in a small degree be invalidated by the reasons which I have just brought forward, in order that there may be nothing at all left beyond what is absolutely certain and indubitable. . . .

. . . Certainty it is no small matter if all these things pertain to my nature. But why should they not so pertain? Am I not that being who now doubts nearly everything, who nevertheless understands certain things, who affirms that one only is true, who denies all the others, who desires to know more, is averse from being deceived, who imagines many things, sometimes indeed despite his will, and who perceives many likewise, as by the intervention of the bodily organs? Is there nothing in all this which is as true as it is certain that I exist, even though I should always sleep and though he who has given me being employed all his ingenuity in deceiving me? Is there likewise anyone of these attributes which can be distinguished from my thought, or which might be said to be separated from myself? For it is so evident of itself that it is I who doubts, who understands, and who desires, that there is no reason here to add anything to explain it. And I have certainly the power of imagining likewise; for although it may happen (as I formerly supposed) that none of the things which I imagine are true, nevertheless this power of imagining does not cease to be really in use, and it forms part of my thought. Finally, I am the same who feels, that is to say, who perceives certain things, as by the organs of sense, since in truth I see light, I hear noise, I feel heat. But it will be said that these phenomena are false and that I am dreaming. Let it be so; still it is at least quite certain that it seems to me that I see light, that I hear noise and that I feel heat. That cannot be false; properly speaking it is what is in me called feeling; and used in this precise sense that is no other thing than thinking. . . .

8

SCEPTICAL DOUBTS CONCERNING THE HUMAN UNDERSTANDING

David Hume

Part I

ALL THE OBJECTS of human reason or inquiry may naturally be divided into two kinds, to wit, "Relations of Ideas," and "Matters of Fact." Of the first kind are the sciences of Geomctry, Algebra, and Arithmetic, and, in short, every affirmation which is either intuitively or demonstratively certain. *That the square of the hypothenuse is equal to the square of the two sides* is a proposition which expresses a relation between these figures. *That three times five is equal to the half of thirty* expresses a relation between these numbers. Propositions of this kind are discoverable by the mere operation of thought, without dependence on what is anywhere existent in the universe. Though there never were a circle or triangle in nature, the truths demonstrated by Euclid would forever retain their certainty and evidence.

Matters of fact, which are the second objects of human reason, are not ascertained in the same manner, nor is our evidence of their truth, however great, of a like nature with the foregoing. The contrary of every matter of fact is still possible, because it can never imply a contradiction and is conceived by the mind with the same facility and distinctness as if ever so conformable to reality. *That the sun will not rise tomorrow* is no less intelligible a proposition and implies no more contradiction than the affirmation *that it will rise*. We should in vain, therefore, attempt to demonstrate its falsehood. Were it demonstratively false, it would imply a contradiction and could never be distinctly conceived by the mind.

[This selection is Section IV of Hume's *An Inquiry Concerning Human Understanding,* a book first published in 1748.]

It may, therefore, be a subject worthy of curiosity to inquire what is the nature of that evidence which assures us of any real existence and matter of fact beyond the present testimony of our senses or the records of our memory. This part of philosophy, it is observable, had been little cultivated either by the ancients or moderns; and, therefore, our doubts and errors in the prosecution of so important an inquiry may be the more excusable while we march through such difficult paths without any guide or direction. They may even prove useful by exciting curiosity and destroying that implicit faith and security which is the bane of all reasoning and free inquiry. The discovery of defects in the common philosophy, if any such there be, will not, I presume, be a discouragement, but rather an incitement, as is usual, to attempt something more full and satisfactory than has yet been proposed to the public.

All reasonings concerning matter of fact seem to be founded on the relation of *cause* and *effect*. By means of that relation alone we can go beyond the evidence of our memory and senses. If you were to ask a man why he believes any matter of fact which is absent, for instance, that his friend is in the country or in France, he would give you a reason, and this reason would be some other fact: as a letter received from him or the knowledge of his former resolutions and promises. A man finding a watch or any other machine in a desert island would conclude that there had once been men in that island. All our reasonings concerning fact are of the same nature. And here it is constantly supposed that there is a connection between the present fact and that which is inferred from it. Were there nothing to bind them together, the inference would be entirely precarious. The hearing of an articulate voice and rational discourse in the dark assures us of the presence of some person. Why? Because these are the effects of the human make and fabric, and closely connected with it. If we anatomize all the other reasonings of this nature, we shall find that they are founded on the relation of cause and effect, and that this relation is either near or remote, direct or collateral. Heat and light are collateral effects of fire, and the one effect may justly be inferred from the other.

If we would satisfy ourselves, therefore, concerning the nature of that evidence which assures us of matters of fact, we must inquire how we arrive at the knowledge of cause and effect.

I shall venture to affirm, as a general proposition which admits of no exception, that the knowledge of this relation is not, in any instance, attained by reasonings *a priori*, but arises entirely from experience, when we find that any particular objects are constantly conjoined with each other. Let an object be presented to a man of ever so strong natural reason and abilities—if that object be entirely new to him, he will not be able, by the most accurate examination of its sensible qualities, to discover any of its causes or effects. Adam, though his rational faculties be supposed, at the very first, entirely perfect, could not have inferred from the fluidity and transparency of water that it would suffocate him, or from the light and warmth of fire that it would consume him. No object ever discovers, by the qualities which appear to the senses, either the causes which produced it or the effects which will arise from it; nor can our reason, unassisted by experience, ever draw any inference concerning real existence and matter of fact.

This proposition, *that causes and effects are discoverable, not by reason, but by experience,* will readily be admitted with regard to such objects as we remember to have once been altogther unknown to us, since we must be conscious of the utter inability which we then lay under of foretelling what would arise from them. Present two smooth pieces of marble to a man who has no tincture of natural philosophy; he will never discover that they will adhere together in such a manner as to require great force to separate them in a direct line, while they make so small a resistance to a lateral pressure. Such events as bear little analogy to the common course of nature are also readily confessed to be known only by experience, nor does any man imagine that the explosion of gunpowder or the attraction of a loadstone could ever be discovered by arguments *a priori.* In like manner, when an effect is supposed to depend upon an intricate machinery or secret structure of parts, we make no difficulty in attributing all our knowledge of it to experience. Who will assert that he can give the ultimate reason why milk or bread is proper nourishment for a man, not for a lion or tiger?

But the same truth may not appear at first sight to have the same evidence with regard to events which have become familiar to us from our first appearance in the world, which bear a close analogy to the whole course of nature, and which are supposed to depend on the simple qualities of objects without any secret structure of parts. We are apt to imagine that we could discover these effects by the mere operation of our reason without experience. We fancy that, were we brought on a sudden into this world, we could at first have inferred that one billiard ball would communicate motion to another upon impulse, and that we needed not to have waited for the event in order to pronounce with certainty concerning it. Such is the influence of custom that where it is strongest it not only covers our natural ignorance but even conceals itself, and seems not to take place, merely because it is found in the highest degree.

But to convince us that all the laws of nature and all the operations of bodies without exception are known only by experience, the following reflections may perhaps suffice. Were any object presented to us, and were we required to pronounce concerning the effect which will result from it without consulting past observation, after what manner, I beseech you, must the mind proceed in this operation? It must invent or imagine some event which it ascribes to the object as its effect; and it is plain that this invention must be entirely arbitrary. The mind can never possibly find the effect in the supposed cause by the most accurate scrutiny and examination. For the effect is totally different from the cause, and consequently can never be discovered in it. Motion in the second billiard ball is a quite distinct event from motion in the first, nor is there anything in the one to suggest the smallest hint of the other. A stone or piece of metal raised into the air and left without any support immediately falls. But to consider the matter *a priori,* is there anything we discover in this situation which can beget the idea of a downward rather than an upward or any other motion in the stone or metal?

And as the first imagination or invention of a particular effect in all natural operations is arbitrary where we consult not experience, so must we also esteem the supposed tie or connection between the cause and effect which binds them together and renders it impossible that any other effect could result from the operation of that cause. When I see, for instance, a billiard ball moving in a straight line toward another, even suppose motion in the second ball should by accident be suggested to me as the result of their contact or impulse, may I not conceive that a hundred different events might as well follow from that cause? May not both these balls remain at absolute rest? May not the first ball return in a straight line or leap off from the second in any line or direction? All these suppositions are consistent and conceivable. Why, then, should we give the preference to one which is no more consistent or conceivable than the rest? All our reasonings *a priori* will never be able to show us any foundation for this preference.

In a word, then, every effect is a distinct event from its cause. It could not, therefore, be discovered in the cause, and the first invention or conception of it, *a priori,* must be entirely arbitrary. And even after it is suggested, the conjunction of it with the cause must appear equally arbitrary, since there are always many other effects which, to reason, must seem fully as consistent and natural. In vain, therefore, should we pretend to determine any single event or infer any cause or effect without the assistance of observation and experience.

Hence we may discover the reason why no philosopher who is rational and modest has ever pretended to assign the ultimate cause of any natural operation, or to show distinctly the action of that power which produces any single effect in the universe. It is confessed that the utmost effort of human reason is to reduce the principles productive of natural phenomena to a greater simplicity, and to resolve the many particular effects into a few general causes, by means of reasonings from analogy, experience, and observation. But as to the causes of these general causes, we should in vain attempt their discovery, nor shall we ever be able to satisfy ourselves by any particular explication of them. These ultimate springs and principles are totally shut up from human curiosity and inquiry. Elasticity, gravity, cohesion of parts, communication of motion by impulse—these are probably the ultimate causes and principles which we shall ever discover in nature; and we may esteem ourselves sufficiently happy if, by accurate inquiry and reasoning, we can trace up the particular phenomena to, or near to, these general principles. The most perfect philosophy of the natural kind only staves off our ignorance a little longer, as perhaps the most perfect philosophy of the moral or metaphysical kind serves only to discover larger portions of it. Thus the observation of human blindness and weakness is the result of all philosophy, and meets us, at every turn, in spite of our endeavors to elude or avoid it.

Nor is geometry, when taken into the assistance of natural philosophy, ever able to remedy this defect or lead us into the knowledge of ultimate causes by all that accuracy of reasoning for which it is so justly celebrated. Every part of mixed mathematics proceeds upon the supposition that certain laws are established by nature in her operations, and abstract reasonings are employed either to assist experience in the discovery of these laws or to determine their influence in particular instances where it depends upon any precise degree of distance and quantity. Thus it is a law of motion, discovered by experience, that the moment or force of any body in motion is in the compound ratio or proportion of its solid contents and its velocity, and, consequently, that a small force may remove the greatest obstacle or raise the greatest weight if by any contrivance or machinery we can increase the velocity of that force so as to make it an overmatch for its antagonist. Geometry assists us in the application of this law by giving us the just dimensions of all the parts and figures which can enter into any species of machine, but still the discovery of the law itself is owing merely to experience; and all the abstract reasonings in the world could never lead us one step toward the knowledge of it. When we reason *a priori* and consider merely any object or cause as it appears to the mind, independent of all observation, it never could suggest to us the notion of any distinct object, such as its effect, much less show us the inseparable and inviolable connection between them. A man must be very sagacious who could discover by reasoning that crystal is the effect of heat, and ice of cold, without being previously acquainted with the operation of these qualities.

Part II

But we have not yet attained any tolerable satisfaction with regard to the question first proposed. Each solution still gives rise to a new question as difficult as the foregoing and leads us on to further inquiries. When it is asked, *What is the nature of all our reasonings concerning matter of fact?* the proper answer seems to be, that they are founded on the relation of cause and effect. When again it is asked, *What is the foundation of all our reasonings and conclusions concerning that relation?* it may be replied in one word, *experience.* But if we still carry on our sifting humor and ask, *What is the foundation of all conclusions from experience?* this implies a new question which may be of more difficult solution and explication. Philosophers that give themselves airs of superior wisdom and sufficiency have a hard task when they encounter persons of inquisitive dispositions, who push them from every corner to which they retreat, and who are sure at last to bring them to some dangerous dilemma. The best expedient to prevent this confusion is to be modest in our pretensions and even to discover the difficulty ourselves before it is objected to us. By this means we may make a kind of merit of our very ignorance.

I shall content myself in this section with an easy task and shall pretend only to give a negative answer to the question here proposed. I say, then, that even after we have experience of the operations of cause and effect, our conclusions from that experience are *not* founded on reasoning or any process of the understanding. This answer we must endeavor both to explain and to defend.

It must certainly be allowed that nature has kept us at a great distance from all her secrets and has afforded us only the knowledge of a few superficial qualities of objects, while she conceals from us those powers and principles on which the influence of these objects entirely depends. Our senses inform us of the color, weight, and consistency of bread, but neither sense nor reason can ever inform us of those qualities which fit it for the nourishment and support of the human body. Sight or feeling conveys an idea of the actual motion of bodies, but as to that wonderful force or power which would carry on a moving body forever in a continued change of place, and which bodies never lose but by communicating it to others, of this we cannot form the most distant conception. But notwithstanding this ignorance of natural powers and principles, we always presume when we see like sensible qualities that they have like secret powers, and expect that effects similar to those which we have experienced will follow from them. If a body of like color and consistency with that bread which we have formerly eaten be presented to us, we make no scruple of repeating the experiment and foresee with certainty like nourishment and support. Now this is a process of the mind or thought of which I would willingly know the foundation. It is allowed on all hands that there is no known connection between the sensible qualities and the secret powers, and, consequently, that the mind is not led to form such a conclusion concerning their constant and regular conjunction by anything which it knows of their nature. As to past *experience,* it can be allowed to give *direct* and *certain* information of those precise objects only, and that precise period of time which fell under its cognizance: But why this experience should be extended to future times and to other objects which, for aught we know, may be only in appearance similar, this is the main question on which I would insist. The bread which I formerly ate nourished me; that is, a body of such sensible qualities was, at that time, endued with such secret powers. But does it follow that other bread must also nourish me at another time, and that like sensible qualities must always be attended with like secret powers? The consequence seems nowise necessary. At least, it must be acknowledged that there is here a consequence drawn by the mind that there is a certain step taken, a process of thought, and an inference which wants to be explained. These two propositions are far from being the same: *I have found that such an object has always been attended with such an effect,* and *I foresee that other objects which are in appearance similar will be attended with similar effects.* I shall allow, if you please, that the one proposition may justly be inferred from the other: I know, in fact, that it always is inferred. But if you insist that the inference is made by a chain of reasoning, I desire you to produce that reasoning. The connection between these propositions is not intuitive. There is required a medium which may enable the mind to draw such an inference, if indeed it be drawn by reasoning and argument. What that medium is I must confess passes my comprehension; and it is incumbent on those to produce it who assert that it really exists and is the original of all our conclusions concerning matter of fact.

This negative argument must certainly, in process of time, become altogether convincing if many penetrating and able philosophers shall turn their inquiries this way, and no one be ever able to discover any connecting proposition or intermediate step which supports the understanding in this conclusion. But as the question is yet new, every reader may not trust so far to his own penetration as to conclude, because an argument escapes his inquiry, that therefore it does not really exist. For this reason it may be requisite to venture upon a more difficult task, and, enumerating all the branches of human knowledge, endeavor to show that none of them can afford such an argument.

All reasonings may be divided into two kinds, namely, demonstrative reasoning, or that concerning relations of ideas, and moral or probable reasoning, or that concerning matter of fact and existence. That there are no demonstrative arguments in the case seems evident, since it implies no contradiction that the course of nature may change and that an object, seemingly like those which we have experienced, may be attended with different or contrary effects. May I not clearly and distinctly conceive that a body, falling from the clouds and which in all other respects resembles snow, has yet the taste of salt or feeling of fire? Is there any more intelligible proposition than to affirm that all the trees will flourish in December and

January, and will decay in May and June? Now, whatever is intelligible and can be distinctly conceived implies no contradiction and can never be proved false by any demonstrative argument or abstract reasoning *a priori.*

If we be, therefore, engaged by arguments to put trust in past experience and make it the standard of our future judgment, these arguments must be probable only, or such as regard matter of fact and real existence, according to the division above mentioned. But that there is no argument of this kind must appear if our explication of that species of reasoning be admitted as solid and satisfactory. We have said that all arguments concerning existence are founded on the relation of cause and effect, that our knowledge of that relation is derived entirely from experience, and that all our experimental conclusions proceed upon the supposition that the future will be conformable to the past. To endeavor, therefore, the proof of this last supposition by probable arguments, or arguments regarding existence, must be evidently going in a circle and taking that for granted which is the very point in question.

In reality, all arguments from experience are founded on the similarity which we discover among natural objects, and by which we are induced to expect effects similar to those which we have found to follow from such objects. And though none but a fool or madman will ever pretend to dispute the authority of experience or to reject that great guide of human life, it may surely be allowed a philosopher to have so much curiosity at least as to examine the principle of human nature which gives this mighty authority to experience and makes us draw advantage from that similarity which nature has placed among different objects. From causes which appear similar, we expect similar effects. This is the sum of all our experimental conclusions. Now it seems evident that, if this conclusion were formed by reason, it would be as perfect at first, and upon one instance, as after ever so long a course of experience; but the case is far otherwise. Nothing so like as eggs, yet no one, on account of this appearing similarity, expects the same taste and relish in all of them. It is only after a long course of uniform experiments in any kind that we attain a firm reliance and security with regard to a particular event. Now, where is that process of reasoning which, from one instance, draws a conclusion so different from that which it infers from a hundred instances that are nowise different from that single one? This question I propose as much for the sake of information as with an intention of raising difficulties. I cannot find, I cannot imagine any such reasoning. But I keep my mind still open to instruction if anyone will vouchsafe to bestow it on me.

Should it be said that, from a number of uniform experiments, we *infer* a connection between the sensible qualities and the secret powers, this, I must confess, seems the same difficulty, couched in different terms.

The question still occurs: On what process of argument is this *inference* founded? Where is the medium, the interposing ideas which join propositions so very wide of each other? It is confessed that the color, consistency, and other sensible qualities of bread appear not of themselves to have any connection with the secret powers of nourishment and support; for otherwise we could infer these secret powers from the first appearance of these sensible qualities without the aid of experience, contrary to the sentiment of all philosophers, and contrary to plain matter of fact. Here, then, is our natural state of ignorance with regard to the powers and influence of all objects. How is this remedied by experience? It only shows us a number of uniform effects resulting from certain objects, and teaches us that those particular objects, at that particular time, were endowed with such powers and forces. When a new object endowed with similar sensible qualities is produced, we expect similar powers and forces, and look for a like effect. From a body of like color and consistency with bread, we expect like nourishment and support. But this surely is a step or progress of the mind which wants to be explained. When a man says, *I have found, in all past instances, such sensible qualities, conjoined with such secret powers,* and when he says, *similar sensible qualities will always be conjoined with similar secret powers,* he is not guilty of a tautology, nor are these propositions in any respect the same. You say that the one proposition is an inference from the other; but you must confess that the inference is not intuitive, neither is it demonstrative. Of what nature is it then? To say it is experimental is begging the question. For all inferences from experience suppose, as their foundation, that the future will resemble the past and that similar powers will be conjoined with similar sensible qualities. If there be any suspicion that the course of nature may change, and that the past may be no rule for the future, all experience becomes useless and can give rise to no inference or conclusion. It is impossible, therefore, that any arguments from experience can prove this resemblance of the past to the future, since all these arguments are founded on the supposition of that resemblance. Let the course of things be allowed hitherto ever so regular, that alone, without some new argument or inference, proves not that for the future it will continue so. In vain do you pretend to have learned the nature of bodies from your past experience. Their secret nature, and consequently all their effects and influence, may change without any change in their sensible qualities. This happens sometimes, and with regard to some objects. Why may it not happen always, and with regard to all objects? What logic, what process of argument secures you against this supposition? My practice, you say, refutes my doubts. But you mistake the purport of my question. As an agent, I am quite satisfied in the point; but as a philosopher who has some share of curiosity, I will not say skepticism, I want to learn the foundation of this inference. No reading, no inquiry has yet been able to remove my difficulty or give me satisfaction in a matter of such importance. Can I do better than propose the difficulty to the public, even though, perhaps, I have small hopes of obtaining a solution? We shall at least, by this means, be sensible of our ignorance, if we do not augment our knowledge.

I must confess that a man is guilty of unpardonable arrogance who concludes, because an argument has escaped his own investigation, that therefore it does not really exist. I must also confess that, though all the learned, for several ages, should have employed themselves in fruitless search upon any subject, it may still, perhaps, be rash to conclude positively that the subject must therefore pass all human comprehension. Even though we examine all the sources of our knowledge and conclude them unfit for such a subject, there may still remain a suspicion that the enumeration is not complete or the examination not accurate. But with regard to the present subject, there are some considerations which seem to remove all this accusation of arrogance or suspicion of mistake.

It is certain that the most ignorant and stupid peasants, nay infants, nay even brute beasts, improve by experience and learn the qualities of natural objects by observing the effects which result from them. When a child has felt the sensation of pain from touching the flame of a candle, he will be careful not to put his hand near any candle, but will expect a similar effect from a cause which is similar in its sensible qualities and appearance. If you assert, therefore, that the understanding of the child is led into this conclusion by any process of argument or ratiocination, I may justly require you to produce that argument, nor have you any pretense to refuse so equitable a demand. You cannot say that the argument is abstruse and may possibly escape your inquiry, since you confess that it is obvious to the capacity of a mere infant. If you hesitate, therefore, a moment or if, after reflection, you produce an intricate or profound argument, you, in a manner, give up the question and confess that it is not reasoning which engages us to suppose the past resembling the future, and to expect similar effects from causes which are to appearance similar. This is the proposition which I intended to enforce in the present section. If I be right, I pretend not to have made any mighty discovery. And if I be wrong, I must acknowledge myself to be indeed a very backward scholar, since I cannot now discover an argument which, it seems, was perfectly familiar to me long before I was out of my cradle.

9

THE GROUND OF INDUCTION

John Stuart Mill

Axiom of the Uniformity of the Course of Nature

INDUCTION, properly so called, as distinguished from those mental operations, sometimes though improperly designated by the name, which I have attempted in the preceding chapter to characterize, may, then, be summarily defined as Generalization from Experience. It consists in inferring from some individual instances in which a phenomenon is observed to occur, that it occurs in all instances of a certain class; namely, in all which resemble the former, in what are regarded as the material circumstances.

In what way the material circumstances are to be distinguished from those which are immaterial, or why some of the circumstances are material and others not so, we are not yet ready to point out. We must first observe that there is a principle implied in the very statement of what Induction is; an assumption with regard to one course of nature and the order of the universe; namely, that there are such things in nature as parallel cases; that what happens once will, under sufficient degree of similarity of circumstance, happen again, and not only again, but as often as the same circumstances recur. This, I say, is an assumption involved in every case of induction. And if we consult the actual course of nature, we find that the assumption is warranted. The universe, as far as known to us, is so constituted, that whatever is true in any one case, is true in all cases of a certain description; the only difficulty is, to find what description.

This universal fact, which is our warrant for all inferences from experience has been decribed by different philosophers in different forms

---

[This selection is taken from Book III of Mill's *A System of Logic*, published in 1843. It comprises the whole of Chapter III and a portion of Chapter XXI.]

of language; that the course of nature is uniform; that the universe is governed by general laws, and the like. One of the most usual of those modes of expression, but also one of the most inadequate, is that which has been brought into familiar use by the metaphysicians of the school of Reid and Stewart. The disposition of the human mind to generalize from experience,—a propensity considered by these philosophers as an instinct of our nature,—they usually describe under some such names as "our intuitive conviction that the future will resemble the past." Now it has been well pointed out by Mr. Bailey, that (whether the tendency be or not an original and ultimate element of your nature) Time, in its modifications of past, present, and future, has no concern either with the belief itself, or with the grounds of it. We believe that fire will burn to-morrow, because it burned to-day and yesterday; but we believe, on precisely the same grounds, that it burned before we were born, and that it burns this very day in Cochin-China. It is not from the past to the future, as past and future, that we infer, but from the known to the un-known; from facts observed to facts unobserved; from what we have perceived, or been directly conscious of, to what has not come within our experience. In this last predicament is the whole region of the future; but also the vastly greater portion of the present and of the past.

Whatever be the most proper mode of expressing it, the proposition that the course of nature is uniform is the fundamental principle, or general axiom, of Induction. It would yet be a great error to offer this large generalization as any explanation of the inductive process. On the contrary, I hold it to be itself an instance of induction, and induction by no means of the most obvious kind. Far from being the first induction we make, it is one of the last, or at all events one of those which are latest in attaining strict philosophical accuracy. As a general maxim, indeed, it has scarcely entered into the minds of any but philosophers; nor even by them, as we shall have many opportunities of remarking, have its extent and limits been always very justly conceived. The truth is that this great generalization is itself founded on prior generalizations. The obscurer laws of nature were discovered by means of it, but the more obvious ones must have been understood and assented to as general truths before it was ever heard of. We should never have thought of affirming that all phenomena take place according to general laws, if we had not first arrived, in the case of a great multitude of phenomena, at some knowledge of the laws themselves; which could be done no otherwise than by induction. In what sense, then, can a principle, which is so far from being our earliest induction, be regarded as our warrant for all the others? In the only sense in which (as we have already seen) the general propositions which we place at the head of our reasonings when we throw them into syllogisms ever really contribute to their validity. As Archbishop Whately remarks, every induction is a syllogism with the major premise suppressed; or (as I prefer expressing it) every induction may be thrown into the form of a syllogism by supplying a major premise. If this be actually done, the principle which we are now considering, that of the uniformity of the course of nature, will appear as the ultimate major premise of all inductions, and will, therefore, stand to all inductions, in the relation in which, as has been shown at so much length, the major proposition of a syllogism always stands to the conclusion; not contributing at all to prove it, but being a necessary condition of its being proved; since no conclusion is proved for which there cannot be found a true major premise.

The statement that the uniformity of the course of nature is the ultimate major premise in all cases of induction may be thought to require some explanation. The immediate major premise in every inductive argument it certainly is not. Of that Archbishop Whately's must be held to be the correct account. The induction, "John, Peter, etc., are mortal, therefore all mankind are mortal," may, as he justly says, be thrown into a syllogism by prefixing as a major premise, (what is at any rate a necessary condition of the validity of the argument), namely, that what is true of John, Peter, etc., is true of all mankind. But how came we by this major premise? It is not self-evident; nay, in all cases of unwarranted generalization it is not true. How, then, is it arrived at? Necessarily either by induction or ratiocination; and if by induction, the process, like all other inductive arguments, may be thrown into the form of a syllogism. This previous syllogism it is, therefore, necessary to construct. There is, in the long run, only one possible construction. The real proof that what is true of John, Peter, etc., is true of all mankind, can only be, that a different supposition would be inconsistent with the uniformity which we know to exist in the course of nature. Whether there would be this inconsistency or not, may be a matter of long and delicate inquiry; but unless there would, we have no sufficient ground for the major of the inductive syllogism. It hence appears, that if we throw the whole course of any inductive argument into a series of syllogisms, we shall arrive by more or fewer steps at an ultimate syllogism, which will have for its major premise the principle or axiom of the uniformity of the course of nature.

It was not to be expected that in the case of this axiom, any more than of other axioms, there should be unanimity among thinkers with respect to the ground on which it is to be received as true. I have already stated that I regard it as itself a generalization from experience. Others hold it to be a principle which, antecedently to any verification by experience, we are compelled by the constitution of our thinking faculty to assume as true. Having so recently, and at so much length, combated a similar doctrine as applied to the axioms of mathematics by arguments which are in a great measure applicable to the present case, I shall defer the more particular discussion of this controverted point in regard to the fundamental axiom of induction until a more advanced period of our inquiry. At present, it is of more importance to understand thoroughly the import of the axiom itself. For the proposition, that the course of nature is uniform, possesses rather the brevity suitable to popular, than the precision requisite in philosophical language: its terms require to be explained, and a stricter than their ordinary signification given to them, before the truth of the assertion can be admitted.

The Axiom Is not True in Every Sense

Every person's consciousness assures him that he does not always expect uniformity in the course of events; he does not always believe that the unknown will be similar to the known, that the future will resemble the past. Nobody believes that the succession of rain and fine weather will be the same in every future year as in the present. Nobody expects to have the same dreams repeated every night. On the contrary, everybody mentions it as something extraordinary if the course of nature is constant, and resembles itself in these particulars. To look for constancy where constancy is not to be expected as, for instance, that a day which has once brought good fortune will always be a fortunate day, is justly accounted superstition.

The course of nature, in truth, is not only uniform, it is also infinitely various. Some phenomena are always seen to recur in the very same combinations in which we met with them at first; others seem altogether capricious; while some, which we had been accustomed to regard as bound down exclusively to a particular set of combinations, we unexpectedly find detached from some of the elements with which we had hitherto found them conjoined, and united to others of quite contrary description. To an inhabitant of Central Africa fifty years ago, no fact probably appeared to rest on more uniform experience than this, that all human beings are black. To Europeans not many years ago, the proposition, All swans are white, appeared an equally unequivocal instance of uniformity in the course of nature. Further experience has proved to both that they were mistaken; but they had to wait fifty centuries for this experience. During that long time, mankind believed in an uniformity of the course of nature where no such uniformity really existed.

According to the notion which the ancients entertained of induction, the foregoing were cases of as legitimate inference as any inductions whatever. In these two instances, in which, the conclusion being false, the ground of inference must have been insufficient, there was nevertheless, as much ground for it as this conception of induction admitted of. The induction of the ancients has been well described by Bacon, under the name of "Inductio per enumerationem simplicem, ubi non reperitur instantia contradictoria." It consists in ascribing the character of general truths to all propositions which are true in every instance that we happen to know of. This is the kind of induction which is natural to the mind when unaccustomed to scientific methods. The tendency, which some call an instinct, and which others account for by association, to infer the future from the past, the known from the unknown, is simply a habit of expecting that what has been found true once or several times, and never yet found false, will be found true again. Whether the instances are few or many, conclusive or inconclusive, does not much affect the matter: these are considerations which occur only on reflection: the unprompted tendency of the mind is to generalize its experience, provided this points all in one direction; provided no other experience of the conflicting character comes unsought. The notion of seeking it, of experimenting for it, of *interrogating* nature (to use Bacon's expression) is of much later growth. The observations of nature by uncultivated intellects is purely passive: they accept the facts which present themselves, without taking the trouble of searching for more: it is a superior mind only which asks itself what facts are needed to enable it to come to a safe conclusion, and then looks out for these.

But though we have always a propensity to generalise from unvarying experience, we are not always warranted in doing so. Before we can be at liberty to conclude that something is universally true because we have never known an instance to the contrary, we must have reason to believe that if there were in nature any instances to the contrary, we should have known of them. This assurance, in the great majority of cases, we cannot have, or can have only in a very moderate degree. The possibility of having it is the foundation on which we shall see hereafter that induction by simple enumeration may in some remarkable cases amount practically to proof. No such assurance, however, can be had on any of the ordinary subjects of scientific inquiry. Popular notions are usually founded on induction by simple enumeration; in science it carries us but a little way. We are forced to begin with it; we must often rely on it provisionally, in the absence of means of more searching investigation. But, for the accurate study of nature, we require a surer and a more potent instrument.

It was, above all, by pointing out the insufficiency of this rude and loose conception of Induction that Bacon merited the title so generally awarded to him of Founder of the Inductive Philosophy. The value of his own contributions to a more philosophical theory of the subject has cretainly been exaggerated. Although (along with some fundamental errors) his writings contain, more or less fully developed, several of the most important principles of the Inductive Method, physical investigation has now far outgrown the Baconian conception of Induction. Moral and political inquiry, indeed, are as yet far behind that conception. The current and improved modes of reasoning on these subjects are still of the same vicious description against which Bacon protested; the method almost exclusively employed by those professing to treat such matter inductively, is the very *inductio per enumerationem simplicem* which he condemns; and the experience which we hear so confidently appealed to by all sects, parties, and interests is still, in his own emphatic words, *mera palpatio.*

The Question of Inductive Logic Stated

In order to a better understanding of the problem which the logician must solve if he would establish a scientific theory of Induction, let us compare a few cases of incorrect inductions with others which are acknowledged to be legitimate. Some, we know, which were believed for centuries to be correct, were nevertheless incorrect. That all swans are white, cannot have been a good induction, since the conclusion has turned out erroneous. The experience, however, on which the conclusion rested was genuine. From the earliest records, the testimony of the inhabitants of the known world was unanimous on the point. The uniform experience, therefore, of the inhabitants of the known world, agreeing in a common result, without one known instance of deviation from that result, is not always sufficient to establish a general conclusion.

But let us now turn to an instance apparently not very dissimilar to this. Mankind were wrong, it seems, in concluding that all swans were white; are we also wrong when we conclude that all men's heads grow above their shoulders, and never below, in spite of the conflicting testimony of the naturalist Pliny? As there were black swans though civilised people had existed for three thousand years on the earth without meeting them, may there not also be "men whose heads do grow beneath their shoulders," notwithstanding a rather less perfect unanimity of negative testimony from observers? Most persons would answer No; it was more credible that a bird should vary in its colour than that men should vary in the relative position of their principal organs. And there is no doubt that in so saying they would be right; but to say why they are right would be impossible, without entering more deeply than is usually done into the true theory of Induction.

Again, there are cases in which we reckon with the most unfailing confidence upon uniformity, and other cases in which we do not count upon it at all. In some we feel complete assurance that the future will resemble the past, the unknown be precisely similar to the known. In others, however invariable may be the result obtained from the instances which have been observed, we draw from them no more than a very feeble presumption that the like result will hold in all other cases. That a straight line is the shortest distance between two points, we do not doubt to be true even in the region of the fixed stars. When a chemist announces the existence and properties of a newly discovered substance, if we confide in his accuracy, we feel assured that the conclusion he has arrived at will hold universally, though the induction be founded but on a single instance. We do not withhold our assent, waiting for a repetition of the experiment; or if we do, it is from a doubt whether the one experiment was properly made, not whether, if properly made, it would be conclusive. Here, then, is a general law of nature, inferred without hesitation from a single instance; an universal proposition from a singular one. Now mark another case, and contrast it with this. Not all the instances which have been observed since the beginning of the world in support of the general proposition that all crows are black would be deemed a sufficient presumption of the truth of the proposition, to outweigh the testimony of one unexceptionable witness who should affirm that in some region of the earth not fully explored he had caught and examined a crow, and had found it to be grey.

Why is a single instance, in some cases, sufficient for a complete induction, while in others myriads of concurring instances, without a single exception known or presumed, go such a very little way towards establishing an universal proposition? Whoever can answer this question knows more of the philosophy of logic than the wisest of the ancients, and has solved the problem of Induction. . . .

The Law of Causality Rests on an Induction
by Simple Enumeration

As was observed in a former place, the belief we entertain in the universality, throughout nature, of the law of cause and effect, is itself an instance of induction, and by no means one of the earliest which any of us, or which mankind in general, can have made. We arrive at this universal law by generalization from many laws of inferior generality. We should never have had the notion of causation (in the philosophical meaning of the term) as a condition of all phenomena, unless many cases of causation, or, in other words, many partial uniformities of sequence, had previously become familiar. The more obvious of the particular uniformities suggest, and give evidence of, the general uniformity, and the general uniformity, once established, enables us to prove the remainder of the particular uniformities of which it is made up. As, however, all rigorous processes of induction presuppose the general uniformity, our knowledge of the particular uniformities from which it was first inferred was not, of course, derived from rigorous induction, but from the loose and uncertain mode of induction *per enumerationem simplicem*; and the law of universal causation, being collected from results so obtained, cannot itself rest on any better foundation.

It would seem, therefore, that induction *per enumerationem simplicem* not only is not necessarily an illicit logical process, but is in reality the only kind of induction possible; since the more elaborate process depends for its validity on a law, itself obtained in that inartificial mode. Is there not then an inconsistency in contrasting the looseness of one method with the rigidity of another, when that other is indebted to the looser method for its own foundation?

The inconsistency, however, is only apparent. Assuredly, if induction by simple enumeration were an invalid process, no process grounded on it could be valid; just as no reliance could be placed on telescopes if we could not trust our eyes. But though a valid process, it is a fallible one, and fallible in very different degrees: if therefore we can substitute for the more fallible forms of the process an operation grounded on the same process in a less fallible form, we shall have effected a very material improvement. And this is what scientific induction does.

A mode of concluding from experience must be pronounced untrustworthy when subsequent experience refuses to confirm it. According to this criterion, induction by simple enumeration—in others words, generalization of an observed fact from the mere absence of any known instance to the contrary—affords in general a precarious and unsafe ground of assurance; for such generalizations are incessantly discovered, on further experience, to be false. Still, however, it affords some assurance, sufficient, in many cases, for the ordinary guidance of conduct. It would be absurd to say that the generalizations arrived at by mankind in the outset of their experience, such as these, Food nourishes, Fire burns, Water drowns, were unworthy of reliance. There is a scale of trustworthiness in the results of the original unscientific Induction; and on this diversity (as observed in the fourth chapter of the present book) depend the rules for improvement of the process. The improvement consists in correcting one of these inartificial generalizations by means of another. As has been already pointed out this is all that art can do. To test generalization, by showing that it either follows from, or conflicts with, some stronger induction, some generalization resting on a broader foundation of experience is the beginning and end of the logic of Induction.

In What Cases Such Induction Is Allowable

Now the precariousness of the method of simple enumeration is in an inverse ratio to the largeness of the generalization. The process is delusive and insufficient, exactly in proportion as the subject-matter of the observation is special and limited in extent. As the sphere widens, this unscientific method becomes less and less liable to mislead; and the most universal class of truths, the law of causation for instance, and the principles of number and of geometry, are duly and satisfactorily proved by that method alone, nor are they susceptible of any other proof. . . .

Now, the most extensive in its subject-matter of all generalisations which experience warrants, respecting the sequences and co-existences of phenomena, is the law of causation. It stands at the head of all observed uniformities in point of universality, and therefore (if the preceding observations are correct) in point of certainty. And if we consider, not what mankind would have been justified in believing in the infancy of their knowledge, but what may rationally be believed in its present more advanced state, we shall find ourselves warranted in considering this fundamental law, though itself obtained by induction from particular laws of causation, as not less certain, but, on the contrary, more so, than any of those from which it was drawn. It adds to them as much proof as it receives from them. For there is probably no one even of the best established laws of causation which is not sometimes counteracted, and to which, therefore, apparent exceptions do not present themselves, which would have necessarily and justly shaken the confidence of mankind in the universality of those laws, if inductive processes founded on the universal law had not enabled us to refer those exceptions to the agency of counteracting causes, and thereby reconcile them with the law with which they apparently conflict. Errors, moreover, may have slipped into the statement of any one of the special laws, through inattention to some material circumstance; and instead of the true proposition, another may have been enunciated, false as an universal law, though leading in all cases hitherto observed, to the same result. To the law of causation, on the contrary, we not only do not know of any exception, but the exceptions which limit or apparently invalidate the special laws, are so far from contradicting the universal one, that they confirm it; since in all cases which are sufficiently open to our observation, we are able to trace the difference of result, either to the absence of a cause which had been present in ordinary cases, or to the presence of one which had been absent. . . .

10

ON INDUCTION

Bertrand Russell

IN ALMOST ALL our previous discussions we have been concerned in the attempt to get clear as to our data in the way of knowledge of existence. What things are there in the universe whose existence is known to us owing to our being acquainted with them? So far, our answer has been that we are acquainted with our sense-data, and, probably, with ourselves. These we know to exist. And past sense-data which are remembered are known to have existed in the past. This knowledge supplies our data.

But if we are to be able to draw inferences from these data—if we are to know of the existence of matter, of other people, of the past before our individual memory begins, or of the future, we must know general principles of some kind by means of which such inferences can be drawn. It must be known to us that the existence of some one sort of thing, A, is a sign of the existence of some other sort of thing, B, either at the same time as A or at some earlier or later time, as, for example, thunder is a sign of the earlier existence of lightning. If this were not known to us, we could never extend our knowledge beyond the sphere of our private experience; and this sphere, as we have seen, is exceedingly limited. The question we have now to consider is whether such an extension is possible, and if so, how it is effected.

Let us take as an illustration a matter about which none of us, in fact, feel the slightest doubt. We are all convinced that the sun will rise tomorrow. Why? Is this belief a mere blind outcome of past experience, or can it be justified as a reasonable belief? It is not easy to find a test by which to judge whether a belief of this kind is reasonable or not, but

---

[This selection is Chapter VI of Russell's *Problems of Philosophy,* which was first published in 1912. It is here reprinted with the kind permission of Bertrand Russell and the Oxford University Press. Mr. Russell has requested that the following note be printed in conjunction with this selection: "What is said about induction in this chapter from my *Problems of Philosophy* seems to me now insufficient, though not erroneous. My present views on the subject are set forth in the last part of *Human Knowledge.*"]

we can at least ascertain what sort of general beliefs would suffice, if true, to justify the judgement that the sun will rise to-morrow, and the many other similar judgements upon which our actions are based.

It is obvious that if we are asked why we believe that the sun will rise to-morrow, we shall naturally answer, "Because it always has risen every day." We have a firm belief that it will rise in the future, because it has risen in the past. If we are challenged as to why we believe that it will continue to rise as heretofore, we may appeal to the laws of motion: the earth, we shall say, is a freely rotating body, and such bodies do not cease to rotate unless something interferes from outside, and there is nothing outside to interfere with the earth between now and to-morrow. Of course it might be doubted whether we are quite certain that there is nothing outside to interfere, but this is not the interesting doubt. The interesting doubt is as to whether the laws of motion will remain in operation until to-morrow. If this doubt is raised, we find ourselves in the same position as when the doubt about the sunrise was first raised.

The *only* reason for believing that the laws of motion will remain in operation is that they have operated hitherto, so far as our knowledge of the past enables us to judge. It is true that we have a greater body of evidence from the past in favour of the laws of motion than we have in favour of the sunrise, because the sunrise is merely a particular case of fulfilment of the laws of motion, and there are countless other particular cases. But the real question is: Do *any* number of cases of a law being fulfilled in the past afford evidence that it will be fulfilled in the future? If not, it becomes plain that we have no ground whatever for expecting the sun to rise to-morrow, or for expecting the bread we shall eat at our next meal not to poison us, or for any of the other scarcely conscious expectations that control our daily lives. It is to be observed that all such expectations are only *probable;* thus we have not to seek for a proof that they *must* be fulfilled, but only for some reason in favour of the view that they are *likely* to be fulfilled.

Now in dealing with this question we must, to begin with, make an important distinction, without which we should soon become involved in hopeless confusions. Experience has shown us that, hitherto, the frequent repetition of some uniform succession or coexistence has been a *cause* of our expecting the same succession or coexistence on the next occasion. Food that has a certain appearance generally has a certain taste, and it is a severe shock to our expectations when the familiar appearance is found to be associated with an unusual taste. Things which we see become associated, by habit, with certain tactile sensations which we expect if we touch them; one of the horrors of a ghost (in many ghost-stories) is that it fails to give us any sensations of touch. Uneducated people who go abroad for the first time are so surprised as to be incredulous when they find their native language not understood.

And this kind of association is not confined to men; in animals also it is very strong. A horse which has been often driven along a certain road resists the attempt to drive him in a different direction. Domestic animals expect food when they see the person who usually feeds them. We know that all these rather crude expectations of uniformity are liable to be misleading. The man who has fed the chicken every day throughout its life at last wrings its neck instead, showing that more refined views as to the uniformity of nature would have been useful to the chicken.

But in spite of the misleadingness of such expectations, they nevertheless exist. The mere fact that something has happened a certain number of times causes animals and men to expect that it will happen again. Thus our instincts certainly cause us to believe that the sun will rise tomorrow, but we may be in no better a position than the chicken which unexpectedly has its neck wrung. We have therefore to distinguish the fact that past uniformities *cause* expectations as to the future, from the question whether there is any reasonable ground for giving weight to such expectations after the question of their validity has been raised.

The problem we have to discuss is whether there is any reason for believing in what is called "the uniformity of nature." The belief in the uniformity of nature is the belief that everything that has happened or will happen is an instance of some general law to which there are *no* exceptions. The crude expectations which we have been considering are all subject to exceptions, and therefore liable to disappoint those who entertain them. But science habitually assumes, at least as a working hypothesis, that general rules which have exceptions can be replaced by general rules which have no exceptions. "Unsupported bodies in air fall" is a general rule to which balloons and aeroplanes are exceptions. But the laws of motion and the law of gravitation, which account for the fact that most bodies fall, also account for the fact that balloons and aeroplanes can rise; thus the laws of motion and the law of gravitation are not subject to these exceptions.

The belief that the sun will rise to-morrow might be falsified if the earth came suddenly into contact with a large body which destroyed its rotation; but the laws of motion and the law of gravitation would not be infringed by such an event. The business of science is to find uniformities, such as the laws of motion and the law of gravitation, to which, so far as our experience extends, there are no exceptions. In this search science has been remarkably successful, and it may be conceded that such uniformities have held hitherto. This brings us back to the question: Have we any reason, assuming that they have always held in the past, to suppose that they will hold in the future?

It has been argued that we have reason to know that the future will resemble the past, because what was the future has constantly become the past, and has always been found to resemble the past, so that we really have experience of the future, namely of times which were formerly future, which we may call past futures. But such an argument really begs the very question at issue. We have experience of past futures, but not of future futures, and the question is: Will future futures resemble past futures? This question is not to be answered by an argument which starts from past futures alone. We have therefore still to seek for some principle which shall enable us to know that the future will follow the same laws as the past.

The reference to the future in this question is not essential. The same question arises when we apply the laws that work in our experience to past things of which we have no experience—as, for example, in geology, or in theories as to the origin of the Solar System. The question we really have to ask is: "When two things have been found to be often associated, and no instance is known of the one occurring without the other, does the occurrence of one of the two, in a fresh instance, give any good ground for expecting the other?" On our answer to this question must depend the validity of the whole of our expectations as to the future, the whole of the results obtained by induction, and in fact practically all the beliefs upon which our daily life is based.

It must be conceded, to begin with, that the fact that two things have been found often together and never apart does not, by itself, suffice to *prove* demonstratively that they will be found together in the next case we examine. The most we can hope is that the oftener things are found together, the more probable it becomes that they will be found together another time, and that, if they have been found together often enough, the probability will amount *almost* to certainty. It can never quite reach certainty, because we know that in spite of frequent repetitions there sometimes is a failure at the last, as in the case of the chicken whose neck is wrung. Thus probability is all we ought to seek.

It might be urged, as against the view we are advocating, that we know all natural phenomena to be subject to the reign of law, and that sometimes, on the basis of observation, we can see that only one law can possibly fit the facts of the case. Now to this view there are two answers. The first is that, even if *some* law which has no exceptions applies to our case, we can never, in practice, be sure that we have discovered that law and not one to which there are exceptions. The second is that the reign of law would seem to be itself only probable, and that our belief that it will hold in the future, or in unexamined cases in the past, is itself based upon the very principle we are examining.

The principle we are examining may be called the *principle of induction,* and its two parts may be stated as follows:

(a) When a thing of a certain sort A has been found to be associated with a thing of a certain other sort B, and has never been found dissociated from a thing of the sort B, the greater the number of cases in which A and B have been associated, the greater is the probability that they will be associated in a fresh case in which one of them is known to be present;

(b) Under the same circumstances, a sufficient number of cases of association will make the probability of a fresh association nearly a certainty, and will make it approach certainty without limit.

As just stated, the principle applies only to the verification of our expectation in a single fresh instance. But we want also to know that there is a probability in favour of the general law that things of the sort A are *always* associated with things of the sort B, provided a sufficient number of cases of association are known, and no cases of failure of association are known. The probability of the general law is obviously less than the probability of the particular case, since if the general law is true, the particular case must also be true, whereas the particular case may be true without the general law being true. Nevertheless the probability of the general law is increased by repetitions, just as the probability of the particular case is. We may therefore repeat the two parts of our principle as regards the general law, thus:

(a) The greater the number of cases in which a thing of the sort A has been found associated with a thing of the sort B, the more probable it is (if no cases of failure of association are known) that A is always associated with B;

(b) Under the same circumstances, a sufficient number of cases of the association of A with B will make it nearly certain that A is always associated with B, and will make this general law approach certainty without limit.

It should be noted that probability is always relative to certain data. In our case, the data are merely the known cases of coexistence of A and B. There may be other data, which *might* be taken into account, which would gravely alter the probability. For example, a man who had seen a great many white swans might argue, by our principle, that on the data it was *probable* that all swans were white, and this might be a perfectly sound argument. The argument is not disproved by the fact that some swans are black, because a thing may very well happen in spite of the fact that some data render it improbable. In the case of the swans, a man might know that color is a very variable characteristic in many species of animals, and that, therefore, an induction as to color is peculiarly liable to error. But this knowledge would be a fresh datum, by no means proving that the probability relatively to our previous data had been wrongly estimated. The fact, therefore, that things often fail to fulfil our expectations is no evidence that our expectations will not *probably* be fulfilled in a given case or a given class of cases. Thus our inductive principle is at any rate not capable of being *disproved* by an appeal to experience.

The inductive principle, however, is equally incapable of being *proved* by an appeal to experience. Experience might conceivably confirm the inductive principle as regards the cases that have been already examined; but as regards unexamined cases, it is the inductive principle alone that can justify any inference from what has been examined to what has not been examined. All arguments which, on the basis of experience, argue as to the future or the unexperienced parts of the past or present, assume the inductive principle; hence we can never use experience to prove the inductive principle without begging the question. Thus we must either accept the inductive principle on the ground of its intrinsic evidence, or forgo all justification of our expectations about the future. If the principle is unsound, we have no reason to expect the sun to rise to-morrow, to expect bread to be more nourishing than a stone, or to expect that if we throw ourselves off the roof we shall fall. When we see what looks like our best friend approaching us, we shall have no reason to suppose that his body is not inhabited by the mind of our worst enemy or of some total stranger. All our conduct is based upon associations which have worked in the past, and which we therefore regard as likely to work in the future; and this likelihood is dependent for its validity upon the inductive principle.

The general principles of science, such as the belief in the reign of law, and the belief that every event must have a cause, are as completely dependent upon the inductive principle as are the beliefs of daily life. All such general principles are believed because mankind have found innumerable instances of their truth and no instances of their falsehood. But this affords no evidence for their truth in the future, unless the inductive principle is assumed.

Thus all knowledge which, on the basis of experience tells us something about what is not experienced, is based upon a belief which experience can neither confirm nor confute, yet which, at least in its more concrete applications, appears to be as firmly rooted in us as many of the facts of experience. The existence and justification of such beliefs —for the inductive principle, as we shall see, is not the only example— raises some of the most difficult and most debated problems of philosophy.

11

WILL THE FUTURE
BE LIKE THE PAST?

F. L. Will

Hume's Scepticism

. . . THE STANDARD ARGUMENT for complete inductive scepticism, for
the belief that inductive procedures have no rational and no empirical
justification whatever, is the one stated in a small variety of ways in the
writings of Hume. If one consults these writings in search of an answer
to the question of inductive validity one finds the same clear answer
argued first in technical detail in the *Treatise,* secondly compressed into
a few non-technical paragraphs in the *Abstract of a Treatise of Human
Nature,* and thirdly, presented again in a non-technical but somewhat
fuller version in a chapter in the *Enquiry Concerning Human Understanding.* There is no basis whatever for any conclusion concerning
future matters, according to this argument; there is no way whatever
in which such conclusions can be established to be certainly true or
even probable. For in the first place no such conclusion can be demonstrated by reasoning alone, since they are all conclusions about matters
of fact, and since it is the case that the denial of any assertion of a
matter of fact is not self-contradictory. But if one gives up the rationalistic aspiration to demonstrate propositions about matters of fact or
existence *a priori,* and turns instead to experience, this road, though apparently more promising at first, likewise ends by leading one exactly
nowhere. Clearly no statement about future matters of fact can be established by observation. Future things cannot be observed. Any event
or state of affairs which can be observed is by definition not in the

[This article originally appeared in *Mind,* 1947. It is here reprinted with slight omissions
by the kind permission of the author and the editor of *Mind.*]

future. The only recourse which remains therefore is the inductive procedure of employing present or past observations and inferring therefrom the nature of the future. But this procedure to which we are all forced, or rather, to which we all should be forced, if we did not, in company with the animals, use it naturally from birth, is in the light of close analysis completely indefensible. For such reasoning assumes, and is quite invalid without the assumption, that the future will be like the past.

> . . . all inferences from experience suppose, as their foundation, that the future will resemble the past, and that similar powers will be conjoined with similar sensible qualities. If there be any suspicion that the course of nature may change, and that the past may be no rule for the future, all experience becomes useless, and can give rise to no inference or conclusion. (*Enquiry*, Section IV.)[1]

Will the future "resemble the past"? Or be "conformable to the past?" These are the ways in which in the *Enquiry* Hume expresses the question concerning the uniformity of nature, restricting to its reference toward the future the question which already had been asked in broader terms in the *Treatise*. There, without the temporal restriction, it is argued that the principle of inductive conclusions, the principle upon which reason would proceed if reason determined us in these matters, is *"that instances, of which we have had no experience, must resemble those, of which we have had experience, and that the course of nature continues always uniformly the same."* (Bk. I, Pt. III, Sect. VI.)

However the principle is stated, the argument about it remains the same. It is indispensable, if inductive conclusions are to be justified; but just as it is absolutely indispensable, so, and this is the measure of our logical misfortune, it cannot be established as certain or as probable in any way. It cannot be established by any demonstrative argument. For it is clearly an assertion of a matter of fact, and therefore the kind of assertion whose denial is non-contradictory and conceivable.

> That there are no demonstrative arguments in the case seems evident; since it implies no contradiction that the course of nature may change, and that an object, seemingly like those which we have experienced, may be attended with different or contrary effects. May I not clearly and distinctly conceive that a body, falling from the clouds, and which, in all other respects, resembles snow, has yet the taste of salt or the feeling of fire? Is there any more intelligible proposition than to affirm, that all the trees will flourish in December and January, and decay in May and June? Now whatever is intelligible, and can be distinctly conceived, implies no contradiction and can never be proved false by any demonstrative argument or abstract reasoning *a priori*. (*Enquiry*, Sect. IV.[2] Cf. *Treatise*, *loc. cit.*)

---

1. See above, p. 114.
2. See above, pp. 112-113.

Any further doubts about the doubtfulness of this principle which is the main-spring of inductive inference are quickly disposed of. No one who understands the principle with its reference to unobserved instances will suggest that it can be simply observed to be true. It is still true that one cannot observe the future, or the unobserved generally. And, finally, no one who has a sound logical conscience and appreciates the indispensability of the principle to induction generally will tolerate the suggestion that the principle may be established by inductions from experience. Such a process would be circular.

> It is impossible, therefore, that any arguments from experience can prove this resemblance of the past to the future; since all these arguments are founded on the supposition of that resemblance.

And again:

> . . . all our experimental conclusions proceed upon the supposition that the future will be conformable to the past. To endeavour, therefore, the proof of this last supposition by probable arguments, or arguments regarding existence, must be evidently going in a circle, and taking that for granted, which is the very point in question. (*Enquiry*, Sect. IV.[3])

On this point the *Treatise* (*loc. cit.*) and the *Abstract* speak with one voice. One final quotation from the latter may serve to summarise the conclusion.

> 'Tis evident that *Adam* with all his science, would never have been able to *demonstrate*, that the course of nature must continue uniformly the same, and that the future must be conformable to the past. What is possible can never be demonstrated to be false; and 'tis possible the course of nature may change, since we can conceive such a change. Nay, I will go farther, and assert, that he could not so much as prove by any *probable* arguments, that the future must be conformable to the past. All probable arguments are built on the supposition, that there is this conformity betwixt the future and the past, and therefore can never prove it. This conformity is a *matter of fact*, and if it must be proved, will admit of no proof but from experience. But our experience in the past can be a proof of nothing for the future, but upon a supposition, that there is a resemblance betwixt them. This therefore is a point, which can admit of no proof at all, and which we take for granted without any proof. (*Abstract*, 1938 ed., p. 15.)

Is Inductive Reasoning Really Circular?

. . . It would be more promising in respect to logical neatness and precision for one to consider the alleged circularity of all inductive procedure, which is the central point of the above argument, while using

---

3. See above, p. 113.

as test case some specific scientific law or principle rather than some affirmation as vague and imprecise as that the future will resemble the past. But, for the purpose of analysing the sceptic's views and meeting the arguments by which these views have been defended, such a pro-- cedure would have this deficiency, that no matter what specific scientific generalisation were chosen, one reply which would be sure to be made would consist of an appeal beyond this generalisation to some general beliefs about uniformity, some general Principle of Uniformity which, it would be urged, is assumed somehow in the inductive establishment of this and other scientific generalisations. Since the sceptical arguments has been presented in terms of general Principles of Uniformity, and it is in these terms that it is alleged to demonstrate the logical circularity of all inductive reasoning, it seems worth while to attempt to deal with this argument, if one can, in the same terms—in terms of some alleged Principle of Uniformity for which it has been claimed in recent philoso- phy that it does serve as a wide and basic inductive assumption.

In his *Treatise on Probability*, J. M. Keynes attempts to formulate a set of principles which, if assumed to be true of a given area of subject- matter, would justify, in accordance with the principles of probability, the employment of inductive methods in that area. One of the principles which he discusses, the simplest and at the same time the one for which it seems, at first view, most plausible to contend that it may serve as a broad inductive assumption, is the one to which he gave the name of the "Principle of the Uniformity of Nature." This Principle affirms that nature is uniform in a specific way; and that is in respect to position in space and time. "It involves," writes Keynes, "the assertion of a general- ised judgment of irrelevance, namely, of the irrelevance of mere position in time and space to generalisations which have no reference to particular positions in time and space." (p. 226. *Cf.* also pp. 255-256, 263, 276) It is this principle, he argues, which

> . . . supplies the answer, if it is correct, to the criticism that the instances, on which generalisations are based, are all alike in being past, and that any generalisation, which is applicable to the future, must be based, for this reason, upon imperfect analogy. We judge directly that the re- semblance between instances, which consists in their being past, is in itself irrelevant, and does not supply a valid ground for impugning a generalisation. (p. 256)

It is, however, difficult to interpret this so-called Principle in such a way that it makes a statement which is both definite and is not at the same time refuted in some areas of experience. Keynes observes that what this Principle affirms is "that the same total cause always produces the same effect" (p. 248), and this is so; but the difficulty here is that of giving a definite meaning to the important adjective "same" as it applies to causes and effects. Unless there is a specifiable meaning applicable to causes in all fields, the formula "same cause—same effect" is not a univocal principle affirming the presence of a specific kind of uniformity in every area of natural phenomena. Yet, when one sets out to specify just what kind of sameness is meant when this formula is employed, one discovers that there is a great variety of interpretations of this word in different fields of inquiry, and that what determines whether a given set of circumstances is regarded as the same cause, for example, varies from field to field, depending upon the nature of the subject-matter as that is revealed in the various generalisations which are regarded as established for that subject-matter. These generalisations exhibit among themselves great differences in scope and precision, as well as in the degree of confidence with which they are accepted. They include, for example, the generalisations about the coherence and constancy of properties which are involved in our belief in and distinctions among various kinds of material objects. And they include the more precise generalisations, frequently expressed in the form of mathematical equations, which would normally be referred to as "scientific laws," as well as broader generalisations formulated in various accepted Principles and Theories. When this is understood, when one sees that in the employment of the Principle of Uniformity what determines the kind of sameness to which the Principle affirms that differences in mere position in space and time are irrelevant is the specific generalisations, the laws, principles, and so on, which have been established in that field, one is in a better position to understand this so-called Principle and its alleged employment as a general inductive assumption. In any given field the Principle of Uniformity states that mere differences in space and time are irrelevant in just this sense, that there are certain generalisations, true of this field, which describe the conditions under which certain objects exist and events occur, and in which differences in mere position in space and time make little or no detectable difference. That this is so, accordingly, is not an inductive assumption in that field in the sense that it is specified and made before all inductive inquiry in the field. It is an inductive assumption in the more usual sense that conclusions of previous experience and inquiries are available for employment in any field as bases for further investigation in that field.

The primary purpose here is not to elucidate and specify the variations of meaning which such a Principle or formula must undergo if it is to be understood as applying to the great variety of fields in which inductive inquiry is carried on, to the great variety in the kinds of uniformity which the generalisations in these fields describe. The primray purpose is to inquire whether the sceptics are right in insisting that it is impossible to provide a genuine evidence for beliefs about uniformity or whether, on the contrary, it is possible to furnish empirical evidence for these beliefs which, in its employment, does not involve circular reasoning. It is granted that what the Principle of Uniformity affirms in any field, if "Principle" it may be called, is that there is uniformity in that field in this sense and no other; that there are certain specific generalisations which apply to that field and in which mere differences of position in time and space are regarded as irrelevant. In the light of this interpretation of uniformity the question briefly is, how can such a broad affirmation be confirmed or verified by induction without circularity?

For purposes of simplicity, in order to secure the clearest statement of the argument in the fewest words, it will be useful in what follows to abbreviate the statement of this Principle of Uniformity and also to consider it only in reference to time. If it can be shown that what the Principle affirms concerning the irrelevance of time in specific generalisations can be confirmed inductively, it can also be shown in exactly the same way that it is possible to confirm the Principle in its spatial reference also. So abbreviated and restricted, the Principle asserts that, in the specific way just defined, differences in time make no difference. Can this interpretation of the assertion that the future will resemble the past be confirmed? What, if any, is the evidence for it?

It follows directly from the interpretation which has just been given of this principle what the evidence for it must be. If the Principle affirms no more for any given area of fact than the validity in that area of certain generalisations which are uniform with respect to space and time, then the evidence for the Principle must be whatever evidence there is for these particular generalisations. This includes all the observations in the past and present which confirm the presence in that area of the uniformities of which these general statements speak. Belief in the uniformity in a given area is not something which is specifiable apart from the laws, principles, and other generalisations regarded as established in that area, but is itself belief in just the kind of uniformities which these generalisations describe and define. If it is correct, then, to say of any generalisation, *e.g.* of any scientific law, that it is confirmed or verified by empirical evidence, is it not correct to say that, to that extent, there is evidence for belief in the uniformity of nature?

Past and Future

The sceptic's answer to this question repeats that final rejoinder of Hume. Granted that there is empirical evidence which has been used to establish various scientific laws, all that it is evidence for, he insists, is the assertion that *in the past* these laws were true, that in the past differences in time have made no difference. This evidence is absolutely worthless for inferences which speak about the future unless it is possible to assume that the future will be like the past. But stop! That is part of what one is trying to show, that is, that mere differences in temporal position, whether past or future, make no difference in these laws of nature. That the future will be like the past means, among other things, that in the future these laws will hold, that in this specific respect differences in time will make no difference. This cannot be inductively confirmed, the sceptic is saying, because any inductive argument for it assumes it and is therefore, as evidence, completely valueless.

One major source of the plausibility of the sceptic's reasoning lies in the analogies which knowing the future easily suggests and in terms of which one is apt to think and be misled. Is this not, one may ask, like any case of sampling? And must one not take care, when reasoning inductively from samples, that one's samples are fair? If a scientist reasons concerning the behavior of oxygen, nitrogen, or hydrogen on Mars, if such elements there be on Mars, on the basis of the known behaviour of these elements on the earth, he is assuming that in some respects the samples of the elements on the other planet are like those we have here. Similarly in reasoning about the future behaviour of these elements on the basis of present and past behaviour one must assume that future samples of these elements will be like present and past ones. Now if it is the case that past samples may be regarded as evidence about future ones only upon such an assumption, then no examination of past samples, however extensive, can be regarded as yielding evidence for the assumption itself. Any reasoning which did attempt to employ such samples as evidence for the assumption would be forced to use the assumption as a principle in the reasoning and would therefore beg the whole question at issue.

A physical representation of the kind of analogy presented here might be as follows: Suppose that there was somewhere in the world an enclosure beyond which it was impossible for anyone ever to go or to make any observations. Nothing could be seen, heard, or in any other way perceived beyond the border. The territory beyond the enclosure, forever barred from human perception, is the land of Future. The territory within the enclosure is the land of Present and Past, but since it is overwhelmingly the latter, it all goes under the name of Past. Now suppose that someone within the enclosure is interested in some proposition about the way things behave beyond the enclosure, say, a simple and homely proposition about chickens, to the effect that beyond the enclosure roosters fight more than hens. And he wonders what evidence, if any, there is for this proposition. Of course he cannot observe this to be true. He must base it upon his observation in the land of Past; and if he does base it upon the observed fact that roosters in the land of Past fight more than hens, he must assume that in this respect chickens beyond the enclosure behave like chickens within it, so that, knowing that in the latter area roosters are the more pugnacious, he may employ this knowledge as evidence that things are this way also in the former area. This is an assumption which no empirical evidence, confined as it must be to evidence in Past, can be employed to support. Any attempt to support it with such evidence must itself assume that in respect to the phenomena involved differences between Past and Future are negligible; and since that is exactly what the reasoning is attempting to establish, the process is patently circular.

This is the kind of metaphor which makes friends, and influences people, in this case, to draw the wrong conclusions. There are several faults in the analogy. The chief one is that, as represented, the border between Past and Future is stationary, while in the temporal situation it is not. To duplicate the temporal situation in this respect the analogy should represent the border as constantly moving, revealing as it does constantly, in territory which has hitherto been Future, hens and roosters similar as regards difference in disposition to those already observed in Past. The matter of evidence for the proposition about hens and roosters is then also different. If this proposition is in a position analogous to the beliefs about uniformity which are represented in modern scientific laws, the situation is something like this. Previously inhabitants in Past had drawn more sweeping conclusions concerning the difference between the disposition to fight of male and female chickens. They have discovered recently that in respect to young chicks and pullets this generalisation did not hold. They have therefore revised the proposition to exclude all the known negative instances and speak only and more surely of the behaviour of hens and roosters, meaning by these latter terms just fully grown and developed female and male chickens.

So far as there is any record, chickens in Past have verified this rule; so far as there is any record, every chicken revealed by the ever-receding border has likewise verified it; so far as there is any record there has not been one negative instance. Is it not the case that the inhabitants of Past do have evidence for the proposition that all chickens obey this rule, those already in Past, which they call "Past-chickens," and those also which are not yet in Past but which will be subsequently revealed by the moving border, and which they call not unnaturally "Future-chickens"? They have a vast number of positive instances of the rule, and no negative instances, except those in respect to which the rule has already been revised. In view of the present evidence that in all cases, year after year and century after century, the progressively revealed chickens have verified and do verify this rule, must one not conclude that the inhabitants of past do have evidence for this proposition, and that anyone is wrong who says that they have actually no evidence one way or other?

The sceptic, however, is still prepared to argue his case, and his argument, in terms of the present analogy, has a now familiar ring. That the inhabitants of Past have no evidence whatsoever about the behaviour of Future-chickens, he will insist; and as grounds he will point out that although the borders does progressively recede and reveal chickens like those previously observed in Past, these are really not Future-chickens. By the very fact that they have been revealed they are no longer Future-chickens, but are now Past-chickens. Observation of them is not observation of Future-chickens, and any attempt to reason from such observation to conclusions about Future-chickens must therefore assume that Future-chickens are like Past-chickens. For the inhabitants of Past, in these efforts to know the land beyond the border, this is both an inescapable and unknowable presumption.

What should one say of an argument of this kind? Only through some logical slip, one feels strongly, would it be possible to arrive at such a conclusion. One would have thought that the receding border was a matter upon which the inhabitants of Past may legitimately congratulate themselves in the light of their interest in learning what Future-chickens, when they become Past, are going to be like. If the border had not yet begun to recede they would indeed be in an unfortunate position for securing such knowledge. But happily this is not the case. The border is constantly receding. And granting that it will constantly recede, revealing always more of the land of Future, and even granting also that this means that there is an inexhaustible area to be revealed, the inhabitants of Past are in the fortunate position that with the progressive recession they may learn more and more about chickens, Past and Future. They may derive hypotheses from their experience of what has already been revealed and proceed further to test these by the progressive revelations of Future, in the light of which they may be confirmed, refuted, or revised. The sceptic's argument amounts to the assertion that all this apparent good fortune is really illusory and that the sorry Pastians are actually in no better position with respect to knowing about Future-chickens and Future-things generally than they would be if the border never moved at all. For the movement of the border does not reveal Future-chickens, since Future is by definition the land beyond the border. No matter how much or how little is revealed, by the very fact that it is revealed and on this side of the border it is not Future but Past, and therefore, since the land of Future always is beyond observation, no empirical method can produce any evidence that what is in that land is in any way similar to what is not. That this rendering of the sceptic's position, though in the language of the above metaphor, is undistorted and fair may be seen by consulting the words of an illustrious modern sceptic and follower of Hume, Bertrand Russell. In his chapter, "On Induction," in *The Problems of Philosophy,* Russell expressed the matter in this fashion:

It has been argued that we have reason to know that the future will resemble the past, because what was the future has constantly become the past, and has always been found to resemble the past, so that we really have experience of the future, namely of times which were formerly future, which we may call past futures. But such an argument really begs the very question at issue. We have experience of past futures, but not of future futures, and the question is: Will future futures resemble past futures? This question is not to be answered by an argument which starts from past futures alone. We have therefore still to seek for some principle which shall enable us to know that the future will follow the same laws as the past.[4]

This is the central difficulty urged by Hume, Russell, and others in arguing that there can never be any empirical evidence that the future will be like the past. Empirically, in Russell's language, it is possible to have evidence only that this has been true of past and possibly present futures, not that it will be true of future futures. It is the situation in the land of Past all over again. There are generalisations which are constantly being confirmed by experience. But every time a confirming instance occurs it is nullified as evidence by the argument that it is not really a confirming instance at all. For by the fact that it has occurred it is an instance of a past future, and therefore it tells nothing whatever about future futures. In treating of the land of Past it was suggested that there is involved in arguing in this manner a logical slip or error. It remains to investigate how this is the case.

Suppose that in 1936, to take but a short span of time, a man says that in the above-defined sense the future will be like the past. In 1936, if he could somehow have shown that 1937 would be like 1936, this would have been evidence for his statement, as even a sceptic would admit. But in 1937, when he does establish that 1937 is like 1936, it has somehow ceased to be evidence. So long as he did not have it, it was evidence; as soon as he gets it it ceases to be. The constant neutralisation of the evidence which is effected in this argument is effected by the same kind of verbal trick which children play upon one another in fun. Child A asks child B what he is going to do to-morrow. B replies that he is going to play ball, go swimming, or what not. Thereupon A says, "You can't do that."

B: Why not?

A: Because to-morrow never comes. When to-morrow comes it won't be to-morrow; it will be to-day. You can never play to-morrow; you can only play to-day.

Again, if a prophet announces that next year will bring a utopia, and if each succeeding year, when the predicted utopia does not come, he defends himself by pointing out that he said "next year" and that

4. See above, pp. 127-128.

obviously this is not next year, no reasonable person would pay much attention to him. Such a person would realise, on a moment's reflexion, that the prophet is being deceptive with the word "next." In 1936 "next year" means "1937;" in 1937 it means "1938." Since every year "next year" means a different year, a year yet to come, what the prophet says can never be verified or disproved. If in 1936 he meant by this phrase 1937, as he sensibly should, then this statement can be verified or refuted in 1937. But if, when 1937 comes, he insists that he did not mean 1937, but "next year," and if in 1938 he again insists that he did not mean that year, and so on, then what he seems to be meaning by "next year" is the $n + 1$th year where n is the ever-progressing number of the present year. No one should alter his present activities or his plans for the future on the basis of such a prediction, for, of course, it really is not a prediction. While in the form of a statement about the future it does not say anything about the future, anything which could possibly be true or false in the infinity of time, if infinity it is, which yet remains to transpire. For what the prophet is saying is that utopia will come next year, and by his own interpretation of the words "next year" he is affirming that next year will never come. In other words, at the time which never comes, and hence when nothing occurs, a utopia will occur. This is not even sensible speech; it is a contradiction.

In a similar though less simple way those who employ the sceptical argument about uniformity to show that there is no evidence whatever for any statement about the future are being themselves deceived and are deceiving others by their use of expressions like "next," "future," "future future," and "past future." The man who said in 1936 that the future would be like the past, that mere differences in temporal position make no difference in the behaviour of nature which is described in scientific laws, meant, as he sensibly should, that this was true of the years 1937, 1938, and so on. He said something of the form "all A's are B's" and it has been possible since 1936 to examine the A's of 1937 to 1946 and to see whether what he said is confirmed or disproved by the available evidence. If, however, now that it is 1946, and all this evidence is in, he should remark that since it is 1946 the years 1937-46 are no longer future and therefore have ceased to be evidence for the proposition, then he is guilty of using, or rather abusing the word "future" in the way in which the prophet in the previous example was abusing the word "next." For the only basis for his contention that the observed A's are not confirming evidence, or what is the same thing, that they are confirming instances only if one assumes quite circularly that the future is like the past, is in his illusive use of the word "future." Time does pass, and, because it does, the present is a constantly changing one; and the point of reference for the use of words like "future" and "past" is accordingly different. The correct conclusion to be drawn from the fact that time passes is that the future is constantly being revealed and that, in consequence, we have had and shall have the opportunity to learn more and more accurately what the laws of nature's behaviour are and how therefore the future will be like the past. But this sceptical man has his eyes fixed in fatal fascination upon the movement of time, the constantly changing present. And seeing that, as the present changes, what was once future is not now future, but present, and will shortly be past, he is led to draw the conclusion that after all, for any present whatever, the future is forever hidden behind a veil. . . .

SELECTED BIBLIOGRAPHY

(ITEMS PROVIDED WITH ASTERISK ARE MORE ADVANCED)

Russell's maturer views on induction may be found, together with a discussion of the theory of probability, in his *Human Knowledge,* (London: Allen and Unwin, New York: Simon and Schuster, 1948). J. M. Keynes, *A Treatise on Probability** (London: Macmillan, 1921) is a classic on the problems of induction and probability. W. Kneale, *Probability and Induction,* (Oxford: Clarendon Press, 1949), Part II, gives a survey of classical theories of induction from Bacon to Keynes. E. Nagel, *Principles of the Theory of Probability* (Int. Encyclopedia of Unified Science, Vol. I. No. 6, University of Chicago Press, 1939) is recommended as an introduction to the technical problems of the theory of probability. R. von Mises, *Probability, Statistics and Truth* (New York: Macmillan, 1939) is an introduction to the theory of probability from the point of view of the interpretation of probability as relative frequency. H. Reichenbach, *Experience and Prediction,* (Chicago: University of Chicago Press, 1938) is a theory of empirical knowledge emphasizing that empirical propositions are never more than highly probable and analyzing probability, like von Mises, in terms of relative frequency. D. Williams, *The Ground of Induction,* (Cambridge: Harvard University Press, 1947) is an attempt to solve Hume's problem by pure logic or the mathematical theory of probability.

Expository and critical discussions of Mill's experimental methods are found in M. Cohen and E. Nagel, *Introduction to Logic and Scientific Method,* (New York: Harcourt, Brace and Co., 1934) Chapter 13, and S. L. Stebbing, *A Modern Introduction to Logic,* (London: Methuen and Co., 1930) Chapters 15 and 17. An introduction to the theory of probability and its application to inductive reasoning may also be found in Chapters 8 and 14 of Cohen and Nagel. The logical foundations of empirical knowledge are dealt with in an elementary way by J. Hospers, *Introduction to Philosophical Analysis,* (New York: Prentice-Hall, 1953) Chapter 3. A. Pap, *Elements of Analytic Philosophy,* (New York: Macmillan, 1949), Chapters 9 and 16, includes a discussion of Hume's problem, of the meaning of probability and of the alleged presuppositions of induction. Chapter 8 of the same book deals with the question of the certainty of empirical propositions.

A critique of philosophical scepticism in terms of the analysis of ordinary language is given in P. Edwards' "Bertrand Russell's Doubts about Induction," *Mind* 1949, reprinted in A. Flew (ed.) *Essays in Logic and Language,* First Series (Oxford: Basil Blackwell, 1951). A similar approach, also including a critique of Russell, is A. Ambrose's "The Problem of Justifying Inductive Inference," *Journal of Philosophy,* 1947, reprinted in S. Hook (ed.), *American Philosophers at Work,* (New York: Criterion Books, 1956). The same kind of view is also defended in Chapter 9 of P. F. Strawson, *Introduction to Logical Theory* (London: Methuen and Co., New York: John Wiley, 1952). The approach of these writers is critically examined in I. O. Urmson's "Some Questions Concerning Validity," which is reprinted in A. Flew (ed.), *Essays in Conceptual Analysis* (London: Macmillan, 1956). For a critique of F. Will's "Will the Future be like the Past?" which is, with minor omissions, reprinted in this section, see D. Williams' "Induction and the Future," *Mind* 1948. A shorter article giving Will's views is entitled "Is there a Problem of Induction?", *Journal of Philosophy,* 1942. A discussion of the views of D. Williams is contained in D. S. Miller's "Professor Donald Williams versus Hume," *Journal of Philosophy,* 1947. For an approach to the problem via an analysis of the meaning of "justification," see M. Black, "The Justification of Induction," in M. Black, *Language and Philosophy,* (Ithaca: Cornell University Press, 1949). Further discussions by Black are his essays "Pragmatic Justification of Induction," "Inductive Support of Inductive Rules," and "How Difficult Might Induction be?" all of which are included in M. Black, *Problems of Analysis,* (Ithaca: Cornell University Press, 1954). The view that the principle of induction is a postulate is presented in H. Feigl's "The Logical Character of the Principle of Induction," reprinted in Feigl and Sellars, *Readings in Philosophical Analysis* (New York: Appleton-Century-Crofts, 1949). G. E. Moore's "Hume's Philosophy," reprinted in Feigl and Sellars, *op. cit.,* is a painstakingly clear analysis of Hume's arguments concerning empirical knowledge. Important articles also to consult are C. D. Broad's "Induction and Probability,"* *Mind,* 1918-1920, and W. Burks' "The Presupposition Theory of Induction,"* *Philosophy of Science,* 1953.

C. I. Lewis, *Mind and the World Order,* (New York: Charles Scribner's, 1929) argues, like Reichenbach, that no proposition asserting an objective fact is conclusively verifiable (see esp. Chapter 9). This thesis is elaborated in Lewis' later book *An Analysis of Knowledge and Valuation** (LaSalle, Illinois: Open Court, 1947), Chapters 7-9. The same view is advocated by A. J. Ayer in *Language, Truth and Logic,* Chapter 5. A comprehensive discussion of the problem of the certainty of empirical propositions was initated by N. Malcolm's "Certainty and Empirical Statements," *Mind,* 1942. This is a criticism of the philosopher's denial of certainty based on the analysis of ordinary language. Malcolm's article was answered by M. Black in a note also called "Certainty and Empirical Statements," *Mind,* 1942. Malcolm continued his criticism in a classic article, "Moore and Ordinary Language," in P. A. Schilpp (ed.) *The Philosophy of G. E. Moore,* (Evanston and Chicago: Northwestern University, 1942). C. A. Campbell entered the debate with his "Common Sense Propositions and Philosophical Paradoxes," *Proceedings of the Aristotelian Society,* 1944-1945. A critique of Campbell is advanced by P. Edwards in "Ordinary Language and Absolute Certainty," *Philosophical Studies,* 1950, which was followed by Campbell's rejoinder, "Mr. Edwards on Absolute Certainty," *ibid.* A revision of Malcolm's views is contained in "On Defending Common Sense," *Philosophical Review,* 1949. A critique of this article is given in C. Rollins' "Ordinary Language and Procrustean Beds," *Mind,* 1951, which is answered in Malcolm's "Moore's Use of 'Know'," *Mind,* 1953. Further exposition of Malcolm's views are given in a symposium in which he participated along with R. M. Chisholm entitled "Philosophy and Ordinary Language," *Philosophical Review,* 1951. The debate is continued in M. Macdonald's "Sleeping and Waking," *Mind,* 1953. Malcolm's latest article on this topic is "Dreaming and Skepticism," *Philosophical Review,* 1956.

A critique of the thesis that no statements asserting existence can be absolutely certain is given in A. Pap's "Indubitable Existential Statements," *Mind,* 1946. There is a reply to Pap by C. Rollins in "Are there Indubitable

Existential Statements?", *Mind,* 1949, and a rejoinder to Rollins by Pap in "Ostensive Definition and Empirical Certainty," *Mind,* 1950. The view that empirical statements can be certain is defended in W. T. Stace's "Are All Empirical Statements Merely Hypotheses?", *Journal of Philosophy,* 1947. There is a reply to Stace in P. Henle's "On the Certainty of Empirical Statements," *ibid.* A critique of the views of C. I. Lewis is given in N. Malcolm's "The Verification Argument," in M. Black (ed.), *Philosophical Analysis,* (Ithaca: Cornell University Press, 1950). A classical attempt to refute Cartesian scepticism in terms of common sense is G. E. Moore's "Proof of an External World," *Proc. of the British Academy,* 1939. For a discussion of Moore's arguments see A. Ambrose's "Moore's Proof of an External World," in *The Philosophy of G. E. Moore, op. cit.* Another relevant article in the same volume is M. Lazerowitz' "Moore's Paradox," which is also reprinted in his book, *The Structure of Metaphysics,* (London: Routledge and Kegan Paul, 1955).

III

Perception and
the Physical World

INTRODUCTION

U<small>NREFLECTIVE PRIMITIVE MEN</small> assume that the things they see and touch exist also at times when they are not seen or touched or perceived in any other way; they further take it for granted that things have just those qualities which they appear to have. Let us dignify this unsophisticated creed with the name "naive realism." Its second part has seemed to various philosophers to involve a patent contradiction. Does not the same penny which appears circular when viewed from directly above, appear elliptical when viewed sideways? Does not the same stick which looks straight in air look crooked when halfway immersed in transparent water? Does not the same volume of water feel warm to one hand and cold to the other hand under certain well-known conditions? But if we assumed that everything really has every quality it appears to have, these facts would force us into the contradictory conclusion that the penny is both circular and elliptical, that the stick is both straight and crooked, that the water is both hot and cold, and so on; thus argue the philosophical critics of naive realism. And up to this point they would probably be joined by educated common sense. But some of them continue to press common sense as follows: If the physical penny is circular, and what we see from certain perspectives is not circular, then it cannot be the physical penny itself which is seen from those perspectives. If the physical stick is straight, and the stick which we see is not, then it cannot be the physical stick that is seen. Further, how can color be a quality "in" the things that appear to be colored in different ways, considering that the apparent color of a thing varies with conditions of illumination as well as organic conditions (think of "jaundice," for example)? Indeed, if whatever we see has some color or other and whatever we touch has some temperature or other, and if color and temperature are not qualities of physical objects at all, then it follows that we never perceive physical objects at all. Nobody would maintain, said Locke, that the pain he feels when in contact with fire is in the fire; why then maintain that the warmth and the color are in the fire? And if you admit that the coldness which we ascribe to snow is only a sensation produced by snow when in contact with a sentient organism, why should you suppose that the snow's whiteness is something "objective," independent of sensation? Conclusion: since physical objects in themselves, i.e., as they are when they are not perceived, have neither color nor temperature, what we directly perceive are *ideas* (modern writers speak of "sense-data" or "sensa" or "percepts"), not physical objects. Whether or not the sense-data resemble the physical objects to which they are believed to "correspond" in some sense, they are at any rate distinct from them. This philosophical theory is commonly called (epistemological) dualism. According to Locke, who held a special form of this theory, we are mistaken in supposing that to all the qualities of our sense-data there correspond similar qualities in the objects. Colors, for example, correspond to certain arrangements of the molecules at the surfaces of physical objects by virtue of which the latter reflect light of a particular wave length into the eyes of sentient organisms, but such structures do not resemble sensations of color. The apparently brown penny "as it is in itself" does not have a color nor a degree of temperature at all, any more than the fire has a quality resembling the pain it produces. On the other hand, said Locke, ideas of shape and size and motion and weight do correspond to similar properties of physical objects. The penny may not have that particular shape which it appears to have under certain conditions, but it does have a shape; and it may not have the particular size it appears to have from such and such a distance (it certainly could not have all the apparent sizes, for that would contradict the assumption of constancy of size), but it does have a size. Those qualities which are in the objects themselves, he called "primary," and those which only characterize our sense-data he called "secondary."

Strangely, Locke seems to have forgotten an elementary distinction in the course of his critique of naive realism, a distinction he himself had made explicitly: that between a quality of a thing and the corresponding idea (sense-datum). "Whatsoever the mind perceives in itself, or is the immediate object of perception, thought, or understanding, that I call 'idea'; and the power to produce any idea in our mind, I call 'quality' of the subject wherein that power is." Does not the snowball have the power to produce a sensation of whiteness, in the sense that an organism endowed with eyesight will see white if it looks at a snowball by daylight? But if this is what we mean by saying that the snowball is white or has the quality we call "white", then the snowball *is* white just as much as it is round. What could be meant by saying, with Locke, that the whiteness is not "in" the snowball? That the snowball does not experience a sensation of whiteness? True enough, but neither does it experience a sensation of roundness. Does it mean that the invisible particles of which the snowball is composed are not themselves white? Evidently Locke had this in mind, for he emphasized that the secondary qualities, unlike the primary qualities, are not possessed by the atoms (the "insensible particles") of which bodies are composed. But if the atoms have no color, no temperature and no smell, does it follow that visible, tangible and smellable aggregates of atoms do not have such qualities either?

The classical critique of Locke's dualism, however, represented in our readings by the selection from Berkeley, took a completely different line: it amounted to an abandonment of the first part of the naive realist creed along with its second part. Berkeley accepted the thesis that the qualities Locke called "secondary" exist "nowhere but in the mind." But he accused Locke of inconsistency in crediting the primary qualities with existence "outside the mind." Locke had argued that it is inconsistent to say that the warmth which is felt at a certain distance from a fire is in the fire but that the pain which is felt as one comes closer to the fire is only in the mind. He had thus called attention to the variation of perceived qualities with variations of the conditions of perception. But Berkeley pointed out that in just the same way the apparent size, shape, weight, velocity of objects varies with conditions of perception. If, for example, the penny appears round from one perspective and elliptical from another perspective, what right do we have to say that the roundness is in the penny or "real" and the ellipticalness only in our mind or "apparent?" Further, he held it to be meaningless to suppose that there exist bodies which have primary qualities but no secondary qualities, on the ground that this is unimaginable: we cannot imagine something that has size and shape without being colored any more than we can imagine something that is colored without having any size or shape. It should be noted that in so arguing Berkeley presupposed the principle that what is intelligible must be imaginable. This principle is the basis of his famous polemic against "abstract general ideas," like triangularity, humanity, materiality etc. (See the discussion of universals, in the introduction to Section I). It is impossible to imagine a triangle which is not a specific kind of triangle, equilateral or isosceles or scalene, large or small; therefore, said Berkeley, an abstract noun like "triangularity" does not stand for an idea at all. General words, like "man," "triangle," "house," are significant not by virtue of standing for an abstract idea, like an idea of a triangle that is not any specific sort of triangle, but by virtue of representing indifferently *any* particular of a certain sort.

Once a philosopher has gone so far, i. e. has deprived physical objects "as they are in themselves" of all specific qualities human beings are acquainted with through sense-perception, two alternatives remain open to him: he may postulate the existence of physical objects while confessing that their nature is completely unknown, that we do not know anything about them. This was the position of Kant who, considerably influenced by Locke, Berkeley and Hume, came to the conclusion that we know nothing about "things in themselves", that empirical knowledge is confined to "phenomena" (his term for Locke's "ideas," meaning literally "appearances"). The second alternative is the thoroughgoing *idealism* of Berkeley, i. e. the doctrine that nothing exists "outside the mind" at all—with the notable exception of minds other than Berkeley's. In order to understand what reasons led Berkeley to such a paradoxical theory, we must take into account his critique of the notion of "substance." Locke had pointed out quite rightly that ordinary men suppose a certain "I know not what" in which the observed qualities inhere, or which "supports" them somehow. We speak of the qualities which a thing "has", implying by our language that the thing is distinct from its qualities. But, said Berkeley, to speak of something, call it "matter," which supports the qualities we sense and is not itself observable, is just to talk nonsense:

> It is said *extension* is a *mode* or accident *of matter,* and that matter is the *substratum* that supports it. Now I desire that you would explain what is meant by matter's *supporting* extension . . . It is evident *support* cannot here be taken in its usual or literal sense, as when we say that pillars support a building: in what sense therefore must it be taken? . . . If we inquire into what the most accurate philosophers declare themselves to mean by *material substance,* we shall find them acknowledge, they have no other meaning annexed to those sounds, but the idea of *being in general,* together *with the relative notion of its supporting accidents.* The

general idea of being appeareth to me the most abstract and incomprehensible of all other; and as for its supporting accidents, this, as we have just now observed, cannot be understood in the common sense of those words; it must therefore be taken in some other sense, but what that is they do not explain. So that when I consider the *two parts* or branches which make the signification of the words *material substance,* I am convinced there is no distinct meaning annexed to them.

If we talk sense, then we cannot mean by a physical object anything else than the very sum-total of qualities which are misleadingly called the qualities of the object. Note how grammatical similarities may mislead: we speak of the possessions, or of the wives, of Mr. Soandso, and here Mr. Soandso is obviously distinct from his possessions and from his wives but it does not follow that a thing is distinct from its qualities though we use the same particle "of." Mr. Soandso can be seen, touched, and in other ways experienced apart from his possessions. But what about the material substance? We cannot perceive it apart from the sense-qualities. In fact, we do not even know what it would be like to experience *it.* The basis of Berkeley's criticism of this theory is a striking anticipation of the later attacks by the logical positivists on metaphysical theories in general. (Cf. the introduction to Section VIII, pp. 544 ff.).

It is thus that Berkeley arrived at his famous thesis *esse est percipi,* to exist is to be perceived. What he meant is that it is just as meaningless, or self-contradictory, to suppose that something which is not a mind exists without being perceived, as to suppose the existence of a husband without a wife. Of course, it does not at all seem self-contradictory to suppose that the earth and the whole solar system existed long before any perceptions, any form of consciousness, emerged in connection with animal life. Indeed, said Berkeley, I can admit all this, for the entire material universe has always existed in the divine consciousness. Berkeley's theology enabled him to reconcile his philosophy with common sense realism.

G. E. Moore, one of the early and influential critics of idealism in England, undertook to refute Berkeleyan idealism. What he set out to prove, however, was not that "esse est percipi" is a *false* proposition, but that it is an *unfounded* proposition. Perhaps, said Moore in his challenging essay "The Refutation of Idealism," consciousness is present everywhere in the universe, as asserted by idealists; but is there any reason for supposing this? Now, Berkeley had maintained that green, the quality, is as indistinguishable from a *sensation of* green as a pain is indistinguishable from a sensation of pain. He might have said that a logically correct language, a language which is not philosophically misleading, would speak of green and round and loud sensations just as ordinary English speaks of painful sensations, not of "sensations of pain." But Moore tried to show that Berkeley confused two demonstrably distinct things: the awareness (the sensation) and the object of awareness (the sense-datum). "Esse is held to be percipi," in Moore's words, "because *what is experienced* is held to be identical with *the experience of it.*" In any sensation, Moore maintains, we must distinguish between two elements—the awareness or consciousness and that of which we are aware, the object of awareness. A sensation of blue and a sensation of red have the common element, awareness, but they differ as regards the object. It certainly would be a self-contradiction to maintain that an *awareness* of blue could exist without a perceiver. From this, however, it does not follow that the *blue* could not exist without a perceiver. It may not be possible to prove that sense-data which no mind is aware of exist but the supposition is not self-contradictory like the supposition that there are husbands that have no wives.

But some modern philosophers, including perhaps Professor Moore himself at the present time, do not find this refutation of idealism convincing. For it rests on an artificial analysis of sensations into an *act* and an *object,* and there is no evidence, they would say, that there are such "acts" that are distinguishable from their "objects." As has been suggested by Professor C. J. Ducasse in the course of a refutation of Moore's refutation of idealism, seeing green may be like dancing a waltz rather than like eating bread: in saying that a couple is dancing a waltz we are *characterizing* the activity of dancing itself (we might say "they are dancing waltzily"), and analogously we are characterizing our sensation when we say we see green, we are not asserting, according to this analysis, a relation of awareness between our mind and an entity that conceivably might exist apart from that relationship. As against Moore, Stace defends idealism, in a rejoinder ironically entitled "The Refutation of Realism," in a diplomatic way: perhaps Berkeley was right in saying that "unsensed sense-datum" (like a patch of blue which is not part of anybody's visual field) is a contradiction in terms, perhaps Moore was right in denying this. But be this as it may, at least nobody could disprove idealism by proving that the things we perceive exist also when they are not perceived. If the realist chooses to believe in the existence of a physical world outside of consciousness, nobody can prevent him, but it should be understood that this belief is faith, not a belief based on reasons.

Is there any reason for believing that physical objects, i. e. such things as stones, chairs, monkeys, mountains, etc., exist at times when they are not perceived? Philosophers who think there is fall into two groups: those who hold that the belief is justifiable by a *causal argument,* and those who attempt to justify it by means of a *phenomenalist* analysis of what is meant by a "physical object" and by the statement that physical objects exist independently of being perceived. The causal argument starts from Locke's dualistic assumption that what we directly perceive are sense-data (or "percepts" in Russell's terminology) which are numerically and qualitively distinct from physical objects; for example, visual sense-data are colored, whereas physical objects are alleged to be colorless. It then alleges that physical objects must be postulated in order to account for the remarkable regularity in the sucession of sense-data and also for the remarkable similarity between the sense-data perceived by different observers. If you come into a room and seem to see a cat there contrary to expectation, you may at first suspect that you are hallucinating. You look again and touch, you look again and touch again, finding that similar visual sense-data recur and are followed by similar tactual sense-data. You ask other observers to look and touch and find that they report similar sense-data. Of course, you cannot perceive sense-data that are not your own. But you infer from the verbal sense-data you perceive ("yes, John, there *is* a cat there") that the mind you are communicating with—however, the belief that there *is* another mind with which you are communicating may be justifiable—perceived feline sense-data similar to those that would cause you under similar circumstances to produce similar sounds. Is it not highly probable, then, that all these similar sense-data are caused by processes originating from a physical cat? In particular, scientists who share the plain man's belief in the existence of a physical world outside the mind tell us that light waves are reflected from the cat's fur into the retina of the observer's eyes and initiate in the optic nerve a process terminating in the visual area of the brain. The cat may not exactly resemble the feline sense-data which it helps produce, but according to this argument it is highly probable that there is a cat at the place and time in question because the occurence of the sense-data would be highly improbable if there were not. Again, we must assume that the reddish-yellowish and warm sense-data we perceive when gazing at a certain spot in the sky are produced by processes originating from the sun the physicist talks about, though the latter is not at all similar to the perceived sun, being neither yellow nor hot. Such is the view held by many physicists and philosophers, among them Sir Arthur Eddington and Bertrand Russell, who in this respect are unmistakably descendants of Locke. Russell even goes to the extreme of affirming that whatever a man *perceives,* in contradistinction to what he *infers* as the external cause of his perceptions, is in his own brain; for it is a percept (sense-datum), not a physical object, and the locus of a man's percepts, says Russell, is his brain. If the reader should, legitimately, be puzzled by this statement, it is advisable that he ponder the semantic question in what sense of "in" perceptions can be said to be in a brain.

The phenomenalist challenges, in the first place, the dualism which underlies the causal argument, the dualism between sense-data and physical objects. Chiefly two arguments have been used to support Locke's claim that we never directly perceive a physical object: a) the argument from illusions, b) the physical argument. a) says that the identification of the perceived object with the physical object in the case of illusions, like those of the bent stick and the elliptical penny, would lead to contradiction, and that it would be arbitrary to distinguish perceived and physical object in the case of illusory perception and to identify them in the case of real perception. But surely this is wrong. It would of course be contradictory to say that the stick we perceive is both straight and bent, but why not say, as is customary, that we see a real stick which *appears* crooked? According to phenomenalism, to ascribe a particular quality to an object is to predict how it would appear under specified conditions of perception. Thus, when we say that the stick is straight though it now appears (to the eye) to be crooked, we are saying that it would feel straight if it were touched, and/or that it would look straight in a relatively non-refracting medium like air. There is no contradiction in saying that a thing appears to have one quality if observed in one way, and appears to have another quality if observed in a different way. b) Physicists have reason to believe that when we see something, light waves that travel at enormous yet finite speed have just reached our eyes after having been reflected or emitted from the thing we see. And physiologists have reason to believe that between the moment when light stimulates the optic nerve and the actual sensation neural energy travels up to the visual area of the brain. Since there is, then, a tiny time-interval separating the sensation from the moment when the described physical process, the external stimulation of the organism, gets started, it is concluded that the sense-datum cannot be identical with the physical object. Now, if by the "sense-datum" is meant *that which* one directly perceives, the conclusion of the physical argument certainly does not follow. For though a visual sensation is an event that is perfectly distinct from any physical events, including reflections of light-waves and stimulations of optic nerves, nobody claims that a visual sensation is ever an *object* of perception: one *has* a visual sensation when one sees something, but it would not even make sense to speak of *seeing* one's visual sensation (or for that matter anyone else's). In other words: sensations are undoubtedly different from physical objects, but since it would be absurd to say that we *perceive* sensations, the distinctness of sensations from physical objects does not justify the contention that we don't perceive physical objects. Furthermore, to deny on the authority of scientific theories that we ever see physical objects or processes would seem to be putting the cart before the horse, since it is hard to see how theories which make assertions about physical objects and processes could be verified if physical objects and processes were never seen at all. How, so a critic of the physical argument for dualism might ask, could physiologists verify their theory about the physiological causation of sensations if they could not at least perceive nervous systems and what goes on in them, but first had to infer their existence from their own "percepts"? Wouldn't this very inference *presuppose* the theory to be verified? If, on the other hand, the physical argument merely purports to establish that the sensation is distinct from the sensed physical object, that is so obvious that no argument is needed to support it. Surely it does not follow that the objects which we sense are not physical. If there were good reasons for denying that the physical sun is red and hot and that the physical table is brown and solid, then, indeed, we could not consistently hold that we see the physical sun and physical tables. But a phenomenalist would deny that there are good reasons for such a denial. He would reject Locke's dualism between secondary and primary qualities. "The sun is red" *means* "the sun appears red under such and such conditions," "the table is solid" *means* "the table feels solid and there are no visible holes in it" (though there may be invisible holes between invisible electrons), which propositions are undeniably true and perfectly compatible with physical theory.

The phenomenalist justification of the common sense belief in the existence of unperceived physical objects is inseparable from the phenomenalist analysis of propositions about physical objects. Berkeley had argued against Locke that when a plain man says "there is a tree in front of me" he does not mean "my present tree-like sense-data are caused by a physical object which cannot be perceived but only inferred, and which is in most respects dissimilar to the sense-data," but just "my present visual field contains tree-like sense-data" (at least Berkeley defended the latter analysis when he was oblivious of God). The phenomenalist agrees with the negative part and disagrees with the positive part of Berkeley's claim. Like Berkeley, he rejects the dualistic conception of physical objects on the ground that it makes propositions about physical objects wholly unverifiable whereas plain men mean something verifiable by such propositions as "there is a tree at this place": for how could one ever find out whether the inference from the sense-data to the physical object is valid? If I see a shadow and infer that there is a man behind me who casts the shadow, the inference can be verified by turning around and seeing the man directly. But according to the dualist no physical object could conceivably be directly perceived; when I turn my head in order to verify my interpretation of the shadow, I still only perceive my sense-data, there is nothing else for me to perceive, according to the dualist. However, the phenomenalist offers an analysis of such propositions which is compatible with the belief that physical objects exist when they are not perceived (not even by God!): "there is a table in room 210" does not entail that table-like sensations actually occur in conjunction with room-210-like sensations; it only entails (and is entailed by) the proposition that table-like sensations *would* occur *if* room-210-like sensations were to occur. When you say "the vase is fragile" you do not mean that it actually breaks at the moment, nor do you even predict that it ever will break; you only make the *conditional* prediction that it would break if it were dropped. Similarly, says the phenomenalist, to assert the existence of a physical object of kind K is not to assert that K-like sensations occur nor that they will ever occur; but it is to assert that K-like sensations would occur if certain conditions, such as sensations of looking in a certain direction at a certain time, were fulfilled.

To be quite accurate, we ought to distinguish two forms of phenomenalism. According to one form, statements about physical objects are to be analysed in terms of *sensations* that occur under specified conditions; according to the other form they are to be analysed in terms of *sense-data* that are perceived under specified conditions. Sensations are commonly regarded as mental events whose occurrence can be known with absolute certainty by one and only one mind; thus many philosophers would characterize my seeing a blue, round patch against a white background as a sensation, and they hold that a proposition asserting its occurrence ("I see a blue, round patch") can be directly known to be true by myself but can only be inferred with probability by other people. Other phenomenalists, however, speak of *perception of sense-data,* where sense-data are not "parts" of any mind though perceptions of sense-data are mental events. The latter form of phenomenalism is obviously bound up with the analysis of sensations into an awareness and a (possibly non-physical) object of awareness in terms of which Moore criticized Berkeley and which some contemporary philosophers of perception reject. It should be noted, however, that the use of the terminology of "sense-data" and "perceptions of sense-data" does not necessarily commit a phenomenalist to such a controversial theory. Sometimes the use of the word "sense-datum" is just a convenient device for indicating that no claim about the physical world is being made, that one is merely describing one's sense-experience. For example, if one says in ordinary language "I see a red apple," one thereby implies that *there is* a red apple in the environment; if it turns out that there is not, one will retract the statement as false, saying "I thought I saw a red apple but since, as it turned out, there is no such thing here, I could not really have seen one." The technical statement "I see a sense-datum of a red apple (a red-apple-like sense-datum)" may simply serve the purpose of annulling, as it were, the implication that the perception is veridical, that there is a physical apple at the place and time in question. In other words, it focuses attention on the character of the sense-experience, and is easily translatable into ordinary, non-technical language: "I seem to see a red apple." Whiteley, for example, uses the terminology of sense-data in formulating and discussing phenomenalism, but it is unlikely that he thereby intends to impute to phenomenalists the awareness-object analysis of sensations which was central in Moore's "Refutation of Idealism."

Phenomenalists are painfully aware of the difficulty to express the "conditions" under which certain kinds of sense-data regularly occur if a certain kind of physical object exists in a language that mentions only sensations, not physical objects and events. For example, a phenomenalist analysis of "a boy will enter the room at exactly 4 P.M. July 17, 1956" would run somewhat as follows: "if sensations of looking at the door occur at 4 P.M. July 17, 1956, then simultaneously sensations of a boy entering will occur." But this analysis is not purely phenomenalistic, because a state of a physical clock is referred to; the phenomenalist would therefore have to go on to translate "it is 4 P.M. July 17, 1956" into the language of sensations. The phenomenalist analysis of physical propositions also runs into the following difficulty. A conditional statement like "if a visually normal observer were to look at the door, he would see a boy entering" contains words that refer to physical objects like "observer," "door," "boy." It therefore does not express an analysis in terms of sense-data exclusively. In order to satisfy this requirement we must, in the first place, refrain from mentioning any sentient organisms with eyes and ears, and secondly replace "looking at the door" by "having a sensation of looking at the door" or "seeming to look at the door," so meant that the statement "a sensation of looking at the door occurs" only characterizes the sensation without entailing that there is a physical door which is involved in a physical stimulation of an organism. Similarly, "there occurs a sensation of a boy entering the door" must be so meant that it could be true even if no boys or doors existed (in the sense in which it could be true that, in a state of delirium, one seems to see a dragon although there are no dragons). But now, if "a boy enters the door at time t" were synonymous with "if a sensation of looking at the door occurred at t, then a sensation of a boy entering would occur at t," then it would be a contradiction to suppose that a boy enters the door at t, a sensation of looking at the door occurs at t yet no sensation of a boy entering the door occurs at t. And this sort of thing clearly might happen, since "a sensation of looking at the door occurs" is not allowed to entail "somebody actually looks at the door." For example, someone might look at a picture of the door which resembles the door so closely that he mistakenly believes that he is looking at the door itself. Clearly he will not see a boy entering the picture of the door and yet a boy may really enter the real door. It seems, then, that a phenomenalist is caught in a dilemma: either he mentions physical objects and physical conditions in his translation or else his translation is demonstrably inadequate. But be this as it may, if such translations into the language of sense-data are feasible, then the phenomenalist can show that common sense realism is justifiable by ordinary inductive reasoning: each time I had sensations of entering room 210, there followed table-like sensations; this is my basis for believing that even now, while I am far from room 210, there is a table there. What is the content of this belief? Just, says the phenomenalist, that if sensations of entering room 210 recurred now, they would again be followed by table-like sensations: same cause, same effect!

Some philosophers, however, feel that this is not the sort of thing plain men (including themselves in their non-academic life) mean when they assert the existence of an unperceived physical object. When they are pressed by the phenomenalist to explain what else is meant by such assertions, they usually cannot do it. But they might counter that there is no more reason to suppose that the physical language must, if it is meaningful, be reducible to the language of sensations than there is for supposing that the language of sensations must, if it is meaningful, be reducible to the physical language. It does not seem possible to express the meanings of such statements describing subjective states as "I see red", "John feels pain in his left hand" in physical language, i. e. language describing publicly observable events like movements of an organism, or physiological processes. Perhaps the converse sort of reduction favored by phenomenalists, a reduction of statements about physical objects and processes to statements about actual and possible sensations, is equally unfeasible.

A. P.

12

SENSE QUALITIES AND
MATERIAL SUBSTANCES

John Locke

The Idea of Material Substance

. . . IDEAS OF SUBSTANCES, HOW MADE.—The mind being, as I have declared, furnished with a great number of the simple ideas, conveyed in by the senses, as they are found in exterior things, or by reflection on its own operations, takes notice also, that a certain number of these simple ideas go constantly together; which being presumed to belong to one thing, and words being suited to common apprehensions, and made use of for quick dispatch, are called, so united in one subject, by one name: which, by inadvertency, we are apt afterward to talk of, and consider as one simple idea, which indeed is a complication of many ideas together; because, as I have said, not imagining how these simple ideas can subsist by themselves, we accustom ourselves to suppose some substratum wherein they do subsist, and from which they do result; which therefore we call substance.

Our idea of substance in general.—So that if any one will examine himself concerning his notion of pure substance in general, he will find he has no other idea of it at all, but only a supposition of he knows not what support of such qualities, which are capable of producing simple ideas in us; which qualities are commonly called accidents. If any one should be asked, what is the subject wherein colour or weight inheres, he would have nothing to say, but the solid extended parts: and if he were demanded, what is it that solidity and extension adhere in, he would not be in a much better case than the Indian, who, saying that the

[This selection consists of sections 1-4 of Chapter XXIII, Book II, and sections 7-19, 23, and 26 of Chapter VIII, Book II, of Locke's *Essay Concerning Human Understanding,* a book first published in 1690.]

world was supported by a great elephant, was asked what the elephant rested on; to which his answer was, a great tortoise. But being again pressed to know what gave support to the broad-backed tortoise, replied, something he knew not what. And thus here, as in all other cases where we use words without having clear and distinct ideas, we talk like children; who being questioned what such a thing is, which they know not, readily give this satisfactory answer, that it is something; which in truth signifies no more, when so used either by children or men, but that they know not what; and that the thing they pretend to know and talk of, is what they have no distinct idea of at all, and so are perfectly ignorant of it, and in the dark. The idea then we have, to which we give the general name substance, being nothing but the supposed, but unknown support of those qualities we find existing, which we imagine cannot subsist, *sine re substante,* without something to support them, we call that support *substantia;* which, according to the true import of the word, is in plain English, standing under or upholding.

Of the sorts of substances.—An obscure and relative idea of substance in general being thus made, we come to have the ideas of particular sorts of substances, by collecting such combinations of simple ideas, as are by experience and observation of men's senses taken notice of to exist together, and are therefore supposed to flow from the particular internal constitution, or unknown essence of that substance. Thus we come to have the ideas of a man, horse, gold, water, etc., of which substances, whether any one has any other clear idea, farther than of certain simple ideas co-existent together, I appeal to every man's own experience. It is the ordinary qualities observable in iron, or a diamond, put together, that make the true complex idea of those substances, which a smith or a jeweller commonly knows better than a philosopher; who, whatever substantial forms he may talk of, has no other idea of those substances, than what is framed by a collection of those simple ideas which are to be found in them; only we must take notice, that our complex ideas of substances, besides all those simple ideas they are made up of, have always the confused idea of something to which they belong, and in which they subsist. And therefore, when we speak of any sort of substances, we say it is a thing having such or such qualities: as body is a thing that is extended, figured, and capable of motion; spirit, a thing capable of thinking; and so hardness, friability, and power to draw iron, we say, are qualities to be found in a loadstone. These, and the like fashions of speaking, intimate, that the substance is supposed always something besides the extension, figure, solidity, motion, thinking, or other observable ideas, though we know not what it is.

No less idea of substance in general.—Hence, when we talk or think of any particular sort of corporeal substances, as horse, stone, etc., though the idea we have of either of them be but the complication or collection of those several simple ideas of sensible qualities, which we used to find united in the thing called horse or stone; yet because we cannot conceive how they should subsist alone, or one in another, we suppose them existing in and supported by some common subject; which support we denote by the name substance, though it be certain we have no clear or distinct idea of that thing we suppose a support. . . .

Primary and Secondary Qualities

Ideas in the mind, qualities in bodies. To discover the nature of our ideas the better, and to discourse of them intelligibly, it will be convenient to distinguish them, as they are ideas or perceptions in our minds, and as they are modifications of matter in the bodies that cause such perceptions in us; that so we may not think (as perhaps usually is done) that they are exactly the images and resemblances of something inherent in the subject; most of those of sensation being in the mind no more the likeness of something existing without us than the names that stand for them are the likeness of our ideas, which yet upon hearing they are apt to excite in us.

Whatsoever the mind perceives in itself, or is the immediate object of perception, thought, or understanding, that I call "idea;" and the power to produce any idea in our mind, I call "quality" of the subject wherein that power is. Thus a snowball having the power to produce in us the ideas of white, cold, and round, the powers to produce those ideas in us as they are in the snowball, I call "qualities;" and as they are sensations or perceptions in our understandings, I call them "ideas;" which ideas, if I speak of them sometimes as in the things themselves, I would be understood to mean those qualities in the objects which produce them in us.

Primary qualities. Qualities thus considered in bodies are, First, such as are utterly inseparable from the body, in what estate soever it be; such as, in all the alterations and changes it suffers, all the force can be used upon it, it constantly keeps; and such as sense constantly finds in every particle of matter which has bulk enough to be perceived, and the mind finds inseparable from every particle of matter, though less than to make itself singly be perceived by our senses: *v.g.,* take a grain of wheat, divide it into two parts, each part has still solidity, extension, figure, and mobility; divide it again, and it retains still the same qualities: and so divide it on till the parts become insensible, they must retain still each of them all those qualities. For, division (which is all that a mill or pestle or any other body does upon another, in reducing it to insensible parts) can never take away either solidity, extension, figure, or mobility from any body, but only makes two or more distinct separate masses of matter of that which was but one before; all which distinct masses, reckoned as so many distinct bodies, after division, make a certain number. These I call *original* or *primary* qualities of body, which I think we may observe to produce simple ideas in us, viz., solidity, extension, figure, motion or rest, and number.

Secondary qualities. Secondly. Such qualities, which in truth are nothing in the objects themselves, but powers to produce various sensations in us by their primary qualities, *i.e.,* by the bulk, figure, texture, and motion of their insensible parts, as colours, sounds, tastes, etc., these I call *secondary* qualities. To these might be added a third sort, which are allowed to be barely powers, though they are as much real qualities in the subject as those which I, to comply with the common way of speaking, call qualities, but, for distinction, *secondary* qualities. For, the power in fire to produce a new colour or consistence in wax or clay by its primary qualities, is as much a quality in fire as the power it has to produce in me a new idea or sensation of warmth or burning, which I felt not before, by the same primary qualities, viz., the bulk, texture, and motion of its insensible parts.

How primary qualities produce their ideas. The next thing to be considered is, how bodies produce ideas in us; and that is manifestly by impulse, the only way which we can conceive bodies operate in.

If, then, external objects be not united to our minds when they produce ideas in it, and yet we perceive these original qualities in such of them as singly fall under our senses, it is evident that some motion must be thence continued by our nerves or animal spirits, by some parts of our bodies, to the brain or the seat of sensation, there to produce in our minds the particular ideas we have of them. And since the extension, figure, number, and motion of bodies of an observable bigness, may be perceived at a distance by the sight, it is evident some singly imperceptible bodies must come from them to the eyes, and thereby convey to the brain some motion which produces these ideas which we have of them in us.

How secondary. After the same manner that the ideas of these original qualities are produced in us, we may conceive that the ideas of secondary qualities are also produced, viz., by the operation of insensible particles on our senses. For it being manifest that there are bodies, and good store of bodies, each whereof are so small that we cannot by any of our senses discover either their bulk, figure, or motion (as is evident in the particles of the air and water, and other extremely smaller than those, perhaps as much smaller than the particles of air or water as the particles of air or water are smaller than pease or hailstones): let us suppose at present that the different motions and figures, bulk and number, of such particles, affecting the several organs of our senses, produce in us those different sensations which we have from the colours and smells of bodies, *v.g.,* that a violet, by the impulse of such insensible particles of matter of peculiar figures and bulks, and in different degrees and modifications of their motions, causes the ideas of the blue colour and sweet scent of that flower to be produced in our minds; it being no more impossible to conceive that God should annex such ideas to such motions with which they have no similitude, than that he should annex the idea of pain to the motion of a piece of steel dividing our flesh, with which that idea hath no resemblance.

What I have said concerning colours and smells may be understood also of tastes and sounds, and other the like sensible qualities; which, whatever reality we by mistake attribute to them, are in truth nothing in the objects themselves, but powers to produce various sensations in us, and depend on those primary qualities, viz., bulk, figure, texture, and motion of parts, as have said.

Ideas of primary qualities are resemblances; of secondary, not. From whence I think it is easy to draw this observation, that the ideas of primary qualities of bodies are resemblances of them, and their patterns do really exist in the bodies themselves; but the ideas produced in us by these secondary qualities have no resemblance of them at all. There is nothing like our ideas existing in the bodies themselves. They are, in the bodies we denominate from them, only a power to produce those sensations in us; and what is sweet, blue, or warm in idea, is but the certain bulk figure, and motion of the insensible parts in the bodies themselves, which we call so.

Flame is denominated *hot* and *light*; snow, *white* and *cold*; and manna, *white* and *sweet,* from the ideas they produce in us which qualities are commonly thought to be the same in those bodies that those ideas are in us, the one the perfect resemblances of the other, as they are in a mirror; and it would by most men be judged very extravagant, if one should say otherwise. And yet he that will consider that the same fire that at one distance produces in us the sensation of warmth, does at a nearer approach produce in us the far different sensation of pain, ought to bethink himself what reason he has to say, that his idea of warmth which was produced in him by the fire, is actually in the fire, and his idea of pain which the same fire produced in him the same way is not in the fire. Why is whiteness and coldness in snow and pain not, when it produces the one and the other idea in us, and can do neither by the bulk, figure, number and motion of its solid parts?

The particular bulk, number, figure, and motion of the parts of fire or snow are really in them, whether any one's senses perceive them or no; and therefore they may be called *real* qualities, because they really exist in those bodies. But light, heat, whiteness, or coldness, are no more really in them than sickness or pain is in manna. Take away the sensation of them; let not the eyes see light or colours, nor the ears hear sounds; let the palate not taste, nor the nose smell; and all colours, tastes, odours, and sounds, as they are such particular ideas, vanish and cease, and are reduced to their causes, *i.e.,* bulk, figure, and motion of parts.

A piece of manna of a sensible bulk is able to produce in us the idea of a round or square figure; and, by being removed from one place to another, the idea of motion. This idea of motion represents it as it really is in the manna moving; a circle or square are the same, whether in idea or existence, in the mind or in the manna; and this both motion and figure are really in the manna, whether we take notice of them or no: this every body is ready to agree to. Besides, manna, by the bulk, figure, texture, and motion of its parts, has a power to produce the sensations of sickness, and sometimes of acute pains or grippings, in us. That these ideas of sickness and pain are not in the manna, but effects of its operations on us, and are nowhere when we feel them not; this also every one readily agrees to. And yet men are hardly to be brought to think that sweetness and whiteness are not really in manna, which are but the effects of the operations of manna by the motion, size, and figure of its particles on the eyes and palate; as the pain and sickness caused by manna, are confessedly nothing but the effects of its operations on the stomach and guts by the size, motion, and figure of its insensible parts (for by nothing else can a body operate, as has been proved): as if it could not operate on the eyes and palate, and thereby produce in the mind particular distinct ideas which in itself it has not, as well as we allow it can operate on the guts and stomach, and thereby produce distinct ideas which in itself it has not. These ideas being all effects of the operations of manna on several parts of our bodies, by the size, figure, number, and motion of its parts, why those produced by the eyes and palate should rather be thought to be really in the manna than those produced by the stomach and guts: or why the pain and sickness, ideas that are the effects of manna, should be thought to be nowhere when they are not felt: and yet the sweetness and whiteness, effects of the same manna on other parts of the body, by ways equally as unknown, should be thought to exist in the manna, when they are not seen nor tasted; would need some reason to explain.

Ideas of primary qualities are resemblances; of secondary, not. Let us consider the red and white colours in porphyry: hinder light but from striking on it, and its colours vanish; it no longer produces any such ideas in us. Upon the return of light, it produces these appearances on us again. Can any one think any real alterations are made in the porphyry by the presence or absence of light, and that those ideas of whiteness and redness are really in porphyry in the light, when it is plain it has no colour in the dark? It has indeed such a configuration of particles, both night and day, as are apt, by the rays of light rebounding from some parts of the hard stone, to produce in us the idea of redness, and from others the idea of whiteness. But whiteness or redness are not in it at any time, but such a texture that hath the power to produce such a sensation in us. . . .

. . . *Three sorts of qualities in bodies.* The qualities then that are in bodies, rightly considered, are of three sorts:

First. The bulk, figure, number, situation, and motion or rest of their solid parts; those are in them, whether we perceive them or no; and when they are of that size that we can discover them, we have by these an idea of the thing as it is in itself, as is plain in artificial things. These I call *primary* qualities.

Secondly. The power that is in any body, by reason of its insensible primary qualities, to operate after a peculiar manner on any of our senses, and thereby produce in us the different ideas of several colours, sounds, smells, tastes, &c. These are usually called *sensible* qualities.

Thirdly. The power that is in any body, by reason of the particular constitution of its primary qualities, to make such a change in the bulk, figure, texture, and motion of another body, as to make it operate on our senses differently from what it did before. Thus the sun has a power to make wax white, and fire, to make lead fluid. These are usually called "powers."

The first of these, as has been said, I think may be properly called real, original, or primary qualities, because they are in the things themselves, whether they are perceived or no; and upon their different modifications it is that the secondary qualities depend.

The other two are only powers to act differently upon other things, which powers result from the different modifications of these primary qualities. . . .

. . . *Secondary qualities twofold: first, immediately perceivable; secondly, mediately perceivable.* To conclude: Besides those before-mentioned primary qualities in bodies, viz., bulk, figure, extension, number, and motion of their solid parts, all the rest whereby we take notice of bodies, and distinguish them one from another, are nothing else but several powers in them depending on those primary qualities, whereby they are fitted, either by immediately operating on our bodies, to produce several different ideas in us; or else by operating on other bodies, so to change their primary qualities as to render them capable of producing ideas in us different from what before they did. The former of these, I think, may be called secondary qualities immediately perceivable; the latter, secondary qualities mediately perceivable.

13

THE FIRST DIALOGUE BETWEEN
HYLAS AND PHILONOUS

George Berkeley

PHILONOUS. Good morrow, Hylas: I did not expect to find you abroad so early.

HYLAS. It is indeed something unusual; but my thoughts were so taken up with a subject I was discoursing of last night, that finding I could not sleep, I resolved to rise and take a turn in the garden.

PHIL. It happened well, to let you see what innocent and agreeable pleasures you lose every morning. Can there be a pleasanter time of the day, or a more delightful season of the year? That purple sky, those wild but sweet notes of birds, the fragrant bloom upon the trees and flowers, the gentle influence of the rising sun, these and a thousand nameless beauties of nature inspire the soul with secret transports; its faculties too being at this time fresh and lively, are fit for those meditations, which the solitude of a garden and tranquillity of the morning naturally dispose us to. But I am afraid I interrupt your thoughts: for you seemed very intent on something.

HYL. It is true, I was, and shall be obliged to you if you will permit me to go on in the same vein; not that I would by any means deprive myself of your company, for my thoughts always flow more easily in conversation with a friend, than when I am alone: but my request is, that you would suffer me to impart my reflexions to you.

PHIL. With all my heart, it is what I should have requested myself if you had not prevented me.

HYL. I was considering the odd fate of those men who have in all ages, through an affectation of being distinguished from the vulgar, or

[This selection comprises the entire first of the *Three Dialogues Between Hylas and Philonous*, a work first published in 1713.]

some unaccountable turn of thought, pretended either to believe nothing at all, or to believe the most extravagant things in the world. This however might be borne, if their paradoxes and scepticism did not draw after them some consequences of general disadvantage to mankind. But the mischief lieth here; that when men of less leisure see them who are supposed to have spent their whole time in the pursuits of knowledge professing an entire ignorance of all things, or advancing such notions as are repugnant to plain and commonly received principles, they will be tempted to entertain suspicions concerning the most important truths, which they had hitherto held sacred and unquestionable.

PHIL. I entirely agree with you, as to the ill tendency of the affected doubts of some philosophers, and fantastical conceits of others. I am even so far gone of late in this way of thinking, that I have quitted several of the sublime notions I had got in their schools for vulgar opinions. And I give it you on my word; since this revolt from metaphysical notions to the plain dictates of nature and common sense, I find my understanding strangely enlightened, so that I can now easily comprehend a great many things which before were all mystery and riddle.

HYL. I am glad to find there was nothing in the accounts I heard of you.

PHIL. Pray, what were those?

The Notion of Material Substance

HYL. You were represented, in last night's conversation, as one who maintained the most extravagant opinion that ever entered into the mind of man, to wit, that there is no such thing as *material substance* in the world.

PHIL. That there is no such thing as what *philosophers* call *material substance,* I am seriously persuaded: but, if I were made to see anything absurd or sceptical in this, I should then have the same reason to renounce this that I imagine I have now to reject the contrary opinion.

HYL. What! can anything be more fantastical, more repugnant to Common Sense, or a more manifest piece of Scepticism, than to believe there is no such thing as *matter?*

PHIL. Softly, good Hylas. What if it should prove that you, who hold there is, are, by virtue of that opinion, a greater sceptic, and maintain more paradoxes and repugnances to Common Sense, than I who believe no such thing?

HYL. You may as soon persuade me, the part is greater than the whole, as that, in order to avoid absurdity and Scepticism, I should ever be obliged to give up my opinion in this point.

PHIL. Well then, are you content to admit that opinion for true, which upon examination shall appear most agreeable to Common Sense, and remote from Scepticism?

HYL. With all my heart. Since you are for raising disputes about the plainest things in nature, I am content for once to hear what you have to say.

PHIL. Pray, Hylas, what do you mean by a *sceptic?*

HYL. I mean what all men mean—one that doubts of everything.

PHIL. He then who entertains no doubt concerning some particular point, with regard to that point cannot be thought a sceptic.

HYL. I agree with you.

PHIL. Whether doth doubting consist in embracing the affirmative or negative side of a question?

HYL. In neither; for whoever understands English cannot but know that *doubting* signifies a suspense between both.

PHIL. He then that denies any point, can no more be said to doubt of it, than he who affirmeth it with the same degree of assurance.

HYL. True.

PHIL. And, consequently, for such his denial is no more to be esteemed a sceptic than the other.

HYL. I acknowledge it.

PHIL. How cometh it to pass then, Hylas, that you pronounce me a *sceptic,* because I deny what you affirm, to wit, the existence of Matter? Since, for aught you can tell, I am as peremptory in my denial, as you in your affirmation.

HYL. Hold, Philonous, I have been a little out in my definition; but every false step a man makes in discourse is not to be insisted on. I said indeed that a *sceptic* was one who doubted of everything; but I should have added, or who denies the reality and truth of things.

PHIL. What things? Do you mean the principles and theorems of sciences? But these you know are universal intellectual notions, and consequently independent of Matter. The denial therefore of this doth not imply the denying them.

HYL. I grant it. But are there no other things? What think you of distrusting the senses, of denying the real existence of sensible things, or pretending to know nothing of them. Is not this sufficient to denominate a man a *sceptic?*

PHIL. Shall we therefore examine which of us it is that denies the reality of sensible things, or professes the greatest ignorance of them; since, if I take you rightly, he is to be esteemed the greatest *sceptic?*

HYL. That is what I desire.

The Nature of Sensible Things

PHIL. What mean you by Sensible Things?

HYL. Those things which are perceived by the senses. Can you imagine that I mean anything else?

PHIL. Pardon me, Hylas, if I am desirous clearly to apprehend your notions, since this may much shorten our inquiry. Suffer me then to ask you this farther question. Are those things only perceived by the senses which are perceived immediately? Or, may those things properly be said to be *sensible* which are perceived mediately, or not without the intervention of others?

HYL. I do not sufficiently understand you.

PHIL. In reading a book, what I immediately perceive are the letters; but mediately, or by means of these, are suggested to my mind the notions of God, virtue, truth, &c. Now, that the letters are truly sensible things, or perceived by sense, there is no doubt: but I would know whether you take the things suggested by them to be so too.

HYL. No, certainly: it were absurd to think *God* or *virtue* sensible things; though they may be signified and suggested to the mind by sensible marks, with which they have an arbitrary connexion.

PHIL. It seems then, that by *sensible things* you mean those only which can be perceived *immediately* by sense?

HYL. Right.

PHIL. Doth it not follow from this, that though I see one part of the sky red, and another blue, and that my reason doth thence evidently conclude there must be some cause of that diversity of colours, yet that cause cannot be said to be a sensible thing, or perceived by the sense of seeing?

HYL. It doth.

PHIL. In like manner, though I hear variety of sounds, yet I cannot be said to hear the causes of those sounds?

HYL. You cannot.

PHIL. And when by my touch I perceive a thing to be hot and heavy, I cannot say, with any truth or propriety, that I feel the cause of its heat or weight?

HYL. To prevent any more questions of this kind, I tell you once for all, that by *sensible things* I mean those only which are perceived by sense; and that in truth the senses perceive nothing which they do not perceive *immediately:* for they make no inferences. The deducing therefore of causes or occasions from effects and appearances, which alone are perceived by sense, entirely relates to reason.

PHIL. This point then is agreed between us—That *sensible things are those only which are immediately perceived by sense*. You will farther inform me, whether we immediately perceive by sight anything beside light, and colours, and figures; or by hearing, anything but sounds; by the palate, anything beside taste; by the smell, beside odours; or by the touch, more than tangible qualities.

HYL. We do not.

PHIL. It seems, therefore, that if you take away all sensible qualities, there remains nothing sensible?

HYL. I grant it.

PHIL. Sensible things therefore are nothing else but so many sensible qualities, or combinations of sensible qualities?

HYL. Nothing else.

PHIL. *Heat* then is a sensible thing?

HYL. Certainly.

PHIL. Doth the *reality* of sensible things consist in being perceived? or, is it something distinct from their being perceived, and that bears no relation to the mind?

HYL. To *exist* is one thing, and to be *perceived* is another.

PHIL. I speak with regard to sensible things only. And of these I ask, whether by their real existence you mean a subsistence exterior to the mind, and distinct from their being perceived?

HYL. I mean a real absolute being, distinct from, and without any relation to, their being perceived.

PHIL. Heat therefore, if it be allowed a real being, must exist without the mind?

HYL. It must.

PHIL. Tell me, Hylas, is this real existence equally compatible to all degrees of heat, which we perceive; or is there any reason why we should attribute it to some, and deny it to others? And if there be, pray let me know that reason.

HYL. Whatever degree of heat we perceive by sense, we may be sure the same exists in the object that occasions it.

PHIL. What! the greatest as well as the least?

HYL. I tell you, the reason is plainly the same in respect of both. They are both perceived by sense; nay, the greater degree of heat is more sensibly perceived; and consequently, if there is any difference, we are more certain of its real existence than we can be of the reality of a lesser degree.

PHIL. But is not the most vehement and intense degree of heat a very great pain?

HYL. No one can deny it.

PHIL. And is any unperceiving thing capable of pain or pleasure?

HYL. No, certainly.

PHIL. Is your material substance a senseless being, or a being endowed with sense and perception?

HYL. It is senseless without doubt.

PHIL. It cannot therefore be the subject of pain?

HYL. By no means.

PHIL. Nor consequently of the greatest heat perceived by sense, since you acknowledge this to be no small pain?

HYL. I grant it.

PHIL. What shall we say then of your external object; is it a material Substance, or no?

HYL. It is a material substance with the sensible qualities inhering in it.

Sensible Things Exist Only in the Mind

PHIL. How then can a great heat exist in it, since you own it cannot in a material substance? I desire you would clear this point.

HYL. Hold, Philonous, I fear I was out in yielding intense heat to be a pain. It should seem rather, that pain is something distinct from heat, and the consequence or effect of it.

PHIL. Upon putting your hand near the fire, do you perceive one simple uniform sensation, or two distinct sensations?

HYL. But one simple sensation.

PHIL. Is not the heat immediately perceived?

HYL. It is.

PHIL. And the pain?

HYL. True.

PHIL. Seeing therefore they are both immediately perceived at the same time, and the fire affects you only with one simple or uncompounded idea, it follows that this same simple idea is both the intense heat immediately perceived, and the pain; and, consequently, that the intense heat immediately perceived is nothing distinct from a particular sort of pain.

HYL. It seems so.

PHIL. Again, try in your thoughts, Hylas, if you can conceive a vehement sensation to be without pain or pleasure.

HYL. I cannot.

PHIL. Or can you frame to yourself an idea of sensible pain or pleasure in general, abstracted from every particular idea of heat, cold, tastes, smells, etc.?

HYL. I do not find that I can.

PHIL. Doth it not therefore follow, that sensible pain is nothing distinct from those sensations or ideas, in an intense degree?

Hyl. It is undeniable; and, to speak the truth, I begin to suspect a very great heat cannot exist but in a mind perceiving it.

Phil. What! are you then in that sceptical state of suspense between affirming and denying?

Hyl. I think I may be positive in the point. A very violent and painful heat cannot exist without the mind.

Phil. It hath not therefore, according to you, any *real* being?

Hyl. I own it.

Phil. Is it therefore certain, that there is no body in nature really hot?

Hyl. I have not denied there is any real heat in bodies. I only say, there is no such thing as an intense real heat.

Phil. But, did you not say before that all degrees of heat were equally real; or, if there was any difference, that the greater were more undoubtedly real than the lesser?

Hyl. True: but it was because I did not then consider the ground there is for distinguishing between them, which I now plainly see. And it is this: because intense heat is nothing else but a particular kind of painful sensation; and pain cannot exist but in a perceiving being; it follows that no intense heat can really exist in an unperceiving corporeal substance. But this is no reason why we should deny heat in an inferior degree to exist in such a substance.

Phil. But how shall we be able to discern those degrees of heat which exist only in the mind from those which exist without it?

Hyl. That is no difficult matter. You know the least pain cannot exist unperceived; whatever, therefore, degree of heat is a pain exists only in the mind. But, as for all other degrees of heat, nothing obliges us to think the same of them.

Phil. I think you granted before that no unperceiving being was capable of pleasure, any more than of pain.

Hyl. I did.

Phil. And is not warmth, or a more gentle degree of heat than what causes uneasiness, a pleasure?

Hyl. What then?

Phil. Consequently, it cannot exist without the mind in an unperceiving substance, or body.

Hyl. So it seems.

Phil. Since, therefore, as well those degrees of heat that are not painful, as those that are, can exist only in a thinking substance; may we not conclude that external bodies are absolutely incapable of any degree of heat whatsoever?

Hyl. On second thoughts, I do not think it so evident that warmth is a pleasure as that a great degree of heat is a pain.

Phil. I do not pretend that warmth is as great a pleasure as heat is a pain. But, if you grant it to be even a small pleasure, it serves to make good my conclusion.

HYL. I could rather call it an *indolence*. It seems to be nothing more than a privation of both pain and pleasure. And that such a quality or state as this may agree to an unthinking substance, I hope you will not deny.

PHIL. If you are resolved to maintain that warmth, or a gentle degree of heat, is no pleasure, I know not how to convince you otherwise than by appealing to your own sense. But what think you of cold?

HYL. The same that I do of heat. An intense degree of cold is a pain; for to feel a very great cold, is to perceive a great uneasiness: it cannot therefore exist without the mind; but a lesser degree of cold may, as well as a lesser degree of heat.

PHIL. Those bodies, therefore, upon whose application to our own, we perceive a moderate degree of heat, must be concluded to have a moderate degree of heat or warmth in them; and those, upon whose application we feel a like degree of cold, must be thought to have cold in them.

HYL. They must.

PHIL. Can any doctrine be true that necessarily leads a man into an absurdity?

HYL. Without doubt it cannot.

PHIL. Is it not an absurdity to think that the same thing should be at the same time both cold and warm?

HYL. It is.

PHIL. Suppose now one of your hands hot, and the other cold, and that they are both at once put into the same vessel of water, in an intermediate state; will not the water seem cold to one hand, and warm to the other?

HYL. It will.

PHIL. Ought we not therefore, by your principles, to conclude it is really both cold and warm at the same time, that is, according to your own concession, to believe an absurdity?

HYL. I confess it seems so.

PHIL. Consequently, the principles themselves are false, since you have granted that no true principle leads to an absurdity.

HYL. But, after all, can anything be more absurd than to say, *there is not heat in the fire?*

PHIL. To make the point still clearer; tell me whether, in two cases exactly alike, we ought not to make the same judgment?

HYL. We ought.

PHIL. When a pin pricks your finger, doth it not rend and divide the fibres of your flesh?

HYL. It doth.

PHIL. And when a coal burns your finger, doth it any more?

HYL. It doth not.

PHIL. Since, therefore, you neither judge the sensation itself occasioned by the pin, nor anything like it to be in the pin; you should not, conformably to what you have now granted, judge the sensation occasioned by the fire, or anything like it, to be in the fire.

HYL. Well, since it must be so, I am content to yield this point, and acknowledge that heat and cold are only sensations existing in our minds. But there still remain qualities enough to secure the reality of external things.

PHIL. But what will you say, Hylas, if it shall appear that the case is the same with regard to all other sensible qualities, and that they can no more be supposed to exist without the mind, than heat and cold?

HYL. Then indeed you will have done something to the purpose; but that is what I despair of seeing proved.

Tastes

PHIL. Let us examine them in order. What think you of *tastes*—do they exist without the mind, or no?

HYL. Can any man in his senses doubt whether sugar is sweet, or wormwood bitter?

PHIL. Inform me, Hylas. Is a sweet taste a particular kind of pleasure or pleasant sensation, or is it not?

HYL. It is.

PHIL. And is not bitterness some kind of uneasiness or pain?

HYL. I grant it.

PHIL. If therefore sugar and wormwood are unthinking corporeal substances existing without the mind, how can sweetness and bitterness, that is, pleasure and pain, agree to them?

HYL. Hold, Philonous, I now see what it was deluded me all this time. You asked whether heat or cold, sweetness and bitterness, were not particular sorts of pleasure and pain; to which I answered simply, that they were. Whereas I should have thus distinguished:—those qualities, as perceived by us, are pleasures or pains; but not as existing in the external objects. We must not therefore conclude absolutely, that there is no heat in the fire, or sweetness in the sugar, but only that heat or sweetness, as perceived by us, are not in the fire or sugar. What say you to this?

PHIL. I say it is nothing to the purpose. Our discourse proceeded altogether concerning sensible things, which you defined to be, *the things we immediately perceive by our senses*. Whatever other qualities, therefore, you speak of, as distinct from these, I know nothing of them, neither do they at all belong to the point in dispute. You may, indeed, pretend to have discovered certain qualities which you do not perceive, and assert those insensible qualities exist in fire and sugar. But what use can be made of this to your present purpose, I am at a loss to conceive. Tell me then once more, do you acknowledge that heat and cold, sweetness and bitterness (meaning those qualities which are perceived by the senses), do not exist without the mind?

HYL. I see it is to no purpose to hold out, so I give up the cause as to those mentioned qualities. Though I profess it sounds oddly, to say that sugar is not sweet.

PHIL. But, for your farther satisfaction, take this along with you: that which at other times seems sweet, shall, to a distempered palate, appear bitter. And, nothing can be plainer than that divers persons perceive different tastes in the same food; since that which one man delights in, another abhors. And how could this be, if the taste was something really inherent in the food?

HYL. I acknowledge I know not how.

Odours

PHIL. In the next place, *odours* are to be considered. And, with regard to these, I would fain know whether what hath been said of tastes doth not exactly agree to them? Are they not so many pleasing or displeasing sensations?

HYL. They are.

PHIL. Can you then conceive it possible that they should exist in an unperceiving thing?

HYL. I cannot.

PHIL. Or, can you imagine that filth and ordure affect those brute animals that feed on them out of choice, with the same smells which we perceive in them?

HYL. By no means.

PHIL. May we not therefore conclude of smells, as of the other forementioned qualities, that they cannot exist in any but a perceiving substance or mind?

HYL. I think so.

Sounds

PHIL. Then as to *sounds,* what must we think of them: are they accidents really inherent in external bodies, or not?

HYL. That they inhere not in the sonorous bodies is plain from hence:

because a bell struck in the exhausted receiver of an air-pump sends forth no sound. The air, therefore, must be thought the subject of sound.

PHIL. What reason is there for that, Hylas?

HYL. Because, when any motion is raised in the air, we perceive a sound greater or lesser, according to the air's motion; but without some motion in the air, we never hear any sound at all.

PHIL. And granting that we never hear a sound but when some motion is produced in the air, yet I do not see how you can infer from thence, that the sound itself is in the air.

HYL. It is this very motion in the external air that produces in the mind the sensation of *sound*. For, striking on the drum of the ear, it causeth a vibration, which by the auditory nerves being communicated to the brain, the soul is thereupon affected with the sensation called *sound*.

PHIL. What! is sound then a sensation?

HYL. I tell you, as perceived by us, it is a particular sensation in the mind.

PHIL. And can any sensation exist without the mind?

HYL. No, certainly.

PHIL. How then can sound, being a sensation, exist in the air, if by the *air* you mean a senseless substance existing without the mind?

HYL. You must distinguish, Philonous, between sound as it is perceived by us, and as it is in itself; or (which is the same thing) between the sound we immediately perceive, and that which exists without us. The former, indeed, is a particular kind of sensation, but the latter is merely a vibrative or undulatory motion in the air.

PHIL. I thought I had already obviated that distinction, by the answer I gave when you were applying it in a like case before. But, to say no more of that, are you sure then that sound is really nothing but motion?

HYL. I am.

PHIL. Whatever therefore agrees to real sound, may with truth be attributed to motion?

HYL. It may.

PHIL. It is then good sense to speak of *motion* as of a thing that is *loud, sweet, acute, or grave.*

HYL. I see you are resolved not to understand me. Is it not evident those accidents or modes belong only to sensible sound, or *sound* in the common acceptation of the word, but not to *sound* in the real and philosophic sense; which, as I just now told you, is nothing but a certain motion of the air?

PHIL. It seems then there are two sorts of sound—the one vulgar, or that which is heard, the other philosophical and real?

HYL. Even so.

PHIL. And the latter consists in motion?

HYL. I told you so before.

PHIL. Tell me, Hylas, to which of the senses, think you, the idea of motion belongs? to the hearing?

HYL. No, certainly; but to the sight and touch.

PHIL. It should follow then, that, according to you, real sounds may possibly be *seen* or *felt,* but never *heard.*

HYL. Look you, Philonous, you may, if you please, make a jest of my opinion, but that will not alter the truth of things. I own, indeed, the inferences you draw me into sound something oddly; but common language, you know, is framed by, and for the use of the vulgar: we must not therefore wonder if expressions adapted to exact philosophic notions seem uncouth and out of the way.

PHIL. Is it come to that? I assure you, I imagine myself to have gained no small point, since you make so light of departing from common phrases and opinions; it being a main part of our inquiry, to examine whose notions are wildest of the common road, and most repugnant to the general sense of the world. But, can you think it no more than a philosophical paradox, to say that *real sounds are never heard,* and that the idea of them is obtained by some other sense? And is there nothing in this contrary to nature and the truth of things?

HYL. To deal ingenuously, I do not like it. And, after the concessions already made, I had as well grant that sounds too have no real being without the mind.

Colours

PHIL. And I hope you will make no difficulty to acknowledge the same of *colours.*

HYL. Pardon me: the case of colours is very different. Can anything be plainer than that we see them on the objects?

PHIL. The objects you speak of are, I suppose, corporeal Substances existing without the mind?

HYL. They are.

PHIL. And have true and real colours inhering in them?

HYL. Each visible object hath that colour which we see in it.

PHIL. How! is there anything visible but what we perceive by sight?

HYL. There is not.

PHIL. And, do we perceive anything by sense which we do not perceive immediately?

HYL. How often must I be obliged to repeat the same thing? I tell you, we do not.

PHIL. Have patience, good Hylas; and tell me once more, whether there is anything immediately perceived by the senses, except sensible qualities. I know you asserted there was not; but I would now be informed, whether you still persist in the same opinion.

HYL. I do.

PHIL. Pray, is your corporeal substance either a sensible quality, or made up of sensible qualities?

HYL. What a question that is! who ever thought it was?

PHIL. My reason for asking was, because in saying, *each visible object hath that colour which we see in it,* you make visible objects to be corporeal substances; which implies either that corporeal substances are sensible qualities, or else that there is something beside sensible qualities perceived by sight: but, as this point was formerly agreed between us, and is still maintained by you, it is a clear consequence, that your *corporeal substance* is nothing distinct from *sensible qualities.*

HYL. You may draw as many absurd consequences as you please, and endeavour to perplex the plainest things; but you shall never persuade me out of my senses. I clearly understand my own meaning.

PHIL. I wish you would make me understand it too. But, since you are unwilling to have your notion of corporeal substance examined, I shall urge that point no farther. Only be pleased to let me know, whether the same colours which we see exist in external bodies, or some other.

HYL. The very same.

PHIL. What! are then the beautiful red and purple we see on yonder clouds really in them? Or do you imagine they have in themselves any other form than that of a dark mist or vapour?

HYL. I must own, Philonous, those colours are not really in the clouds as they seem to be at this distance. They are only apparent colours.

PHIL. *Apparent* call you them? how shall we distinguish these apparent colours from real?

HYL. Very easily. Those are to be thought apparent which, appearing only at a distance, vanish upon a nearer approach.

PHIL. And those, I suppose, are to be thought real which are discovered by the most near and exact survey.

HYL. Right.

PHIL. Is the nearest and exactest survey made by the help of a microscope, or by the naked eye?

HYL. By a microscope, doubtless.

PHIL. But a microscope often discovers colours in an object different from those perceived by the unassisted sight. And, in case we had microscopes magnifying to any assigned degree, it is certain that no object whatsoever, viewed through them, would appear in the same colour which it exhibits to the naked eye.

HYL. And what will you conclude from all this? You cannot argue that there are really and naturally no colours on objects: because by artificial managements they may be altered, or made to vanish.

PHIL. I think it may evidently be concluded from your own concessions, that all the colours we see with our naked eyes are only apparent as those on the clouds, since they vanish upon a more close and accurate inspection which is afforded us by a microscope. Then, as to what you say by way of prevention: I ask you whether the real and natural state of an object is better discovered by a very sharp and piercing sight, or by one which is less sharp?

HYL. By the former without doubt.

PHIL. Is it not plain from *Dioptrics* that microscopes make the sight more penetrating, and represent objects as they would appear to the eye in case it were naturally endowed with a most exquisite sharpness?

HYL. It is.

PHIL. Consequently the microscopical representation is to be thought that which best sets forth the real nature of the thing, or what it is in itself. The colours, therefore, by it perceived are more genuine and real than those perceived otherwise.

HYL. I confess there is something in what you say.

PHIL. Besides, it is not only possible but manifest, that there actually are animals whose eyes are by nature framed to perceive those things which by reason of their minuteness escape our sight. What think you of those inconceivably small animals perceived by glasses? must we suppose they are all stark blind? Or, in case they see, can it be imagined their sight hath not the same use in preserving their bodies from injuries, which appears in that of all other animals? And if it hath, is it not evident they must see particles less than their own bodies; which will present them with a far different view in each object from that which strikes our senses? Even our own eyes do not always represent objects to us after the same manner. In the jaundice every one knows that all things seem yellow. Is it not therefore highly probable those animals in whose eyes we discern a very different texture from that of ours, and whose bodies abound with different humours, do not see the same colours in every object that we do? From all which, should it not seem to follow that all colours are equally apparent, and that none of those which we perceive are really inherent in any outward object?

HYL. It should.

PHIL. The point will be past all doubt, if you consider that, in case colours were real properties or affections inherent in external bodies, they could admit of no alteration without some change wrought in the very bodies themselves: but, is it not evident from what hath been said that, upon the use of microscopes, upon a change happening in the humours of the eye, or a variation of distance, without any manner of real alteration in the thing itself, the colours of any object are either changed, or totally disappear? Nay, all other circumstances remaining the same, change but the situation of some objects, and they shall present different colours to the eye. The same thing happens upon viewing an object in various degrees of light. And what is more known than that the same bodies appear differently coloured by candlelight from what they do in the open day? Add to these the experiment of a prism which, separating the heterogeneous rays of light, alters the colour of any object, and will cause the whitest to appear of a deep blue or red to the naked eye. And now tell me whether you are still of opinion that every body hath its true real colour inhering in it; and, if you think it hath, I would fain know farther from you, what certain distance and position of the object, what peculiar texture and formation of the eye, what degree or kind of light is necessary for ascertaining that true colour, and distinguishing it from apparent ones.

HYL. I own myself entirely satisfied, that they are all equally apparent, and that there is no such thing as colour really inhering in external bodies, but that it is altogether in the light. And what confirms me in this opinion is, that in proportion to the light colours are still more or less vivid; and if there be no light, then are there no colours perceived. Besides, allowing there are colours on external objects, yet, how is it possible for us to perceive them? For no external body affects the mind, unless it acts first on our organs of sense. But the only action of bodies is motion; and motion cannot be communicated otherwise than by impulse. A distant object therefore cannot act on the eye; nor consequently make itself or its properties perceivable to the soul. Whence it plainly follows that it is immediately some contiguous substance, which, operating on the eye, occasions a perception of colours: and such is light.

PHIL. How! is light then a substance?

HYL. I tell you, Philonous, external light is nothing but a thin fluid substance, whose minute particles being agitated with a brisk motion, and in various manners reflected from the different surfaces of outward objects to the eyes, communicate different motions to the optic nerves; which, being propagated to the brain, cause therein various impressions; and these are attended with the sensations of red, blue, yellow, etc.

PHIL. It seems then the light doth no more than shake the optic nerves.

HYL. Nothing else.

PHIL. And consequent to each particular motion of the nerves, the mind is affected with a sensation, which is some particular colour.

HYL. Right.

PHIL. And these sensations have no existence without the mind.

HYL. They have not.

PHIL. How then do you affirm that colours are in the light; since by *light* you understand a corporeal substance external to the mind?

HYL. Light and colours, as immediately perceived by us, I grant cannot exist without the mind. But in themselves they are only the motions and configurations of certain insensible particles of matter.

PHIL. Colours then, in the vulgar sense, or taken for the immediate objects of sight, cannot agree to any but a perceiving substance.

HYL. That is what I say.

PHIL. Well then, since you give up the point as to those sensible qualities which are alone thought colours by all mankind beside, you may hold what you please with regard to those invisible ones of the philosophers. It is not my business to dispute about *them;* only I would advise you to bethink yourself, whether, considering the inquiry we are upon, it be prudent for you to affirm—*the red and blue which we see are not real colours, but certain unknown motions and figures which no man ever did or can see are truly so.* Are not these shocking notions, and are not they subject to as many ridiculous inferences, as those you were obliged to renounce before in the case of sounds?

Are the Primary Qualities Really in Bodies?

HYL. I frankly own, Philonous, that it is in vain to stand out any longer. Colours, sounds, tastes, in a word all those termed *secondary qualities,* have certainly no existence without the mind. But by this acknowledgment I must not be supposed to derogate anything from the reality of Matter, or external objects; seeing it is no more than several philosophers maintain, who nevertheless are the farthest imaginable from denying Matter. For the clearer understanding of this, you must know sensible qualities are by philosophers divided into *Primary* and *Secondary.* The former are Extension, Figure, Solidity, Gravity, Motion, and Rest; and these they hold exist really in bodies. The latter are those above enumerated; or, briefly, *all sensible qualities beside the Primary;* which they assert are only so many sensations or ideas existing nowhere but in the mind. But all this, I doubt not, you are apprised of. For my part, I have been a long time sensible there was such an opinion current among philosophers, but was never thoroughly convinced of its truth until now.

Extension and Figures

PHIL. You are still then of opinion that *extension* and *figures* are inherent in external unthinking substances?

HYL. I am.

PHIL. But what if the same arguments which are brought against Secondary Qualities will hold good against these also?

HYL. Why then I shall be obliged to think, they too exist only in the mind.

PHIL. Is it your opinion the very figure and extension which you perceive by sense exist in the outward object or material substance?

HYL. It is.

PHIL. Have all other animals as good grounds to think the same of the figure and extension which they see and feel?

HYL. Without doubt, if they have any thought at all.

PHIL. Answer me, Hylas. Think you the senses were bestowed upon all animals for their preservation and well-being in life? or were they given to men alone for this end?

HYL. I make no question but they have the same use in all other animals.

PHIL. If so, is it not necessary they should be enabled by them to perceive their own limbs, and those bodies which are capable of harming them?

HYL. Certainly.

PHIL. A mite therefore must be supposed to see his own foot, and things equal or even less than it, as bodies of some considerable dimension; though at the same time they appear to you scarce discernible, or at best as so many visible points?

HYL. I cannot deny it.

PHIL. And to creatures less than the mite they will seem yet larger?

HYL. They will.

PHIL. Insomuch that what you can hardly discern will to another extremely minute animal appear as some huge mountain?

HYL. All this I grant.

PHIL. Can one and the same thing be at the same time in itself of different dimensions?

HYL. That were absurd to imagine.

PHIL. But, from what you have laid down it follows that both the extension by you perceived, and that perceived by the mite itself, as likewise all those perceived by lesser animals, are each of them the true extension of the mite's foot; that is to say, by your own principles you are led into an absurdity.

HYL. There seems to be some difficulty in the point.

PHIL. Again, have you not acknowledged that no real inherent property of any object can be changed without some change in the thing itself?

HYL. I have.

PHIL. But, as we approach to or recede from an object, the visible extension varies, being at one distance ten or a hundred times greater

than at another. Doth it not therefore follow from hence likewise that
it is not really inherent in the object?

HYL. I own I am at a loss what to think.

PHIL. Your judgment will soon be determined, if you will venture to
think as freely concerning this quality as you have done concerning the
rest. Was it not admitted as a good argument, that neither heat nor cold
was in the water, because it seemed warm to one hand and cold to the
other?

HYL. It was.

PHIL. Is it not the very same reasoning to conclude, there is no extension or figure in an object, because to one eye it shall seem little,
smooth, and round, when at the same time it appears to the other, great,
uneven, and angular?

HYL. The very same. But does this latter fact ever happen?

PHIL. You may at any time make the experiment, by looking with
one eye bare, and with the other through a microscope.

HYL. I know not how to maintain it; and yet I am loath to give up
extension, I see so many odd consequences following upon such a concession.

PHIL. Odd, say you? After the concessions already made, I hope
you will stick at nothing for its oddness. But, on the other hand, should
it not seem very odd, if the general reasoning which includes all other
sensible qualities did not also include extension? If it be allowed that
no idea, nor anything like an idea, can exist in an unperceiving substance,
then surely it follows that no figure, or mode of extension, which we can
either perceive, or imagine, or have any idea of, can be really inherent
in Matter; not to mention the peculiar difficulty there must be in conceiving a material substance, prior to and distinct from extension, to be
the *substratum* of extension. Be the sensible quality what it will—figure,
or sound, or colour, it seems alike impossible it should subsist in that
which doth not perceive it.

Motion

HYL. I give up the point for the present, reserving still a right to
retract my opinion, in case I shall hereafter discover any false step in
my progress to it.

PHIL. That is a right you cannot be denied. Figures and extension
being despatched, we proceed next to *motion.* Can a real motion in any
external body be at the same time both very swift and very slow?

HYL. It cannot.

PHIL. Is not the motion of a body swift in a reciprocal proportion to the time it takes up in describing any given space? Thus a body that describes a mile in an hour moves three times faster than it would in case it described only a mile in three hours.

HYL. I agree with you.

PHIL. And is not time measured by the succession of ideas in our minds?

HYL. It is.

PHIL. And is it not possible ideas should succeed one another twice as fast in your mind as they do in mine, or in that of some spirit of another kind?

HYL. I own it.

PHIL. Consequently the same body may to another seem to perform its motion over any space in half the time that it doth to you. And the same reasoning will hold as to any other proportion: that is to say, according to your principles (since the motions perceived are both really in the object) it is possible one and the same body shall be really moved the same way at once, both very swift and very slow. How is this consistent either with common sense, or with what you just now granted?

HYL. I have nothing to say to it.

Solidity

PHIL. Then as for *solidity;* either you do not mean any sensible quality by that word, and so it is beside our inquiry: or if you do, it must be either hardness or resistance. But both the one and the other are plainly relative to our senses: it being evident that what seems hard to one animal may appear soft to another, who hath greater force and firmness of limbs. Nor is it less plain that the resistance I feel is not in the body.

HYL. I own the very *sensation* of resistance, which is all you immediately perceive, is not in the body; but the *cause* of that sensation is.

PHIL. But the causes of our sensations are not things immediately perceived, and therefore are not sensible. This point I thought had been already determined.

HYL. I own it was; but you will pardon me if I seem a little embarrassed: I know not how to quit my old notions.

PHIL. To help you out, do but consider that if *extension* be once acknowledged to have no existence without the mind, the same must necessarily be granted of motion, solidity, and gravity; since they all evidently suppose extension. It is therefore superfluous to inquire particularly concerning each of them. In denying extension, you have denied them all to have any real existence.

HYL. I wonder, Philonous, if what you say be true, why those philosophers who deny the Secondary Qualities any real existence should yet attribute it to the Primary. If there is no difference between them, how can this be accounted for?

PHIL. It is not my business to account for every opinion of the philosophers. But, among other reasons which may be assigned for this, it seems probable that pleasure and pain being rather annexed to the former than the latter may be one. Heat and cold, tastes and smells, have something more vividly pleasing or disagreeable than the ideas of extension, figure, and motion affect us with. And, it being too visibly absurd to hold that pain or pleasure can be in an unperceiving Substance, men are more easily weaned from believing the external existence of the Secondary than the Primary Qualities. You will be satisfied there is something in this, if you recollect the difference you made between an intense and more moderate degree of heat; allowing the one a real existence, while you denied it to the other. But, after all, there is no rational ground for that distinction; for, surely an indifferent sensation is as truly *a sensation* as one more pleasing or painful; and consequently should not any more than they be supposed to exist in an unthinking subject.

Absolute and Sensible Extension and Motion

HYL. It is just come into my head, Philonous, that I have somewhere heard of a distinction between absolute and sensible extension. Now, though it be acknowledged that *great* and *small,* consisting merely in the relation which other extended beings have to the parts of our own bodies, do not really inhere in the substances themselves; yet nothing obliges us to hold the same with regard to *absolute extension,* which is something abstracted from *great* and *small,* from this or that particular magnitude or figure. So likewise as to motion; *swift* and *slow* are altogether relative to the succession of ideas in our own minds. But, it doth not follow, because those modifications of motion exist not without the mind, that therefore absolute motion abstracted from them doth not.

PHIL. Pray what is it that distinguishes one motion, or one part of extension, from another? Is it not something sensible, as some degree of swiftness or slowness, some certain magnitude or figure peculiar to each?

HYL. I think so.

PHIL. These qualities, therefore, stripped of all sensible properties, are without all specific and numerical differences, as the schools call them.

HYL. They are.

PHIL. That is to say, they are extension in general, and motion in general.

HYL. Let it be so.

Abstract Ideas

PHIL. But it is a universally received maxim that *Everything which exists is particular.* How then can motion in general, or extension in general, exist in any corporeal substance?

HYL. I will take time to solve your difficulty.

PHIL. But I think the point may be speedily decided. Without doubt you can tell whether you are able to frame this or that idea. Now I am content to put our dispute on this issue. If you can frame in your thoughts a distinct *abstract idea* of motion or extension, divested of all those sensible modes, as swift and slow, great and small, round and square, and the like, which are acknowledged to exist only in the mind, I will then yield the point you contend for. But if you cannot, it will be unreasonable on your side to insist any longer upon what you have no notion of.

HYL. To confess ingenuously, I cannot.

PHIL. Can you even separate the ideas of extension and motion from the ideas of all those qualities which they who make the distinction term *secondary?*

HYL. What! is it not an easy matter to consider extension and motion by themselves, abstracted from all other sensible qualities? Pray how do the mathematicians treat of them?

PHIL. I acknowledge, Hylas, it is not difficult to form general propositions and reasonings about those qualities, without mentioning any other; and, in this sense, to consider or treat of them abstractedly. But, how doth it follow that, because I can pronounce the word *motion* by itself, I can form the idea of it in my mind exclusive of body? or, because theorems may be great of extension and figures, without any mention of *great* or *small,* or any other sensible mode of quality, that therefore it is possible such an abstract idea of extension, without any particular size or figure, or sensible quality, should be distinctly formed, and apprehended by the mind? Mathematicians treat of quantity, without regarding what other sensible qualities it is attended with, as being altogether indifferent to their demonstrations. But, when laying aside the words, they contemplate the bare ideas, I believe you will find, they are not the pure abstracted ideas of extension.

HYL. But what say you to *pure intellect?* May not abstracted ideas be framed by that faculty?

PHIL. Since I cannot frame abstract ideas at all, it is plain I cannot frame them by the help of *pure intellect,* whatsoever faculty you understand by those words. Besides, not to inquire into the nature of pure intellect and its spiritual objects, as *virtue, reason, God,* or the like, thus much seems manifest—that sensible things are only to be perceived by sense, or represented by the imagination. Figures, therefore, and extension, being originally perceived by sense, do not belong to pure intellect: but, for your farther satisfaction, try if you can frame the idea of any figure, abstracted from all particularities of size, or even from other sensible qualities.

HYL. Let me think a little— I do not find that I can.

PHIL. And can you think it possible that should really exist in nature which implies a repugnancy in its conception?

HYL. By no means.

PHIL. Since therefore it is impossible even for the mind to disunite the ideas of extension and motion from all other sensible qualities, doth it not follow, that where the one exist there necessarily the other exist likewise?

HYL. It should seem so.

PHIL. Consequently, the very same arguments which you admitted as conclusive against the Secondary Qualities are, without any farther application of force, against the Primary too. Besides, if you will trust your senses, is it not plain all sensible qualities coexist, or to them appear as being in the same place? Do they ever represent a motion, or figure, as being divested of all other visible and tangible qualities?

HYL. You need say no more on this head. I am free to own, if there be no secret error or oversight in our proceedings hitherto, that *all* sensible qualities are alike to be denied existence without the mind. But, my fear is that I have been too liberal in my former concessions, or overlooked some fallacy or other. In short, I did not take time to think.

PHIL. For that matter, Hylas, you may take what time you please in reviewing the progress of our inquiry. You are at liberty to recover any slips you might have made, or offer whatever you have omitted which makes for your first opinion.

Sensation and Objects

HYL. One great oversight I take to be this—that I did not sufficiently distinguish the *object* from the *sensation.* Now, though this latter may not exist without the mind, yet it will not thence follow that the former cannot.

PHIL. What object do you mean? the object of the senses?

HYL. The same.

PHIL. It is then immediately perceived?

HYL. Right.

PHIL. Make me to understand the difference between what is immediately perceived and a sensation.

HYL. The sensation I take to be an act of the mind perceiving; besides which, there is something perceived; and this I call the *object*. For example, there is red and yellow on that tulip. But then the act of perceiving those colours is in me only, and not in the tulip.

PHIL. What tulip do speak of? Is it that which you see?

HYL. The same.

PHIL. And what do you see beside colour, figure, and extension?

HYL. Nothing.

PHIL. What you would say then is that the red and yellow are coexistent with the extension; is it not?

HYL. That is not all; I would say they have a real existence without the mind, in some unthinking substance.

PHIL. That the colours are really in the tulip which I see is manifest. Neither can it be denied that this tulip may exist independent of your mind or mine; but, that any immediate object of the senses—that is, any idea, or combination of ideas—should exist in an unthinking substance, or exterior to *all* minds, is in itself an evident contradiction. Nor can I imagine how this follows from what you said just now, to wit, that the red and yellow were on the tulip *you saw,* since you do not pretend to *see* that unthinking substance.

HYL. You have an artful way, Philonous, of diverting our inquiry from the subject.

PHIL. I see you have no mind to be pressed that way. To return then to your distinction between *sensation* and *object*; if I take you right, you distinguish in every perception two things, the one an action of the mind, the other not.

HYL. True.

PHIL. And this action cannot exist in, or belong to, any unthinking thing; but, whatever beside is implied in a perception may?

HYL. That is my meaning.

PHIL. So that if there was a perception without any act of the mind, it were possible such a perception should exist in an unthinking substance?

HYL. I grant it. But it is impossible there should be such a perception.

PHIL. When is the mind said to be active?

HYL. When it produces, puts an end to, or changes, anything.

PHIL. Can the mind produce, discontinue, or change anything, but by an act of the will?

HYL. It cannot.

PHIL. The mind therefore is to be accounted *active* in its perceptions so far forth as *volition* is included in them?

HYL. It is.

PHIL. In plucking this flower I am active; because I do it by the motion of my hand, which was consequent upon my volition; so likewise in applying it to my nose. But is either of these smelling?

HYL. No.

PHIL. I act too in drawing the air through my nose; because my breathing so rather than otherwise is the effect of my volition. But neither can this be called *smelling*: for, if it were, I should smell every time I breathed in that manner?

HYL. True.

PHIL. Smelling then is somewhat consequent to all this?

HYL. It is.

PHIL. But I do not find my will concerned any farther. Whatever more there is—as that I perceive such a particular smell, or any smell at all—this is independent of my will, and therein I am altogether passive. Do you find it otherwise with you, Hylas?

HYL. No, the very same.

PHIL. Then, as to seeing, is it not in your power to open your eyes, or keep them shut; to turn them this or that way?

HYL. Without doubt.

PHIL. But, doth it in like manner depend on *your* will that in looking on this flower you perceive *white* rather than any other colour? Or, directing your open eyes towards yonder part of the heaven, can you avoid seeing the sun? Or is light or darkness the effect of your volition?

HYL. No, certainly.

PHIL. You are then in these respects altogether passive?

HYL. I am.

PHIL. Tell me now, whether *seeing* consists in perceiving light and colours, or in opening and turning the eyes?

HYL. Without doubt, in the former.

PHIL. Since therefore you are in the very perception of light and colours altogether passive, what is become of that action you were speaking of as an ingredient in every sensation? And, doth it now follow from your own concessions, that the perception of light and colours, including no action in it, may exist in an unperceiving substance? And is not this a plain contradiction?

HYL. I know not what to think of it.

PHIL. Besides, since you distinguish the *active* and *passive* in every perception, you must do it in that of pain. But how is it possible that pain, be it as little active as you please, should exist in an unperceiving substance? In short, do but consider the point, and then confess ingenuously, whether light and colours, tastes, sounds, etc., are not all equally passions or sensations in the soul. You may indeed call them *external objects,* and give them in words what subsistence you please. But, examine your own thoughts, and then tell me whether it be not as I say?

HYL. I acknowledge, Philonous, that upon a fair observation of what passes in my mind, I can discover nothing else but that I am a thinking being, affected with variety of sensations; neither is it possible to conceive how a sensation should exist in an unperceiving substance. —But then, on the other hand, when I look on sensible things in a different view, considering them as so many modes and qualities, I find it necessary to suppose a *material substratum,* without which they cannot be conceived to exist.

The Material Substratum

PHIL. *Material substratum* call you it? Pray, by which of your senses came you acquainted with that being?

HYL. It is not itself sensible; its modes and qualities only being perceived by the senses.

PHIL. I presume then it was by reflexion and reason you obtained the idea of it?

HYL. I do not pretend to any proper positive *idea* of it. However, I conclude it exists, because qualities cannot be conceived to exist without a support.

PHIL. It seems then you have only a relative *notion* of it, or that you conceive it not otherwise than by conceiving the relation it bears to sensible qualities?

HYL. Right.

PHIL. Be pleased therefore to let me know wherein that relation consists.

HYL. Is it not sufficiently expressed in the term *substratum,* or *substance?*

PHIL. If so, the word *substratum* should import that it is spread under the sensible qualities or accidents?

HYL. True.

PHIL. And consequently under extension?

HYL. I own it.

PHIL. It is therefore somewhat in its own nature entirely distinct from extension?

HYL. I tell you, extension is only a mode, and Matter is something that supports modes. And is it not evident the thing supported is different from the thing supporting?

PHIL. So that something distinct from, and exclusive of, extension is supposed to be the *substratum* of extension?

HYL. Just so.

PHIL. Answer me, Hylas. Can a thing be spread without extension? or is not the idea of extension necessarily included in *spreading?*

HYL. It is.

PHIL. Whatsoever therefore you suppose spread under anything must have in itself an extension distinct from the extension of that thing under which it is spread?

HYL. It must.

PHIL. Consequently, every corporeal substance, being the *substratum* of extension, must have in itself another extension, by which it is qualified to be a *substratum*: and so on to infinity? And I ask whether this be not absurd in itself, and repugnant to what you granted just now, to wit, that the *substratum* was something distinct from and exclusive of extension?

HYL. Aye but, Phinolous, you take me wrong. I do not mean that Matter is *spread* in a gross literal sense under extension. The word *substratum* is used only to express in general the same thing with *substance*.

PHIL. Well then, let us examine the relation implied in the term *substance*. Is it not that it stands under accidents?

HYL. The very same.

PHIL. But, that one thing may stand under or support another, must it not be extended?

HYL. It must.

PHIL. Is not therefore this supposition liable to the same absurdity with the former?

HYL. You still take things in a strict literal sense. That is not fair, Philonous.

PHIL. I am not for imposing any sense on your words: you are at liberty to explain them as you please. Only, I beseech you, make me understand something by them. You tell me Matter supports or stands under accidents. How! is it as your legs support your body?

HYL. No; that is the literal sense.

PHIL. Pray let me know any sense, literal or not literal, that you understand it in.—How long must I wait for an answer, Hylas?

HYL. I declare I know not what to say. I once thought I understood well enough what was meant by Matter's supporting accidents. But now, the more I think on it the less can I comprehend it: in short I find that I know nothing of it.

PHIL. It seems then you have no idea at all, neither relative nor positive, of Matter; you know neither what it is in itself, nor what relation it bears to accidents?

HYL. I acknowledge it.

PHIL. And yet you asserted that you could not conceive how qualities or accidents should really exist, without conceiving at the same time a material support of them?

HYL. I did.

PHIL. That is to say, when you conceive the *real* existence of qualities, you do withal conceive Something which you cannot conceive?

HYL. It was wrong, I own. But still I fear there is some fallacy or other. Pray what think you of this? It is just come into my head that the ground of all our mistake lies in your treating of each quality by itself. Now, I grant that each quality cannot singly subsist without the mind. Colour cannot without extension, neither can figure without some other sensible quality. But, as the several qualities united or blended together form entire sensible things, nothing hinders why such things may not be supposed to exist without the mind.

PHIL. Either, Hylas, you are jesting, or have a very bad memory. Though indeed we went through all the qualities by name one after another, yet my arguments, or rather your concessions, nowhere tend to prove that the Secondary Qualities did not subsist each alone by itself; but, that they were not *at all* without the mind. Indeed, in treating of figure and motion we concluded they could not exist without the mind, because it was impossible even in thought to separate them from all secondary qualities, so as to conceive them existing by themselves. But then this was not the only argument made use of upon that occasion. But (to pass by all that hath been hitherto said, and reckon it for nothing, if you will have it so) I am content to put the whole upon this issue. If you can conceive it possible for any mixture or combination of qualities, or any sensible object whatever, to exist without the mind, then I will grant it actually to be so.

Is the Existence of Unperceived
Objects Conceivable?

HYL. If it comes to that the point will soon be decided. What more easy than to conceive a tree or house existing by itself, independent of, and unperceived by, any mind whatsoever? I do at this present time conceive them existing after that manner.

PHIL. How say you, Hylas, can you see a thing which is at the same time unseen?

HYL. No, that were a contradiction.

PHIL. Is it not as great a contradiction to talk of *conceiving* a thing which is *unconceived?*

HYL. It is.

PHIL. The tree or house therefore which you think of is conceived by you?

HYL. How should it be otherwise?

PHIL. And what is conceived is surely in the mind?

HYL. Without question, that which is conceived is in the mind.

PHIL. How then came you to say, you conceived a house or tree existing independent and out of all minds whatsoever?

HYL. That was I own an oversight; but stay, let me consider what led me into it.—It is a pleasant mistake enough. As I was thinking of a tree in a solitary place, where no one was present to see it, methought that was to conceive a tree as existing unperceived or unthought of; not considering that I myself conceived it all the while. But now I plainly see that all I can do is to frame ideas in my own mind. I may indeed conceive in my own thoughts the idea of a tree, or a house, or a mountain, but that is all. And this is far from proving that I can conceive them *existing out of the minds of all Spirits*.

PHIL. You acknowledge then that you cannot possibly conceive how any one corporeal sensible thing should exist otherwise than in a mind?

HYL. I do.

PHIL. And yet you will earnestly contend for the truth of that which you cannot so much as conceive?

HYL. I profess I know not what to think; but still there are some scruples remain with me. Is it not certain I *see things at a distance?* Do we not perceive the stars and moon, for example, to be a great way off? Is not this, I say, manifest to the senses?

PHIL. Do you not in a dream too perceive those or the like objects?

HYL. I do.

PHIL. And have they not then the same appearance of being distant?

HYL. They have.

PHIL. But you do not thence conclude the apparitions in a dream to be without the mind?

HYL. By no means.

PHIL. You ought not therefore to conclude that sensible objects are without the mind, from their appearance, or manner wherein they are perceived.

HYL. I acknowledge it. But doth not my sense deceive me in those cases?

The Idea of Distance

PHIL. By no means. The idea or thing which you immediately perceive, neither sense nor reason informs you that *it* actually exists without the mind. By sense you only know that you are affected with such certain sensations of light and colours, etc. And these you will not say are without the mind.

HYL. True: but, beside all that, do you not think the sight suggests something of *outness* or *distance?*

PHIL. Upon approaching a distant object, do the visible size and figure change perpetually, or do they appear the same at all distances?

HYL. They are in a continual change.

PHIL. Sight therefore doth not suggest, or any way inform you, that the visible object you immediately perceive exists at a distance,[1] or will be perceived when you advance farther onward; there being a continued series of visible objects succeeding each other during the whole time of your approach.

HYL. It doth not; but still I know, upon seeing an object, what object I shall perceive after having passed over a certain distance: no matter whether it be exactly the same or no: there is still something of distance suggested in the case.

PHIL. Good Hylas, do but reflect a little on the point, and then tell me whether there be any more in it than this: From the ideas you actually perceive by sight, you have by experience learned to collect what other ideas you will (according to the standing order of nature) be affected with, after such a certain succession of time and motion.

HYL. Upon the whole, I take it to be nothing else.

PHIL. Now, is it not plain that if we suppose a man born blind was on a sudden made to see, he could at first have no experience of what may be *suggested* by sight?

HYL. It is.

PHIL. He would not then, according to you, have any notion of distance annexed to the things he saw; but would take them for a new set of sensations, existing only in his mind?

HYL. It is undeniable.

PHIL. But, to make it still more plain: is not *distance* a line turned endwise to the eye?

HYL. It is.

PHIL. And can a line so situated be perceived by sight?

HYL. It cannot.

PHIL. Doth it not therefore follow that distance is not properly and immediately perceived by sight?

HYL. It should seem so.

PHIL. Again, is it your opinion that colours are at a distance?

HYL. It must be acknowledged they are only in the mind.

PHIL. But do not colours appear to the eye as coexisting in the same place with extension and figures?

HYL. They do.

PHIL. How can you then conclude from sight that figures exist with-

---

1. [See the *Essay towards a New Theory of Vision,* and its *Vindication.*] Note added by Berkeley in the 1734 edition.

out, when you acknowledge colours do not; the sensible appearance being the very same with regard to both?

HYL. I know not what to answer.

PHIL. But, allowing that distance was truly and immediately perceived by the mind, yet it would not thence follow it existed out of the mind. For, whatever is immediately perceived is an idea: and can any idea exist out of the mind?

HYL. To suppose that were absurd: but, inform me, Philonous, can we perceive or know nothing beside our ideas?

PHIL. As for the rational deducing of causes from effects, that is beside our inquiry. And, by the senses you can best tell whether you perceive anything which is not immediately perceived. And I ask you, whether the things immediately perceived are other than your own sensations or ideas? You have indeed more than once, in the course of this conversation, declared yourself on those points; but you seem, by this last question, to have departed from what you then thought.

Do Ideas Represent External Objects

HYL. To speak the truth, Philonous, I think there are two kinds of objects:—the one perceived immediately, which are likewise called *ideas;* the other are real things or external objects, perceived by the mediation of ideas, which are their images and representations. Now, I own ideas do not exist without the mind; but the latter sort of objects do. I am sorry I did not think of this distinction sooner; it would probably have cut short your discourse.

PHIL. Are those external objects perceived by sense, or by some other faculty?

HYL. They are perceived by sense.

PHIL. How! Is there anything perceived by sense which is not immediately perceived?

HYL. Yes, Philonous, in some sort there is. For example, when I look on a picture or statue of Julius Cæsar, I may be said after a manner to perceive him (though not immediately) by my senses.

PHIL. It seems then you will have our ideas, which alone are immediately perceived, to be pictures of external things: and that these also are perceived by sense, inasmuch as they have a conformity or resemblance to our ideas?

HYL. That is my meaning.

PHIL. And, in the same way that Julius Cæsar, in himself invisible, is nevertheless perceived by sight; real things, in themselves imperceptible, are perceived by sense.

HYL. In the very same.

PHIL. Tell me, Hylas, when you behold the picture of Julius Cæsar, do you see with your eyes any more than some colours and figures, with a certain symmetry and composition of the whole?

HYL. Nothing else.

PHIL. And would not a man who had never known anything of Julius Cæsar see as much?

HYL. He would.

PHIL. Consequently he hath his sight, and the use of it, in as perfect a degree as you?

HYL. I agree with you.

PHIL. Whence comes it then that your thoughts are directed to the Roman emperor, and his are not? This cannot proceed from the sensations or ideas of sense by you then perceived; since you acknowledge you have no advantage over him in that respect. It should seem therefore to proceed from reason and memory: should it not?

HYL. It should.

PHIL. Consequently, it will not follow from that instance that anything is perceived by sense which is not immediately perceived. Though I grant we may, in one acceptation, be said to perceive sensible things mediately by sense: that is, when, from a frequently perceived connexion, the immediate perception of ideas by one sense *suggests* to the mind others, perhaps belonging to another sense, which are wont to be connected with them. For instance, when I hear a coach drive along the streets, immediately I perceive only the sound; but, from the experience I have had that such a sound is connected with a coach, I am said to hear the coach. It is nevertheless evident that, in truth and strictness, nothing can be *heard* but *sound;* and the coach is not then properly perceived by sense, but suggested from experience. So likewise when we are said to see a red-hot bar of iron; the solidity and heat of the iron are not the objects of sight, but suggested to the imagination by the colour and figure which are properly perceived by that sense. In short, those things alone are actually and strictly perceived by any sense, which would have been perceived in case that same sense had then been first conferred on us. As for other things, it is plain they are only suggested to the mind by experience, grounded on former conceptions. But, to return to your comparison of Cæsar's picture, it is plain, if you keep to that, you must hold the real things, or archetypes of our ideas, are not perceived by sense, but by some internal faculty of the soul, as reason or memory. I would therefore fain know what arguments you can draw from reason for the existence of what you call *real things* or *material objects*. Or, whether you remember to have seen them formerly as they are in themselves; or, if you have heard or read of any one that did.

HYL. I see, Philonous, you are disposed to raillery; but that will never convince me.

PHIL. My aim is only to learn from you the way to come at the knowledge of *material beings*. Whatever we perceive is perceived immediately or mediately: by sense, or by reason or reflexion. But, as you have excluded sense, pray shew me what reason you have to believe their existence; or what *medium* you can possibly make use of to prove it, either to mine or your own understanding.

HYL. To deal ingenuously, Philonous, now I consider the point, I do not find I can give you any good reason for it. But, thus much seems pretty plain, that it is at least possible such things may really exist. And, as long as there is no absurdity in supposing them, I am resolved to believe as I did, till you bring good reasons to the contrary.

PHIL. What! Is it come to this, that you only *believe* the existence of material objects, and that your belief is founded barely on the possibility of its being true? Then you will have me bring reasons against it: though another would think it reasonable the proof should lie on him who holds the affirmative. And, after all, this very point which you are now resolved to maintain, without any reason, is in effect what you have more than once during this discourse seen good reason to give up. But, to pass over all this; if I understand you rightly, you say our ideas do not exist without the mind, but that they are copies, images, or representations, of certain originals that do?

HYL. You take me right.

PHIL. They are then like external things?

HYL. They are.

PHIL. Have those things a stable and permanent nature, independent of our senses; or are they in a perpetual change, upon our producing any motions in our bodies—suspending, exerting, or altering, our faculties or organs of sense?

HYL. Real things, it is plain, have a fixed and real nature, which remains the same notwithstanding any change in our senses, or in the posture and motion of our bodies; which indeed may affect the ideas in our minds; but it were absurd to think they had the same effect on things existing without the mind.

PHIL. How then is it possible that things perpetually fleeting and variable as our ideas should be copies or images of anything fixed and constant? Or, in other words, since all sensible qualities, as size, figure, colour, &c., that is, our ideas, are continually changing, upon every alteration in the distance, medium, or instruments of sensation; how can any determinate material objects be properly represented or painted forth by several distinct things, each of which is so different from and unlike the rest? Or, if you say it resembles some one only of our ideas, how shall we be able to distinguish the true copy from all the false ones?

HYL. I profess, Philonous, I am at a loss. I know not what to say to this.

PHIL. But neither is this all. Which are material objects in themselves—perceptible or imperceptible?

HYL. Properly and immediately nothing can be perceived but ideas. All material things, therefore, are in themselves insensible, and to be perceived only by our ideas.

PHIL. Ideas then are sensible, and their archetypes or originals insensible?

HYL. Right.

PHIL. But how can that which is sensible be *like* that which is insensible? Can a real thing, in itself *invisible*, be like a *colour;* or a real thing, which is not *audible,* be like a *sound?* In a word, can anything be like a sensation or idea, but another sensation or idea?

HYL. I must own, I think not.

PHIL. Is it possible there should be any doubt on the point? Do you not perfectly know your own ideas?

HYL. I know them perfectly; since what I do not perceive or know can be no part of my idea.

PHIL. Consider, therefore, and examine them, and then tell me if there be anything in them which can exist without the mind: or if you can conceive anything like them existing without the mind.

HYL. Upon inquiry, I find it is impossible for me to conceive or understand how anything but an idea can be like an idea. And it is most evident that *no idea can exist without the mind.*

PHIL. You are therefore, by your principles, forced to deny the *reality* of sensible things; since you made it to consist in an absolute existence exterior to the mind. That is to say, you are a downright sceptic. So I have gained by point, which was to shew your principles led to Scepticism.

HYL. For the present I am, if not entirely convinced, at least silenced.

PHIL. I would fain know what more you would require in order to a perfect conviction. Have you not had the liberty of explaining yourself all manner of ways? Were any little slips in discourse laid hold and insisted on? Or were you not allowed to retract or reinforce anything you had offered, as best served your purpose? Hath not everything you could say been heard and examined with all the fairness imaginable? In a word, have you not in every point been convinced out of your own mouth? And, if you can at present discover any flaw in any of your former concessions, or think of any remaining subterfuge, any new distinction, colour, or comment whatsoever, why do you not produce it?

HYL. A little patience, Philonous. I am at present so amazed to see myself ensnared, and as it were imprisoned in the labyrinths you have drawn me into, that on the sudden it cannot be expected I should find my way out. You must give me time to look about me and recollect myself.

PHIL. Hark; is not this the college bell?

HYL. It rings for prayers.

PHIL. We will go in then, if you please, and meet here again to-morrow morning. In the meantime, you may employ your thoughts on this morning's discourse, and try if you can find any fallacy in it, or invent any new means to extricate yourself.

HYL. Agreed.

14

THE REFUTATION OF REALISM

W. T. Stace

MORE THAN THIRTY YEARS have now elapsed since Professor Moore published in *Mind* his famous article, "The Refutation of Idealism." Therewith the curtain rose upon the episode of contemporary British realism. After three decades perhaps the time is now ripe for the inauguration of another episode. And it is but fitting that "The Refutation of Realism" should appear on the same stage as its famous predecessor.

I shall not gird at realism because its exponents disagree among themselves as to what precisely their philosophy teaches. But disagreements certainly exist, and they make it difficult for a would-be refuter to know precisely what is the proposition which he ought to refute. It is far from certain that all idealists would agree that the idealism which Professor Moore purported to refute represented adequately, or even inadequately, their views. And it may be that a similar criticism will be urged by realists against what I shall here have to say. But I must take my courage in my hands. Realists, it seems to me, agree in asserting that "some entities sometimes exist without being experienced by any finite mind." This, at any rate, is the proposition which I shall undertake to refute.

I insert the word "finite" in this formula because if I wrote "some entities exist without being experienced by any mind," it might be objected that the proposition so framed would imply that some entities exist of which God is ignorant, if there is such a being as God, and that it is not certain that all realists would wish to assert this. I think that we can very well leave God out of the discussion. In front of me is a piece of paper. I assume that the realist believes that this paper will continue to exist when it is put away in my desk for the night, and when

---

["The Refutation of Realism" originally appeared in *Mind*, 1934. It is here reproduced with a slight omission by the kind permission of the author and the editor of *Mind*.]

no finite mind is experiencing it. He *may* also believe that it will continue to exist even if God is not experiencing it. But he must *at least* assert that it will exist when no finite mind is experiencing it. That, I think, is essential to his position. And therefore to refute that proposition will be to refute realism. In what follows, therefore, when I speak of minds I must be understood as referring to finite minds.

Possibly I shall be told that although realists probably do as a matter of fact believe that some entities exist unexperienced, yet this is not the essence of realism. Its essence, it may be said, is the belief that the relation between knowledge and its object is such that the knowledge makes no difference to the object, so that the object *might* exist without being known, whether as a matter of fact it does so exist or not.

But it would seem that there could be no point in asserting that entities *might* exist unexperienced, unless as a matter of fact they at least sometimes do so exist. To prove that the universe *might* have the property X, if as a matter of fact the universe has no such property, would seem to be a useless proceeding which no philosophy surely would take as its central contribution to truth. And I think that the only reason why realists are anxious to show that objects are such, and that the relation between knowledge and object is such, that objects might exist unexperienced, is that they think that this will lead on to the belief that objects actually do exist unexperienced. They have been anxious to prove that the existence of objects is not dependent on being experienced by minds because they wished to draw the conclusion that objects exist unexperienced. Hence I think that I am correct in saying that the essential proposition of realism, which has to be refuted, is that "some entities sometimes exist without being experienced by any finite mind."

Now, lest I should be misunderstood, I will state clearly at the outset that I cannot prove that no entities exist without being experienced by minds. For all I know completely unexperienced entities may exist, but what I shall assert is that we have not the slightest reason for believing that they do exist. And from this it will follow that the realistic position that they do exist is perfectly groundless and gratuitous, and one which ought not to be believed. It will be in exactly the same position as the proposition "there is a unicorn on the planet Mars." I cannot prove that there is no unicorn on Mars. But since there is not the slightest reason to suppose that there is one, it is a proposition which ought not to be believed.

And still further to clarify the issue, I will say that I shall not be discussing in this paper whether sense-objects are "mental." My personal opinion is that this question is a pointless one, but that if I am forced to answer it with a "yes" or "no," I should do so by saying that they are not mental; just as, if I were forced to answer the pointless question whether the mind is an elephant, I should have to answer that it is not an elephant. I will, in fact, assume for the purposes of this paper that sense-objects, whether they be color patches or other sense-data, or objects, are not mental. My position will then be as follows: There is absolutely no reason for asserting that these non-mental, or physical, entities ever exist except when they are being experienced, and the proposition that they do so exist is utterly groundless and gratuitous, and one which ought not to be believed.

The refutation of realism will therefore be sufficiently accomplished if it can be shown that we do *not* know that any single entity exists unexperienced. And that is what I shall in this paper endeavor to show. I shall inquire how we could possibly know that unexperienced entities exist, even if, as a matter of fact, they do exist. And I shall show that there is no possible way in which we could know this, and that therefore we do *not* know it, and have no reason to believe it.

For the sake of clearness, let us take once again the concrete example of the piece of paper. I am at this moment experiencing it, and at this moment it exists, but how can I know that it existed last night in my desk when, so far as I know, no mind was experiencing it? How can I know that it will continue to exist tonight when there is no one in the room? The knowledge of these alleged facts is what the realists assert that they possess. And the question is, Whence could such knowledge have been obtained, and how can it be justified? What I assert is that it is absolutely impossible to have any such knowledge.

There are only two ways in which it could be asserted that the existence of any sense-object can be established. One is by sense-perception, the other by inference from sense-perception. I know of the existence of this paper *now* because I see it. I am supposed to know of the existence of the other side of the moon, which no one has ever seen, by inference from various actual astronomical observations, that is, by inference from things actually experienced. There are no other ways of proving the existence of a sense-object. Is either of them possible in the present case?

1. *Sense-perception.* I obviously cannot know by perception the existence of the paper when no one is experiencing it. For that would be self-contradictory. It would amount to asserting that I can experience the unexperienced.

2. *Inference.* Nor is it possible to prove by inference the existence of the paper when no mind is experiencing it. For how can I possibly pass by inference from the particular fact of the existence of the paper now, when I am experiencing it, to the quite different particular fact of the existence of the paper yesterday or tomorrow, when neither I nor any other mind is experiencing it? Strictly speaking, the onus of proving that such an inference is impossible is not on me. The onus of proving that it is possible is upon anyone who asserts it, and I am entitled to sit back and wait until someone comes forward with such an alleged proof. Many

realists who know their business admit that no valid inference from an experienced to an unexperienced existence is possible. Thus Mr. Russell says, "Belief in the existence of things outside my own biography must, from the stand-point of theoretical logic, be regarded as a prejudice, not as a well-grounded theory."[1]

I might therefore adopt the strategy of masterly inaction. But I prefer to carry the war into the enemy's camp. I propose to *prove* that no proof of the existence of unexperienced objects is possible.

It is clear in the first place that any supposed reasoning could not be inductive. Inductive reasoning proceeds always upon the basis that what has been found in certain observed cases to be true will also be true in unobserved cases. But there is no single case in which it has been observed to be true that an experienced object continues to exist when it is not being experienced; for, by hypothesis, its existence when it is not being experienced cannot be observed. Induction is generalization from observed facts, but there is not a single case of an unexperienced existence having been observed on which could be based the generalization that entities continue to exist when no one is experiencing them. And there is likewise not a single known instance of the existence of an unexperienced entity which could lead me to have even the slightest reason for supposing that this paper ever did exist, or will exist, when no one is experiencing it.

Since inductive reasoning is ruled out, the required inference, if there is to be an inference, must be of a formal nature. But deductive inference of all kinds depends upon the principle of consistency. If $P \supset Q$, then we can only prove Q, *if* P is admitted. From $P \supset Q$, therefore, all that can be deduced is that P and not-Q are inconsistent, and that we cannot hold both P and not-Q together, though we may hold either of them separately.

Hence, if it is alleged that a deductive inference can be drawn from the existence of the paper now, when I am experiencing it, to its existence when no one is experiencing it, this can only mean that to assert together the two propositions, (1) that it exists now, and (2) that it does not exist when no one is experiencing it, is an internally inconsistent position. But there is absolutely no inconsistency between these two propositions. If I believe that nothing whatever exists or ever did or will exist, except my own personal sense-data, this may be a view of the universe which no one would ever hold, but there is absolutely nothing internally inconsistent in it. Therefore, no deductive inference can prove the existence of an unexperienced entity. Therefore, by no reasoning at all, inductive or deductive, can the existence of such an entity be proved.

Nevertheless, arguments have been put forward from time to time by realists which are apparently intended to prove this conclusion. I will deal shortly with those with which I am acquainted. I am not bound to do this, since I have already proved that no proof of the realists' con-

1. *Analysis of Mind*, p. 133.

clusion is possible. And for the same reason, if there are any arguments of this kind with which I am not acquainted, I am under no obligation to disprove them. But it will be better to meet at least the most well-known arguments.

(a) It was Mr. Perry, I believe, who invented the phrase "egocentric predicament." The egocentric predicament was supposed to indicate where lay a fallacy committed by idealists. It consisted in arguing from the fact that it is impossible to discover anything which is not known to the conclusion that all things are known. That any competent idealist ever did use such an argument may well be doubted, but I will waive that point. Mr. Perry's comment was that the egocentric predicament, as employed by idealists, appeared to imply that from our ignorance of unexperienced entities we could conclude to their non-existence, and that to do so is a fallacy.

No doubt such a procedure would be a fallacy. But though Mr. Perry's argument may refute a supposed idealistic argument, *it does not prove anything whatever in favor of realism*. It would be a fallacy to argue that, because we have never observed a unicorn on Mars, therefore there is no unicorn there; but by pointing out this fallacy, one does not prove the existence of a unicorn there. And by pointing out that our ignorance of the existence of unexperienced entities does not prove their non-existence, one does nothing whatever towards proving that unexperienced entities do exist. As regards the unicorn on Mars, the correct position, as far as logic is concerned, is obviously that if anyone asserts that there is a unicorn there, the onus is on him to prove it; and that until he does prove it, we ought not to believe it to be true. As regards the unexperienced entities, the correct position, as far as logic is concerned, is that if realists assert their existence, the onus is on them to prove it; and that until they do prove it, we ought not to believe that they exist. Mr. Perry's argument, therefore, proves nothing whatever in favour of realism.

Possibly all this is admitted and understood by realists. But there seems, nevertheless, to have been a tendency to think that the overthrow of the supposed idealistic argument was a very important matter in forwarding the interests of realism. To point out, therefore, that it actually accomplishes nothing seems desirable.

(b) Mr. Lovejoy, in his recent book, *The Revolt Against Dualism*, argues that we can infer, or at least render probable, the existence of things during interperceptual intervals by means of the law of causation. He writes, "The same uniform causal sequences of natural events which may be observed within experience appear to go on in the same manner when not experienced. You build a fire in your grate of a certain quantity of coal, of a certain chemical composition. Whenever you remain in the room there occurs a typical succession of sensible phenomena according to an approximately regular schedule of clock-time; in, say, half an hour the coal is half consumed; at the end of the hour the grate contains only ashes. If you build a fire of the same quantity of the same material under the same conditions, leave the room, and return after any given time has elapsed, you get approximately the same sense-experiences as you would have had at the corresponding moment if you had remained in the room. You infer, therefore, that the fire has been burning as usual during your absence, and that being perceived is not a condition necessary for the occurrence of the process."[2]

This argument is simply a *petitio principii*. It assumes that we must believe that the law of causality continues to operate in the universe when no one is observing it. But the law of causality is one aspect of the universe, the unobserved existence of which is the very thing to be proved.

Why must we believe that causation continues to operate during interperceptual intervals? Obviously, the case as regards unexperienced processes and laws is in exactly the same position as the case regarding unexperienced *things*. Just as we cannot perceive unexperienced things, so we cannot perceive unexperienced processes and laws. Just as we cannot infer from anything which we experience the existence of unexperienced things, so we cannot infer from anything we experience the existence of unexperienced processes and laws. There is absolutely no evidence (sense-experience) to show that the fire went on burning during your absence, nor is any inference to that alleged fact possible. Any supposed inference will obviously be based upon our belief that the law of causation operates continuously through time whether observed or unobserved. But this is one of the very things which has to be proved. Nor is there the slightest logical inconsistency in believing that, when you first observed the phenomena, unburnt coal existed, that there followed an interval in which nothing existed, not even a law, and that at the end of the interval ashes began to exist.

No doubt this sounds very absurd and contrary to what we usually believe, but that is nothing to the point. We usually believe that things go on existing when no one is aware of them. But if we are inquiring how this can be *proved,* we must, of course, begin from the position that we do not know it, and therefore that it might not be true.

(c) The distinction between sense-data and our awareness of them, which was first emphasized, so far as I know, by Professor Moore, has been made the basis of an argument in favor of realism. Green, it is said, is not the same thing as awareness of green. For if we compare a green sense-datum with a blue sense-datum, we find a common element, namely awareness. The awareness must be different from the green because awareness also exists in the case of awareness of blue, and *that* awareness, at any rate, is not green. Therefore, since green is not the same thing as awareness of green, green might exist without awareness. Connected with

2. *The Revolt Against Dualism,* p. 268.

this argument, too, is the assertion of a special kind of relationship between the awareness and the green.

Possibly this argument proves that green is not "mental." I do not know whether it proves this or not, but the point is unimportant, since I have already admitted that sense-data are not "mental." But whatever the argument proves, it certainly does *not* prove that unexperienced entities exist. For suppose that it proves that green has the predicate *x* (which may be "non-mental" or "independent of mind," or anything else you please), it still can only prove that green has the predicate *x* during the period when green is related to the awareness in the alleged manner, that is, when some mind is aware of the green. It cannot possibly prove anything about green when no mind is aware of it. Therefore, it cannot prove that green exists when no mind is aware of it.

For the sake of clearness, I will put the same point in another way. Suppose we admit that green and awareness of green are two quite different things, and suppose we admit that the relation between them is *r*—which may stand for the special relation asserted in the argument. Now it is not in any way inconsistent with these admissions to hold that green begins to exist only when awareness of green begins to exist, and that when awareness of green ceases to exist, green ceases to exist. It may be the case that these two quite different things always co-exist, always accompany each other, and are co-terminous in the sense that they always begin and end simultaneously, and that while they co-exist, they have the relation *r*. And this will be so *whatever* the relation *r* may be. And not only is this supposition that they always co-exist not at all absurd or arbitrary. It is on the contrary precisely the conclusion to which such evidence as we possess points. For we never have evidence that green exists except when some mind is aware of green. And it will not be asserted that awareness of green exists when green does not exist.

The argument from the distinction between green and the awareness of it, therefore, does nothing whatever towards proving the realist conclusion that some entities exist unexperienced. . . .

15

PHYSICS AND PERCEPTION

Bertrand Russell

WHEN WE CONSIDER PERCEPTION—visual or auditory—of an external event, there are three different matters to be examined. There is first the process in the outside world, from the event to the percipient's body; there is next the process in his body, in so far as this can be known by an outside observer; lastly, there is the question, which must be faced sooner or later, whether the percipient can perceive something of the process in his body which no other observer could perceive. We will take these points in order.

If it is to be possible to "perceive" an event not in the percipient's body, there must be a physical process in the outer world such that, when a certain event occurs, it produces a stimulus of a certain kind at the surface of the percipient's body. Suppose, for example, that pictures of different animals are exhibited on a magic lantern to a class of children, and all the children are asked to say the name of each animal in turn. We may assume that the children are sufficiently familiar with animals to say "cat," "dog," "giraffe," "hippopotamus," etc., at the right moments. We must then suppose—taking the physical world for granted—that some process travels from each picture to the eyes of the various children, retaining throughout these journeys such peculiarities that, when the process reaches their eyes, it can in one case stimulate the word "cat" and in another the word "dog." All this the physical theory of light provides for. But there is one interesting point about language that should be noticed in this connection. If the usual physical theory of light is correct, the various children will receive stimuli which differ greatly according to their distance and direction from the picture, and

[This selection consists of parts of Chapters XII and XIII of *The Outline of Philosophy* published by George Allen and Unwin in 1927. The book was published in the United States by W. W. Norton and Co., under the title *Philosophy*. The extracts are reproduced with the kind permission of Bertrand Russell and the publishers.]

according to the way the light falls. There are also differences in their reactions, for, though they all utter the word "cat," some say it loud, others soft, some in a soprano voice, some in a contralto. But the differences in their reactions are much less than the differences in the stimuli. . . .

The fact that it is possible for a number of people to perceive the same noise or the same colored pattern obviously depends upon the fact that a physical process can travel outward from a center and retain certain of its characteristics unchanged, or very little changed. The most notable of such characteristics is frequency in a wave-motion. That, no doubt, affords a biological reason for the fact that our most delicate senses, sight and hearing, are sensitive to frequencies, which determine color in what we see and pitch in what we hear. If there were not, in the physical world, processes spreading out from centers and retaining certain characters practically unchanged, it would be impossible for different percipients to perceive the same object from different points of view, and we should not have been able to discover that we all live in a common world.

We come now to the process in the percipient's body, in so far as this can be perceived by an outside observer. This raises no new philosophical problems, because we are still concerned, as before, with the perception of events outside the observer's body. The observer, now, is supposed to be a physiologist, observing, say, what goes on in the eye when light falls upon it. His means of knowing are, in principle, exactly the same as in the observation of dead matter. An event in an eye upon which light is falling causes light-waves to travel in a certain manner until they reach the eye of the physiologist. They there cause a process in the physiologist's eye and optic nerve and brain, which ends in what he calls "seeing what happens in the eye he is observing." But this event, which happens in the physiologist, is not what happened in the eye he was observing; it is only connected with this by a complicated causal chain. Thus our knowledge of physiology is no more direct or intimate than our knowledge of processes in dead matter; we do not know any more about our eyes than about the trees and fields and clouds that we see by means of them. The event which happens when a physiologist observes an eye is an event in him, not on the eye that he is observing.

. . . It may be said that we do not in fact proceed to *infer* the physical world from our perceptions, but that we begin at once with a rough-and-ready knowledge of the physical world, and only at a late stage of sophistication compel ourselves to regard our knowledge of the physical world as an inference. What is valid in this statement is the fact that our knowledge of the physical world is not at first inferential, but that is only because we take our percepts to *be* the physical world. Sophistication and philosophy come in at the stage at which we realize that the physical world cannot be identified with our percepts. When my boy was three years old, I showed him Jupiter, and told him that Jupiter was larger than earth. He insisted that I must be speaking of some other Jupiter, because, as he patiently explained, the one he was seeing was obviously quite small. After some efforts, I had to give it up and leave him unconvinced. In the case of the heavenly bodies, adults have got used to the idea that what is really there can only be *inferred* from what they see; but where rats in mazes are concerned, they still tend to think that they are seeing what is happening in the physical world. The difference, however, is only one of degree, and naive realism is as untenable in the one case as in the other. There are differences in the perceptions of two persons observing the same process; there are sometimes no discoverable differences between two perceptions of the same persons observing different processes, e.g., pure water and water full of bacilli. The subjectivity of our perceptions is thus of practical as well as theoretical importance.

. . . A lamp at the top of a tall building might produce the same visual stimulus as Jupiter, or at any rate one practically indistinguishable from that produced by Jupiter. A blow on the nose might make us "see stars." Theoretically, it should be possible to apply a stimulus direct to the optic nerve, which should give us a visual sensation. Thus when we think we see Jupiter, we may be mistaken. We are less likely to be mistaken if we say that the surface of the eye is being stimulated in a certain way, and still less likely to be mistaken if we say that the optic nerve is being stimulated in a certain way. We do not eliminate the risk of error completely unless we confine ourselves to saying that an event of a certain sort is happening in the brain; this statement may still be true if we see Jupiter in a dream.

But, I shall be asked, what do you know about what is happening in the brain? Surely nothing. Not so, I reply. I know what is happening in the brain exactly what naive realism thinks it knows about what is happening in the outside world. But this needs explaining, and there are other matters that must be explained first.

When the light from a fixed star reaches me, I see the star if it is night and I am looking in the right direction. The light started years ago, probably many years ago, but my reaction is primarily something that is happening *now*. When my eyes are open, I see the star; when they are shut, I do not. Children discover at a fairly early age that they see nothing when their eyes are shut. They are aware of the difference between seeing and not seeing, and also of the difference between eyes open and eyes shut; gradually they discover that these two differences are correlated—I mean that they have expectations of which this is the intellectualist transcription. Again, children learn to name the colors, and to state correctly whether a thing is blue or red or yellow or whatnot. They ought not to be sure that light of the appropriate wave-length started from the object. The sun looks red in a London fog, grass looks blue through blue spectacles, everything looks yellow to a person suffering from jaundice. But suppose you ask: What color are you seeing? The person who answers, In these cases, red for the sun, blue for the grass, and yellow for the sick-room of the jaundiced patient, is answering quite truly. And in each of these cases he is stating something that he *knows*. What he knows in such cases is what I call a "percept." I shall contend later that, from the standpoint of physics, a percept is in the brain; for the present, I am only concerned to say that a percept is what is most indubitable in our knowledge of the world.

I do not in fact entertain any doubts that physics is true in its main lines. The interpretation of physical formulae is a matter as to which a considerable degree of uncertainty is possible; but we cannot well doubt that there is an interpretation which is true roughly and in the main. I shall come to the question of interpretation later; for the present, I shall assume that we may accept physics in its broad outlines, without troubling to consider how it is to be interpreted. On this basis, the above remarks on perception seem undeniable. We are often misled as to what is happening, either by peculiarities of the medium between the object and our bodies, or by unusual states of our bodies, or by a temporary or permanent abnormality in the brain. But in all these cases *something* is really happening, as to which, if we turn our attention to it, we can obtain knowledge that is not misleading. At one time when, owing to illness, I had been taking a great deal of quinine, I became hypersensitive to noise, so that when the nurse rustled the newspaper I thought she was spilling a scuttle of coals on the floor. The interpretation was mistaken, but it was quite true that I heard a loud noise. It is commonplace that a man whose leg has been amputated can still feel pains in it; here again, he does really feel the pains, and is only mistaken in his belief that they come from his leg. A percept is an observable event, but its interpretation as knowledge of this or that event in the physical world is liable to be mistaken, for reasons which physics and physiology can make fairly clear.

Perhaps there is nothing so difficult for the imagination as to teach it to feel about space as modern science compels us to think. This is the task which must now be attempted. . . . The gist of the matter is that percepts . . . are in our heads; that percepts are what we can know with most certainty; and that percepts contain what naive realism thinks it knows about the world.

But when I say that my percepts are in my head, I am saying something which is ambiguous until the different kinds of space have been explained, for the statement is only true in connection with *physical* space. There is also a space in our percepts, and of this space the statement would not be true. When I say that there is space in our percepts, I mean nothing at all difficult to understand. I mean—to take the sense of sight, which is the most important in this connection—that in what we see at one time there is up and down, right and left, inside and outside. If we see, say, a circle on a blackboard, all these relations exist within what we see. The circle has a top half and a bottom half, a right-hand half and a left-hand half, an inside and an outside. Those relations alone are enough to make up a space of sorts. But the space of every-day life is filled out with what we derive from touch and movement—how a thing feels when we touch it, and what movements are necessary in order to grasp it. Other elements also come into the genesis of the space in which everybody believes who has not been troubled by philosophy; but it is unnecessary for our purposes to go into this question any more deeply. The point that concerns us is that a man's percepts are private to himself: what I see, no one else sees; what I hear, no one else hears; what I touch, no one else touches; and so on. True, others hear and see something very like what I hear and see, if they are suitably placed; but there are always differences. Sounds are less loud at a distance; objects change their visual appearance according to the laws of perspective. Therefore it is impossible for two persons at the same time to have exactly identical percepts. It follows that the space of percepts, like the percepts, must be private; there are as many perceptual spaces as there are percipients. My percept of a table is outside my percept of my head, in my perceptual space; but it does not follow that it is outside my head as a physical object in physical space. Physical space is neutral and public: in this space, all my percepts are in my head, even the most distant star *as I see it*. Physical and perceptual space have relations, but they are not identical, and failure to grasp the difference between them is a potent source of confusion.

To say that you see a star when you see the light that has come from it is no more correct than to say that you see New Zealand when you see a New Zealander in London. Your perception when (as we say) you see a star is causally connected, in the first instance, with what happens in the brain, the optic nerve, and the eye, then with a light-wave which, according to physics, can be traced back to the star as its source. Your sensations will be closely similar if the light comes from a lamp at the top of a mast. The physical space in which you believe the "real" star to be is an elaborate inference; what is given is the private space in which the speck of light you see is situated. It is still an open question whether the space of sight has depth, or is merely a surface, as Berkeley contended. This does not matter for our purposes. Even if we admit that sight alone shows a difference between an object a few inches from the eyes and an object several feet distant, yet you certainly cannot, by sight alone, see that a cloud is less distant than a fixed star, though you may *infer* that it is, because it can hide the star. The world of astronomy, from the point of view of sight, is a surface. If you were put in a dark room with little holes cut in the ceiling in the pattern of the stars letting light come through, there would be nothing in your immediate visual data to show that you were not "seeing the stars." This illustrates what I mean by saying that what you see is *not* "out there" in the sense of physics.

We learn in infancy that we can sometimes touch objects we see, and sometimes not. When we cannot touch them at once, we can sometimes do so by walking to them. That is to say, we learn to correlate sensations of sight with sensations of touch, and sometimes with sensations of movement followed by sensations of touch. In this way we locate our sensations in a three-dimensional world. Those which involve sight alone we think of as "external," but there is no justification for this view. What you see when you see a star is just as internal as what you feel when you feel a headache. That is to say, it is internal from the standpoint of *physical* space. It is distant in your private space, because it is not associated with sensations of touch, and cannot be associated with them by means of any journey you can perform.

To make the matter definite, let us suppose that a physiologist is observing a living brain—no longer an impossible supposition, as it would have been formerly. It is natural to suppose that what the physiologist sees is in the brain he is observing. But if we are speaking of physical space, what the physiologist sees is in his own brain. It is in no sense in the brain that he is observing, though it is in the percept of that brain, which occupies part of the physiologist's perceptual space. Causal continuity makes the matter perfectly evident: light-waves travel from the brain that is being observed to the eye of the physiologist, at which they only arrive after an interval of time, which is finite though short. The physiologist sees what he is observing only after the light-waves have reached his eye; therefore the event which constitutes his seeing comes at the end of a series of events which travel from the observed brain into the brain of the physiologist. We cannot, without a preposterous kind of discontinuity, suppose that the physiologist's percept, which comes at the end of this series, is anywhere else but in the physiologist's head.

It is extraordinarily difficult to divest ourselves of the belief that the physical world is the world we perceive by sight and touch; even if, in our philosophic moments, we are aware that this is an error, we nevertheless fall into it again as soon as we are off our guard. The notion that what we see is "out there" in physical space is one which cannot survive while we are grasping the difference between what physics supposes to be really happening, and what our senses show us as happening; but it is sure to return and plague us when we begin to forget the argument. Only long reflection can make a radically new point of view familiar and easy.

Our illustrations hitherto have been taken from the sense of sight; let us now take one from the sense of touch. Suppose that, with your eyes shut, you let your finger-tip press against a hard table. What is really happening? The physicist says that your finger-tip and the table consist, roughly speaking, of vast numbers of electrons and protons; more correctly, each electron and proton is to be thought of as a collection of processes of radiation, but we can ignore this for our present purposes. Although you think you are touching the table, no electron or proton in your finger ever really touches an electron or proton in the table, because this would develop an infinite force. When you press, repulsions are set up between parts of your finger and parts of the table. If you try to press upon a liquid or a gas, there is room in it for the parts that are repelled to get away. But if you press a hard solid, the electrons and protons that try to get away, because electrical forces from your finger repel them, are unable to do so, because they are crowded close to others which elbow them back to more or less their original position, like people in a dense crowd. Therefore the more you press the more they repel your finger. The repulsion consists of electrical forces, which set up in the nerves a current whose nature is not very definitely known. This current runs into the brain, and there has effects which, so far as the physiologist is concerned, are almost wholly conjectural. But there is one effect which is not conjectural, and that is the sensation of touch. This effect, owing to physiological inference or perhaps to a reflex, is associated by us with the finger-tip. But the sensation is the same if, by artificial means, the parts of the nerve nearer the brain are suitably stimulated—e.g., if your hand has been amputated and the right nerves are skilfully manipulated. Thus our confidence that touch affords evidence of the existence of bodies at the place which we think is being touched is quite misplaced. As a rule we are right, but we can be wrong; there is nothing of the nature of an infallible revelation about the matter. And even in the most favorable case, the perception of touch is something very different from the mad dance of electrons and protons trying to jazz out of each other's way, which is what physics maintains is really taking place at your finger-tip. . . .

16

PHENOMENALISM

C. H. Whiteley

The Meaning of Words

. . . WHEN I AM TEACHING a child the meaning of the word "table," I point to the table, so that he sees it; I put his hand to it, so that he feels it; that is, I cause him to sense certain sense-data. Surely it is with these sense-data that he thereupon associates the sound "table"; when he sees and feels similar sense-data, he repeats "table." It is by the differences in what they look like and feel like that he distinguishes tables from chairs and apples and half-crowns. It is natural to conclude that when he uses the word "table" or "apple," he is using it to describe what he sees, feels, tastes, etc., rather than to propound some theory about an invisible and intangible material substance.

The word "table" *means* a certain visible squareness and brownness, a certain tangible hardness; i.e., it means a certain type of sense-experience. When I say "There is a table in this room" I am describing the sense-data which I am now sensing, and if I do not sense such sense-data, then, being a truthful person, I do not say that there is a table in the room. If someone else says that there is, I test his statement by looking and feeling, i.e., by finding out whether the appropriate sense-data are available; if they are not, I dismiss his statement as false. If I say "Socrates drank his companions under the table," I am not describing any sense-experiences which I have now, but I am describing sense-experiences which I suppose Socrates and his companions to have had at another time and place.

We cannot, of course, identify "the table" with any one single sense-datum; an experience which was entirely unique and did not recur would

[This selection consists of portions of Chapters VI and VII of C. H. Whiteley's *An Introduction to Metaphysics,* a book published in 1949 by Methuen and Co., Ltd., London. It is reproduced here with the kind permission of Professor Whiteley and the publisher.]

not be worth naming. The function of words is not to name everything we see or hear, but to pick out the recurrent patterns in our experience. They identify our present sense-data as being of the same group or type as others which we have sensed before. A word, then, describes, not a single experience, but a group or type of experiences; the word "table" describes all the various sense-data which we normally refer to as appearances or sensations "of" the table. So a material thing is not indeed identical with any sense-datum; but neither is it something different in kind from sense-data. It is a group, or class, or system of sense-data; and nothing but sense-data goes to constitute it. So this doctrine may be expressed by saying that every statement we make about a material thing is equivalent to another statement about sense-data.

The Advantages of Phenomenalism

This analysis of the notion of a material thing is called Phenomenalism, since it makes of a material thing a group of phenomena, appearances, instead of a transcendent reality distinct from appearances. It is a widespread view, and has been accepted by many philosophers who do not call themselves Idealists and are far from accepting Berkeley's view that the fundamental reality is Mind. The term "idealism" itself, however, though it has shifted in meaning since, does properly denote just this part of Berkeley's theory, that the material world—"the whole choir of heaven and furniture of the earth" says Berkeley—consists of what he calls "ideas" and I have been calling "sense-data." The word in this sense has nothing to do with ideals, and the theory would have been called "ideaism" but for considerations of pronunciation.

Phenomenalism, then, is the doctrine that all statements about material objects can be completely analyzed into statements about sense-data. The analysis of any such statement must be very complex; and the value of the "material-object language" is that it enables us to refer in one word, such as "table," to a vast number of sense-data differing very much among themselves. The group of sense-data constituting the table includes all the different views I can obtain at different distances, from different angles, in different lights, no two of them exactly alike, but all of them variations on one central pattern; it includes sense-data of touch, and those of sound (though these last seem somewhat more loosely connected with the main visuo-tactual group); and with other kinds of material things, such as apples, sense-data of taste and smell form important constituents of the thing.

This type of theory has certain clear advantages. On the representative theory, the very existence of a material world or of any given material object must always be in principle doubtful. I am directly aware of my sense-data, and so can be certain of their existence and character: but "material objects" are quite different—their existence and character can be known only by an inference, which cannot give the complete certainty which comes from observation. Descartes, for example, accepts this consequence of the theory, and will not allow himself to believe that there is a material world at all, until he has convinced himself that there exists an omnipotent and benevolent God who would never have led him to believe in the material world if it had not been real. But if Descartes really succeeded in keeping up this attitude of doubt for more than a moment, few men have been able to imitate him. We *cannot* believe that the existence of the table is in any way subject to doubt.

The phenomenalist theory, by making the existence of the table *the same thing* as the occurrence of certain sense-data, removes that doubt; for the system of sense-data constituting the table has beyond doubt come under my observation.

The theory not only removes the doubt, but makes it clear why we cannot seriously entertain it. The Plain Man was right after all: material things are seen and touched, are objects of direct awareness, and it is by seeing and touching that we know that they exist, though no material thing is straightforwardly identical with what I am seeing and touching *at this particular moment.*

So, by accepting the phenomenalist analysis, we escape being involved in any reference to an unobservable Matter. We can preserve our empiricism inviolate, and talk about the things we see and hear and smell and touch, and not about other hypothetical things beyond the reach of our observation. Science, the knowledge of nature, on this view becomes the recording, ordering and forecasting of human experiences. Therein lies its interest for us. If the physical world lay outside our experience, why should we be concerned with it?

Criticisms of Phenomenalism

But these advantages of phenomenalism are purchased at a cost. Along several different lines the phenomenalist interpretation of our statements about material things seems to conflict with our usual beliefs, and produces paradoxes not very easy to accept.

(1) In ordinary speech we are accustomed to draw a distinction between "appearance" and "reality," and to allow that a thing may appear to be what it is not, as Descartes' stick half under water may appear bent although it is really straight. Hence we reckon some of our perceptions as "real" or "true" or "genuine," and others as illusions."

The representative theory of perception is in accordance with this way of thinking; for on that theory our sense-data are in some respects copies of material things; some are accurate copies, and so are genuine and true, others are inaccurate copies, and so false and illusory. The representative theory differs from common sense mainly in holding that the discrepancies between the sense-datum and the material object which it represents are greater than we realize.

But what is the phenomenalist to make of this distinction? He can admit no essential difference between appearance and reality; for on his view the appearances *are* the reality. Material things consist of appearances—sense-data—and of nothing else. And these sense-data all actually occur and so are equally real. Moreover, they are what they appear to be; their reality consists in appearing, and the suggestion that they might "really" have qualities which they do not appear to have is without meaning. Thus the phenomenalist has no justification for classifying them into "real" and "unreal," or "genuine" and "counterfeit." The various sense-data which go to constitute a material object, such as my table, are of many different shapes and colours. All of them are equally real, and none of them can be *the* "real shape" or "real color" of the table. Evidently tables are more versatile objects than we thought, and may have as many different shapes and colors as there are occasions of observing them. Why then should we come by the idea that there is only one "real shape," and the rest are mere appearances?

The phenomenalist solution of this difficulty is to allow that in a strict philosophical sense of the word "real," the distinction between reality and appearance cannot be drawn. But the purpose of the common-sense distinction between appearance and reality is not to pry into the ultimacies of metaphysics, but to enable us to deal with the experiences we encounter. What causes us to condemn an experience as an "illusion" is that it leads us astray. A mirage is an illusion because it causes us to make a mistake. But what kind of mistake? Surely, not the mistake of thinking that we now see trees and water, but the mistake of expecting that we shall soon be able to have a drink and sit in the shade. The mistake consists in the false expectation of certain other sense-data. Thus the illusoriness is not in the sense-datum itself, but in the expectation which we form when we sense it.

Error of this sort is possible because sense-data are not chaotic, but in the main are arranged in orderly series. Normally, when the visual sense-data belonging to water are obtainable, so are the gustatory sense-data of drinking water and relieving one's thirst. The mirage deceives us because, abnormally, we get the visual sense-data without the gustatory ones. Mirror-images may deceive us because the things seen in a mirror cannot be observed from the back and cannot be touched. Thus a "real" table consists of a complete set of sense-data of different senses related to one another in certain systematic ways (e.g., visual sense-data become continuously smaller and auditory ones continuously fainter as we move away from a certain region of space). When, as in the case of a table seen in a mirror, you have some members of the set but not others, you say that what is seen in the mirror is not a "real" table, or is not "really" there.

Again, the stick in water may lead us into error because sticks that "look bent" usually "feel bent" as well; and so we are surprised to find that it "feels straight," and say that though it "looks bent" it is not "really bent."

The precise interpretation of the word "real" is different in different contexts. But in general, say phenomenalists, it will be found that what we call the "real world" is not a world different from that of appearances; it is a selection from the world of appearances, a collection of appearances which are normal, systematic, and so reliable. The "unreal" consists of eccentric appearances which in one way or another fail to fit in with the normal type of sets of sense-data, and therefore cause us to form false expectations.

(2) Sensations come and go. Few of them last for very long, and none of them lasts for ever. If we add up all the occasions in my life on which I have been looking at this table, we get a very short period indeed. And, like the rest of my species, I frequently go to sleep, and cease to perceive any material object whatsoever. That is to say, if a material thing consists of sense-data, its existence must be intermittent. Sense-data belonging to the thing exist only now and again, and most of the time they do not exist at all. But material objects such as tables are normally supposed to be permanent things, which endure uninterruptedly for very long periods. How can a permanent object be made out of momentary sense-data?

If I am alone in the room and close my eyes, there are then no sense-data belonging to the table; are we to suppose that I can annihilate so substantial a material object simply by shutting my eyes? It seems as though the phenomenalist must deny that any such statement as "There is a table in the room" can be true unless there is someone there seeing or touching it; and he must also deny that any such statement as "The table has been here for twenty years" can be true, unless (what seems most improbable) gangs of watchers have been observing it in relays for the whole of that time.

The phenomenalist answer to these difficulties involves a radical reinterpretation of the whole notion of a permanent material thing. That the existence of the table should be permanent in the way in which my waking experience is uninterrupted, that the table should last for twenty years in the way that my hearing a performance of a symphony can last for three-quarters of an hour, is of course impossible on a phenomenalist view. Whatever kind of permanence is attributed to the table must be understood in another sense.

Clearly, when I say that there is a table in the now uninhabited attic, I am not describing the sense-data of anyone. But, though the statement cannot be a description of *actual* sense-data, it can be a description of *possible* sense-data; and this is what it is according to phenomenalists. To say that there is a table there now is to say that *if* there were anyone in the room he *would* be having the kind of experience which we call seeing a table. "There is a table" means "Go and look and you will see a table." And to say that it has been there twenty years means that if at any time during those years anyone had been in the room, he could have seen or touched a table.

So we must modify our original account of the nature of a material thing. It consists not merely of actual sense-data, but also of possible sense-data; or, more precisely, of the fact that under certain conditions sense-data are obtainable. What is permanent is then not any sense-datum or group of sense-data, but the possibility of obtaining sense-data of a certain kind. Hence J. S. Mill defined matter as "the permanent possibility of sensation."

I think this much at least must be admitted: if it is true that there is a table in the attic, it is also true that if anyone with the use of normal eyes in a good light were to be in the attic now, he would have the experience of seeing the table; if it is true that the table has been there for twenty years, it is also true that if anyone has been there under those conditions at any time during those twenty years, he would have had the experience of seeing the table. That is to say, the statement about sense-data is involved in or implied by the statement about the table. According to the phenomenalist, such statements about possible sense-data constitute the whole of what the statement about the table means. All statements about material objects are equivalent to statements about what people have experienced, or would have experienced if circumstances had been different.

He points out that if we try to imagine the presence of the table in the attic, what we do is to imagine what it would look like and feel like. If we want to test the statement that it is there, we go and look. Statements which are not, in the final analysis, about actual or possible experiences, cannot be tested at all, and are therefore without meaning for us.

Berkeley himself gives another explanation of the permanence of material things. According to his theory, God is eternally perceiving everything, and therefore, at times when neither I nor any other human being or animal is perceiving the table, God is still perceiving it. But whether or not this is really the case, it is obviously not a correct interpretation of what we mean when we attribute continuous existence in time to the table. For if it were, we should not believe in permanent material things at all unless we believed, not only in God, but in an omnisentient God such as Berkeley believed in.

(3) According to our ordinary notions of them, material objects are causally active: they do things. The table supports the tablecloth, the fire warms the room. Material objects exercise force, have influences on one another and incidentally on ourselves, causing, among other things, our sensations of them. This continually active causal interplay makes up the system of nature, which it is the business of science to study and reduce to laws. Does not science explain what happens by referring events to their causes, which in the material realm at least are material things, exercising physical force? Surely, the room cannot be warmed by my visual sense-datum of a fire! Still less can it be warmed by the possibility of a visual sense-datum of a fire during my absence, when I am not looking at the fire but the room gets warmed all the same. When we all sit round the table and sense sense-data very similar in shape, size and color, what is the explanation of this fact, if not that there is an independent table which is the common cause of all our similar sense-data? Berkeley himself admits, or rather insists, that an "idea" is "inert," and can *do* nothing.

Phenomenalist Analysis of Causation

To deal with this problem, we need a fresh analysis and re-interpretation of the notion of cause, parallel to the phenomenalist re-interpretation of the notion of "substance" or "thing." Such an analysis was given in David Hume's *Treatise of Human Nature* (1739), and modern phenomenalists in the main follow his line of thought. Hume's aim is to interpret statements about cause and effect in such a way that the relation between a cause and its effect shall be an observable fact, and shall contain nothing mysterious or occult. For unless the words "cause and effect" described something we could observe, they would not, according to Hume, be intelligible to us.

What, then, do I observe in cases in which I should naturally use causal language? I am watching a game of billiards. I observe the event which I might naturally describe by saying that one ball A moved across the table and made or caused another ball B to roll into a pocket. What do I actually *see*? I see a certain sequence of events: first the movement of A, then the touching of A and B, then the movement of B. This temporal sequence of movements, the one which I call the effect following on the one I call the cause, seems to be all the visible relation there is between them.

But obviously, mere temporal sequence is not the same thing as causation; *post hoc* is not the same as *propter hoc;* plenty of other things preceded the movement of my billiard-ball in time which were not causes of it. Yet nothing seems to be observable but temporal sequence—first one event, then the other. Whence do I get this notion of the ball being made or caused or forced to move?

If I were pushing the ball myself, I should be aware of myself making a certain muscular effort, *trying* to make it move; and, when I observe the collision of the two balls and the ensuing movement of B, I may perhaps have a vague image of a similar kind of pushing going on between the balls. But if I do, it is clear that this feeling of muscular effort is not observed in the situation presented to my senses, but is a "projection" of my own past feelings in similar situations. For billiard-balls do not have muscles, or make efforts, and even if they did, I could not observe what efforts they were making, I could only observe their movements.

Certainly when I see the collision, I expect that the second ball will move—there is a "felt tendency of the mind" to pass from the "cause" to the "effect," but this is a psychological fact about me, not a physical fact about the balls. There seems nothing in the observed situation corresponding to the words "cause," "power," "force," which I am inclined to apply to it; only the observed sequence of one event on the other. But how, then, do I distinguish between those temporal antecedents of an event which are its causes, and those which are not? How do I establish the difference between *post hoc* and *propter hoc*?

The answer is plain enough; I repeat the experiment, and if the same sequence of events recurs, I conclude that it was a causal and not an accidental sequence. The reason I believe that the movement of the ball was caused by the impact of the other ball, and not by somebody lighting a cigarette at the same time, is that I know by long experience that balls always move when they are struck by other balls moving fairly quickly, whereas they do not usually move when men light cigarettes in their neighborhood. When medical men inquire into the cause of cancer, what they are looking for is something which always happens to a man before he becomes ill with cancer, just as, when they say that malaria is caused by the bite of a mosquito, they mean that a man has always been bitten by a mosquito before developing malaria. The observable fact which leads us to say that C is the cause of E is the fact that events of the kind C are followed by events of the kind E, not once or sometimes, but whenever they occur.

Causality, as a fact about the world, is then, according to Hume, a relation of invariable sequence. What is required to convert *post hoc* into *propter hoc* is regular repetition. To say that every event has a cause is to say that for any event E there is another event (or complex of "conditions") C such that whenever an event of the kind C occurs, an event of the kind E follows. It is to say that the sequence of phenomena is patterned, systematic; that there are in nature discoverable regularities.

But these regularities are discoverable among the observed phenomena themselves, and not between phenomena and something transcending phenomena. Causation, thus interpreted, is a relation between sense-data. The causes, that is to say, the invariable antecedents, of sense-experiences, are other sense-experiences.

Of course, not all causes are actually observed phenomena. In the analysis of cause, as in the analysis of substance, we must sometimes refer to possible sense-data which are not actual. But to say, for example, that a burst pipe was caused by the formation of a lump of ice which I have not seen, is not to desert the realm of sense-data; it is only to refer to sense-data which were not actually observed, but which might, in principle, have been observed; if I had been in a position to look at the interior of the pipe, I should have seen a lump of ice there.

Thus Hume and his followers do not deny that the relation of cause and effect is a real feature of the world; but they interpret it as a relation between sense-data, actual or possible. So the principle of causality does not carry us beyond the sphere of the observed and the observable, or compel us to admit the existence of "material substance" over and above systems of sense-data.

Thus, on this theory, the material world consists of sets of sense-experiences, together with the fact that an indefinitely large number of other similar sense-experiences might be had under certain specified conditions. Its "substances" are orderly groups of sense-data; and its causal relations are relations of regular sequence between sense-data of specified kinds. The main business of science is to discover causal laws, i.e., to reveal the patterns in that complex of experiences we call Nature. Science tells us what experiences to expect as the sequel to the experiences we are now having, and so renders our knowledge of the world systematic. . . .

The Paradoxes of Phenomenalism

. . . If we adopt phenomenalism, let us not do so without being clearly and fully aware of what it involves. (1) It involves the denial that physical objects are permanent, or exist unperceived. It must be granted to the phenomenalists that when I say "There is a table upstairs," I am at least implying that if you were to go upstairs and look (given normal eyesight, normal lighting, etc.) you would have certain visual sense-data. But it seems quite clear to me that this is not the whole nor the essential part of what I am asserting. For when I say that the table is there, I am stating something about what exists or happens *in fact, now;* my statement is about the actual present, and not, as the phenomenalists make it, about the possible future. And if the phenomenalist account is to be accepted, we must say that this statement is a mistake. There is nothing at all in the attic now; there is no attic now at all; for there is nobody perceiving it.

(2) We must very seriously revise our opinions about the nature of causality. As a rule, we are in the habit of believing that a cause is something which actually exists or occurs, and that something which does not actually exist or occur can have no effects. This opinion must be given up if we accept the phenomenalist view. For on that view, to say that the bursting of pipes is caused by the formation of ice in them is to say that whenever one observes or could observe sense-data of the set constituting a burst pipe, one either has or could have previously observed sense-data of the set constituting a lump of ice inside that pipe. But quite clearly, in practically every instance of this rule, nobody does actually observe the ice; the sense-data of the ice are possible, not actual. That is to say, causality in such a case is a relation between something and nothing, between an actually observed burst, and a hypothetical proposition to the effect that if something had happened which did not happen and in practice could not have happened, then something else would have happened which also did not happen. This interpretation flouts our usual assumption that what might have happened but did not happen can have no effects. The actual material agents of physics and common sense must be replaced by a set of hypothetical facts relating to unfulfilled conditions. If this is so, it is difficult to see why we should suppose that these hypothetical propositions are true. If I leave a fire in my room, I expect it to be warm on my return; but is this not because I believe that the fire is still now burning, a real present fire exercising an influence on a real present atmosphere? I cannot see what reason can be given for expecting the room to be warmed, independently of my reasons for supposing that the fire *is* burning *now* (and not that, *if* I went and looked, I should see flame). I can see reason for believing in regularities in nature holding between one event and another; but no reason at all for believing in regularities holding between one event which happened and another which might have happened but did not.

(3) A similar paradox arises with regard to other persons. According to the phenomenalist theory, all the statements I make about the consciousnesses of other people must be interpreted in terms of actual or possible observations of my own. A statement like "Jones is bored but he is not giving any sign of it" is a contradiction in terms, for on this

theory the boredom *is* the signs. The only experiences I can intelligibly talk about or think about are my own, and whatever is not expressible in terms of actual or possible observations of mine is not intelligible to me. That is, there is no good argument for phenomenalism which is not an equally good argument for solipsism—the doctrine that the only experience in the world is my experience, and the only person existing in the universe is myself.

These paradoxical conclusions have been accepted by able philosophers, and one cannot therefore say that they are beyond belief. But they are markedly at variance with the ordinary assumptions, not only of common sense, but also of scientific investigation (for, whatever some scientists may manage to persuade themselves, they are not concerned only with the cataloguing and ordering of phenomena, but believe themselves to be dealing with permanent and independent objects). Hence we must demand very strong reasons indeed for accepting them. . . .

SELECTED BIBLIOGRAPHY

(ITEMS PROVIDED WITH ASTERISK ARE MORE ADVANCED)

Plato's dialogue *Theaetetus* contains the first evaluation, in the history of philosophy, of perception as a means to knowledge. Berkeley's *The Principles of Human Knowledge,* which covers similar ground as the *Three Dialogues between Hylas and Philonous,* is a classic of British empiricism which every student of philosophy ought to know. The same holds for Hume's *Treatise of Human Nature,* Book I, Part IV, esp. Section 2. This is a classical formulation of phenomenalism though it is controversial whether Hume was consistently a phenomenalist. A close commentary on Hume's theory of perception and physical reality may be found in H. H. Price, *Hume's Theory of the External World** (Oxford: Clarendon Press, 1940). Bertrand Russell, *The Problems of Philosophy* (London: Oxford University Press, 1912), Chapters 1-4, provides a beautifully lucid and simple introduction to the problems of Locke and Berkeley, including a critique of Berkeleyan idealism. Elementary expositions and critiques of the theories of Berkeley and Locke may also be found in C. H. Whiteley, *An Introduction to Metaphysics* (London: Methuen and Co., 1950), Chapter 5; A. C. Ewing, *The Fundamental Questions of Philosophy* (London: Routledge and Kegan Paul, 1951), Chapter 4; A. Pap, *Elements of Analytic Philosophy* (New York: Macmillan, 1949), Chapter 7, and J. Hospers, *Introduction to Philosophical Analysis* (New York: Prentice-Hall, 1953), Chapter 6.

Fuller statements of Russell's views on perception may be found in his books *Our Knowledge of the External World* (London: Allen and Unwin, second edition, 1926), *Mysticism and Logic* (London: Allen and Unwin, 1917), *Human Knowledge* (London: Allen and Unwin, New York: Simon and Schuster, 1948), Part III, and *The Analysis of Matter** (London: Allen and Unwin, 1927; New York: Dover Publications, 1954). The latter book is more difficult, but Chapter XX presents the case for the "causal theory of perception" clearly and intelligibly. S. L. Stebbing, *Philosophy and the Physicists* (London: Methuen and Co., 1937), Part II, is a critique of Lockean dualism and the contention of such thinkers as Eddington and Russell that it is supported by physics. The critique is based on the analysis of ordinary language and is most profitably studied in conjunction with our selection from Russell's *Outline of Philosophy.* Views similar to those of Stebbing are expressed in Chapter V of Gilbert Ryle, *Dilemmas* (Cambridge: University Press, 1954). Another important criticism of Russell's dualism is E. Nagel's "Russell's Philosophy of Science," in P. Schilpp (ed.), *The Philosophy of Bertrand Russell* (Evanston and Chicago: Northwestern University, 1944). Russell has a reply in the same volume. The relationship between physics and epistemology is intensively explored in the symposium, "Realism and Modern Physics,"* *Proceedings of the Aristotelian Society,* Suppl. Vol. IX, 1929.

For a discussion of the physical argument for epistemological dualism in historical perspective see Lovejoy, *The Revolt against Dualism* (New York: Norton and Co., 1930). A defense of epistemological dualism may also be found in Durant Drake, *An Invitation to Philosophy* (New York: Houghton Mifflin Co., 1933). Criticisms of all the traditional forms of dualism are advanced in J. Dewey, *Logic: The Theory of Inquiry** (Henry Holt and Co., 1939), Chapter XXV. A pragmatic critique of epistemological dualism is given by the same author in "Conduct and Experience" in C. Murchison (ed.) *Psychologies of 1930,* (Worcester: Clark University Press, 1930). Dewey's views on perception are also stated in his essays "Naive Realism versus Presentative Realism," "Epistemological Realism: The Alleged Ubiquity of the Knowledge Relation," and "The Existence of the World as a Logical Problem," all of which are contained in his *Essays in Experimental Logic* (Chicago: University of Chicago Press, 1916). A highly stimulating article presenting views akin to those of Dewey is E. B. McGilvary's "Perceptual and Memory Perspectives,"* *Journal of Philosophy,* 1933.

An especially illuminating analysis of the "argument from illusions" for dualism is found in Chapter 1 of A. J. Ayer, *The Foundations of Empirical Knowledge* (London: Macmillan, 1940). Ayer's most recent views on perception are expressed in his book, *The Problem of Knowledge* (London: Pelican Books, 1956). For the views of one of the founders of logical positivism see M. Schlick's "Positivism and Realism," reprinted in English translation in A. J. Ayer (ed.), *Logical Positivism* (Glencoe, Illinois: Free Press, 1957). Discussions of the issues raised by Schlick can be found in F. Will's "Verifiability and the External World," *Philosophy of Science,* 1940, and W. Barrett's "On the Existence of an External World," *Journal of Philosophy,* 1939. The argument from illusion is also discussed by H. H. Price in his contribution to H. D. Lewis (ed.) *Contemporary British Philosophy,* Third Series, (London: Allen and Unwin, 1956).

Classical writings in the idealist tradition, including selections from Berkeley, G. E. Moore's celebrated "The Refutation of Idealism,"* and H. Rashdall's *Philosophy and Religion,* Chapter 1 (which is an attempt to strengthen Berkeley's arguments for epistemological idealism), are collected in A. C. Ewing (ed.), *The Idealist Tradition from Berkeley to Blanshard* (Glencoe, Illinois: Free Press, 1957). This work also contains a very extensive bibliography. For statements of the position of the American realists who reacted against the idealist tradition in Britain and the United States (which was influenced by both Berkeley and the German idealists), see Perry, Holt, *et alia, The New Realism* (New York: Macmillan, 1912), Drake Lovejoy, Pratt, *et alia, Essays in Critical Realism** (New York: Macmillan, 1920), R. W. Sellars, *The Philosophy of Physical Realism* (New York: Macmillan, 1932), and W. P. Montahue, *The Ways of Knowing* (New York, Macmillan, 1925), Part II and Postscript. Moore's "The Refutation of Idealism," can also be found in his *Philosophical Studies* (London: Kegan Paul, 1922). For a critique of Moore see C. J. Ducasse's "Moore's Refutation of Idealism"* in P. Schilpp (ed.), *The Philosophy of G. E. Moore* (Evanston and Chicago: Northwestern University, 1942). In the same volume there is Moore's reply to Ducasse to which Ducasse in turn replied in his book *Nature, Mind and Death* (LaSalle, Illinois: Open Court, 1951), Chapter 13. Another influential critique of idealism is R. B. Perry's "The Egocentric Predicament," *Journal of Philosophy, Psychology and Scientific Methods,* 1910. A defense of idealism is given in J. E. Creighton's "Two Types of Idealism," *Philosophical Review,* 1917. In three articles in the *Monist,* 1933 and 1934, entitled respectively "The A Priori

Argument for Subjectivism," "The Inductive Argument for Subjectivism," and "The Inductive Argument for Realism," Donald Williams dissects in great deal the various arguments put forward by the idealists and defends realism as the best-supported of all scientific hypotheses. Moore's famous paper "A Defence of Common Sense," in J. H. Muirhead (ed.), *Contemporary British Philosophy, Second Series* (London: Allen and Unwin, 1925), may also be mentioned here. It contains a critique of philosophical paradoxes in general of which idealism, at least in some of its forms, is a prominent example.

The following books are classics on "phenomenalism" in a broad sense: John Stuart Mill, *An Examination of Sir William Hamilton's Philosophy,* (London: Longmans, Green and Co., 1872), Karl Pearson, *The Grammar of Science* (first published 1892, Everyman edition, 1937), Chapters 2-5, and Ernst Mach, *Contributions towards the Analysis of Sensations* (Chicago: Open Court, 1897). The latter is criticized by Lenin in *Materialism and Empirio-Criticism* (Moscow: Foreign Languages Publishing House, 1952). Lenin is answered in G. A. Paul's "Lenin's Theory of Perception," in M. Macdonald (ed.), *Philosophy and Analysis* (Oxford: Basil Blackwell, 1954), and by H. B. Acton, *The Illusion of the Epoch* (London: Cohen and West, 1955).

Of more recent origin is the defense of phenomenalism found in Chapter V of A. J. Ayer, *The Foundations of Empirical Knowledge, op. cit.,* and the same writer's "Phenomenalism," *Proceedings of the Aristotelian Society,* 1947, which is reprinted in A. J. Ayer, *Philosophical Essays* (London: Macmillan, 1953). The theory is also closely examined in P. Marhenke's "Phenomenalism," in M. Black (ed.), *Philosophical Analysis* (Ithaca: Cornell University Press, 1950), and C. D. Broad's "Phenomenalism," *Proc. of the Arist. Soc.,* 1914/15. A causal argument for the existence of physical objects is combined with a critique of phenomenalism in A. C. Ewing's book, *Idealism, a Critical Survey* (London: Methuen and Co., 1934) Chapter VII. A paper dealing especially with the question of phenomenalist versus realist interpretations of scientific theory is H. Feigl's "Existential Hypotheses,"* *Philosophy of Science,* 1950. Phenomenalism is also discussed in R. B. Braithwaite's "Propositions about Material Objects," *Proc. of the Arist. Soc.,* 1937/38, and I. Berlin's "Empirical Propositions and Hypothetical Statements," *Mind,* 1950. Perhaps the most sophisticated and detailed defense of phenomenalism is C. I. Lewis, *An Analysis of Knowledge and Valuation,** (LaSalle, Illinois: Open Court, 1947), Chapters 7-9. A critique of Lewis' phenomenalism is given in R. M. Chisholm's "The Problem of Empiricism,"* *Journal of Philosophy,* 1948. In the same volume is Lewis' reply, "Professor Chisholm and Empiricism."* R. Firth refers to the Lewis-Chisholm debate and sides with phenomenalism in his "Radical Empiricism and Perceptual Relativity," *Philosophical Review,* 1950. There are valuable discussions of the notion of substance in Bertrand Russell, *Human Knowledge* (London: Allen and Unwin, New York: Simon and Schuster, 1948), Chapter 3*, in C. D. Broad's "Berkeley's Argument about Material Substance," *Proceedings of the British Academy,* 1942; and in M. Lazerowitz' "Substratum," in M. Black (ed.), *Philosophical Analysis, op. cit.* The latter is reprinted in M. Lazerowitz, *The Structure of Metaphysics* (London: Routledge and Kegan Paul, 1955).

A theory of sense-data, or "sensa," as non-mental and non-physical entities that are directly perceived is worked out by C. D. Broad in his books, *Perception, Physics and Reality* (Cambridge: University Press, 1914), *Scientific Thought** (London: Routledge and Kegan Paul, 1923) and *The Mind and Its Place in Nature** (London: Routlege and Kegan Paul, 1925), Chapter 4. The latter chapter aims to demonstrate that no consistent theory of perception can be reconciled with all common sense beliefs about perception. Broad's most recent discussion of this subject is a series of articles entitled "Professor Marc-Wogau's *Theorie der Sinnesdaten,*" *Mind,* 1947. Broad's views on perception are the subject of a minute critique in terms of the analysis of ordinary language by M. Lean, *Sense-Perception and Matter* (London: Routledge and Kegan Paul, 1953). A somewhat similar critique of this notion of sense-data may be found in G. Ryle, *The Concept of Mind* (London: Hutchinson and Co., 1949), Chapter 7. It is also criticized, though in a different context, by C. J. Ducasse, in *Nature, Mind and Death, op. cit.,* Chapter 13. Two essays that deal especially with the question whether we perceive physical objects directly are G. E. Moore's "The Nature and Reality of Objects of Perception,"* and the same author's "Some Judgments of Perception,"* both reprinted in Moore's *Philosophical Studies, op. cit.* For a discussion of Moore's views see O. K. Bouwsma's "Moore's Theory of Sense-Data," in P. A. Schilpp (ed.) *The Philosophy of G. E. Moore, op. cit.,* and P. Marhenke's "Moore's Analysis of Sense-Perception,"* *ibid.* Replies by Moore are contained in the same volume. Two valuable symposia are "The Nature of Sensible Appearances,"* *Proc. of the Arist. Soc.,* Suppl. Vol. VI, 1926; and "The Status of Sense-data,"* *ibid.* Another critique of the sense-data theory is given in W. H. F. Barnes "The Myth of Sense-data," *Proc. of the Arist. Soc.,* 1945. There is a more recent paper by the same author entitled "On Seeing and Hearing," in H. D. Lewis (ed.) *Contemporary British Philosophy,* Third Series, *op. cit.* This volume contains also G. Ryle's essay, "Sensation." Naive realism, the arguments from illusions against it and the causal argument from sense-data to physical objects, are dealt with very carefully by H. H. Price, in *Perception* (London: Methuen and Co., 1932) especially Chapters 1-4. Important also to consult for discussions of the sense-data theory are G. A. Paul's, "Is there a Problem about Sense-data?" in A. Flew (ed.), *Essays in Logic and Language,* First Series (Oxford: Basil Blackwell, 1951), R. Firth's "Sense-data and the Percept Theory," *Mind,* 1949, and 1950, and A. J. Ayer's "The Terminology of Sense-data," *Mind,* 1945, reprinted in his *Philosophical Essays, op. cit.*

IV

Body, Mind and Death

INTRODUCTION

Sᴏᴍᴇ ᴘʜɪʟᴏsᴏᴘʜᴇʀs have maintained that a human being is simply his body and nothing else besides. Thus Nietzsche once remarked: "Body am I entirely, and nothing more; and soul is only the name of something in the body." The same view is also expressed in an epigram coined by the German philosopher Feuerbach. "A man," he said, "is what he eats." However, the great majority of philosophers, and especially those with a religious background, have agreed that human beings are something more than their bodies; and this something more has variously been referred to as the mind, the self, or the soul. Is a human being really a mind in addition to his body? If he is, what exactly is this mind and how is it related to the body? Finally, are there any good grounds for supposing that his mind survives the disintegration of his body? These are the main questions discussed in the selections contained in the present section.

At least at first sight, it seems exceedingly plausible to contend that a human being is something over and above his body. Things like houses and mountains and also of course human and animal bodies are publicly observable. All these "physical" objects have extension and occupy positions in space. By contrast, only a person himself can experience his feelings, sensations, dreams, or thoughts. A dentist can observe the cavity which causes his patient's pain, but only the patient himself can feel the pain. If I am angry and shake my fist, an outsider can see this manifestation of my anger but not the anger itself. Assuming that a person's dreams or thoughts can be correlated with certain specific movements of brain-molecules, it is theoretically feasible that scientists might one day perceive these molecular motions. But they would not even then be experiencing the dreams or thoughts of the person whose brain they were observing. Feelings, sensations, dreams, and thoughts are the sort of phenomena which are usually classified as "mental." In calling them mental, philosophers usually mean that, unlike physical objects, they are "private" or directly knowable by one person only. Some philosophers also include having no extension and no spatial location in the meaning of "mental." This, however, might prove a confusing definition since certain sensations and feelings do seem to have extension and a location in space.

It is plausible, then, to maintain that a human being possesses a mind as well as a body. It seems just as reasonable to hold, in the absence of special considerations to the contrary, that there are causal connections between body and mind. To give a few simple illustrations: cavities in teeth cause pain, the impact of light-waves on the retina leads to visual sensations, contact of the tongue with food causes taste-sensations, indigestion gives rise to morbid feelings, consumption of large quantities of alcohol produces hallucinations, some drugs make us calm, others more excited. All these are instances of causal influence by the body on the mind, but there seems just as ample evidence of causal relations in the opposite direction: a person who is ill but has nothing to live for is far less likely to recover than one who has many interests and is filled with hope. Expectations of pleasant encounters affect our body in one way, expectations of unpleasant encounters in quite another. Embarrassment causes us to blush, fear to tremble, happiness to smile and sometimes to cry. Perhaps the plainest cases of mind-body causation are "voluntary movements." A man intends to see the tennis-matches at Forest Hills and, other things being equal, he really gets there. It would seem very odd indeed to maintain that in this and similar situations the intention or volition was not part of the cause of the person's action.

Philosophers who first make a distinction between the body and the mind and who then proceed to assert that there are causal influences in both directions are known as "dualistic interactionists." They are divided among themselves according to their views about the nature of the body and of the mind respectively. Confining ourselves to the latter topic, we have to distinguish between those who, like the scholastics and Descartes, adopt a "substance" theory and those who, following Hume, adopt a "bundle" conception. The point here at issue may be explained by the following question: is a human being something additional to (a) his body, (b) the various experiences he goes through, (c) the relations between these experiences such as similarity, causation, and memory, and (d) his capacities, habits, temperament, and ideals—that is, his dispositions to act and react in certain ways and have certain experiences if exposed to certain stimuli? According to the substance-theory there is something in human beings over and above these items and something of great importance at that. This extra something is variously referred to as the "subject" or "owner" of the experiences, as the "spiritual substance" which "underlies" them and which gives a human being the unity he possesses.

Among those holding this type of theory there are differences of opinion as to the manner in which the underlying subject is known and also as to how much we can know about it. According to one group, including Sir William Hamilton (1788-1856) and many other philosophers influenced by Kant, no such spiritual substance is given in introspective experience. Its existence has to be *inferred* in order to account for such facts as our personal identity which could not otherwise be explained. Writers who adopt this point of view are usually rather modest in their claims of how much can be known about the attributes of the underlying self. Other philosophers maintain that the substance-self is *given* in experience. In fact it is given in *every* experience. The German philosopher Lotze (1807-1881) was a prominent defender of this position. In a well-known passage he wrote:

It has been required of any theory which starts without presuppositions and from the basis of experience, that in the beginning it should speak only of sensations and ideas, without mentioning the soul to which, it is said, we hasten without justification to ascribe them. I should maintain, on the contrary, that such a mode of setting out involves a wilful departure from that which is actually given in experience. A mere sensation without a subject is nowhere to be met with as a fact. It is impossible to speak of a bare movement without thinking of the mass whose movement it is; and it is just as impossible to conceive a sensation existing without the accompanying of that which has it—or rather, of that which feels it, for this also is included in the given fact of experience that the relation of the feeling subject to its feeling, whatever its other characteristics may be, is in any case something different from the relation of the moved element to its movement. It is thus and thus only, that the sensation is a given fact; and we have no right to abstract from its relations to its subject because this relation is puzzling, and because we wish to obtain a starting-point which looks more convenient, but is utterly unwarranted by experience.

Many, though not all, of the writers holding this position believe that the self which is thus given in every experience is not only simple and "abiding the same during all the varying modes of consciousness," but is furthermore indestructible and therefore immortal.

According to the bundle-theory a human being is nothing over and above factors (a), (b), (c) and (d) listed above. There are no facts which warrant the inference to a permanent underlying spiritual substance. Nor is such a self ever given in experience. We are apt to mistake as an "owner" of our experiences certain background feelings or sensations which generally accompany them. We are angry against a "background mood" of depression, or we read a letter against a background feeling of delight or disappointment, as the case may be. And practically all our experiences are accompanied by some "marginal" bodily sensations—of our breathing, our eye-ball movements, our stationary or moving limbs, our hunger or satiety, our bodily tensions, and many more. Bertrand Russell has been one of the outstanding champions of the bundle-theory in our own day. "We think and feel and act," he writes in one place,

> but there is not, in addition to thoughts and feelings and actions, a bare entity, the mind or the soul, which does or suffers these occurrences. The mental continuity of a person is a continuity of habit and memory: there was yesterday one person whose feelings I can remember, and that person I regard as myself of yesterday; but in fact, myself of yesterday was only certain mental occurrences which are now remembered, and are regarded as part of the person who now recollects them.

The classical formulation of this view is found in Hume's *Treatise of Human Nature*:

> For my part, when I enter most intimately into what I call myself, I always stumble on some particular perception or other, of heat or cold, light or shade, love or hatred, pain or pleasure. I never can catch myself at any time without a perception, and never can observe anything but the perception. When my perceptions are removed for any time, as by sound sleep, so long am I insensible of myself, and may truly be said not to exist. And were all my perceptions removed by death, and could I neither think, nor feel, nor see, nor love, nor hate, after the dissolution of my body, I should be entirely annihilated, nor do I conceive what is further requisite to make me a perfect nonentity. If any one, upon serious and

unprejudiced reflection, thinks he has a different notion of himself, I must confess I can reason no longer with him. All I can allow him is, that he may be in the right as well as I, and that we are essentially different in this particular. He may, perhaps, perceive something simple and continued, which he calls himself; though I am certain there is no such principle in me.

But setting aside some metaphysicians of this kind, I may venture to affirm of the rest of mankind, that they are nothing but a bundle or collection of different perceptions, which succeed each other with an inconceivable rapidity, and are in a perpetual flux and movement.

It should be added that some contemporary philosophers go further than Russell and Hume and declare that the substance-theory is *meaningless*. The spiritual substance is not like a mythical animal which we could recognize if we came across it but which as a matter of fact does not exist. We don't even know what it would be like to come across it. "The point is not," in Ayer's words, "that the vast majority of men are unable to perform the difficult feat of experiencing themselves as substances. It is rather that such a feat is not conceivable. There is nothing that would count as stumbling upon oneself, as opposed to some particular perception."

To many philosophers it has seemed that interactionism is open to a number of fatal objections, regardless of whether it conceives the mind as a substance or as a bundle. It is easy enough, the critics have declared, to speak of interaction between body and mind in general terms. As soon, however, as we try to visualize concretely the manner in which the supposed interaction takes place, we are utterly baffled. How exactly, for example, is the last member in the physiological series following the impact of light-rays on the retina transformed into a visual sensation? What exactly does a volition do to the brain-molecules to set in motion the train of events culminating in the person's overt reaction? It is evident that the brain-molecules must somehow be moved for this purpose, but how can something which does not occupy space and which has no extension move a material particle? In the words of W. K. Clifford, a 19th century mathematician and philosopher:

> . . . if anybody says that the will influences matter, the statement is not untrue, but it is nonsense. The will is not a material thing, it is not a mode of material motion. . . . The only thing which influences matter is the position of surrounding matter or the motion of surrounding matter.

There is an "enormous gulf," an "impassable chasm," "a gap which cannot be bridged" between phenomena as radically different as brain-events on the one hand and psychological events like sensations or volitions on the other.

Moreover, interactionism seems to these philosophers inconsistent with the continuity of physiological processes and also with certain well-established principles of physics. From the point of view of physiology and physics, it is argued, mental events which cause or are caused by bodily events are disturbing and unwanted interlopers for which there is no room. If the causal story were what the interactionist believes it to be, then we should expect a break in the physiological sequences in the body at certain times. The last brain-event, for instance, would be followed not by another brain-event but by a non-physical event—the sensation; this by another non-physical event—the volition; and this then by the outgoing physiological sequence. In actual fact, however, the critics claim, no such interruption or discontinuity in the physiological processes is ever found.

Even worse, perhaps, interaction appears to be in conflict with the law of the Conservation of Energy. This principle, in one of its most familiar formulations, maintains that the amount of energy in the universe is always constant. This means that energy can be neither created nor destroyed. Yet, if interaction occurs, then energy would be lost when the body affects the mind and energy would be gained when the mind affects the body. We should in all such cases have exceptions to the Conservation of Energy. There is, however, no evidence that such violations of the principle take place. The occurrence of sensations, for example, is not, as far as we know, accompanied by decreases of energy in the body. Nor are volitions followed by increases of energy.

In the light of these and similar considerations numerous philosophers regard interactionism as untenable. They have put forward several alternative theories which would avoid the difficulties we mentioned. Perhaps the simplest of these is the theory known as "monistic" or "reductive" materialism. On this view all psychological terms really refer to some kind of physiological events or processes. It maintains, to use another formulation, that matter alone is real, that a human being is simply his body. This is the position to which we briefly referred at the beginning of this introduction.

Reductive materialism has been held in many different forms. The 18th century physiologist Cabanis asserted that "thought is a secretion of the brain," a view echoed by the German biologist Vogt who wrote that "the relation between thought and the brain is roughly of the same order as that between bile and the liver or urine and the bladder." Hobbes and some German materialists of the 19th century believed that thought is nothing more than the movement of particles in the brain and the Danish physiologist Lange claimed that emotions are really nothing but functional disturbances of the body. However, most of these writers also expressed more moderate views not compatible with reductive materialism. Early in the 20th century the German chemist Ostwald and his followers claimed that mental processes are a form of physical energy. In our own day the favorite type of reductive materialism is behaviorism, or at any rate, certain specially radical forms of it. Some behaviorists, it is true, do not maintain that consciousness is identical with any bodily processes. But others, or the same behaviorists on other occasions, maintain that all psychological terms really refer to nothing more than bodily reactions of some kind—to actual bodily responses or to dispositions to respond in certain ways.

Reductive or monistic materialism is in many respects a highly attractive theory. Like other "monistic" theories it would satisfy the widespread intellectual craving to reduce everything to one ultimate reality. It presents the universe as all "of one piece." It also appeals to those who wish to do away with mystery and who fear that once something immaterial is allowed to exist anywhere in the world, the door has been opened to let in such unwelcome guests as the immortal soul or even God. But most important of all, the theory undoubtedly avoids all the supposed difficulties of interactionism. We now no longer have the problem of bridging the "chasm" between body and mind or of visualizing the causal influence of volitions on brain-molecules; we no longer need to postulate a gap in the physiological processes of the organism; and of course we no longer have any violations of the Conservation of Energy.

In spite of these attractive features the great majority of philosophers reject reductive materialism. They maintain that it is simply not a true account of our experience. To talk of thought as a "secretion" is absurd. Bile and urine are substances which can be publicly observed, which occupy space, which can be weighed and even bottled. None of this is true of our thoughts. If for example I think of Freud's theory of the death-instinct or of the assassination of Abraham Lincoln, my thoughts are not publicly observable; they do not occupy space; they cannot be weighed or bottled. It is no less absurd to identify thought with movement of brain-molecules or emotions with contractions and dilations of blood-vessels. It may well be the case that thoughts are always accompanied by certain molecular motions and that emotions always occur along with certain contractions and dilations of blood-vessels, but this does not mean that the mental events *are* the bodily processes. To say that thought is really nothing but a certain movement, as the German philosopher Friederich Paulsen put it in his celebrated critique of reductive materialism, is about as sensible as to say that iron is really made of wood:

> Turn it which way you will, you will never find thought in movement. The common man knows nothing whatever of the motion in the brain or of the vasomotor process, but he knows what anger is, and what thought is, and he means these, when he speaks of them, and not something else of which the physiologist alone knows or thinks he knows.

It is also not the case that sensations are identical with any kind of bodily process or reaction. A person's awareness of red, for example, cannot be the same thing as a molecular movement. It makes sense to ask about the molecular movement such questions as "Is it swift or slow, straight or circular?" But, as Broad has pointed out, it would make no sense at all to raise these questions about the awareness of red. Conversely, it makes perfectly good sense to ask about the awareness whether it is clear or confused, but such a question could not sensibly be asked about a molecular movement. If a person touches a piece of red-hot iron, to use an illustration given by Ewing, the throb of pain he feels is not at all like the act of withdrawing his hand nor "like anything described in textbooks of physiology as happening in the nervous system or the brain." The difference between sensations and bodily events, Ewing insists, is not a question of *a priori* speculative metaphysics, but "as much an empirical matter as that between sight and sound."

Another rival to interactionism is the theory known as "epiphenomenalism" (See T. H. Huxley: "The Automaton Theory," Selection 17). On this view mental events are distinct from any kind of physical substances or movements. They are, however, powerless to interfere with anything in the physical world. Mental states are caused by brain-processes, but do not in turn exert any causal influence. They are mere by-products ("epiphenomenon" is the Greek for "by-product"), mere accompanying echoes or shadows of bodily events.

Only material structures, including of course human bodies and their parts, are causally active. In the words of Santayana, one of the most famous advocates of this theory:

> There are not two parallel streams, but one stream which, in slipping over certain rocks or dropping into certain pools, begins to babble a wanton music; not thereby losing any part of its substance or changing its course, but unawares enriching the world with a new beauty.
> . . . Consciousness is a lyric cry in the midst of business.

Epiphenomenalism is usually considered a form of "materialism" and perhaps a few words of explanation are needed about the meanings of this term in philosophical discussion. We may distinguish a narrower and a broader sense. In the narrower sense materialism asserts that whatever exists is material or physical. In this view "mental" events, in so far as they really exist, are a sub-class of physical occurrences. In the broader sense materialism merely asserts that matter is in some way the "primary" or "most fundamental" reality. In the latter sense, somebody could be a materialist and at the same time allow that there are mental processes which are not a sub-class of physical occurrences. In this sense dualism and materialism are not contradictory theories. Epiphenomenalism is not a form of materialism in the narrower sense, but it clearly is a form of materialism in the broader sense. In the broader sense even quite a number of dualistic interactionists could be regarded as materialists. There are many interactionists who, after conceding that mind is distinct from body and that there is causal influence both ways, proceed to maintain that matter can exist without mind but that mind cannot exist without matter, or at least that this is highly probable on the basis of a great deal of empirical evidence. Bertrand Russell and Hume (See Selection 21, pp. 301 ff.) adopt such a position in several places. Thus Russell likens the relation between mental events and the brain to that between a river and a river-bed. When the brain is dissolved at death there is no more reason to suppose that mental events will continue than that a river "will persist in its old course after an earthquake has raised a mountain where a valley used to be." Moreover, a river-bed can exist without a river but a river cannot exist without a river-bed; and the same holds for the mind and the body. Writers like Russell may be considered materialists in the broader sense, since they do assert that matter is more "basic" in the way just explained.

Some philosophers, usually classified as materialists, have proposed a theory which is at least fairly similar to epiphenomenalism and which may or may not coincide with it, depending on how the notions of "thing" and "quality" are interpreted. On this view, mental processes are not a species of physical occurences; and to this extent the theory is dualistic. On the other hand, mental processes cannot be described as "things." Only physical objects are "things." Mental processes are *qualities or attributes of physical organisms*. A human body not only has size and shape and a certain weight and certain colors; it also has certain intellectual and emotional attributes. This view is found, among others, in the writings of the French physician and philosopher Lamettrie (1709-1751) and the English chemist and religious reformer, Joseph

Priestley (1733-1804). Both Lamettrie and Priestley strenuously opposed the view that matter is essentially "passive" or "inert" and maintained that feeling and thought could be attributed as "powers" to human and animal bodies on the basis of the same kind of evidence by which we attribute "powers" of attraction and repulsion to matter in general. "Thought is so little incompatible with organized matter," wrote Lamettrie, "that it seems to be one of its properties on a par with electricity, the faculty of motion, impenetrability, and extension."

However, to return to epiphenomenalism. It does not identify mental events with any kind of physiological processes and therefore circumvents the main difficulty of reductive materialism. But in the opinion of many philosophers, it, too, is open to a number of serious objections. In the first place, since it allows causal influence in the direction from body to mind, epiphenomenalism escapes only half of whatever difficulties beset interactionism. Secondly, it has been charged that epiphenomenalism is a "self-stultifying" theory: if it were true we could never be justified in believing that it is true. For if it were true then all our beliefs are entertained not because of any prior awareness of good grounds or adequate evidence, but solely because of physical changes in the brain and nervous system. None of our conclusions, including epiphenomenalism itself, would be based on logic. We would always think, in Pratt's words, "the way our mechanical brains constrain us to think"; and if in any given case our thought is true, this is so because the brain molecules happened "to shake down in a lucky fashion."

Perhaps the most momentous objection to epiphenomenalism consists in the enormous quantity of *prima facie* evidence that the mental processes of human beings do make a difference to their lives and indirectly to inanimate nature as well. It is said that epiphenomenalism implies a truly staggering paradox in this connection. Father Maher, a scholastic critic, has stated this objection very forcefully:

> But reflection discovers consequences still more surprising. The whole past history of the world, the building of cities, the invention of machinery, the commerce of nations, the emigrations of peoples, the rise and fall of civilizations, all that has been done on this planet by human beings, might have happened in precisely the same way if there had never awoke to consciousness a single human mind! All the pain and sorrow, all the joy and gladness, all the love and anger that we suppose have governed the world's history might never have been, and that history *might have run exactly the same course!* The neural groupings, the cerebral movements, which were the true, ultimate, and *only* causes of the various actions of human beings, have never once been interrupted, modified, or interfered with by those "aspects" or "phases" which constitute the "parallel" series of conscious states, since the first man appeared on the earth. Given the original collocation of the material atoms from which the present cosmos has evolved, and every event, down to the least incident of our daily life, was therein rigidly and sufficiently determined, even though no single act of intelligence or volition had ever wakened into life!

Interactionism may have its problems; but according to a number of philosophers they are small when compared with this paradox of epiphenomenalism.

Epiphenomenalists would probably retort that this criticism is based on a misunderstanding of their theory. They would maintain that terms like "willing," "reasoning," "knowing," or "forecasting" really have a double meaning. They do indeed refer to certain conscious states, but they also refer to certain states of the organism. They also refer, that is, to the bodily processes which cause the mental epiphenomena. The reductive materialists are wrong in denying the conscious accompaniments. Critics like Father Maher are guilty of the opposite error—of tacitly equating "ourselves" with our mental states exclusively. To give a simple illustration: A person may quite properly be said to know how to drive a car even if on a given occasion he makes all the appropriate responses without consciously attending to them. The question at issue, an epiphenomenalist would contend, is not whether willing, reasoning, knowing, forecasting and the rest are causally relevant to what happens in the world. For this much is admitted by him no less than by the interactionist. The question is whether we need to bring in something over and above the *body's* knowledge, willing, reasoning or forecasting—whether we have to attribute causal relevance to the conscious side of these phenomena *as well*. If it is maintained that the body alone could never bring about such splendid results as Mozart's operas or the feats of modern engineering, an epiphenomenalist would answer, following Spinoza, that nobody has ever discovered the body's limitations and that this criticism rests therefore on a gratuitous assumption. He would perhaps conclude his answer with the recommendation that we should cease to identify "ourselves" so exclusively with our conscious lives.

Another alternative to interactionism is the view known as "parallelism" which agrees with epiphenomenalism in denying any influence of mental states over our bodies, but which goes further in also denying causal relations in the other direction. The life of a human being on this view consists of two distinct series which never intersect. When light strikes my eye and this is followed by a visual sensation, there is no causal connection between these processes, since the former belongs to the physical and the latter to the mental series of my life. Again, if I eat a chocolate éclair filled with whipped cream, this is usually followed by a feeling of pleasure. But according to parallelism the two events are not causally related. In both of these and in all similar instances there is only a relation of concomitance or of temporal succession.

Most parallelists have not been satisfied to let the matter rest here. They felt obliged to explain the universal correlations between certain kinds of bodily and certain kinds of mental events—e.g., between certain stimulations of the sense organs and the sensations following these, or between volitions and movements of the body. Although these correlations are not causal, parallelists generally conceded that they are not accidental either. Historically, there are three major attempts on the part of parallelists to explain such correlations. The first is that of Malebranche (1638-1715) and the occasionalists who maintain that "corresponding" physical and mental events are "occasions" for God to become active. The physical contact between my tongue and the chocolate éclair is the occasion for God to produce pleasure in me, and my volition to pick up a fork is the occasion for God's production of this motion. Leibniz (1646-1716), who was also a parallelist, did not believe in the *immediate* intervention of God on all these occasions, but believed instead that a "pre-established harmony" exists between the two series. He compared the body and the mind to two clocks which "agree perfectly" and which were from the start made with such "art and accuracy that we can be assured of their future accordance." Similarly, by a "divine prevenient contrivance" body and mind were from the beginning formed "so perfect and regulated with so much accuracy" that although they follow merely their respective laws, they nevertheless always agree with each other "just as if there were mutual influence, or as if God in addition to His general cooperation constantly put His hand thereto."

Not all parallelists, however, have been believers in God or have considered it necessary to bring in God's immediate or remote causal activity to explain the correlations between bodily and mental states. Probably the explanation most popular among them has been some form of "identity" or "double aspect" theory which goes back to Spinoza and which had many outstanding advocates in later centuries, including Fechner, Wundt, Höffding, Paulsen, and Clifford. On this view bodily and mental processes are really "at bottom" or "ultimately" the same events. They are two "aspects" of the same reality; they are the same thing "viewed" from different angles or known in different ways. Our mental states are the private or "inner" nature or "side" and the corresponding brain processes the publicly observable or "outer" nature of the same phenomena. Numerous illustrations have been adduced to indicate how on this theory the regular concomitance of mental and physical events would be explained. Fechner gave the example of a curved line which is on one side convex and on the other concave. No matter how many turns and twists are found in such a line, a concavity will always correspond to a convexity although there is no causal connection between them. Another illustration, given by the German philosopher Lasswitz, is that of a loan of money: the same sum is an asset for one of the parties and a debit for the other. Feigl compares the body-mind relation to that kind of identity which is discovered by two explorers who "may unwittingly have observed the same mountain from different directions, and only after comparing notes come to realize that it was really identically the same mountain."

Most parallelists would go on to assert that brain-processes are not the only phenomena which also have an "inner nature." All things in the universe, including not only human beings and animals, but even plants and what we normally consider inanimate objects, have such an additional inner side. None of them is a purely material structure. All have an aspect which in varying degrees resembles our mental states. "Even in the very lowest organisms, even in the amoeba which swims about in our own blood," writes Clifford, "along with every motion of matter, whether organic or inorganic . . . there is something or other, inconceivably simple to us, which is of the same nature with our own consciousness, although not of the same complexity." Just as our bodies are made up of atoms so our minds are made up of the rudimentary bits of feeling which are attached to each atom and which are its "inner nature." This theory is usually known as "panpsychism," but some parallelists do not like the term because it suggests that they claim *consciousness* for sticks and stones and stars and atoms, whereas they merely claim some resemblance to consciousness. They do not claim self-awareness or introspection for inanimate phenomena. Only human beings and possibly some animals can *know* their inner nature.

Many writers who have adopted this position prefer the term "universal parallelism." The assumption that some kind of inner process accompanies every physical event enables them, they assert, to give a consistent causal explanation of all mental states without in any way introducing special divine interferences. Supposing I hear a loud noise, of thunder, for example. What is the cause of this sensation? A certain excitation of the auditory nerve and a certain stimulation of the brain, say both the epiphenomenalist and the interactionist. But this answer is not open to the parallelists. Surely the sensation has a cause. Is it then some state of consciousness? This answer is in most cases ruled out because the sensation may follow no state of consciousness, as when a person awakes from dreamless sleep, or it may follow a state of consciousness which cannot possibly be the cause. For example, my sensation of a loud noise may follow a feeling of pleasure of which it can hardly be the effect. It is at this stage that writers like Paulsen and Fechner appeal to their "hypothesis" of universal parallelism. The causes of the sensation are the inner processes accompanying the excitation of the auditory nerve. The cause of "psychical states" like sensations, writes Paulsen, are other psychical processes "which are unknown to us but whose physical equivalents are physical or chemical processes."

Contemporary philosophers tend to be repelled by wild speculations about God's constant interventions in the universe or a pre-established harmony or a universal "mind-stuff," as Clifford called the "inner side" of physical events. Those philosophers today who are opposed to materialism in all its more radical varieties incline therefore to interactionism in spite of the difficulties with which this theory appears to be confronted. Some of them, like Lord Samuel, may be termed "agnostic interactionists." Their position is roughly that while interaction in both directions is a plain and undeniable fact, the "how" of interaction is still a mystery. The "meeting place" between mind and brain, and exactly "what the mind takes over" at the meeting place, as Lord Samuel puts it, has not yet been discovered. In this belief he is supported by many eminent scientists. Thus Sir Charles Sherrington, who was probably the greatest physiologist of this century, declared that "we have to regard the relation of mind to brain as still not merely unsolved, but still devoid of a basis for the very beginning [of a solution]. . . ." Professor Le Gros Clark, a distinguished Oxford anatomist, writes that physiology and anatomy are unable "even to suggest how the physico-chemical phenomena associated with the passage of nervous impulses from one part of the brain to another can be translated into a mental experience."

Other contemporary interactionists adopt a more confident approach. They claim that most if not all the traditional difficulties of interactionism are altogether spurious. Thus Ducasse rejects as meaningless the question of *how* brain-processes produce mental events or how mental events produce modifications in the brain. He insists that in general the question as to how one events causes another is meaningful "only as regards *remote* causation since what the problem 'how' asks for is an account of the causal steps intermediary between the two events concerned." If, for example, it is asserted that a diet rich in animal fats is one of the causal factors responsible for coronary heart attacks, it makes perfectly good sense to ask how this diet produces such results. The cause and the effect are not here "proximate members" of the same causal series, and the "how" asks for information about intermediate members in the series, such as the exact processes in the circulatory system consequent upon the consumption of animal fats. On the other hand, the sensation and the last member of the physiological series prior to its occurrence are proximate, and the same is true of the volition and the first member of the physiological series following it. Here the nature of the case makes it impossible to obtain intermediate members, and hence the question "how" the cause leads to the effect is meaningless.

Broad and others (see Selection 18, pp. 264 ff.) also maintain that many of the apparent difficulties of interactionism arise from the tendency to approach the body-mind problem with inappropriate and misleading images. We tend to think of the mind as a little man inside the brain, and of introspection as a kind of looking with eyes turned to the inside of our bodies. We then try to "visualize" the "meeting place" of mind and body and the "impact" of one on the other. When such attempts end in failure we feel utterly perplexed. According to Broad, the demand to visualize such an "impact" is illegitimate and shows that its authors, if they are dualists, did not have the courage of their initial conviction to regard mental processes as having no spatial location. The use of words like "gap," "chasm," or "hiatus," furthermore, suggests difficulties which do not really exist. The "gap" of the agnostic interactionists cannot be bridged. Nothing less than a "rope" or a "fluid" consisting first of pure matter, then of 90% matter and 10% mind, then of 80% matter and 20% mind . . . and finally of pure mind would satisfy them once the "gap-and-bridge" picture has come to dominate their thinking on this subject. The gap cannot be bridged because there is really no such gap in the first place: the mind is not another physical object, and its relation to the brain cannot be compared to the relation between the banks of a river. Nor does it make sense to speak of "translations" or "transformations" of neural impulses into thought, since thought is not another kind of bodily process or physical energy.

As to the difficulty based on the Conservation of Energy, some writers deny that interaction is in any way incompatible with this principle (see Broad, Selection 18, pp. 262 ff.). Others like Pratt concede that interaction is incompatible with the Conservation of Energy and that the influence of the mind on the body can be saved only on the assumption that it is a "genuine creator of energy." Although he is therefore willing to deny the universal application of the Conservation principle, Pratt insists that the breach is only a very minor one:

If we refuse to admit that the laws which control inorganic matter also absolutely dominate that small portion of the material world in which matter comes into relation with personality, how many of the claims of physical science will thereby be undermined? In the whole realm of physics and of chemistry, of astronomy and geology, not one. Mechanical science will be forced to give up its claims to absolute sway only in that tiny realm where personality, or perhaps where life, begins to have influence. In this connection it is interesting to note that the demand for the absolute universality of physical laws comes, as a rule, not from the physicists, not from the *chemists*, but from a small number of biologists, a large number of psychologists, and most of all from the naturalistic school of the philosophers. The mechanistic philosophers are much more royalist than their king, and the demand for the universal sway of the mechanical seems to vary directly with the square of the distance from headquarters.

Quite a number of philosophers are satisfied with answers along one or other of these lines and rest content in interactionism. To many others interaction between the mind and the body remains something incredible. Some of the latter have fallen back on materialist theories. Quite a few are sympathetic to behaviorism. John Dewey and some of his disciples appear to favor a theory along the lines of Lamettrie and Priestley, according to which mental processes are attributes of the body. Yet other philosophers believe that many of the puzzles on this subject are the result of trying to squeeze the relations between body and mind into some standard pattern. It is a unique relation which one can help to describe by *comparisons* and *contrasts* with other relations. But once it is *identified* with any of these relations we have insoluble problems on our hands, since our customer simply will not fit into the clothes which we have tailored for him.

P. E.

17

THE AUTOMATON THEORY

T. H. Huxley

. . . There remains a doctrine to which Descartes attached great weight, so that full acceptance of it became a sort of note of a thoroughgoing Cartesian, but which, nevertheless, is so opposed to ordinary prepossessions that it attained more general notoriety, and gave rise to more discussion, than almost any other Cartesian hypothesis. It is the doctrine that brute animals are mere machines or automata, devoid not only of reason, but of any kind of consciousness, which is stated briefly in the *Discourse on Method,* and more fully in the "Replies to the Fourth Objections," and in the correspondence with Henry More.

The process of reasoning by which Descartes arrived at this startling conclusion is well shown in the following passage of the "Réponses:"

> But as regards the souls of beasts, although this is not the place for considering them, and though, without a general exposition of physics, I can say no more on this subject than I have already said in the fifth part of my Treatise on Method; yet, I will further state, here, that it appears to me to be a very remarkable circumstance that no movement can take place, either in the bodies of beasts, or even in our own, if these bodies have not in themselves all the organs and instruments by means of which the very same movements would be accomplished in a machine. So that, even in us, the spirit, or the soul, does not directly move the limbs, but only determines the course of that very subtle liquid which is called the animal spirits, which, running continually from the heart by the brain into the muscles, is the cause of all the movements of our limbs, and often may cause many different motions, one as easily as the other.
>
> And it does not even always exert this determination; for among the movements which take place in us, there are many which do not depend on the mind at all, such as the beating of the heart, the digestion of food,

[This selection consists of the major parts of Huxley's article, "On the Hypothesis that Animals are Automata and its History," which was first published in 1874. The entire essay can be found in Huxley's volume *Methods and Results,* published by D. Appleton and Co., New York and London.]

the nutrition, the respiration of those who sleep; and even in those who are awake, walking, singing, and other similar actions, when they are performed without the mind thinking about them. And, when one who falls from a height throws his hands forward to save his head, it is in virtue of no ratio-cination that he performs this action; it does not depend upon his mind, but takes place merely because his senses being affected by the present danger, some change arises in his brain which determines the animal spirits to pass thence into the nerves, in such a manner as is required to produce this motion, in the same way as in a machine, and without the mind being able to hinder it. Now since we observe this in ourselves, why should we be so much astonished if the light reflected from the body of a wolf into the eye of a sheep has the same force to excite in it the motion of flight?

After having observed this, if we wish to learn by reasoning, whether certain movements of beasts are comparable to those which are effected in us by the operation of the mind, or, on the contrary, to those which depend only on the animal spirits and the disposition of the organs, it is necessary to consider the difference between the two, which I have explained in the fifth part of the *Discourse on Method* (for I do not think that any others are discoverable), and then it will easily be seen, that all the actions of beasts are similar only to those which we perform without the help of our minds. For which reason we shall be forced to conclude, that we know of the existence in them of no other principle of motion than the disposition of their organs and the continual affluence of animal spirits produced by the heat of the heart, which attenuates and subtilises the blood; and, at the same time, we shall acknowledge that we have had no reason for assuming any other principle, except that, not having distinguished these two principles of motion, and seeing that the one, which depends only on the animal spirits and the organs, exists in beasts as well as in us, we have hastily concluded that the other, which depends on mind and on thought, was also possessed by them.

Reflex Action and Consciously Motivated Behavior

Descartes' line of argument is perfectly clear. He starts from reflex action in man, from the unquestionable fact that, in ourselves, co-ordinate, purposive, actions may take place, without intervention of consciousness or volition, or even contrary to the latter. As actions of a certain degree of complexity are brought about by mere mechanism, why may not actions of still greater complexity be the result of a more refined mechanism? What proof is there that brutes are other than a superior race of marionettes, which eat without pleasure, cry without pain, desire nothing, know nothing, and only simulate intelligence as a bee simulates a mathematician?

The Port Royalists adopted the hypothesis that brutes are machines, and are said to have carried its practical applications so far as to treat doinestic animals with neglect, if not with actual cruelty. . . . Modern research has brought to light a great multitude of facts, which not only show that Descartes' view is defensible, but render it far more defensible than it was in his day.

It must be premised, that it is wholly impossible absolutely to prove the presence or absence of consciousness in anything but one's own brain, though, by analogy, we are justified in assuming its existence in other men. Now if, by some accident, a man's spinal cord is divided, his limbs are paralysed, so far as his volition is concerned, below the point of injury; and he is incapable of experiencing all those states of consciousness which, in his uninjured state, would be excited by irritation of those nerves which come off below the injury. If the spinal cord is divided in the middle of the back, for example, the skin of the feet may be cut, or pinched, or burned, or wetted with vitriol, without any sensation of touch, or of pain, arising, in consciousness. So far as the man is concerned, therefore, the part of the central nervous system which lies beyond the injury is cut off from consciousness. It must indeed be admitted, that, if any one think fit to maintain that the spinal cord below the injury is conscious, but that it is cut off from any means of making its consciousness known to the other consciousness in the brain, there is no means of driving him from his position by logic. But assuredly there is no way of proving it, and in the matter of consciousness, if in anything, we may hold by the rule, *De non apparentibus et de non existentibus eadem est ratio.** However near the brain the spinal cord is injured, consciousness remains intact, except that the irritation of parts below the injury is no longer represented by sensation. On the other hand, pressure upon the anterior division of the brain, or extensive injuries to it, abolish consciousness. Hence, it is a highly probable conclusion, that consciousness in man depends upon the integrity of the anterior division of the brain, while the middle and hinder divisions of the brain, and the rest of the nervous centres, have nothing to do with it. And it is further highly probable, that what is true for man is true for other vertebrated animals.

We may assume, then, that in a living vertebrated animal, any segment of the cerebro-spinal axis (or spinal cord and brain) separated from that anterior division of the brain which is the organ of consciousness, is as completely incapable of giving rise to consciousness as we know it to be incapable of carrying out volitions. Nevertheless, this separated segment of the spinal cord is not passive and inert. On the contrary, it is the seat of extremely remarkable powers. In our imaginary case of injury, the man would, as we have seen, be devoid of sensation in his legs, and would have not the least power of moving them.

---

* "That what is not given in experience may be treated as non-existent." (Eds.)

But, if the soles of his feet were tickled, the legs would be drawn up just as vigorously as they would have been before the injury. We know exactly what happens when the soles of the feet are tickled; a molecular change takes place in the sensory nerves of the skin, and is propagated along them and through the posterior roots of the spinal nerves, which are constituted by them, to the grey matter of the spinal cord. Through that grey matter the molecular motion is reflected into the anterior roots of the same nerves, constituted by the filaments which supply the muscles of the legs, and, travelling along these motor filaments, reaches the muscles, which at once contract, and cause the limbs to be drawn up.

In order to move the legs in this way, a definite co-ordination of muscular contractions is necessary; the muscles must contract in a certain order and with duly proportioned force; and moreover, as the feet are drawn away from the source of irritation, it may be said that the action has a final cause, or is purposive.

Thus it follows, that the grey matter of the segment of the man's spinal cord, though it is devoid of consciousness, nevertheless responds to a simple stimulus by giving rise to a complex set of muscular contractions, co-ordinated towards a definite end, and serving an obvious purpose.

Effect of Brain Damage in a Lower Animal

If the spinal cord of a frog is cut across, so as to provide us with a segment separated from the brain, we shall have a subject parallel to the injured man, on which experiments can be made without remorse; as we have a right to conclude that a frog's spinal cord is not likely to be conscious, when a man's is not.

Now the frog behaves just as the man did. The legs are utterly paralysed, so far as voluntary movement is concerned; but they are vigorously drawn up to the body when any irritant is applied to the foot. But let us study our frog a little farther. Touch the skin of the side of the body with a little acetic acid, which gives rise to all the signs of great pain in an uninjured frog. In this case, there can be no pain, because the application is made to a part of the skin supplied with nerves which come off from the cord below the point of section; nevertheless, the frog lifts up the limb of the same side, and applies the foot to rub off the acetic acid; and, what is still more remarkable, if the limb be held so that the frog cannot use it, it will, by and by, move the limb of the other side, turn it across the body, and use it for the same rubbing process. It is impossible that the frog, if it were in its entirety and could reason, should perform actions more purposive than these: and yet we have most complete assurance that, in this case, the frog is not acting from purpose, has no consciousness, and is a mere insensible machine.

But now suppose that, instead of making a section of the cord in the middle of the body, it had been made in such a manner as to separate the hindermost division of the brain from the rest of the organ, and suppose the foremost two-thirds of the brain entirely taken away. The frog is then absolutely devoid of any spontaneity; it sits upright in the attitude which a frog habitually assumes; and it will not stir unless it is touched; but it differs from the frog which I have just described in this, that, if it be thrown into the water, it begins to swim, and swims just as well as the perfect frog does. But swimming requires the combination and successive co-ordination of a great number of muscular actions. And we are forced to conclude, that the impression made upon the sensory nerves of the skin of the frog by the contact with the water into which it is thrown, causes the transmission to the central nervous apparatus of an impulse which sets going a certain machinery by which all the muscles of swimming are brought into play in due co-ordination. If the frog be stimulated by some irritating body, it jumps or walks as well as the complete frog can do. The simple sensory impression, acting through the machinery of the cord, gives rise to these complex combined movements.

It is possible to go a step farther. Suppose that only the anterior division of the brain—so much of it as lies in front of the "optic lobes"—is removed. If that operation is performed quickly and skillfully, the frog may be kept in a state of full bodily vigour for months, or it may be for years; but it will sit unmoved. It sees nothing: it hears nothing. It will starve sooner than feed itself, although food put into its mouth is swallowed. On irritation, it jumps or walks; if thrown into the water it swims. If it be put on the hand, it sits there, crouched, perfectly quiet, and would sit there for ever. If the hand be inclined very gently and slowly, so that the frog would naturally tend to slip off, the creature's fore paws are shifted on to the edge of the hand, until he can just prevent himself from falling. If the turning of the hand be slowly continued, he mounts up with great care and deliberation, putting first one leg forward and then another, until he balances himself with perfect precision upon the edge; and if the turning of the hand is continued, he goes through the needful set of muscular operations, until he comes to be seated in security, upon the back of the hand. The doing of all this requires a delicacy of co-ordination, and a precision of adjustment of the muscular apparatus of the body, which are only comparable to those of a rope-dancer. To the ordinary influences of light, the frog, deprived of its cerebral hemispheres, appears to be blind. Nevertheless, if the animal be put upon a table, with a book at some little distance between it and the light, and the skin of the hinder part of its body is then irritated, it will jump forward, avoiding the book by passing to the right or left of it. Therefore, although the frog appears to have no sensation of light, visible objects act through its brain upon the motor mechanism of its body.

It is obvious, that had Descartes been acquainted with these remarkable results of modern research, they would have furnished him with far more powerful arguments than he possessed in favour of his view of the automatism of brutes. The habits of a frog, leading its natural life, involve such simple adaptations to surrounding conditions, that the machinery which is competent to do so much without the intervention of consciousness, might well do all. And this argument is vastly strengthened by what has been learned in recent times of the marvellously complex operations which are performed mechanically, and to all appearance without consciousness, by men, when, in consequence of injury or disease, they are reduced to a condition more or less comparable to that of a frog, in which the anterior part of the brain has been removed. A case has recently been published by an eminent French physician, Dr. Mesnet, which illustrates this condition so remarkably, that I make no apology for dwelling upon it at considerable length.

The Case of Sergeant F.

A sergeant of the French army, F——, twenty-seven years of age, was wounded during the battle of Bazeilles, by a ball which fractured his left parietal bone. He ran his bayonet through the Prussian soldier who wounded him, but almost immediately his right arm became paralysed; after walking about two hundred yards, his right leg became similarly affected, and he lost his senses. When he recovered them, three weeks afterwards, in a hospital at Mayence, the right half of the body was completely paralysed, and remained in this condition for a year. At present, the only trace of the paralysis which remains is a slight weakness of the right half of the body. Three or four months after the wound was inflicted, periodical disturbances of the functions of the brain made their appearance, and have continued ever since. The disturbances last from fifteen to thirty hours; the intervals at which they occur being from fifteen to thirty days.

For four years, therefore, the life of this man has been divided into alternating phases—short abnormal states intervening between long normal states.

In the periods of normal life, the ex-sergeant's health is perfect; he is intelligent and kindly, and performs, satisfactorily, the duties of a hospital attendant. The commencement of the abnormal state is ushered in by uneasiness and a sense of weight about the forehead, which the patient compares to the constriction of a circle of iron; and, after its termination, he complains, for some hours, of dullness and heaviness of the head. But the transition from the normal to the abnormal state takes place in a few minutes, without convulsions or cries, and without anything to indicate the change to a bystander. His movements remain free and his expression calm, except for a contraction of the brow, an incessant movement of the eyeballs, and a chewing motion of the jaws. The eyes are wide open, and their pupils dilated. If the man happens to be in a place to which he is accustomed, he walks about as usual; but, if he is in a new place, or if obstacles are intentionally placed in his way, he stumbles gently against them, stops, and then, feeling over the objects with his hands, passes on one side of them. He offers no resistance to any change of direction which may be impressed upon him, or to the forcible acceleration or retardation of his movements. He eats, drinks, smokes, walks about, dresses and undresses himself, rises and goes to bed at the accustomed hours. Nevertheless, pins may be run into his body, or strong electric shocks may be sent through it, without causing the least indication of pain; no odorous substance, pleasant or unpleasant, makes the least impression; he eats and drinks with avidity whatever is offered, and takes asafoetida, or vinegar, or quinine, as readily as water; no noise affects him; and light influences him only under certain conditions. Dr. Mesnet remarks, that the sense of touch alone seems to persist, and indeed to be more acute and delicate than in the normal state: and it is by means of the nerves of touch, almost exclusively, that his organism is brought into relation with the external world. Here a difficulty arises. It is clear from the facts detailed, that the nervous apparatus by which, in the normal state, sensations of touch are excited, is that by which external influences determine the movements of the body, in the abnormal state. But does the state of consciousness, which we term a tactile sensation, accompany the operation of this nervous apparatus in the abnormal state? or is consciousness utterly absent, the man being reduced to an insensible mechanism?

It is impossible to obtain direct evidence in favour of the one conclusion or the other; all that can be said is, that the case of the frog shows that the man may be devoid of any kind of consciousness.

A further difficult problem is this. The man is insensible to sensory impressions made through the ear, the nose, the tongue, and, to a great extent, the eye; nor is he susceptible of pain from causes operating during his abnormal state. Nevertheless, it is possible so to act upon his tactile apparatus, as to give rise to those molecular changes in his sensorium, which are ordinarily the causes of associated trains of ideas. I give a striking example of this process in Dr. Mesnet's words:—

> He was taking a walk in the garden under a bunch of trees. We placed in his hand his walking stick which he had let fall a few minutes before.

He feels it, passes his hand over the bent handle a few times, becomes attentive, seems to extend his ear, and suddenly calls out, "Henry," then, "Here they are. There are about twenty to our two! We have reached our end." And then, with his hand behind his back, as if about to leap, he prepares to attack with his weapon. He crouches in the level, green grass, his head concealed by a tree, in the position of a hunter, and follows all the short-distance movements of the enemy which he believes he sees, with accompanying movements of his hands and shoulders.

In a subsequent abnormal period, Dr. Mesnet caused the patient to repeat this scene by placing him in the same conditions. Now, in this case, the question arises whether the series of actions constituting this singular pantomime was accompanied by the ordinary states of consciousness, the appropriate train of ideas, or not? Did the man dream that he was skirmishing? Or was he in the condition of one of Vaucauson's automata—a senseless mechanism worked by molecular changes in his nervous system? The analogy of the frog shows that the latter assumption is perfectly justifiable.

The ex-sergeant has a good voice, and had, at one time, been employed as a singer at a café. In one of his abnormal states he was observed to begin humming a tune. He then went to his room, dressed himself carefully, and took up some parts of a periodical novel, which lay on his bed, as if he were trying to find something. Dr. Mesnet, suspecting that he was seeking his music, made up one of these into a roll and put it into his hand. He appeared satisfied, took his cane and went downstairs to the door. Here Dr. Mesnet turned him round, and he walked quite contentedly, in the opposite direction, towards the room of the concierge. The light of the sun shining through a window now happened to fall upon him, and seemed to suggest the foot-lights of the stage on which he was accustomed to make his appearance. He stopped, opened his roll of imaginary music, put himself into the attitude of a singer, and sang, with perfect execution, three songs, one after the other. After which he wiped his face with his handkerchief and drank, without a grimace, a tumbler of strong vinegar and water which was put into his hand.

Innate and Automatic Behavior Patterns

An experiment which may be performed upon the frog deprived of the fore part of its brain, well known as Goltz's "Quak-versuch," affords a parallel to this performance. If the skin of a certain part of the back of such a frog is gently stroked with the finger, it immediately croaks. It never croaks unless it is so stroked, and the croak always follows the stroke, just as the sound of a repeater follows the touching of the spring.

In the frog, this "song" is innate—so to speak *a priori*—and depends upon a mechanism in the brain governing the vocal apparatus, which is set at work by the molecular change set up in the sensory nerves of the skin of the back by the contact of a foreign body.

In man there is also a vocal mechanism, and the cry of an infant is in the same sense innate and *a priori*, inasmuch as it depends on an organic relation between its sensory nerves and the nervous mechanism which governs the vocal apparatus. Learning to speak, and learning to sing, are processes by which the vocal mechanism is set to new tunes. A song which has been learned has its molecular equivalent, which potentially represents it in the brain, just as a musical box, wound up, potentially represents an overture. Touch the stop and the overture begins; send a molecular impulse along the proper afferent nerve and the singer begins his song.

Again, the manner in which the frog, though apparently insensible to light, is yet, under some circumstances, influenced by visual images, finds a singular parallel in the case of the ex-sergeant.

Sitting at a table, in one of his abnormal states, he took up a pen, felt for paper and ink, and began to write a letter to his general, in which he recommended himself for a medal, on account of his good conduct and courage. It occurred to Dr. Mesnet to ascertain experimentally how far vision was concerned in this act of writing. He therefore interposed a screen between the man's eyes and his hands; under these circumstances he went on writing for a short time, but the words became illegible, and he finally stopped, without manifesting any discontent. On the withdrawal of the screen he began to write again where he had left off. The substitution of water for ink in the inkstand had a similar result. He stopped, looked at his pen, wiped it on his coat, dipped it in the water, and began again with the same effect.

On one occasion, he began to write upon the topmost of ten superimposed sheets of paper. After he had written a line or two, this sheet was suddenly drawn away. There was a slight expression of surprise, but he continued his letter on the second sheet exactly as if it had been the first. This operation was repeated five times, so that the fifth sheet contained nothing by the writer's signature at the bottom of the page. Nevertheless, when the signature was finished, his eyes turned to the top of the blank sheet, and he went through the form of reading over what he had written, a movement of the lips accompanying each word; moreover, with his pen, he put in such corrections as were needed, in that part of the blank page which corresponded with the position of the words which required correction, in the sheets which had been taken away. If the five sheets had been transparent, therefore, they would, when superposed, have formed a properly written and corrected letter.

Immediately after he had written his letter, F—— got up, walked down to the garden, made himself a cigarette, lighted and smoked it. He was about to prepare another, but sought in vain for his tobacco-pouch, which had been purposely taken away. The pouch was now thrust before his eyes and put under his nose, but he neither saw nor smelt it; yet, when it was placed in his hand, he at once seized it, made a fresh cigarette, and ignited a match to light the latter. The match was blown out, and another lighted match placed close before his eyes, but he made no attempt to take it; and, if his cigarette was lighted for him, he made no attempt to smoke. All this time the eyes were vacant, and neither winked, nor exhibited any contraction of the pupils. From these and other experiments, Dr. Mesnet draws the conclusion that his patient sees some things and not others; that the sense of sight is accessible to all things which are brought into relation with him by the sense of touch, and, on the contrary, insensible to things which lie outside this relation. He sees the match he holds and does not see any other.

Just so the frog "sees" the book which is in the way of his jump, at the same time that isolated visual impressions take no effect upon him.

As I have pointed out, it is impossible to prove that F—— is absolutely unconscious in his abnormal state, but it is no less impossible to prove the contrary; and the case of the frog goes a long way to justify the assumption that, in the abnormal state, the man is a mere insensible machine.

If such facts as these had come under the knowledge of Descartes, would they not have formed an apt commentary upon that remarkable passage in the *Traité de l'Homme*, which I have quoted elsewhere, but which is worth repetition:

> All the functions which I have attributed to this machine (the body), as the digestion of food, the pulsation of the heart and of the arteries; the nutrition and the growth of the limbs; respiration, wakefulness, and sleep; the reception of light, sounds, odours, flavours, heat, and such like qualities, in the organs of the external senses; the impression of the idea of these in the organ of common sensation and in the imagination; the retention or the impression of these ideas on the memory; the internal movements of the appetites and the passions; and lastly the external movements of all the limbs, which follow so aptly, as well the action of the objects which are presented to the senses, as the impressions which meet in the memory, that they imitate as nearly as possible those of a real man; I desire, I say, that you should consider that these functions in the machine naturally proceed from the mere arrangement of its organs, neither more nor less than do the movements of a clock, or other automaton, from that of its weights and its wheels; so that, so far as these are concerned, it is not necessary to conceive any other vegetative or sensitive soul, nor any other principle of motion or of life, than the blood and the spirits agitated by the fire which burns continually in the heart, and which is no wise essentially different from all the fires which exist in inanimate bodies.

And would Descartes not have been justified in asking why we need deny that animals are machines, when men, in a state of unconsciousness, perform, mechanically, actions as complicated and as seemingly rational as those of any animals?

Animals Are Conscious *Automata*

But though I do not think that Descartes' hypothesis can be positively refuted, I am not disposed to accept it. The doctrine of continuity is too well established for it to be permissible to me to suppose that any complex natural phenomenon comes into existence suddenly, and without being preceded by simpler modifications; and very strong arguments would be needed to prove that such complex phenomena as those of consciousness, first make their appearance in man. We know, that, in the individual man, consciousness grows from a dim glimmer to its full light, whether we consider the infant advancing in years or the adult emerging from slumber and swoon. We know, further, that the lower animals possess, though less developed, that part of the brain which we have every reason to believe to be the organ of consciousness in man; and as, in other cases, function and organ are proportional, so we have a right to conclude it is with the brain; and that the brutes, though they may not possess our intensity of consciousness, and though from the absence of language, they can have no trains of thoughts, but only trains of feelings, yet have a consciousness which, more or less distinctly, foreshadows our own.

I confess that, in view of the struggle for existence which goes on in the animal world, and of the frightful quantity of pain with which it must be accompanied, I should be glad if the probabilities were in favour of Descartes' hypothesis; but, on the other hand, considering the terrible practical consequences to domestic animals which might ensue from any error on our part, it is as well to err on the right side, if we err at all, and deal with them as weaker brethren, who ae bound, like the rest of us, to pay their toll for living, and suffer what is needful for the general good. As Hartley finely says, "We seem to be in the place of God to them"; and we may justly follow the precedents He sets in nature in our dealings with them.

But though we may see reason to disagree with Descartes' hypothesis that brutes are unconscious machines, it does not follow that he was wrong in regarding them as automata. They may be more or less conscious, sensitive, automata; and the view that they are such conscious machines is that which is implicitly, or explicitly, adopted by most persons. When we speak of the actions of the lower animals being guided by instinct and not by reason, what we really mean is that, though they feel as we do, yet their actions are the results of their physical organisation. We believe, in short, that they are machines, one part of which (the nervous system) not only sets the rest in motion, and co-ordinates its movements in relation with changes in surrounding bodies, but is provided with special apparatus, the function of which is the calling into existence of those states of consciousness which are termed sensations, emotions, and ideas. I believe that this generally accepted view is the best expression of the facts at present known.

It is experimentally demonstrable—any one who cares to run a pin into himself may perform a sufficient demonstration of the fact—that a mode of motion of the nervous system is the immediate antecedent of a state of consciousness. All but the adherents of "Occasionalism," or of the doctrine of "Pre-established Harmony" (if any such now exist), must admit that we have as much reason for regarding the mode of motion of the nervous system as the cause of the state of consciousness, as we have for regarding any event as the cause of another. How the one phenomenon causes the other we know, as much or as little, as in any other case of causation; but we have as much right to believe that the sensation is an effect of the molecular change, as we have to believe that motion is an effect of impact; and there is as much propriety in saying that the brain evolves sensation, as there is in saying that an iron rod, when hammered, evolves heat.

As I have endeavored to show, we are justified in supposing that something analogous to what happens in ourselves takes place in the brutes, and that the affections of their sensory nerves give rise to molecular changes in the brain, which again give rise to, or evolve, the corresponding states of consciousness. Nor can there be any reasonable doubt that the emotions of brutes, and such ideas as they possess, are similarly dependent upon molecular brain changes. Each sensory impression leaves behind a record in the structure of the brain—an "ideagenous" molecule, so to speak, which is competent, under certain conditions, to reproduce, in a fainter condition, the state of consciousness which corresponds with that sensory impression; and it is these "ideagenous molecules" which are the physical basis of memory.

It may be assumed, then, that molecular changes in the brain are the causes of all the states of consciousness of brutes. Is there any evidence that these states of consciousness may, conversely, cause those molecular changes which give rise to muscular motion? I see no such evidence. The frog walks, hops, swims, and goes through his gymnastic performances quite as well without consciousness, and consequently without volition, as with it; and, if a frog, in his natural state, possesses anything corresponding with what we call volition, there is no reason to think that it is anything but a concomitant of the molecular changes in the brain which form part of the series involved in the production of motion.

The consciousness of brutes would appear to be related to the mechanism of their body simply as a collateral product of its working, and to be as completely without any power of modifying that working as the steam-whistle which accompanies the work of a locomotive engine is without influence upon its machinery. Their volition, if they have any, is an emotion indicative of physical changes, not a cause of such changes.

This conception of the relations of states of consciousness with molecular changes in the brain—of *psychoses* with *neuroses*—does not prevent us from ascribing free will to brutes. For an agent is free when there is nothing to prevent him from doing that which he desires to do. If a greyhound chases a hare, he is a free agent, because his action is in entire accordance with his strong desire to catch the hare; while so long as he is held back by the leash he is not free, being prevented by external force from following his inclination. And the ascription of freedom to the greyhound under the former circumstances is by no means inconsistent with the other aspect of the facts of the case—that he is a machine impelled to the chase, and caused, at the same time, to have the desire to catch the game by the impression which the rays of light proceeding from the hare make upon his eyes, and through them upon his brain.

Much ingenious argument has at various times been bestowed upon the question: How is it possible to imagine that volition, which is a state of consciousness, and, as such, has not the slightest community of nature with matter in motion, can act upon the moving matter of which the body is composed, as it is assumed to do in voluntary acts? But if, as is here suggested, the voluntary acts of brutes—or, in other words, the acts which they desire to perform—are as purely mechanical as the rest of their actions, and are simply accompanied by the state of consciousness called volition, the inquiry, so far as they are concerned, becomes superfluous. Their volitions do not enter into the chain of causation of their actions at all. . . . .

The Same Conclusion Applies to Human Beings

It will be said, that I mean that the conclusions deduced from the study of the brutes are applicable to man, and that the logical consequences of such application are fatalism, materialism, and atheism—whereupon the drums will beat the *pas de charge*.

One does not do battle with drummers; but I venture to offer a few remarks for the calm consideration of thoughtful persons, untrammelled by foregone conclusions, unpledged to shore-up tottering dogmas, and anxious only to know the true bearings of the case.

It is quite true that, to the best of my judgment, the argumentation which applies to brutes holds equally good of men; and, therefore, that all states of consciousness in us, as in them, are immediately caused by molecular changes of the brain-substance. It seems to me that in men, as in brutes, there is no proof that any state of consciousness is the cause of change in the motion of the matter of the organism. If these positions are well based, it follows that our mental conditions are simply the symbols in consciousness of the changes which takes place automatically in the organism; and that, to take an extreme illustration, the feeling we call volition is not the cause of a voluntary act, but the symbol of that state of the brain which is the immediate cause of that act. We are conscious automata, endowed with free will in the only intelligible sense of that much-abused term—inasmuch as in many respects we are able to do as we like—but none the less parts of the great series of causes and effects which, in unbroken continuity, composes that which is, and has been, and shall be—the sum of existence.

As to the logical consequences of this conviction of mine, I may be permitted to remark that logical consequences are the scarecrows of fools and the beacons of wise men. The only question which any wise man can ask himself, and which any honest man will ask himself, is whether a doctrine is true or false. Consequences will take care of themselves; at most their importance can only justify us in testing with extra care the reasoning process from which they result.

So that if the view I have taken did really and logically lead to fatalism, materialism, and atheism, I should profess myself a fatalist, materialist, and atheist; and I should look upon those who, while they believed in my honesty of purpose and intellectual competency, should raise a hue and cry against me, as people who by their own admission preferred lying to truth, and whose opinions therefore were unworthy of the smallest attention.

But, as I have endeavored to explain on other occasions, I really have no claim to rank myself among fatalistic, materialistic, or atheistic philosophers. Not among the fatalists, for I take the conception of necessity to have a logical, and not a physical foundation; not among materialists, for I am utterly incapable of conceiving the existence of matter if there is no mind in which to picture that existence; not among atheists, for the problem of the ultimate cause of existence is one which seems to me to be hopelessly out of reach of my poor powers. Of all the senseless babble I have ever had occasion to read, the demonstrations of these philosophers who undertake to tell us all about the nature of God would be the worst, if they were not surpassed by the still greater absurdities of the philosophers who try to prove that there is no God. . . .

18

THE TRADITIONAL PROBLEM
OF BODY AND MIND

C. D. Broad

. . . THERE IS A QUESTION which has been argued about for some centuries now under the name of "Interaction"; this is the question whether minds really do act on the organisms which they animate, and whether organisms really do act on the minds which animate them. (I must point out at once that I imply no particular theory of mind or body by the word "to animate." I use it as a perfectly neutral name to express the fact that a certain mind is connected in some peculiarly intimate way with a certain body, and, under normal conditions with no other body. This is a fact even on a purely behaviouristic theory of mind; on such a view to say that the mind M animates the body B would mean that the body B, in so far as it behaves in certain ways, is the Mind M. A body which did not act in these ways would be said not to be animated by a mind. And a different body B', which acted in the same general way as B, would be said to be animated by a different mind M').

The problem of Interaction is generally discussed at the level of enlightened common-sense; where it is assumed that we know pretty well what we mean by "mind," by "matter" and by "causation." Obviously no solution which is reached at that level can claim to be ultimate. If what we call "matter" should turn out to be a collection of spirits of low intelligence, as Leibniz thought, the argument that mind and body are so unlike that their interaction is impossible would become irrelevant. Again, if causation be nothing but regular sequence and concomitance, as some philosophers have held, it is ridiculous to regard psychoneural parallelism and interaction as mutually exclusive alternatives. For

---

[This selection consists of extracts from Chapter III of Broad's *The Mind and Its Place in Nature* which was published in 1925. It is here reprinted with the kind permission of Routledge and Kegan Paul, London.]

interaction will mean no more than parallelism, and parallelism will mean no less than interaction. Nevertheless I am going to discuss the arguments here at the common-sense level, because they are so incredibly bad and yet have imposed upon so many learned men.

We start then by assuming a developed mind and a developed organism as two distinct things, and by admitting that the two are now intimately connected in some way or other which I express by saying that "this mind animates this organism." We assume that bodies are very much as enlightened common-sense believes them to be; and that, even if we cannot define "causation," we have some means of recognising when it is present and when it is absent. The question then is: "Does a mind ever act on the body which it animates, and does a body ever act on the mind which animates it?" The answer which common-sense would give to both questions is: "Yes, certainly." On the face of it my body acts on my mind whenever a pin is stuck into the former and a painful sensation thereupon arises in the latter. And, on the face of it, my mind acts on my body whenever a desire to move my arms arises in the former and is followed by this movement in the latter. Let us call this common-sense view "Two-sided Interaction." Although it seems so obvious it has been denied by probably a majority of philosophers and a majority of physiologists. So the question is: "Why should so many distinguished men, who have studied the subject, have denied the apparently obvious fact of Two-sided Interaction?"

The arguments against Two-sided Interaction fall into two sets:— Philosophical and Scientific. We will take the philosophical arguments first; for we shall find that the professedly scientific arguments come back in the end to the principles or prejudices which are made explicit in the philosophical arguments.

Philosophical Arguments against Two-Sided Interaction

No one can deny that there is a close correlation between certain bodily events and certain mental events, and conversely. Therefore anyone who denies that there is action of mind on body and of body on mind must presumably hold (a) that concomitant variation is not an adequate criterion of causal connexion, and (b) that the other feature which is essential for causal connexion is absent in the case of body and mind. Now the common philosophical argument is that minds and mental states are so extremely unlike bodies and bodily states that it is inconceivable that the two should be causally connected. It is certainly true that, if minds and mental events are just what they seem to be to introspection and nothing more, and if bodies and bodily events are just what enlightened common-sense thinks them to be and nothing more, the two are extremely unlike. And this fact is supposed to show that, however closely correlated certain pairs of events in mind and body respectively may be, they cannot be causally connected.

Evidently the assumption at the back of this argument is that concomitant variation, together with a high enough degree of likeness, is an adequate test for causation; but that no amount of concomitant variation can establish causation in the absence of a high enough degree of likeness. Now I am inclined to admit part of this assumption. I think it is practically certain that causation does not simply mean concomitant variation (and, if it did, *cadit quæstio*). Hence the existence of the latter is not *ipso facto,* a proof of the presence of the former. Again, I think it is almost certain that concomitant variation between A and B is not in fact a sufficient sign of the presence of a direct causal relation between the two (I think it may perhaps be a sufficient sign of either a direct causal relation between A and B or of several causal relations which indirectly unite A and B through the medium of other terms C, D, etc.). So far I agree with the assumptions of the argument. But I cannot see the least reason to think that the other characteristic, which must be added to concomitant variation before we can be sure that A and B are causally connected, is a high degree of likeness between the two. One would like to know just how unlike two events may be before it becomes impossible to admit the existence of a causal relation between them. No one hesitates to hold that draughts and colds in the head are causally connected, although the two are extremely unlike each other. If the unlikeness of draughts and colds in the head does not prevent one from admitting a causal connexion between the two, why should the unlikeness of volitions and voluntary movements prevent one from holding that they are causally connected? To sum up. I am willing to admit that an adequate criterion of causal connexion needs some other relation between a pair of events beside concomitant variation; but I do not believe for a moment that this other relation is that of qualitative likeness. . . .

Scientific Arguments against Two-Sided Interaction

There are, so far as I know, two of these. One is supposed to be based on the physical principle of the Conservation of Energy, and on certain experiments which have been made on human bodies. The other is based on the close analogy which is said to exist between the structures of the physiological mechanism of reflex action and that of voluntary action. I will take them in turn.

(1) *The Argument from Energy.* It will first be needful to state

clearly what is asserted by the principle of the Conservation of Energy. It is found that, if we take certain material systems, e.g., a gun, a cartridge, and a bullet, there is a certain magnitude which keeps approximately constant throughout all their changes. This is called "Energy." When the gun has not been fired it and the bullet have no motion, but the explosive in the cartridge has great chemical energy. When it has been fired the bullet is moving very fast and has great energy of movement. The gun, though not moving fast in its recoil, has also great energy of movement because it is very massive. The gases produced by the explosion have some energy of movement and some heat-energy, but much less chemical energy than the unexploded charge had. These various kinds of energy can be measured in common units according to certain conventions. To an innocent mind there seems to be a good deal of "cooking" at this stage, i.e., the conventions seem to be chosen and various kinds and amounts of concealed energy seem to be postulated in order to make the principle come out right at the end. I do not propose to go into this in detail, for two reasons. In the first place, I think that the conventions adopted and the postulates made, though somewhat suggestive of the fraudulent company-promoter, can be justified by their coherence with certain experimental facts, and that they are not simply made *ad hoc*. Secondly, I shall show that the Conservation of Energy is absolutely irrelevant to the question at issue, so that it would be waste of time to treat it too seriously in the present connexion. Now it is found that the total energy of all kinds in this system, when measured according to these conventions, is approximately the same in amount though very differently distributed after the explosion and before it. If we had confined our attention to a part of this system and its energy this would not have been true. The bullet, e.g., had no energy at all before the explosion and a great deal afterwards. A system like the bullet, the gun, and the charge, is called a "Conservative System"; the bullet alone, or the gun and the charge, would be called "Non-conservative Systems." A conservative system might therefore be defined as one whose total energy is redistributed, but not altered in amount, by changes that happen within it. Of course a given system might be conservative for some kinds of change and not for others.

So far we have merely defined a "Conservative System," and admitted that there are systems which, for some kinds of change at any rate, answer approximately to our definition. We can now state the Principle of the Conservation of Energy in terms of the conceptions just defined. The principle asserts that every material system is either itself conservative, or, if not, is part of a larger material system which is conservative. We may take it that there is good inductive evidence for this proposition.

The next thing to consider is the experiments on the human body. These tend to prove that a living body, with the air that it breathes and the food that it eats, forms a conservative system to a high degree of approximation. We can measure the chemical energy of the food given to a man, and that which enters his body in the form of Oxygen breathed in. We can also, with suitable apparatus, collect, measure and analyse the air breathed out, and thus find its chemical energy. Similarly, we can find the energy given out in bodily movement, in heat, and in excretion. It is alleged that, on the average, whatever the man man do, the energy of his bodily movements is exactly accounted for by the energy given to him in the form of food and of Oxygen. If you take the energy put in food and Oxygen, and subtract the energy given out in waste-products, the balance is almost exactly equal to the energy put out in bodily movements. Such slight differences as are found are as often on one side as on the other, and are therefore probably due to unavoidable experimental errors. I do not propose to criticize the interpretation of these experiments in detail, because, as I shall show soon, they are completely irrelevant to the problem of whether mind and body interact. But there is just one point that I will make before passing on. It is perfectly clear that such experiments can tell us only what happens on the average over a long time. To know whether the balance was accurately kept at every moment we should have to kill the patient at each moment and analyse his body so as to find out the energy present then in the form of stored-up products. Obviously we cannot keep on killing the patient in order to analyse him, and then reviving him in order to go on with the experiment. Thus it would seem that the results of the experiment are perfectly compatible with the presence of quite large excesses or defects in the total bodily energy at certain moments, provided that these average out over longer periods. However, I do not want to press this criticism; I am quite ready to accept for our present purpose the traditional interpretation which has been put on the experiments.

We now understand the physical principle and the experimental facts. The two together are generally supposed to prove that mind and body cannot interact. What precisely is the argument, and is it valid? I imagine that the argument, when fully stated, would run somewhat as follows: "I will to move my arm, and it moves. If the volition has anything to do with causing the movement we might expect energy to flow from my mind to my body. Thus the energy of my body ought to receive a measurable increase, not accounted for by the food that I eat and the Oxygen that I breathe. But no such physically unaccountable increases of bodily energy are found. Again, I tread on a tin-tack, and a painful sensation arises in my mind. If treading on the tack has anything to do with causing the sensation we might expect energy to flow from my body to my mind. Such energy would cease to be measurable. Thus there ought to be a noticeable decrease in my bodily energy not balanced by increases anywhere in the physical system. But such unbalanced decreases of bodily energy are not found." So it is concluded that the volition has nothing to do with causing my arm to move, and that treading on the tack has nothing to do with causing the painful sensation.

Is this argument valid? In the first place it is important to notice that the conclusion does not follow from the Conservation of Energy and the experimental facts alone. The real premise is a tacitly assumed proposition about causation; viz., that, if a change in A has anything to do with causing a change in B, energy must leave A and flow into B. This is neither asserted nor entailed by the Conservation of Energy. What it says is that, if energy leaves A, it must appear in something else, say B; so that A and B together form a conservative system. Since the Conservation of Energy is not itself the premise for the argument against Interaction, and since it does not entail that premise, the evidence for the Conservation of Energy is not evidence against Interaction. Is there any independent evidence for the premise? We may admit that it is true of many, though not of all, transactions within the physical realm. But there are cases where it is not true even of purely physical transactions; and even if it were always true in the physical realm, it would not follow that it must always be true of trans-physical causation. Take the case of a weight swinging at the end of a string hung from a fixed point. The total energy of the weight is the same at all positions in its course. It is thus a conservative system. But at every moment the direction and velocity of the weight's motion are different, and the proportion between its kinetic and its potential energy is constantly changing. These changes are caused by the pull of the string, which acts in a different direction at each different moment. The string makes no difference to the total energy of the weight; but it makes all the difference in the world to the particular way in which the weight moves and the particular way in which the energy is distributed between the potential and the kinetic forms. This is evident when we remember that the weight would begin to move in an utterly different course if at any moment the string were cut.

Here, then, we have a clear case even in the physical realm where a system is conservative but is continually acted on by something which affects its movement and the distribution of its total energy. Why should not the mind act on the body in this way? If you say that you can see how a string can affect the movement of a weight, but cannot see how a volition could affect the movement of a material particle, you have deserted the scientific argument and have gone back to one of the philosophical arguments. Your real difficulty is either that volitions are so very unlike movements, or that the volition is in your mind whilst the movement belongs to the physical realm. And we have seen how little weight can be attached to these objections.

The fact is that, even in purely physical systems, the Conservation of Energy does not explain what changes will happen or when they will happen. It merely imposes a very general limiting condition on the changes that are possible. The fact that the system composed of bullet, charge, and gun, in our earlier example, is conservative does not tell us that the gun ever will be fired, or when it will be fired, if at all, or what will cause it to go off, or what forms of energy will appear if and when it does go off. The change in this case is determined by pulling the trigger. Likewise the mere fact that the human body and its neighbourhood form a conservative system does not explain any particular bodily movement; it does not explain why I ever move at all, or why I sometimes write, sometimes walk, and sometimes swim. To explain the happening of these particular movements at certain times it seems to be essential to take into account the volitions which happen from time to time in my mind; just as it is essential to take the string into account to explain the particular behaviour of the weight, and to take the trigger into account to explain the going off of the gun at a certain moment. The difference between the gun-system and body-system is that a little energy does flow into the former when the trigger is pulled, whilst it is alleged that none does so when a volition starts a bodily movement. But there is not even this amount of difference between the body-system and the swinging weight.

Thus the argument from energy has no tendency to disprove Two-sided Interaction. It has gained a spurious authority from the august name of the Conservation of Energy. But this impressive principle proves to have nothing to do with the case. And the real premise of the argument is not self-evident, and is not universally true even in purely intra-physical transactions. In the end this scientific argument has to lean on the old philosophic arguments; and we have seen that these are but bruised reeds. Nevertheless, the facts brought forward by the argument from energy do throw some light on the nature of the interaction between mind and body, assuming this to happen. They do suggest that all the energy of our bodily actions comes out of and goes back into the physical world, and that minds neither add energy to nor abstract it from the latter. What they do, if they do anything, is to determine that at a given moment so much energy shall change from the chemical form to the form of bodily movement; and they determine this so far as we can see, without altering the total amount of energy in the physical world.

(2) *The Argument from the Structure of the Nervous System.* There are purely reflex actions, like sneezing and blinking, in which there is no reason to suppose that the mind plays any essential part. Now we know the nervous structure which is used in such acts as these. A stimulus is given to the outer end of an efferent nerve; some change or other runs up this nerve, crosses a synapsis between this and an afferent nerve, travels down the latter to a muscle, causes the muscle to contract,

and so produces a bodily movement. There seems no reason to believe that the mind plays any essential part in this process. The process may be irreducibly vital, and not merely physico-chemical; but there seems no need to assume anything more than this. Now it is said that the whole nervous system is simply an immense complication of inter-connected nervous arcs. The result is that a change which travels in-wards has an immense number of alternative paths by which it may travel outwards. Thus the reaction to a given stimulus is no longer one definite movement, as in the simple reflex. Almost any movement may follow any stimulus according to the path which the afferent disturbance happens to take. This path will depend on the relative resistance of the various synapses at the time. Now a variable response to the same stimu-lus is characteristic of deliberate as opposed to reflex action.

These are the facts. The argument based on them runs as follows. It is admitted that the mind has nothing to do with the causation of purely reflex actions. But the nervous structure and the nervous processes in-volved in deliberate action do not differ in kind from those involved in reflex action; they differ only in degree of complexity. The variability which characterises deliberate action is fully explained by the variety of alternative paths and the variable resistances of the synapses. So it is unreasonable to suppose that the mind has any more to do with causing deliberate actions than it has to do with causing reflex actions.

I think that this argument is invalid. In the first place I am pretty sure that the persons who use it have before their imagination a kind of picture of how mind and body must interact if they interact at all. They find that the facts do not answer to this picture, and so they conclude that there is no interaction. The picture is of the following kind. They think of the mind as sitting somewhere in a hole in the brain, surrounded by telephones. And they think of the efferent disturbance as coming to an end at one of these telephones and there affecting the mind. The mind is then supposed to respond by sending an efferent impulse down another of these telephones. As no such hole, with efferent nerves stopping at its walls and afferent nerves starting from them, can be found, they conclude that the mind can play no part in the transaction. But another alternative is that this picture of how the mind must act if it acts at all is wrong. To put it shortly, the mistake is to confuse a gap in an explanation with a spatio-temporal gap, and to argue from the absence of the latter to the absence of the former.

The Interactionist's contention is imply that there is a gap in any purely physiological explanation of deliberate action; i.e., that all such explanations fail to account completely for the facts because they leave out one necessary condition. It does not follow in the least that there must be a spatio-temporal breach of continuity in the physiological con-ditions, and that the missing condition must fill this gap in the way in which the movement of a wire fills the spatio-temporal interval between the pulling of a bell-handle and the ringing of a distant bell. To assume this is to make the mind a kind of physical object, and to make its action a kind of mechanical action. Really, the mind and its actions are not literally in Space at all, and the time which is occupied by the mental event is no doubt also occupied by some part of the physiological process. Thus I am inclined to think that much of the force which this argument actually exercises on many people is simply due to the presupposition about the modus operandi of interaction, and that it is greatly weakened when this presupposition is shown to be a mere prejudice due to our limited power of envisaging unfamiliar alternative possibilities.

We can, however, make more detailed objections to the argument than this. There is a clear introspective difference between the mental accompaniment of voluntary action and that of reflex action. What goes on in our minds when we decide with difficulty to get out of a hot bath on a cold morning is obviously extremely different from what goes on in our minds when we sniff pepper and sneeze. And the difference is qualitative; it is not a mere difference of complexity. This difference has to be explained somehow; and the theory under discussion gives no plausible explanation of it. The ordinary view that, in the latter case, the mind is not acting on the body at all; whilst, in the former, it is acting on the body in a specific way, does at least make the intro-spective difference between the two intelligible.

Again, whilst it is true that deliberate action differs from reflex action in its greater variability of response to the same stimulus, this is certainly not the whole or the most important part of the difference be-tween them. The really important difference is that, in deliberate action, the response is varied appropriately to meet the special circumstances which are supposed to exist at the time or are expected to arise later; whilst reflex action is not varied in this way, but is blind and almost mechanical. The complexity of the nervous system explains the possi-bility of variation; it does not in the least explain why the alternative which actually takes place should as a rule be appropriate and not merely haphazard. And so again it seems as if some factor were in operation in deliberate action which is not present in reflex action; and it is reasonable to suppose that this factor is the volition in the mind.

It seems to me that this second scientific argument has no tendency to disprove interaction; but that the facts which it brings forward do tend to suggest the particular form which interaction probably takes if it happens at all. They suggest that what the mind does to the body in voluntary action, if it does anything, is to lower the resistance of certain synapses and to raise that of others. The result is that the nervous current follows such a course as to produce the particular movement which the mind judges to be appropriate at the time. On such a view the difference

between reflex, habitual, and deliberate actions for the present purpose
becomes fairly plain. In pure reflexes the mind cannot voluntarily affect
the resistance of the synapses concerned, and so the action takes place
in spite of it. In habitual action it deliberately refrains from interfering
with the resistance of the synapses, and so the action goes on like a
complicated reflex. But it can affect these resistances if it wishes, though
often only with difficulty; and it is ready to do so if it judges this to be
expedient. Finally, it may lose the power altogether. This would be what
happens when a person becomes a slave to some habit, such as drug-
taking.

I conclude that, at the level of enlightened common-sense at which
the ordinary discussion of Interaction moves, no good reason has been
produced for doubting that the mind acts on the body in volition, and
that the body acts on the mind in sensation. The philosophic arguments
are quite inconclusive; and the scientific arguments, when properly understood, are quite compatible with Two-sided Interaction. At most they
suggest certain conclusions as to the form which interaction probably
takes if it happens at all.

Difficulties in the Denial of Interaction

I propose now to consider some of the difficulties which would attend
the denial of Interaction, still keeping the discussion at the same common-
sense level. If a man denies the action of body on mind he is at once in
trouble over the causation of new sensations. Suppose that I suddenly
tread on an unsuspected tin-tack. A new sensation suddenly comes into
my mind. This is an event, and it presumably has some cause. Now,
however carefully I introspect and retrospect, I can find no other mental
event which is adequate to account for the fact that just that sensation
has arisen at just that moment. If I reject the common-sense view that
treading on the tack is an essential part of the cause of the sensation,
I must suppose either that it is uncaused, or that it is caused by other
events in my mind which I cannot discover by introspection or retro-
spection, or that it is caused telepathically by other finite minds or by
God. Now enquiry or my neighbors would show that it is not caused
telepathically by any event in their minds which they can introspect or
remember. Thus anyone who denies the action of body on mind, and
admits that sensations have causes, must postulate either (a) immense
numbers of unobservable states in his own mind; or (b) as many unobservable states in his neighbors' minds, together with telepathic action;
or (c) some non-human spirit together with telepathic action. I must
confess that the difficulties which have been alleged against the action of

body on mind seem to be mild compared with those of the alternative hypotheses which are involved in the denial of such action.

The difficulties which are involved in the denial of the action of mind on body are at first sight equally great; but I do not think that they turn out to be so serious as those which are involved in denying the action of body on mind. The *prima facie* difficulty is this. The world contains many obviously artificial objects, such as books, bridges, clothes, etc. We know that, if we go far enough back in the history of their production, we always do in fact come on the actions of some human body. And the minds connected with these bodies did design the objects in question, did will to produce them, and did believe that they were initiating an guiding the physical process by means of these designs and volitions. If it be true that the mind does not act on the body, it follows that the designs and volitions in the agents' minds did not in fact play any part in the production of books, bridges, clothes, etc. This appears highly paradoxical. And it is an easy step from it to say that anyone who denies the action of mind on body must admit that books, bridges, and other such objects *could* have been produced even though there had been no minds, no thought of these objects and no desire for them. This consequence seems manifestly absurd to common-sense, and it might be argued that it reflects its absurdity back on the theory which entails it.

The man who denies that mind can act on body might deal with this difficulty in two ways: (1) He might deny that the conclusion *is* intrinsically absurd. He might say that human bodies are extraordinarily complex physical objects, which probably obey irreducible laws of their own, and that we really do not know enough about them to set limits to what their unaided powers could accomplish. This is the line which Spinoza took. The conclusion, it would be argued, *seems* absurd only because the state of affairs which it contemplates is so very unfamiliar. We find it difficult to imagine a body like ours without a mind like ours; but, if we could get over this defect in our powers of imagination, we might have no difficulty in admitting that such a body could do all the things which our bodies do. I think it must be admitted that the difficulty is not so great as that which is involved in denying the action of body on mind. There we had to postulate *ad hoc* utterly unfamiliar entities and modes of action; here it is not certain that we should have to do this.

(2) The other line of argument would be to say that the alleged consequence does not necessarily follow from denying the action of mind on body. I assume that both parties admit that causation is something more than mere *de facto* regularity of sequence and concomitance. If they do not, of course the whole controversy between them becomes futile; for there will certainly be causation between mind and body and between body and mind, in the only sense in which there is causation

anywhere. This being presupposed, the following kind of answer is logically possible. When I say that B could not have happened unless A had happened, there are two alternative possibilities. (a) A may itself be an indispensable link in any chain of causes which ends up with B. (b) A may not itself be a link in any chain of causation which ends up in B. But there may be an indispensable link α in any such chain of causation, and A may be a necessary accompaniment or sequent of α. These two possibilities may be illustrated by diagrams. (a) is represented by the figure below:—

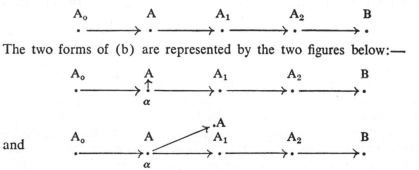

The two forms of (b) are represented by the two figures below:—

and

Evidently, if B cannot happen unless a precedes, and if α cannot happen without A accompanying or immediately following it, B will not be able to happen unless A precedes it. And yet A will have had no part in causing B. It will be noticed that, on this view, α has a complex effect AA_1, of which a certain part, viz., A_1 is sufficient by itself to produce A_2 and ultimately B. Let us apply this abstract possibility to our present problem. Suppose that B is some artificial object, like a book or a bridge. If we admit that this could not have come into existence unless a certain design and volition had existed in a certain mind, we could interpret the facts in two ways. (a) We could hold that the design and volition are themselves an indispensable link in the chain of causation which ends in the production of a bridge or a book. This is the common view, and it requires us to admit the action of mind on body. (b) We might hold that the design and the volition are not themselves a link in the chain of causation which ends in the production of the artificial object; but that they are a necessary accompaniment or sequent of something which is an indispensable link in this chain of causation. On this view the chain consists wholly of physical events; but one of these physical events (viz., some event in the brain) has a complex consequent. One part of this consequent is purely physical, and leads by purely physical causation to the ultimate production of a bridge or a book. The other is purely mental, and consists of a certain design and volition in the mind which animates the human body concerned. If this has any consequences they are purely mental. Each part of this complex consequent follows with equal necessity; this particular brain-state could no more have existed without such and such a mental state accompanying or following it than it could have existed without such and such a bodily movement following it. If we are willing to take some such view as this, we can admit that certain objects could not have existed unless there had been designs of them and desires for them; and yet we could consistently deny that these desires and designs have any effect on the movements of our bodies.

It seems to me then that the doctrine which I will call "One-sided Action of Body on Mind" is logically possible; i.e., a theory which accepts the action of body on mind but denies the action of mind on body. But I do not see the least reason to accept it, since I see no reason to deny that mind acts on body in volition. One-sided Action has, I think, generally been held in the special form called "Epiphenomenalism." I take this doctrine to consist of the following four propositions: (1) Certain bodily events cause certain mental events. (2) No mental event plays any part in the causation of any bodily event. (3) No mental event plays any part in the causation of any other mental event. Consequently (4) all mental events are caused by bodily events and by them only. Thus Epiphenomenalism is just One-sided Action of Body on Mind, together with a special theory about the nature and structure of mind. This special theory does not call for discussion here, where I am dealing only with the relations between minds and bodies, and am not concerned with a detailed analysis of mind. . . .

Arguments in Favor of Interaction

The only arguments *for* One-sided Action of Body on Mind or for Parallelism are the arguments *against* Two-sided Interaction; and these, as we have seen, are worthless. Are there any arguments in favour of Two-sided Interaction? I have incidentally given two which seem to me to have considerable weight. In favour of the action of mind on body is the fact that we seem to be immediately aware of a causal relation when we voluntarily try to produce a bodily movement, and that the arguments to show that this cannot be true are invalid.* In favour of the action of body on mind are the insuperable difficulties which I have pointed out in accounting for the happening of new sensations on any other hypothesis. There are, however, two other arguments which have

---

* Broad here refers to a discussion on pp. 100-103 of *The Mind and Its Place in Nature* which is not reproduced in our selection. (Eds.)

often been thought to prove the action of mind on body. These are (1) an evolutionary argument, first used, I believe, by William James; and (2) the famous "telegram argument." They both seem to me to be quite obviously invalid.

(1) The evolutionary argument runs as follows: It is a fact, which is admitted by persons who deny Two-sided Interaction, that minds increase in complexity and power with the growth in complexity of the brain and nervous system. Now, if the mind makes no difference to the actions of the body, this development on the mental side is quite unintelligible from the point of view of natural selection. Let us imagine two animals whose brains and nervous systems were of the same degree of complexity; and suppose, if possible, that one had a mind and the other had none. If the mind makes no difference to the behavior of the body the chance of survival and of leaving descendants will clearly be the same for the two animals. Therefore natural selection will have no tendency to favor the evolution of mind which has actually taken place. I do not think that there is anything in this argument. Natural selection is a purely negative process; it simply tends to eliminate individuals and species which have variations unfavourable to survival. Now, by hypothesis, the possession of a mind is not *unfavorable* to survival; it simply makes no difference. Now it may be that the existence of a mind of such and such a kind is an inevitable consequence of the existence of a brain and nervous system of such and such a degree of complexity. Indeed we have seen that some such view is essential if the opponent of Two-sided Interaction is to answer the common-sense objection that artificial objects could not have existed unless there had been a mind which designed and desired them. On this hypothesis there is no need to invoke natural selection twice over, once to explain the evolution of the brain and nervous system, and once to explain the evolution of the mind. If natural selection will account for the evolution of the brain and nervous system, the evolution of the mind will follow inevitably, even though it adds nothing to the survival-value of the organism. The plain fact is that natural selection does not account for the origin or for the growth in complexity of anything whatever; and therefore it is no objection to any particular theory of the relations of mind and body that, if it were true, natural selection would not explain the origin and development of mind.

(2) The "telegram argument" is as follows: Suppose there were two telegrams, one saying "Our son has been killed," and the other saying: "Your son has been killed." And suppose that one or other of them was delivered to a parent whose son was away from home. As physical stimuli they are obviously extremely alike, since they differ only in the fact that the letter "Y" is present in one and absent in the other. Yet we know that the reaction of the person who received the telegram

might be very different according to which one he received. This is supposed to show that the reactions of the body cannot be wholly accounted for by bodily causes, and that the mind must intervene causally in some cases. Now I have very little doubt that the mind does play a part in determining the action of the recipient of the telegram; but I do not see why this argument should prove it to a person who doubted or denied it. If two very similar stimuli are followed by two very different results, we are no doubt justified in concluding that these stimuli are not the complete causes of the reactions which follow them. But of course it would be admitted by every one that the receipt of the telegram is not the complete cause of the recipient's reaction. We all know that his brain and nervous system play an essential part in any reaction that he may make to the stimulus. The question then is whether the minute structure of his brain and nervous system, including in this the supposed traces left by past stimuli and past reactions, is not enough to account for the great difference in his behaviour on receiving two very similar stimuli. Two keys may be very much alike, but one may fit a certain lock and the other may not. And, if the lock be connected with the trigger of a loaded gun, the results of "stimulating" the system with one or other of the two keys will be extremely different. We know that the brain and nervous system are very complex, and we commonly suppose that they contain more or less permanent traces and linkages due to past stimuli and reactions. If this be granted, it is obvious that two very similar stimuli may produce very different results, simply because one fits in with the internal structure of the brain and nervous system whilst the other does not. And I do not see how we can be sure that anything more is needed to account for the mere difference of reaction adduced by the "telegram argument." . . .

19

TEN REASONS FOR
BELIEVING IN IMMORTALITY

John Haynes Holmes

NOBODY CAN SPEAK on the immortality of the soul at this late date without being acutely conscious of the fact that there is nothing new that can be said. Since the time of Plato, at least, five hundred years before the birth of Jesus, the discussion of immortality has been conducted by the greatest minds upon the highest levels of human thought. Theology, philosophy, psychology and science have all been called upon to make their contributions to the theme. Poetry has offered its voice and religion its faith, with the result that every corner of knowledge has been explored, every depth of truth uncovered and revealed! There is always the possibility, of course, that the veil which hangs over every grave to divide this life from the mystery that lies beyond, may some day be lifted to our gaze. There are those who claim—not without some reason, it seems to me—that they have penetrated this veil, and thus have looked upon the reality of survival after death. But short of some such remarkable discovery as this, there is nothing new to be anticipated in this field. Everything has been said that can be said. The case for immortality is in!

Now it is this case which I want to present to you this morning. Since I cannot hope to say anything that is new, I want to see what I can do in the way of saying something that is old. I cannot say much, to be sure, for no discourse however merciless in length, can compass the range and beauty of the argument for immortality. But since ten is a goodly number, I take ten of the reasons which have brought conviction to the minds of men and offer these as the case for immortality today. I

[This essay was first delivered as a sermon at the Community Church in 1929 and published in the *Community Pulpit* for 1929-1930. It is here reprinted with the kind permission of Dr. Holmes.]

trust that it may be interesting, and also persuasive, especially to the members of our younger generation, to be reminded of what has been thought upon this question for many years.

By way of introduction, may I make mention of some two or three reasons for believing in immortality which do not concern me. I speak of these not because they are important, but because some of you may wonder, if I am silent, why they do not appear in my list of ten.

Thus I do not see any reason for believing in immortality because Jesus is reputed to have risen from the dead. In the first place, I do not believe that he rose from the dead. There is no evidence to substantiate this miracle. In the second place, even if he did break the barriers of the tomb, I fail to see what the resurrection of the body has to do with the immortality of the soul. The two things are irrelevant, the one to the other. What we have here is one of the myths of Christianity which, even if it were true, would have nothing seriously to do with our question.

Again, I find no argument for immortality in the succession of the seasons, the revival of nature in the spring, the blossoming of the flowers after the winter's cold. Poets are fond of this idea, as Shelley, for example, when he wrote his famous line,

> If winter comes, can spring be far behind.

I think we may see in it a pretty parable, a rather beautiful poetic concept. But as an argument for immortality, it is what Ruskin called an instance of the "pathetic fallacy." The flowers that blossom in the spring are not the flowers that died the preceding autumn. The tide of life that flows on through nature, season after season, is the same tide that flows on through humanity, generation after generation, and it touches as little in the one case as in the other the survival of the individual. Like most parables, this does not hold when applied rigorously to the issue that is involved.

Again, I must confess that I am not convinced by the argument that men must be immortal because the heart demands it. It is natural that we should cling to those we love. It is inevitable that we should believe that providence, if it be beneficent, must give answer to our plea that we have not permanently separated from our friends and kindred. Whittier was yielding to the deepest impulses of the soul when he suggested in his "Snow Bound" that "Life is ever Lord of Death," because "Love can never lose its own." This is the cry of the human heart, and I personally believe that it is not destined to go unanswered. But a longing is one thing, and a reason is another. I see no evidence, in the scheme of things, that what we want we are therefore going to have. On the contrary, Felix Adler has taught us that frustration is the basic principle of life, that experience is "permeated with the sense of incompleteness," and that this "sense of incompleteness" is a perpetual doom that is laid upon us as "a necessary instrument of spiritual development." Whether this be true or not I do not know, but in either case I still believe that love gives no guarantee of its own survival.

But there are arguments for immortality which seem to suggest that it is true. Surveying all the field, I find myself agreeing with William James that, while we are under no compulsion to believe in immortality, as we are under a compulsion, for example, to believe that "things equal to the same thing are equal to each other," yet we are free to believe, if we so desire, without being guilty of superstition. "You may believe henceforward," said Professor James, "whether you care to profit by the permission or not." There are perfectly good and sufficient reasons, in other words, why an intelligent man may intelligently believe in immortality. Ten of these reasons I propose to submit to you this morning, beginning with those which open up the question, so to speak, and ending with those which close it as a conviction of the soul.

(1) First of all, may I offer the suggestion, not important in itself and yet of real significance to the thinking mind, that we may believe in immortality because there is no reason for *not* believing in it. In discussions of this question we are constantly reminded that immortality has never been proved. To which there is the immediate and inevitable reply that immortality has never been disproved! As there is no positive testimony to prove it true, so is there no negative testimony to prove it untrue. What we have here is an absence of testimony, and such "absence of testimony," says John Fiske, "does not even raise a negative presumption, except in cases where testimony is accessible." In this case, testimony is not accessible. Therefore the question is open "for those general considerations of philosophic analogy and moral probability which are the grounds upon which we can call for help in this arduous inquiry." As the question is open, so must our minds be open. My first reason, therefore, for believing in immortality or for being ready to believe in immortality, is the primarily interesting fact that there is no reason for not believing in immortality. My mind is absolutely at one with that of John Stuart Mill when he said upon his question, "To anyone who feels it conducive either to his satisfaction or to his usefulness to hope for a future state, . . . there is no hindrance to his indulging that hope."

(2) My second reason for believing in immortality is to be found in the universality of the idea. In saying this, I am not seeking to substantiate my position by taking a majority vote upon the question. I am not arguing that a proposition is necessarily true because most persons have believed it. All too many beliefs have clung pertinaciously to the human mind, only in the end to be revealed as superstitions, and it may very well be that this concept of immortality is one of them.

What I have in mind here is the very different consideration that immortality is not merely a belief to be accepted but an idea to be explained. "Here is this wonderful thought," says Emerson, "Wherever man ripens, this audacious belief presently appears. . . . As soon as thought is exercised, this belief is inevitable. . . . Whence came it? Who put it in the mind?" In itself it is remarkable, this idea that the death of the body is not the extinction of personality. Who has ever looked upon a dead body without marvelling that man has ever thought of survival beyond the grave? Emerson could not explain the fact, as it has appeared in all ages and among all peoples, except upon the supposition that the thought of immortality is "not sentimental" but "elemental"—elemental in the sense that it is "grounded in the necessities and forces we possess."

That this idea is something more than idle speculation is shown by the whole philosophy of evolution, which has given to us that fundamental interpretation of life as "the continuous adjustment of inner relations to outer relations." An organism lives by successfully adjusting itself to the conditions of its environment, by developing itself inwardly in such a way as to meet the conditions of reality. When we find in plant or animal some inner faculty or attitude which is universally present, and which persists from generation to generation, we may be perfectly sure that it represents some correspondence with reality which has made survival possible. Life, in other words, is so definitely a matter of the successful coordination of inner relations with outer relations, that it is altogether impossible to conceive that in any specific relation the subjective term is real and the objective term is non-existent. What exists within is the sign and symbol, and guarantee, of what exists without.

Now man has never existed without the thought of immortality. From the earliest period of his life upon the earth, he has been profoundly concerned with this idea. He has never been able to live without it; even when he has tried to deny it, he has not been able to get rid of it. The immortal life is part of his being, as a line on the surface of a coin is a part of the pattern of its design. And as the line upon the coin could not have been set there except as the impression of the die which stamped its mark upon the metal, so the idea of immortality could not have appeared within the consciousness of man, except as the impression of the reality which made it what it is. Our faculties, our attributes, our ideas, as we have seen, are the reflection of the environment to which we adapt ourselves as the condition of survival. What we feel within is the reaction upon what exists without. As the eye proves the existence of light, and the ear the existence of sound, so the immortal hope may not unfairly be said to prove the existence of the immortal life. It is this that we mean when we say that the universality of the idea is an argument for the acceptance of the idea. In his great essay on "Immortality," Emerson tells us of two men who early in life spent much of their time together in earnest search for some proof of immortality. An accident separated them, and they did not meet again for a quarter of a century. They said nothing, "but shook hands long and cordially. At last his friend said, 'Any light, Albert?' 'None,' replied Albert. 'Any light,' Lewis?' 'None,' he replied." And Emerson comments "that the impulse which drew these two minds to this inquiry through so many years was a better affirmative evidence for immortality than their failure to find a confirmation was a negative."

(3) This universal diffusion of the idea of immortality takes on an added significance when I come to my third reason for believing in immortality. I refer to the fact so memorably stated by Cicero. "There is in the minds of men," he says, "I know not how, a certain presage, as it were, of a future existence; and this takes deepest root in the greatest geniuses and the most exalted souls." The leaders of the race, in other words, have always believed in immortality. They are not separated in this case, as in so many cases, from the masses of ignorant and superstitous men by doctrines of dissent. On the contrary, in this case the ideas of the highest are at one with the hopes of the humblest among mankind.

In referring thus to the great names that are attached to the idea of immortality, I would not have you believe that I am making any blind appeal to the concept of authority. I have never seen any reason for arbitrarily separating our minds from the companionship of other minds. There is such a thing, even for the independent thinker, as a consensus of best opinion which can not be defied without the weightiest of reasons. And in this matter of immortality there is a consensus of best opinion which constitutes, to my mind, one of the most remarkable phenomena in the whole history of human thinking. I have no time this morning to list the names of those who have believed in the immortality of the soul. If I did so, I should have to include the names of scientists from Aristotle to Darwin and Eddington, of philosophers from Plato to Kant and Bergson, of poets from Sophocles to Goethe and Robert Browning, of ethical teachers and public leaders from Socrates to Tolstoi and Mahatma Gandhi. There are dissenters from the doctrine, like Epictetus yesterday and Bernard Shaw to-day, but the consensus of opinion the other way is remarkable. Even the famous heretics stand in awe before this conception of eternity. Thus, Voltaire declared that "reason agrees with revelation . . . that the soul is immortal." Thomas Paine affirmed that he did not "trouble (himself) about the manner of future existence," so sure he was that "the Power which gave existence is able to continue it in any form." Even Robert G. Ingersoll confessed, as he stood by his brother's grave, that love could "hear the rustle of an angel's wing." In the light of such testimony as this, are we not justified in believing that there is reason for believing in immortality? If not, then we know, with James Martineau, "who are those who are mistaken. Not the mean and grovelling souls who never reached to so great a thought. . . . No, the deceived are the great and holy, whom all men revere; the men who have lived for something better than their happiness and spent themselves on the altar of human good. Whom are we to reverence, and what can we believe, if the inspirations of the highest nature are but cunningly-devised fables?"

(4) This conviction of immortality as rooted in the minds of men, and the greatest men, brings us immediately to the consideration of human nature itself as evidence for its own survival. Thus, my fourth reason this morning for believing in immortality is found in what I would call man's over-endowment as a creature of this earth, his surplus equipment for the adventure of his present life. If we want to know what is needed for successful existence upon this planet, we have only to look at any animal. His equipment of physical attributes and powers seems perfectly adapted to the necessities of his natural environment. The outfit of man, on the contrary, seems to constitute something like "a vast over-provision" for his necessities. If this life is all, in other words, what need has man for all these mental faculties, moral aspirations, spiritual ideals, which make him to be distinctly a man as contrasted with the animal? If existence upon the earth is his only destiny, why should man not prefer the swiftness of the deer, the strength of the lion, the vision of the eagle, to any endowment of mind and heart, as more adequate provision for the purely physical task of physical survival in a physical world? What we have here is a fundamental discrepancy between the endowment of man and the life he has to live; and this constitutes, if this life be all, an unparalleled violation of the creative economy of the universe. In every other form of life, an organism is equipped to meet the exactions of its immediate environment. Man is equipped for this environment, and also for something more. Why is this not proof that he is destined for something more? As we estimate the length of the voyage of a ship by the character of its equipment, never confusing a little coasting vessel with a transatlantic liner or an arctic exploration steamer, why should we not estimate the length of man's voyage upon the seas of life in exactly the same way? What man bears within himself is evidence that he is destined for some farther port than any upon these shores. What he is in mind and heart and spirit, in the range of his interests and the lift of his soul, can only be explained on the supposition that he is preparing for another and a vaster life. I believe that man is immortal because already the signs of immortality are upon him.

(5) This consideration is basic, and sums up our whole case for immortality as rooted in human nature. But it opens out into other considerations which may well be taken as other reasons for believing in immortality. Thus, I would specify as my fifth reason for believing in immortality the lack of coordination, or proportion, between a man's

body and a man's mind. If these two are to be regarded as aspects of a single organism, adapted only to the conditions of this present life, why do they so early begin to pull apart, and the weakness of the one to retard and at last to defeat the other? For a while, to be sure, there seems to be a real coordination between soul and body, between the personality, on the one hand, and the physical frame which it inhabits, on the other. Thus the child is in nothing so delightful as in the fact that it is a perfect animal. Then, as maturity approaches, two exactly opposite processes begin to take place within the life of the human being. On the one hand, the body begins to lose its resiliency and harden, to stop its growth and become static, then to decay and at last to dissolve. There is a definite cycle, in other words, in the physical life of the individual. There is a beginning, then a pause, and then an end. It is from first to last a process of completion. But there is no completion in the life of the soul. "Who dares speak the word 'completed,'" says Professor Munsterberg, the great psychologist. "Do not our purposes grow? Does not every newly-created value give us the desire for further achievement? Is our life ever so completely done that no desire has still a meaning?" The personality of man is an enduring thing. As the body weakens through the years, so the soul only grows the stronger and more wonderful. As the body approaches irrevocably to its end, so the soul only mounts to what seems to be a new beginning. We come to death, in other words, only to discover within ourselves exhaustless possibilities. The aged have testified again and again to this amazing truth that as the body turns to ashes, the spirit mounts as to a flame. Victor Hugo, protesting against the waning of his powers, said, "For half a century I have been writing my thoughts in prose and verse . . . but I feel that I have not said a thousandth part of what is in me." Said James Martineau, on his 80th birthday, "How small a part of my plans have I been able to carry out! Nothing is so plain as that life at its fullest on earth is but a fragment." Robert Browning catches this thought in his poem, "Cleon," where he makes his hero say,

> . . . Every day my sense of joy
> Grows more acute, my soul . . . enlarged, more keen,
> While every day my hairs fall more and more,
> My hand shakes, and the heavy years increase
> The horror quickening still from year to year,
> When I shall know most, and yet least enjoy.

What to do, in such emergency, except what Cleon did,

> . . . imagine to (our) need
> Some future state . . .

(6) But there is a lack of coordination not only between our personalities and our physical bodies, but also between our personalities and

the physical world. This is my sixth reason for believing in immortality—that our souls have potentialities and promises which should not, as indeed they cannot, be subject to the chance vicissitudes of earthly fortune. What are we going to say, for example, when we see some life of eminent utility, of great achievement, of character and beauty and noble dedication to mankind, not merely borne down by the body, but cut off sharply before its time by an automobile accident, a disease germ, a bit of poisoned food: What shall we think when we see a Shelley drowned in his thirtieth year by the heedless sea, a Phillips Brooks stricken in the prime of his manhood by a diptheric sore-throat, a Captain Scott frozen in mid-career by an accident of weather? Is it possible that these lives of ours are dependent upon a fall of snow, a grain of dust, a passing breeze upon the sea? Is it conceivable that our personalities, with all their potencies of spirit, can be destroyed, as our bodies can be broken, by the material forces of the world? Are we to believe that eternal powers can be annihilated by transient accidents? I cannot think so! Rather must I think, as Professor George Herbert Palmer thought, as he looked upon the dead body of his wife, one of the greatest and most beautiful women of her time, stricken ere her years were ripe. "Though no regrets are proper for the manner of her death," said this noble husband, "yet who can contemplate the fact of it and not call the world irrational if, out of deference to a few particles of disordered matter, it excludes so fair a spirit?"

(7) But this question of the irrationality of a world which would allow death to exercise mastery over a radiant spirit, has application not merely to the individual but also to the race. This brings me to my seventh reason for believing in immortality—a reason drawn from the logic of evolution. There is nothing more familiar, of course, than the fact that this world is the result of a natural process of development which has been going on for unnumbered millions of years. If this process is rational, as man's processes are rational, it must have been working all these aeons of time to the achievement of some permanent and worthy end. What is this end? It is not the physical world itself, for the day must come when this earth will be swallowed up by the sun, and all the universe be merged again into the original fire-mist from which it sprang. It is not the works of man, for these perish even as man lives, and must vanish utterly in the last cataclysm of ruin. It is not man himself, for man, like the earth on which he lives, must finally disappear. Is there nothing that will remain as the evidence and vindication of this cosmic process? Or must we believe that, from the beginning, it has been like a child's tower of blocks built up only to be thrown down?

It was the challenge of this contingency, of evolution coming in the end to naught that moved no less a man than Charles Darwin, agnostic though he was, to proclaim the conviction that "it is an intolerable thought that (man) and all other sentient beings are doomed to complete annihilation after such long-continued slow process." Unless the universe is crazy, something must remain. The process must justify itself by producing something that endures. And what can this thing be but the spiritual essence of man's nature—the soul which is immortal? "The more thoroughly we comprehend the process of evolution," says John Fiske, in an unforgettable statement, "the more we are likely to feel that to deny the everlasting persistence of the spiritual element in man is to rob the whole process of its meaning. It goes far toward putting us to permanent intellectual confusion." Which led him to his famous verdict upon all the evidence: "I believe in the immortality of the soul as a supreme act of faith in the reasonableness of God's work."

(8) This leads us deep into the realm of science—to a fundamental principle that provides my eighth reason for believing in immortality. I refer to the principle of persistence or conservation. The gist of this doctrine is that nothing in the universe is ever lost. All energy is conserved. No matter what changes take place in any particular form of energy, that energy persists, if not in the old form then in a new, and the sum total of energy in the universe remains the same. "Whatever is," says Sir Oliver Lodge, speaking of forms of energy in the physical universe, "whatever is, both was and shall be." And he quotes the famous statement of Professor Tait, that "persistence, or conservation, is the test or criterion of real existence."

Now if this principle applies to the "real existence" of the material world, why not to the "real existence" of the spiritual world as well? If it is impossible to think of physical energy as appearing and disappearing, coming into and going out of existence, why is it not equally impossible to think of intellectual or moral or spiritual energy as acting in this same haphazard fashion? We would laugh at a man who contended that the heat in molten metal, which disappears under the cooling action of air or water, had thereby been destroyed. Why should we not similarly laugh at a man who argues that the personality of a human being, which disappears under the chilling influence of death, has thereby been annihilated? What the personality may be, I do not know. Whether it is a form of energy itself, as some scientists assert, or "belongs to a separate order of existence," as Sir Oliver Lodge, for example, argues, I cannot say. But of this thing I am sure—that the soul of man is just as much a force in the world as magnetism or steam, or electricity, and that if the cosmic law of conservation forbids the destruction of the latter, it must as well forbid the destruction of the former. Anything else is inconceivable. The universe cannot be so thrifty of its physical, and so wasteful of its spiritual, resources. It is madness to conceive that the heat of an engine must be preserved, while the love of a heart may be thrown away. What prevails in the great realm of matter can be only an anticipation of what must equally prevail in the greater realm of spirit. For the universe is one. Its laws are everywhere the same. What science has discovered about the conservation of energy is only the physical equivalent of what religion has discovered about the immortality of the soul.

(9) We are coming now to ultimate things—to those first and last questions of origins and meanings. This brings me to my ninth reason for believing in immortality—the fact, namely, that all the values of life exist in man, and in man alone. For the world as we know it and love it is not the world as we receive it, but the world as we make it by the creative genius of the inward spirit. Consider this earthly scene with man eliminated! The sun would be here, and the stars. Mountains would still lift themselves to the skies, and oceans spread afar to vast horizons. Birds would sing, and leaves rustle, and sunsets glow. But what would it all mean without man to see and hear, to interpret? What do the stars mean to the eagle, or the sea to the porpoise, or the mountain to the goat? It is man's ear which has heard the cuckoo as a "wandering voice," his eye which has seen "the floor of heaven thick inlaid with patines of bright gold," his mind which has found "sermons in stone, books in the running brooks, and good in everything." All that is precious in the world—all its beauty, its wonder, its meaning—exists in man, and by man, and for man. The world is what man has done with it in the far reaches of his soul. And we are asked to believe that the being who sees and glorifies shall perish, while the world which he has seen and glorified endures! Such a conclusion is irrational. The being who created the world must himself be greater than the world. The soul which conceives Truth, Goodness and Beauty, must itself be as eternal as the Truth, Goodness, and Beauty which it conceives. Nothing has any value without man. Man, therefore, is the supreme value. Which is the essence of the Platonic philosophy of eternal life for man!

"Tell me, then," says Socrates in the "Phaedo," "what is that the inherence of which renders the body alive?

"The soul, Cebes replied . . .

"Then whatever the soul possesses, to that she comes bearing life?

"Yes, certainly.

"And is there any opposite to life?

"There is . . . Death.

"And will the soul . . . ever receive the opposite of what she brings?

"Impossible, replied Cebes.

"Then, said Socrates, the soul is immortal!"

(10) These, now, are my main reasons for believing in immortality. I have but one more, the tenth to add. It is the pragmatic argument that faith in an eternal life beyond the grave justifies itself in terms of the life that we are now living upon this side of the grave. For immortality does not concern the future alone; it concerns, also, the present. We are immortal today, if we are ever going to be immortal tomorrow. And this means that we have the chance to put to the test, even now and here, the belief

to which we hold. It is the essence of the pragmatic philosophy that what is true will conduce to life, as food conduces to health, and that what is false will destroy life, as poison the body. Whatever is true enlarges and lifts and strengthens the life of man; whatever is false represses and weakens and disintegrates his life. Now what does immortality do when we puts its affirmation to this test? What are the consequences which follow if we live as though we were eternal spirits? Can there be any doubt as to the answer?

We see a universe where spiritual values, not material forces, prevail; where personality, whether in ourselves or in others, is precious, and therefore to be conserved; where principles, not possessions, are the supreme concern of life; where man is equal to his task, and labors not in vain for the high causes of humanity; where sacrifice is not foolish but wise, and love "the greatest thing in the world." The man who lives an immortal life takes on immortal qualities. His character assumes the proportions of his faith, and his work the range of his high destiny. "Immortality makes great living," says Dr. Fosdick. Therefore I believe in immortality.

Ten reasons! Are these all? No, they are not all! They are simply ten of the many reasons for the most persistent faith which has ever beset the heart of man. In choosing these ten, I have sought to gather reasons which were reasons, and not mere superstitions—arguments which appeal to intellect rather than emotion, and which are based upon experience rather than credulity. That these reasons prove the idea of immortality to be true, I cannot claim. But there is many an idea which we accept for good reasons, even though it be not proved, as there is many a verdict in court which is returned for good reasons, even though it be not proved, and immortality is one of them. What impresses me, as I follow the course of this great argument through the ages, is what impressed the mind of James Martineau when he said, "We do not believe immortality because we have proved it, but we forever try to prove it because we believe it." Hence the judgment of the poet, Tennyson—

> O, yet we trust that somehow good
>   Will be the final goal of ill,
>   To pangs of nature, sins of will,
> Defects of doubt, and taints of blood.
>
> That nothing walks with aimless feet;
>   That not one life shall be destroyed,
>   Or cast as rubbish to the void,
> When God hath made the pile complete. . . .
>
> I stretch lame hands of faith, and grope
>   And gather dust and chaff, and call
>   To what I feel is Lord of all,
> And faintly trust the larger hope.

20

IS LIFE AFTER
DEATH POSSIBLE?

C. J. Ducasse

THE QUESTION whether human personality survives death is sometimes asserted to be one upon which reflection is futile. Only empirical evidence, it is said, can be relevant, since the question is purely one of fact.

But no question is purely one of fact until it is clearly understood; and this one is, on the contrary, ambiguous and replete with tacit assumptions. Until the ambiguities have been removed and the assumptions critically examined, we do not really know just what it is we want to know when we ask whether a life after death is possible. Nor, therefore, can we tell until then what bearing on this question various facts empirically known to us may have.

To clarify its meaning is chiefly what I now propose to attempt. I shall ask first why a future life is so generally desired and believed in. Then I shall state, as convincingly as I can in the time available, the arguments commonly advanced to prove that such a life is impossible. After that, I shall consider the logic of these arguments, and show that they quite fail to establish, the impossibility. Next, the tacit but arbitrary assumption, which makes them nevertheless appear convincing, will be pointed out. And finally, I shall consider briefly a number of specific forms which a life after death might take, if there is one.

Let us turn to the first of these tasks.

Why Man Desires Life After Death

To begin with, let us note that each of us here has been alive and conscious at all times in the past which he can remember. It is true that

[This selection is the Agnes E. and Constantine E. A. Foerster Lecture delivered at the University of Califorma at Berkeley in May, 1947. The concluding section, dealing with the forms which the after-life might take, has been omitted. The lecture is here reprinted with the kind permission of Professor Ducasse.]

sometimes our bodies are in deep sleep, or made inert by anesthetics or injuries. But even at such times we do not experience unconsciousness in ourselves, for to experience it would mean being conscious of being unconscious, and this is a contradiction. The only experience of unconsciousness in ourselves we ever have is, not experience of total unconsciousness, but of unconsciousness *of this or that;* as when we report: "I am not conscious of any pain," or "of any bell-sound," or "of any difference between those two colors," etc. Nor do we ever experience unconsciousness in another person, but only the fact that, sometimes, some or all of the ordinary activities of his body cease to occur. That consciousness itself is extinguished at such times is thus only a hypothesis which we construct to account for certain changes in the behavior of another person's body or to explain in him or in ourselves the eventual lack of memories relating to the given period.

Being alive and conscious is thus, with all men, a lifelong experience and habit; and conscious life is therefore something they naturally— even if tacitly—expect to continue. As J. B. Pratt has pointed out, the child takes the continuity of life for granted. It is the fact of death that has to be taught him. But when he has learned it, and the idea of a future life is then put explicitly before his mind, it seems to him the most natural thing in the world.[1]

The witnessing of death, however, is a rare experience for most of us, and, because it breaks so sharply into our habits, it forces on us the question whether the mind, which until then was manifested by the body now dead, continues somehow to live on, or, on the contrary, has become totally extinct. This question is commonly phrased as concerning "the immortality of the soul," and immortality, strictly speaking, means survival forever. But assurance of survival for some considerable period —say a thousand, or even a hundred, years—would probably have almost as much present psychological value as would assurance of survival strictly forever. Most men would be troubled very little by the idea of extinction at so distant a time—even less troubled than is now a healthy and happy youth by the idea that he will die in fifty or sixty years. Therefore, it is survival for some time, rather than survival specifically forever, that I shall alone consider.

The craving for continued existence is very widespread. Even persons who believe that death means complete extinction of the individual's consciousness often find comfort in various substitute conceptions of survival. They may, for instance, dwell on the continuity of the individual's germ plasm in his descendants. Or they find solace in the thought that, the past being indestructible, their individual life remains eternally an intrinsic part of the history of the world. Also—and more satisfying to one's craving for personal importance—there is the fact that since

1. J. B. Pratt, *The Religious Consciousness*, p. 225.

the acts of one's life have effects, and these in turn further effects, and so on, therefore what one has done goes on forever influencing remotely, and sometimes greatly, the course of future events.

Gratifying to one's vanity, too, is the prospect that, if the achievements of one's life have been great or even only conspicuous, or one's benefactions or evil deeds have been notable, one's name may not only be remembered by acquaintances and relatives for a little while, but may live on in recorded history. But evidently survival in any of these senses is but a consolation prize—but a thin substitute for the continuation of conscious individual life, which may not be a fact, but which most men crave nonetheless.

The roots of this craving are certain desires which death appears to frustrate. For some, the chief of these is for reunion with persons dearly loved. For others, whose lives have been wretched, it is the desire for another chance at the happiness they have missed. For others yet, it is desire for further opportunity to grow in ability, knowledge or character. Often, there is also the desire, already mentioned, to go on counting for something in the affairs of men. And again, a future life for oneself and others is often desired in order that the redressing of the many injustices of this life shall be possible. But it goes without saying that, although desires such as these are often sufficient to cause belief in a future life, they constitute no evidence at all that it is a fact.

In this connection, it may be well to point out that, although both the belief in survival and the belief in the existence of a god or gods are found in most religions, nevertheless there is no necessary connection between the two beliefs. No contradiction would be involved in supposing either that there is a God but no life after death or that there is a life after death but no God. The belief that there is a life after death may be tied to a religion, but it is no more intrinsically religious than would be a belief that there is life on the planet Mars. The after-death world, if it exists, is just another region or dimension of the universe.

But although belief in survival of death is natural and easy and has always been held in one form or another by a large majority of mankind, critical reflection quickly brings forth a number of apparently strong reasons to regard that belief as quite illusory. Let us now review them.

The Arguments Against Survival

There are, first of all, a number of facts which definitely suggest that both the existence and the nature of consciousness wholly depend on the presence of a functioning nervous system. It is pointed out, for example, that wherever consciousness is observed, it is found associated with a living and functioning body. Further, when the body dies, or the head is struck a heavy blow, or some anesthetic is administered, the familiar outward evidences of consciousness terminate, permanently or temporarily. Again, we know well that drugs of various kinds—alcohol, caffein, opium, heroin, and many others—cause specific changes at the time in the nature of a person's mental states. Also, by stimulating in appropriate ways the body's sense organs, corresponding states of consciousness—namely, the various kinds of sensations—can be caused at will. On the other hand, cutting a sensory nerve immediately eliminates a whole range of sensations.

Again, the contents of consciousness, the mental powers, or even the personality, are modified in characteristic ways when certain regions of the brain are destroyed by disease or injury or are disconnected from the rest by such an operation as prefrontal lobotomy. And that the nervous system is the indispensable basis of mind is further suggested by the fact that, in the evolutionary scale, the degree of intelligence of various species of animals keeps pace closely with the degree of development of their brain.

That continued existence of mind after death is impossible has been argued also on the basis of theoretical considerations. It has been contended, for instance, that what we call states of consciousness—or more particularly, ideas, sensations, volitions, feelings, and the like—are really nothing but the minute physical or chemical events which take place in the tissues of the brain. For, it is urged, it would be absurd to suppose that an idea or a volition, if it is not itself a material thing or process, could cause material effects such as contractions of muscles.

Moreover, it is maintained that the possibility of causation of a material event by an immaterial, mental cause is ruled out *a priori* by the principle of the conservation of energy; for such causation would mean that an additional quantity of energy suddenly pops into the nervous system out of nowhere.

Another conception of consciousness, which is more often met with today than the one just mentioned, but which also implies that consciousness cannot survive death, is that "consciousness" is only the name we give to certain types of behavior, which differentiate the higher animals from all other things in nature. According to this view, to say, for example, that an animal is conscious of a difference between two stimuli means nothing more than that it responds to each by different behavior. That is, the difference of *behavior* is what consciousness of difference between the stimuli *consists in;* and is not, as is commonly assumed, only the behavioral *sign* of something mental and not public, called "consciousness that the stimuli are different."

Or again, consciousness, of the typically human sort called thought, is identified with the typically human sort of behavior called speech; and this, again not in the sense that speech *expresses* or *manifests* something different from itself, called "thought," but in the sense that speech—whether uttered or only whispered—*is* thought itself. And obviously, if thought, or any mental activity, is thus but some mode of behavior of the living body, the mind cannot possibly survive death.

Still another difficulty confronting the hypothesis of survival becomes evident when one imagines in some detail what survival would have to include in order to satisfy the\ desires which cause man to crave it. It would, of course, have to include persistence not alone of consciousness, but also of personality; that is, of the individual's character, acquired knowledge, cultural skills and interests, memories, and awareness of personal identity. But even this would not be enough, for what man desires is not bare survival, but to go on living in some objective way. And this means to go on meeting new situations and, by exerting himself to deal with them, to broaden and deepen his experience and develop his latent capacities.

But it is hard to imagine this possible without a body and an environment for it, upon which to act and from which to receive impressions. And, if a body and an environment were supposed, but not material and corruptible ones, then it is paradoxical to think that, under such radically different conditions, a given personality could persist.[2]

To take a crude but telling analogy, it is past belief that, if the body of any one of us were suddenly changed into that of a shark or an octopus, and placed in the ocean, his personality could, for more than a very short time, if at all, survive intact so radical a change of environment and of bodily form.

The Arguments Examined

Such, in brief, are the chief reasons commonly advanced for holding that survival is impossible. Scrutiny of them, however, will, I think, reveal that they are not as strong as they first seem and far from strong enough to show that there can be no life after death.

Let us consider first the assertion that "thought," or "consciousness," is but another name for subvocal speech, or for some other form of behavior, or for molecular processes in the tissues of the brain. As Paulsen and others have pointed out,[3] no evidence ever is or can be offered to support that assertion, because it is in fact but a disguised proposal to

2. Cf. Gardner Murphy, "Difficulties Confronting the Survival Hypothesis," *Journal of the American Society for Psychical Research* for April, 1945, p. 72; Corliss Lamont, "The Illusion of Immortality" (New York, 1935), pp. 26 ff.

3. F. Paulsen, "Introduction to Philosophy" (trans. by F. Thilly, 2d ed.), pp. 82-83.

make the words "thought," "feeling," "sensation," "desire," and so on,
denote facts quite different from those which these words are commonly
employed to denote. To say that those words are but other names for
certain chemical or behavioral events is as grossly arbitrary as it would
be to say that "wood" is but another name for glass, or "potato" but
another name for cabbage. What thought, desire, sensation, and other
mental states are like, each of us can observe directly by introspection;
and what introspection reveals is that they do not in the least resemble
muscular contraction, or glandular secretion, or any other known bodily
events. No tampering with language can alter the observable fact that
thinking is one thing and muttering quite another; that the feeling called
anger has no resemblance to the bodily behavior which usually goes
with it; or that an act of will is not in the least like anything we find
when we open the skull and examine the brain. Certain mental events
are doubtless connected in some way with certain bodily events, but
they are not those bodily events themselves. The connection is not identity.

This being clear, let us next consider the arguments offered to show
that mental processes, although not identical with bodily processes,
nevertheless depend on them. We are told, for instance, that some head
injuries, or anesthetics, totally extinguish consciousness for the time
being. As already pointed out, however, the strict fact is only that the
usual bodily signs of consciousness are then absent. But they are also
absent when a person is asleep; and yet, at the same time, dreams, which
are states of consciousness, may be occurring.

It is true that when the person concerned awakens, he often remembers his dreams, whereas the person that has been anesthetized or
injured has usually no memories relating to the period of apparent
blankness. But this could mean that his consciousness was, for the time,
dissociated from its ordinary channels of manifestation, as was reported
of the co-conscious personalities of some of the patients of Dr. Morton
Prince.[4] Moreover, it sometimes occurs that a person who has been in
an accident reports lack of memories not only for the period during
which his body was unresponsive but also for a period of several hours
before the accident, during which he had given to his associates all the
ordinary external signs of being conscious as usual.

But, more generally, if absence of memories relating to a given period
proved unconsciousness for that period, this would force us to conclude
that we were unconscious during the first few years of our lives, and
indeed have been so most of the time since; for the fact is that we have
no memories whatever of most of our days. That we are alive and conscious on any long past specific date is, with only a few exceptions, not
something we actually remember, but only something which we infer
must be true.

---

4. "My Life as a Dissociated Personality" (edited by Morton Prince; Boston: Badger).

Evidence from Psychical Research

Another argument advanced against survival was, it will be remembered, that death must extinguish the mind, since all manifestations of it then cease. But to assert that they invariably then cease is to ignore altogether the considerable amount of evidence to the contrary, gathered over many years and carefully checked by the Society for Psychical Research. This evidence, which is of a variety of kinds, has been reviewed by Professor Gardner Murphy in an article published in the Journal of the Society.[5] He mentions first the numerous well-authenticated cases of apparition of a dead person to others as yet unaware that he had died or even been ill or in danger. The more strongly evidential cases of apparition are those in which the apparition conveys to the person who sees it specific facts until then secret. An example would be that of the apparition of a girl to her brother nine years after her death, with a conspicuous scratch on her cheek. Their mother then revealed to him that she herself had made that scratch accidentally while preparing her daughter's body for burial, but that she had then at once covered it with powder and never mentioned it to anyone.

Another famous case is that of a father whose apparition some time after death revealed to one of his sons the existence and location of an unsuspected second will, benefiting him, which was then found as indicated. Still another case would be the report by General Barter, then a subaltern in the British Army in India, of the apparition to him of a lieutenant he had not seen for two or three years. The lieutenant's apparition was riding a brown pony with black mane and tail. He was much stouter than at their last meeting, and, whereas formerly clean-shaven, he now wore a peculiar beard in the form of a fringe encircling his face. On inquiry the next day from a person who had known the lieutenant at the time he died, it turned out that he had indeed become very bloated before his death; that he had grown just such a beard while on the sick list; and that he had some time before bought and eventually ridden to death a pony of that very description.

Other striking instances are those of an apparition seen simultaneously by several persons. It is on record that an apparition of a child was perceived first by a dog, that the animal's rushing at it, loudly barking, interrupted the conversation of the seven persons present in the room, thus drawing their attention to the apparition, and that the latter

---

5. "An Outline of Survival Evidence," *Journal of the American Society for Psychical Research* for January, 1945.

then moved through the room for some fifteen seconds, followed by the barking dog.[6]

Another type of empirical evidence of survival consists of communications, purporting to come from the dead, made through the persons commonly called sensitives, mediums, or automatists. Some of the most remarkable of these communications were given by the celebrated American medium, Mrs. Piper, who for many years was studied by the Society for Psychical Research, London, with the most elaborate precautions against all possibility of fraud. Twice, particularly, the evidences of identity supplied by the dead persons who purportedly were thus communicating with the living were of the very kinds, and of the same precision and detail, which would ordinarily satisfy a living person of the identity of another living person with whom he was not able to communicate directly, but only through an intermediary, or by letter or telephone.[7]

Again, sometimes the same mark of identity of a dead person, or the same message from him, or complementary parts of one message, are obtained independently from two mediums in different parts of the world.

Of course, when facts of these kinds are recounted, as I have just done, only in abstract summary, they make little if any impression upon us. And the very word "medium" at once brings to our minds the innumerable instances of demonstrated fraud perpetrated by charlatans to extract money from the credulous bereaved. But the modes of trickery and sources of error, which immediately suggest themselves to us as easy, natural explanations of the seemingly extraordinary facts, suggest themselves just as quickly to the members of the research committees of the Society for Psychical Research. Usually, these men have had a good deal more experience than the rest of us with the tricks of conjurers and fraudulent mediums, and take against them precautions far more strict and ingenious than would occur to the average sceptic.[8]

But when, instead of stopping at summaries, one takes the trouble to study the detailed, original reports, it then becomes evident that they cannot all be just laughed off; for to accept the hypothesis of fraud or mal-observation would often require more credulity than to accept the facts reported.

---

6. The documents obtained by the Society for Psychical Research concerning this case, that of the lieutenant's apparation, and that of the girl with the scratch, are reproduced in Sir Ernest Bennett's "Apparitions and Haunted Houses" (London: Faber and Faber, 1945), pp. 334-337, 28-35, and 145-150 respectively.

7. A summary of some of the most evidential facts may be found in the book by M. Sage, entitled "Mrs. Piper and the Society for Psychical Research" (New York: Scott-Thaw Co., 1904); others of them are related in some detail in Sir Oliver Lodge's "The Survival of Man," Sec. IV (New York, Moffat, Yard and Co., 1909) and in A. M. Robbins' "Both Sides of the Veil," Part II (Boston: Sherman, French, and Co., 1909). The fullest account is in the *Proceedings of the Society for Psychical Research*.

8. Cf. H. Carrington, "The Physical Phenomena of Spiritualism, Fraudulent and Genuine" (Small, Maynard & Co., Boston, 1908).

To *explain* those facts, however, is quite another thing. Only two hypotheses at all adequate to do so have yet been advanced. One is that the communications really come, as they purport to do, from persons who have died and have survived death. The other is the hypothesis of telepathy—that is, the supposition, itself startling enough, that the medium is able to gather information directly from the minds of others, and that this is the true source of the information communicated. To account for all the facts, however, this hypothesis has to be stretched very far, for some of them require us to suppose that the medium can tap the minds even of persons far away and quite unknown to him, and can tap even the subconscious part of their minds.

Diverse highly ingenious attempts have been made to devise conditions that would rule out telepathy as a possible explanation of the communications received; but some of the most critical and best-documented investigators still hold that it has not yet been absolutely excluded. Hence, although some of the facts recorded by psychical research constitute, prima facie, strong empirical evidence of survival, they cannot be said to establish it beyond question. But they do show that we need to revise rather radically in some respects our ordinary ideas of what is and is not possible in nature.

Can Mental States Cause Bodily Events?

Let us now turn to another of the arguments against survival. That states of consciousness entirely depend on bodily processes, and therefore cannot continue when the latter have ceased, is proved, it is argued, by the fact that various states of consciousness—in particular, the several kinds of sensations—can be caused at will be appropriately stimulating the body.

Now, it is very true that sensations and some other mental states can be so caused; but we have just as good and abundant evidence that mental states can cause various bodily events. John Laird mentions, among others, the fact that merely willing to raise one's arm normally suffices to cause it to rise; that a hungry person's mouth is caused to water by the idea of food; that feelings of rage, fear or excitement cause digestion to stop; that anxiety causes changes in the quantity and quality of the milk of a nursing mother; that certain thoughts cause tears, pallor, blushing or fainting; and so on.[9] The evidence we have that the relation is one of cause and effect is exactly the same here as where bodily processes cause mental states.

9. John Laird, "Our Minds and Their Bodies" (London, 1925), pp. 16-19.

It is said, of course, that to suppose something non-physical, such as thought, to be capable of causing motion of a physical object, such as the body, is absurd. But I submit that if the heterogeneity of mind and matter makes this absurd, then it makes equally absurd the causation of mental states by stimulation of the body. Yet no absurdity is commonly found in the assertion that cutting the skin causes a feeling of pain, or that alcohol, caffein, bromides, and other drugs, cause characteristic states of consciousness. As David Hume made clear long ago, no kind of causal connection is intrinsically absurd. Anything might cause anything; and only observation can tell us what in fact can cause what.

Somewhat similar remarks would apply to the allegation that the principle of the conservation of energy precludes the possibility of causation of a physical event by a mental event. For if it does, then it equally precludes causation in the converse direction, and this, of course, would leave us totally at a loss to explain the occurrence of sensations. But, as Keeton and others have pointed out,[10] that energy is conserved is not something observation has revealed or could reveal, but only a postulate—a defining postulate for the notion of an "isolated physical system."

That is, conservation of energy is something one has to have if, but only if, one insists on conceiving the physical world as wholly self-contained, independent, isolated. And just because the metaphysics which the natural sciences tacitly assume does insist on so conceiving the physical world, this metaphysics compels them to save conservation by postulations *ad hoc* whenever dissipation of energy is what observation reveals. It postulates, for instance, that something else, which appears at such times but was not until then regarded as energy, is energy too, but it is then said, "in a different form."

Furthermore, as Broad has emphasized, all that the principle of conservation requires is that when a quantity Q of energy disappears at one place in the physical world an equal quantity of it should appear at some other place there. And the supposition that, in some cases, what causes it to disappear here and appear there is some mental event, such perhaps as a volition, does not violate at all the supposition that energy is conserved.[11]

A word, next, on the parallelism between the degree of development of the nervous systems of various animals and the degree of their intelligence. This is alleged to prove that the latter is the product of the former. But the facts lend themselves equally well to the supposition that, on the contrary, an obscurely felt need for greater intelligence in the cir-

10. M. T. Keeton, "Some Ambiguities in the Theory of the Conservation of Energy," *Philosophy of Science*, Vol. 8, No. 3, July 1941.
11. C. D. Broad, "The Mind and Its Place in Nature," pp. 103 ff. (See Selection 18 above, pp 262 ff.)

cumstances the animal faced was what brought about the variations which eventually resulted in a more adequate nervous organization.

In the development of the individual, at all events, it seems clear that the specific, highly complex nerve connections which become established in the brain and cerebellum of, for instance, a skilled pianist are the results of his will over many years to acquire the skill.

We must not forget in this context that there is a converse, equally consistent with the facts, for the theory, called epiphenomenalism, that mental states are related to the brain much as the halo is to the saint, that is, as effects but never themselves as causes. The converse theory, which might be called hypophenomenalism, and which is pretty well that of Schopenhauer, is that the instruments which the various mechanisms of the body constitute are the objective products of obscure cravings for the corresponding powers; and, in particular, that the organization of the nervous system is the effect and material isomorph of the variety of mental functions exercised at a given level of animal or human existence.

The Initial Assumption Behind
the Arguments Against Survival

We have now scrutinized all but the last of the reasons mentioned earlier for rejecting the possibility of survival, and we have found them all logically weak. Before examining the one which remains, it will be useful for us to pause a moment and inquire why so many of the persons who advance those reasons nevertheless think them convincing.

It is, I believe, because these persons approach the question of survival with a certain unconscious metaphysical bias. It derives from a particular initial assumption which they tacitly make. It is that *to be real is to be material*. And to be material, of course, is to be some process or part of the perceptually public world, that is, of the world we all perceive by means of our so-called five senses.

Now the assumption that to be real is to be material is a useful and appropriate one for the purpose of investigating the material world and of operating upon it; and this purpose is a legitimate and frequent one. But those persons, and most of us, do not realize that the validity of that assumption is strictly relative to that specific purpose. Hence they, and most of us, continue making the assumption, and it continues to rule judgment, even when, as now, the purpose in view is a different one, for which the assumption is no longer useful or even congruous.

The point is all-important here and therefore worth stressing. Its essence is that the conception of the nature of reality that proposes to define the real as the material is not the expression of an observable fact to which everyone would have to bow, but is the expression only of a certain direction of interest on the part of the persons who so define reality—of interest, namely, which they have chosen to center wholly in the material, perceptually public world. This specialized interest is of course as legitimate as any other, but it automatically ignores all the facts, commonly called facts of mind, which only introspection reveals. And that specialized interest is what alone compels persons in its grip to employ the word "mind" to denote, instead of what it commonly does denote, something else altogether, namely, the public behavior of bodies that have minds.

Only so long as one's judgment is swayed unawares by that special interest do the logically weak arguments against the possibility of survival, which we have examined, seem strong.

It is possible, however, and just as legitimate, as well as more conducive to a fair view of our question, to center one's interest at the start on the facts of mind as introspectively observable, ranking them as most real in the sense that they are the facts the intrinsic nature of which we most directly experience, the facts which we most certainly know to exist; and moreover; that they are the facts without the experiencing of which we should not know any other facts whatever—such, for instance, as those of the material world.

The sort of perspective one gets from this point of view is what I propose now to sketch briefly. For one thing, the material world is then seen to be but one among other objects of our consciousness. Moreover, one becomes aware of the crucially important fact that it is an object postulated rather than strictly given. What this means may be made clearer by an example. Suppose that, perhaps in a restaurant we visit for the first time, an entire wall is occupied by a large mirror and we look into it without realizing that it is a mirror. We then perceive, in the part of space beyond it, various material objects, notwithstanding that in fact they have no existence there at all. A certain set of the vivid color images which we call visual sensations was all that was strictly given to us, and these we construed, automatically and instantaneously, but nonetheless erroneously, as signs or appearances of the existence of certain material objects at a certain place.

Again, and similarly, we perceive in our dreams various objects which at the time we take as physical but which eventually we come to believe were not so. And this eventual conclusion, let it be noted, is forced upon us not because we then detect that something, called "physical substance," was lacking in those objects, but only because we notice, as we did not at the time, that their behavior was erratic—incoherent with their ordinary one. That is, their appearance was a *mere* appearance, deceptive in the sense that it did not then predict truly, as ordinarily it does, their later appearances. This, it is important to notice, is the *only* way in which we ever discover that an object we perceive was not really physical, or was not the particular sort of physical object we judged it to be.

These two examples illustrate the fact that our perception of physical objects is sometimes erroneous. But the essential point is that, even when it is veridical instead of erroneous, *all* that is literally and directly given to our minds is still only *some set of sensations*. These, on a given occasion, may be only color sensations; but they often include also tactual sensations, sounds, odors, and so on. It is especially interesting, however, to remark here in passing that, with respect to almost all the many thousands of persons and other "physical" objects we have perceived in a life time, *vivid color images* were the only data our perceiving strictly had to go by; so that, if the truth should happen to have been that those objects, like ghosts or images in a mirror, were actually intangible—that is, were *only* color images—we should never have discovered that this was the fact. For all we *directly* know, it *may* have been the fact!

To perceive a physical object, then, instead of merely experiencing passively certain sensations (something which perhaps hardly ever occurs), is always to *interpret,* that is, to *construe,* given sensations as signs of, and appearances to us of, a postulated something other than themselves, which we believe is causing them in us and is capable of causing in us others of specific kinds. We believe this because we believe that our sensations too must have some cause, and we find none for them among our other mental states.

Such a postulated extramental something we call "a physical object." We say that we observe physical objects, and this is true. But it is important for the present purpose to be clear that we "observe" them never in any more direct or literal manner than is constituted by the process of interpretive postulation just described—never, for example, in the wholly direct and literal manner in which we are able to observe our sensations themselves and our other mental states.

That perception of a physical object is thus always the product of two factors—one, a set of sensations simply given to us, and the other an act of interpretation of these, performed by us—is something which easily escapes notice and has even been denied. This, however, is only because the interpretive act is almost always automatic, instantaneous, and correct—like, for instance, that of thinking of the meaning of any familiar word we hear. But that an interpretive act does occur is forced on our attention when, in a particular case, we discover that we misconstrued the meaning of the sensations. Or, again, the interpretive act is noticeable when, because the sensations are too scant and therefore ambiguous, we catch ourselves hesitating between two or more possible interpretations of them and say that we are not sure what object it is we see.

"Our Own" Bodies

To complete the sketch of the view of the universe obtained when we conceive ourselves primarily as minds rather than primarily as bodies, attention must now be directed to a particular one of the objects which, in the sense described, we perceive in the world external to our minds. This especially interesting object is the one we call "our own body"; and the question we must now ask is: How do we identify it among the thousands of human bodies we perceive? What peculiarities mark it from all others and make us call it our own?

One of them, of course, is that we never directly see certain parts of it; for instance, most of its back, or any part of its head except a certain aspect of its nose and orbital arch. This aspect, moreover, we always see when it is illuminated if we see anything at all.

But there are four other and more important peculiarities which mark a human body as our own. One is that it is the only physical object we can directly cause to move by a mere act of will. This statement, however, probably needs to be slightly qualified, since the results of the many experiments at Duke University and elsewhere have provided strong evidence of the reality of the so-called psychokinetic effect (as well as of clairvoyance).[12] These experiments appear to show that it is sometimes possible for a human volition to cause directly at least minute alterations in the behavior of physical objects other than one's own body. If so, we could then conceive a willed motion of our own body as simply a psychokinetic effect in maximum degree. It is well to remember in this connection that causation, directly by an act of will, of some alteration in the behavior of a molecule, is neither more nor less intrinsically intelligible, nor *a priori* more probable or improbable, when the molecule happens to be part of a brain than when it happens instead to be part of a physical object of some other kind, such as a piece of wood or a stone.

Another of the marks of the body we call our own is that it is the only one the stimulation of which causes directly in us sensations of the corresponding kinds. This statement, too, may turn out to need slight qualification if full confirmation should be obtained that vivid images are sometimes received by the mind *directly* from physical objects or events, that is, received without intermediary stimulation of the sense organs of one's body.

Cases of this kind would be examples of what is meant by clairvoyance as distinguished from telepathy, and if the reality of it can be regarded as firmly established, then sensation could be viewed as a spe-

---

12. For a summary of these experiments, see J. B. Rhine's book, "The Reach of the Mind" (New York, 1947).

cial instance of clairvoyance, and the sense organs, together with the corresponding nerves and brain regions, as specialized transmitters, which, like microscopes, magnify what they transmit, but transmit at all only what occurs at relatively short distances and in circumstances of special kinds. Here, as before, we should not forget that it is neither more nor less intelligible or probable *a priori* that a color experience, for example, should have for its immediate cause a molecular event in the visual cortex of the brain, than a molecular event in some physical object other than the brain or even the body.[13]

Besides the two marks just mentioned, there are two others likewise peculiar to the body we call our own. They are less obvious to casual observation, but quite as important theoretically. And they, too, consist of unique capacities in respect to causation, but causation now of changes in the structure, instead of only the states, of conscious mind and of brain.

One of them is that the body we call our own is the only one in which certain mutilations of the brain ever directly cause specific alterations in the dispositions or capacities our mind manifests. An example would be the effects upon the mind of the brain operation called prefrontal lobotomy, mentioned earlier. It notably alters the conscious personality.

The other mark relates to causation in the converse direction: the body we call our own is the only one in which certain elaborate connections among the nerve cells in the association areas of the brain can be directly caused by a mental event—for instance, by that mental event which consists of a firm and persistent volition to acquire some particular bodily skill, such as skill to play a given musical instrument.

These remarks have been intended to provide a perspective by virtue of which the relation of body to mind can be observed without the distortion otherwise imposed by the tacit assumption we mentioned, which is commonly made, but which has validity and relevance strictly limited to the purpose of studying and controlling the material world. That enlarged and fairer perspective, I now submit, makes clear that no paradox at all is really involved in the supposition that some forms of consciousness may exist independently of connection with animal or human bodies; and, therefore, that survival is at least theoretically possible. . . .

---

13. It is interesting to note that essentially the same suggestion as that made above— that voluntary activity is a special case of psychokinesis, and sensory perception a special case of clairvoyance—was independently made and developed by R. H. Thouless and B. P. Wiesner in an article, "The Psi Processes in Normal and 'Paranormal' Psychology" (*Procs. Soc. for Psychical Research*, December 1947) where they wrote: "The hypothesis we wish to suggest is that, in normal thinking and perceiving I am in the same sort of relation to what is going on in the sensory part of my brain and nervous system as that of the successful clairvoyant to some external event, and that this relation is established by the same means," and "We suggest also that there is a similar identity of relation in normal motor control of the body on the one hand and the 'paranormal' process of psychokinesis on the other." (pp. 180-81)

21

OF THE IMMORTALITY
OF THE SOUL

David Hume

BY THE MERE LIGHT OF REASON it seems difficult to prove the Immortality of the Soul. The arguments for it are commonly derived either from *metaphysical* topics, or *moral,* or *physical.* But in reality, it is the gospel, and the gospel alone, that has brought life and immortality to light.

I. Metaphysical topics suppose that the soul is immaterial, and that it is impossible for thought to belong to a material substance.

But just metaphysics teach us, that the notion of substance is wholly confused and imperfect, and that we have no other idea of any substance, than as an aggregate of particular qualities inhering in an unknown something. Matter, therefore, and spirit, are at bottom equally unknown; and we cannot determine what qualities inhere in the one or in the other.

They likewise teach us, that nothing can be decided *a priori* concerning any cause or effect; and that experience, being the only source of our judgments of this nature, we cannot know from any other principle, whether matter, by its structure or arrangement, may not be the cause of thought. Abstract reasonings cannot decide any question of fact or existence.

But admitting a spiritual substance to be dispersed throughout the universe, like the ethereal fire of the *Stoics,* and to be the only inherent subject of thought, we have reason to conclude from *analogy,* that nature uses it after the manner she docs the other substance, matter. She employs it as a kind of paste or clay; modifies it into a variety of forms and existences; dissolves after a time each modification, and from its sub-

---

[This essay was written by Hume in 1755 and was not published until after his death.]

stance erects a new form. As the same material substance may successively compose the bodies of all animals, the same spiritual substance may compose their minds: their consciousness, or that system of thought, which they formed during life, may be continually dissolved by death; and nothing interests them in the new modification. The most positive assertors of the mortality of the soul, never denied the immortality of its substance. And that an immaterial substance, as well as a material, may lose its memory or consciousness, appears, in part, from experience, if the soul be immaterial.

Reasoning from the common course of nature, and without supposing any new interposition of the Supreme Cause, which ought always to be excluded from philosophy; what is incorruptible must also be ingenerable. The soul, therefore, if immortal, existed before our birth: And if the former existence noways concerned us, neither will the latter.

Animals undoutedly feel, think, love, hate, will, and even reason, though in a more imperfect manner than man. Are their souls also immaterial and immortal?

II. Let us now consider the *moral* arguments, chiefly those derived from the justice of God, which is supposed to be further interested in the further punishment of the vicious and reward of the virtuous.

But these arguments are grounded on the supposition, that God has attributes beyond what he has exerted in this universe, with which alone we are acquainted. Whence do we infer the existence of these attributes?

'Tis very safe for us to affirm, that, whatever we know the Deity to have actually done, is best; but it is very dangerous to affirm, that he must always do what to us seems best. In many instances would this reasoning fail us with regard to the present world.

But, if any purpose of nature be clear, we may affirm, that the whole scope and intention of man's creation, so far as we can judge by natural reason, is limited to the present life. With how weak a concern, from the original, inherent structure of the mind and passions, does he ever look further? What comparison either for steadiness or efficacy, betwixt so floating an idea, and the most doubtful persuasion of any matter of fact, that occurs in common life?

There arise, indeed, in some minds, some unaccountable terrors with regard to futurity: But these would quickly vanish, were they not artificially fostered by precept and education. And those, who foster them: what is their motive? Only to gain a livelihood, and to acquire power and riches in this world. Their very zeal and industry, therefore, are an argument against them.

What cruelty, what iniquity, what injustice in nature, to confine thus all our concern, as well as all our knowledge, to the present life, if there be another scene still waiting us, of infinitely greater consequence? Ought this barbarous deceit to be ascribed to a beneficent and wise Being?

Observe with what exact proportion the task to be performed, and the performing powers, are adjusted throughout all nature. If the reason of man gives him a great superiority above other animals, his necessities are proportionably multiplied upon him. His whole time, his whole capacity, activity, courage, passion, find sufficient employment, in fencing against the miseries of his present condition. And frequently, nay almost always, are too slender for the business assigned them.

A pair of shoes, perhaps, was never yet wrought to the highest degree of perfection, which that commodity is capable of attaining. Yet it is necessary, at least very useful, that there should be some politicians and moralists, even some geometers, poets, and philosophers among mankind.

The powers of men are no more superior to their wants, considered merely in this life, than those of foxes and hares are, compared to *their* wants and *their* period of existence. The inference from parity of reason is therefore obvious.

On the theory of the soul's mortality, the inferiority of women's capacity is easily accounted for: Their domestic life requires no higher faculties either of mind or body. This circumstance vanishes and becomes absolutely insignificant, on the religious theory: The one sex has an equal task to perform as the other: Their powers of reason and resolution ought also to have been equal, and both of them infinitely greater than at present.

As every effect implies a cause, and that another, till we reach the first cause of all, which is the *Deity;* everything that happens, is ordained by Him; and nothing can be the object of His punishment or vengeance.

By what rule are punishments and rewards distributed? What is the Divine standard of merit and demerit? Shall we suppose, that human sentiments have place in the Deity? However bold that hypothesis, we have no conception of any other sentiments.

According to human sentiments, sense, courage, good manners, industry, prudence, genius, etc., are essential parts of personal merits. Shall we therefore erect an elysium for poets and heroes, like that of the ancient mythology? Why confine all rewards to one species of virtue?

Punishment, without any proper end or purpose, is inconsistent with *our* ideas of goodness and justice; and no end can be served by it after the whole scene is closed.

Punishment, according to *our* conception, should bear some proportion to the offence. Why then eternal punishment for the temporary offences of so frail a creature as man? Can any one approve of *Alexander's* rage, who intended to exterminate a whole nation, because they had seized his favourite horse, Bucephalus?

Heaven and hell suppose two distinct species of men, the good and the bad. But the greatest part of mankind float betwixt vice and virtue.

Were one to go round the world with an intention of giving a good supper to the righteous and a sound drubbing to the wicked, he would frequently be embarrassed in his choice, and would find, that the merits and demerits of most men and women scarcely amount to the value of either.

To suppose measures of approbation and blame, different from the human, confounds every thing. Whence do we learn, that there is such a thing as moral distinctions, but from our own sentiments?

What man, who has not met with personal provocation (or what good-natur'd man who has), could inflict on crimes, from the sense of blame alone, even the common, legal, frivolous punishments? And does anything steel the breast of judges and juries against the sentiments of humanity but reflections on necessity and public interest?

By the Roman law, those who had been guilty of parricide, and confessed their crime, were put into a sack, along with an ape, a dog, and a serpent; and thrown into the river: Death alone was the punishment of those, who denied their guilt, however fully proved. A criminal was tried before *Augustus,* and condemned after a full conviction: but the humane emperor, when he put the last interrogatory, gave it such a turn as to lead the wretch into a denial of his guilt. *"You surely,* said the prince, *did not kill your father?"* This lenity suits our natural ideas of RIGHT, even towards the greatest of all criminals, and even though it prevents so inconsiderable a sufferance. Nay, even the most bigoted priest would naturally, without reflection, approve of it; provided the crime was not heresy or infidelity. For as these crimes hurt himself in his *temporal* interest and advantages; perhaps he may not be altogether so indulgent to them.

The chief source of moral ideas is the reflection on the interests of human society. Ought these interests, so short, so frivolous, to be guarded by punishments, eternal and infinite? The damnation of one man is an infinitely greater evil in the universe, than the subversion of a thousand millions of kingdoms.

Nature has rendered human infancy peculiarly frail and mortal; as it were on purpose to refute the notion of a probationary state. The half of mankind die before they are rational creatures.

III. The *physical* arguments from the analogy of nature are strong for the mortality of the soul: and these are really the only philosophical arguments, which ought to be admitted with regard to this question, or indeed any question of fact.

Where any two objects are so closely connected, that all alterations, which we have seen in the one, are attended with proportionable alterations in the other: we ought to conclude, by all rules of analogy, that, when there are still greater alterations produced in the former, and it is totally dissolved, there follows a total dissolution of the latter.

Sleep, a very small effect on the body, is attended with a temporary extinction: at least, a great confusion in the soul.

The weakness of the body and that of the mind in infancy are exactly proportioned; their vigour in manhood, their sympathetic disorder in sickness, their common gradual decay in old age. The step further seems unavoidable; their common dissolution in death.

The last symptoms, which the mind discovers, are disorder, weakness, insensibility, and stupidity; the forerunners of its annihilation. The further progress of the same causes, increasing the same effects, totally extinguish it.

Judging by the usual analogy of nature, no form can continue, when transferred to a condition of life very different from the original one, in which it was placed. Trees perish in the water; fishes in the air; animals in the earth. Even so small a difference as that of climate is often fatal. What reason then to imagine, that an immense alteration, such as is made on the soul by the dissolution of its body, and all its organs of thought and sensation, can be effected without the disolution of the whole?

Everything is in common betwixt soul and body. The organs of the one are all of them the organs of the other. The existence therefore of the one must be dependent on the other.

The souls of animals are allowed to be mortal: and these bear so near a resemblance to the souls of men, that the analogy from one to the other forms a very strong argument. Their bodies are not more resembling: yet no one rejects the argument drawn from comparative anatomy. The *Metempsychosis* is therefore the only system of this kind, that philosophy can hearken to.

Nothing in this world is perpetual; Everything, however seemingly firm, is in continual flux and change: The world itself gives symptoms of frailty and dissolution: How contrary to analogy, therefore, to imagine, that one single form, seeming the frailest of any, and subject to the greatest disorders is immortal and indissoluble! What a daring theory is that! How lightly, not to say how rashly, entertained!

How to dispose of the infinite number of posthumous existences ought also to embarrass the religious theory. Every planet, in every solar system, we are at liberty to imagine peopled with intelligent, mortal beings: At least we can fix on no other supposition. For these, then, a new universe must, every generation, be created beyond the bounds of the present universe: or one must have been created at first so prodigiously wide as to admit of this continual influx of beings. Ought such bold suppositions to be received by philosophy: and that merely on the pretext of a bare possibility?

When it is asked, whether *Agamemnon, Thersites, Hannibal, Nero,* and every stupid clown, that ever existed in *Italy, Scythia, Bactria, or Guinea,* are now alive; can any man think, that a scrutiny of nature will furnish arguments strong enough to answer so strange a question in the affirmative? The want of argument, without revelation, sufficiently establishes the negative. *Quanto facilius,* says Pliny, *certiusque sibi quemque credere, ac specimen accuritatis antegenitali sumere experimento.** Our insensibility, before the composition of the body, seems to natural reason a proof of a like state after dissolution.

Were our horrors of annihilation an original passion, not the effect of our general love of happiness, it would rather prove the mortality of the soul: For as nature does nothing in vain, she would never give us a horror against an impossible event. She may give us a horror against an unavoidable event, provided our endeavours, as in the present case, may often remove it to some distance. Death is in the end unavoidable; yet the human species could not be preserved, had not nature inspired us with an aversion towards it. All doctrines are to be suspected which are favoured by our passions. And the hopes and fears which give rise to this doctrine, are very obvious.

'Tis an infinite advantage in every controversy, to defend the negative. If the question be out of the common experienced course of nature, this circumstance is almost, if not altogether, decisive. By what arguments or analogies can we prove any state of existence, which no one ever saw, and which no way resembles any that ever was seen? Who will repose such trust in any pretended philosophy, as to admit upon its testimony the reality of so marvelous a scene? Some new species of logic is requisite for that purpose; and some new faculties of the mind, that they may enable us to comprehend that logic.

Nothing could set in a fuller light the infinite obligations which mankind have to Divine revelation; since we find, that no other medium could ascertain this great and important truth.

---

* Hume's quotation is the last sentence of a discussion of the belief in an after-life in Pliny's *Natural History,* Book VII, Section 55. It reads as follows: "All men are in the same state from their last day onward as they were before their first day, and neither body nor mind possesses any sensation after death, any more than it did before birth—for the same vanity prolongs itself also into the future and fabricates for itself a life lasting even into the period of death, sometimes bestowing on the soul immortality, sometimes transfiguration, sometimes giving sensation to those below, and worshipping ghosts and making a god of one who has already ceased to be even a man—just as if man's mode of breathing were in any way different from that of the other animals, or as if there were not many animals found of greater longevity, for which nobody prophesies a similar immortality! But what is the substance of the soul taken by itself? What is its material? Where is its thought located? How does it see and hear, and with what does it touch? What use does it get from these senses, so what good can it experience without them? Next, what is the abode, or how great is the multitude of the souls or shadows in all these ages? These are fictions of childish absurdity and belong to a mortality greedy for life unceasing. . . . What repose are the generations ever to have if the soul retains permanent sensation in the upper world and the ghost in the lower? Assuredly this sweet but credulous fancy ruins nature's chief blessing, death, and doubles the sorrow of one about to die by the thought of sorrow to come hereafter also. . . . But how much easier and safer for each to trust in himself, and for us to derive our idea of future tranquillity from our experience of it before birth!" The English translation just quoted is by H. Rackham. (Eds.)

SELECTED BIBLIOGRAPHY

(ITEMS PROVIDED WITH ASTERISK ARE MORE ADVANCED)

There are several works which are devoted entirely to the body-mind problem in its various ramifications. Of these the best known are John Laird, *Our Minds and Their Bodies* (London: Oxford University Press, 1925), C. D. Broad, *The Mind and Its Place in Nature* (London: Routledge and Kegan Paul, 1925), John Wisdom, *Problems of Mind and Matter* (Cambridge: Cambridge University Press, 1934), J. B. Pratt, *Matter and Spirit* (New York: Macmillan, 1926), Durant Drake, *The Mind and Its Place in Nature* (New York: Macmillan, 1925), C. J. Ducasse, *Nature, Mind and Death* (LaSalle, Illinois: Open Court, 1951), and Alexander Bain, *Mind and Body* (London: Henry King, 1873). In Chapter VII of Bain's book there is a valuable historical survey of the different theories on the subject. The books by Laird, Broad, Pratt and Ducasse contain defenses of interactionism. The classic formulation of this theory is found in Descartes' *Meditations* and in his correspondence. Many editions of Descartes' works contain also Gassendi's objections to his theory and Descartes' answer. A very detailed defense of interactionism from a Catholic viewpoint is found in M. Maher, *Psychology* (London: Longmans, Green and Co., 1940).

Reductive materialism of the older variety is expounded in Ludwig Büchner, *Force and Matter* (London: Asher and Co., 1884). The works by Cabanis, Vogt, and Moleschott in which similar views are advocated have not been translated into English. It should be noted that all these writers frequently shift to some milder form of materialism. F. A. Lange's magnificent *History of Materialism* (London: Kegan Paul, 1925, with an introduction by Bertrand Russell) is a mine of information on this subject. Paul Janet, *Materialism of the Present Day* (London, 1867) is an informative critical work. The historical development of materialism is also sympathetically sketched in the famous "Belfast Address" by the nineteenth century physicist John Tyndall which is reprinted in his *Lectures and Essays* (London: Watts and Co., 1903). Materialism is also defended by J. M. Robertson, the great historian of freethought, in *Explorations* (London: Watts and Co., 1909). More recent writings in support of materialism are Hugh Elliot, *Modern Science and Materialism* (London: Longmans, Green and Co., 1919), Chapman Cohen, *Materialism Restated* (London: The Pioneer Press, 1927), Donald Williams' "Naturalism and the Nature of Things," *Philosophical Review,* 1944, and T. Kotarbinski's "The Fundamental Ideas of Pansomatism,"* *Mind,* 1955.

There are several varieties of what is called "behaviorism." Some psychologists who call themselves behaviorists do not at all deny the existence of "consciousness" but merely exclude it as a proper subject-matter of scientific research. Others and sometimes the same writers in less guarded moments go further and deny consciousness altogether. Many eminent American psychologists have expressed one or other of these views. The following are some of their most influential writings: J. B. Watson, *Psychology from the Standpoint of a Behaviorist* (Philadelphia: Lippincott, 1919), J. B. Watson, *Behaviorism* (New York: Norton and Co., 1924), A. P. Weiss, *A Theoretical Basis of Human Behavior* (Columbus, Ohio: Adams, 1925), W. S. Hunter, *Human Behavior* (Chicago: University of Chicago Press, 1928), E. C. Tolman, *Purposive Behavior in Animals and Men* (New York: Appleton-Century, 1932), and C. L. Hull, *Principles of Behavior** (New York: Appleton-Century-Crofts, 1943). H. H. Bawden's "The Presuppositions of a Behaviorist Psychology," *Psychological Review,* 1918, is a particularly lucid statement of the more radical form of behaviorism mentioned above.

There is also a theory known as "logical behaviorism" which is not concerned to advocate and justify a certain program of psychological research but which offers an analysis of the so-called psychological predicates in terms of "behavior" alone. This view is stated in C. G. Hempel's "The Logical Analysis of Psychology," reprinted in H. Feigl and W. Sellars (eds.), *Readings in Philosophical Analysis* (New York: Appleton-Century-Crofts, 1949) and in Rudolf Carnap's "Psychologie in Physikalischer Sprache," *Erkenntnis,* 1932. Gilbert Ryle, *The Concept of Mind* (London: Hutchinson and Co., 1949) is also regarded by many reviewers as a defense of logical behaviorism. The papers by Carnap and Hempel are from the early days of logical positivism. Both these writers referred to their views as "physicalism." Moritz Schlick also called himself a physicalist in his paper "On the Relation Between Psychological and Physical Concepts," reprinted in Feigl and Sellars, *op. cit.* Schlick's position is, however, clearly dualistic and thus not equivalent to logical behaviorism. Hempel and Carnap in later years also abandoned their earlier extreme viewpoint. Carnap's later views are sketched in "Logical Foundations of the Unity of Science," reprinted in Feigl and Sellars, *op. cit.* Herbert Feigl's "The Mind-Body Problem in the Development of Logical Empiricism,"* reprinted in Feigl and Brodbeck (eds.), *Readings in the Philosophy of Science* (New York: Appleton-Century-Crofts, 1953), contains a survey of the various theories advocated on this topic by the logical positivists, in addition to presenting Feigl's own view. There are criticisms of some or all varieties of behaviorism in the above-mentioned books by Broad, Ducasse, Pratt, and Drake. Other criticisms of behaviorism will be found in Bertrand Russell, *The Outline of Philosophy* (London: Allen and Unwin, New York: Norton and Co., 1927), in B. Blanshard, *The Nature of Thought,* Vol. I (London: Allen and Unwin, 1939), the same writer's article "Behaviorism and the Theory of Knowledge," *Philosophical Review,* 1928, in A. O. Lovejoy's "The Paradox of the Thinking Behaviorist," *Philosophical Review,* 1922, and in W. Köhler, *Gestalt Psychology* (New York: Horace Liveright, 1929). There are interesting critical discussions of Ryle's *Concept of Mind* by A. Hofstadter, D. S. Miller, M. Weitz, and H. King in the *Journal of Philosophy,* 1951. Other important criticisms of Ryle's views are A. C. Ewing's "Professor Ryle's Attack on Dualism," *Proc. of the Arist. Soc.,* 1952/53, A. Pap's "Semantic Analysis and Psycho-Physical Dualism," *Mind,* 1952, and A. C. Garnett's "Mind as Minding," *ibid.*

Epiphenomenalism is defended in Shadworth Hodgson, *The Metaphysics of Experience,** Vol. II (London: Longmans, Green, and Co., 1898), in G. Santayana, *The Realm of Essence** (Charles Scribner's Sons, 1927), the same author's *Reason and Common Sense* (Charles Scribner's Sons, 1922), and in H. C. Warren's "The Mechanics of Intelligence," *Philosophical Review,* 1917. It is criticized by Broad, Pratt, Maher, also in T. H. Herbert, *Modern Realism Examined* (London: Macmillan, 1879), and in A. O. Lovejoy's "Pragmatism as Interactionism," *Journal of Philosophy,* 1920. The classical statement of the theory that psychological phenomena are attributes of the body is found in Lamettrie, *Man as a Machine* (LaSalle, Illinois: Open Court, 1912) and in Joseph Priestley, *Disquisitions Relating to Matter and Spirit* (London, 1777). Holbach in *The System of Nature* also at times inclines to this view and so does Diderot in several of his works which are unfortunately not available in English. Ernest Nagel's "Are Naturalists Materialists?", reprinted in Ernest Nagel, *Logic Without Metaphysics* (Glencoe, Illinois: Free Press, 1957) is a highly stimulating modern presentation of the same general position. Similar views are also expressed by Y. Krikorian in "A Naturalistic View of Mind," which is included in Y. Krikorian (ed.), *Naturalism and the Human Spirit* (New York: Columbia University Press, 1944). The views of Krikorian and other naturalists are criticized in W. H. Sheldon's "Critique of Naturalism," *Journal of Philosophy,* 1945.

The classic exposition of occasionalism is that of Malebranche in his *Dialogue on Metaphysics and Religion** (London: Allen and Unwin, 1923). A more recent defense of occasionalism is given in Vol. I, Book III, Chapter I of Lotze's *Microcosmus* (Edinburgh: T. R. T. Clark, 1885). The illustration of the two clocks and the parallelism of Leibniz are found in his *Exposition and Defense of the New System* which is reprinted in most popular editions of his works. More recent defenses of this theory are contained in H. Höffding, *The Problems of Philosophy* (New York: Macmillan, 1905), W. K. Clifford's articles "Body and Mind" and "Things-in-Themselves," which are reprinted in Vol. II of his *Lectures and Essays* (London and New York: Macmillan, 1879), and in Friedrich Paulsen, *Introduction to Philosophy* (New York: Henry Holt and Co., 1906). G. T. Fechner who was the leading parallelist and panpsychist of the nineteenth century wrote a number of works which deal with various aspects of the body-mind problem, but very few of these have been translated into English. The most valuable collection of his writings in English is *Religion of a Scientist* (New York: Pantheon Books, 1946, ed. W. Lowrie). G. S. Fullerton in *A System of Metaphysics* (New York: Macmillan, 1904) and again in *An Introduction to Philosophy* (New York: Macmillan, 1906) champions a form of parallelism, but he admits that his disagreement with interactionists concerns the use of the best language for the body-mind relation rather than the existence of any facts.

Hume's statement of his "bundle" theory of the self is given in *The Treatise of Human Nature,* Book I, Section VI. Substantially similar views are expressed by John Stuart Mill in Chapter XII of *An Examination of Sir William Hamilton's Philosophy* (London: Longmans, Green and Co., 1872) and in various books by Bertrand Russell, most recently in *Portraits from Memory and Other Essays* (London: Allen and Unwin, New York: Simon and Schuster, 1956). There is also a discussion of this topic from a viewpoint basically akin to Hume's in Chapter 5 of A. J. Ayer, *The Problem of Knowledge* (London: Pelican Books, 1956). T. Penelhum's "Hume on Personal Identity," *Philosophical Review,* 1955, contains a particularly valuable discussion of the notion of "sameness." Penelhum accepts the bundle-theory without however endorsing Hume's paradoxical conclusions concerning self-identity. Supplementary Vol. XV of the *Proceedings of the Aristotelian Society* (1939), entitled "David Hume, 1739-1939," contains a symposium on "Self-Identity," with J. N. Wright and C. M. Mace as contributors. Substance-views are defended by Lotze, *Metaphysic* (Oxford: Clarendon Press, 1887), in Chapter V of Pratt, *op cit.,* in Chapter XXI of Maher, *op. cit.,* and in Chapter 5 of J. McCosh, *An Examination of J. S. Mill's Philosophy* (New York: R. Carter, 1880). I. Gallie's "Is the Self a Substance?",* *Mind,* 1936, and H. P. Grice's "Personal Identity,"* *Mind,* 1941, are two recent articles on this subject. There is also an elaborate and highly suggestive discussion in Volume I of W. James, *The Principles of Psychology* (New York: Henry Holt and Co., 1890).

A very full exposition of the traditional arguments for immortality is contained in Chapter XXIV of Maher's book. Plato defended this belief in the *Phaedo.* The German-Jewish philosopher of the Enlightenment, Moses Mendelsohn, defended the same conclusion in his dialogue, *Phaidon,* which was modeled after Plato. Bishop Butler in the eighteenth century produced an "inductive" argument for immortality in Chapter I of *The Analogy of Religion.* John Fiske, *The Destiny of Man* (Boston and New York: Houghton, Mifflin and Co., 1884), the same author's *Life Everlasting* (Boston and New York: Houghton, Mifflin and Co., 1901), H. E. Fosdick, *The Assurance of Immortality* (New York: Macmillan, 1926), and A. E. Taylor, *The Christian Hope of Immortality* (London: Unicorn Press, 1938) all favor the belief in an afterlife. Sympathetic also is William James, *Human Immortality* (Boston and New York: Houghton Mifflin and Co., 1898, second edition with an answer to critics, 1917). Corliss Lamont, *The Illusion of Immortality* (London: Watts and Co., New York: G. P. Putnam's, 1935) and C. Cohen, *The Other Side of Death* (London: The Pioneer Press, 1922) are detailed presentations of the unbeliever's viewpoint. Briefer statements of the same outlook are found in several chapters of Bertrand Russell, *Why I am not a Christian and Other Essays* (London: Allen and Unwin, New York: Simon and Schuster, 1957) and in Chapter 43 of Clarence Darrow, *The Story of My Life* (New York: Charles Scribner's Sons, 1932). A rebuttal of the moral argument for immortality is contained in Section D of C. D. Broad, *The Mind and Its Place in Nature, op. cit.* The same book discusses also the view that what is called "psychical research" provides evidence for human survival. Broad's most recent contribution to this subject is his lecture, "Human Personality and the Possibility of Its Survival," (Berkeley and Los Angeles: University of California Press, 1955). Gardner Murphy's articles "An Outline of Survival Evidence," and "Difficulties Confronting the Survival Hypothesis," in the *Journal of the American Society for Psychical Research,* 1945, contain much interesting information. Chapters 20 and 21 of C. J. Ducasse, *Nature, Mind and Death, op. cit.,* give a more detailed statement of Ducasse's views than the selection included in the present work. Ducasse, Aldous Huxley, H. H. Price, and J. B. Rhine are some of the contributors to a special issue of *"Tomorrow"* (Autumn, 1956) devoted to the question "Does Man Survive Death?" W. R. Alger, *Critical History of the Doctrine of a Future Life* (New York, W. I. Widdleton, 1871) is a book of vast bulk giving a great deal of information on the history of the belief in immortality.

The problems concerning the nature of the mind and its relation to the body have been given a great deal of attention in recent years. There are many suggestive remarks in Wittgenstein's posthumously published *Philosophical Investigations** (Oxford: Basil Blackwell, 1953). Another influential book is John Wisdom, *Other Minds** (Oxford: Basil Blackwell, 1952). Peter Laslett (ed.), *The Physical Basis of Mind* (Oxford: Basil Blackwell, 1951) is a collection of talks given over the Third Program of the B. B. C. The majority of these are by scientists who summarize what physiology and anatomy have taught us about the brain. The last three addresses present the views of three distinguished philosophers—Lord Samuel, A. J. Ayer, and Gilbert Ryle. Samuel defends a form of "agnostic" interactionism, Ayer discusses what he takes to be the confusions behind Samuel's position, and Ryle briefly repeats the views more fully developed in his *Concept of Mind, op. cit.* During the last few years numerous valuable articles have appeared in philosophical periodicals, many of them provoked or inspired by Ryle's book. There is an article by A. C. Ewing entitled "Mental Acts" in *Mind*, 1948, an answer by W. B. Gallie in the same volume which in turn is followed by Ewing's rejoinder in *Mind*, 1949. J. R. Jones' "The Self in Sensory Cognition," *Mind*, 1949, was criticized in the same volume by A. Flew and this criticism was answered by Jones in *Mind*, 1950. Behaviorism is discussed in C. A. Mace's "Some Implications of Analytical Behaviorism,"* *Proc. of the Arist. Soc.*, 1949, in B. A. Farrell's "Experience,"* *Mind*, 1950, and in A. Peters' "Observationalism in Psychology," *Mind*, 1951. In "Recommendations regarding the Language of Introspection," *Philosophy and Phenomenological Research*, 1948, and "Linguistic Approach to Psycho-Physics," *Proc. of the Arist. Soc.*, 1950, J. N. Findlay defends dualism as against theories like Ryle's. The topic of introspection and self-knowledge which is the main subject of the former of these articles is also discussed in W. Kneale's "Experience and Introspection," *Proc. of the Arist. Soc.*, 1951 and by J. R. Jones and T. R. Miles in a symposium entitled "Self-Knowledge," in the *Proc. of the Arist. Soc.*, Supp. Vol. XXX, 1956. Problems concerning our knowledge of other minds are dealt with in M. Shearn's "Other People's Sense-Data,"* *Proc. of the Arist. Soc.*, 1951, P. Alexander's "Other People's Experiences,"* *ibid.*, R. Wollhein's "Privacy," *ibid.*, Stuart Hampshire's "The Analogy of Feeling,"* *Mind*, 1952, A. J. Ayer's "One's Knowledge of Other Minds," which is reprinted in his *Philosophical Essays* (London: Macmillan, 1954), and by John Wisdom, J. L. Austin, and A. J. Ayer in a celebrated symposium entitled "Other Minds,"* in the *Proc. of the Arist. Soc.*, Suppl. Vol. XX, 1946. Wisdom's contribution was reprinted in his book, *Other Minds, op. cit.*, Austin's in A. Flew (ed.), *Logic and Language*, Second Series (Oxford: Basil Blackwell, 1953). Immortality is discussed by A. H. Basson in a dialogue entitled "The Immortality of the Soul," *Mind*, 1950. There are answers to Basson by N. A. Nikan in *Mind*, 1951 and by C. B. Martin in *Mind*, 1955. Other discussions of related topics by analytic philosophers are A. C. MacIntyre's "A Note on Immortality," *Mind*, 1955 and C. Lewy's "Is the Notion of Disembodied Existence Self-Contradictory," *Proc. of the Arist. Soc.*, 1943. The most recent comprehensive discussion of the whole body-mind problem is H. Feigl's "The 'Mental' and the 'Physical',"* in Feigl and Scriven (eds.), *Minnesota Studies in the Philosophy of Science*, Vol. II (Minneapolis: University of Minnesota Press, 1957). Feigl's article contains also an extremely valuable, up-to-date bibliography.

V

Determinism, Freedom, and Moral Responsibility

INTRODUCTION

D ETERMINISM is the theory that everything in the universe is entirely governed by causal laws. It asserts that whatever happens at some specific moment is the outcome of something that happened at a previous moment, i.e., that the present is always "determined" by the past. It may be difficult or impossible to prove that this theory is true. But most people accept it, or something very close to it, in their daily activities. They do so whether they are dealing with inanimate objects or with living organisms; whether they are concerned with involuntary or "voluntary" human behavior.

Let us suppose, for example, that a doctor, after carefully examining a patient, announces that unfortunately he cannot offer any assistance since the patient suffers from a mysterious ailment—one, in fact, which has no cause. The patient would in these circumstances undoubtedly be justified in angrily telling the doctor to keep his jokes for some academic discussion group and in turning to somebody else for help. If the doctor had merely said that he had never come across this kind of illness before and that he knew of no cure for it or that the cause of it had not yet been discovered, we would not necessarily consider his statement absurd. On the contrary, we might even admire him for his candor. We are ready to admit that there are illnesses whose causes are unknown. We are not ready to admit that there are illnesses without a cause.

Let us take another illustration. In Melbourne, Australia, whether forecasts for a period of twenty-four hours are exceedingly reliable. That is to say, the predictions based on the available atmospheric data and the known meteorological laws are almost always correct. In New York City, on the other hand, the official forecasts for a period of twenty-four hours in advance are more often wrong than right. Supposing someone came along and said, "There is an easy explanation for the successes of the Australian and the lack of successes of the New York weather forecasts. In Melbourne the weather is caused —there it is the outcome of preceding conditions; but in New York, more often than not, the weather has no cause. It is 'cut off from,' it is 'disconnected with' what happened before." We would assuredly question the sanity of this man. For we all believe that the failures of the New York meteorologists are to be explained quite differently. We all believe that the weather in New York is just as much the outcome of preceding conditions as the weather in Melbourne. The forecasts are less reliable because of the greater complexities of the factors which have to be taken into account and the greater difficulty of observing them, but certainly not because no causal factors exist.

It is exactly the same with human behavior. We all of us believe, to use Mill's words, that,

> given the motives which are present to an individual's mind, and given likewise the character and disposition of the individual, the manner in which he will act might be unerringly inferred; that if we knew the person thoroughly, and knew all the inducements which are acting upon him, we could foretell his conduct with as much certainty as we can predict any physical event. . . . No one who believed that he knew thoroughly the circumstances of any case, and the characters of the different persons concerned, would hesitate to foretell how all of them would act. Whatever degree of doubt he may in fact feel, arises from the uncertainty whether he really knows the circumstances, or the character of some one or other of the persons, with the degree of accuracy required; but by no means from thinking that if he did know these things, there could be any uncertainty what the conduct would be.

We do indeed occasionally say about people that they did or felt certain things without a cause, e.g., "He was in a dreadful mood after an argument with his wife and took out his anger on his secretary, insulting her quite without cause," or "Suddenly he went beserk without cause and in a frightful rampage shot his mother and all his seven children" or "He hates the Jews without cause." However, we do not really in such situations mean literally that the actions or feelings are uncaused. We mean, rather, that they lack adequate justification or that their cause is unknown to us. We do not mean, for instance, that the Jew-baiter's feelings have no cause, but that they have no good ground. We do not mean that the sudden epileptic fury came from nowhere. We mean that we don't know what caused it, and perhaps, also, that on the basis of what we knew about the man's previous record we could not have predicted the attack.

We believe that human actions are caused regardless of whether they are "in" or "out" of character, regardless of whether a person surprises us or acts in accordance with our expectations. Perhaps the following example will help to make this clear. A determinist once engaged in a public debate with an "indeterminist"—i.e., a person who rejects determinism. The debate took place in a college classroom. By the rules of the college everybody had to be out of the building not later than 11 P.M. In the course of his talk the determinist predicted that his opponent would not be in the room or in the building at 2 o'clock the following morning. The indeterminist defied this prediction. He stayed on, presumably spent a miserable night, had himself discovered in the morning by the cleaning woman, and made sure that he was reported to the dean in charge of such matters for breaking the rules of the college. His action of course falsified the determinist's prediction and greatly surprised all who had been present at the debate. Nevertheless, everyone who heard of the indeterminist's bizarre performance had no doubt that it was just as much due to a cause as any of his other, less unusual actions. Moreover, if it had been known that he was eager to defy the prediction, and furthermore that this desire was stronger than his desire for a comfortable night, the outcome could have been predicted. Or, what for our purposes amounts to the same thing: in retrospect we can explain his extraordinary behavior in terms of preceding conditions just as completely as the more customary conduct of other people who in similar circumstances would prefer sleep to defiance.

Although we thus accept determinism at least in our practical activities, the vast majority of people in our culture also indulge in judgments of moral responsibility; and at first sight it seems that these could never be justified, if determinism were true. For we hold people responsible only for those actions which they performed "freely" in the sense that they could have done something other than what they did. But if determinism is true, then everything people do is completely caused; and, given the causal antecedents in any particular case, nothing could happen except what does happen. It seems to follow that nobody can act differently from the way he acts, and hence that freedom must be an illusion and that human beings are never properly accountable for their conduct. Alternatively, if freedom is not an illusion, determinism must be false.

The apparent conflict between determinism and freedom has also been formulated in the following way: Let us consider some example of a momentous choice in recent history, e.g., Harry Truman's decision to drop the atomic bomb on Hiroshima. We would normally say that Harry Truman was a free agent in this matter, that there were several alternative courses open to him. Some people have praised him for what he did, while others have cursed him. But all of them, including Harry Truman himself, agree that he carries the responsibility for the decision. Now if determinism is true, it has been argued, it would be absurd to hold Harry Truman responsible, since all he did was predetermined long before he was born. If determinism is true, then the whole future of the universe is in principle predictable. As the result of our imperfect knowledge of the existing conditions at any particular moment and our imperfect knowledge of causal connections, our predictive ability is in practice severely limited. This, however, does not affect the point at issue. Supposing there were a "Superscientist" who knew absolutely everything happening in the universe at one particular moment—say, at 8 A.M. on January 1, 1800. Let us suppose further that the Superscientist knew absolutely every causal law. If determinism were true, he could predict the entire future of the universe, including Harry Truman's instructions to drop the atomic bomb. But in that case Harry Truman's choice was a bogus affair. If the outcome was known, or rather knowable, in advance, he cannot properly be said to have been choosing. And what is true of Harry Truman's "decision" applies equally to all apparent choices of all other human beings. They are merely apparent and not genuine, if determinism is true. When determinism is stated in this way it appears as a paralyzing doctrine which implies that human efforts are quite pointless. As Edington put it: "What significance is there to my mental struggle tonight whether I shall or shall not give up smoking, if the laws which govern the matter of the physical universe already preordain for the morrow a configuration of matter consisting of pipe, tobacco and smoke connected to my lips?"

In the light of these and similar considerations, philosophers have asked themselves: Which is true, determinism or freedom? Or can we perhaps believe in both and show that there is no conflict between them? There are three possible answers to these questions, and important writers can be quoted in support of all three. There are, to begin with, philosophers who accept determinism and reject freedom. They usually reason somewhat along the following lines: All the objective, scientific evidence favors determinism. It is true that human beings have a feeling or an "intuition" of freedom. A rational person, however, must be guided by objective evidence and not by intuitions. In our book this position is represented by Holbach (Selection 22). Among the great philosophers Spinoza and Schopenhauer may be cited as supporters of a view of this kind, and many celebrated thinkers outside the fold of professional philosophers adopted it. Einstein held it, and so did Freud. Many famous novelists and poets held it, including Melville, Arthur Schnitzler, A. E. Houseman, and Thomas Hardy. The greatest lawyer the United States ever produced, Clarence Darrow, made this view the basis of many of his successful court pleas, as well as of revolutionary suggestions concerning the treatment of criminals.

Secondly, there are philosophers who, agreeing that determinism is not compatible with freedom and moral responsibility, accept freedom and reject determinism. This position has been justified in many different ways, but perhaps the most common defense proceeds along these lines: Nothing can be more certain than what is given in immediate experience. If, for instance, I see a white patch or feel pleasure, this is more certain than any complicated theory, no matter how eminent the supporters of that theory may be. Now, our experience of freedom is a datum of immediate experience, while determinism is at best a complicated theory. If the two conflict, this indicates that there must be something wrong with determinism. It is true that sometimes we make erroneous judgments of perception. For instance, we might, looking at an object from a distance, judge it to be black, although on closer examination it turns out to be red. But the case of freedom is different. Here further experience only serves to confirm our conviction. On every new occasion when I am confronted with several alternatives, I once again experience my freedom. In the words of Henry Sidgwick:

> It is impossible for me to think at such a moment that my volition is completely determined by my formed character and the motives acting upon it. The opposite conviction is so strong as to be absolutely unshaken by the evidence brought against it; I cannot believe it to be illusory. So far it is unlike the erroneous intuitions which occur in the exercise of the senses; as e.g., the imperfections of sight and hearing. For experience soon teaches me to regard these as appearances whose suggestions are misleading; but no amount of experience of the sway of motives even tends to make me distrust my intuitive consciousness that in resolving after deliberation I exercise free choice as to which of the motives acting on me shall prevail.

Moreover, our moral consciousness must not be denied a hearing, and an adequate philosophy ought to do justice to it. If a scientific theory conflicts with the revelations of our moral consciousness, this, in the last analysis, may be so much the worse for the scientific theory. Among the philosophers represented in the present book William James (Selection 23) and C. A. Campbell (Selection 27) take a view of this kind. It is also found in many religious philosophers, especially those with a Catholic background. The same conclusion, thought partly for different reasons, was defended by the great English physicist, Sir Arthur Eddington, who believed that recent discoveries in quantum physics had important bearings on the problem of freedom and determinism.

There are, finally, philosophers who maintain that both determinism and our belief in freedom are true, and that any appearance of conflict is deceptive. A reconciling position of this kind was advocated by Kant, in whose work, however, it depends on a highly speculative bifurcation of the universe into the world of "noumena" and the world of "phenomena," which is accepted by very few contemporaries. Hegel and his disciples, notably the British philosophers Green and Bradley, also put forward a theory which attempted to reconcile determinism and freedom. The same theory, incidentally, is found in Engels and other Marxist writers who followed Hegel completely on this subject. But this attempt at reconciliation, like Kant's, has few adherents today, at least in the English-speaking world. There is, however, a third variety of this general position which is very widely held. This view goes back at least as far as Hobbes and was given its classic statement by Hume and Mill. It is therefore sometimes called the "Hume-Mill theory." In our book it is represented by the extracts from Mill (Selection 24), Schlick (Selection 25), and Ducasse (Selection 26).

The main idea behind this theory is very simple. If by "free" we meant "uncaused," then of course determinism would imply that nobody is ever a free agent. But when we call an action "free" in ordinary life, we never mean "uncaused"; and this most emphatically includes the kind of conduct about which we pass moral judgments. By calling an action "free" we mean that the agent was not coerced, that he was acting from or in accordance with his own unimpeded desire. Thus if I take a ride in a car because I have been kidnapped, what I do is not free since I act under a threat. Again, if I hand over money to somebody as the result of a post-hypnotic suggestion—something I would not have done but for the hypnotic influence—I am not free since my action springs from somebody else's desire and not my own. But if I take a car-ride or give money to a beggar not because I am threatened or because I am under hypnotic suggestion but because I like to do these things and decided to do them, then my actions are free. My actions are free although they are just as much caused as any unfree action. They are free although anybody knowing my general disposition and the state of my body and mind at the preceding moments could have predicted them without difficulty.

Contemporary defenders of this view who are familiar with the facts concerning compulsion neurosis would be inclined to qualify the definition of "free" mentioned in the last paragraph. An action is free, they would say, if it comes from an unimpeded *rational* desire on the part of the agent. While it may not be easy to give a general definition of "rational desire" in this context, there would be up to a point very general agreement as to which desires are rational and which are not. For example, if a rich kleptomaniac steals an article he does not need, he is not a free agent, because the desire from which he is acting is not rational. But if I go into a restaurant and order a steak not because I suffer from a compulsion neurosis (at least not concerning steaks) but simply because I desire to eat a juicy, tender and nourishing steak, my action is free. I am acting in accordance with an unimpeded rational desire.

Philosophers who adopt this position emphatically deny that they are fatalists and that determinism, as they understand it, is a paralyzing doctrine. There is a famous dilemma which may help to illustrate the difference. According to this dilemma, if a person falls off a ship into the sea it is senseless for him to make any attempt to be saved. For he is either fated to drown or else fated to be saved. In the former case efforts are of no avail, in the latter they are unnecessary. This is the position of fatalism. An advocate of the Hume-Mill theory, on the other hand, would maintain that there is a third alternative which has been omitted: the man who fell into the sea may be saved *because of his efforts*—because, for instance, others may hear his cries. The fact that his efforts are themselves caused in no way cancels out the fact that the efforts were, in the case imagined, the cause of his rescue.

Determinism, on the Hume-Mill theory, does indeed claim that all human actions are in principle *predictable*. It does not claim that all actions are *predetermined,* if this means that what human beings do is independent of their desires, choices, deliberations, and other psychological states and aspirations. The Superscientist, on this view, could have predicted Harry Truman's order to drop the atomic bomb on Hiroshima. But he could have made the prediction only by taking into account Harry Truman's desires and interests and hopes and fears and reflections on the consequences of alternative courses of action. The Superscientist in this picturesque formulation of determinism is not, it should be noted, a super-blackmailer or a super-hypnotist. He is not influencing or constraining Harry Truman. He is only predicting what will be done.

Most defenders of the Hume-Mill theory trace back the belief that determinism and freedom are incompatible to two factors—to certain confused anthropomorphic notions about causation and also to certain unrecognized ambiguities in ordinary speech. The latter would be said to occur particularly in connection with expressions like "nothing *could* have happened except what actually happened" or "this event *had* to happen." These expressions are commonly used in two very different senses. In one sense which may be called the "regularity" sense, they merely designate certain invariable sequences. Thus if one billiard ball strikes another with a certain force and the second ball moves, we might easily say that, given the impact of the first ball upon the second, given the application of an unbalanced force, the second ball "had to move"; "it could have done nothing else." But this means no more than that there is an invariable sequence between the application of net forces and the motion or, strictly, the acceleration of the bodies to which the forces are applied. It means that if we know the magnitude and direction of the unbalanced force it is possible to predict that the ball will move in a certain way and not stay at rest or move in any other way. When we say, "the second ball had to move," we do not mean the presence of a constraining or compelling influence such as may occur in a situation involving human beings. We do not mean that the first billiard ball said to the second, "Listen here, you scoundrel, move or I'll knock your brains out!" Nor do we mean that the second ball suffered from a compulsive urge of the kind which makes us say in the case of the kleptomaniac that he had to act the way he did. However, when we say about a human being that he had to act the way he did or that he could have done nothing else, we do as a rule mean to assert the presence of a constraining influence like a threat or a compulsive urge. This may be called the "constraint" sense of the ambiguous expressions we are discussing. Now, a defender of the Hume-Mill theory would argue that determinism properly understood does indeed entail that nothing in the universe, including all human actions, could have been different from what it is. But determinism applies this only in the regularity-sense which does not at all exclude freedom. Determinism is taken to negate freedom when it is tacitly *mis*understood to claim that no human action could ever have been different in the constraint-sense.

According to these writers the regularity-sense of "nothing else could have happened" or "this had to happen" or "it was necesssarily so" and similar expressions must also be carefully distinguished from the sense in which they designate *logical* necessity, as when we say for example that two plus two "has" to equal four or that the sum of the interior angles of a Euclidian triangle "must necessarily" equal 180 degrees. When a defender of the Hume-Mill theory asserts that no event in the universe could have failed to occur he implies: *given* the total set of preceding events. If C is the total set of relevant conditions preceding an event E, the occurrence of E was necessary in the sense, and *only* in the sense, that whenever and wherever conditions like C obtain, an event like E follows. The law connecting C and E is not logically necessary in the sense that it would be self-contradictory to suppose exceptions to it. Nor is the occurrence of any particular event asserted to be logically necessary.

There is something very attractive about all reconciling theories, since they allow us to go on believing both in freedom and in determinism. The Hume-Mill theory in particular, as already noted, has many adherents among contemporary philosophers. It is, however, far from universally accepted. The opposition to the theory is represented in our book by C. A. Campbell (Selection 27). Among the arguments used by the critics, the following is perhaps the most powerful. The reconcilers, it is said, do not pursue the subject far enough. They stop arbitrarily at the desires or volitions which are the causes of some of our actions. We must not stop there. We must go on to ask where our desires come from. If determinism is true there can be no doubt about the answer to this question. Ultimately our desires and our whole character are derived from our inherited equipment and from the environmental influences to which we were subjected at the beginning of our lives. It is clear that we had no hand in shaping either of these and we cannot rationally be held responsible for them. Hence if determinism is true we are ultimately not really free—at least not in the sense required for moral responsibility. Schopenhauer expressed this thought in a telling epigram: "A man can surely do what he wills to do, but he cannot determine what he wills."

P. E.

22

THE ILLUSION OF FREE WILL

Baron Holbach

Motives and the Determination of the Will

. . . IN WHATEVER manner man is considered, he is connected to universal nature, and submitted to the necessary and immutable laws that she imposes on all the beings she contains, according to their peculiar essences or to the respective properties with which, without consulting them, she endows each particular species. Man's life is a line that nature commands him to describe upon the surface of the earth, without his ever being able to swerve from it, even for an instant. He is born without his own consent; his organization does innowise depend upon himself; his ideas come to him involuntarily; his habits are in the power of those who cause him to contract them; he is unceasingly modified by causes, whether visible or concealed, over which he has no control, which necessarily regulate his mode of existence, give the hue to his way of thinking, and determine his manner of acting. He is good or bad, happy or miserable, wise or foolish, reasonable or irrational, without his will being for anything in these various states. Nevertheless, in spite of the shackles by which he is bound, it is pretended he is a free agent, or that independent of the causes by which he is moved, he determines his own will, and regulates his own condition.

However slender the foundation of this opinion, of which everything ought to point out to him the error, it is current at this day and passes for an incontestable truth with a great number of people, otherwise extremely enlightened; it is the basis of religion, which, supposing relations between man and the unknown being she has placed above nature, has been incapable of imagining how man could merit reward or deserve

[This selection consists of extracts from Chapter XI and XII of Holbach's *System of Nature*, a book first published in 1770. The translation used is that of H. D. Robinson.]

punishment from this being, if he was not a free agent. Society has been believed interested in this system; because an idea has gone abroad, that if all the actions of man were to be contemplated as necessary, the right of punishing those who injure their associates would no longer exist. At length human vanity accommodated itself to a hypothesis which, unquestionably, appears to distinguish man from all other physical beings, by assigning to him the special privilege of a total independence of all other causes, but of which a very little reflection would have shown him the impossibility. . . .

The will, as we have elsewhere said, is a modification of the brain, by which it is disposed to action, or prepared to give play to the organs. This will is necessarily determined by the qualities, good or bad, agreeable or painful, of the object or the motive that acts upon his senses, or of which the idea remains with him, and is resuscitated by his memory. In consequence, he acts necessarily, his action is the result of the impulse he receives either from the motive, from the object, or from the idea which has modified his brain, or disposed his will. When he does not act according to this impulse, it is because there comes some new cause, some new motive, some new idea, which modifies his brain in a different manner, gives him a new impulse, determines his will in another way, by which the action of the former impulse is suspended: thus, the sight of an agreeable object, or its idea, determines his will to set him in action to procure it; but if a new object or a new idea more powerfully attracts him, it gives a new direction to his will, annihilates the effect of the former, and prevents the action by which it was to be procured. This is the mode in which reflection, experience, reason, necessarily arrests or suspends the action of man's will: without this he would of necessity have followed the anterior impulse which carried him towards a then desirable object. In all this he always acts according to necessary laws from which he has no means of emancipating himself.

If when tormented with violent thirst, he figures to himself in idea, or really perceives a fountain, whose limpid streams might cool his feverish want, is he sufficient master of himself to desire or not to desire the object competent to satisfy so lively a want? It will no doubt be conceded, that it is impossible he should not be desirous to satisfy it; but it will be said—if at this moment it is announced to him that the water he so ardently desires is poisoned, he will, notwithstanding his vehement thirst, abstain from drinking it: and it has, therefore, been falsely concluded that he is a free agent. The fact, however, is, that the motive in either case is exactly the same: his own conservation. The same necessity that determined him to drink before he knew the water was deleterious upon this new discovery equally determined him not to drink; the desire of conserving himself either annihilates or suspends the former impulse; the second motive becomes stronger than the preceding, that is, the fear of death, or the desire of preserving himself, necessarily prevails over the painful sensation caused by his eagerness to drink: but, it will be said, if the thirst is very parching, an inconsiderate man without regarding the danger will risk swallowing the water. Nothing is gained by this remark: in this case, the anterior impulse only regains the ascendency; he is persuaded that life may possibly be longer preserved, or that he shall derive a greater good by drinking the poisoned water than by enduring the torment, which, to his mind, threatens instant dissolution: thus the first becomes the strongest and necessarily urges him on to action. Nevertheless, in either case, whether he partakes of the water, or whether he does not, the two actions will be equally necessary; they will be the effect of that motive which finds itself most puissant; which consequently acts in the most coercive manner upon his will.

This example will serve to explain the whole phenomena of the human will. This will, or rather the brain, finds itself in the same situation as a bowl, which, although it has received an impulse that drives it forward in a straight line, is deranged in its course whenever a force superior to the first obliges it to change its direction. The man who drinks the poisoned water appears a madman; but the actions of fools are as necessary as those of the most prudent individuals. The motives that determine the voluptuary and the debauchee to risk their health, are as powerful, and their actions are as necessary, as those which decide the wise man to manage his. But, it will be insisted, the debauchee may be prevailed on to change his conduct: this does not imply that he is a free agent; but that motives may be found sufficiently powerful to annihilate the effect of those that previously acted upon him; then these new motives determine his will to the new mode of conduct he may adopt as necessarily as the former did to the old mode. . . .

The errors of philosophers on the free agency of man, have arisen from their regarding his will as the *primum mobile,* the original motive of his actions; for want of recurring back, they have not perceived the multiplied, the complicated causes which, independently of him, give motion to the will itself; or which dispose and modify his brain, whilst he himself is purely passive in the motion he receives. Is he the master of desiring or not desiring an object that appears desirable to him? Without doubt it will be answered, no: but he is the master of resisting his desire, if he reflects on the consequences. But, I ask, is he capable of reflecting on these consequences, when his soul is hurried along by a very lively passion, which entirely depends upon his natural organization, and the causes by which he is modified? Is it in his power to add to these consequences all the weight necessary to counterbalance his desire? Is he the master of preventing the qualities which render an object desirable from residing in it? I shall be told: he ought to have learned to resist his passions; to contract a habit of putting a curb on his desires.

I agree to it without any difficulty. But in reply, I again ask, is his nature susceptible of this modification? Does his boiling blood, his unruly imagination, the igneous fluid that circulates in his veins, permit him to make, enable him to apply true experience in the moment when it is wanted? And even when his temperament has capacitated him, has his education, the examples set before him, the ideas with which he has been inspired in early life, been suitable to make him contract this habit of repressing his desires? Have not all these things rather contributed to induce him to seek with avidity, to make him actually desire those objects which you say he ought to resist.

The *ambitious man* cries out: you will have me resist my passion; but have they not unceasingly repeated to me that rank, honours, power, are the most desirable advantages in life? Have I not seen my fellow citizens envy them, the nobles of my country sacrifice every thing to obtain them? In the society in which I live, am I not obliged to feel, that if I am deprived of these advantages, I must expect to languish in contempt; to cringe under the rod of oppression?

The *miser* says: you forbid me to love money, to seek after the means of acquiring it: alas! does not every thing tell me that, in this world, money is the greatest blessing; that it is amply sufficient to render me happy? In the country I inhabit, do I not see all my fellow citizens covetous of riches? but do I not also witness that they are little scrupulous in the means of obtaining wealth? As soon as they are enriched by the means which you censure, are they not cherished, considered and respected? By what authority, then, do you defend me from amassing treasure? what right have you to prevent my using means, which, although you call them sordid and criminal, I see approved by the sovereign? Will you have me renounce my happiness?

The *voluptuary* argues: you pretend that I should resist my desires; but was I the maker of my own temperament, which unceasingly invites me to pleasure? You call my pleasures disgraceful; but in the country in which I live, do I not witness the most dissipated men enjoying the most distinguished rank? Do I not behold that no one is ashamed of adultery but the husband it has outraged? do not I see men making trophies of their debaucheries, boasting of their libertinism, rewarded with applause?

The *choleric man* vociferates: you advise me to put a curb on my passions, and to resist the desire of avenging myself: but can I conquer my nature? Can I alter the received opinions of the world? Shall I not be forever disgraced, infallibly dishonoured in society, if I do not wash out in the blood of my fellow creatures the injuries I have received?

The *zealous enthusiast* exclaims: you recommend me mildness; you advise me to be tolerant; to be indulgent to the opinions of my fellow men; but is not my temperament violent? Do I not ardently love my

God? Do they not assure me, that zeal is pleasing to him; that sanguinary inhuman persecutors have been his friends? As I wish to render myself acceptable in his sight, I therefore adopt the same means.

In short, the actions of man are never free; they are always the necessary consequence of his temperament, of the received ideas, and of the notions, either true or false, which he has formed to himself of happiness; of his opinions, strengthened by example, by education, and by daily experience. So many crimes are witnessed on the earth only because every thing conspires to render man vicious and criminal; the religion he has adopted, his government, his education, the examples set before him, irresistibly drive him on to evil: under these circumstances, morality preaches virtue to him in vain. In those societies where vice is esteemed, where crime is crowned, where venality is constantly recompensed, where the most dreadful disorders are punished only in those who are too weak to enjoy the privilege of committing them with impunity, the practice of virtue is considered nothing more than a painful sacrifice of happiness. Such societies chastise, in the lower orders, those excesses which they respect in the higher ranks; and frequently have the injustice to condemn those in the penalty of death, whom public prejudices, maintained by constant example, have rendered criminal.

Man, then, is not a free agent in any one instant of his life; he is necessarily guided in each step by those advantages, whether real or fictitious, that he attaches to the objects by which his passions are roused: these passions themselves are necessary in a being who unceasingly tends towards his own happiness; their energy is necessary, since that depends on his temperament; his temperament is necessary, because it depends on the physical elements which enter into his composition; the modification of this temperament is necessary, as it is the infallible and inevitable consequence of the impulse he receives from the incessant action of moral and physical beings.

Choice Does Not Prove Freedom

In spite of these proofs of the want of free agency in man, so clear to unprejudiced minds, it will, perhaps be insisted upon with no small feeling of triumph, that if it be proposed to any one, to move or not to move his hand, an action in the number of those called indifferent, he evidently appears to be the master of choosing; from which it is concluded that evidence has been offered of free agency. The reply is, this example is perfectly simple; man in performing some action which he is resolved on doing, does not by any means prove his free agency: the very desire of displaying this quality, excited by the dispute, becomes a necessary motive, which decides his will either for the one or the other of these actions: What deludes him in this instance, or that which persuades him he is a free agent at this moment, is, that he does not discern the true motive which sets him in action, namely, the desire of convincing his opponent: if in the heat of the dispute he insists and asks, "Am I not the master of throwing myself out of the window?" I shall answer him, no; that whilst he preserves his reason there is no probability that the desire of proving his free agency, will become a motive sufficiently powerful to make him sacrifice his life to the attempt: if, notwithstanding this, to prove he is a free agent, he should actually precipitate himself from the window, it would not be a sufficient warranty to conclude he acted freely, but rather that it was the violence of his temperament which spurred him on to this folly. Madness is a state, that depends upon the heat of the blood, not upon the will. A fanatic or a hero, braves death as necessarily as a more phlegmatic man or a coward flies from it.

There is, in point of fact, no difference between the man that is cast out of the window by another, and the man who throws himself out of it, except that the impulse in the first instance comes immediately from without whilst that which determines the fall in the second case, springs from within his own peculiar machine, having its more remote cause also exterior. When Mutius Scaevola held his hand in the fire, he was as much acting under the influence of necessity (caused by interior motives) that urged him to this strange action, as if his arm had been held by strong men: pride, despair, the desire of braving his enemy, a wish to astonish him, an anxiety to intimidate him, etc., were the invisible chains that held his hand bound to the fire. The love of glory, enthusiasm for their country, in like manner caused Codrus and Decius to devote themselves for their fellow-citizens. The Indian Colanus and the philosopher Peregrinus were equally obliged to burn themselves, by desire of exciting the astonishment of the Grecian assembly.

It is said that free agency is the absence of those obstacles competent to oppose themselves to the actions of man, or to the exercise of his faculties: it is pretended that he is a free agent whenever, making use of these faculties, he produces the effect he has proposed to himself. In reply to this reasoning, it is sufficient to consider that it in nowise depends upon himself to place or remove the obstacles that either determine or resist him; the motive that causes his action is no more in his own power than the obstacle that impedes him, whether this obstacle or motive be within his own machine or exterior of his person: he is not master of the thought presented to his mind, which determines his will; this thought is excited by some cause independent of himself.

To be undeceived on the system of his free agency, man has simply to recur to the motive by which his will is determined; he will always find this motive is out of his own control. It is said: that in consequence of an idea to which the mind gives birth, man acts freely if he encounters no obstacle. But the question is, what gives birth to this idea in his brain? was he the master either to prevent it from presenting itself, or from renewing itself in his brain? Does not this idea depend either upon objects that strike him exteriorly and in despite of himself, or upon causes, that without his knowledge, act within himself and modify his brain? Can he prevent his eyes, cast without design upon any object whatever, from giving him an idea of this object, and from moving his brain? He is not more master of the obstacles; they are the necessary effects of either interior or exterior causes, which always act according to their given properties. A man insults a coward; this necessarily irritates him against his insulter; but his will cannot vanquish the obstacle that cowardice places to the object of his desire, because his natural conformation, which does not depend upon himself, prevents his having courage. In this case, the coward is insulted in spite of himself; and against his will is obliged patiently to brook the insult he has received.

Absence of Restraint Is Not Absence of Necessity

The partisans of the system of free agency appear ever to have confounded constraint with necessity. Man believes he acts as a free agent, every time he does not see any thing that places obstacles to his actions; he does not perceive that the motive which causes him to will, is always necessary and independent of himself. A prisoner loaded with chains is compelled to remain in prison; but he is not a free agent in the desire to emancipate himself; his chains prevent him from acting, but they do not prevent him from willing; he would save himself if they would loose his fetters; but he would not save himself as a free agent; fear or the idea of punishment would be sufficient motives for his action.

Man may, therefore, cease to be restrained, without, for that reason, becoming a free agent: in whatever manner he acts, he will act necessarily, according to motives by which he shall be determined. He may be compared to a heavy body that finds itself arrested in its descent by any obstacle whatever: take away this obstacle, it will gravitate or continue to fall; but who shall say this dense body is free to fall or not? Is not its descent the necessary effect of its own specific gravity? The virtuous Socrates submitted to the laws of his country, although they were unjust; and though the doors of his jail were left open to him, he would not save himself; but in this he did not act as a free agent: the invisible chains of opinion, the secret love of decorum, the inward respect for the laws, even when they were iniquitous, the fear of tarnishing his glory, kept him in his prison; they were motives sufficiently powerful with this enthusiast for virtue, to induce him to wait death with tranquillity; it was not in his power to save himself, because he could find no potential motive to bring him to depart, even for an instant, from those principles to which his mind was accustomed.

Man, it is said, frequently acts against his inclination, from whence it is falsely concluded he is a free agent; but when he appears to act contrary to his inclination, he is always determined to it by some motive sufficiently efficacious to vanquish this inclination. A sick man, with a view to his cure, arrives at conquering his repugnance to the most disgusting remedies: the fear of pain, or the dread of death, then become necessary motives; consequently this sick man cannot be said to act freely.

When it is said, that man is not a free agent, it is not pretended to compare him to a body moved by a simple impulsive cause: he contains within himself causes inherent to his existence; he is moved by an interior organ, which has its own peculiar laws, and is itself necessarily determined in consequence of ideas formed from perception resulting from sensation which it receives from exterior objects. As the mechanism of these sensations, of these perceptions, and the manner they engrave ideas on the brain of man, are not known to him; because he is unable to unravel all these motions; because he cannot perceive the chain of operations in his soul, or the motive principle that acts within him, he supposes himself a free agent; which literally translated, signifies, that he moves himself by himself; that he determines himself without cause: when he rather ought to say, that he is ignorant how or why he acts in the manner he does. It is true the soul enjoys an activity peculiar to itself: but it is equally certain that this activity would never be displayed, if some motive or some cause did not put it in a condition to exercise itself: at least it will not be pretended that the soul is able either to love or to hate without being moved, without knowing the objects, without having some idea of their qualities. Gunpowder has unquestionably a particular activity, but this activity will never display itself, unless fire be applied to it; this, however, immediately sets it in motion.

The Complexity of Human Conduct and
the Illusion of Free Agency

It is the great complication of motion in man, it is the variety of his action, it is the multiplicity of causes that move him, whether simultaneously or in continual succession, that persuades him he is a free agent: if all his motions were simple, if the causes that move him did not confound themselves with each other, if they were distinct, if his machine

were less complicated, he would perceive that all his actions were necessary, because he would be enabled to recur instantly to the cause that
made him act. A man who should be always obliged to go towards the
west, would always go on that side; but he would feel that, in so going,
he was not a free agent: if he had another sense, as his actions or his
motion, augmented by a sixth, would be still more varied and much
more complicated, he would believe himself still more a free agent than
he does with his five senses.

It is, then, for want of recurring to the causes that move him; for
want of being able to analyze, from not being competent to decompose
the complicated motion of his machine, that man believes himself a
free agent: it is only upon his own ignorance that he founds the profound yet deceitful notion he has of his free agency; that he builds those
opinions which he brings forward as a striking proof of his pretended
freedom of action. If, for a short time, each man was willing to examine
his own peculiar actions, search out their true motives to discover their
concatenation, he would remain convinced that the sentiment he has of
his natural free agency, is a chimera that must speedily be destroyed by
experience.

Nevertheless it must be acknowledged that the multiplicity and diversity
of the causes which continually act upon man, frequently without even
his knowledge, render it impossible, or at least extremely difficult for him
to recur to the true principles of his own peculiar actions, much less the
actions of others: they frequently depend upon causes so fugitive, so
remote from their effects, and which, superficially examined, appear to
have so little analogy, so slender a relation with them, that it requires
singular sagacity to bring them into light. This is what renders the study
of the moral man a task of such difficulty; this is the reason why his
heart is an abyss, of which it is frequently impossible for him to fathom
the depth. . . .

If he understood the play of his organs, if he were able to recall to
himself all the impulsions they have received, all the modifications they
have undergone, all the effects they have produced, he would perceive
that all his actions are submitted to that fatality, which regulates his own
particular system, as it does the entire system of the universe: no one
effect in him, any more than in nature, produces itself by chance; this,
as has been before proved, is word void of sense. All that passes in him;
all that is done by him; as well as all that happens in nature, or that is
attributed to her, is derived from necessary causes, which act according
to necessary laws, and which produce necessary effects from whence
necessarily flow others.

Fatality, is the eternal, the immutable, the necessary order, established in nature; or the indispensable connexion of causes that act, with
the effects they operate. Conforming to this order, heavy bodies fall;

light bodies rise; that which is analogous in matter reciprocally attracts; that which is heterogeneous mutually repels; man congregates himself in society, modifies each his fellow; becomes either virtuous or wicked; either contributes to his mutual happiness, or reciprocates his misery; either loves his neighbour, or hates his companion necessarily, according to the manner in which the one acts upon the other. From whence it may be seen, that the same necessity which regulates the physical, also regulates the moral world, in which every thing is in consequence submitted to fatality. Man, in running over, frequently without his own knowledge, often in spite of himself, the route which nature has marked out for him, resembles a swimmer who is obliged to follow the current that carries him along: he believes himself a free agent, because he sometimes consents, sometimes does not consent, to glide with the stream, which, notwithstanding, always hurries him forward; he believes himself the master of his condition, because he is obliged to use his arms under the fear of sinking. . . .

23

THE DILEMMA OF DETERMINISM

William James

Rationality and the Free Will Controversy

A COMMON OPINION prevails that the juice has ages ago been pressed out of the free-will controversy, and that no new champion can do more than warm up stale arguments which everyone has heard. This is a radical mistake. I know of no subject less worn out, or in which inventive genius has a better chance of breaking open new ground—not, perhaps, of forcing a conclusion or of coercing assent, but of deepening our sense of what the issue between the two parties really is, and of what the ideas of fate and of free will imply. At our very side almost, in the past few years, we have seen falling in rapid succession from the press works that present the alternative in entirely novel lights. Not to speak of the English disciples of Hegel, such as Green and Bradley; not to speak of Hinton and Hodgson, nor of Hazard here—we see in the writings of Renouvier, Fouillée, and Delboeuf how completely changed and refreshed is the form of the old disputes. I cannot pretend to vie in originality with any of the masters I have named, and my ambition limits itself to just one little point. If I can make two of the necessarily implied corollaries of determinism clearer to you than they have been made before, I shall have made it possible for you to decide before or against that doctrine with a better understanding of what you are about. And if you prefer not to decide at all, but to remain doubters, you will at least see more plainly what the subject of your hesitation is. I thus declaim openly on the threshold all pretension to prove to you that the freedom of the will is true. The most I hope is to induce some of you to follow my own example in assuming it true, and acting as if it were true. If it be true, it seems to

[This selection is reprinted, with omissions, from "The Dilemma of Determinism," an essay which first appeared in 1884.]

me that this is involved in the strict logic of the case. Its truth ought not to be forced willy-nilly down our indifferent throats. It ought to be freely espoused by men who can equally well turn their backs upon it. In other words, our first act of freedom, if we are free, ought in all inward propriety to be to affirm that we are free. This should exclude, it seems to me, from the free-will side of the question all hope of a coercive demonstration—a demonstration which I, for one, am perfectly contented to go without.

With thus much understood at the outset, we can advance. But, not without one more point understood as well. The arguments I am about to urge all proceed on two suppositions: first, when we make theories about the world and discuss them with one another, we do so in order to attain a conception of things which shall give us subjective satisfaction; and, second, if there be two conceptions, and the one seems to us, on the whole, more rational than the other, we are entitled to suppose that the more rational one is truer of the two. I hope that you are all willing to make these suppositions with me; for I am afraid that if there be any of you here who are not, they will find little edification in the rest of what I have to say. I cannot stop to argue the point; but I myself believe that all the magnificent achievements of mathematical and physical science —our doctrines of evolution, of uniformity of law, and the rest—proceed from our indomitable desire to cast the world into a more rational shape in our minds than the shape into which it is thrown there by the crude order of our experience. The world has shown itself, to a great extent, plastic to this demand of ours for rationality. How much farther it will show itself plastic no one can say. Our only means of finding out is to try; and I, for one, feel as free to try conceptions of moral as of mechanical or of logical rationality. If a certain formula for expressing the nature of the world violates my moral demand, I shall feel free to throw it overboard, or at least to doubt it, as if it disappointed my demand for uniformity of sequence, for example; the one demand being, so far as I can see, quite as subjective and emotional as the other is. The principle of causality, for example—what is it but a postulate, an empty name covering simply a demand that the sequence of events shall some day manifest a deeper kind of belonging of one thing with another than the mere juxtaposition which now phenomenally appears? It is as much an altar to an unknown god as the one that Saint Paul found at Athens. All our scientific and philosophic ideals are altars to unknown gods. Uniformity is as much so as is free will. If this be admitted, we can debate on even terms. But if any one pretends that while freedom and variety are, in the first instance, subjective demands, necessity and uniformity are something altogether different, I do not see how we can debate at all.

To begin, then, I must suppose you acquainted with all the usual arguments on the subject. I cannot stop to take up the old proofs from causation, from statistics, from the certainty with which we can foretell one another's conduct, from the fixity of character, and all the rest. But there are two *words* which usually encumber these classical arguments, and which we must immediately dispose of if we are to make any progress. One is the eulogistic word *freedom,* and the other is the opprobrious word *chance.* The word "chance" I wish to keep, but I wish to get rid of the word "freedom." Its eulogistic associations have so far overshadowed all the rest of its meaning that both parties claim the sole right to use it, and determinists today insist that they alone are freedom's champions. Old-fashioned determinism was what we may call *hard* determinism. It did not shrink from such words as fatality, bondage of the will, necessitation, and the like. Nowadays, we have a *soft* determinism which abhors harsh words, and, repudiating fatality, necessity, and even predetermination, says that its real name is freedom; for freedom is only necessity understood, and bondage to the highest is identical with true freedom. Even a writer as little used to making capital out of soft words as Mr. Hodgson hesitates not to call himself a "free-will determinist."

Now, all this is a quagmire of evasion under which the real issue of fact has been entirely smothered. Freedom in all these senses presents simply no problem at all. No matter what the soft determinist mean by it—whether he mean the acting without external constraint; whether he mean the acting rightly, or whether he mean the acquiescing in the law of the whole—who cannot answer him that sometimes we are free and sometimes we are not? But there *is* a problem, an issue of fact and not of words, an issue of the most momentous importance, which is often decided without discussion in one sentence—nay, in one clause of a sentence—by those very writers who spin out whole chapters in their efforts to show what "true" freedom is; and that is the question of determinism, about which we are to talk tonight.

Possibilities and Actualities

Fortunately, no ambiguities hang about this word or about its opposite, indeterminism. Both designate an outward way in which things may happen, and their cold and mathematical sound has no sentimental associations that can bribe our partiality either way in advance. Now, evidence of an external kind to decide between determinism and indeterminism is, as I intimated a while back, strictly impossible to find. Let us look at the difference between them and see for ourselves. What does determinism profess?

It professes that those parts of the universe already laid down absolutely appoint and decree what the other parts shall be. The future has no ambiguous possibilities hidden in its womb: the part we call the present is compatible with only one totality. Any other future complement than the one fixed from eternity is impossible. The whole is in each and every part, and welds it with the rest into an absolute unity, an iron block, in which there can be no equivocation or shadow of turning.

> With earth's first clay they did the last man knead,
> And there of the last harvest sowed the seed.
> And the first morning of creation wrote
> What the last dawn of reckoning shall read.

Indeterminism, on the contrary, says that the parts have a certain amount of loose play on one another, so that the laying down of one of them does not necessarily determine what the others shall be. It admits that possibilities may be in excess of actualities, and that things not yet revealed to our knowledge may really in themselves be ambiguous. Of two alternative futures which we conceive, both may now be really possible; and the one become impossible only at the very moment when the other excludes it by becoming real itself. Indeterminism thus denies the world to be one unbending unit of fact. It says there is a certain ultimate pluralism in it; and, so saying, it corroborates our ordinary unsophisticated view of things. To that view, actualities seem to float in a wider sea of possibilities from out of which they are chosen; and, somewhere, indeterminism says, such possibilities exist, and form a part of truth.

Determinism, on the contrary, says they exist *nowhere,* and that necessity on the one hand and impossibility on the other are the sole categories of the real. Possibilities that fail to get realized are, for determinism, pure illusions: they never were possibilities at all. There is nothing inchoate, it says, about this universe of ours, all that was or is or shall be actual in it having been from eternity virtually there. The cloud of alternatives our minds escort this mass of actuality withal is a cloud of sheer deceptions, to which "impossibilities" is the only name which rightfully belongs.

The issue, it will be seen, is a perfectly sharp one, which no eulogistic terminology can smear over or wipe out. The truth *must* lie with one side or the other, and its lying with one side makes the other false.

The question relates solely to the existence of possibilities, in the strict sense of the term, as things that may, but need not, be. Both sides admit that a volition, for instance, has occurred. The indeterminists say another volition might have occurred in its place: the determinists swear that nothing could possibly have occurred in its place. Now, can science be called in to tell us which of these two point-blank contradicters of each other is right? Science professes to draw no conclusions but such as are based on matters of fact, things that have actually happened; but how can any amount of assurance that something actually happened give us the least grain of information as to whether another thing might or might not have happened in its place? Only facts can be proved by other facts. With things that are possibilities and not facts, facts have no concern. If we have no other evidence than the evidence of existing facts, the possibility-question must remain a mystery never to be cleared up.

And the truth is that facts practically have hardly anything to do with making us either determinists or indeterminists. Sure enough, we make a flourish of quoting facts this way or that; and if we are determinists, we talk about the infallibility with which we can predict one another's conduct; while if we are indeterminists, we lay great stress on the fact that it is just because we cannot foretell one another's conduct, either in war or statecraft or in any of the great and small intrigues and businesses of men, that life is so intensely anxious and hazardous a game. But who does not see the wretched insufficiency of this so-called objective testimony on both sides? What fills up the gaps in our minds is something not objective, not external. What divides us into *possibility* men and *anti-possibility* men is different faiths or postulates—postulates of rationality. To this man the world seems more rational with possibilities in it—to that man more rational with possibilities excluded; and talk as we will about having to yield to evidence, what makes us monists or pluralists, determinists or indeterminists, is at bottom always some sentiment like this.

The Idea of Chance

The stronghold of the deterministic sentiment is the antipathy to the idea of chance. As soon as we begin to talk indeterminism to our friends, we find a number of them shaking their heads. This notion of alternative possibility, they say, this admission that any one of several things may come to pass, is, after all, only a round-about name for chance; and chance is something the notion of which no sane mind can for an instant tolerate in the world. What is it, they ask, but barefaced crazy unreason, the negation of intelligibility and law? And if the slightest particle of it exists anywhere, what is to prevent the whole fabric from falling together, the stars from going out, and chaos from recommencing her topsy-turvy reign?

Remarks of this sort about chance will put an end to discussion as quickly as anything one can find. I have already told you that "chance" was a word I wished to keep and use. Let us then examine exactly what it means, and see whether it ought to be such a terrible bugbear to us. I fancy that squeezing the thistle boldly will rob it of its sting.

The sting of the word "chance" seems to lie in the assumption that it means something positive, and that if anything happens by chance, it must needs be something of an intrinsically irrational and preposterous sort. Now, chance means nothing of the kind. It is a purely negative and relative term, giving us no information about that of which it is predicated, except that it happens to be disconnected with something else— not controlled, secured, or necessitated by other things in advance of its own actual presence. As this point is the most subtle one of the whole lecture, and at the same time the point on which all the rest hinges, I beg you to pay particular attention to it. What I say is that it tells us nothing about what a thing may be in itself to call it "chance." It may be a bad thing, it may be a good thing. It may be lucidity, transparency, fitness incarnate, matching the whole system of other things, when it has once befallen, in an unimaginably perfect way. All you mean by calling it "chance" is that this is not guaranteed, that it may also fall out otherwise. For the system of other things has no positive hold on the chance-thing. Its origin is in a certain fashion negative: it escapes, and says, "Hands off!" coming, when it comes, as a free gift, or not at all.

This negativeness, however, and this opacity of the chance-thing when thus considered *ab extra,* or from the point of view of previous things or distant things, do not preclude its having any amount of positiveness and luminosity from within, and at its own place and moment. All that its chance-character asserts about it is that there is something in it really of its own, something that is not the unconditional property of the whole. If the whole wants this property, the whole must wait till it can get it, if it be a matter of chance. That the universe may actually be a sort of joint-stock society of this sort, in which the sharers have both limited liabilities and limited powers, is of course a simple and conceivable notion.

Nevertheless, many persons talk as if the minutest dose of disconnectedness of one part with another, the smallest modicum of independence, the faintest tremor of ambiguity about the future, for example, would ruin everything, and turn this goodly universe into a sort of insane sand-heap or nulliverse—no universe at all. Since future human volitions are, as a matter of fact, the only ambiguous things we are tempted to believe in, let us stop for a moment to make ourselves sure whether their independent and accidental character need be fraught with such direful consequences to the universe as these.

What is meant by saying that my choice of which way to walk home after the lecture is ambiguous and matter of chance as far as the present moment is concerned? It means that both Divinity Avenue and Oxford

Street are called; but that only one, and that one *either* one shall be chosen. Now, I ask you seriously to suppose that this ambiguity of my choice is real; and then to make the impossible hypothesis that the choice is made twice over, and each time falls on a different street. In other words, imagine that I first walk through Divinity Avenue, and then imagine that the powers governing the universe annihilate ten minutes of time with all that it contained, and set me back at the door of this hall just as I was before the choice was made. Imagine then that, everything else being the same, I now make a different choice and traverse Oxford Street. You, as passive spectators, look on and see the two alternative universes—one of them with me walking through Divinity Avenue in it, the other with the same me walking through Oxford Street. Now, if you are determinists you believe one of these universes to have been from eternity impossible: you believe it to have been impossible because of the intrinsic irrationality or accidentality somewhere involved in it. But looking outwardly at these universes, can you say which is the impossible and accidental one, and which the rational and necessary one? I doubt if the most iron-clad determinist among you could have the slightest glimmer of light at this point. In other words, either universe *after the fact* and once there would, to our means of observation and understanding, appear just as rational as the other. There would be absolutely no criterion by which we might judge one necessary and the other matter of chance. Suppose now we relieve the gods of their hypothetical task and assume my choice, once made, to be made forever. I go through Divinity Avenue for good and all. If, as good determinists, you now begin to affirm, what all good determinists punctually do affirm, that in the nature of things I couldn't have gone through Oxford Street—had I done so it would have been chance, irrationality, insanity, a horrid gap in nature—I simply call your attention to this, that your affirmation is what the Germans call a *Machtspruch,* a mere conception fulminated as a dogma and based on no insight into details. Before my choice, either street seemed as natural to you as to me. Had I happened to take Oxford Street, Divinity Avenue would have figured in your philosophy as the gap in nature; and you would have so proclaimed it with the best deterministic conscience in the world.

But what a hollow outcry, then, is this against a chance which, if it were present to us, we could by no character whatever distinguish from a rational necessity! I have taken the most trivial of examples, but no possible example could lead to any different result. For what are the alternatives which, in point of fact, offer themselves to human volition? What are those futures that now seem matters of chance? Are they not one and all like the Divinity Avenue and Oxford Street of our example? Are they not all of them *kinds* of things already here and based in the existing frame of nature? Is any one ever tempted to produce an *absolute* accident, something utterly irrelevant to the rest of the world? Do not all the motives that assail us, all the futures that offer themselves to our choice, spring equally from the soil of the past; and would not either one of them, whether realized through chance or through necessity, the moment it was realized, seem to us to fit that past, and in the completest and most continuous manner to interdigitate with the phenomena already there?

A favorite argument against free will is that if it be true, a man's murderer may as probably be his best friend as his worst enemy, a mother be as likely to strangle as to suckle her first-born, and all of us be as ready to jump from fourth-story windows as to go out of front doors, etc. Users of this argument should probably be excluded from debate till they learn what the real question is. "Free-will" does not say that everything that is physically conceivable is also morally possible. It merely says that of alternatives that really *tempt* our will more than one is really possible. Of course, the alternatives that do thus tempt our will are vastly fewer than the physical possibilities we can coldy fancy. Persons really tempted often do murder their best friends, mothers do strangle their first-born, people do jump out of fourth stories, etc.

The more one thinks of the matter, the more one wonders that so empty and gratuitous a hubbub as this outcry against chance should have found so great an echo in the hearts of men. It is a word which tells us absolutely nothing about what chances, or about the *modus operandi* of the chancing; and the use of it as a war-cry shows only a temper of intellectual absolutism, a demand that the world shall be a solid block, subject to one control—which temper, which demand, the world may not be bound to gratify at all. In every outwardly verifiable and practical respect, a world in which the alternatives that now actually distract *your* choice were decided by pure chance would be by *me* absolutely undistinguished from the world in which I now live. I am, therefore, entirely willing to call it, so far as your choices go, a world of chance for me. To *yourselves,* it is true, those very acts of choice, which to me are so blind, opaque, and external, are the opposites of this, for you are within them and effect them. To you they appear as decisions; and decisions, for him who makes them, are altogether peculiar psychic facts. Self-luminous and self-justifying at the living moment in which they occur, they appeal to no outside moment to put its stamp upon them or make them continuous with the rest of nature. Themselves it is rather who seem to make nature continuous; and in their strange and intense function of granting consent to one possibility and withholding it from another, to transform an equivocal and double future into an inalterable and simple past.

But with the psychology of the matter we have no concern this evening. The quarrel which determinism has with chance fortunately has

nothing to do with this or that phychological detail. It is a quarrel altogether metaphysical. Determinism denies the ambiguity of future volitions, because it affirms that nothing future can be ambiguous. But we
have said enough to meet the issue. Indeterminate future volitions *do*
mean chance. Let us not fear to shout it from the house-tops if need be;
for we now know that the idea of chance is, at bottom, exactly the same
thing as the idea of gift—the one simply being a disparaging, and the
other a eulogistic, name for anything on which we have no effective *claim*.
And whether the world be the better or the worse for having either chances
or gifts in it will depend altogether on *what* these uncertain and unclaim-
able things turn out to be.

The Moral Implications of Determinism

And this at last brings us within sight of our subject. We have seen
what determinism means: we have seen that indeterminism is rightly
described as meaning chance; and we have seen that chance, the very
name of which we are urged to shrink from as from a metaphysical pestilence, means only the negative fact that no part of the world, however
big, can claim to control absolutely the destinies of the whole. But although, in discussing the word "chance," I may at moments have seemed
to be arguing for its real existence, I have not meant to do so yet. We
have not yet ascertained whether this be a world of chance or no; at
most, we have agreed that it seems so. And I now repeat what I said at
the outset, that, from any strict theoretical point of view, the question is
insoluble. To deepen our theoretic sense of the *difference* between a
world with chances in it and a deterministic world is the most I can
hope to do; and this I may now at last begin upon, after all our tedious
clearing of the way.

I wish first of all to show you just what the notion that this is a
deterministic world implies. The implications I call your attention to are
all bound up with the fact that it is a world in which we constantly have
to make what I shall, with your permission, call judgments of regret.
Hardly an hour passes in which we do not wish that something might be
otherwise; and happy indeed are those of us whose hearts have never
echoed the wish of Omar Khayam—

> That we might clasp, ere closed, the book of fate,
>   And make the writer on a fairer leaf
> Inscribe our names, or quite obliterate.
>
> Ah! Love, could you and I with fate conspire
> To mend this sorry scheme of things entire,

> Would we not shatter it to bits, and then
> Remould it nearer to the heart's desire?

Now, it is undeniable that most of these regrets are foolish, and quite on a par in point of philosophic value with the criticisms on the universe of that friend of our infancy, the hero of the fable, "The Atheist and the Acorn"—

> Fool! had that bough a pumpkin bore,
> Thy whimsies would have worked no more, etc.

Even from the point of view of our own ends, we should probably make a botch of remodelling the universe. How much more then from the point of view of ends we cannot see! Wise men therefore regret as little as they can. But still some regrets are pretty obstinate and hard to stifle— regrets for acts of wanton cruelty or treachery, for example, whether performed by others or by ourselves. Hardly any one can remain *entirely* optimistic after reading the confession of the murderer at Brockton the other day: how, to get rid of the wife whose continued existence bored him, he inveigled her into a deserted spot, shot her four times, and then, as she lay on the ground and said to him, "You didn't do it on purpose, did you, dear?" replied, "No, I didn't do it on purpose," as he raised a rock and smashed her skull. Such an occurrence, with the mild sentence and self-satisfaction of the prisoner, is a field for a crop of regrets, which one need not take up in detail. We feel that, although a perfect mechanical fit to the rest of the universe, it is a bad moral fit, and that something else would really have been better in its place.

But for the deterministic philosophy the murder, the sentence, and the prisoner's optimism were all necessary from eternity; and nothing else for a moment had a ghost of a chance of being put in their place. To admit such a chance, the determinists tell us, would be to make a suicide of reason; so we must steel our hearts against the thought. And here our plot thickens, for we see the first of those difficult implications of determinism and monism which it is my purpose to make you feel. If this Brockton murder was called for by the rest of the universe, if it had come at its preappointed hour, and if nothing else would have been consistent with the sense of the whole, what are we to think of the universe? Are we stubbornly to stick to our judgment of regret, and say, though it *couldn't* be, yet it *would* have been a better universe with something different from this Brockton murder in it? That, of course, seems the natural and spontaneous thing for us to do; and yet it is nothing short of deliberately espousing a kind of pessimism. The judgment of regret calls the murder bad. Calling a thing bad means, if it means anything at all, that the thing ought not be, that something else ought to be in its stead. Determinism, in denying that anything else can be in its stead, virtually defines the universe as a place in which what ought to be is impossible—in other words, as an organism whose constitution is afflicted with an incurable taint, and irremediable flaw. The pessimism of a Schopenhauer says no more than this—that the murder is a symptom; and that it is a vicious symptom because it belongs to a vicious whole, which can express its nature no otherwise than by bringing forth just such a symptom as that at this particular spot. Regret for the murder must transform itself, if we are determinists and wise, into a larger regret. It is absurd to regret the murder alone. Other things being what they are, *it* could not be different. What we should regret is that whole frame of things of which the murder is one member. I see no escape whatever from this pessimistic conclusion if, being determinists, our judgment of regret is to be allowed to stand at all.

The only deterministic escape from pessimism is everywhere to abandon the judgment of regret. That this can be done, history shows to be not impossible. The devil, *quoad existentiam,* may be good. That is, although he be a *principle* of evil, yet the universe, with such a principle in it, may practically be a better universe than it could have been without. On every hand, in a small way, we find that a certain amount of evil is a condition by which a higher form of good is brought. There is nothing to prevent anybody from generalizing this view, and trusting that if we could but see things in the largest of all ways, even such matters as this Brockton murder would appear to be paid for by the uses which follow in their train. An optimism *quand même,* a systematic and infatuated optimism like that ridiculed by Voltaire in his *Candide,* is one of the possible ideal ways in which a man may train himself to look upon life. Bereft of dogmatic hardness and lit up with the expression of a tender and pathetic hope, such an optimism has been the grace of some of the most religious characters that ever lived.

> Throb thine with Nature's throbbing breast,
> And all is clear from east to west.

Even cruelty and treachery may be among the absolutely blessed fruits of time, and to quarrel with any of their details may be blasphemy. The only real blasphemy, in short, may be that pessimistic temper of the soul which lets it give away to such things as regrets, remorse, and grief.

Thus, our deterministic pessimism may become a deterministic optimism at the price of extinguishing our judgments of regret.

But does not this immediately bring us into a curious logical predicament? Our determinism leads us to call our judgments of regret wrong, because they are pessimistic in implying that what is impossible yet ought to be. But how then about the judgments of regret themselves? If they are wrong, other judgments, judgments of approval presumably, ought to be in their place. But as they are necessitated, nothing else *can* be in their place; and the universe is just what it was before—namely, a place in which what ought to be appears impossible. We have got one foot out of the pessimistic bog, but the other one sinks all the deeper. We have rescued our actions from the bonds of evil, but our judgments are now held fast. When murders and treacheries cease to be sins, regrets are theoretic absurdities and errors. The theoretic and the active life thus play a kind of see-saw with each other on the ground of evil. The rise of either sends the other down. Murder and treachery cannot be good without regret being bad: regret cannot be good without treachery and murder being bad. Both, however, are supposed to have been foredoomed; so something must be fatally unreasonable, absurd, and wrong in the world. It must be a place of which either sin or error forms a necessary part. From this dilemma there seems at first sight no escape. Are we then so soon to fall back into the pessimism from which we thought we had emerged? And is there no possible way by which we may, with good intellectual consciences, call the cruelties and the treacheries, the reluctances and the regrets, *all* good together?

Certainly there is such a way, and you are probably most of you ready to formulate it yourselves. But, before doing so, remark how inevitably the question of determinism and indeterminism slides us into the question of optimism and pessimism, or, as our fathers called it, the question of optimism and pessimism, or, as our fathers called it, simplest and the deepest, the form from which there is the least escape —not because, as some have sarcastically said, remorse and regret are clung to with a morbid fondness by the theologians as spiritual luxuries, but because they are existing facts in the world, and as such must be taken into account in the deterministic interpretation of all that is fated to be. If they are fated to be error, does not the bat's wing of irrationality cast its shadow over the world? . . .

Morality and Indeterminism

The only consistent way of representing a pluralism and a world whose parts may affect one another through their conduct being either good or bad is the indeterministic way. What interest, zest, or excitement can there be in achieving the right way, unless we are enabled to feel that the wrong way is also a possible and a natural way—nay, more, a menacing and an imminent way? And what sense can there be in condemning ourselves for taking the wrong way, unless we need have done nothing of the sort, unless the right way was open to us as well? I cannot understand the willingness to act, no matter how we feel, without the belief that acts are really good and bad. I cannot understand the belief that an act is bad, without regret at its happening. I cannot understand regret without the admission of real, genuine possibilities in the world. Only then is it other than a mockery to feel, after we have failed to do our best, that an irreparable opportunity is gone from the universe, the loss of which it must forever after mourn.

If you insist that this is all superstition, that possibility is in the eye of science and reason impossibility, and that if I act badly 'tis that the universe was foredoomed to suffer this defect, you fall right back into the dilemma, the labyrinth, of pessimism and subjectivism, from out of whose toils we have just wound our way.

Now, we are of course free to fall back, if we please. For my own part, though, whatever difficulties may beset the philosophy of objective right and wrong, and the indeterminism it seems to imply, determinism, with its alternative pessimism or romanticism, contains difficulties that are greater still. But you will remember that I expressly repudiated awhile ago the pretension to offer any arguments which could be coercive in a so-called scientific fashion in this matter. And I consequently find myself, at the end of this long talk, obliged to state my conclusions in an altogether personal way. This personal method of appeal seems to be among the very conditions of the problem; and the most any one can do is to confess as candidly as he can the grounds for the faith that is in him, and leave his example to work on others as it may.

Let me, then, without circumlocution say just this. The world is enigmatical enough in all conscience, whatever theory we may take up toward it. The indeterminism I defend, the free-will theory of popular sense based on the judgment of regret, represents that world as vulnerable, and liable to be injured by certain of its parts if they act wrong. And it represents their acting wrong as a matter of possibility or accident, neither inevitable nor yet to be infallibly warded off. In all this, it is a theory devoid either of transparency or of stability. It gives us a pluralistic, restless universe, in which no single point of view can ever take in the whole scene; and to a mind possessed of the love of unity at any cost, it will, no doubt, remain forever inacceptable. A friend with such a mind once told me that the thought of my universe made him sick, like the sight of the horrible motion of a mass of maggots in their carrion bed.

But while I freely admit that the pluralism and the restlessness are repugnant and irrational in a certain way, I find that every alternative to them is irrational in a deeper way. The indeterminism with its maggots, if you please to speak so about it, offends only the native absolutism of my intellect—an absolutism which, after all, perhaps, deserves to be snubbed and kept in check. But the determinism with its necessary carrion, to continue the figure of speech, and with no possible maggots to eat the latter up, violates my sense of moral reality through and through. When, for example, I imagine such carrion as the Brockton murder, I cannot conceive it as an act by which the universe, as a whole, logically and necessarily expresses its nature without shrinking from complicity with such a whole. And I deliberately refuse to keep on terms of loyalty with the universe by saying blankly that the murder, since it does flow from the nature of the whole, is not carrion. There are *some* instinctive reactions which I, for one, will not tamper with. The only remaining alternative, the attitude of gnostical romanticism, wrenches my personal instincts in quite as violent a way. It falsifies the simple objectivity of their deliverance. It makes the goose-flesh the murder excites in me a sufficient reason for the perpetration of the crime. It transforms life from a tragic reality into an insincere melodramatic exhibition, as foul or as tawdry as any one's diseased curiosity pleases to carry it out. And with its consecration of the *roman naturaliste* state of mind, and its enthronement of the baser crew of Parisian *litterateurs* among the eternally indispensable organs by which the infinite spirit of things attains to that subjective illumination which is the task of its life, it leaves me in presence of a sort of subjective carrion considerably more noisome than the objective carrion I called it in to take away.

No! better a thousand times, than such systematic corruption of our moral sanity, the plainest pessimism, so that it be straightforward; but better far than that, the world of chance. Make as great an uproar about chance as you please, I know that chance means pluralism and nothing more. If some of the members of the pluralism are bad, the philosophy of pluralism, whatever broad views it may deny me, permits me, at least, to turn to the other members with a clean breast of affection and an unsophisticated moral sense. And if I still wish to think of the world as a totality, it lets me feel that a world with a chance in it of being altogether good, even if the chance never come to pass, is better than a world with no such chance at all. That "chance" whose very notion I am exhorted and conjured to banish from my view of the future as the suicide of reason concerning it, that "chance" is—what? Just this—the chance that in moral respects the future may be other and better than the past has been. This is the only chance we have any motive for supposing to exist. Shame, rather, on its repudiation and its denial! For its presence is the vital air which lets the world live, the salt which keeps it sweet. . . .

24

OF LIBERTY AND NECESSITY

John Stuart Mill

Are Human Actions Subject to the Law of Causality?

THE QUESTION whether the law of causality applies in the same strict sense to human actions as to other phenomena, is the celebrated controversy concerning the freedom of the will, which, from at least as far back as the time of Pelagius, has divided both the philosophical and the religious world. The affirmative opinion is commonly called the doctrine of Necessity, as asserting human volitions and actions to be necessary and inevitable. The negative maintains that the will is not determined, like other phenomena, by antecedents, but determines itself; that our volitions are not, properly speaking, the effects of causes, or at least have no causes which they uniformly and implicitly obey.

I have already made it sufficiently apparent that the former of these opinions is that which I consider the true one; but the misleading terms in which it is often expressed, and the indistinct manner in which it is usually apprehended, have both obstructed its reception and perverted its influence when received. The metaphysical theory of free-will, as held by philosophers (for the practical feeling of it, common in a greater or less degree to all mankind, is in no way inconsistent with the contrary theory), was invented because the supposed alternative of admitting human actions to be *necessary* was deemed inconsistent with every one's instinctive consciousness, as well as humiliating to the pride, even degrading to the moral nature of man. Nor do I deny that the doctrine, as sometimes held, is open to these imputations; for the misapprehension in which I shall be able to show that they originate unfortunately is not confined to the opponents of the doctrine, but is participated in by many, perhaps we might say by most, of its supporters.

[This selection comprises all of Chapter 2, Book VI, of *A System of Logic,* which was published in 1843.]

The Doctrine of Philosophical Necessity

Correctly conceived, the doctrine entitled Philosophical Necessity is simply this: that, given the motives which are present to an individual's mind, and given likewise the character and disposition of the individual, the manner in which he will act might be unerringly inferred; that if we knew the person thoroughly, and knew all the inducements which are acting upon him, we could foretell his conduct with as much certainty as we can predict any physical event. This proposition I take to be a mere interpretation of universal experience, a statement in words of what every one is internally convinced of. No one who believed that he knew thoroughly the circumstances of any case, and the characters of the different persons concerned, would hesitate to foretell how all of them would act. Whatever degree of doubt he may in fact feel arises from the uncertainty whether he really knows the circumstances, or the character of some one or other of the persons, with the degree of accuracy required; but by no means from thinking that if he did know these things, there could be any uncertainty what the conduct should be. Nor does this full assurance conflict in the smallest degree with what is called our feeling of freedom. We do not feel ourselves the less free because those to whom we are intimately known are well assured how we shall will to act in a particular case. We often, on the contrary, regard the doubt what our conduct will be as a mark of ignorance of our characters, and sometimes even resent it as an imputation. The religious metaphysicians who have asserted the freedom of the will have always maintained it to be consistent with divine foreknowledge of our actions; and if with divine, then with any other foreknowledge. We may be free, and yet another may have reason to be perfectly certain what use we shall make of our freedom. It is not, therefore, the doctrine that our volitions and actions are invariable consequents of our antecedent states of mind, that is either contradicted by our consciousness or felt to be degrading.

But the doctrine of causation, when considered as obtaining between our volitions and their antecedents, is almost universally conceived as involving more than this. Many do not believe, and very few practically feel, that there is nothing in causation but invariable, certain, and unconditional sequence. There are few to whom mere constancy of succession appears a sufficiently stringent bond of union for so peculiar a relation as that of cause and effect. Even if the reason repudiates, the imagination retains, the feeling of some more intimate connection, of some peculiar tie or mysterious constraint exercised by the antecedent over the consequent. Now this it is which, considered as applying to the human will, conflicts with our consciousness and revolts our feelings. We are certain that, in the case of our volitions, there is not this mysterious constraint. We know that we are not compelled, as by a magical spell, to obey any particular motives. We feel that if we wished to prove that we have the power of resisting the motive, we could do so, (that wish being, it needs scarcely be observed, a *new antecedent;*) and it would be humiliating to our pride, and (what is of more importance) paralyzing to our desire of excellence, if we thought otherwise. But neither is any such mysterious compulsion now supposed, by the best philosophical authorities, to be exercised by any other cause over its effect. Those who think that causes draw their effects after them by a mystical tie are right in believing that the relation between volitions and their antecedents is of another nature. But they should go farther, and admit that this is also true of all other effects and their antecedents. If such a tie is considered to be involved in the word necessity, the doctrine is not true of human actions; but neither is it then true of inanimate objects. It would be more corect to say that matter is not bound by necessity, than that mind is so.

That the free-will metaphysicians, being mostly of the school which rejects Hume's and Brown's analysis of Cause and Effect, should miss their way for want of the light which that analysis affords, cannot surprise us. The wonder is, that the Necessitarians, who usually admit that philosophical theory, should in practice equally lose sight of it. The very same misconception of the doctrine called Philosophical Necessity which prevents the opposite party from recognising its truth, I believe to exist more or less obscurely in the minds of most Necessitarians, however they may in words disavow it. I am much mistaken if they habitually feel that the necessity which they recognise in actions is but uniformity of order, and capability of being predicted. They have a feeling as if there were at bottom a stronger tie between the volitions and their causes: as if, when they asserted that the will is governed by the balance of motives, they meant something more cogent that if they had only said, that whoever knew the motives, and our habitual susceptibilities to them, could predict how we should will to act. They commit, in opposition to their own scientific system, the very same mistake which their adversaries commit in obedience to theirs; and in consequence do really in some instances suffer those depressing consequences which their opponents erroneously impute to the doctrine itself.

Pernicious Effect of the Term "Necessity"

I am inclined to think that this error is almost wholly an effect of the associations with a word, and that it would be prevented by forebearing to employ, for the expression of the simple fact of causation, so extremely inappropriate term as Necessity. That word, in its other acceptations, involves much more than mere uniformity of sequence: it implies irresistibleness. Applied to the will, it only means that the given cause will be followed by the effect, subject to all possibilities of counteraction by other causes; but in common use it stands for the operation of those causes exclusively, which are supposed too powerful to be counteracted at all. When we say that all human actions take place of necessity, we only mean that they will certainly happen if nothing prevents:—when we say that dying of want, to those who cannot get food, is a necessity, we mean that it will certainly happen, whatever may be done to prevent it. The application of the same term to the agencies on which human actions depend as is used to express those agencies of nature which are really uncontrollable, cannot fail, when habitual, to create a feeling of uncontrollableness in the former also. This, however, is a mere illusion. There are physical sequences which we call necessary as death for want of food or air; there are others which, though as much cases of causation as the former, are not said to be necessary, as death from poison, which an antidote, or the use of the stomach pump, will sometimes avert. It is apt to be forgotten by people's feelings, even if remembered by their understandings, that human actions are in this last predicament: they are never (except in some cases of mania) ruled by any one motive with such absolute sway that there is no room for the influence of any other. The causes, therefore, on which action depends are never uncontrollable, and any given effect is only necessary provided that the causes tending to produce it are not controlled. That whatever happens could not have happened otherwise unless something had taken place which was capable of preventing it, no one surely needs hesitate to admit. But to call this by the name necessity is to use the term in a sense so different from its primitive and familiar meaning, from that which it bears in the common occasions of life, as to amount almost to a play upon words. The associations derived from the ordinary sense of the term will adhere to it in spite of all we can do; and though the doctrine of Necessity, as stated by most who hold it, is very remote from fatalism, it is probable that most Necessitarians are Fatalists, more or less, in their feelings.

A Fatalist believes, or half believes (for nobody is a consistent Fatalist), not only that whatever is about to happen will be the infallible result of the causes which produce it (which is the true Necessitarian doctrine), but, moreover, that there is no use in struggling against it; that it will happen however we may strive to prevent it. Now, a Necessitarian, believing that our actions follow from our characters, and that our characters follow from our organisation, our education, and our circumstances, is apt to be, with more or less of consciousness on his part, a Fatalist as to his own actions, and to believe that his nature is such, or that his education and circumstances have so moulded his characters, that nothing can now prevent him from feeling and acting in a particular way, or at least that no effort of his own can hinder it. In the words of the sect* which in our own day has most perseveringly inculcated and most perversely misunderstood this great doctrine, his character is formed *for* him, and not *by* him; therefore his wishing that it had been formed differently is of no use; he has no power to alter it. But this is a grand error. He has, to a certain extent, a power to alter his character. Its being, in the ultimate resort, formed for him, is not inconsistent with its being, in part, formed *by* him as one of the intermediate agents. His character is formed by his circumstances (including among these his particular organisation), but his own desire to mould it in a particular way is one of these circumstances, and by no means one of the least influential. We cannot, indeed, directly will to be different from what we are; but neither did those who are supposed to have formed our characters directly will that we should be what we are. Their will had no direct power except over their own actions. They made us what they did make us by willing, not the end, but the requisite means; and we, when our habits are not too inveterate, can, by similarly willing the requisite means, make ourselves different. If they could place us under the influence of certain circumstances, we in like manner can place ourselves under the influence of other circumstances. We are exactly as capable of making our own character, *if we will,* as others are of making it for us.

Yes (answers the Owenite), but these words, "if we will," surrender the whole point, since the will to alter our own character is given us, not by any efforts of ours, but by circumstances which we cannot help; it comes to us either from external causes or not at all. Most true: if the Owenite stops here, he is in a position from which nothing can expel him. Our character is formed by us as well as for us; but the wish which induces us to attempt to form it is formed for us; and how? Not, in general, by our organisation, nor wholly by our education, but by our experience—experience of the painful consequences of the character we previously had, or by some strong feeling of admiration or aspiration accidentally aroused. But to think that we have no power of altering our character, and to think that we shall not use our power unless we desire to use it, are very different things, and have a very different effect on the mind. A person who does not wish to alter his character cannot be the person who is supposed to feel discouraged or paralysed by thinking himself unable to do it. The depressing effect of the Fatalist doctrine can only be felt where there *is* a wish to do what that doctrine represents

---

* Mill here refers to the social reformer Robert Owen (1771-1858) and his followers. (Eds.)

as impossible. It is of no consequence what we think forms our character, when we have no desire of our own about forming it, but it is of great consequence that we should not be prevented from forming such a desire by thinking the attainment impracticable, and that if we have the desire we should know that the work is not so irrevocably done as to be incapable of being altered.

And, indeed, if we examine closely, we shall find that this feeling, of our being able to modify our own character *if we wish,* is itself the feeling of moral freedom which we are conscious of. A person feels morally free who feels that his habits or his temptations are not his masters, but he theirs: who even in yielding to them knows that he could resist; that were he desirous of altogether throwing them off, there would not be required for that purpose a stronger desire than he knows himself to be capable of feeling. It is of course necessary, to render our consciousness of freedom complete, that we should have succeeded in making our character all we have hitherto attempted to make it; for if we have wished and not attained, we have, to that extent, not power over our own character—we are not free. Or at least, we must feel that our wish, if not strong enough to alter our character, is strong enough to conquer our character when the two are brought into conflict in any particular case of conduct. And hence it is said with truth, that none but a person of confirmed virtue is completely free.

The application of so improper a term as Necessity to the doctrine of cause and effect in the matter of human character seems to me one of the most signal instances in philosophy of the abuse of terms, and its practical consequences one of the most striking examples of the power of language over our associations. The subject will never be generally understood until that objectionable term is dropped. The free-will doctrine, by keeping in view precisely that portion of the truth which the word Necessity puts out of sight, namely, the power of the mind to co-operate in the formation of its own character, has given to its adherents a practical feeling much nearer to the truth than has generally (I believe) existed in the minds of Necessitarians. The latter may have had a stronger sense of the importance of what human beings can do to shape the characters of one another; but the free-will doctrine has, I believe, fostered in its supporters a much stronger spirit of self-culture.

A Motive not Always the Anticipation of
Pleasure or Pain

There is still one fact which requires to be noticed (in addition to the existence of a power of self-formation) before the doctrine of the causation of human actions can be freed from the confusion and misapprehensions which surround it in many minds. When the will is said to be determined by motives, a motive does not mean always, or solely, the anticipation of a pleasure or of a pain. I shall not here inquire whether it be true that, in the commencements, all our voluntary actions are mere means consciously employed to obtain some pleasure or avoid some pain. It is at least certain that we gradually, through the influence of association, come to desire the means without thinking of the end: the action itself becomes an object of desire, and is performed without reference to any motive beyond itself. Thus far, it may still be objected, that the action having through association become pleasurable, we are, as much as before, moved to act by the anticipation of a pleasure, namely, the pleasure of the action itself. But granting this, the matter does not end here. As we proceed in the formation of habits, and become accustomed to will a particular act or a particular course of conduct because it is pleasurable, we at last continue to will it without any reference to its being pleasurable. Although, from some change in us or in our circumstances, we have ceased to find any pleasure in the action, or perhaps to anticipate any pleasure as the consequence of it, we still continue to desire the action, and consequently to do it. In this manner it is that habits of hurtful excess continue to be practised although they have ceased to be pleasurable; and in this manner also it is that the habit of willing to persevere in the course which he has chosen does not desert the moral hero, even when the reward, however real, which he doubtless receives from the consciousness of well-doing, is anything but an equivalent for the sufferings he undergoes or the wishes which he may have to renounce.

A habit of willing is commonly called a purpose; and among the causes of our volitions, and of the actions which flow from them, must be reckoned not only likings and aversions, but also purposes. It is only when our purposes have become independent of the feelings of pain or pleasure from which they originally took their rise that we are said to have a confirmed character. "A character," says Novalis, "is a completely fashioned will;" and the will, once so fashioned, may be steady and constant, when the passive susceptibilities of pleasure and pain are greatly weakened or materially changed.

With the corrections and explanations now given, the doctrine of the causation of our volitions by motives, and of motives by the desirable objects offered to us, combined without particular susceptibilities of desire, may be considered, I hope as sufficiently established for the purposes of this treatise.

25

WHEN IS A MAN RESPONSIBLE?

Moritz Schlick

WITH HESITATION AND RELUCTANCE I prepare to add this chapter to the discussion of ethical problems. For in it I must speak of a matter which, even at present, is thought to be a fundamental ethical problem, but which got into ethics and has become a much discussed problem only because of a misunderstanding. This is the so-called problem of the freedom of the will. Moreover, this pseudo-problem has long since been settled by the efforts of certain sensible persons; and, above all, the state of affairs just described has been often disclosed—with exceptional clarity by Hume. Hence it is really one of the greatest scandals of philosophy that again and again so much paper and printer's ink is devoted to this matter, to say nothing of the expenditure of thought, which could have been applied to more important problems (assuming that it would have sufficed for these). Thus I should truly be ashamed to write a chapter on "freedom." In the chapter heading, the word "responsible" indicates what concerns ethics, and designates the point at which misunderstanding arises. Therefore the concept of responsibility constitutes our theme, and if in the process of its clarification I must also speak of the concept of freedom I shall, of course, say only what others have already said better; consoling myself with the thought that in this way alone can anything be done to put an end at last to that scandal.

The main task of ethics is to explain moral behavior. To explain means to refer back to laws: every science, including psychology, is possible only in so far as there are such laws to which the events can be referred. Since the assumption that all events are subject to universal

[This selection consists of Chapter 7 of Schlick's *Problems of Ethics*, with the omission of one short paragraph. It is here reprinted with the kind permission of Prentice-Hall Inc., New York. The translation is by David Rynin. The English translation of this book appeared in 1939, the book itself was published in Vienna in 1931.]

laws is called the principle of causality, one can also say, "Every science presupposes the principle of causality." Therefore every explanation of human behavior must also assume the validity of causal laws; in this case the existence of psychological laws. All of our experience strengthens us in the belief that this presupposition is realized, at least to the extent required for all purposes of practical life in intercourse with nature and human beings, and also for the most precise demands of technique. Whether, indeed, the principle of causality holds universally, whether, that is, determinism is true, we do not know; no one knows. But we do know that it is impossible to settle the dispute between determinism and indeterminism by mere reflection and speculation, by the consideration of so many reasons for and so many reasons against (which collectively and individually are but pseudo-reasons). Such an attempt becomes especially ridiculous when one considers with what enormous expenditure of experimental and logical skill contemporary physics carefully approaches the question of whether causality can be maintained for the most minute intra-atomic events. . . .

Fortunately, it is not necessary to lay claim to a final solution of the causal problem in order to say what is necessary in ethics concerning responsibility; there is required only an analysis of the concept, the careful determination of the meaning which is in fact joined to the words "responsibility" and "freedom," as these are actually used. If men had made clear to themselves the sense of these propositions, which we use in everyday life, that pseudo-argument which lies at the root of the pseudo-problem, and which recurs thousands of times within and outside philosophical books, would never have arisen.

The argument runs as follows: "If determinism is true, if, that is, all events obey immutable laws, then my will too is always determined, by my innate character and my motives. Hence my decisions are necessary, not free. But if so, then I am not responsible for my acts, for I would be accountable for them only if I could do something about the way my decisions went; but I can do nothing about it, since they proceed with necessity from my character and the motives. And I have made neither, and have no power over them: the motives come from without, and my character is the necessary product of the innate tendencies and the external influences which have been effective during my lifetime. Thus determinism and moral responsibility are incompatible. Moral responsibility presupposes freedom, that is, exemption from causality."

This process of reasoning rests upon a whole series of confusions, just as the links of a chain hang together. We must show these confusions to be such, and thus destroy them.

Two Meanings of the Word "Law"

It all begins with an erroneous interpretation of the meaning of "law." In practice this is understood as a rule by which the state prescribes certain behavior to its citizens. These rules often contradict the natural desires of the citizens (for if they did not do so, there would be no reason for making them), and are in fact not followed by many of them; while others obey, but under compulsion. The state does in fact compel its citizens by imposing certain sanctions (punishment) which serve to bring their desires into harmony with the prescribed laws.

In natural science, on the other hand, the word "law" means something quite different. The natural law is not a prescription as to how something should behave, but a formula, a description of how something does in fact behave. The two forms of "laws" have only this in common: both tend to be expressed in formulae. Otherwise they have absolutely nothing to do with one another, and it is very blameworthy that the same word has been used for two such different things; but even more so that philosophers have allowed themselves to be led into serious errors by this usage. Since natural laws are only descriptions of what happens, there can be in regard to them no talk of "compulsion." The laws of celestial mechanics do not prescribe to the planets how they have to move, as though the planets would actually like to move quite otherwise, and are only forced by these burdensome laws of Kepler to move in orderly paths; no, these laws do not in any way "compel" the planets, but express only what in fact planets actually do.

If we apply this to volition, we are enlightened at once, even before the other confusions are discovered. When we say that a man's will "obeys psychological laws," these are not civic laws, which compel him to make certain decisions, or dictate desires to him, which he would in fact prefer not to have. They are laws of nature, merely expressing which desires he actually has under given conditions; they describe the nature of the will in the same manner as the astronomical laws describe the nature of planets. "Compulsion" occurs where man is prevented from realizing his natural desires. How could the rule according to which these natural desires arise itself be considered as "compulsion?"

Compulsion and Necessity

But this is the second confusion to which the first leads almost inevitably: after conceiving the laws of nature, anthropomorphically, as order imposed nolens volens upon the events, one adds to them the concept of "necessity." This word, derived from "need," also comes to us from practice, and is used there in the sense of inescapable compulsion. To apply the word with this meaning to natural laws is of course senseless, for the presupposition of an opposing desire is lacking, and it is then confused with something altogether different, which is actually an attribute of natural laws. That is, universality. It is of the essence of natural laws to be universally valid, for only when we have found a rule which holds of events without exception do we call the rule a law of nature. Thus when we say "a natural law holds necessarily" this has but one legitimate meaning: "It holds in all cases where it is applicable." It is again very deplorable that the word "necessary" has been applied to natural laws (or, what amounts to the same thing, with reference to causality), for it is quite superfluous, since the expression "universally valid" is available. Universal validity is something altogether different from "compulsion;" these concepts belong to spheres so remote from each other that once insight into the error has been gained one can no longer conceive the possibility of a confusion.

The confusion of two concepts always carries with it the confusion of their contradictory opposites. The opposite of the universal validity of a formula, of the existence of a law, is the nonexistence of a law, indeterminism, acausality; while the opposite of compulsion is what in practice everyone calls "freedom." Here emerges the nonsense, trailing through centuries, that freedom means "exemption from the causal principle," or "not subject to the laws of nature." Hence it is believed necessary to vindicate indeterminism in order to save human freedom.

Freedom and Indeterminism

This is quite mistaken. Ethics has, so to speak, no moral interest in the purely theoretical question of "determinism or indeterminism?," but only a theoretical interest, namely: in so far as it seeks the laws of conduct, and can find them only to the extent that causality holds. But the question of whether man is morally free (that is, has that freedom which, as we shall show, is the presupposition of moral responsibility) is altogether different from the problem of determinism. Hume was especially clear on this point. He indicated the inadmissable confusion of the concepts of "indeterminism" and "freedom;" but he retained, inappropriately, the word "freedom" for both, calling the one freedom of "the will," the other genuine kind, "freedom of conduct." He showed that morality is interested only in the latter, and that such freedom, in general, is unquestionably to be attributed to mankind. And this is quite correct. Freedom means the opposite of compulsion; a man is free if he does not act under compulsion, and he is compelled or unfree when he is hindered from without in the realization of his natural desires. Hence he is unfree when he is locked up, or chained, or when someone forces him at the point of a gun to do what otherwise he would not do. This is quite clear, and everyone will admit that the everyday or legal notion of the lack of freedom is thus correctly interpreted, and that a man will be considered quite free and responsible if no such external compulsion is exerted upon him. There are certain cases which lie between these clearly described ones, as, say, when someone acts under the influence of alcohol or a narcotic. In such cases we consider the man to be more or less unfree, and hold him less accountable, because we rightly view the influence of the drug as "external," even though it is found within the body; it prevents him from making decisions in the manner peculiar to his nature. If he takes the narcotic of his own will, we make him completely responsible for this act and transfer a part of the responsibility to the consequences, making, as it were, an average or mean condemnation of the whole. In the case of a person who is mentally ill we do not consider him free with respect to those acts in which the disease expresses itself, because we view the illness as a disturbing factor which hinders the normal functioning of his natural tendencies. We make not him but his disease responsible.

The Nature of Responsibility

But what does this really signify? What do we mean by this concept of responsibility which goes along with that of "freedom," and which plays such an important role in morality? It is easy to attain complete clarity in this matter; we need only carefully determine the manner in which the concept is used. What is the case in practice when we impute "responsibility" to a person? What is our aim in doing this? The judge has to discover who is responsible for a given act in order that he may punish him. We are inclined to be less concerned with the inquiry as to who deserves reward for an act, and we have no special officials for this; but of course the principle would be the same. But let us stick to punishment in order to make the idea clear. What is punishment, actually? The view still often expressed, that it is a natural retaliation for past wrong, ought no longer to be defended in cultivated society; for the opinion that an increase in sorrow can be "made good again" by further sorrow is altogether barbarous. Certainly the origin of punishment may lie in an impulse of retaliation or vengeance; but what is such an impulse except the instinctive desire to destroy the cause of the deed to be avenged, by the destruction of or injury to the malefactor? Punishment is concerned only with the institution of causes, of motives of conduct, and this alone is its meaning. Punishment is an educative measure, and as such is a means to the formation of motives, which are in part to prevent the wrongdoer from repeating the act (reformation) and in part to prevent others from committing a similar act (intimidation). Analogously, in the case of reward we are concerned with an incentive.

Hence the question regarding responsibility is the question: Who in a given case, is to be punished? Who is to be considered the true wrong-doer? This problem is not identical with that regarding the original instigator of the act; for the great-grandparents of the man, from whom he inherited his character, might in the end be the cause, or the states-men who are responsible for his social milieu, and so forth. But the "doer" is the one upon whom the motive must have acted in order, with certainty, to have prevented the act (or called it forth, as the case may be). Consideration of remote causes is of no help here, for in the first place their actual contribution cannot be determined, and in the second place they are generally out of reach. Rather, we must find the person in whom the decisive junction of causes lies. The question of who is responsible is the question concerning the correct point of application of the motive. And the important thing is that in this its meaning is completely exhausted; behind it there lurks no mysterious connection between transgression and requital, which is merely indicated by the described state of affairs. It is a matter only of knowing who is to be punished or rewarded, in order that punishment and reward function as such—be able to achieve their goal.

Thus, all the facts connected with the concepts of responsibility and imputation are at once made intelligible. We do not charge an insane person with responsibility, for the very reason that he offers no unified point for the application of motive. It would be pointless to try to affect him by means of promises or threats, when his confused soul fails to respond to such influence because its normal mechanism is out of order. We do not try to give him motives, but try to heal him (metaphorically, we make his sickness responsible, and try to remove its causes). When a man is forced by threats to commit certain acts we do not blame him, but the one who held the pistol at his breast. The reason is clear: the act would have been prevented had we been able to restrain the person who threatened him; and this person is the one whom we must influence in order to prevent similar acts in the future.

The Consciousness of Responsibility

But much more important than the question of when a man is said to be responsible is that of when he himself feels responsible. Our whole treatment would be untenable if it gave no explanation of this. It is, then, a welcome confirmation of the view here developed that the sub-jective feeling of responsibility coincides with objective judgment. It is a fact of experience that, in general, the person blamed or condemned is conscious of the fact that he was "rightly" taken to account—of course, under the supposition that no error has been made, that the assumed state of affairs actually occurred. What is this consciousness of having been the true doer of the act, the actual instigator? Evidently not merely that it was he who took the steps required for its performance; but there must be added the awareness that he did it "independently," "of his own initiative," or however it be expressed. This feeling is simply the consciousness of freedom, which is merely the knowledge of having acted on one's own desires. And "one's own desires" are those which have their origin in the regularity of one's character in the given situa-tion, and are not imposed by an external power, as explained above. The absence of the external power expresses itself in the well-known feeling (usually considered characteristic of the consciousness of free-dom) that one could also have acted otherwise. How this indubitable experience ever came to be an argument in favor of determinism is in-comprehensible to me. It is of course obvious that I should have acted differently had I willed something else; but the feeling never says that I could also have willed something else, even though this is true, if, that is, other motives had been present. And it says even less that under exactly the same inner and outer conditions I could also have willed something else. How could such a feeling inform me of anything regard-ing the purely theoretical question of whether the principle of causality holds or not? Of course, after what has been said on the subject, I do not undertake to demonstrate the principle, but I do deny that from any such fact of consciousness the least follows regarding the principle's validity. This feeling is not the consciousness of the absence of a cause, but of something altogether different, namely, of freedom, which con-sists in the fact that I can act as I desire.

Thus the feeling of responsibility assumes that I acted freely, that my own desires impelled me; and if because of this feeling I willingly suffer blame for my behavior or reproach myself, and thereby admit that I might have acted otherwise, this means that other behavior was compatible with the laws of volition—of course granted other motives. And I myself desire the existence of such motives and bear the pain (regret and sorrow) caused me by my behavior so that its repetition will be prevented. To blame oneself means just to apply a motive of improvement to oneself, which is usually the task of the educator. But if, for example, one does something under the influence of torture, feelings of guilt and regret are absent, for one knows that according to the laws of volition no other behavior was possible—no matter what ideas, because of their feeling tones, might have functioned as motives.

The important thing, always, is that the feeling of responsibility means the realization that one's self, one's own psychic processes constitute the point at which motives must be applied in order to govern the acts of one's body.

Causality as the Presupposition of Responsibility

We can speak of motives only in a causal context; thus it becomes clear how very much of the concept of responsibility rests upon that of causation, that is, upon the regularity of volitional decisions. In fact if we should conceive of a decision as utterly without any cause (this would in all strictness be the indeterministic presupposition) then the act would be entirely a matter of chance, for chance is identical with the absence of a cause; there is no other opposite of causality. Could we under such conditions make the agent responsible? Certainly not. Imagine a man, always calm, peaceful and blameless, who suddenly falls upon and begins to beat a stranger. He is held and questioned regarding the motive of his actions, to which he answers, in his opinion truthfully, as we assume: "There was no motive for my behavior. Try as I may I can discover no reason. My volition was without any cause—I desired to do so, and there is simply nothing else to be said about it." We should shake our heads and call him insane, because we have to believe that there was a cause, and lacking any other we must assume some mental disturbance as the only cause remaining; but certainly no one would hold him to be responsible. If decisions were causeless there would be no sense in trying to influence men; and we see at once that this is the reason why we could not bring such a man to account, but would always have only a shrug of the shoulders in answer to his behavior. One can easily determine that in practice we make an agent the more responsible the more motives we can find for his conduct. If a man guilty of an atrocity was an enemy of his victim, if previously he had shown violent tendencies, if some special circumstance angered him, then we impose severe punishment upon him; while the fewer the reasons to be found for an offense the less do we condemn the agent, but make "unlucky chance," a momentary aberration, or something of the sort, responsible. We do not find the causes of misconduct in his character, and therefore we do not try to influence it for the better: this and only this is the significance of the fact that we do not put the responsibility upon him. And he too feels this to be so, and says, "I cannot understand how such a thing could have happened to me."

In general we know very well how to discover the causes of conduct in the characters of our fellow men; and how to use this knowledge in the prediction of their future behavior, often with as much certainty as that with which we know that a lion and a rabbit will behave quite differently in the same situation. From all this it is evident that in practice no one thinks of questioning the principle of causality, that, thus, the attitude of the practical man offers no excuse to the metaphysician for confusing freedom from compulsion with the absence of a cause. If one makes clear to himself that a causeless happening is identical with a chance happening, and that, consequently, an indetermined will would destroy all responsibility, then every desire will cease that might be father to an indeterministic thought. No one can prove determinism, but it is certain that we assume its validity in all our practical life, and that in particular we can apply the concept of responsibility to human conduct only in as far as the causal principle holds of volitional processes.

For a final clarification I bring together again a list of those concepts which tend, in the traditional treatment of the "problem of freedom," to be confused. In the place of these concepts on the left are put, mistakenly, those of the right, and those in the vertical order form a chain, so that sometimes the previous confusion is the cause of that which follows:

NATURAL LAW   LAW OF STATE
DETERMINISM (CAUSALITY)   COMPULSION
(UNIVERSAL VALIDITY)   (NECESSITY)
INDETERMINISM (CHANCE)   FREEDOM
(NO CAUSE)   (NO COMPULSION)

26

"PREPERCEPTION" AND FREEDOM

C. J. Ducasse

WERE PREVISION, as distinguished from predictive inference, only a postulated faculty of a hypothetical omniscient being, there would be little reason for discussion of it outside theological works which take as known the existence of such a being. But there is considerable empirical evidence that some human beings at times have experiences which depict future or past events veridically, and yet do not come under the heading of predictive inference or of memory.

For these experiences, the names Precognition and Retrocognition are generally used rather than Prevision and Retrovision, because the experiences do not always consist of visual images. But in relation to our present problem, Precognition and Retrocognition are terms even more unsatisfactory because they categorize the experiences concerned as *cognitive*, whereas the truth is that, even when the experiences are veridical, they are not themselves cognitive at all. This assertion may seem paradoxical, but is not really so because (*a*) "cognition" means knowledge—here, knowledge that something is (or was, or will be) a fact; and (*b*) knowledge does not consist simply in belief of something which truly is (or was, or will be) a fact, but in belief of it *based on evidence sufficient to show* that it is (or was, or will be) a fact. For example, I might now believe—whether or not as result of a vision or dream—that the Pope has died; and it might be a fact that he has died. But this would not mean that I *know* he has died. I could be said to know it only if my belief, in addition to its happening to be true, were *based on adequate evidence* that he has died. Precognition or Retrocognition are bad terms for the kind of experience they are used to designate because they tacitly postulate not only (*a*) that the experience is veridical, but also

[This selection is part of Chapter XI of Ducasse's *Nature, Mind, and Death*, published in 1951 by the Open Court Publishing Co. It is here reprinted with the kind permission of Professor Ducasse and the publishers.]

(*b*) that it includes evidence of it own veridicality; whereas the fact is that experiences of the kind referred to are sometimes erroneous, and that, even when they are veridical, their veridicality does not become evident until afterwards. Hence, even when veridical, the experiences called Precognition and Retrocognition are not in themselves really cognitions at all.

The best names for them would seem to be Preperception and Retro-perception; for the general process of interpretation of sensory images, called Perception, is as we know fallible; and we therefore customarily distinguish between *veridical* perception and *erroneous* perception (the latter being technically called illusion, or hallucination, according as the sensory images interpreted are caused normally or abnormally). More-over, a veridical perception does not contain evidence of its own veridi-cality, nor does an illusion or hallucination contain evidence that it is only this. The evidence either way comes only afterwards, consisting as it does of the coherence or incoherence of the given perception with the rest of our experience. And it is because these features of perception are also features of the kind of experience now in view that I propose for it the names Preperception and Retroperception.

The instances where preperception and freedom at first sight seem incompatible are those presenting together the three following features:

(*a*) the preperception turns out to have been veridical;

(*b*) the person whose freedom is in question is the prepercipient him-self;

(*c*) the event preperceived is either an act of the prepercipient, or an external event of a kind capable of being caused or prevented at will by human beings in circumstances such as those in which the preper-cipient is between the time of his preperception and the time of the event's occurence.

The apparent incompatibility arises from the fact that the event *E* preperceived eventually occurs; and yet that if this event is of a kind which, in the circumstances, the prepercipient would prevent if he could, and which he could prevent if he would, then preperception of it would motivate him so to act as to prevent it.

Let us consider the logic of the situation in terms of a concrete in-stance—one which has often been referred to in discussions of veridical preperception. It was reported by the late F. W. H. Myers in the *Pro-ceedings of the Society for Physical Research for 1895,* Vol. XI, pp. 487-8. The person concerned was Mrs. Atlay, wife of the Bishop of Hereford. In March 1893 she wrote Myers as follows:

> I dreamt that the Bishop being from home, we were unable to have family prayers as usual in the chapel, but that I read them in the large hall of the Palace, out of which, on one side, a door opens into the dining room. In my dream, prayers being ended, I left the hall, opened the dining

room door, and there saw, to my horror, standing between the table and the sideboard, an enormous pig. The dream was very vivid, and amused me much.

The Bishop being from home, when dressed I went down into the hall to read prayers. The servants had not come in, so I told my governess and children, who were already there, about my dream, which amused them as much as it had done me. The servants came in and I read prayers, after which the party dispersed. I opened the dining room door, where, to my amazement, stood the pig in the very spot in which I had seen him in my dream.

The governess, Emily Nimmo, appended her own written statement that Mrs. Atlay had related the dream when she came into the hall before prayers. And inquiries by Myers brought out the fact that the pig escaped from its sty while prayers were being read; its escape having been due to the fact that the gardener, who was at that time cleaning the sty, left it imperfectly secured, so that, the servants "having left every door open, the pig met with no obstacle on his voyage of discovery."

Since there can be no doubt that the presence of a pig between the table and sideboard of the dining room of an episcopal palace is an exceedingly rare if not unique event, chance coincidence is not a plausible explanation of the dream. The fact that the dream was recounted to other persons before its fulfillment excludes the possibility of explaining it away as an instance of the familiar illusion of *deja vu;* and the fact that the pig did not escape until after the dream had ended and been reported to the governess excludes the possibility that noise made by the pig in the dining room should have caused the dream. The episode thus is about as clear-cut a case as one could have, in terms of which to consider the theoretical bearing of veridical preperception on freedom; although for this purpose the case would of course be just as good if, instead of real, it were imaginary.

Obviously, if recollection of the dream had caused Mrs. Atlay to have had the entrances to the dining room, or the gate of the sty, securely fastened and kept so until she went into the dining room, the pig would not have been there. But if the dream had caused her to take these precautions, *it would not have constituted veridical preperception* since the event preperceived would then not have occurred. The fact, however, was that the dream was regarded by Mrs. Atlay as a ridiculous mere dream and therefore did not cause her to take the precautions which would have prevented its fulfillment; so that the dream did turn out to be veridical. The situation is then this: for the dream to have caused her to take these precautions, it would have been necessary *that she should have considered the dreamed event a real contingency*—something that would or might happen unless she acted to prevent it. But this very belief would have resulted in non-veridicality of the dream.

On the other hand, for the dream to have been *veridical* (as in fact it was), one or the other of two things were necessary: either (*a*) that the event preperceived should *not have been believed a risk* and those precautions therefore not taken; or else (*b*) that, although believed a risk and those precautions taken, *they should have turned out insufficient* through some accident too extraordinary to have been thought of or guarded against, and the dream therefore fulfilled. This, however, would have meant, not that Mrs. Atlay had no freedom of efficacy, but only that—as we pointed out earlier is the case—there are limits to such human freedom, especially when what a person wills is not merely an *act* but is a *deed, i.e.,* some event external to the act, and which he intends the act to cause (or as the case may be to prevent) either directly or mediately. Man's freedom to do what he would is limited sometimes by his ignorance of means; and sometimes by lack of means, for example, by his lack of the necessary bodily strength or dexterity, or of the necessary tools, or helpers, etc. Obviously, no plausible conception of man's freedom can imply that his volition suffices to cause or prevent every event he wills to cause or prevent, for we know perfectly well that it fails to do it in many cases; and this quite irrespective of whether the eventual outcome of the volition was or was not veridically preperceived or susceptible of being so.

Aside, then, from events over which man, through ignorance or lack of means, has no control, and limiting ourselves to those he can—*i.e.,* is free to—cause or prevent at will, the essential point is that, *at the time he preperceives an event E, he cannot know whether his preperception is, or is not, veridical;* and that its turning out eventually to have been the one or the other *depends in part on whether he did not, or did, consider E a contingency,* and therefore, respectively, did *not* so act as to prevent occurrence of *E* and thereby made his preperception veridical; or on the contrary *did* so act as to prevent *E* and thereby made his preperception non-veridical. It is true that, even in cases where *E* does occur, he could have prevented it, *i.e.,* he was free to prevent it if he would. But as we have seen, this means only that volition by him to prevent *E* would have sufficed to prevent *E*. But *E* occurs because he believed there was no risk it would occur and he therefore did not will to prevent it. The fact that his not having willed to prevent it was determined—determined by his belief that there was no risk *E* would occur, and this belief itself determined by the rarity of *E*—that fact is perfectly consistent with the other fact that he was free to prevent *E, i.e.,* once more, that volition by him to prevent *E* would have prevented *E*.

The appearance of incompatibility in the cases we are considering, between veridical preperception and "free will," is thus due only to failure to analyze the several senses of this ambiguous and emotion-laden term, or to failure to realize that although man has some freedom in each of the several legitimate senses of this term his freedom always has limits.

To conclude our discussion of the relation between preperception and freedom, it will be interesting to consider briefly another recorded instance. It is one peculiar in that although the preperception was veridical in the broad sense that it was preperception of a danger which eventually did occur, nevertheless some features of the preperception were non-veridical; and, because the preperception was remembered at the time of that danger, the accident preperceived was averted, and the preperception was therefore to this extent erroneous.

The case is that of the dream of a lady, whom Myers states he knows but to whom he refers only as Lady Z. Her letter to him, which appears on p. 497 of the volume of the S. P. R. Proceedings already cited, is rather long, so I shall quote only portions, and summarize the rest.

On a certain day, Lady Z resolved to have her coachman drive her the next day, with her child and the nurse, to visit a relative. "During the night," she says, "I had a painfully clear dream in vision of the brougham turning up one of the streets from Piccadilly; and then of myself standing on the pavement and holding my child, our old coachman falling on his head on the road—his hat smashed in." This dream so distressed her that she almost decided to go by train instead of driving; but she finally decided to drive. On the return journey, at about the place visioned, she saw other coachmen looking at hers, and then noticed that he was leaning back in his seat as if the horses had been pulling violently, which, however, they were not doing. Then "my dream flashed back upon me. I called to him to stop, jumped out, caught hold of my child, and called to a policeman to catch the coachman. Just as he did so the coachman swayed and fell off the box. If I had been in the least less prompt, he would have fallen just as I saw him in my dream." It turned out that he had fainted because of illness, of which he had said nothing. The dream proved to have differed from the reality in only two points: "In my dream we approached Down-street from the west; in reality we came from the east. In my dream the coachman actually fell on his head; . . . in reality this was just averted by the prompt action which my anxious memory of the dream inspired."

It is obvious that no incompatibility exists either between those features of the preperception which were veridical, or those which were not, and the prepercipient's freedom to act as she chose at the time.

How the possibility of veridical preperception is to be explained is of course a separate question, and one which we are not called upon to speculate about in the present connection. But that veridical preperception, not explicable as imaged expectation or as chance coincidence, sometimes occurs is something which cannot be left out of account when the nature of time and the notions of pastness, presentness, and futureness are the subject of inquiry.[1]

---

1. The two cases of verdical preperception quoted are selected from the many reported by F. W. H. Myers in the *Proceedings of the* (English) *Society for Psychical Research,* Vol. XI, pp. 485-585. For a critical survey of the evidence for spontaneous precognition, see H. F. Saltmarsh, "Report on Cases of Apparent Precognition," *ditto,* Vol. XLII, 1934-5, pp. 49-103. As regards experimental evidence for precognition, see S. G. Soal and K. M. Goldney, "Experiments in Precognitive Telepathy," *Proceedings S.P.R.,* Vol. XLVII, 1943, pp. 21-150. Also, J. B. Rhine's "Precognition Reconsidered," *Journal of Parapsychology,* Vol. 9, Dec. 1945, pp. 264-277. See also, Gardner Murphy, "An Approach to Precognition," *Journal of the American Society for Psychical Research,* Vol. XLII, Jan. 1948, pp. 3-14.

27

IS "FREE WILL" A PSEUDO-PROBLEM?

C. A. Campbell

Schlick's Account of Moral Responsibility Examined

. . . LET US NOW EXAMINE Schlick's theory. In the first place, it is surely quite unplausible to suggest that the common assumption that moral freedom postulates some breach of causal continuity arises from a confusion of two different types of law. Schlick's distinction between descriptive and prescriptive law is, of course, sound. It was no doubt worth pointing out, too that descriptive laws cannot be said to "compel" human behaviour in the same way as prescriptive laws do. But it seems to me evident that the usual reason why it is held that moral freedom implies some breach of causal continuity, is not a belief that causal laws "compel" as civil laws "compel," but simply the belief that the admission of unbroken causal continuity entails a *further* admission which is directly incompatible with moral responsibility; *viz.,* the admission that no man could have acted otherwise than he in fact did. Now it may, of course, be an error thus to assume that a man is not morally responsible for an act, a fit subject for moral praise and blame in respect of it, unless he could have acted otherwise than he did. Or, if *this* is not an error, it may still be an error to assume that a man could not have acted otherwise than he did, in the sense of the phrase that is crucial for moral responsibility, without there occurring some breach of causal continuity. Into these matters we shall have to enter very fully at a later stage. But the relevant point at the moment is that these (not *prima facie* absurd) assumptions about the conditions of moral responsi-

---

[This article originally appeared in *Mind*, 1951. It is republished, with some omissions, by the kind permission of the author and editor of *Mind.* The references to Schlick are to the chapter in *Problem of Ethics* which is reprinted in this book as Selection 25, pp. 348 ff. By the "pseudo-problem theory" Campbell means the view of writers like Hume, Mill and Schlick that there is no conflict between determinism and freedom.]

bility have very commonly, indeed normally, been made, and that they are entirely adequate to explain why the problem of Free Will finds its usual formulation in terms of partial exemption from causal law. Schlick's distinction between prescriptive and descriptive laws has no bearing at all upon the truth or falsity of these assumptions. Yet if these assumptions are accepted, it is (I suggest) really inevitable that the Free Will problem should be formulated in the way to which Schlick takes exception. Recognition of the distinction upon which Schlick and his followers lay so much stress can make not a jot of difference.

As we have seen, however, Schlick does later proceed to the much more important business of disputing these common assumptions about the conditions of moral responsibility. He offers us an analysis of moral responsibility which flatly contradicts these assumptions; an analysis according to which the only freedom demanded by morality is a freedom which is compatible with Determinism. If this analysis can be sustained, there is certainly no problem of "Free Will" in the traditional sense.

But it seems a simple matter to show that Schlick's analysis is untenable. Let us test it by Schlick's own claim that it gives us what we mean by "moral responsibility" in ordinary linguistic usage.

We do not ordinarily consider the lower animals to be morally responsible. But *ought* we not to do so if Schlick is right about what we mean by moral responsibility? It is quite possible, by punishing the dog who absconds with the succulent chops designed for its master's luncheon, favourably to influence its motives in respect of its future behaviour in like circumstances. If moral responsibility is to be linked with punishment as Schlick links it, and punishment conceived as a form of education, we should surely hold the dog morally responsible? The plain fact, of course, is that we don't. We don't, because we suppose that the dog "couldn't help it": that its action (unlike what we usually believe to be true of human beings) was simply a link in a continuous chain of causes and effects. In other words, we do commonly demand the contracausal sort of freedom as a condition of moral responsibility.

Again, we do ordinarily consider it proper, in certain circumstances, to speak of a person no longer living as morally responsible for some present situation. But *ought* we to do so if we accept Schlick's essentially "forward-looking" interpretation of punishment and responsibility? Clearly we cannot now favourably affect the dead man's motives. No doubt they could *at one time* have been favourably affected. But that cannot be relevant to our judgment of responsibility if, as Schlick insists, the question of who is responsible "is a matter only of knowing who is to be punished or rewarded." Indeed he expressly tells us, as we saw earlier, that in asking this question we are not concerned with a "great-grand-parent" who may have been the "original instigator," because, for one reason, this "remote cause" is "out of reach." We cannot bring the appropriate educative influence to bear upon it. But the plain fact, of course, is that we do frequently assign moral responsibility for present situations to persons who have long been inaccessible to any punitive action on our part. And Schlick's position is still more paradoxical in respect of our apportionment of responsibility for occurrences in the distant past. Since in these cases there is no agent whatsoever whom we can favorably influence by punishment, the question of moral responsibility here should have no meaning for us. But of course it has. Historical writings are studded with examples.

Possibly the criticism just made may seem to some to result from taking Schlick's analysis too much *au pied de la lettre*. The absurd consequences deduced, it may be said, would not follow if we interpreted Schlick as meaning that a man is morally responsible where his motive is such as can *in principle* be favourably affected by reward or punishment—whether or not we who pass the judgment are in a position to take such action. But with every desire to be fair to Schlick, I cannot see how he could accept this modification and still retain the essence of his theory. For the essence of his theory seems to be that moral responsibility has its whole meaning and importance for us in relation to our potential control of future conduct in the interests of society. (I agree that it is hard to believe that anybody *really* thinks this. But it is perhaps less hard to believe to-day than it has ever been before in the history of modern ethics.)

Again, we ordinarily consider that, in certain circumstances, the *degree* of a man's moral responsibility for an act is affected by considerations of his inherited nature, or of his environment, or of both. It is our normal habit to "make allowances" (as we say) when we have reason to believe that a malefactor had a vicious heredity, or was nurtured in his formative years in a harmful environment. We say in say cases "Poor chap, he is more to be pitied than blamed. We could scarcely expect him to behave like a decent citizen with *his* parentage or upbringing." But this extremely common sort of judgment has no point at all if we mean by moral responsibility what Schlick says that we mean. On *that* meaning the degree of a man's moral responsibility must presumably be dependent upon the degree to which we can favourably affect his future motives, which is quite another matter. Now there is no reason to believe that the motives of a man with a bad heredity or a bad upbringing are either less or more subject to educative influence than those of his more fortunate fellows. Yet it is plain matter of fact that we do commonly consider the degree of a man's moral responsibility to be affected by these two factors.

A final point. The extremity of paradox in Schlick's identification of the question "Who is morally blameworthy?" with the question "Who is to be punished?" is apt to be partially concealed from us just because it is our normal habit to include in the meaning of "punishment" an element of "requital for moral transgression" which Schlick expressly denies to it. On that account we commonly think of "punishment," in its strict sense, as implying moral blameworthiness in the person punished. But if we remember to mean by punishment what Schlick means by it, a purely "educative measure," with no retributive ingredients, his identification of the two questions loses such plausibility as it might otherwise have. For clearly we often think it proper to "punish" a person, in *Schlick's* sense, where we are not at all prepared to say that the person is morally blameworthy. We may even think him morally commendable. A case in point would be the unmistakably sincere but muddle-headed person who at the cost of great suffering to himself steadfastly pursues as his "duty" a course which, in our judgment is fraught with danger to the common weal. We should most of us feel entitled, in the public interest, to bring such action to bear upon the man's motives as might induce him to refrain in future from his socially injurious behaviour: in other words, to inflict upon him what Schlick would call "punishment." But we should most of us feel perfectly clear that in so "punishing" this misguided citizen we are not proclaiming his moral blameworthiness or moral wickedness.

Adopting Schlick's own criterion, then, looking simply "to the manner in which the concept is used,"[1] we seem bound to admit that constantly people do assign moral responsibility where Schlick's theory says they shouldn't, don't assign moral responsibility where Schlick's theory says they should, and assign degrees of moral responsibility where on Schlick's theory there should be no difference in degree. I think we may reasonably conclude that Schlick's account of what we mean by moral responsibility breaks down.

The rebuttal of Schlick's arguments, however, will not suffice of itself to refute the pseudo-problem theory. The indebtedness to Schlick of most later advocates of the theory may be conceded; but certainly it does not comprehend all of significance that they have to say on the problem. There are recent analyses of the conditions of moral responsibility containing sufficient new matter, or sufficient old matter in a more precise and telling form, to require of us now something of a fresh start. In the section which follows I propose to consider some representative samples of these analyses—all of which, of course, are designed to show that the freedom which moral responsibility implies is not in fact a contra-causal type of freedom.

But before reopening the general question of the nature and conditions of moral responsibility there is a *caveat* which it seems to me worth while to enter. The difficulties in the way of a clear answer are not slight; but they are apt to seem a good deal more formidable than they

---

1. See p. 349 above.

really are because of a common tendency to consider in unduly close association two distinct questions: the question "Is a contra-causal type of freedom implied by moral responsibility?" and the question "Does a contra-causal type of freedom anywhere exist?" It seems to me that many philosophers (and I suspect that Moritz Schlick is among them) begin their inquiry with so firm a conviction that the contra-causal sort of freedom nowhere exists, that they find it hard to take very seriously the possibility that it is *this* sort of freedom that moral responsibility implies. For they are loth to abandon the commonsense belief that moral responsibility itself is something real. The implicit reasoning I take to be this. Moral responsibility is real. If moral responsibility is real, the freedom implied in it must be a fact. But contra-causal freedom is not a fact. Therefore contra-causal freedom is not the freedom implied in moral responsibility. I think we should be on our guard against allowing this or some similar train of reasoning (whose premises, after all, are far from indubitable) to seduce us into distorting what we actually find when we set about a direct analysis of moral responsibility and its conditions.

"Ought" Imples "Can"

The pseudo-problem theorists usually, and naturally, develop their analysis of moral responsibility by way of contrast with a view which, while it has enjoyed a good deal of philosophic support, I can perhaps best describe as the common view. It will be well to remind ourselves, therefore, of the main features of this view.

So far as the *meaning,* as distinct from the *conditions,* of moral responsibility is concerned, the common view is very simple. If we ask ourselves whether a certain person is morally responsible for a given act (or it may be just "in general"), what we are considering, it would be said, is whether or not that person is a fit subject upon whom to pass moral judgment; whether he can fittingly be deemed morally good or bad, morally praiseworthy or blameworthy. This does not take us any great way: but (*pace* Schlick) so far as it goes it does not seem to me seriously disputable. The really interesting and controversial question is about the *conditions* of moral responsibility, and in particular the question whether freedom of a contra-causal kind is among these conditions.

The answer of the common man to the latter question is that it most certainly *is* among the conditions. Why does he feel so sure about this? Not, I argued earlier, because the common man supposes that causal law exercises "compulsion" in the sense that prescriptive laws do, but simply because he does not see how a person can be deemed morally praiseworthy or blameworthy in respect of an act which he could not help performing. From the stand-point of moral praise and blame, he would say—though not necessarily from other stand-points—it is a matter of indifference whether it is by reason of some external constraint or by reason of his own given nature that the man could not help doing what he did. It is quite enough to make moral praise and blame futile that in either case there were no genuine alternatives, no open possibilities, before the man when he acted. He could not have acted otherwise than he did. And the common man might not unreasonably go on to stress the fact that we all, even if we are linguistic philosophers, do in our actual practice of moral judgment appear to accept the common view. He might insist upon the point alluded to earlier in this paper, that we do all, in passing moral censure, "make allowances" for influences in a man's hereditary nature or environmental circumstances which we regard as having made it more than ordinarily difficult for him to act otherwise than he did: the implication being that if we supposed that the man's heredity and environment made it not merely very *difficult* but actually *impossible* for him to act otherwise than he did, we could not properly assign moral blame to him at all.

Let us put the argument implicit in the common view a little more sharply. The moral "ought" implies "can." If we say that A morally ought to have done X, we imply that in our opinion, he could have done X. But we assign moral blame to a man only for failing to do what we think he morally ought to have done. Hence if we morally blame A for not having done X, we imply that he could have done X even though in fact he did not. In other words, we imply that A could have acted otherwise than he did. And that means that we imply, as a necessary condition of a man's being morally blameworthy, that he enjoyed a freedom of a kind not compatible with unbroken causal continuity.

The Reflective and the Unreflective Conception of Moral Responsibility

Now what is it that is supposed to be wrong with this simple piece of argument?—For, of course, it must be rejected by all these philosophers who tell us that the traditional problem of Free Will is a mere pseudo-problem. The argument looks as though it were doing little more than reading off necessary implications of the fundamental categories of our moral thinking. One's inclination is to ask "If one is to think morally at all, how else than this *can* we think?"

In point of fact, there is pretty general agreement among the contemporary critics as to what is wrong with the argument. Their answer in general terms is as follows. No doubt A's moral responsibility does imply that he could have acted otherwise. But this expression "could have acted otherwise" stands in dire need of analysis. When we analyse it, we find that it is not, as is so often supposed, simple and unambiguous, and we find that in *some* at least of its possible meanings it implies *no* breach of causal continuity between character and conduct. Having got this clear, we can further discern that only in one of these *latter* meanings is there any compulsion upon our moral thinking to assert that if A is morally blameworthy for an act, A "could have acted otherwise than he did." It follows that, contrary to common belief, our moral thinking does *not* require us to posit a contra-causal freedom as a condition of moral responsibility.

So much of importance obviously turns upon the validity or otherwise of this line of criticism that we must examine it in some detail and with express regard to the *ipsissima verba* of the critics.

In the course of a recent article in MIND[2] entitled "Free Will and Moral Responsibility," Mr. Nowell Smith (having earlier affirmed his belief that "the traditional problem has been solved") explains very concisely the nature of the confusion which, as he thinks, has led to the demand for a contra-causal freedom. He begins by frankly recognising that "It is evident that one of the necessary conditions of moral action is that the agent 'could have acted otherwise' " and he adds "it is to this fact that the Libertarian is drawing attention."[3] Then, after showing (unexceptionably, I think) how the relationship of "ought" to "can" warrants the proposition which he has accepted as evident, and how it induces the Libertarian to assert the existence of action that is "uncaused," he proceeds to point out, in a crucial passage, the nature of the Libertarian's error:

> The fallacy in the argument (he contends) lies in supposing that when we say "A could have acted otherwise" we mean that A, *being what he was and being placed in the circumstances in which he was placed*, could have done something other than what he did. But in fact we never do mean this.[4]

What then *do* we mean here by "A could have acted otherwise"? Mr. Nowell Smith does not tell us in so many words, but the passage I have quoted leaves little doubt how he would answer. What we really mean by the expression, he implies, is not a *categorical* but a *hypothetical* proposition. We mean "A could have acted otherwise, *if he did not happen to be what he in fact was, or if he were placed in circumstances other than those in which he was in fact placed.*" Now, *these* propositions, it is easy to see, are in no way incompatible with acceptance of the causal principle in its full rigour. Accordingly the claim that our

2. January, 1948.
3. *Loc. cit.*, p. 49.
4. *Loc. cit.*, p. 49.

fundamental moral thinking obliges us to assert a contra-causal freedom as a condition of moral responsibility is disproved.

Such is the "analytical solution" of our problem offered (with obvious confidence) by one able philosopher of to-day, and entirely representative of the views of many other able philosophers. Yet I make bold to say that its falsity stares one in the face. It seems perfectly plain that the hypothetical propositions which Mr. Nowell Smith proposes to substitute for the categorical proposition cannot express "what we really mean" in this context by "A could have acted otherwise," for the simple reason that these hypothetical propositions have no bearing whatsoever upon the question of the moral responsibility of A. And it is A whose moral responsibility we are talking about—a definite person A with a definitive character and in a definitive set of circumstances. What conceivable significance could it have for our attitude to A's responsibility to know that someone with a *different* character (or A with a different character, if that collocation of words has any meaning), or A in a different set of circumstances from those in which A as we are concerned with him was in fact placed, "could have acted otherwise"? No doubt this supposititious being *could* have acted otherwise than the definitive person A acted. But the point is that where we are reflecting, as we are supposed in this context to be reflecting, upon the question of A's moral responsibility, our interest in this supposititious being is precisely *nil*.

The two hypothetical propositions suggested in Mr. Nowell Smith's account of the matter do not, however, exhaust the speculations that have been made along these lines. Another very common suggestion by the analysts is that what we really mean by "A could have acted otherwise" is "A could have acted otherwise *if he had willed, or chosen, otherwise.*" This was among the suggestions offered by G. E. Moore in the well-known chapter on Free Will in his *Ethics*. It is, I think, the suggestion he most strongly favoured: though it is fair to add that neither about this nor about any other of his suggestions is Moore in the least dogmatic. He does claim, for, I think, convincing reasons, that "we *very often* mean by 'could' merely 'would, *if* so-and-so had chosen.' "[5] And he concludes "I must confess that I cannot feel certain that this may not be all that we usually mean and understand by the assertion that we have Free Will."[6]

This third hypothetical proposition appears to enjoy also the support of Mr. C. L. Stevenson. Mr. Stevenson begins the chapter of *Ethics and Language* entitled "Avoidability-Indeterminism" with the now familiar pronouncement of his School that "controversy about freedom and determinism of the will . . . presents no permanent difficulty to

5. *Ethics*, p. 212.
6. *Loc. cit.*, p. 217.

ethics, being largely a product of confusions." A major confusion (if I understand him rightly) he takes to lie in the meaning of the term "avoidable," when we say "A's action was avoidable"—or, I presume, "A could have acted otherwise." He himself offers the following definition of "avoidable"—" 'A's action was avoidable' has the meaning of 'If A had made a certain choice, which in fact he did not make, his action would not have occurred.' "[7] This I think we may regard as in substance identical with the suggestion that what we really mean by "A could have acted otherwise" is "A could have acted otherwise *if* he had chosen (or willed) otherwise." For clarity's sake we shall here keep to this earlier formulation. In either formulation the special significance of the third hypothetical proposition, as of the two hypothetical propositions already considered, is that it is compatible with strict determinism. If this be indeed all that we mean by the "freedom" that conditions moral responsibility, then those philosophers are certainly wrong who hold that moral freedom is of the contra-causal type.

Now this third hypothetical proposition does at least possess the merit, not shared by its predecessors, of having a real relevance to the question of moral responsibility. If, *e.g.,* A had promised to meet us at 2 P.M., and he chanced to break his leg at 1 P.M., we should not blame him for his failure to discharge his promise. For we should be satisfied that he *could not* have acted otherwise, even if he had so chosen; or *could not,* at any rate, in a way which would have enabled him to meet us at 2 P.M. The freedom to translate one's choice into action, which we saw earlier is for Schlick the *only* freedom required for moral responsibility, is without doubt *one* of the conditions of moral responsibility.

But it seems easy to show that this third hypothetical proposition does not exhaust what we mean, and *some*times is not even *part* of what we mean, by the expression "could have acted otherwise" in its moral context. Thus it can hardly be even part of what we mean in the case of that class of wrong actions (and it is a large class) concerning which there is really no question whether the agent could have acted otherwise, *if* he had chosen otherwise. Take lying, for example. Only in some very abnormal situation could it occur to one to doubt whether A, whose power of speech was evinced by his telling a lie, was in a position to tell what he took to be the truth *if* he had so chosen. Of *course* he was. Yet it still makes good sense for one's moral thinking to ask whether A, when lying, "could have acted otherwise": and we still require an affirmative answer to this question if A's moral blameworthiness is to be established. It seems apparent, therefore, that in this class of cases at any rate one does *not* mean by "A could have acted otherwise," "A could have acted otherwise *if* he had so chosen."

---

7. *Ethics and Language,* p. 298.

What then *does* one mean in this class of cases by "A could have acted otherwise"? I submit that the expression is taken in its simple, categorical meaning, without any suppressed "if" clause to qualify it. Or perhaps, in order to keep before us the important truth that it is only as expressions of *will* or *choice* that acts are of moral import, it might be better to say that a condition of A's moral responsibility is that he could have *chosen* otherwise. We saw that there is no real question whether A who told a lie could have acted otherwise *if* he had chosen otherwise. But there is a very real question, at least for any person who approaches the question of moral responsibility at a tolerably advanced level of reflexion, about whether A could have *chosen* otherwise. Such a person will doubtless be acquainted with the claims advanced in some quarters that causal law operates universally: or/and with the theories of some philosophies that the universe is throughout the expression of a single supreme principle; or/and with the doctrines of some theologians that the world is created, sustained and governed by an Omniscient and Omnipotent Being. Very understandably such world-views awaken in him doubts about the validity of his first, easy, instinctive assumption that there are genuinely open possibilities before a man at the moment of moral choice. It thus becomes for him a real question whether a man could have chosen otherwise than he actually did, and, in consequence, whether man's moral responsibility is really defensible. For how can a man be morally responsible, he asks himself, if his choices, like all other events in the universe, could not have been otherwise than they in fact were? It is precisely against the background of world-views such as these that for reflective people the problem of moral responsibility normally arises.

Furthermore, to the man who has attained this level of reflexion, it will in *no* class of cases be a sufficient condition of moral responsibility for an act that one could have acted otherwise *if* one had chosen otherwise—not even in these cases where there *was* some possibility of the operation of "external constraint." In these cases he will, indeed, expressly recognize freedom from external constraint as a *necessary condition,* but not as a *sufficient* condition. For he will be aware that, even granted *this* freedom, it is still conceivable that the agent had no freedom to choose otherwise than he did, and he will therefore require that the latter sort of freedom be added if moral responsibility for the act is to be established.

I have been contending that, for persons at a *tolerably advanced level of reflexion,* "A could have acted otherwise," as a condition of A's moral responsibility, means "A could have chosen otherwise." The qualification italicised is of some importance. The unreflective or unsophisticated person, the ordinary "man in the street," who does not know or much care what scientists and theologians and philosophers have said about the world, sees well enough that A is morally responsible only if he could have acted otherwise, but in his intellectual innocence he will, very probably, envisage nothing capable of preventing A from having acted otherwise except some material impediment—like the broken leg in the example above. Accordingly, for the unreflective person, "A could have acted otherwise, as a condition of moral responsibility, *is* apt to mean no more than "A could have acted otherwise *if* he had so chosen."

It would appear, then, that the view now favoured by many philosophers, that the freedom required for moral responsibility is merely freedom from external constraint, is a view which they share only with the less reflective type of layman. Yet it should be plain that on a matter of this sort the view of the unreflective person is of little value by comparison with the view of the reflective person. There are some contexts, no doubt, in which lack of sophistication is an asset. But this is not one of them. The question at issue here is as to the kind of impediments which might have prevented a man from acting otherwise than he in fact did: and on this question knowledge and reflexion are surely prerequisites of any answer that is worth listening to. It is simply on account of the limitations of his mental vision that the unreflective man interprets the expression "could have acted otherwise," in its context as a condition of moral responsibility, solely in terms of external constraint. He has failed (as yet) to reach the intellectual level at which one takes into account the implications for moral choices of the world-views of science, religion, and philosophy. If on a matter of this complexity the philosopher finds that his analysis accords with the utterances of the uneducated he has, I suggest, better cause for uneasiness than for self-congratulation.

This concludes the main part of what it seems to me necessary to say in answer to the pseudo-problem theorists. My object so far has been to expose the falsity of those innovations (chiefly Positivist) in the way of argument and analysis which are supposed by many to have made it impossible any longer to formulate the problem of Free Will in the traditional manner. My contention is that, at least so far as these innovations are concerned, the simple time-honoured argument still holds from the nature of the moral ought to the conclusion that moral responsibility implies a contra-causal type of freedom. The attempts to avoid that conclusion by analyzing the proposition "A could have acted otherwise" (acknowledged to be implied in *some* sense in A's moral responsibility) into one or other of certain hypothetical propositions which are compatible with unbroken causal continuity, break down hopelessly when tested against the touchstone of actual moral thinking. It is, I think, not necessary to defend the procedure of testing hypotheses in the ethical field by bringing to bear upon them our actual moral thinking. If there is any other form of test applicable, I should be much interested to learn what it is supposed to be. Certainly "logical analysis" *per se* will not do. That has a function, but a function that can only be ancillary. For what we are seeking to know is the meaning of the expression "could have acted otherwise" not *in the abstract,* but in the context of the question of man's *moral responsibility.* Logical analysis *per se* is impotent to give us this information. It can be of value only in so far as it operates within the orbit of "the moral consciousness." One may admit, with some qualifications, that on a matter of this sort the moral consciousness without logical analysis is blind: but it seems to me to be true without any qualification whatsoever that, on the same problem, logical analysis without the moral consciousness is empty.

Contra-Causal Freedom and Creative Activity

There are times when what seems to a critic the very strength of his case breeds mistrust in the critic's own mind. I confess that in making the criticisms that have preceded I have not been altogether free from uncomfortable feelings of this kind. For the arguments I have criticised, and more particularly the analyses of the conditions of moral responsibility, seem to me to be in many cases quite desperately unplausible. Such a state of affairs ought, I think, to give the critic pause. The thought must at least enter his mind (unless he be a total stranger to modesty) that perhaps, despite his best efforts to be fair, he has after all misrepresented what his opponents are saying. No doubt a similar thought will enter, and perhaps find lodgment in, the minds of many readers.

In this situation there is, however, one course by which the critic may reasonably hope to allay these natural suspicions. He should consider whether there may not be certain predisposing influences at work, extrinsic to the specific arguments, which could have the effect of blinding the proponents of these arguments to their intrinsic demerits. If so, he need not be too much disquieted by the seeming weakness of the case against him. For it is a commonplace that, once in the grip of general prepossessions, even very good philosophers sometimes avail themselves of very bad arguments.

Actually, we can, I think, discern at least two such influences operating powerfully in the case before us. One is sympathy with the general tenets of Positivism. The other is the conviction already alluded to, that man does not in fact possess a contra-causal type of freedom; whence follows a strong presumption that no such freedom is necessary to moral responsibility. . . .

. . . Of far wider and more permanent interest, in my judgment, is the second of the "predisposing influences"—the conviction that there just *is* no contra-causal freedom such as is commonly alleged to be a condition of moral responsibility. A natural desire to "save" moral responsibility issues, logically enough, in attempts to formulate its conditions in a manner compatible with unbroken causal continuity. The consequent analyses may be, as I have urged, very unsatisfactory. But there is no doubt that the conviction that motivates the analysis is supported by reasons of great weight: well-known arguments that are the property of no particular school and which most of us learned in our philosophical cradles. A very brief summary of what I take to be the most influential of these arguments will suffice for the comments I wish to make upon them.

A contra-causal freedom, it is argued, such as is implied in the "categorical" interpretation of the proposition "A could have chosen otherwise than he did," posits a breach of causal continuity between a man's character and his conduct. Now apart from the general presumption in favour of the universality of causal law, there are special reasons for disallowing the breach that is here alleged. It is the common assumption of social intercourse that our acquaintances will act "in character"; that their choices will exhibit the "natural" response of their characters to the given situation. And this assumption seems to be amply substantiated, over a wide range of conduct, by the actual success which attends predictions made on this basis. Where there should be, on the contra-causal hypothesis, chaotic variability, there is found in fact a large measure of intelligible continuity. Moreover, what is the alternative to admitting that a person's choices flow from his character? Surely just that the so-called "choice" is not *that person's* choice at all: that, relatively to the person concerned, it is a mere "accident." Now we cannot really believe this. But if it *were* the case, it would certainly not help to establish *moral* freedom, the freedom required for *moral* responsibility. For clearly a man cannot be morally responsible for an act which does not express his own choice but is, on the contrary, attributable simply to chance.

These are clearly considerations worthy of all respect. It is not surprising if they have played a big part in persuading people to respond sympathetically to the view that "Free Will," in its usual contra-causal formulation, is a pseudo-problem. A full answer to them is obviously not practicable in what is little more than an appendix to the body of this paper; but I am hopeful that something can be said, even in a little space, to show that they are very far from being as conclusive against a contra-causal freedom as they are often supposed to be.

To begin with the less troublesome of the two main objections indicated—the objection that the break in causal continuity which free will involves is inconsistent with the predictability of conduct on the basis of the agent's known character. All that is necessary to meet this objection,

I suggest, is the frank recognition, which is perfectly open to the Libertarian, that there is a wide area of human conduct, determinable on clear general principles, within which free will does not effectively operate. The most important of these general principles (I have no space to deal here with the others) has often enough been stated by Libertarians. Free will does not operate in these practical situations in which no conflict arises in the agent's mind between what he conceives to be his "duty" and what he feels to be his "strongest desire." It does not operate here because there just is no occasion for it to operate. There is no reason whatever why the agent should here even contemplate choosing any course other than that prescribed by his strongest desire. In all such situations, therefore, he naturally wills in accordance with strongest desire. But his "strongest desire" is simply the specific *ad hoc* expression of that system of conative and emotive dispositions which we call his "character." In all such situations, therefore, whatever may be the case elsewhere, his will is in effect determined by his character as so far formed. Now when we bear in mind that there are an almost immeasurably greater number of situations in a man's life that conform to *this* pattern than there are situations in which an agent is aware of a conflict between strongest desire and duty, it is apparent that a Libertarianism which accepts the limitation of free will to the *latter* type of situation is not open to the stock objection on the score of "predictability." For there still remains a vast area of human behaviour in which prediction on the basis of known character may be expected to succeed: an area which will accommodate without difficulty, I think, all these empirical facts about successful prediction which the critic is apt to suppose fatal to Free Will.

So far as I can see, such a delimitation of the field of effective free will denies to the Libertarian absolutely nothing which matters to him. For it is precisely that small sector of the field of choices which our principle of delimitation still leaves open to free will—the sector in which strongest desire clashes with duty—that is crucial for moral responsibility. It is, I believe, with respect to such situations, and in the last resort to such situations alone, that the agent himself recognises that moral praise and blame are appropriate. They are appropriate, according as he does or does not "rise to duty" in the face of opposing desires; always granted, that is, that he is free to choose between these courses as genuinely open possibilities. If the reality of freedom be conceded *here,* everything is conceded that the Libertarian has any real interest in securing.

But, of course, the most vital question is, can the reality of freedom be conceded even here? In particular, can the standard objection be met which we stated, that if the person's choice does not, in these situations as elsewhere, flow from his *character,* then it is not *that person's* choice at all.

This is, perhaps, of all the objections to a contra-causal freedom, the one which is generally felt to be the most conclusive. For the assumption upon which it is based, *viz.,* that no intelligible meaning can attach to the claim that an act which is not an expression of the self's *character* may nevertheless be the *self's* act, is apt to be regarded as self-evident. The Libertarian is accordingly charged with being in effect an *In*determinist, whose "free will," in so far as it does not flow from the agent's character, can only be a matter of "chance." Has the Libertarian—who invariably repudiates this charge and claims to be a *Self*-determinist— any way of showing that, contrary to the assumption of his critics, we *can* meaningfully talk of an act as the self's act even though, in an important sense, it is not an expression of the self's "character"?

I think that he has. I want to suggest that what prevents the critics from finding a meaning in this way of talking is that they are looking for it in the wrong way; or better, perhaps, with the wrong orientation. They are looking for it from the stand-point of the *external observer;* the stand-point proper to, because alone possible for, apprehension of the physical world. Now from the external stand-point we may observe processes of change. But one thing which, by common consent, *cannot* be observed from without is *creative activity.* Yet—and here lies the crux of the whole matter—it is precisely creative activity which we are trying to understand when we are trying to understand what is traditionally designated by "free will." For if there should be an act which is genuinely the self's act and is nevertheless not an expression of its character, such an act, in which the self "transcends" its character as so far formed, would seem to be essentially of the nature of creative activity. It follows that to look for a meaning in "free will" from the external stand-point is absurd. It is to look for it in a way that ensures that it will not be found. Granted that a creative activity of any kind is at least *possible* (and I know of no ground for its *a priori* rejection), there is one way, and one way only, in which we can hope to apprehend it, and that is from the *inner* stand-point of direct participation.

It seems to me therefore, that if the Libertarian's claim to find a meaning in a "free" will which is genuinely the self's will, though not an expression of the self's character, is to be subjected to any test that is worth applying, that test must be undertaken from the inner stand-point. We ought to place ourselves imaginatively at the stand-point of the agent engaged in the typical moral situation in which free will is claimed, and ask ourselves whether from *this* stand-point the claim in question does or does not have meaning for us. That the appeal must be to introspection is no doubt unfortunate. But he would be a very doctrinaire critic of introspection who declined to make use of it when in the nature of the case no other means of apprehension is available. Everyone must make the introspective experiment for himself: but I may perhaps venture to report, though at this late stage with extreme brevity, what I at least seem to find when I make the experiment myself.

In the situation of moral conflict, then, I (as agent) have before my mind a course of action X, which I believe to be my duty; and also a course of action Y, incompatible with X, which I feel to be that which I most strongly desire. Y is, as it is sometimes expressed, "in the line of least resistance" for me—the course which I am aware I should take if I let my purely desiring nature operate without hindrance. It is the course towards which I am aware that my *character,* as so far formed, naturally inclines me. Now, as actually engaged in this situation, I find that I cannot help believing that I *can* rise to duty and choose X; the "rising to duty" being effected by what is commonly called "effort of will." And I further find, if I ask myself just what it is I am believing when I believe that I "can" rise to duty, that I cannot help believing that it lies with me here and now, quite absolutely, which of two genuinely open possibilities I adopt; whether, that is, I make the effort of will and choose X, or, on the other hand, let my desiring nature, my character as so far formed, "have its way," and choose Y, the course "in the line of least resistance." These beliefs may, of course, be illusory, but that is not at present in point. For the present argument all that matters is whether beliefs of this sort are in fact discoverable in the moral agent in the situation of "moral temptation." For my own part, I cannot doubt the introspective evidence that they are.

Now here is the vital point. No matter which course, X or Y, I choose in this situation, I cannot doubt, *qua* practical being engaged in it, that my choice is *not* just the expression of my formed character, and yet *is* a choice made by my *self.* For suppose I make the effort and choose X (my "duty"). Since my very purpose in making the "effort" is to enable me to act against the existing "set" of desire, which is the expression of my character as so far formed, I cannot possibly regard the act itself as the expression of my *character.* On the other hand, introspection makes it equally clear that I am certain that it is *I* who choose; that the act is not an "accident," but is genuinely *my* act. Or suppose that I choose Y (the end of "strongest desire"). The course chosen here is, it is true, in conformity with my "character." But since I find myself unable to doubt that I *could* have made the effort and chosen X, I cannot possibly regard the choice of Y as *just* the expression of my character. Yet here again I find that I cannot doubt that the choice is *my* choice, a choice for which *I* am justly to be blamed.

What this amounts to is that I *can* and *do* attach meaning, *qua* moral agent, to an act which is not the self's character and yet is genuinely the self's act. And having no good reason to suppose that other persons have a fundamentally different mental constitution, it seems to me probable that anyone else who undertakes a similar experiment will be obliged to submit a similar report. I conclude, therefore, that the argument against "free will" on the score of its "meaninglessness" must be held to fail. "Free Will" does have meaning; though, because it is of the nature of a creative activity, its meaning is discoverable only in an intuition of the practical consciousness of the participating agent. To the agent making a moral choice in the situation where duty clashes with desire, his "self" is known to him as a creatively active self, a self which declines to be identified with his "character" as so formed. Not, of course, that the self's character—let it be added to obviate misunderstanding—either is, or is supposed by the agent to be, devoid of bearing upon his choices, even in the "sector" in which free will is held to operate. On the contrary, such a bearing is manifest in the empirically verifiable fact that we find it "harder" (as we say) to make the effort of will required to "rise to duty" in proportion to the extent that the "dutiful" course conflicts with the course to which our character as so far formed inclines us. It is only in the polemics of the critics that a "free" will is supposed to be incompatible with recognising the bearing of "character" upon choice.

"But what" (it may be asked) "of the all-important question of the value of this 'subjective certainty'? Even if what you say is sound as 'phenomenology,' is there any reason to suppose that the conviction on which you lay so much stress is in fact true?" I agree that the question is important; far more important, indeed, than is always realised, for it is not always realised that the only direct evidence there could be for a creative activity like "free will" is an intuition of the practical consciousness. But this question falls outside the purview of the present paper. The aim of the paper has not been to offer a constructive defence of free will. It has been to show that the problem as traditionally posed is a real, and not a pseudo, problem. A serious threat to that thesis, it was acknowledged, arises from the apparent difficulty of attaching meaning to an act which is not the expression of the self's character and yet is the self's own act. The object of my brief phenomenological analysis was to provide evidence that such an act does have meaning for us in the one context in which there is any sense in expecting it to have meaning.

My general conclusion is, I fear, very unexciting. It is merely that it is an error to suppose that the "Free Will" problem, when correctly formulated, turns out not to be a "problem" at all. Labouring to reinstate an old problem is dull work enough. But I am disposed to think that the philosophic situation to-day calls for a good deal more dull work of a similar sort.

SELECTED BIBLIOGRAPHY

(ITEMS PROVIDED WITH ASTERISK ARE MORE ADVANCED)

There are several books which contain surveys of the various positions which philosophers and others have adopted on this subject. The most recent of these are M. Cranston, *Freedom—A New Analysis* (London: Longmans, Green and Co., 1953) and M. Davidson, *The Free Will Controversy* (London: Watts and Co., 1942). Older works covering the same territory are H. Wildon Carr, *The Free Will Problem* (London: Ernest Benn, 1928) and G. H. Palmer, *The Problem of Freedom* (New York: Houghton Mifflin and Co., 1911). There is also a valuable historical survey in Chapter XI, Book IV, of Alexander Bain, *Mental and Moral Science* (London: Longmans, Green, and Co., 1872).

There is perhaps no other philosophical problem in which there exists so much terminological confusion and discrepancy and it is for this reason frequently not easy to classify different writers. It is often for example difficult to be sure whether a philosopher adopts what James calls "soft" determinism —the "reconciling" position represented in our selections by Mill, Schlick, and Ducasse—or whether he is a "hard" determinist like Holbach. In the case of some writers fortunately there is no doubt. Thus Hobbes, Locke and Hume may be considered as the earliest reconcilers. Hobbes discusses the subject briefly in Chapter XXI of the *Leviathan* and more fully in his booklet, *Of Liberty and Necessity*. Locke's treatment is found in Book II, Chapter XXI of the *Essay Concerning Human Understanding* and Hume's in the *Treatise of Human Nature,* Book II, Part III as well as in Section VIII of the *Inquiry Concerning Human Understanding*. There are numerous contemporary developments of this form of soft determinism. In this connection mention should be made of G. S. Fullerton, *A System of Metaphysics,* Chapter XXXIII (New York: Macmillan, 1904), R. B. Hobart's "Free-Will as Involving Determination and Inconceivable Without It," *Mind,* 1934, Chapter XIV of C. L. Stevenson, *Ethics and Language,* (New Haven: Yale University Press, 1944), A. J. Ayer's "Freedom and Necessity," reprinted in his *Philosophical Essays* (London: Macmillan, 1954), Chapter 2 of Arthur Pap, *Elements of Analytic Philosophy* (New York: Macmillan, 1949), Chapter 4 of John Hospers, *An Introduction to Philosophical Analysis* (New York: Prentice-Hall, 1953), and Adolf Grünbaum's "Causality and the Science of Human Behavior," reprinted in Feigl and Brodbeck, *Readings in the Philosophy of Science* (New York: Appleton-Century-Crofts, 1953). John Laird, *On Human Freedom* (London: Allen and Union, 1947) is a very detailed discussion of the subject from the same general viewpoint. The first essay in Gilbert Ryle, *Dilemmas* (Cambridge: University Press, 1954) tries to remove one of the "conceptual roadblocks" encountered in reflections on freedom and determinism. Mill whose discussion in his *System of Logic* is reprinted as our Selection 24, returned to the subject in Chapter XXVI of *An Examination of Sir William Hamilton's Philosophy* (London: Longmans, Green and Co., 1872).

The Hegelian variety of reconciliation is stated in the first essay of F. H. Bradley, *Ethical Studies** (Oxford: Clarendon Press, 1927) and in T. H. Green, *Prolegomena to Ethics** (Oxford: Clarendon Press, 1906). It is also supported by Engels in his *Anti-Dühring,* Part I, Chapter XI and by Lenin *Materialism and Empirio-Criticism,* Chapter III, Section 6. The standard texts of both of these books are printed by the Foreign Languages Publishing House, Moscow. Similar positions are forcibly defended in Chapter V of J. M. E. McTaggart, *Some Dogmas of Religion* (London: Edward Arnold, 1906) and in Chapter III of Book III of Hastings Rashdall, *The Theory of Good and Evil* (Oxford: Oxford University Press, 1924). The latter book contains also a particularly detailed and fair discussion of the arguments for indeterminism. Kant, who also considered himself a kind of reconciler, offers his resolution in the *Critique of Pure Reason** and more fully in *The Groundwork of the Metaphysics of Morals* and the *Critique of Practical Reason.* Useful discussions of this feature of Kant's philosophy may be found in A. C. Ewing, *Kant's Treatment of Causality* (London: Routledge and Kegan Paul, 1924), in the same author's *A Short Commentary on Kant's Critique of Pure Reason* (Chicago: University of Chicago Press, 1950) and in W. T. Jones, *Morality and Freedom in the Philosophy of Kant* (London: Oxford University Press, 1940).

Schopenhauer in his essay, "Free-Will and Fatalism" (*Complete Essays,* Book VI, tr. T. B. Saunders) approximates to "hard" determinism and so does Spinoza in Part III of the *Ethics.* Among recent writers the most fervent hard determinist was probably Clarence Darrow who stated without any qualifications that no human being is ever morally responsible for any of his actions. Darrow's views are found in his book, *Crime, Its Cause and Treatment* (New York: Thomas Crowell Co., 1922) and in numerous pamphlets published by the Haldeman-Julius Co. of Girard, Kansas. The most moving of these is Darrow's plea in defense of the boy-murderers, Loeb and Leopold. There are many literary works, including the poems of A. E. Houseman and the novels of Melville, Thomas Hardy, and Schnitzler in which similar views are expressed. Anthony Collins, one of the most important of the English deists, Voltaire, Jonathan Edwards, and Joseph Priestley are usually regarded as determinists who denied freedom, but a careful reading of their works suggests that they are really determinists of the reconciling variety.

A famous defense of indeterminism is contained in Henri Bergson, *Time and Free Will** (New York: Macmillan, 1921). This theory is also supported by Lotze in his books *Microcosmus** (New York: Charles Scribner's Sons, 1894) and *Outlines of the Philosophy of Religion* (Boston: Ginn, 1885), by James Martineau in his *Study of Religion,* Vol. II (Oxford: Clarendon Press, 1888), by Charles Peirce in his essay "The Doctrine of Necessity Examined," which is reprinted both in Peirce, *Chance, Love and Logic* (New York: Harcourt, Brace and Co., 1923, ed. M. R. Cohen) and in J. Buchler (ed.), *The Philosophy of Peirce* (New York: Harcourt, Brace and Co., 1950), and Henry Sidgwick in *The Methods of Ethics* (New York: Macmillan, 1907). The last-mentioned book contains a valuable and very balanced discussion of all the main arguments on both sides. Samuel Clarke and the Scotch philosopher of "common sense," Thomas Reid, are earlier philosophers who wrote in opposition to determinism. Clarke's discussion is found in his *Discourse Upon Natural Religion,* Reid's forms a large part of his *Active Powers.** C. A. Campbell, whose critique of Schlick and other reconcilers is Selection 27 of our book, develops his own theory in *Scepticism and Construction** (London: Allen and Unwin, 1931) and in his inaugural lecture "In Defence of Free Will" (Glasgow: Jackson, Son, and Co., 1938). There are interesting discussions of James' defense of "chance" in some of the correspondence between him and diverse philosophers reprinted in R. B. Perry, *The Thought and Character of William James* (Cambridge: Harvard University Press, 1935). The notion of "chance" is discussed in some detail in S. Hook's article "determinism" in *The Encyclopedia of the Social Sciences* (New York: Macmillan, 1935). A recent defense of "limited" indeterminism is found in Corliss Lamont, *Humanism as a Philosophy* (New York: Philosophical Library, 1949) and in an article by the same writer in "The Humanist" for June, 1948. This article gave rise to a discussion in later issues of the same periodical. W. P. Montague and Gardner Williams were among those who participated. A vigorous attack on all forms of determinism is contained in I. Berlin, *Historical Inevitability* (London: Oxford University Press, 1954).

The late Sir Arthur Eddington attacked determinism in numerous books and articles, basing his criticisms chiefly on the quantum-theory and Heisenberg's so-called "principle of indeterminacy." The main statements of Eddington's position are found in Chapter XIV of his *Nature of the Physical World* (New York: Macmillan, 1928), in Chapter XI of *The Philosophy of Physical Science* (New York: Macmillan, 1939) and in his address "The Decline of Determinism," published in the *Mathematical Gazette* of May, 1932. Eddington's views are criticized by Lord Samuel in an article, "Cause, Effect, and Professor Eddington" in *The Nineteenth Century and After,* April 1933, by Bertrand Russell in Chapter VI of *Religion and Science* (London: Oxford University Press, 1935) and in a lecture on "Determinism and Physics" (University of Durham Philosophical Society, 1936), and most fully by L. S. Stebbing, *Philosophy and the Physicists* (London: Methuen and Co., 1937). Eddington replied to some of these criticisms in Chapter XIII of *New Pathways in Science* (Cambridge: University Press, 1935). Other discussions of determinism in relation to recent physical theory are found in Max Planck, *Where is Science Going?* (New York: Norton and Co., 1932), in Phillip Frank's classical work, *Das Kausalgesetz und seine Grenzen* (Vienna: Julius Springer, 1932), Ernst Cassirer, *Determinism and Indeterminism in Modern Physics** (New Haven: Yale University Press, 1956), in Karl Popper's article "Indeterminism in Quantum Physics," published in *The British Journal for the Philosophy of Science,* 1950, and Ernest Nagel's "The Causal Character of Modern Physical Theory," which is reprinted in Feigl and Brodbeck, *Readings in the Philosophy of Science, op. cit.* There is a very stimulating review of Stebbing's book by G. A. Paul in *Mind,* 1938.

A discussion from a Catholic point of view and opposed to determinism is found in Chapter XIX of M. Maher, *Psychology* (London: Longmans, Green and Co., 1940). Other discussions of the problem by writers with a religious background are contained in E. W. Barnes, *Scientific Theory and Religion** (Cambridge: University Press, 1935), W. Bennett, *Religion and Free Will* (Oxford: Clarendon Press, 1913), C. F. d'Arcy, *God and Freedom in Human Experience* (London: Edward Arnold, 1915), and D. Von Hildebrand, *Christian Ethics* (New York: David McKay Co., 1953). Antony Flew, an unbeliever, discusses "Divine Omnipotence and Human Freedom" in an article reprinted in Flew and Macintyre (eds.), *New Essays in Philosophical Theology* (New York: Macmillan, 1955).

In recent years numerous articles have appeared discussing the implications (if any) of psychoanalytic theories on the question of whether human beings are ever free and morally responsible. In this connection mention should be made of John Hospers' "Free-Will and Psychoanalysis," reprinted in W. Sellars and J. Hospers (eds.) *Readings in Ethical Theory* (New York:

Appleton-Century-Crofts, 1952), P. H. Nowell-Smith's "Psychoanalysis and Moral Language," *The Rationalist Annual*, 1954, H. Fingarette's "Psychoanalytic Perspectives on Moral Guilt and Responsibility," *Philosophy and Phenomenological Research*, 1955, and a symposium on "The Problem of Guilt" in the *Proceedings of the Aristotelian Society*, Suppl. Vol. XXI, 1947.

There are many valuable articles discussing determinism in a more general way in recent numbers of philosophical periodicals. These include Ledger Wood's "The Free-Will Controversy," *Philosophy*, 1941, S. S. Browne's "Paralogisms of the Free-Will Problem," and P. Crissman's "Freedom in Determinism," both in the *Journal of Philosophy*, 1942, D. J. O'Connor's "Is there a Problem about Free-Will?", *Proc. of the Arist. Soc.*, 1948, C. A. Baylis' "Rational Preference, Determinism and Moral Obligation," *Journal of Philosophy*, 1950, H. L. A. Hart's "The Ascription of Responsibility and Rights,"* reprinted in A. Flew (ed.) *Essay in Logic and Language*, First Series (Oxford: Basil Blackwell, 1951), P. H. Nowell-Smith's "Free Will and Moral Responsibility,"* *Mind*, 1948, and the same author's "Determinists and Libertarians," *Mind*, 1954, F. B. Ebersole's "Free-Choice and the Demands of Morals," *Mind*, 1952, F. V. Raab's "Free Will and the Ambiguity of 'Could'," *Philosophical Review*, 1955, W. I. Matson's "On the Irrelevance of Free-Will to Moral Responsibility," *Mind*, 1956, R. Taylor's "The Problem of Future Contingencies,"* *Philosophical Review*, 1957, P. Herbst's "Freedom and Prediction," *Mind*, 1957, A. C. MacIntyre's "Determinism," *ibid.*, and W. F. R. Hardie's "My Own Free Will,"* *Philosophy*, 1957.

There are important treatments of our topic which cannot easily be classified in C. D. Broad's inaugural lecture "Determinism, Indeterminism and Libertarianism,"* which is reprinted in his book, *Ethics and the History of Philosophy* (New York: Harcourt, Brace and Co., 1952) and in Chapter VIII of John Wisdom, *Problems of Mind and Matter* (Cambridge: Cambridge University Press, 1934). Chapman Cohen, *Determinism or Free Will?* (London: The Pioneer Press, 1943) contains a defense of determinism by a gifted amateur and in H. L. Mencken, *A Treatise of Right and Wrong* (New York: Alfred Knopf, 1934) there is a thought-provoking discussion by the great American heretic which ends with a confession of bewilderment.

VI

Moral Judgments

INTRODUCTION

People constantly use terms like "good" and "evil," "right" and "wrong," "virtuous and sinful," "ought," "duty," "obliged," and many others, all of which seem to have a fairly similar function in our discourse. It is customary to refer to them as the "moral" or "ethical" predicates and to say that the sentences in which they occur express "moral" or "ethical" judgments. When people apply opposite moral predicates to the same thing, philosophers say that there is "moral disagreement" between them.

It seems plain at first sight that there is a great deal of difference between moral judgments and straightforward statements of fact. If someone says "Mercy-killing is widely practiced by the medical profession in Connecticut," it is fairly clear what observations, what sort of facts would make his statement true. If, however, he went on to say "and all these mercy-killings are *wrong,* whatever their motives may be," it is not clear, at least not at first sight, what facts would establish the truth or falsehood of his judgment. In fact, it is not obvious that there are *any* facts which could make his claim either true or false. Again, if I say "Several hundred thousand persons from the New York area are at present serving in the armed forces," no one has any doubt about the kind of observations which would prove or disprove what I asserted. But if I said "It is the *duty* of every able-bodied American citizen to serve in the armed forces if called upon to do so," it is far from evident what facts, if any, would prove or disprove my statement.

When philosophers have written on the subject of "ethics" they have, among other things, discussed the question, "What (if any) is the meaning of the moral predicates and the moral judgments in which they occur?" and the related question, "What is the nature of moral disagreement?" They have also discussed a great many other questions, but the two just mentioned are perhaps the most basic. Philosophers have also concerned themselves, for instance, with the question, "What is the greatest good, or the so-called 'summum bonum'?" And they have given widely conflicting answers to this question. But before this question can be approached in an intelligent fashion, we must have a clear idea as to what the word "good" means. Moreover, if certain theories about the meaning or function of the moral predicates were true, it would be pointless to ask the question about the summum bonum—at least, it would be a mistake to suppose that a true answer can be obtained to questions of this kind. Unfortunately, many writers on ethics neglected this very obvious consideration and raised all sorts of questions—about the summum bonum, about what we ought and ought not to do, about our unconditional duties, and what have you—without first making any attempt to determine the meaning of the moral predicates.

In this section we are exclusively concerned with the two fundamental questions about the meaning of moral judgments and the nature of moral disagreement. All our selections present various answers to these questions. Theories which attempt to answer these questions are nowadays called "metamoral" or "metaethical" theories. It should be noted that metamoral theories are interpretations of moral judgments but are not themselves moral judgments. This point may be made clear by considering briefly the metamoral theory called "subjectivism," which will be discussed more fully later on. A subjectivist maintains that all moral judgments are really only about the feelings or attitudes of the person who makes the moral judgment. Let us suppose that a certain person, A, has said, "Joseph McCarthy is a good man," and someone else, B, has said that McCarthy is an evil man. Let us next suppose that C is a subjectivist. Now, C's subjectivism does not commit him to endorsing either A's favorable or B's unfavorable moral judgment about McCarthy. It does commit him to a certain *interpretation* of both of their judgments. It commits him to holding that both A and B were merely referring to their own liking or disliking, their own love or hate, approval or disapproval, of Senator McCarthy. The same is true of all other metamoral theories. None of them logically implies a particular moral code or a specific moral judgment. All of them are, in this respect, perfectly neutral.

Before explaining the more important metamoral theories, it will be helpful to introduce some technical terms without which a fruitful discussion of this subject can hardly be carried on. To begin with, it is necessary to define the terms "subjective" and "objective" as applied to statements. A subjective statement, in our present context, is one in which the speaker or writer is referring to his own feeling or attitude or, in general, to a state of his own mind. In an objective statement, on the other hand, the speaker is talking about something other than the state of his own mind. If I say, "I feel angry now," this is a subjective statement in the sense just defined. If I say, "New York has eight million inhabitants," or "Mount Everest is the highest mountain on earth," these are objective statements. If I say, "General MacArthur is full of resentment and bitterness," this is in our sense an objective statement. I am indeed speaking about feelings, but the feelings which are the subject matter of my statement are MacArthur's and not my own. To say that a statement is objective in this sense does not necessarily imply that it is true or that it is supported by strong evidence or that it is made in an unbiased spirit. It merely means that the statement's *subject matter* is someting other than the state of the speaker's own mind. The words "subjective" and "objective" are of course commonly used also in other senses. However, it will help to bring out the contrast between the rival metamoral theories if we use these terms here only in the sense just defined.

Next we must distinguish two senses in which people may be said to disagree. Supposing A says, "Eisenhower will be reelected in 1956," and B retorts, "No, he will be defeated by a candidate of the Socialist Workers' Party." It is plain that A and B cannot both be right in this case, though they can both be mistaken. Following C. L. Stevenson, contemporary philosophers label this kind of disagreement "disagreement in belief," meaning by this that the two parties have made mutually incompatible assertions.

Let us consider another illustration. A now says, "I like Ike," to which B retorts, "I detest him." Here, too, it would be natural to describe the situation as a case of disagreement. But here the two parties are making mutually compatible statements. It may well be the case that A really likes Ike, while B really detests him. A and B disagree in the sense of entertaining opposite feelings or attitudes towards the same person. Again following Stevenson, philosophers refer to disagreement of this kind as "disagreement in attitude." It is evident that many cases of disagreement in attitude are the consequence of disagreement in belief. Whether this is always so is a much debated question which we do not need to discuss here.

The last distinction which has to be explained concerns two very different senses in which we may talk about the "settlement" or "resolution" of a dispute. Stalin and Trotzky, for example, disagreed as to whether socialism could exist in one country while all the rest of the world remained capitalist. In one sense Stalin very effectively settled this dispute in his favor by having Trotzky assassinated. But although the elimination of Trotzky from the scene settled the dispute in the sense of leaving the field to one of the parties, it did not settle the dispute in another sense—it did not prove that Stalin was right and Trotzky wrong. Again, I may be arguing with somebody whether Beria or Slansky or Zinoviev or Bukharin were "imperialist spies," and by means of forged documents and perjured witnesses I may convince my opponent that the accusations were true. In one sense this would constitute a settlement of our dispute, since we no longer disagree. In another sense, however, it would not mean a resolution of the dispute at all: I would not have proved the charges. These examples are meant to illustrate the distinction between settling or resolving a dispute in the sense of *terminating* it, whether by silencing one of the parties or by achieving agreement, and settling or resolving a dispute in the sense of *proving* one party right and the other party wrong. It will be convenient from now on to refer to the former as the "termination" and to the latter as the "resolution" of a dispute. There can be no doubt that while resolution and termination frequently go together, this is by no means always the case. It certainly happens that people are not convinced although adequate and more than adequate evidence has been presented, and, conversely, that people are convinced when adequate evidence has not been presented.

In surveying the major metamoral theories it is perhaps best to begin with the simplest. This is the theory already mentioned, according to which moral judgments are always nothing more than subjective statements. Moral judgments on this view always assert that the author of the judgment has or tends to have a certain feeling or attitude. This theory is usually known as "subjectivism." Sometimes, to differentiate it from other fairly similar theories, it is called "private subjectivism," sometimes "naive subjectivism." It is found in the writings of Hume and Westermarck and Bertrand Russell, though Russell occasionally inclines more to the emotive theory. It is also a very popular view among people without philosophical training, especially students of psychology and anthropology. It is implicit in such sayings as "Morality is just a matter of taste" or "There is no good, but thinking makes it so." According to subjectivism, moral disagreement is disagreement in attitude and not in belief, and moral disputes can be settled, if at all, only in the sense of being terminated. If I say "Abraham Lincoln was a better man than Joseph McCarthy," and you say "McCarthy is a better man than Lincoln," I can win the argument in the sense of silencing you or by getting you to share my feelings on the subject, but not in the sense of proving that I am right and that you are mistaken.

It is sometimes said that subjectivists are inconsistent in making moral judgments. Bertrand Russell, for instance, has written many books in which he makes all sorts of moral judgments—about marriage and divorce and birth-control, about socialism and communism and capitalism, about envy and cruelty and fear and love. His critics maintain that as a subjectivist he has no right to make these moral judgments, or any others for that matter. It is easy to see that this is not a valid objection. If I first say "There is nothing objectively superior or inferior about the works of different composers—it's all a matter of taste," I am not at all inconsistent in adding "and I happen to like Schubert better than Sibelius, that windy bore." I would be inconsistent if I added that my preference for Schubert is superior to your preference for Sibelius. Similarly, a subjectivist is not inconsistent in making moral judgments. He would be inconsistent if he claimed a special, non-subjective character for his own moral judgments. He would be inconsistent if he said, "Your moral judgments are merely statements about how you feel, while mine are objective truths."

If this is not a valid objection, there are others, however, which in the opinion of most contemporary philosophers amount to a decisive refutation of subjectivism. Thus, to mention only one standard argument, it is pointed out that whenever two sentences have the same meaning, any facts proving or disproving one of them *ipso facto* prove or disprove the other. For instance, whatever facts are sufficient to prove that Betrand Russell is an atheist equally prove that Bertrand Russell denies the existence of God. Conversely, if there are facts which prove or disprove one of a pair of sentences without proving or disproving the other, the two sentences cannot mean the same. Thus the facts which prove that Eisenhower is a general do not *ipso facto* prove that he believes in the existence of God; and the sentences "Eisenhower is a general" and "Eisenhower believes in God" do not mean the same. Now, according to subjectivism, moral judgments really mean the same as statements by the speaker about his own feelings. For instance, if A says "Birth-control is an evil practice" it is claimed that he means no more than "I, A, disapprove of birth-control." Let us call the former sentence "p" and the latter sentence "q." It is easy to see that facts which would prove q would certainly not prove p. To prove that he really disapproved of birth-control, A could with perfect relevance point to his record, e.g., his membership in a society opposed to birth-control." Let us call the former sentence "p" and the latter sentence "q." of "Moral Protection Leagues," and other things of the same kind. But nobody in his senses, neither A himself nor anybody else, would consider these autobiographical facts relevant to the truth of p. Whatever facts would prove p (assuming there are any), they are not the facts which would prove q. Hence p does not mean the same as q; and this holds equally for all moral judgments. It would follow that subjectivism does not give an adequate account of what we mean by the moral predicates: whatever we do mean, we don't just mean that we ourselves have a certain feeling or attitude.

This argument and other similar standard arguments (see the selection from Ewing, pp. 401 ff.) have convinced most contemporary writers that subjectivism as here defined is an untenable theory. Many contemporary philosopers are nevertheless persuaded that subjectivism was getting at some important truth. They have tried to formulate theories which would escape the difficulties of subjectivism while embodying what is sound in it. Thus, according to Richard Brandt, when a man claims that X is good he means something like "If I had all the facts about X clearly in mind and if I were ethically consistent, I would approve of X." Then there is the very similar "ideal observer" theory of Adam Smith and others which maintains that "X is good" can be translated into some such statement as "If there were an omniscient, disinterested and dispassionate observer he would approve of X." Another interesting theory was proposed by the Australian philosopher John Mackie. On his view we constantly "objectify" our feelings of approval and disapproval. When we say about something that it is good we mean that it possesses a certain objective quality and in this respect subjectivists did not offer a correct account of moral judgments. However, although we *mean* more by "X is good" than that we approve it, there exists no such objective quality of goodness as we assert. All we *have a right* to assert is that we approve of X. In so far as subjectivism denies the *existence* of any special qualities of good and bad it is a sound theory. Finally, the emotive theory may be mentioned in this context. It, too, may be regarded as an attempt to restate whatever is worth saving in the contentions of the subjectivists. We shall say more about it a little later.

There are two types of "objectivism" which have been opposed to all the metamoral theories mentioned so far. On all these views moral judgments are objective claims and moral disagreements are essentially disagreements in belief. While they agree up to this point, the two types of objectivism differ very greatly on what they take to be the detailed meaning of moral judgments. The first type of objectivism maintains that the subject matter of moral judgments is always something "natural," that is, something or other which is or can be the object of somebody's experience. On views of this kind there is no such thing as a special moral faculty. The truth or falsehood of moral judgments can always in principle be established by the use of observation and the kind of method used in the natural sciences. Philosophers who adopt this position are called "objective naturalists." Perhaps the most famous form of objective naturalism is the theory known as "utilitarianism." Interpreted as a metamoral theory rather than as a moral judgment, utilitarianism maintains that "X is right" means the same as "X produces the greatest possible happiness for the greatest number of people."

The other type of objectivism asserts that in addition to the senses and to introspection we possess the further faculty of "moral intuition" or "moral insight," and it is by means of this faculty that we recognize the truth, at any rate, of the most basic moral judgments. Philosophers holding this view are referred to as "objective non-naturalists" or "intuitionists." Most, though not all, intuitionists would identify this special moral faculty with the "under-standing" or the "*a priori*" insight." The moral intuition is not a "hunch" but a rational faculty and the basic moral principles are usually conceived by these writers to have the same status as mathematical and logical principles. They are claimed to be necessary and not merely contingent truths. At the same time they are not definitions but describe real relations in the universe. In the words of Samuel Clarke (1675-1729), an early exponent of this theory:

> These things (the basic moral principles) are so notoriously plain and self-evident, that nothing but the extremest stupidity of mind, corruption of Manners, or perverseness of Spirit can possibly make any Man entertain the least doubt concerning them. For Man endowed with Reason to deny the Truth of these things, is the very same thing as if . . . a Man that understands Geometry or Arithmetic, should deny the most obvious and known proportions of Lines or Numbers, and perversely contend that the Whole is not equal to all its parts, or that a square is not double to a triangle of equal base and height.

In our own day, views of this general kind have been held, among many others, by Sir David Ross, A. C. Ewing (see Selection 29), and Nicolai Hartmann. It is not clear whether G. E. Moore (see Selection 30), who has probably been the most influential writer on ethics during the last fifty years, is to be included in this group. When writing his great book, *Principia Ethica,* Moore certainly believed that "good" and "bad" designated objective qualities of some kind which are not given in ordinary sense-experience, but he nowhere identified our means of coming to know moral principles with the "*a priori* faculty.*" His view seems closer to the "moral sense" philosophers of the 18th century who believed that human beings came to know moral principles in a special way which was not identical either with introspection or the familiar physical senses. However, they considered themselves empiricists and regarded the special moral faculty as much more like the senses than the *a priori* faculty of the Rationalists.

There is a famous argument against all forms of objective naturalism which has persuaded many philosophers that theories of this kind cannot be true. The argument is already found in some early writers, especially in Richard Price (1723-1792), but it has been stated most forcefully in our own day by G. E. Moore (Selection 30). It is sometimes called the argument of the "open question." Moore himself calls it the "argument against the naturalistic fallacy." The argument is based on a certain technique which Moore devised for testing the correctness of proposed definitions. The technique can be explained most easily by considering a correct and incorrect definition respec-tively and by constructing a question in each case which contains both the term to be defined and the defining expression. For example, it is undoubtedly correct to say that "atheist" means the same as "person who denies the exist-ence of God," while it would not be correct to say that "atheist" means "wealthy wholesale butcher with a country home in Scarsdale." Supposing now somebody were to ask "I know that Bertrand Russell denies the existence of God, but is he an atheist?" It is clear that this would be a silly or senseless question. We might also very appropriately call it a "closed" question. The question is silly or senseless or closed because the first part of the sentence has already supplied the answer. On the other hand, if somebody said "I know that Ballanti is a wealthy wholesale butcher with a home in Scarsdale, but is he an atheist?" this would not be silly or senseless in the same sense as the earlier question. We could properly call it an "open" question. It is open because in asserting that Ballanti is a wholesale butcher with a home in Scarsdale, the questioner did not assert or imply anything one way or another about Ballanti's views on religion. In general: when we have a correct definition the question we construct must be senseless or closed; when we have an incorrect definition the question must be sensible or open. And the converse must also be true: if a question is closed this can only be so because the two expressions (in our instance "atheist" and "person who denies the existence of of God") really have the same meaning; if the question is open this can only be because the two expressions ("atheist" and "wealthy wholesale butcher with a home in Scarsdale") do not mean the same, i.e., because the definition is not correct.

Moore then applied this test to the various definitions of "good" which had been suggested. Thus he examined the utilitarian definition by raising the question "Is producing the greatest happiness a good thing?" This, Moore maintained, is plainly a sensible or open question. Hence "good" and "producing the greatest happiness" do not have the same meaning and the utilitarian defiinition must be mistaken. Other attempts to define "good" fare no better. The question "Is it a good thing to aid the struggle for survival?" is a sensible question and hence a definition of "good" in terms of "promoting evolution" is incorrect. Again it makes sense to ask "Is obedience to the will of God a good thing?" and hence the corresponding theological definition of "good" is in error.

Moore concludes that "good" is indefinable. This does not mean that it is meaningless. It is indefinable for the same reason that terms like "yellow" or "bitter" or "pleasure" are indefinable. These terms are indefinable because they designate the simplest kind of quality which cannot be analyzed into anything simpler. Other terms can be defined in terms of "yellow" or "bitter" or "pleasure," but these most basic terms can have their meaning explained only by pointing to instances of the qualities they designate. Like them, Moore maintains, "good" designates a simple quality which cannot be analysed into anything simpler. Philosophers who tried to find definitions of "good" had missed this crucial fact. But the quality designated by "good" is not given to the senses, like colors and tastes, or to introspection like love or anger. To mark this difference Moore called it a "non-natural" quality.

When enumerating theories which try to embody whatever is sound in subjectivism, reference was made to the "emotive" theory which is the meta-moral theory favored by most of the "logical positivists." The proponents of this theory accept Moore's open-question argument and agree with him that "good" is indefinable. However, they explain this fact differently. The word "good" is indefinable not because it designates a simple quality disclosed by some special moral faculty, but because it is meaningless—because it designates nothing at all. Or rather: "good" and the other moral predicates have "emotive" but lack "descriptive" or "cognitive" meaning. The defenders of the emotive theory maintain that the function of moral judgments has been radically misconceived by the other theories in the field. Moral judgments are not the sort of thing which can be true or false. They are not statements of fact. Their function is not to give information about anything—not about our own feelings, not about production of the greatest possible happiness and certainly not about some nebulous realm of non-natural qualities. The function of moral judgments is "dynamic": we use them either, like exclamations, to *vent* our emotions, or else, like commands, to *arouse* emotions and *influence* people's actions. If I say "Harry Truman is a good man" this is roughly equivalent to "Harry Truman Hurrah!" or "Long live Harry Truman!" If I say "One ought not to cheat in making out one's income tax return" this is like saying "Don't cheat on your income tax return," but in a certain special subtle tone which avoids the directness of a straightforward command.

So far the emotive theory has been stated in its earlier and more radical form. In this form it resembles subjectivism in maintaining that moral disagreement is disagreement in attitude and that moral disputes can be terminated but not resolved. In later years the theory was modified in several ways. Many recent writers would say that moral judgments have both descriptive *and* emotive meaning and that moral disagreement is both disagreement in attitude *and* disagreement in belief. (See Stevenson, Selection 32). For example if somebody says "Harry Truman is a good man" he is said to express his favorable feelings towards Harry Truman and also to make some such factual assertions as that Harry Truman is courageous, sincere, loyal, etc. If I say "One ought not to cheat in making out one's income tax" I am issuing a kind of command, but I am also making or implying some such factual assertion as that cheating on one's income tax return has a tendency to undermine the basis of organized society.

While thus allowing that moral judgments have descriptive meaning, these writers insist that what we here assert is always something "natural"—something whose existence can in principle be ascertained without having to resort to a special moral faculty. To determine for instance whether Harry Truman is courageous or loyal, sense-observations of some kind are all that is required. These later versions of the emotive theory have aptly been referred to as "emotive naturalism."

The emotive theory, sometimes with additions which were not mentioned in the preceding survey, has won widespread acceptance among the younger philosophers in Britain and the United States. There are also, however, distinguished philosophers who think it mistaken. The selection from Blanshard (Selection 33) contains some arguments against the emotive theory. Others will be found in articles and books mentioned in the bibliography at the end of this section.

P. E.

28

SCIENCE AND ETHICS

Bertrand Russell

. . . THE FRAMING of moral rules, so long as the ultimate Good is supposed known, is a matter for science. For example: should capital punishment be inflicted for theft, or only for murder, or not at all? Jeremy Bentham, who considered pleasure to be the Good, devoted himself to working out what criminal code would most promote pleasure, and concluded that it ought to be much less severe than that prevailing in his day. All this, except the proposition that pleasure is the Good, comes within the sphere of science.

But when we try to be definite as to what we mean when we say that this or that is "the Good," we find ourselves involved in very great difficulties. Bentham's creed that pleasure is the Good roused furious opposition, and was said to be a pig's philosophy. Neither he nor his opponents could advance any argument. In a scientific question, evidence can be adduced on both sides, and in the end one side is seen to have the better case—or, if this does not happen, the question is left undecided. But in a question as to whether this or that is the ultimate Good, there is no evidence either way; each disputant can only appeal to his own emotions, and employ such rhetorical devices as shall rouse similar emotions in others.

Take, for example, a question which has come to be important in practical politics. Bentham held that one man's pleasure has the same ethical importance as another man's, provided the quantities are equal; and on this ground he was led to advocate democracy. Nietzsche, on the contrary, held that only the great man can be regarded as important on his own account, and that the bulk of mankind are only means to his well-being. He viewed ordinary men as many people view animals: he

[This selection consists of the major parts of Chapter IX of Russell's *Religion and Science*, which was first published in 1935. It is here reprinted with the kind permission of Bertrand Russell and the Oxford University Press.]

thought it justifiable to make use of them, not for their own good, but for that of the superman, and this view has since been adopted to justify the abandonment of democracy. We have here a sharp disagreement of great practical importance, but we have absolutely no means, of a scientific or intellectual kind, by which to persuade either party that the other is in the right. There are, it is true, ways of altering men's opinions on such subjects, but they are all emotional, not intellectual.

Questions as to "values"—that is to say, as to what is good or bad on its own account, independently of its effects—lie outside the domain of science, as the defenders of religion emphatically assert. I think that in this they are right, but I draw the further conclusion, which they do not draw, that questions as to "values" lie wholly outside the domain of knowledge. That is to say, when we assert that this or that has "value," we are giving expressions to our own emotions, not to a fact which would still be true if our personal feelings were different. To make this clear, we must try to analyzse the conception of the Good.

It is obvious, to begin with, that the whole idea of good and bad has some connection with desire. *Prima facie,* anything that we all desire is "good," and anything that we all dread is "bad." If we all agreed in our desires, the matter could be left there, but unfortunately our desires conflict. If I say "what I want is good," my neighbor will say "No, what I want." Ethics is an attempt—though not, I think, a successful one—to escape from this subjectivity. I shall naturally try to show, in my dispute with my neighbor, that my desires have some quality which makes them more worthy of respect than his. If I want to preserve a right of way, I shall appeal to the landless inhabitants of the district; but he, on his side, will appeal to the landowners. I shall say: "What use is the beauty of the countryside if no one sees it?" He will retort: "What beauty will be left if trippers are allowed to spread devastation?" Each tries to enlist allies by showing that his own desires harmonize with those of other people. When this is obviously impossible, as in the case of a burglar, the man is condemned by public opinion, and his ethical status is that of a sinner.

Ethics is thus closely related to politics: it is an attempt to bring the collective desires of a group to bear upon individuals; or, conversely, it is an attempt by an individual to cause his desires to become those of his group. This latter is, of course, only possible if his desires are not obviously opposed to the general interest: the burglar will hardly attempt to persuade people that he is doing them good, though plutocrats make similar attempts, and often succeed. When our desires are for things which all can enjoy in common, it seems not unreasonable to hope that others may concur; thus the philosopher who values Truth, Goodness and Beauty seems, to himself, to be not merely expressing his own desires, but pointing the way to the welfare of all mankind. Unlike the burglar, he is able to believe that his desires are for something that has value in an impersonal sense.

Ethics is an attempt to give universal, and not merely personal, importance to certain of our desires. I say "certain" of our desires, because in regard to some of them this is obviously impossible, as we saw in the case of the burglar. The man who makes money on the Stock Exchange by means of some secret knowledge does not wish others to be equally well informed: Truth (in so far as he values it) is for him a private possession, not the general human good that it is for the philosopher. The philosopher may, it is true, sink to the level of the stock-jobber, as when he claims priority for a discovery. But this is a lapse: in his purely philosophic capacity, he wants only to enjoy the contemplation of Truth in doing which he in no way interferes with others who wish to do likewise. . . .

. . . Every attempt to persuade people that something is good (or bad) in itself, and not merely in its effects, depends upon the art of rousing feelings, not upon an appeal to evidence. In every case the preacher's skill consists in creating in others emotions similar to his own —or dissimilar, if he is a hypocrite. I am not saying this as a criticism of the preacher, but as an analysis of the essential character of his activity.

When a man says "this is good in itself," he seems to be making a statement, just as much as if he said "this is square" or "this is sweet." I believe this to be a mistake. I think that what the man really means is: "I wish everybody to desire this," or rather "Would that everybody desired this." If what he says is interpreted as a statement, it is merely an affirmation of his own personal wish; if, on the other hand, it is interpreted in a general way, it states nothing, but merely desires something. The wish, as an occurrence, is personal, but what it desires is universal. It is, I think, this curious interlocking of the particular and the univeral which has caused so much confusion in ethics.

The matter may perhaps become clearer by contrasting an ethical sentence with one which makes a statement. If I say "all Chinese are Buddhists," I can be refuted by the production of a Chinese Christian or Mohammedan. If I say "I believe that all Chinese are Buddhists," I cannot be refuted by any evidence from China, but only by evidence that I do not believe what I say; for what I am asserting is only something about my own state of mind. If, now, a philosopher says "Beauty is Good," I may interpret him as meaning either "Would that everybody loved the beautiful" (which corresponds to "all Chinese are Buddhists") or "I wish that everybody loved the beautiful" (which corresponds to "I believe that all Chinese are Buddhists"). The first of these makes no assertion, but expresses a wish; since it affirms nothing, it is logically impossible that there should be evidence for or against it, or for it to possess either truth or falsehood. The second sentence, instead of being merely optative, does make a statement, but is one about the philosopher's state of mind, and it could only be refuted by evidence that he does not have the wish that he says he has. This second sentence does not belong to ethics, but to psychology or biography. The first sentence, which does belong to ethics, expresses a desire for something, but asserts nothing.

Ethics, if the above analysis is correct, contains no statements, whether true or false, but consists of desires of a certain general kind, namely such as are concerned with the desires of mankind in general— and of gods, angels, and devils, if they exist. Science can discuss the causes of desires, and the means for realizing them, but it cannot contain any genuinely ethical sentences, because it is concerned with what is true or false.

The theory which I have been advocating is a form of the doctrine which is called the "subjectivity" of values. This doctrine consists in maintaining that, if two men differ about values, there is not a disagreement as to any kind of truth, but a difference of taste. If one man says "oysters are good" and another says "I think they are bad," we recognize that there is nothing to argue about. The theory in question holds that all differences as to values are of this sort, although we do not naturally think them so when we are dealing with matters that seem to us more exalted than oysters. The chief ground for adopting this view is the complete impossibility of finding any arguments to prove that this or that has intrinsic value. If we all agreed, we might hold that we know values by intuition. We cannot prove, to a color-blind man, that grass is green and not red. But there are various ways of proving to him that he lacks a power of discrimination which most men possess, whereas in the case of values there are no such ways, and disagreements are much more frequent than in the case of colors. Since no way can be even imagined for deciding a difference as to values, the conclusion is forced upon us that the difference is one of tastes, not one as to any objective truth.

The consequences of this doctrine are considerable. In the first place, there can be no such thing as "sin" in any absolute sense; what one man calls "sin" another may call "virtue," and though they may dislike each other on account of this difference, neither can convict the other of intellectual error. Punishment cannot be justified on the ground that the criminal is "wicked," but only on the ground that he has behaved in a way which others wish to discourage. Hell, as a place of punishment for sinners, becomes quite irrational.

In the second place, it is impossible to uphold the way of speaking about values which is common among those who believe in Cosmic

Purpose. Their argument is that certain things which have been evolved are "good," and therefore the world must have had a purpose which was ethically admirable. In the language of subjective values, this argument becomes: "Some things in the world are to our liking, and therefore they must have been created by a Being with our tastes, Whom, therefore, we also like, and Who, consequently, is good." Now it seems fairly evident that, if creatures having likes and dislikes were to exist at all, they were pretty sure to like some things in their environment, since otherwise they would find life intolerable. Our values have been evolved along with the rest of our constitution, and nothing as to any original purpose can be inferred from the fact that they are what they are.

Those who believe in "objective" values often contend that the view which I have been advocating has immoral consequences. This seems to me to be due to faulty reasoning. There are, as has already been said, certain ethical consequences of the doctrine of subjective values, of which the most important is the rejection of vindictive punishment and the notion of "sin." But the more general consequences which are feared, such as the decay of all sense of moral obligation, are not to be logically deduced. Moral obligation, if it is to influence conduct, must consist not merely of a belief, but of a desire. The desire, I may be told, is the desire to be "good" in a sense which I no longer allow. But when we analyze the desire to be "good" it generally resolves itself into a desire to be approved, or, alternatively, to act so as to bring about certain general consequences which we desire. We have wishes which are not purely personal, and, if we had not, no amount of ethical teaching would influence our conduct except through fear of disapproval. The sort of life that most of us admire is one which is guided by large impersonal desires; now such desires can, no doubt, be encouraged by example, education, and knowledge, but they can hardly be created by the mere abstract belief that they are good, nor discouraged by an analysis of what is meant by the word "good."

When we contemplate the human race, we may desire that it should be happy, or healthy, or intelligent, or warlike, and so on. Any one of these desires, if it is strong, will produce its own morality; but if we have no such general desires, our conduct, whatever our ethic may be, will only serve social purposes in so far as self-interest and the interests of society are in harmony. It is the business of wise institutions to create such harmony as far as possible, and for the rest, whatever may be our theoretical definition of value, we must depend upon the existence of impersonal desires. When you meet a man with whom you have a fundamental ethical disagreement—for example, if you think that all men count equally, while he selects a class as alone important—you will find yourself no better able to cope with him if you believe in objective values than if you do not. In either case, you can only influence his conduct through influencing his desires: if you succeed in that, his ethic will change, and if not, not.

Some people feel that if a general desire, say for the happiness of mankind, has not the sanction of absolute good, it is in some way "irrational." This is due to a lingering belief in objective values. A desire cannot, in itself, be either rational or irrational. It may conflict with other desires, and therefore lead to unhappiness; it may rouse opposition in others, and therefore be incapable of gratification. But it cannot be considered "irrational" merely because no reason can be given for feeling it. We may desire A because it is a means to B, but in the end, when we have done with mere means, we must come to something which we desire for no reason, but not on that account "irrationally." All systems of ethics embody the desires of those who advocate them, but this fact is concealed in a mist of words. Our desires are, in fact, more general and less purely selfish than most moralists imagine; if it were not so, no theory of ethics would make moral improvement possible. It is, in fact, not by ethical theory, but by the cultivation of large and generous desires through intelligence, happiness, and freedom from fear, that men can be brought to act more than they do at present in a manner that is consistent with the general happiness of mankind. Whatever our definition of the "Good," and whether we believe it to be subjective or objective, those who do not desire the happiness of mankind will not endeavor to further it, while those who do desire it will do what they can to bring it about. . . .

29

THE OBJECTIVITY
OF MORAL JUDGMENTS

A. C. Ewing

ONE CLASS OF ANSWER to the question how "good" is to be defined is given by the subjectivists. But, before we consider this type of answer, we must try to make clear to ourselves what could be meant by the "objectivity" of ethical judgments or of value judgments in general. It obviously does not mean that they ascribe value properties to physical objects. These clearly do not possess ethical qualities. It might indeed be held that they possessed the property of beauty and therefore the property of intrinsic goodness quite independently of being perceived. This view does not seem to me obviously false, but it is plain that most philosophers who have asserted the objectivity of value judgments did not wish to commit themselves to it, still less to maintain that all value judgments were objective in precisely the same sense as that in which judgments about physical objects are. We can therefore rule out at once the sense of "objective" as referring to what exists independently of being experienced. What then does "objective" mean when used in reference to ethics?

It may mean "claiming to be true." Obviously in this sense judgments about psychological events and dispositions are objective, though they do not refer to what exists independently of experience, and in this sense ethical judgments may be objective. To say they are is indeed to say no more than that they are judgments and not merely something else which we have confused with judgments. But even this much is denied by some who maintain that so-called ethical judgments are only exclamations, commands, or wishes.

However, a person who admitted the occurrence of ethical judg-

[This selection consists of parts of Chapter I of Ewing's *The Definition of Good*, which appeared in 1947. The American edition was published by the Macmillan Co., the British edition by Routledge and Kegan Paul. The selection is here reprinted with the kind permission of the author and the publishers.]

ments, but denied that they were ever in fact true or that we could ever have any justification for believing them to be true, would not usually be described as holding an objective view of ethics. So "objective" here may be taken as implying that ethical judgments in particular and value judgments in general are sometimes true and can be sometimes known or at least justifiably believed to be true. An objective view involves the rejection of scepticism in ethics.

But this would not by itself be sufficient to satisfy the holders of the view that ethical judgments are objectives. Suppose "A is good" simply meant "I have a certain feeling about A." It would then be a judgment and could perfectly well be true and known to be true, yet anybody who maintained such a position would be said to be holding a subjective and not an objective view of ethics. The proposition that ethical judgments are objective, therefore, besides asserting that they are judgments, asserts of them a certain independence of the feelings or attitude of the person judging. They are not merely judgments about his feelings, or for that matter his thoughts. Even if partly based on feeling, they are not about the feeling itself but about something to which the feeling points, and something which cannot adequately be described in terms merely of the man's own psychology.

The view that "ethical judgments are objective" therefore excludes the following views: (a) that they are not really judgments at all, (b) that they are all false or that we are never justified in thinking them true, (c) that they are merely judgments about one's own psychological state or dispositions. Any of these three alternative views may be called "subjective."

The Difficulties of Subjectivism

The simplest form of the subjectivist view is that according to which ethical judgments, though genuine judgments, assert only that the person who makes the judgment has or tends to have certain feelings. "This is good" or "right" on such a view becomes "I have (or tend to have) an emotion of approval on considering this." A number of incredibly paradoxical consequences would follow from the adoption of this view. Firstly, the judgments could not be false unless the person judging had made a mistake about his own psychology. Secondly, two different people would never mean the same thing when they made such a judgment, since each would mean "This is approved by *me*." Indeed the same person would never mean the same by it on two different occasions, because each time he would mean "I *now* feel (or tend to feel) approval of this."

Thirdly, if I judge something to be good and you judge it to be bad, our judgments would never be logically incompatible with each other. It is not a sufficient reply to point out that they can still be incompatible with each other in some different sense, for example in the sense that they express attitudes which are in conflict with each other or lead to incompatible policies. For we do not see merely that A's judgment "This is good" and B's judgment "This is bad" (in the corresponding sense of the word) lead to or express incompatible policies like A's judgment "I desire to further X" and B's judgment "I desire to oppose X." We see that the two judgments logically contradict each other so that it is logically impossible that they could both be true. No doubt, since "good" and "bad" can each be used in different senses, "this is bad" may not always contradict "this is good," because, for example, "good" may mean "instrumentally good" and "bad" may mean "intrinsically bad;" but at any rate they sometimes do so, and on the view under discussion they could, when asserted by different people, never do so. Fourthly, no argument or rational discussion, nor indeed any citation of empirical facts, could be in any degree relevant to supporting or casting doubt on any ethical judgment unless it could be directed to showing that the person who makes the judgment has made a mistake about his own feelings or tendencies to have feelings. It is true that argument or fresh knowledge about the circumstances and likely consequences of an act might lead me to have different feelings about it and so judge it right while I had judged it wrong before, or vice versa; but it would not in any way indicate that my previous judgment was false. The judgments would be different; but since they referred only to my feelings at different times they would not contradict each other any more than "I was ill on January 1" contradicts "I was well on February 1." Yet it is clear that argument can really cast doubt on propositions in ethics.

Fifthly, I could not, while asserting an ethical belief, conceive that I might possibly be wrong in this belief and yet be certain that I now feel (or tend to feel) disapproval. Since it is quite clear that I can conceive this in some cases at least, this argument provides another *reductio ad absurdum* of the theory. To think that an ethical belief now expressed by me may possibly be wrong is not the same as thinking that I may come in the future to have different feelings, for I think that the present judgment may be wrong and not a future one. To put the objection in another way, it would follow from the theory that to say "If I feel approval of A, A is always right (good)" is to utter a tautology. But it is not, it is a piece of gross conceit, if made in any ordinary context. Even if it were true that, if I feel approval of A, I shall always at the time judge A to be right (good), this is quite a different statement. I need not always be certain that my judgments are correct (unless judgment is so defined as to cover only cases of *knowledge*).

Sixthly, it would follow from the theory under discussion that, when I judge that Hitler was bad or acted wrongly, I am not really talking about Hitler at all but about my own psychology.

To me the consequences that I have mentioned are all quite incredible and constitute a fully sufficient *reductio ad absurdum* of the theory from which they are deduced. They hold whether it is applied both to "good" and to "right" or only to one of them. . . .

The Case Against Objectivism

Let us now examine the case against the objectivity of ethical judgments. If it is conclusive we shall have to be subjectivists in the sense that we shall have to admit the impossibility of making any true or at least any justified ethical judgments, even if we do not admit that ethical judgments are of such a nature that they could not conceivably be true at all or true of anything but the mental state or dispositions of the speaker.

One argument is based on the striking differences in ethical views between different people. But the differences between the views of savages and those of modern scientists about eclipses, or between the views of different politicians as to the causes and likely effects of contemporary events, are as great as the differences between the views of savages and of Christians, or the views of democrats and of Nazis, as to ethics. Are we to conclude from this that the scientists are no more right than the savages or that the political events about which the disputes turn have not objectively any causes or effects? If we do not draw this conclusion here, why draw the corresponding conclusion about ethics? There are also various ways of explaining the differences of view that exist without casting doubt on the objectivity of ethics. In the first place, acts which bear the same name may be very different acts in different states of society, because the circumstances and the psychology of the people concerned are very different. So it might be the case that, for example, slavery or polygamy was right, as the course which involved least evil, in certain more primitive societies and wrong in ours. This is quite compatible with the objectivity of ethical judgments. The proposition that slavery was right in ancient Egypt would not contradict the proposition that it was wrong in the United States in 1850 A.D. Both we and the ancient Egyptians may be right in our ethical judgments. Let us, however, take cases where one party is wrong. Now it is important to note that differences in ethical beliefs are often due to differences of opinion as to matters of fact. If A and B differ as to the likely consequences of an action, they may well differ as to whether the action is right or wrong, and this is perhaps the most fertile source of disputes as to what is right. But it is not an ethical difference at all; it is a difference such as arises between rival scientific predictions based on inductive evidence. Differences or apparent differences of opinion of these two kinds obviously constitute no possible argument against the objectivity of ethics.

But there are also genuine ethical differences—that is, differences as to our judgments not of fact but of value. These may sometimes be explained by differences in people's experience of life. If I never experience A, I cannot realize the intrinsic goodness of A and may therefore wrongly subordinate it to something less good. And we must remember that what is intrinsically good is not a physical thing or a physical act, but the experience or state of mind associated with it. Even a long study of philosophical books would not qualify a person to pass a judgment on the intrinsic value of philosophy if he were hopelessly bad at the subject, because then, however many books he read, he would not have a genuinely philosophical experience. Two persons who differ as to the aesthetic value of a picture may really be judging about different things, their several experiences of it. Or at least their judgments will be based on different data. Other differences of view may be due to the misapplication of principles previously accepted, or to genuine intellectual confusions such as the philosopher or even the man of common sense who is not a philosopher could remove. For instance a man may confuse badness and wrongness and conclude or assume, for example, that, because he really sees lying to be always bad (an evil), he sees it to be always wrong, while it may be a case of choosing the lesser evil rather than the greater. Often a man will think that he knows intuitively P to be R when he really only sees it to be Q but confuses Q with R.

Or the judgment that something is good or bad on the whole may have been due to concentrating attention on one side of it while ignoring or underestimating the other sides, as, for instance, militarists concentrate their attention on the unselfish heroism which war brings out in men and forget or underestimate war's evils. Lesser degrees of such onesidedness it is impossible to avoid, and yet they may detrimentally influence ethical judgments. To decide what is right in a particular case is often a difficult matter of balancing the good or evil likely to be produced by one proposed act against that likely to be produced by others. For, even if we do not hold the view that the rightness of an act depends solely on its consequences, we cannot in any case deny that such balancing of the consequences should play the predominant part in at least many ethical decisions. Perhaps, if we foresaw all the consequences clearly as they would be in their factual character and could keep our attention fixed equally on them all, we should always be in agreement as to the degree in which they were good or evil as compared with the consequences of the other possible acts. But, apart from the difficulty of estimating what the consequences of an act will be, it is practically impossible in cases which are at all complex to keep our attention sufficiently fixed at the same time on all the foreseeable consequences likely to be seriously relevant for good or evil, and so we are likely through lack of attention to underestimate the value or disvalue of some as compared to that of others.

The lack of attention I have mentioned is in some degree inevitable, but it is greatly enhanced by the influence of desire and prejudice. It is a commonplace that ethical mistakes are often due to non-intellectual factors. Whether these act only through affecting the attention or whether they can lead to mistaken valuations even in the presence of full attention to the object valued we need not discuss. Their influence is certainly not confined to ethical mistakes; we may note the different conclusions as to the factual consequences of a policy which members of different political parties may draw from the same evidence. There is, in any case, a large class of errors for which some form of "psychoanalysis" (I do not say necessarily the Freudian) is required rather than argument, and another (probably much larger) of which it can be said only that the person in question fell into error because he did not steadfastly will to seek the truth and therefore did not fix his attention on points which displeased him. The convictions of some people as to the objectivity of ethics appear to have been shaken by the fact that enthusiastic Nazis seem to have believed that it was their duty to do things which we are convinced are completely wrong, such as ill-treating the Jews; but is there any reason to think that these Nazis really wanted to arrive at the truth regarding the question whether it was right or wrong to send Jews to concentration camps? If not, we need not be so surprised that they did not attain the truth which they did not seek.

So it may well be the case that all differences in people's judgments whether certain actions are right or wrong or certain things good or bad are due to factors other than an irreducible difference in ethical intuition. But, even if they should not be, we must remember that ethical intuition, like our other capacities, is presumably a developing factor and therefore may be capable of error. But in any case we have said enough to show that great differences of opinion as to ethics are quite compatible with the objectivity of ethical judgments.

Differences between philosophers about the general theory of ethics are remarkably great; but experience shows that very wide philosophical differences are quite compatible with striking agreement as regards the kind of action judged right or wrong, just as radical differences between philosophers in their theory of perception and of physical objects are quite compatible with complete agreement in ordinary life as to what particular physical objects are in a particular place at a particular time.

The differences between philosophers are differences not mainly as to their ethical judgments in concrete ethical situations, but as to the general theory explaining these. We may add that the differences between different peoples and different civilizations as to concrete ethical judgments are commonly exaggerated. David Livingstone says that nowhere had he need to teach the African savages at any rate the ethical, as opposed to the religious, portion of the Decalogue. But there is of course a great inconsistency (not only among savages) in confining to a limited group rules which demand universal extension.

The Argument from the Psychological Origin of Ethical Beliefs

Another argument is that ethical beliefs can be explained psychologically as having originated from non-ethical factors such as fear of punishment. Now there must be a psychological history of the origin of any beliefs, and there must have been a time when no ethical ideas or beliefs yet existed, both in the history of the individual and in the history of the race. But this does not prove that ethical beliefs originated solely from the pre-existing ideas through a sort of confusion and were not due to a genuine cognition of properties really present. There was also a time when there were no logical or mathematical ideas, but nobody would entertain a similar argument against logic or mathematics.

Further, to be sceptical about ethics on the strength of a theory as to the origin of ethical ideas would be to give up the more for the far less certain, indeed the extremely uncertain. For such a sceptical theory would rest on the psychology of children if applied to individual development, and the psychology of savages if applied to evolutionary development of the race. But, owing to the impossibility of obtaining reliable introspective evidence, the psychology of children and savages, at least when we consider their higher mental processes or the beginnings of such, is speculative in the extreme. To quote from Broad, "Of all branches of empirical psychology that which is concerned with what goes on in the minds of babies must, from the nature of the case, be one of the most precarious. Babies, whilst they remain such, cannot tell us what their experiences are; and all statements made by grown persons about their own infantile experiences on the basis of ostensible memory are certainly inadequate and probably distorted. The whole of this part of psychology therefore is, and will always remain, a mere mass of speculations about infantile mental processes, put forward to explain certain features in the lives of grown persons and incapable in principle of any independent check or verification. Such speculations are of the weakest kind known to science." The psychology of primitive savages is in an equally or almost equally weak position. Some of our ethical judgments, on the other hand, I should insist, are quite or almost as certain as any judgment, and, even if the reader is not prepared to go so far, he must admit that they are at any rate far more certain than could be any theory founded on the psychology of children and savages which explained them away. The same uncertainty must attach to any theory of ethics or analysis of ethical terms based on the way in which children learn the use of the terms. Such a theory is irrelevant unless it is based on a study of what children exactly have in mind and what their mental processes are when they use the words, and how can we possibly have a well founded idea of that when they cannot introspect or adequately report introspections?

Westermarck contends that objectivity is disproved by the fact that ethical judgments are based on emotion; but he does not even try, as far as I can see, to disprove the view that emotions only provide a psychological condition in the absence of which we should not have been in a fit state ever to intuit the characteristic of goodness or the relation of obligation. I certainly should not admit that the emotion was normally or originally prior to at least a confused apprehension of good or evil, rightness or wrongness; but even if I, like some even among the objectivists and non-naturalists, admitted this and made the feeling of the emotion a necessary prior condition of the apprehension, Westermarck's conclusion would not follow. The making of an ethical judgment will in any case presuppose various psychological conditions, but it does not follow that the judgment must be about these conditions. Nobody would argue that ethical judgments must all really be about breathing because breathing is a necessary condition without which we could not have made the judgments. . . .

The Role of Intuition

. . . Probably the principal reason which makes people inclined to deny the objectivity of ethics is the fact that in ethical argument we are very soon brought to a point where we have to fall back on intuition, so that disputants are placed in a situation where there are just two conflicting intuitions between which there seem to be no means of deciding. However, it is not only ethics but all reasoning which presupposes intuition. I cannot argue A, ∴ B, ∴ C without seeing that A entails B and B entails C, and this must either be seen immediately or require a further argument. If it is seen immediately, it is a case of intuition; if it has to be established by a further argument, this means that another term, D, must be interpolated between A and B such that A entails D and D entails B, and similarly with B and C, but then the same question arises about A entailing D, so that sooner or later we must come to something which we see intuitively to be true, as the process of interpolation cannot go on *ad infinitum*. We cannot therefore, whatever we do, get rid of intuition if we are to have any valid inference at all. It may, however, be said that in subjects other than ethics people at any rate agree in their intuitions. But outside mathematics or formal logic this is by no means universally true. There is frequent disagreement about matters of fact as to what has happened or will happen or concerning the causes of something, and when we have exhausted the arguments on a given point in these matters there still remains a difference between the ways in which these arguments are regarded by the disputants. In any science where you cannot prove your conclusions but only make them more or less probable there will be different estimates as to the balance of probability. As in ethics you have to balance different values against each other in order to decide what you ought to do, so here you have to balance different probable arguments, and in order to do this you must rely at some point or other on an estimate of their strength which cannot itself be further justified by mediate reasoning. Yet, when everything has been said in the way of argument, people may not all agree. Some will attribute more weight to one consideration, others to another, as they do in ethical questions about what is the right action in a given case. Our decision as to which of two probable arguments is the stronger may be influenced by other arguments in turn; but in order to deal with the situation rationally we must also estimate the weight of these other arguments, so that in the last resort it is a matter of insight into their nature which cannot be settled by other arguments *ad infinitum*. Just as in a demonstrative argument you must see intuitively how each step follows from the preceding one, so in the case of a probable argument you must rely on estimates of the degree of probability given by the argument as compared to that given by arguments on the other side, and these estimates, unless the degree of probability can be mathematically calculated, must either be themselves intuitive or be deduced from other estimates which are intuitive. I do not wish to maintain that reasoning in these matters is altogether analogous to that which occurs in dealing with ethical questions, but at any rate it is the case here that, as in ethics, we are often confronted with a situation in which we either see or do not see, and cannot logically prove, that what we seem to see is true. Yet we cannot surely therefore conclude that the scientific or historical propositions under discussion are really only propositions about the state of mind of the people who assert them, or that they are neither true nor false, or that we have no justification whatever for believing any of them!

We must therefore have intuition, and in a subject where infallibility is not attainable, intuitions will sometimes disagree. Some philosophers indeed prefer not to call them intuitions when they are wrong, but then the problem will be to distinguish real from ostensible intuitions, since people certainly sometimes think they see intuitively what is not true. Now Lord Russell says: "Since no way can be even imagined for deciding a difference as to values, the conclusion is forced upon us that the difference is one of tastes, not one as to any objective truth;"[1] but what I have said shows that we can imagine plenty of ways. I have indicated that errors as to judgments of value may arise (a) from lack of the requisite experience, (b) from intellectual confusions of some sort, (c) from failure to attend adequately to certain aspects of the situation or of the consequences, or (d) from psychological causes such as those with which the psychoanalyst deals. Therefore to remove errors we may (a) supply the lacking experience, or failing this, if possible, describe it in a way which will make its nature clear to the other party; we may (b) dispel intellectual confusions by making adequate distinctions or exposing actual fallacies such as make a person think he has seen that A is C when he has really only seen that A is B and mistakenly identified B with C; we may (c) suggest the direction of attention to the neglected points, or we may (d) use psychological methods. And we shall, if we are wise, also look out to see whether we ourselves have tripped up in any of these ways. Further, even when inference cannot completely prove or disprove, we may use it to confirm or cast doubt on ostensible intuition. The large class of errors which result mainly from an unwillingness really to seek for the truth can hardly be used as an argument against objectivity, since they are due to the moral fault of the persons who are in error and could have been removed if the latter had tried. In these cases the trouble is not that there are no means of deciding but that the means are not used.

The methods I have suggested will not always be successful, but then is there any sphere in which human efforts always do succeed? Even the methodology of physical science cannot lay down rules which will guarantee that any scientist can make discoveries or show him in detail in advance how to prove to others the truth of the discoveries when made. I am not claiming that it is possible in practice to remove all ethical differences, but how do we know that it could not be done if there were a will on each side to listen to what the other had to say and an intelligence to discern the best methods to adopt in order to facilitate a decision? A person cannot be brought into agreement even with the established truths of science if he will not listen to what the scientist says, and there is no reason to think even with ethical intuitions

---

1. See above, p. 397.

that there are not describable processes by which any cause of error can on principle be removed. I insert the words "on principle" simply because it will still often be the case that none of the disputants thinks of the right way of removing the error or that the person in error will not or cannot take it, as also occurs in disputes about questions of fact outside ethics.

Where the intuitive belief is due to non-intellectual factors of a kind which vitiate it, there seem to be two possibilities of cure. First, the person concerned may lose all tendency to hold the intuitive conviction when its alleged cause is clearly pointed out to him. The alleged cause is then in his case probably at least an essential part of the real cause. If, on the other hand, the intuitive belief remains unimpaired, and the man does not react to the causal explanation in a way which suggests that it has really touched a sore point, this is presumptive evidence that the explanation is mistaken. But, secondly, the cure from a false belief due to non-intellectual factors is more likely to arise because the man has been induced to approach the subject in a new spirit than merely because the true causation of the belief has been suggested to him. After all it is impossible to prove even to an unprejudiced person that such a causal theory as to the origin of a person's belief is really correct. How to induce a person to make such a new approach is a question not of logical argument but of practical psychology.

We must not think of intuition as something quite by itself, uninfluenced by inference; it is helped by inference but sees beyond what could be proved by inference. And, when intuitive ethical views differ, use may be made of inference to support one or other of the clashing views, especially by showing that it fits well into a coherent ethical system. This will not settle the question absolutely conclusively, but it can help toward settlement. Perhaps as the result of the inference one of the parties to the dispute may realize that he does not see by intuition what he claimed to see, but something rather different. It would thus be a great mistake to say that, when two men disagree on an ethical question, there is nothing to be done about it or that there is no scope in ethics for inference. No argument is available which could prove the subjectivity or fallaciousness of all ethics without establishing a similar conclusion about all other branches of study except mathematics and formal logic. . . .

30

THE INDEFINABILITY OF GOOD

G. E. Moore

"Good" Is a Simple Notion

. . . WHAT, THEN, IS GOOD? How is good to be defined? Now, it may be thought that this is a verbal question. A definition does indeed often mean the expressing of one word's meaning in other words. But this is not the sort of definition I am asking for. Such a definition can never be of ultimate importance in any study except lexicography. If I wanted that kind of definition I should have to consider in the first place how people generally used the word "good," but my business is not with its proper usage, as established by custom. I should, indeed, be foolish, if I tried to use it for something which it did not usually denote: if, for instance, I were to announce that, whenever I used the word "good," I must be understood to be thinking of that object which is usually denoted by the word "table." I shall, therefore, use the word in the sense in which I think it is ordinarily used; but at the same time I am not anxious to discuss whether I am right in thinking that it is so used. My business is solely with that object or idea, which I hold, rightly or wrongly, that the word is generally used to stand for. What I want to discover is the nature of the object or idea, and about this I am extremely anxious to arrive at an agreement.

But, if we understand the question in this sense, my answer to it may seem a very disappointing one. If I am asked "What is good?" my answer is that good is good, and· that is the end of the matter. Or if I am asked "How is good to be defined?" my answer is that it cannot be defined, and that is all I have to say about it. But disappointing as these answers may appear, they are of the very last importance. To readers

[This selection is part of Chapter I of Moore's *Principia Ethica*, published by the Cambridge University Press in 1903. It is reproduced here with the kind permission of Professor Moore and the publishers.]

who are familiar with philosophic terminology, I can express their importance by saying that they amount to this: That propositions about the good are all of them synthetic and never analytic; and that is plainly no trivial matter. And the same thing may be expressed more popularly, by saying that, if I am right, then nobody can foist upon us such an axiom as that "Pleasure is the only good" or that "The good is the desired" on the pretence that this is the very meaning of the word.

Let us, then, consider this position. My point is that "good" is a simple notion, just as "yellow" is a simple notion; that, just as you cannot, by any manner of means, explain to any one who does not already know it, what yellow is, so you cannot explain what good is. Definitions of the kind that I was asking for, definitions which describe the real nature of the object or notion denoted by a word, and which do not merely tell us what the word is used to mean, are only possible when the object or notion in question is something complex. You can give a definition of a horse, because a horse has many different properties and qualities, all of which you can enumerate. But when you have enumerated them all, when you have reduced a horse to his simplest terms, then you can no longer define those terms. They are simply something which you think of or perceive, and to any one who cannot think of or perceive them, you can never, by any definition, make their nature known. It may perhaps be objected to this that we are able to describe to others, objects which they have never seen or thought of. We can, for instance, make a man understand what a chimaera is, although he has never heard of one or seen one. You can tell him that it is an animal with a lioness's head and body, with a goat's head growing from the middle of its back, and with a snake in place of a tail. But here the object which you are describing is a complex object; it is entirely composed of parts, with which we are all perfectly familiar—a snake, a goat, a lioness; and we know, too, the manner in which those parts are to be put together, because we know what is meant by the middle of a lioness's back, and where her tail is wont to grow. And so it is with all objects, not previously known, which we are able to define; they are all complex; all composed of parts, which may themselves, in the first instance be capable of similar definition, but which must in the end be reducible to simplest parts, which can no longer be defined. But yellow and good, we say, are not complex: they are notions of that simple kind, out of which definitions are composed and with which the power of further defining ceases.

When we say, as Webster says, "The definition of horse is a 'hoofed quadruped of the genus Equus,'" we may, in fact, mean three different things. (1) We may mean merely: "When I say 'horse,' you are to understand that I am talking about a hoofed quadruped of the genus Equus." This might be called the arbitrary verbal definition: and I do not mean that good is indefinable in that sense. (2) We may mean, as Webster ought to mean: "When most English people say 'horse,' they mean a hoofed quadruped of the genus Equus." This may be called the verbal definition proper, and I do not say that good is indefinable in this sense either; for it is certainly possible to discover how people use a word: otherwise, we could never have known that "good" may be translated by "gut" in German and by "bon" in French. But (3) we may, when we define horse, mean something much more important. We may mean that a certain object, which we all of us know, is composed in a certain manner: that it has four legs, a head, a heart, a liver, etc., etc., all of them arranged in definite relations to one another. It is in this sense that I deny good to be definable. I say that it is not composed of any parts, which we can substitute for it in our minds when we are thinking of it. We might think just as clearly and correctly about a horse, if we thought of all its parts and their arrangement instead of thinking of the whole: we could, I say, think how a horse differed from a donkey just as well, just as truly, in this way, as now we do, only not so easily; but there is nothing whatsoever which we could so substitute for good; and that is what I mean, when I say that good is indefinable.

But I am afraid I have still not removed the chief difficulty which may prevent acceptance of the proposition that good in indefinable. I do not mean to say that *the* good, that which is good, is thus indefinable; if I did think so, I should not be writing on Ethics, for my main object is to help towards discovering that definition. It is just because I think there will be less risk of error in our search for a definition of "the good," that I am now insisting that *good* is indefinable. I must try to explain the difference between these two. I suppose it may be granted that "good" is an adjective. Well "the good," "that which is good," must therefore be the substantive to which the adjective "good" will apply: it must be the whole of that to which the adjective will apply, and the adjective must *always* truly apply to it. But if it is that to which the adjective will apply, it must be something different from that adjective itself; and the whole of that something different, whatever it is, will be our definition of *the* good. Now it may be that this something will have other adjectives, besides "good," that will apply to it. It may be full of pleasure, for example; it may be intelligent: and if these two adjectives are really part of its definition, then it will certainly be true, that pleasure and intelligence are good. And many people appear to think that, if we say "Pleasure and intelligence are good," or if we say "Only pleasure and intelligence are good," we are defining "good." Well, I cannot deny that propositions of this nature may sometimes be called definitions; I do not know well enough how the word is generally used to decide upon this point. I only wish it to be understood that that is not what I mean when I say there is no possible definition of good, and that I shall not mean this if I use the word again. I do most fully believe that some true proposition of the form "Intelligence is good and intelligence alone is good" can be found; if none could be found, our definition of *the* good would be impossible. As it is, I believe *the* good to be definiable; and yet I still say that good itself is indefinable.

"Good," then, if we mean by it that quality which we assert to belong to a thing, when we say that the thing is good, is incapable of any definition, in the most important sense of that word. The most important sense of "definition" is that in which a definition states what are the parts which invariably compose a certain whole; and in this sense "good" has no definition because it is simple and has no parts. It is one of those innumerable objects of thought which are themselves incapable of definition, because they are the ultimate terms by reference to which whatever *is* capable of definition must be defined. That there must be an indefinite number of such terms is obvious, on reflection; since we cannot define anything except by an analysis, which, when carried as far as it will go, refers us to something, which is simply different from anything else, and which by that ultimate difference explains the peculiarity of the whole which we are defining: for every whole contains some parts which are common to other wholes also. There is, therefore, no intrinsic difficulty in the contention that "good" denotes a simple and indefinable quality. There are many other instances of such qualities.

Consider yellow, for example. We may try to define it, by describing its physical equivalent; we may state what kind of light-vibrations must stimulate the normal eye, in order that we may perceive it. But a moment's reflection is sufficient to show that those light-vibrations are not themselves what we mean by yellow. *They* are not what we perceive. Indeed we should never have been able to discover their existence, unless we had first been struck by the patent difference of quality between the different colours. The most we can be entitled to say of those vibrations is that they are what corresponds in space to the yellow which we actually perceive.

The Naturalistic Fallacy

Yet a mistake of this simple kind has commonly been made about "good." It may be true that all things which are good are *also* something else, just as it is true that all things which are yellow produce a certain kind of vibration in the light. And it is a fact, that Ethics aims at discovering what are those other properties belonging to all things which are good. But far too many philosophers have thought that when they named those other properties they were actually defining good; that these properties, in fact, were simply not "other," but absolutely and entirely the same with goodness. This view I propose to call the "naturalistic fallacy" and of it I shall now endeavor to dispose . . .

Suppose a man says "I am pleased"; and suppose that is not a lie or a mistake but the truth. Well, if it is true, what does that mean? It means that his mind, a certain definite mind, distinguished by certain definite marks from others, has at this moment a certain definite feeling called pleasure. "Pleased" *means* nothing but having pleasure, and though we may be more pleased or less pleased, and even, we may admit for the present, have one or another kind of pleasure; yet in so far as it is pleasure we have, whether there be more or less of it, and whether it be of one kind or another, what we have is one definite thing, absolutely indefinable, some one thing that is the same in all the various degrees and in all the various kinds of it that there may be. We may be able to say how it is related to other things: that, for example, it is in the mind, that it causes desire, that we are conscious of it, etc., etc. We can, I say, describe its relations to other things, but define it we can *not*. And if anybody tried to define pleasure for us as being any other natural object; if anybody were to say, for instance, that pleasure *means* the sensation of red, and were to proceed to deduce from that that pleasure is a colour, we should be entitled to laugh at him and to distrust his future statements about pleasure. Well, that would be the same fallacy which I have called the naturalistic fallacy. That "pleased" does not mean "having the sensation of red," or anything else whatever, does not prevent us from understanding what it does mean. It is enough for us to know that "pleased" does mean "having the sensation of pleasure," and though pleasure is absolutely indefinable, though pleasure is pleasure and nothing else whatever, yet we feel no difficulty in saying that we are pleased. The reason is, of course, that when I say "I am pleased," I do *not* mean that "I" am the same thing as "having pleasure." And similarly no difficulty need be found in my saying that "pleasure is good" and yet not meaning that "pleasure" is the same thing as "good," that pleasure *means* good, and that good *means* pleasure. If I were to imagine that when I said "I am pleased," I meant that I was exactly the same thing as "pleased," I should not indeed call that a naturalistic fallacy, although it would be the same fallacy as I have called naturalistic with reference to Ethics. The reason for this is obvious enough. When a man confuses two natural objects with one another, defining the one by the other, if for instance, he confuses himself, who is one natural object, with "pleased" or with "pleasure" which are others, then there is no reason to call the fallacy naturalistic. But if he confuses "good" which is not in the same sense a natural object, with any natural object whatever, then there is a reason for calling that a naturalistic fallacy; its being made with regard to "good" marks it as something quite specific, and this specific mistake deserves a name because it is so common. As for the reasons why good is not to be considered a natural object, they may be reserved for discussion in another place. But, for the present, it is sufficient to notice this: Even if it were a natural object, that would not alter the nature of the fallacy nor diminish its importance one whit. All that I have said about it would remain quite equally true: only the name which I have called it would not be so appropriate as I think it is. And I do not care about the name: what I do care about is the fallacy. It does not matter what we call it, provided we recognize it when we meet with it. It is to be met with in almost every book on Ethics; and yet it is not recognized: and that is why it is necessary to multiply illustrations of it, and convenient to give it a name. It is a very simple fallacy indeed. When we say that an orange is yellow, we do not think our statement binds us to hold that "orange" means nothing else than "yellow," or that nothing can be yellow but an orange. Supposing the orange is also sweet! Does that bind us to say that "sweet" is exactly the same thing as "yellow" that "sweet" must be defined as "yellow?" And supposing it be recognized that "yellow" just means "yellow" and nothing else whatever, does that make it any more difficult to hold that oranges are yellow? Most certainly it does not· on the contrary, it would be absolutely meaningless to say that oranges were yellow, unless yellow did in the end mean just "yellow" and nothing else whatever—unless it was absolutely indefinable. We should not get any very clear notion about things, which are yellow—we should not get very far with our science, if we were bound to hold that everything which was yellow, *meant* exactly the same thing as yellow. We should find we had to hold that an orange was exactly the same thing as a stool, a piece of paper, a lemon anything you like. We could prove any number of absurdities; but should we be the nearer to the truth? Why then, should it be different with "good?" Why, if good is good and indefinable, should be held to deny that pleasure is good? Is there any difficulty in holding both to be true at once? On the contrary, there is no meaning in saying that pleasure is good, unless good is something different from pleasure. It is absolutely useless, so far as Ethics is concerned, to prove, as Mr. Spencer tries to do, that increase of pleasure coincides with increase of like, unless good *means* something different from either life or pleasure. He might just as well try to prove that an orange is yellow by showing that it always is wrapped up in paper.

In fact, if it is not the case that "good" denotes something simple and indefinable, only two alternatives are possible: either it is a complex, a given whole, about the correct analysis ot which there may be disagreement; or else it means nothing at all, and there is no such subject as Ethics. In general, however, ethical philosophers have attempted to define good without recognizing what such an attempt must mean. . . .

It is very natural to make the mistake of supposing that what is universally true is of such a nature that its negation would be self-contradictory: the importance which has been assigned to analytic propositions in the history of philosophy shows how easy such a mistake is. And thus it is very easy to conclude that what seems to be a universal ethical principle is in fact an identical proposition; that, if, for example, whatever is called "good" seems to be pleasant, the proposition "Pleasure is the good" does not assert a connection between two different notions, but involves only one, that of pleasure, which is easily recognized as a distinct entity. But whoever will attentively consider with himself what is actually before his mind when he asks the question "Is pleasure (or whatever it may be) after all good?" can easily satisfy himself that he is not merely wondering whether pleasure is pleasant. And if he will try this experiment with each suggested definition in succession, he may become expert enough to recognize that in every case he has before his mind a unique object, with regard to the connection of which with any other object, a distinct question may be asked. Every one does in fact understand the question "Is this good?" When he thinks of it, his state of mind is different from what it would be, were he asked "Is this pleasant, or desired, or approved?" It has a distinct meaning for him, even though he may not recognize in what respect it is distinct. Whenever he thinks of "intrinsic value," or "intrinsic worth," or says that a thing "ought to exist," he has before his mind the unique object—the unique property of things—which I mean by "good." Everybody is constantly aware of this notion, although he may never become aware at all that it is different from other notions of which he is also aware. But, for correct ethical reasoning, it is extremely important that he should become aware of this fact; and as soon as the nature of the problem is clearly understood, there should be little difficulty in advancing so far in analysis.

"Good," then, is indefinable; and yet, so far as I know, there is only one ethical writer, Prof. Henry Sidgwick, who has clearly recognized and stated this fact. . . .

31

CRITIQUE OF ETHICS

A. J. Ayer

The Task of Ethical Philosophy

. . . IT IS OUR BUSINESS to give an account of "judgments of value" which is both satisfactory in itself and consistent with our general empiricist principles. We shall set ourselves to show that in so far as statements of value are significant, they are ordinary "scientific" statements; and that in so far as they are not scientific, they are not in the literal sense significant, but are simply expressions of emotion which can be neither true nor false. In maintaining this view, we may confine ourselves for the present to the case of ethical statements. What is said about them will be found to apply, *mutatis mutandis,* to the case of æsthetic statements also.

The ordinary system of ethics, as elaborated in the works of ethical philosophers, is very far from being a homogeneous whole. Not only is it apt to contain pieces of metaphysics, and analyses of non-ethical concepts: its actual ethical contents are themselves of very different kinds. We may divide them, indeed, into four main classes. There are, first of all, propositions which express definitions of ethical terms, or judgments about the legitimacy or possibility of certain definitions. Secondly, there are propositions describing the phenomena of moral experience, and their causes. Thirdly, there are exhortations to moral virtue. And, lastly, there are actual ethical judgments. It is unfortunately the case that the distinction between these four classes, plain as it is, is commonly ignored by ethical philosophers; with the result that it is often very difficult to tell from their works what it is that they are seeking to discover or prove.

In fact, it is easy to see that only the first of our four classes, namely

[This selection is taken from Chapter VI of Ayer's *Language, Truth and Logic,* published in Great Britain by Victor Gollancz, Ltd., and in the United States by Dover Publications, Inc. It is here reprinted with the kind permission of Professor Ayer and the publishers.]

that which comprises the propositions relating to the definitions of ethical terms, can be said to constitute ethical philosophy. The propositions which describe the phenomena of moral experience, and their causes, must be assigned to the science of psychology, or sociology. The exhortations to moral virtue are not propositions at all, but ejaculations or commands which are designed to provoke the reader to action of a certain sort. Accordingly, they do not belong to any branch of philosophy or science. As for the expressions of ethical judgments, we have not yet determined how they should be classified. But inasmuch as they are certainly neither definitions nor comments upon definitions, nor quotations, we may say decisively that they do not belong to ethical philosophy. A strictly philosophical treatise on ethics should therefore make no ethical pronouncements. But it should, by giving an analysis of ethical terms, show what is the category to which all such pronouncements belong. And this is what we are now about to do.

A question which is often discussed by ethical philosophers is whether it is possible to find definitions which would reduce all ethical terms to one or two fundamental terms. But this question, though it undeniably belongs to ethical philosophy, is not relevant to our present enquiry. We are not now concerned to discover which term, within the sphere of ethical terms, is to be taken as fundamental; whether, for example, "good" can be defined in terms of "right" or "right" in terms of "good," or both in terms of "value." What we are interested in is the possibility of reducing the whole sphere of ethical terms to non-ethical terms. We are enquiring whether statements of ethical value can be translated into statements of empirical fact.

Subjectivism and Utilitarianism

That they can be so translated is the contention of those ethical philosophers who are commonly called subjectivists, and of those who are known as utilitarians. For the utilitarian defines the rightness of actions, and the goodness of ends, in terms of the pleasure, or happiness, or satisfaction, to which they give rise; the subjectivist, in terms of the feelings of approval which a certain person, or group of people, has towards them. Each of these types of definition makes moral judgments into a sub-class of psychological or sociological judgments; and for this reason they are very attractive to us. For, if either was correct, it would follow that ethical assertions were not generically different from the factual assertions which are ordinarily contrasted with them; and the account which we have already given of empirical hypotheses would apply to them also.

Nevertheless we shall not adopt either a subjectivist or a utilitarian analysis of ethical terms. We reject the subjectivist view that to call an action right, or a thing good, is to say that it is generally approved of, because it is not self-contradictory to assert that some actions which are generally approved of are not right, or that some things which are generally approved of are not good. And we reject the alternative subjectivist view that a man who asserts that a certain action is right, or that a certain thing is good, is saying that he himself approves of it, on the ground that a man who confessed that he sometimes approved of what was bad or wrong would not be contradicting himself. And a similar argument is fatal to utilitarianism. We cannot agree that to call an action right is to say that of all the actions possible in the circumstances it would cause, or be likely to cause, the greatest happiness, or the greatest balance of pleasure over pain, or the greatest balance of satisfied over unsatisfied desire, because we find that it is not self-contradictory to say that it is sometimes wrong to perform the action which would actually or probably cause the greatest happiness, or the greatest balance of pleasure over pain, or of satisfied over unsatisfied desire. And since it is not self-contradictory to say that some pleasant things are not good, or that some bad things are desired, it cannot be the case that the sentence "x is good" is equivalent to "x is pleasant," or to "x is desired." And to every other variant of utilitarianism with which I am acquainted the same objection can be made. And therefore we should, I think, conclude that the validity of ethical judgments is not determined by the felicific tendencies of actions, any more than by the nature of people's feelings; but that it must be regarded as "absolute" or "intrinsic," and not empirically calculable.

If we say this, we are not, of course, denying that it is possible to invent a language in which all ethical symbols are definable in non-ethical terms, or even that it is desirable to invent such a language and adopt it in place of our own; what we are denying is that the suggested reduction of ethical to non-ethical statements is consistent with the conventions of our actual language. That is, we reject utilitarianism and subjectivism, not as proposals to replace our existing ethical notions by new ones, but as analyses of our existing ethical notions. Our contention is simply that, in our language, sentences which contain normative ethical symbols are not equivalent to sentences which express psychological propositions, or indeed empirical propositions of any kind.

It is advisable here to make it plain that it is only normative ethical symbols, and not descriptive ethical symbols, that are held by us to be indefinable in factual terms. There is a danger of confusing these two types of symbols, because they are commonly constituted by signs of the same sensible form. Thus a complex sign of the form "x is wrong" may constitute a sentence which expresses a moral judgment concerning a certain type of conduct, or it may constitute a sentence which states that a certain type of conduct is repugnant to the moral sense of a particular society. In the latter case, the symbol "wrong" is a descriptive ethical symbol, and the sentence in which it occurs expresses an ordinary sociological proposition; in the former case, the symbol "wrong" is a normative ethical symbol, and the sentence in which it occurs does not, we maintain, express an empirical proposition at all. It is only with normative ethics that we are at present concerned; so that whenever ethical symbols are used in the course of this argument without qualifications, they are always to be interpreted as symbols of the normative type.

Intuitionism

In admitting that normative ethical concepts are irreducible to empirical concepts, we seem to be leaving the way clear for the "absolutist" view of ethics—that is, the view that statements of value are not controlled by observation, as ordinary empirical propositions are, but only by a mysterious "intellectual intuition." A feature of this theory, which is seldom recognized by its advocates, is that it makes statements of value unverifiable. For it is notorious that what seems intuitively certain to one person may seem doubtful, or even false, to another. So that unless it is possible to provide some criterion by which one may decide between conflicting intuitions, a mere appeal to intuition is worthless as a test of a proposition's validity. But in the case of moral judgments, no such criterion can be given. Some moralists claim to settle the matter by saying that they "know" that their own moral judgments are correct. But such an assertion is of purely psychological interest, and has not the slightest tendency to prove the validity of any moral judgment. For dissentient moralists may equally well "know" that their ethical views are correct. And, as far as subjective certainty goes, there will be nothing to choose between them. When such differences of opinion arise in connection with an ordinary empirical proposition, one may attempt to resolve them by referring to, or actually carrying out, some relevant empirical test. But with regard to ethical statements, there is, on the "absolutist" or "intuitionist" theory, no relevant empirical test. We are therefore justified in saying that on this theory ethical statements are held to be unverifiable. They are, of course, also held to be genuine synthetic propositions.

Considering the use which we have made of the principle that a synthetic proposition is significant only if it is empirically verifiable, it is clear that the acceptance of an "absolutist" theory of ethics would undermine the whole of our main argument. And as we have already rejected the "naturalistic" theories which are commonly supposed to provide the only alternative to "absolutism" in ethics, we seem to have reached a difficult position. We shall meet the difficulty by showing that the correct treatment of ethical statements is afforded by a third theory, which is wholly compatible with our radical empiricism.

Assertions of Value Are Not Scientific but "Emotive"

We begin by admitting that the fundamental ethical concepts are unanalysable, inasmuch as there is no criterion by which one can test the validity of the judgments in which they occur. So far we are in agreement with the absolutists. But, unlike the absolutists, we are able to give an explanation of this fact about ethical concepts. We say that the reason why they are unanalysable is that they are mere pseudo-concepts. The presence of an ethical symbol in a proposition adds nothing to its factual content. Thus if I say to someone, "You acted wrongly in stealing that money," I am not stating anything more than if I had simply said, "You stole that money." In adding that this action is wrong I am not making any further statement about it. I am simply evincing my moral disapproval of it. It is as if I had said, "You stole that money," in a peculiar tone of horror, or written it with the addition of some special exclamation marks. The tone, or the exclamation marks, adds nothing to the literal meaning of the sentence. It merely serves to show that the expression of it is attended by certain feelings in the speaker.

If now I generalize my previous statement and say, "Stealing money is wrong," I produce a sentence which has no factual meaning—that is, expresses no proposition which can be either true or false. It is as if I had written "Stealing money!!"—where the shape and thickness of the exclamation marks show, by a suitable convention, that a special sort of moral disapproval is the feeling which is being expressed. It is clear that there is nothing said here which can be true or false. Another man may disagree with me about the wrongness of stealing, in the sense that he may not have the same feelings about stealing as I have, and he may quarrel with me on account of my moral sentiments. But he cannot, strictly speaking, contradict me. For in saying that a certain type of action is right or wrong, I am not making any factual statement, not even a statement about my own state of mind. I am merely expressing certain moral sentiments. And the man who is ostensibly contradicting me is merely expressing his moral sentiments. So that there is plainly no sense in asking which of us is in the right. For neither of us is asserting a genuine proposition.

What we have just been saying about the symbol "wrong" applies to all normative ethical symbols. Sometimes they occur in sentences which record ordinary empirical facts besides expressing ethical feeling about those facts: sometimes they occur in sentences which simply express ethical feeling about a certain type of action, or situation, without making any statement of fact. But in every case in which one would commonly be said to be making an ethical judgment, the function of the relevant ethical word is purely "emotive." It is used to express feeling about certain objects, but not to make any assertion about them.

It is worth mentioning that ethical terms do not serve only to express feeling. They are calculated also to arouse feeling, and so to stimulate action. Indeed some of them are used in such a way as to give the sentences in which they occur the effect of commands. Thus the sentence "It is your duty to tell the truth" may be regarded both as the expression of a certain sort of ethical feeling about truthfulness and as the expression of the command "Tell the truth." The sentence "You ought to tell the truth" also involves the command "Tell the truth," but here the tone of the command is less emphatic. In the sentence "It is good to tell the truth" the command has become little more than a suggestion. And thus the "meaning" of the word "good," in its ethical usage, is differentiated from that of the word "duty" or the word "ought." In fact we may define the meaning of the various ethical words in terms both of the different feelings they are ordinarily taken to express, and also the different responses which they are calculated to provoke.

We can now see why it is impossible to find a criterion for determining the validity of ethical judgments. It is not because they have an "absolute" validity which is mysteriously independent of ordinary sense-experience, but because they have no objective validity whatsoever. If a sentence makes no statement at all, there is obviously no sense in asking whether what it says is true or false. And we have seen that sentences which simply express moral judgments do not say anything. They are pure expressions of feeling and as such do not come under the category of truth and falsehood. They are unverifiable for the same reason as a cry of pain or a word of command is unverifiable—because they do not express genuine propositions.

The Difference Between the Emotive Theory
and Orthodox Subjectivism

Thus, although our theory of ethics might fairly be said to be radically subjectivist, it differs in a very important respect from the orthodox subjectivist theory. For the orthodox subjectivist does not deny, as we do, that the sentences of a moralizer express genuine propositions. All he denies is that they express propositions of a unique non-empirical character. His own view is that they express propositions about the speaker's feelings. If this were so, ethical judgments clearly would be capable of being true or false. They would be true if the speaker had the relevant feelings, and false if he had not. And this is a matter which is, in principle, empirically verifiable. Furthermore they could be significantly contradicted. For I say, "Tolerance is a virtue," and someone answers, "You don't approve of it," he would, on the ordinary subjectivist theory, be contradicting me. On our theory, he would not be contradicting me, because, in saying that tolerance was a virtue, I should not be making any statement about my own feelings or about anything else. I should simply be evincing my feelings, which is not at all the same thing as saying that I have them.

The distinction between the expression of feeling and the assertion of feeling is complicated by the fact that the assertion that one has a certain feeling often accompanies the expression of that feeling, and is then, indeed, a factor in the expression of that feeling. Thus I may simultaneously express boredom and say that I am bored, and in that case my utterance of the words, "I am bored," is one of the circumstances which make it true to say that I am expressing or evincing boredom. But I can express boredom without actually saying that I am bored. I can express it by my tone and gestures, while making a statement about something wholly unconnected with it, or by an ejaculation, or without uttering any words at all. So that even if the assertion that one has a certain feeling always involves the expression of that feeling, the expression of a feeling assuredly does not always involve the assertion that one has it. And this is the important point to grasp in considering the distinction between our theory and the ordinary subjectivist theory. For whereas the subjectivist holds that ethical statements actually assert the existence of certain feelings, we hold that ethical statements are expressions and excitants of feeling which do not necessarily involve any assertions.

We have already remarked that the main objection to the ordinary subjectivist theory is that the validity of ethical judgments is not determined by the nature of their author's feelings. And this is an objection which our theory escapes. For it does not imply that the existence of any feelings is a necessary and sufficient condition of the validity of an ethical judgment. It implies, on the contrary, that ethical judgments have no validity.

Do We Ever Dispute About Questions of Value?

There is, however, a celebrated argument against subjectivist theories which our theory does not escape. It has been pointed out by Moore that if ethical statements were simply statements about the speaker's feelings, it would be impossible to argue about questions of value.[1] To take a typical example: if a man said that thrift was a virtue, and another replied that it was a vice, they would not, on this theory, be disputing with one another. One would be saying that he approved of thrift, and the other that *he* didn't; and there is no reason why both these statements should not be true. Now Moore held it to be obvious that we do dispute about questions of value, and accordingly concluded that the particular form of subjectivism which he was discussing was false.

It is plain that the conclusion that it is impossible to dispute about questions of value follows from our theory also. For as we hold that such sentences as "Thrift is a virtue" and "Thrift is a vice" do not express propositions at all, we clearly cannot hold that they express incompatible propositions. We must therefore admit that if Moore's argument really refutes the ordinary subjectivist theory, it also refutes ours. But, in fact, we deny that it does refute even the ordinary subjectivist theory. For we hold that one really never does dispute about questions of value.

This may seem, at first sight, to be a very paradoxical assertion. For we certainly do engage in disputes which are ordinarily regarded as disputes about questions of value. But, in all such cases, we find, if we consider the matter closely, that the dispute is not really about a question of value, but about a question of fact. When someone disagrees with us about the moral value of a certain action or type of action, we do admittedly resort to argument in order to win him over to our way of thinking. But we do not attempt to show by our arguments that he has the "wrong" ethical feeling towards a situation whose nature he has correctly apprehended. What we attempt to show is that he is mistaken about the facts of the case. We argue that he has misconceived the agent's motive: or that he has misjudged the effects of the action, or its probable effects in view of the agent's knowledge; or that he has failed to take into account the special circumstances in which the agent was placed. Or else we employ more general arguments about the effects which actions of a certain type tend to produce, or the qualities which are usually manifested in their performance. We do this in the hope that we have only to get our opponent to agree with us about the nature of the empirical facts for him to adopt the same moral attitude towards them as we do. And as the people with whom we argue have generally received the same moral education as ourselves, and live in the same social order, our expectation is usually justified. But if our opponent happens to have undergone a different process of moral "conditioning" from ourselves, so that, even when he acknowledges all the facts, he still disagrees with us about the moral value of the actions under discussion, then we abandon the attempt to

---

1. Cf. *Philosophical Studies*, "The Nature of Moral Philosophy."

convince him by argument. We say that it is impossible to argue with him because he has a distorted or undeveloped moral sense; which signifies merely that he employs a different set of values from our own. We feel that our own system of values is superior, and therefore speak in such derogatory terms of his. But we cannot bring forward any arguments to show that our system is superior. For our judgment that it is so is itself a judgment of value, and accordingly outside the scope of argument. It is because argument fails us when we come to deal with pure questions of value, as distinct from questions of fact, that we finally resort to mere abuse.

In short, we find that argument is possible on moral questions only if some system of values is presupposed. If our opponent concurs with us in expressing moral disapproval of all actions of a given type *t*, then we may get him to condemn a particular action A, by bringing forward arguments to show that A is of type *t*. For the question whether A does or does not belong to that type is a plain question of fact. Given that a man has certain moral principles, we argue that he must, in order to be consistent, react morally to certain things in a certain way. What we do not and cannot argue about is the validity of these moral principles. We merely praise or condemn them in the light of our own feelings.

If anyone doubts the accuracy of this account of moral disputes, let him try to construct even an imaginary argument on a question of value which does not reduce itself to an argument about a question of logic or about an empirical matter of fact. I am confident that he will not succeed in producing a single example. And if that is the case, he must allow that its involving the impossibility of purely ethical arguments is not, as Moore thought, a ground of objection to our theory, but rather a point in favour of it.

Having upheld our theory against the only criticism which appeared to threaten it, we may now use it to define the nature of all ethical enquiries. We find that ethical philosophy consists simply in saying that ethical concepts are pseudo-concepts and therefore unanalysable. The further task of describing the different feelings that the different ethical terms are used to express, and the different reactions that they customarily provoke, is a task for the psychologist. There cannot be such a thing as ethical science, if by ethical science one means the elaboration of a "true" system of morals. For we have seen that, as ethical judgments are mere expressions of feeling, there can be no way of determining the validity of any ethical system, and, indeed no sense in asking whether any such system is true. All that one may legitimately inquire in this connection is, What are the moral habits of a given person or group of people, and what causes them to have precisely those habits and feelings? And this inquiry falls wholly within the scope of the existing social sciences. . . .

32

THE NATURE
OF ETHICAL DISAGREEMENT

C. L. Stevenson

WHEN PEOPLE DISAGREE about the value of something—one saying that it is good or right, and another that it is bad or wrong—by what methods of argument or inquiry can their disagreement be resolved? Can it be resolved by the methods of science, or does it require methods of some other kind, or is it open to no rational solution at all?

The question must be clarified before it can be answered. And the word that is particularly in need of clarification, as we shall see, is the word "disagreement."

Let us begin by noting that "disagreement" has two broad senses: In the first sense it refers to what I shall call "disagreement in belief." This occurs when Mr. A believes p, when Mr. B believes not-p, or something incompatible with p, and when neither is content to let the belief of the other remain unchallenged. Thus doctors may disagree in belief about the causes of an illnes; and friends may disagree in belief about the exact date on which they last met.

In the second sense, the word refers to what I shall call "disagreement in attitude." This occurs when Mr. A has a favorable attitude to something, when Mr. B has an unfavorable or less favorable attitude to it, and when neither is content to let the other's attitude remain unchanged. The term "attitude" is here used in much the same sense that R. B. Perry uses "interest;" it designates any psychological disposition of being for or against something. Hence love and hate are relatively specific kinds of attitudes, as are approval and disapproval, and so on.

This second sense can be illustrated in this way: Two men are plan-

[This article is reprinted, with the kind permission of the author and the Centro di Metodologia, Milano.]

ning to have dinner together. One is particularly anxious to eat at a certain restaurant, but the other doesn't like it. Temporarily, then, the men cannot "agree" on where to dine. Their argument may be trivial, and perhaps only half serious; but in any case it represents a disagreement *in attitude*. The men have divergent preferences, and each is trying to redirect the preference of the other.

Further examples are readily found. Mrs. Smith wishes to cultivate only the four hundred; Mr. Smith is loyal to his old poker-playing friends. They accordingly disagree, in attitude, about whom to invite to their party. The progressive mayor wants modern school-buildings and large parks; the older citizens are against these "new-fangled" ways; so they disagree on civic policy. These cases differ from the one about the restaurant only in that the clash of attitudes is more serious, and may lead to more vigorous argument.

The difference between the two senses of "disagreement" is essentially this: the first involves an opposition of beliefs, both of which cannot be true, and the second involves an opposition of attitudes, both of which cannot be satisfied.

Let us apply this distinction to a case that will sharpen it. Mr. A believes that most voters will favor a proposed tax, and Mr. B disagrees with him. The disagreement concerns attitudes—those of the voters—but note that A and B are *not* disagreeing in attitude. Their disagreement is *in belief* about attitudes. It is simply a special kind of disagreement in belief, differing from disagreement in belief about head colds only with regard to subject matter. It implies not an opposition of the actual attitudes of the speakers, but only of their beliefs about certain attitudes. Disagreement *in* attitude, on the other hand, implies that the very attitudes of the speakers are opposed. A and B may have opposed beliefs about attitudes without having opposed attitudes, just as they may have opposed beliefs about head colds without having opposed head colds. Hence we must not, from the fact that an argument is concerned with attitudes, infer that it necessarily involves disagreement *in* attitude.

We may now turn more directly to disagreement about values, with particular reference to normative ethics. When people argue about what is good, do they disagree in belief, or do they disagree in attitude? A long tradition of ethical theorists strongly suggests, whether they always intend to or not, that the disagreement is one *in belief*. Naturalistic theorists, for instance, identify an ethical judgment with some sort of scientific statement, and so make normative ethics a branch of science. Now a scientific argument typically exemplifies disagreement in belief, and if an ethical argument is simply a scientific one, then it too exemplifies disagreement in belief. The usual naturalistic theories of ethics that stress attitudes—such as those of Hume, Westermarck, Perry, Richards, and so many others—stress disagreement in belief no less than the rest.

They imply, of course, that disagreement about what is good is disagreement *in belief* about attitudes; but we have seen that that is simply one sort of disagreement in belief, and by no means the same as disagreement *in* attitude. Analyses that stress disagreement *in* attitude are extremely rare.

If ethical arguments, as we encounter them in everyday life, involved disagreement in belief exclusively—whether the beliefs were about attitudes or about something else—then I should have no quarrel with the ordinary sort of naturalistic analysis. Normative judgments could be taken as scientific statements, and amenable to the usual scientific proof. But a moment's attention will readily show the disagreement in belief has not the exclusive role that theory has so repeatedly ascribed to it. It must be readily granted that ethical arguments usually involve disagreement in belief; but they *also* involve disagreement in attitude. And the conspicuous role of disagreement in attitude is what we usually take, whether we realize it or not, as the distinguishing feature of ethical arguments. For example: suppose that the representative of a union urges that the wage level in a given company ought to be higher—that it is only right that the workers receive more pay. The company representative urges in reply that the workers ought to receive no more than they get. Such argument clearly represents a disagreement in attitude. The union is *for* higher wages; the company is *against* them, and neither is content to let the other's attitude remain unchanged. *In addition* to this disagreement in attitude, of course, the argument may represent no little disagreement in belief. Perhaps the parties disagree about how much the cost of living has risen, and how much the workers are suffering under the present wage scale. Or perhaps they disagree about the company's earnings, and the extent to which the company could raise wages and still operate at a profit. Like any typical ethical argument, then, this argument involves both disagreement in attitude and disagreement in belief.

It is easy to see, however, that the disagreement in attitude plays a unifying and predominating role in the argument. This is so in two ways:

In the first place, disagreement in attitude determines what beliefs are *relevant* to the argument. Suppose that the company affirms that the wage scale of fifty years ago was far lower than it is now. The union will immediately urge that this contention, even though true, is irrelevant. And it is irrelevant simply because information about the wage level of fifty years ago, maintained under totally different circumstances, is not likely to affect the present attitudes of either party. To be relevant, any belief that is introduced into the argument must be one that is likely to lead one side or the other to have a different attitude, and so reconcile disagreement in attitude. Attitudes are often functions of beliefs. We often change our attitudes to something when we change our beliefs about it; just as a child ceases to *want* to touch a live coal when he comes to *believe* that it will burn him. Thus in the present argument, any beliefs that are at all likely to alter attitudes, such as those about the increasing cost of living or the financial state of the company, will be considered by both sides to be relevant to the argument. Agreement in belief on these matters may lead to agreement in attitude toward the wage scale. But beliefs that are likely to alter the attitudes of neither side will be declared irrelevant. They will have no bearing on the disagreement in attitude, with which both parties are primarily concerned.

In the second place, ethical argument usually terminates when disagreement in attitude terminates, even though a certain amount of disagreement in belief remains. Suppose, for instance, that the company and the union continue to disagree in belief about the increasing cost of living, but that the company, even so, ends by favoring the higher wage scale. The union will then be content to end the argument, and will cease to press its point about living costs. It may bring up that point again, in some future argument of the same sort, or in urging the righteousness of its victory to the newspaper columnists; but for the moment the fact that the company has agreed in attitude is sufficient to terminate the argument. On the other hand: suppose that both parties agreed on all beliefs that were introduced into the argument, but even so continued to disagree in attitude. In that case neither party would feel that their dispute had been successfully terminated. They might look for other beliefs that could be introduced into the argument. They might use words to play on each other's emotions. They might agree (in attitude) to submit the case to arbitration, both feeling that a decision, even if strongly adverse to one party or the other, would be preferable to a continued impasse. Or, perhaps, they might abandon hope of settling their dispute by any peaceable means.

In many other cases, of course, men discuss ethical topics without having the strong, uncompromising attitudes that the present example has illustrated. They are often as much concerned with redirecting their own attitudes, in the light of greater knowledge, as with redirecting the attitudes of others. And the attitudes involved are often altruistic, rather than selfish. Yet the above example will serve, so long as that is understood, to suggest the nature of ethical disagreement. Both disagreement in attitude and disagreement in belief are involved, but the former predominates in that (1) it determines what sort of disagreement in belief is relevantly disputed in a given ethical argument, and (2) it determines, by its continued presence or its resolution, whether or not the argument has been settled. We may see further how intimately the two sorts of disagreement are related: since attitudes are often functions of beliefs, an agreement in belief may lead people, as a matter of psychological fact, to agree in attitude.

Having discussed disagreement, we may turn to the broad question that was first mentioned, namely: By what methods or argument or inquiry may disagreement about matters of value be resolved?

It will be obvious that to whatever extent an argument involves disagreement in belief, it is open to the usual methods of the sciences. If these methods are the *only* rational methods for supporting beliefs— as I believe to be so, but cannot now take time to discuss—then scientific methods are the only rational methods for resolving the disagreement in *belief* that arguments about values may include.

But if science is granted an undisputed sway in reconciling beliefs, it does not thereby acquire, without qualification, an undisputed sway in reconciling attitudes. We have seen that arguments about values include disagreement in attitude, no less than disagreement in belief, and that in certain ways the disagreement in attitude predominates. By what methods shall the latter sort of disagreement be resolved?

The methods of science are still available for that purpose, but only in an indirect way. Initially, these methods have only to do with establishing agreement in belief. If they serve further to establish agreement in attitude, that will be due simply to the psychological fact that altered beliefs may cause altered attitudes. Hence scientific methods are conclusive in ending arguments about values only to the extent that their success in obtaining agreement in belief will in turn lead to agreement in attitude.

In other words: the extent to which scientific methods can bring about agreement on values depends on the extent to which a commonly accepted body of scientific beliefs would cause us to have a commonly accepted set of attitudes.

How much is the development of science likely to achieve, then, with regard to values? To what extent *would* common beliefs lead to common attitudes? It is, perhaps, a pardonable enthusiasm to *hope* that science will do everything—to hope that in some rosy future, when all men know the consequences of their acts, they will all have common aspirations, and live peaceably in complete moral accord. But if we speak not from our enthusiastic hopes, but from our present knowledge, the answer must be far less exciting. We usually *do not know,* at the beginning of any argument about values, whether an agreement in belief, scientifically established, will lead to an agreement in attitude or not. It is logically possible, at least, that two men should continue to disagree in attitude even though they had all their beliefs in common, and even though neither had made any logical or inductive error, or omitted any relevant evidence. Differences in temperament, or in early training, or in social status, might make the men retain different attitudes even though both were possessed of the complete scientific truth. Whether this logical possibility is an empirical likelihood I shall not presume to say; but it is unquestionably a possibility that must not be left out of account.

To say that science can always settle arguments about value, we have seen, is to make this assumption: Agreement in attitude will always be consequent upon complete agreement in belief, and science can always bring about the latter. Taken as purely heuristic, this assumption has its usefulness. It leads people to discover the discrepancies in their beliefs, and to prolong enlightening argument that *may* lead, as a matter of fact, from commonly accepted beliefs to commonly accepted attitudes. It leads people to reconcile their attitudes in a rational, permanent way, rather than by rhapsody or exhortation. But the assumption is *nothing more,* for present knowledge, than a heuristic maxim. It is wholly without proper foundation of probability. I conclude, therefore, that scientific methods cannot be guaranteed the definite role in the so-called "normative sciences" that they may have in the natural sciences. Apart from a heuristic assumption to the contrary, it is possible that the growth of scientific knowledge may leave many disputes about values permanently unsolved. Should these disputes persist, there are nonrational methods for dealing with them, of course, such as impassioned, moving oratory. But the purely intellectual methods of science, and, indeed, *all* methods of reasoning, may be insufficient to settle disputes about values, even though they may greatly help to do so.

For the same reasons, I conclude that normative ethics is not a branch of any science. It deliberately deals with a type of disagreement that science deliberately avoids. Ethics is not psychology, for instance; for although psychologists may, of course, agree or disagree in belief about attitudes, they need not, as psychologists, be concerned with whether they agree or disagree with one another *in* attitude. Insofar as normative ethics draws from the sciences, in order to change attitudes *via* changing people's beliefs, it *draws* from *all* the sciences; but a moralist's peculiar aim—that of *redirecting* attitudes—is a type of activity, rather than knowledge, and falls with no science. Science may study that activity, and may help indirectly to forward it; but it is not *identical* with that activity.

I have only a moment to explain why the ethical terms, such as "good," "wrong," "ought," and so on, are so habitually used to deal with disagreement in attitude. On account of their repeated occurrence in emotional situations they have acquired a strong emotive meaning. This emotive meaning makes them serviceable in initiating changes in a hearer's attitudes. Sheer emotive impact is not likely, under many circumstances, to change attitudes in any permanent way; but it *begins* a process that can then be supported by other means.

There is no occasion for saying that the meaning of ethical terms is *purely* emotive, like that of "alas" or "hurrah." We have seen that ethical *arguments* include many expressions of *belief;* and the rough rules of ordinary language permit us to say that some of these beliefs are expressed by an ethical judgment itself. But the beliefs so expressed are by no means always the same. Ethical terms are notable for their ambiguity, and opponents in an argument may use them in different senses. Sometimes this leads to artificial issues; but it usually does not. So long as one person says "This is good" with emotive praise, and another says "No, it is bad," with emotive condemnation, a disagreement in attitude is manifest. Whether or not the beliefs that these statements express are logically incompatible may not be discovered until later in the argument; but even if they are actually compatible, disagreement in attitude will be preserved by emotive meaning; and this disagreement, so central to ethics, may lead to an argument that is certainly not artificial in its issues, so long as it is taken for what it is.

The many theorists who have refused to identify ethical statements with scientific ones have much to be said in their favor. They have seen that ethical judgments mold or alter attitudes, rather than describe them, and they have seen that ethical judgments can be guaranteed no definitive scientific support. But one need not, on that account, provide ethics with any extramundane, sui generis *subject matter.* The distinguishing features of an ethical judgment can be preserved by a recognition of emotive meaning and disagreement in attitude, rather than by some non-natural quality—and with far greater intelligibility. If an unique subject is *postulated,* as it usually is, to preserve the important distinction between normative ethics, and science, it serves no purpose that is not served by the very simple analysis I have here suggested. Unless non-natural qualities can be defended by positive arguments, rather than as an "only resort" from the acknowledged weakness of ordinary forms of naturalism, they would seem nothing more than the invisible shadows cast by emotive meaning.

33

THE NEW SUBJECTIVISM IN ETHICS

Brand Blanshard

BY THE NEW SUBJECTIVISM in ethics I mean the view that when anyone says "this is right" or "this is good," he is only expressing his own feeling; he is not asserting anything true or false, because he is not asserting or judging at all; he is really making an exclamation that expresses a favorable feeling.

This view has recently come into much favor. With variations of detail, it is being advocated by Russell, Wittgenstein and Ayer in England, and by Carnap, Stevenson, Feigl, and others, in this country. Why is it that the theory has come into so rapid a popularity? It is because moralists of insight have been making a fresh and searching examination of moral experience and its expression? No, I think not. A consideration of the names just mentioned suggests a truer reason. All these names belong, roughly speaking, to a single school of thought in the theory of knowledge. If the new view has become popular in ethics, it is because certain persons who were at work in the theory of knowledge arrived at a new view *there,* and found, on thinking it out, that it required the new view in ethics; the view comes less from ethical analysis than from logical positivism.

As positivists, these writers held that every judgment belongs to one or other of two types. On the one hand, it may be *a priori* or necessary. But then it is always analytic, i.e., it unpacks in its predicate part or all of its subject. Can we safely say that $7+5$ make 12? Yes, because 12 is what we mean by "$7+5$." On the other hand, the judgment may be empirical, and then, if we are to verify it, we can no longer look to our meanings only; it refers to sense experience and there we must look for

[This article is reprinted with the kind permission of the author and the editor of *Philosophy and Phenomenological Research,* where it first appeared in 1949.]

its warrant. Having arrived at this division of judgments, the positivists raised the question where value judgments fall. The judgment that knowledge is good, for example, did not seem to be analytic; the value that knowledge might have did not seem to be part of our concept of knowledge. But neither was the statement empirical, for goodness was not a quality like red or squeaky that could be seen or heard. What were they to do, then, with these awkward judgments of value? To find a place for them in their theory of knowledge would require them to revise the theory radically, and yet that theory was what they regarded as their most important discovery. It appeared that the theory could be saved in one way only. If it could be shown that judgments of good and bad were not judgments at all, that they asserted nothing true or false, but merely expressed emotions like "Hurrah" or "Fiddlesticks," then these wayward judgments would cease from troubling and weary heads could be at rest. This is the course the positivists took. They explained value judgments by explaining them away.

Now I do not think their view will do. But before discussing it, I should like to record one vote of thanks to them for the clarity with which they have stated their case. It has been said of John Stuart Mill that he wrote so clearly that he could be found out. This theory has been put so clearly and precisely that it deserves criticism of the same kind, and this I will do my best to supply. The theory claims to show by analysis that when we say, "That is good," we do not mean to assert a character of the subject of which we are thinking. I shall argue that we do mean to do just that.

Let us work through an example, and the simpler and commoner the better. There is perhaps no value statement on which people would more universally agree than the statement that intense pain is bad. Let us take a set of circumstances in which I happen to be interested on the legislative side and in which I think every one of us might naturally make such a statement. We come upon a rabbit that has been caught in one of the brutal traps in common use. There are signs that it has struggled for days to escape and that in a frenzy of hunger, pain, and fear, it has all but eaten off its own leg. The attempt failed: the animal is now dead. As we think of the long and excruciating pain it must have suffered, we are very likely to say: "It was a bad thing that the little animal should suffer so." The positivist tells us that when we say this we are only expressing our present emotion. I hold, on the contrary, that we mean to assert something of the pain itself, namely, that it was bad—bad when and as it occurred.

Consider what follows from the positivist view. On that view, nothing good or bad happened in the case until I came on the scene and made my remark. For what I express in my remark is something going on in me at the time, and that of course did not exist until I did come on the scene.

The pain of the rabbit was not itself bad; nothing evil was happening when that pain was being endured; badness, in the only sense in which it is involved at all, waited for its appearance till I came and looked and felt. Now that this is at odds with our meaning may be shown as follows. Let us put to ourselves the hypothesis that we had not come on the scene and that the rabbit never was discovered. Are we prepared to say that in that case nothing bad occurred in the sense in which we said it did? Clearly not. Indeed we should say, on the contrary, that the accident of our later discovery made no difference whatever to the badness of the animal's pain, that it would have been every whit as bad whether a chance passer-by happened later to discover the body and feel repugnance or not. If so, then it is clear that in saying the suffering was bad we are not expressing our feelings only. We are saying that the pain was bad when and as it occurred and before anyone took an attitude toward it.

The first argument is thus an ideal experiment in which we use the method of difference. It removes our present expression and shows that the badness we meant would not be affected by this, whereas on positivist grounds it should be. The second argument applies the method in the reverse way. It ideally removes the past event, and shows that this would render false what we mean to say, whereas on positivist grounds it should not. Let us suppose that the animal did not in fact fall into the trap and did not suffer at all, but that we mistakenly believe it did, and say as before that its suffering was an evil thing. On the positivist theory, everything I sought to express by calling it evil in the first case is still present in the second. In the only sense in which badness is involved at all, whatever was bad in the first case is still present in its entirety, since all that is expressed in either case is a state of feeling, and that feeling is still there. And our question is, is such an implication consistent with what we meant? Clearly it is not. If anyone asked us, after we made the remark that the suffering was a bad thing, whether we should think it was relevant to what we said to learn that the incident had never occurred and no pain had been suffered at all, we should say that it made all the difference in the world, that what we were asserting to be bad was precisely the suffering we thought had occurred back there, that if this had not occurred, there was nothing left to be bad, and that our assertion was in that case mistaken. The suggestion that in saying something evil had occurred we were after all making no mistake, because we had never meant anyhow to say anything about the past suffering, seems to me merely frivolous. If we did not mean to say this, why should we be so relieved on finding that the suffering had not occurred? On the theory before us, such relief would be groundless, for in that suffering itself there was nothing bad at all, and hence in its non-occurrence there would be nothing to be relieved about. The positivist theory would here distort our meaning beyond recognition.

So far as I can see, there is only one way out for the positivist. He holds that goodness and badness lie in feelings of approval or disapproval. And there is a way in which he might hold that badness did in this case precede our own feeling of disapproval without belonging to the pain itself. The pain in itself was neutral; but unfortunately the rabbit, on no grounds at all, took up toward this neutral object an attitude of disapproval, and that made it for the first time, and in the only intelligible sense, bad. This way of escape is theoretically possible, but since it has grave difficulties of its own and has not, so far as I know, been urged by positivists, it is perhaps best not to spend time over it.

I come now to a third argument, which again is very simple. When we come upon the rabbit and make our remark about its suffering being a bad thing, we presumably make it with some feeling; the positivists are plainly right in saying that such remarks do usually express feeling. But suppose that a week later we revert to the incident in thought and make our statement again. And suppose that the circumstances have now so changed that the feeling with which we made the remark in the first place has faded. The pathetic evidence is no longer before us; and we are now so fatigued in body and mind that feeling is, as we say, quite dead. In these circumstances, since what was expressed by the remark when first made is, on the theory before us, simply absent, the remark now expresses nothing. It is as empty as the word "Hurrah" would be when there was no enthusiasm behind it. And this seems to me untrue. When we repeat the remark that such suffering was a bad thing, the feeling with which we made it last week may be at or near the vanishing point, but if we were asked whether we meant to say what we did before, we should certainly answer Yes. We should say that we made our point with feeling the first time and little or no feeling the second time, but that it was the same point we were making. And if we can see that what we meant to say remains the same, while the feeling varies from intensity to near zero, it is not the feeling that we primarily meant to express.

I come now to a fourth consideration. We all believe that toward acts or effects of a certain kind one attitude is fitting and another not; but on the theory before us such a belief would not make sense. Broad and Ross have lately contended that this fitness is one of the main facts of ethics, and I suspect they are right. But that is not exactly my point. My point is this: whether there is such fitness or not, we all assume that there is, and if we do, we express in moral judgments more than the subjectivists say we do. Let me illustrate.

In his novel *The House of the Dead,* Dostoevsky tells of his experiences in a Siberian prison camp. Whatever the unhappy inmates of such camps are like today, Dostoevsky's companions were about as grim a lot as can be imagined. "I have heard stories," he writes, "of the most terrible, the most unnatural actions, of the most monstrous murders, told with the most spontaneous, childishly merry laughter." Most of us would say that in this delight at the killing of others or the causing of suffering there is something very unfitting. If we were asked why we thought so, we should say that these things involve great evil and are wrong, and that to take delight in what is evil or wrong is plainly unfitting. Now on the subjectivist view, this answer is ruled out. For before someone takes up an attitude toward death, suffering, or their infliction, they have no moral quality at all. There is therefore nothing about them to which an attitude of approval or condemnation could be fitting. They are in themselves neutral, and, so far as they get a moral quality, they get it only through being invested with it by the attitude of the onlooker. But if that is true, why is any attitude more fitting than any other? Would applause, for example, be fitting if, apart from the applause, there were nothing good to applaud? Would condemnation be fitting if, independently of the con-demnation, there were nothing bad to condemn? In such a case, any attitude would be as fitting or unfitting as any other, which means that the notion of fitness has lost all point.

Indeed we are forced to go much farther. If goodness and badness lie in attitudes only and hence are brought into being by them, those men who greeted death and misery with childishly merry laughter are taking the only sensible line. If there is nothing evil in these things, if they get their moral complexion only from our feeling about them, why shouldn't they be greeted with a cheer? To greet them with repulsion would turn what before was neutral into something bad; it would needlessly bring badness into the world; and even on subjectivist assumptions that does not seem very bright. On the other hand, to greet them with delight would convert what before was neutral into something good; it would bring goodness into the world. If I have murdered a man and wish to remove the stain, the way is clear. It is to cry, "Hurrah for murder."

What is the subjectivist to reply? I can only guess. He may point out that the inflicting of death is *not* really neutral before the onlooker takes his attitude, for the man who inflicted the death no doubt himself took on attitude, and thus the act had a moral quality derived from this. But that makes the case more incredible still, for the man who did the act pre-sumably approved it, and if so it was good in the only sense in which any-thing is good, and then our conviction that the laughter is unfit is more unaccountable still. It may be replied that the victim, too, had his at-titude and that since this was unfavorable, the act was not unqualifiedly good. But the answer is plain. Let the killer be expert at his job; let him despatch his victim instantly before he has time to take an attitude, and then gloat about his perfect crime without ever telling anyone. Then, so far as I can see, his act will be good without any qualification. It would become bad only if someone found out about it and disliked it. And that would be a curiously irrational procedure, since the man's approving of his own killing is in itself as neutral as the killing that it approves. Why then should anyone dislike it?

It may be replied that we can defend our dislike on this ground that, if the approval of killing were to go unchecked and spread, most men would have to live in insecurity and fear, and these things are undesirable. But surely this reply is not open; these things are not, on the theory, undesirable, for nothing is; in themselves they are neutral. Why then should I disapprove men's living in this state? The answer may come that if other men live in insecurity and fear, I shall in time be infected myself. But even in my own insecurity and fear there is, on the theory before us, nothing bad whatever, and therefore, if I disapprove them, it is without a shadow of ground and with no more fitness in my attitude than if I cordially cheered them. The theory thus conflicts with our judgments of fitness all along the line.

I come now to a fifth and final difficulty with the theory. It makes mistakes about values impossible. There is a whole nest of inter-connected criticisms here, some of which have been made so often that I shall not develop them again, such as that I can never agree or disagree in opinion with anyone else about an ethical matter, and that in these matters I can never be inconsistent with others or with myself. I am not at all content with the sort of analysis which says that the only contradictions in such cases have regard to facts and that contradictions about value are only differences of feeling. I think that if anyone tells me that having a bicuspid out without an anaesthetic is not a bad experience and I say it is a very nasty experience indeed, I am differing with him in opinion, and differing about the degrees of badness of the experience. But without pressing this further, let me apply the argument in what is perhaps a fresh direction.

There is an old and merciful distinction that moralists have made for many centuries about conduct—the distinction between what is subjectively and what is objectively right. They have said that in any given situation there is some act which, in view of all the circumstances, would be the best act to do; and this is what would be objectively right. The notion of an objectively right act is the ground of our notion of duty: our duty is always to find and do this act if we can. But of course we often don't find it. We often hit upon and do acts that we think are the right ones, but we are mistaken; and then our act is only subjectively right. Between these two acts the disparity may be continual; Professor Prichard suggested that probably few of us in the course of our lives ever succeed in doing *the* right act.

Now so far as I can see, the new subjectivism would abolish this difference at a stroke. Let us take a case. A boy abuses his small brother. We should commonly say, "That is wrong, but perhaps he doesn't know any better. By reason of bad teaching and a feeble imagination, he may see nothing wrong in what he is doing, and may even be proud of it. If so, his act may be subjectively right, though it is miles away from what is objectively right." What concerns me about the new subjectivism is that it prohibits this distinction. If the boy feels this way about his act, then it is right in the only sense in which anything is right. The notion of an objective right lying beyond what he has discovered, and which he ought to seek and do is meaningless. There might, to be sure, be an act that would more generally arouse favorable feelings in others, but that would not make it right for him unless he thought of it and approved it, which he doesn't. Even if he did think of it, it would not be obligatory for him to feel about it in any particular way, since there is nothing in any act, as we have seen, which would make any feeling more suitable than any other.

Now if there is no such thing as an objectively right act, what becomes of the idea of duty? I have suggested that the idea of duty rests on the idea of such an act, since it is always our duty to find that act and do it if we can. But if whatever we feel approval for at the time is right, what is the point of doubting and searching further? Like the little girl in Boston who was asked if she would like to travel, we can answer, "Why should I travel when I'm already there?" If I am reconciled in feeling to my present act, no act I could discover by reflection could be better, and therefore why reflect or seek at all? Such a view seems to me to break the mainspring of duty, to destroy the motive for self-improvement, and to remove the ground for self-criticism. It may be replied that by further reflection I can find an act that would satisfy my feelings more widely than the present one, and that this is the act I should seek. But this reply means either that such general satisfaction is objectively better, which would contradict the theory, or else that, if at the time I don't feel it better, it isn't better, in which case I have no motive for seeking it. When certain self-righteous persons took an inflexible line with Oliver Cromwell, his very Cromwellian reply was, "Bethink ye, gentlemen, by the bowels of Christ, that ye may be mistaken." It was good advice. I hope nobody will take from me the privilege of finding myself mistaken. I should be sorry to think that the self of thirty years ago was as far along the path as the self of today, merely because he was a smug young jackanapes, or even that the paragon of today has as little room for improvement as would be allowed by his myopic complacency.

One final remark. The great problems of the day are international problems. Has the new subjectivism any bearing upon these problems? I think it has, and a somewhat sinister bearing. I would not suggest, of course, that those who hold the theory are one whit less public-spirited than others; surely there are few who could call themselves citizens of the world with more right (if "rights" have meaning any longer) than Mr. Russell. But Mr. Russell has confessed himself discontented with his ethical theory, and in view of his breadth of concern, one cannot wonder.

For its general acceptance would, so far as one can see, be an international disaster. The assumption behind the old League and the new United Nations was that there is such a thing as right and wrong in the conduct of a nation, a right and wrong that do not depend on how it happens to feel at the time. It is implied, for example, that when Japan invaded Manchuria in 1931 she might be wrong, and that by discussion and argument she might be shown to be wrong. It was implied that when the Nazis invaded Poland they might be wrong, even though German public sentiment overwhelmingly approved it. On the theory before us, it would be meaningless to call these nations mistaken; if they felt approval for what they did, then it was right with as complete a justification as could be supplied for the disapproval felt by the rest of the world. In the present dispute between Russia and our own country over southeast Europe, it is nonsense to speak of the right or rational course for either of us to take; if with all the facts before the two parties, each feels approval for its own course, both attitudes are equally justified or unjustified; neither is mistaken; there is no common reason to which they can take an appeal; there are no principles by which an international court could pronounce on the matter; nor would there be any obligation to obey the pronouncement if it were made. This cuts the ground from under any attempt to establish one's case as right or anyone else's case as wrong. So if our friends the subjectivists still hold their theory after I have applied my little ruler to their knuckles, which of course they will, I have but one request to make of them: Do keep it from Mr. Molotov and Mr. Vishinsky.

SELECTED BIBLIOGRAPHY

(ITEMS PROVIDED WITH ASTERISK ARE MORE ADVANCED)

Several English philosophers of the 17th and 18th centuries may be consulted for statements of the Rationalist theory concerning the nature of moral judgments. The most important of these are Samuel Clarke, John Balguy, Ralph Cudworth, and Richard Price. Selections from all these writers are contained in Vol. II of L. A. Selby-Bigge (ed.), *British Moralists* (Oxford: Clarendon Press, 1897). A new edition of Price's *Review of Morals,* with a valuable preface by D. D. Raphael, was brought out by the Clarendon Press in 1948. Contemporary defenses of Rationalism are given in Ross, *The Right and the Good* (London: Oxford University Press, 1931), the same author's *Foundations of Ethics* (Oxford: Clarendon Press, 1939), and in D. D. Raphael, *The Moral Sense* (London: Oxford University Press, 1947). Ross and Raphael are criticized in P. F. Strawson's "Ethical Intuitionism," which is reprinted in W. Sellars and J. Hospers (eds.), *Readings in Ethical Theory* (New York: Appleton-Century-Crofts, 1952).

The classical formulation of the "moral sense" theory is Hutcheson's *Inquiry Concerning the Original of Our Ideas of Virtue or Moral Good.* Extracts from this and other of Hutcheson's works are given in Vol. I of L. A. Selby-Bigge (ed.), *British Moralists, op. cit.* There are helpful commentaries in the above-mentioned book by Raphael and a searching examination in C. D. Broad's "Some Reflections On Moral-Sense Theories in Ethics" which is reprinted in Sellars and Hospers, *op. cit.* G. E. Moore's intuitionism is stated in *Principia Ethica* (Cambridge: Cambridge University Press, 1903), in his smaller book, *Ethics* (London: Oxford University Press, 1912), and in the last two essays of his book, *Philosophical Studies* (London: Kegan Paul, 1922). There are several critical articles in P. A. Schilpp (ed.), *The Philosophy of G. E. Moore* (Evanston and Chicago: Northwestern University, 1942), which also contains Moore's reply to his critics. W. K. Frankena's "The Naturalistic Fallacy" and G. C. Field's "The Place of Definition In Ethics" are two well-known answers to Moore's open-question argument. Both are reprinted in Sellars and Hospers, *op. cit.* The history of this argument is traced in A. N. Prior, *Logic and The Basis of Ethics* (Oxford: Clarendon Press, 1948).

Theories which, by our classification, would be considered forms of objective naturalism, are defended by Jeremy Bentham in *The Principles of Morals and Legislation,* John Stuart Mill in his *Utilitarianism,* Herbert Spencer in *The Data of Ethics,* John Dewey in *Human Nature and Conduct* (New York: Henry Holt and Co., 1922) and in *The Theory of Valuation* (Chicago: Chicago University Press, 1939), R. B. Perry in his *General Theory of Value* (Cambridge: Harvard University Press, 1926), and W. T. Stace in *The Concept of Morals* (New York: Macmillan, 1937).

Subjectivism is defended by Hume in Book III of *A Treatise Of Human*

Nature and also in *An Inquiry Concerning the Principles of Morals.* His position, however, is not always consistent and in places he writes like a utilitarian. More modern defenses of subjectivism are found in E. Westermarck, *The Origin and Development of Moral Ideas* (London: Macmillan, 1912), in the same author's *Ethical Relativity* (New York: Harcourt, Brace and Co., 1932), in Bertrand Russell's essay, "What I Believe" which forms part of *Why I am not a Christian and Other Essays* (London: Allen and Unwin, New York: Simon and Schuster, 1957) and in his *Human Society in Ethics and Politics* (London: Allen and Unwin, New York: Simon and Schuster, 1955). There are articles by J. Buchler and S. Hook criticizing Russell's subjectivism in P. A. Schilpp (ed.), *The Philosophy of Bertrand Russell* (Evanston and Chicago: Northwestern University, 1944). At the end of this volume Russell replies to his critics but concedes that he does not feel altogether satisfied with his own theory. Ewing's attack on subjectivism which forms part of Selection 29 of the present book was answered by H. W. B. Acton in an article entitled "Moral Subjectivism," in *Analysis,* 1948, which is followed by Ewing's reply in the same volume. The "ideal observer" theory received its first formulation in Adam Smith, *The Theory of Moral Sentiments.* Parts of this work are reprinted in Vol. I of Selby-Bigge (ed.), *British Moralists, op. cit.* In recent years the theory was discussed by R. Firth in, "Ethical Absolutism and The Ideal Observer,"* *Philosophy and Phenomenological Research,* 1952, and R. Brandt in, "The Definition of an 'Ideal Observer' in Ethics,"* *ibid.,* 1955. Brandt's own version of subjectivism is given in "The Status of Empirical Assertion Theories In Ethics," *Mind,* 1952. The "error-theory" is stated by John Mackie in "The Refutation of Morals," *Australasian Journal of Psychology and Philosophy,* 1946.

The earliest formulation of the emotive theory is found in C. K. Ogden and I. A. Richards, *The Meaning of Meaning* (London: Kegan Paul, 1923), but it is not developed there in any detail. Other early statements are found in Rudolf Carnap, *Philosophy and Logical Syntax* (London: Kegan Paul, 1935) and in a short article by W. F. H. Barnes entitled "A Suggestion About Value," *Analysis,* 1933. Probably the most celebrated statement of the theory is C. L. Stevenson's "The Emotive Meaning of Ethical Terms," reprinted in Sellars and Hospers, *op. cit.* Stevenson subsequently developed the theory in great detail in *Ethics and Language** (New Haven: Yale University Press, 1943). Ayer replied to some of his critics in his introduction to the second edition of *Language, Truth and Logic.* He restated his position in an article entitled "On the Analysis of Moral Judgments," which is included in his *Philosophical Essays* (London: Macmillan, 1954). Other valuable articles in support of the emotive theory are A. Kaplan's "Are Moral Judgments Assertions?", *Philosophical Review,* 1942 and A. I. Melden's "On the Method of Ethics," *Journal of Philosophy,* 1948. The emotive theory is criticized in A. Stroll, *The Emotive Theory of Ethics* (Berkeley and Los Angeles: University of California Press, 1954), in Chapter II of W. D. Ross, *The Foundations of Ethics, op. cit.,* in C. E. M. Joad, *A Critique of Logical Positivism* (Chicago: University of Chicago Press, 1950) and from a Marxist point of view in B. Dunham, *Man Against Myth* (Boston: Brown, Little and Co., 1947). Among articles in which the emotive theory is attacked, mention may be made of R. Brandt's "The Emotive Theory of Ethics," *Philosophical Review,* 1950, H. J. Paton's "The Emotive Theory of Ethics," *Proceedings of the Aristotelian Society,* Supplem. Vol. XXII, 1948, A. Moore's "The Emotive Theory in Moral Controversy," *Mind,* 1951, V. Tomas' "Ethical Disagreements and the Emotive Theory of Values," *Mind,* 1951, and C. A. Campbell's, "Ethics

Without Proposition,"* *Mind,* 1950, which is an answer to W. F. H. Barnes',
"Ethics Without Propositions,"* *Proc. of the Arist. Soc.,* Supplem. Vol. XXII,
1948. The *Philosophical Review,* 1950, also contains Stevenson's answer to
Brandt and Brandt's rejoinder to Stevenson's answer. Several recent books,
while not exactly following the emotive theory, express viewpoints which are
on certain crucial issues closely akin to it. Among works of this kind are S. E.
Toulmin, *The Place of Reason in Ethics** (Cambridge: Cambridge University
Press, 1950), R. M. Hare, *The Language Of Morals** (Oxford: Clarendon
Press, 1952), P. H. Nowell-Smith, *Ethics** (London: Penguin Books, 1954)
and Paul Edwards, *The Logic of Moral Discourse* (Glencoe, Illinois: Free
Press, 1955). Important recent articles which are not easily classified are
Stuart Hampshire's "The Fallacies of Moral Philosophy,"* *Mind,* 1949, J. N.
Findlay's "Morality by Convention,"* *Mind,* 1944 and the same writer's "The
Justification of Attitudes," *ibid.,* 1954, K. Baier's "Decisions and Descriptions,"
Mind, 1951, R. M. Hare's contribution to the symposium on "The Freedom of
the Will,"* *Proc. of the Arist. Soc.,* Suppl. Vol. XXV, 1951, W. D. Falk's
"Goading and Guiding," *Mind,* 1953, J. O. Urmson's "On Grading,"* which
is reprinted in A. Flew (ed.), *Logic and Language,* Second Series (Oxford:
Basil Blackwell, 1953), Morton G. White's "Value and Obligation in Dewey
and Lewis," *Philosophical Review,* 1949, Gail Kennedy's "The Hidden Link
in Dewey's Theory of Evaluation," *Journal of Philosophy,* 1955, and E. M.
Adams' "The Nature of Ought," *Philosophical Studies,* 1956. Important recent
books which are not easy to classify include E. W. Hall, *What is Value?**
(New York: Humanities Press, 1952), A. Edel, *Ethical Judgment** (Glencoe,
Illinois: Free Press, 1955), M. Mandelbaum, *The Phenomenology of Moral
Experience** (Glencoe, Illinois: Free Press, 1955) and D. D. Raphael,
Moral Judgment (London: Allen and Unwin, 1955).

There are helpful surveys of the different theories about the nature of
moral judgments and disagreement in T. E. Hill, *Contemporary Ethical
Theories* (New York: Macmillan, 1952), in Chapter 7 of John Hospers, *An
Introduction to Philosophical Analysis* (New York: Prentice-Hall, 1953),
in Chapter 2 of A. Pap, *Elements of Analytic Philosophy* (New York: Macmillan, 1949), and in W. K. Frankena's "Moral Philosophy at Mid-Century,"
Philosophical Review, 1951.

VII

The Existence of God

INTRODUCTION

THE WORD "GOD" has been used in a great many senses. For our purposes it will be convenient to consider somebody a believer in God if he asserts the existence of a supreme personal being who is the creator of the universe or at least the designer of some of its prominent features. He may claim more, but he must not claim less. Thus pantheists, who deny that God and the universe are distinct and who therefore cannot believe in creation, will not be counted as believers in God. Certain idealistic philosophers who believed in an "Absolute Reality," but who refused to characterize that Reality as personal, would also be excluded from the class of believers by this criterion. However, all of the writers whose work is represented in this section, whether they are believers or unbelievers, include in their concept of God the characteristics listed above. Christian believers, of course, go a great deal further. They would also claim that God is eternal, all-powerful, all-knowing, perfectly good and that He possesses many other admirable characteristics. Philosophers like J. S. Mill and W. P. Montague, who believe in a finite god, would not go this far, but they too can be classified as believers by our definition.

Believers in the existence of God differ among themselves not only in how much they claim about the divine attributes. There is also disagreement about the relation between God and the universe. Some philosophers merely claim that God created the universe and reject any belief in subsequent divine interferences in the course of nature, such as miracles, answers to prayer, or special revelations of the kind related in the Bible. This view is known as "deism." Voltaire, the most famous deist, argued that the belief in miracles was really blasphemous. For it implies that God bungled, to some extent at least, his original job of creation and had to step in subsequently to make repairs.

Opposed to the deists are the more orthodox believers who claim that God originally created the universe and who go on to assert that he does on occasions work miracles, answer prayers, and reveal himself to specific human beings. God is supposed to take an active interest in the good and evil deeds of human being and divine interventions usually have a moral purpose of some kind. The word "theism" is sometimes used to designate this more orthodox position, but there is no very consistent linguistic usage on this point.

Deism was the first powerful rebellion against traditional theology in Western Europe and the United States; and many of the outstanding philosophers of the 17th and 18th centuries inclined to a view of this kind. During the last hundred years or so, more radical rejections of theology have become fairly common. Probably the most widespread form of unbelief at the present time is "agnosticism." This theory maintains that it is impossible for human beings to know whether there is a God or not. Agnosticism is to be distinguished from atheism which denies the existence of God. It should be noted that, in denying the existence of God, an atheist does not necessarily claim to know the answers to such questions as "What is the origin of life?" or "Where does the universe come from?" He merely rules out as false theological answers to these questions. There has been a great deal of confusion on this subject. Clarence Darrow, for example, based his agnosticism partly on the premise that "whether the universe had an origin—and if it had—what the origin is will never be known by men." An atheist, however, could quite consistently admit that this is an insoluble problem. If somebody asked me "who killed Carlo Tresca?" I could answer "I don't know and it will probably never be discovered" and I could then quite consistently add "But I know some people who certainly did not kill him—e.g., Julius Caesar or General Eisenhower or Bertrand Russell."

During the last thirty years a number of philosophers have gone even further in rejecting the claims of theology. They would say that atheists made an unjustified concession to believers in calling their theory *false*. The theological sentences found in the writings of such philosophers as Aquinas or Leibniz or Descartes, as distinct from the anthropomorphic theology of children and many ordinary believers, are really *meaningless*. This is the position of the "logical positivists" who base their opposition to theology on the so-called "Verifiability Principle." A sentence is meaningful or makes sense, according to this principle, only if we can at least describe what it would be like to test it in experience. It is then maintained that in the case of the theological sentences of Aquinas and many other philosophers such tests cannot even be described and that hence all the sentences in question are senseless. If this were true there would be no need to investigate the arguments which these philosophers offered in support of the existence of God. If the conclusion is meaningless, then the arguments cannot possibly be sound.

At first sight, the view of the logical positivists may seem to be identical with agnosticism. For if theism is a meaningless theory, then so is atheism. If I say, to make up a deliberate piece of nonsense, "There are six pirods under the desk," then a person who counters with a denial, i.e., with the sentence "There are no pirods under the desk," is just as much guilty of nonsense. In thus ruling out theism as well as atheism, the logical positivists do indeed to this extent agree with the agnostics. However, they go further and also declare agnosticism to be a meaningless theory. For if the sentence "There is a God" is nonsensical, then it is meaningless to doubt as well as to deny it. It is just as meaningless to say that we shall never know whether or not there are any pirods under the desk as it is to assert or to deny their existence.

The views of the logical positivists are considered in detail not in the present but in the last section of this book. It may be worth mentioning here that quite a number of philosophers, who do not go along with the logical positivists in condemning theological conclusions as meaningless, do agree that some of the *questions* raised in discussions of the existence of God are meaningless. Bertrand Russell, for instance, is not a logical positivist; but he emphatically condemns as senseless such questions as "Why does the universe exist?" or "Why is there something rather than nothing?" He would say that while it makes sense to ask for the "why" of this or that specific thing, the word loses all meaning when applied to the universe as a whole. It makes sense to demand an explanation of this or that specific phenomenon, but it does not make sense to demand an explanation of the universe. "Every man who exists has a mother," he writes in one place. It does not follow from this that "the human race has a mother—This is a different logical sphere." The question "What is the explanation of the universe?" is in Russell's view as senseless as the question "Who is the mother of the human race?"

Many famous philosophers have advanced arguments which, they hoped, would serve as a rational justification of the belief in God and such arguments form an important chapter in the history of Western philosophy. Since the days of Hume and Kant the majority of these arguments have not been widely accepted among philosophers. They are, however, far from dead and some of them have, to this day, the support of writers whose ability is unquestioned. In any event, even if one concludes that all these arguments are fallacious, a study of them is worth while since in most cases they raise logical issues of much wider application.

The more common arguments may be conveniently divided into six varieties: (1) the ontological argument; (2) the cosmological argument; (3) the teleological argument or the argument from design; (4) the moral argument; (5) the argument from the common consent of mankind and the related argument from a religious instinct; and (6) the appeal to what is called "religious experience." In the course of these introductory comments nothing will be said about (3), (4) and (5). It is difficult to say anything useful about (4) or (5) in a short space. In the case of the design argument, which is probably the most popular of all, our selections cover it so comprehensively both on the affirmative (Aquinas, p. 474, Copleston, p. 482, and Paley, pp. 483 ff.) and on the negative side (Smart, pp. 506 ff., Darrow, pp. 510 ff.) that any comments on it here are quite superfluous. However, our selections dealing with the ontological and the cosmological arguments and with the appeal to religious experience are not as extensive as one might wish and a few further remarks here may be of some help. This is particularly true of the cosmological proof which is historically the most important next to the design argument. Much of this introduction will therefore be taken up with the cosmological argument and especially the difficulties confronting its advocates.

The ontological argument was first put forward by the medieval theologian St. Anselm of Canterbury (1035-1109) and was subsequently defended by a number of distinguished philosophers including Descartes (Selection 34, pp. 469 ff.). It was rejected by Aquinas, by many of Descartes' contemporaries, notably Gassendi, and was exhaustively criticized by Kant. The argument begins by defining "God" as an all-perfect Being, that is, as a Being containing all conceivable perfections. Now, if, in addition to possessing omnipotence, omniscience, and various other admirable qualities, this being did not also possess existence it would be less perfect than if it possessed this additional attribute. If it lacked existence it would not be all-perfect. But by definition God is all-perfect. Hence, among other things, He must exist. The existence of God can thus be established, according to this argument, simply by explicating our concept of God. The definition, or using scholastic language, the "essence" of God guarantees His existence just as the definition or essence of a "triangle" guarantees that all triangles must have three sides. To say that God exists is *necessarily* true just as it is necessarily true that a triangle must have three sides. To say that there is no God is not false but *self-contradictory* the way it would be self-contradictory to say "here is a triangle with four sides."

Kant objected to the ontological argument mainly on the ground that it treats existence as if it were a quality or characteristic or property. To suppose this, however, is to be misled by grammatical similarities. The word "exists" is not indeed meaningless, but it has quite a different function from "property-words" like "green" or "pleased" or "all-powerful" or "having three sides." The following illustration will perhaps serve to bring out the difference. Suppose I am an explorer and claim to have discovered a new species of animal which I call "gangle." I have been asked to explain what I mean by calling an animal a "gangle" and I have given this answer: "By a gangle I mean a mammal with eleven noses, seven blue eyes, bristly hair, sharp teeth and wheels in the place of feet." Let us now constrast two supplementary remarks I might make. The first time I add "furthermore a gangle has three long tails." The second time I add "furthermore, let me insist that gangles exist." It is evident that these are two radically different additions. In the first case I was adding to the definition of "gangle"; I was enlarging the concept; I was mentioning a further property which a thing must possess before I would call it a "gangle." The second time I was doing something quite different. I was not enlarging the concept of gangle. I was saying that there is something to which the concept applies, that the combination of characteristics or qualities *previously* mentioned belong to something.

Only characteristics or qualities can enlarge a concept. Since existence is not a characteristic or quality it follows that it cannot be part of any concept. It cannot be part of the concept of God any more than of the concept of cat or gangle. It may well be true that God exists, but this conclusion cannot be derived from the concept of the all-perfect Being any more than the existence of centaurs or hippogriffs or leprechauns could be deduced from an analysis of the corresponding concepts. It has also been pointed out that if the ontological argument were sound we could, with equal justice, prove the existence of a perfect scientist, a perfect singer, and any other number of perfect beings. This alone is sufficient to indicate that there is something drastically wrong with it.

We next turn to the cosmological proof. This has taken a number of forms, the most important of which are known as the "causal argument" and "the argument from contingency," respectively. In some writers, like Samuel Clarke, they are combined, but it is best to keep them apart as far as possible. The causal argument is the second of the "five ways" of Aquinas (Selection 35, p. 473, see also Copleston, Selection 36, pp. 476 ff.) and roughly proceeds as follows: we find that the things around us come into being as the result of the activity of other things. These causes are themselves the result of the activity of yet other things. But such a causal series cannot "go back to infinity." Hence there must be a first member, a member which is not itself caused by any preceding member—an uncaused or "first" cause.

It has frequently been pointed out that even if this argument were sound it would not establish the existence of *God*. It would not show that the first cause is all-powerful or all-good or that it is in any sense personal. Somebody believing in the eternity of atoms or of matter generally could quite consistently accept the conclusion. Defenders of the causal argument usually concede this and insist that the argument is not in itself meant to prove the existence of God. Supplementary arguments are required to show that the first cause must have the attributes assigned to the deity. They claim, however, that the argument, if valid, would at least be an important step towards a complete proof of the existence of God.

Does the argument succeed in proving so much as a first cause? This will depend mainly on the soundness of the premise that an infinite series of causes is impossible. Aquinas supports this premise by maintaining that the opposite belief involves a plain absurdity. To suppose that there is an infinite series of causes logically implies that nothing exists now; but we know that plenty of things do exist now; and hence any theory which implies that nothing exists now must be wrong. Let us take some causal series and refer to its members by the letters of the alphabet:

$$A \longrightarrow B \qquad \ldots \ldots \ldots W \longrightarrow X \longrightarrow Y \longrightarrow Z$$

Z stands here for something presently existing, e.g., Margaret Truman. Y represents the cause or part of the cause of Z, say Harry Truman. X designates the cause or part of the cause of Y, say Harry Truman's father, etc. Now, Aquinas reasons, whenever we take away the cause, we also take away the effect: if Harry Truman had never lived, Margaret Truman would never have been born. If Harry Truman's father had never lived, Harry Truman and Margaret Truman would never have been born. If A had never existed none of the subsequent members of the series would have come into existence. But it is precisely A that the believer in the infinite series is "taking away." For in maintaining that the series is infinite he is denying that it has a first member; he is dening that there is such a thing as a first cause; he is, in other words, denying the existence of A. Since without A, Z could not have existed, his position implies that Z does not exist now; and that is plainly false.

Critics of the argument would object that it does not do justice to the supporter of the infinite series of causes. They would say that Aquinas had failed to distinguish between the two statements

> (1) A did not exist, and
> (2) A is not uncaused.

To say that the series is infinite implies (2), but it does not imply (1). The following parallel may be helpful here: Suppose Captain Spaulding had said "I am the greatest explorer who ever lived" and somebody replied "No, you are not." This answer would be denying that the Captain possessed the exalted attribute he had claimed for himself, but it would not be denying his existence. It would not be "taking him away." Similarly, the believer in the infinite series is not "taking A away." He is taking away the privileged status of A; he is taking away its "first causiness," if you like. He does not deny the existence of A or of any particular member of the series. He denies that A or anything else is the first member of the series. Since he is not taking A away, he is not taking B away and thus he is also not taking X, Y, or Z away. His view, then, does not commit him to the absurdity that nothing exists now or, more specifically, that Margaret Truman does not exist now. It may be noted in this connection that a believer in the infinite series is not necessarily denying the existence of supernatural beings. He is merely committed to denying that such a being, if it exists, is uncaused. He is committed to holding that whatever other impressive attributes a supernatural being might possess, the attribute of being a first cause is not among them.

The causal argument has also been criticized on many other counts. Thus it has been asserted that, even if otherwise valid, the argument would not prove a *single* first cause. For there does not seem to be any good ground for supposing that all the various causal series in the universe ultimately merge. Hence even if it is granted that no series of causes can be infinite, the possibility of a plurality of first members has not been ruled out. Nor does the argument, according to some critics, establish the *present* existence of the first cause. It does not prove this since experience clearly shows that an effect may exist long after its cause has been destroyed. There are also other objections and some of these will be discussed further on in this introduction.

Many defenders of the causal argument would contend that at least some of these criticisms rest on a misunderstanding. They would probably go further and contend that the argument was not quite fairly stated in the first place— or at any rate that if it was fair to some of its adherents, it was not fair to others. They would in this connection distinguish between two types of causes —what they call "causes *in fieri*" and what they call "causes *in esse.*" A cause *in fieri* is a factor which brought or helped to bring an effect into existence. A cause *in esse* is a factor which "sustains" or helps to sustain the effect "in being." The parents of a human being would be an example of a cause *in fieri*. If somebody puts a book in my hand and I keep holding it up, his putting it there would be the cause *in fieri,* and my holding it would be the cause *in esse* of the books' position. The builder of a house is its cause *in fieri;* the materials which, in virtue of their rigidity, keep it in existence are its cause *in esse*. Sometimes the cause in *fieri* and the cause in *esse* are identical. In this connection Father Joyce gives the example of a candle which produces light in a room in the first place and whose further presence is required if the illumination is to continue.

Using this distinction, a defender of the argument now reasons in the following way. To say that there is an infinite series of causes *in fieri* does not lead to any absurd conclusion. But Aquinas is concerned only with causes *in esse* and an infinite series of *such* causes is impossible. In the words of the contemporary American Thomist, R. P. Phillips:

> . . . Each member of the series of causes possesses being solely by virtue of the actual present operation of a superior cause. . . . Life is dependent, *inter alia,* on a certain atmospheric pressure, this again on the continual operation of physical forces, whose being and operation depends on the position of the earth in the solar system, which itself must endure relatively unchanged, a state of being which can only be continuously produced by a definite—if unknown—constitution of the material universe. This constitution, however, cannot be its own cause. That a thing should

cause itself is impossible: for in order that it may cause it is necessary for it to exist, which it cannot do, on the hypothesis, until it has been caused. So it must *be* in order to cause itself, and it cannot *be* until it has caused itself. Thus, not being uncaused nor yet its own cause, it must be caused by another, which produces and preserves it. It is plain, then, that as no member of this series possesses being except in virtue of the actual present operation of a superior cause, if there be no first cause actually operating none of the dependent causes could operate either. We are thus irresistibly led to posit a first efficient cause which, while itself uncaused, shall impart causality to a whole series. . . .

The series of causes which we are considering is not one which stretches back into the past; so that we are not demanding a beginning of the world at some definite moment reckoning back from the present, but an actual cause now operating, to account for the present being of things.

The supporter of the infinite series of causes, in the words of Father Joyce,

. . . is asking us to believe that although each link in a suspended chain is prevented from falling simply because it is attached to the one above it, yet if only the chain be long enough, it will, taken as a whole, need no support, but will hang loose in the air suspended from nothing.

This formulation of the causal argument unquestionably circumvents one of the objections mentioned previously. If Y is the cause *in esse* of an effect, Z, then it must exist as long as Z exists. If the argument were valid in this form it would therefore prove the present and not merely the past existence of a first cause. In this form the argument is, however, less convincing in another respect. To maintain that all "natural" or "phenomenal" objects— things like tables and mountains and human beings—require a cause *in fieri* is not implausible, though even here Mill and others have argued that strictly speaking only *changes* require a causal explanation. It is far from plausible on the other hand to claim that all natural objects require a cause *in esse*. It may be granted that the air around us is a cause *in esse* of human life and further that certain gravitational forces are among the causes *in esse* of the air being where it is. But when we come to gravitational forces or at any rate to material particles like atoms or electrons, it is difficult to see what cause *in esse* they require. To those not already convinced of the need for a supernatural First Cause some of the remarks by the supporters of the argument in this connection appear merely dogmatic and question-begging. Most people would grant that particles like atoms did not cause themselves, since they would in that event have had to exist before they began existing. It is not at all evident, however, that these particles cannot be uncaused. Professor Phillips and all other supporters of the causal argument immediately proceed to claim that there *is* something else which needs no cause *in esse*. They themselves admit thus, a critic would say, that there is nothing self-evident about the proposition that everything must have a cause *in esse*. Their entire procedure here incidentally, seems to lend substance to Schopenhauer's gibe that supporters of the cosmological argument treat the law of universal causation like "a hired cab which we dismiss when we have reached our destination."

But waiving this and all similar objections, an opponent would maintain that the restatement of the argument in terms of causes *in esse* in no way avoids the main difficulty which was previously mentioned. A believer in the infinite series would insist that his position was just as much misrepresented now as before. He is no more removing the member of the series which is supposed to be the first cause *in esse* than he was removing the member which had been declared to be the first cause *in fieri*. He is again merely denying a privileged status to it. He is not denying the reality of the cause *in esse* labelled "A." He is not even necessarily denying that it possesses supernatural attributes. He is again merely taking away its "first causiness."

To many critics it appears that the advocates of the causal argument in either form frequently confuse in their own minds an infinite series with one which is long but finite. If a book, Z, is to remain in its position, say 100 miles up in the air, there must be another object, say another book, Y, underneath it, to serve as its support. If Y is to remain where it is, it will need another support, X, beneath it. Suppose that this series of supports, one below the other, continues for a long time but, eventually, say after 100,000 members, comes to a first book which is not resting on any other book or indeed on any other support. In that event the whole collection would come crashing down. What we seem to need is a first member of the series, a first support (like the earth) which does not need another member as *its* support, which in other words is "self-supporting."

This is evidently the sort of picture that supporters of the First Cause argument have before their minds when they rule out the possibility of an infinite series. A critic of the argument would counter that such a picture is not a fair representation of the theory of the infinite series. A *finite* series of books would indeed come crashing down since the first or lowest member would not have a predecessor on which it could be supported. If the series, were infinite, however, this would not be the case. In that event every member *would* have a predecessor to support itself on and there would be no crash. That is to say: a crash can be avoided either by a finite series with a first self-supporting member or by an infinite series. Similarly, the present existence of motion is equally compatible with the theory of a first unmoved mover and with the theory of an infinite series of moving objects; and the present existence of causal activity is compatible with the theory of a first cause *in esse* as much as with the theory of an infinite series of such causes.

No staunch defender of the cosmological argument would give up at this stage. Even if there were an infinite series of causes *in fieri* or *in esse,* he would contend, this still would not do away with the need for an ultimate, a first cause. As Father Copleston put it in his debate with Bertrand Russell (see also the debate with A. J. Ayer, Selection 46, pp. 590 ff.).

> Every object has a phenomenal cause, if you insist on the infinity of the series. But the series of phenomenal causes is an insufficient explanation of the series. Therefore, the series has not a phenomenal cause, but a transcendent cause. . . . An infinite series of contingent beings will be, to my way of thinking, as unable to cause itself as one contingent being.

A critic would retort that the demand to find the cause of the series as a whole rests on the erroneous assumption that the series is something over and above the members of which it is composed. It is tempting to suppose this, at least by implication, because the word "series" is a noun like "dog" or "man." Like the expression "this dog" or "this man" the phrase "this series" is easily taken to designate an individual object. But reflection shows this to be an error. If we have explained the individual members there is nothing additional left to be explained. Supposing I see a group of five Eskimos standing on the corner of Sixth Avenue and 50th Street and I wish to explain why the group came to New York. Investigation reveals the following stories:

> Eskimo No. 1 did not enjoy the extreme cold in the polar region and decided to move to a warmer climate;
> No. 2 is the husband of Eskimo No. 1. He loves her dearly and did not wish to live without her;
> No. 3 is the son of Eskimos 1 and 2. He is too small and too weak to oppose his parents;
> No. 4 saw an advertisement in the *New York Times* for an Eskimo to appear on television;
> No. 5 is a private detective engaged by the Pinkerton Agency to keep an eye on Eskimo No. 4.

Let us assume that we have now explained in the case of each of the five Eskimos why he or she is in New York. Somebody then asks: "All right, but what about the group as a whole, why is *it* in New York?" This would plainly be an absurd question. There is no group over and above the five members and if we have explained why each of the five members is in New York, we have *ipso facto* explained why the group is there. A critic of the cosmological argument would claim that it is just as absurd to ask for the cause of the series as a whole, as distinct from asking for the causes of individual members.

It is most unlikely that a determined defender of the cosmological line of reasoning would surrender even here. He would probably admit that the series is not a thing over and above its members and that it does not make sense to ask for the cause of the series if the cause of each member has already been found. He would insist, however, that when he asked for the explanation of the entire series, he was not asking for its *cause*. He was really saying that a series, finite or infinite, is not "intelligible" or "explained" if it consists of nothing but "contingent" members. To quote Father Copleston once more:

> What we call the world is intrinsically unintelligible apart from the existence of God. The infinity of the series of events, if such an infinity could be proved, would not be in the slightest degree relevant to the situation. If you add up chocolates, you get chocolates after all, and not a sheep. If you add up chocolates to infinity, you presumably get an infinite number of chocolates. So, if you add up contingent beings to infinity, you still get contingent beings, not a necessary being.

This last quotation is really a summary of the "contingency argument," the other main form of the cosmological proof. This is the third of the five ways of Aquinas (see Selection 35, p. 473). It may be stated more fully in these words: All around us we perceive contingent beings. This includes all physical objects and also all human minds. In calling them "contingent" we mean that they might not have existed. We mean that the universe can be *conceived* without this or that physical object, without this or that human being, however certain their actual existence may be. These contingent beings we can trace back to other contingent beings—e.g., a human being to his parents. However, since these other beings are also contingent, they do not provide a real or full explanation. The contingent beings we originally wanted explained have not yet become intelligible, since the beings to which they have been traced back are no more necessary than they were. It is just as true of our parents, for example, as it is of ourselves, that they might not have existed. We can, then, properly explain the contingent beings around us only by tracing them back ultimately to some necessary being, to something which exists necessarily, which has "the reason for its existence within itself." The existence of contingent beings, in other words, implies the existence of a necessary being.

This argument, according to many philosophers, is even more beset with difficulties than the causal form of the cosmological proof. In the first place, Kant and many other writers contend that it really commits the same error as the ontological argument in tacitly regarding existence as an attribute or characteristic (see Smart, Selection 38, pp. 503 ff.). To say that there is a necessary being is to say that it would be a self-contradiction to deny its existence. This would mean that at least one existential statement is a necessary truth; and this in turn presupposes that in at least one case existence is contained in a concept. But, for reasons outlined in connection with the ontological argument, it seems plain to very many philosophers that existence is not a characteristic, that it can hence never be contained in a concept and that no existential statement can ever be a necessary truth. To talk about anything "existing necessarily" is in their view about as sensible as to talk about round squares. They conclude that the contingency-argument is quite absurd. Scholastic philosophers like Father Copleston would reply that existence *is* a characteristic and would thus also reject the Kantian criticism of the ontological argument. They do reject the ontological argument but not as radically as Kant and for different reasons.

Let us assume that this difficulty can somehow be surmounted and that the expression "necessary being," as it is intended by the champions of the contingency-argument, might conceivably apply to something. There remain other objections which are of great weight in the opinion of many writers. One of these may perhaps be best explained by first quoting again from the debate between Bertrand Russell and Father Copleston:

RUSSELL: . . . It all turns on this question of sufficient reason, and I must say you havn't defined "sufficient reason" in a way that I can understand—what do you mean by sufficient reason? You don't mean cause?

COPLESTON: Not necessarily. Cause is a kind of sufficient reason. Only contingent being can have a cause. God is his own sufficient reason; and he is not cause of himself. By sufficient reason in the full sense I mean an explanation adequate for the existence of some particular being.

RUSSELL: But when is an explanation adequate? Suppose I am about to make a flame with a match. You may say that the adequate explanation of that is that I rub it on the box.

COPLESTON: Well for practical purposes—but theoretically, that is only a partial explanation. An adequate explanation must ultimately be a total explanation, to which nothing further can be added.

RUSSELL: Then I can only say that you're looking for something which can't be got, and which one ought not to expect to get.

COPLESTON: To say that one has not found it is one thing; to say that one should not look for it seems to me rather dogmatic.

RUSSELL: Well, I don't know. I mean, the explanation of one thing is another thing which makes the other thing dependent on yet another, and you have to grasp this sorry scheme of things entire to do what you want, and that we can't do.

Russell's criticism may be expanded in the following way. The contingency argument rests on a misconception of what an explanation is and does, and similarly on what it is that makes phenomena "intelligible." Or else it involves an obscure and arbitrary redefinition of "explanation," "intelligible," and related terms. Normally, we are satisfied that we have explained a phenomenon if we have found its cause or if we have exhibited some other uniform connection between it and something else. Confining ourselves to the former case, which is probably the most common, we might say that a phenomenon, Z, has been explained if it has been traced back to a group of factors, a, b, c, d, etc., which are its cause. These factors are the full and real explanation of Z quite regardless of whether they are pleasing or displeasing, admirable or contemptible, necessary or contingent. The explanation would not be adequate only if the factors listed are not really the cause of Z. If they are the cause of Z, the explanation would be adequate even though each of the factors is merely a "contingent being."

Let us suppose that we have been asked to explain why General Eisenhower won the elections of 1952. "He was an extremely popular general," we might answer, "while Stevenson was relatively little known; moreover there was a great deal of resentment over the scandals in the Truman Administration." If somebody complained that this was only a partial explanation we might mention additional antecedents such as the widespread belief that the Democrats had allowed Communist agents to infiltrate the State Department, that Eisenhower was a man with a winning smile, and that unlike Stevenson he had shown the good sense to say one thing on race relations in the North and quite another in the South. Theoretically, we might go further and list the motives of all American voters during the weeks or months preceding the elections. If we could do this we would have explained Eisenhower's victory. We would have made it intelligible. We would "understand" why he won and why Stevenson lost. Perhaps there is a sense in which we might make Eisenhower's victory even more intelligible if we went further back and discussed such matters as the origin of American views on Communism or of racial attitudes in the North and South. However, to explain the outcome of the election in any ordinary sense, loose or strict, it would not be necessary to go back to pre-historic days or to the amoeba or to a first cause, if such a first cause exists. Nor would our explanation be considered in any way defective because each of the factors mentioned was a "contingent" and not a necessary being. The only thing that matters is whether the factors were really the cause of Eisenhower's election. If they were then it has been explained although they are contingent beings. If they were not the cause of Eisenhower's victory we would have failed to explain it even if each of the factors were a necessary being.

If it is granted that in order to explain a phenomenon or to make it intelligible we need not bring in a necessary being, the contingency-argument breaks down. For a series, as was already pointed out, is not something over and above its members; and every contingent member of it could in that case be explained by reference to other contingent beings. It is evident from Russell's remarks that he would go further in his criticisms. Even if it were granted, he would argue, both that the phrase "necessary being" is meaningful and that all explanations are defective unless the phenomena to be explained are traced back to a necessary being the conclusion would not have been established. The conclusion that a necessary being actually exists does not follow from the premise that phenomena have not been really or fully explained without the introduction of a necessary being. The conclusion follows from this premise together with the additional premise that *there are* explanations of phenomena in this special sense of the word. It is this further premise which Russell and many other philosophers would question. They do not merely question whether human beings can ever obtain explanations in this sense, but whether they exist. To assume without further ado that phenomena have explanations or an explanation in this sense is to beg the very point at issue. The use of the same word "explanation" in two crucially different ways, a critic might argue, may lend the second premise a plausibility it does not really possess. It may indeed be highly plausible to assert that phenomena have explanations, whether we have found them or not, in the ordinary sense in which this usually means that they have causes. It is then tempting to suppose, because of the use of the same word, that they also have explanations in a sense in which this implies dependence on a necessary being. But this, a critic would insist, does not follow in the least.

Kant, who rejected the ontological, the cosmological and also the teleological argument, produced an argument of his own which belongs to the species known as moral arguments for the existence of God. Moral arguments enjoyed much popularity in the 19th century both among writers who followed Kant in the rejection of the other arguments and also among Catholic philosophers who remained unmoved by Kant's criticisms. In recent years, however, the popularity of moral arguments appears to have greatly declined and today among philosophers with a Protestant background the appeal to religious experience is perhaps the most widespread method of supporting belief in God.

The main point at issue in this argument may be stated as follows: There are human beings who claim to have experiences in the course of which they have immediate knowledge of God. In these "religious" experiences they claim to have as direct a "contact" with the "Creator and Sustainer of the universe" as we ordinarily have with physical objects when we see or touch them. Of course God is not physical and He is not known by means of the physical senses; but the contact is just as real, perhaps even more so. Cardinal Newman, for instance, referring to his conversion through a religious experience many years after it had taken place, wrote that he was still more certain of its veracity than that he had "hands and feet."

That experiences take place in which people *believe* to have contact with God can hardly be questioned. It has, however, been debated whether any of these experiences are "veridical," whether any of those who have religious experiences *really make contact* with the deity. There are roughly three points of view on this whole topic. Firstly, there is the affirmative position which maintains that while no doubt some religious experiences have to be classified as "delusive," in others human beings are really in touch with the ultimate spiritual Cause of the universe. There is, secondly, the negative position which, in its more radical form, maintains that all religious experiences are of the same nature as either illusions or hallucinations. Bertrand Russell and Freud are among those who endorse this view. "From a scientific point of view," Russell remarks, "we can make no distinction between the man who eats little and sees heaven and the man who drinks much and sees snakes." There is also a more modest version of the negative position which contends merely that the veridical character of religious experiences cannot be established. Finally, there is a middle-of-the-road position according to which human beings do, in some of these religious experiences, come into contact with "an aspect of reality" not given in more ordinary types of experience. But it is held that this aspect is probably misdescribed by the use of theological language. Broad and Stace are perhaps the most eminent exponents of views of this kind.

In the case of sense-experiences we possess certain fairly precise criteria which enable us to discriminate between those which are veridical and those which are deceptive. Supposing one day I come home at nine in the evening and see, or think I see, the tenor Jussi Bjoerling in my living room, although he has been announced to sing Manrico in *Trovatore* at that very moment. I could determine whether my visual experience is veridical or not by looking more closely and by making use of senses other than sight. I could for instance try to start a conversation with what I take to be Jussi Bjoerling and I could try to put my hands in the place where he would be if my visual experience were veridical. I could also call in other observers, preferably such as are sane and sober and not dominated by conscious or unconscious wishes for the presence of distinguished Swedish tenors. Again I could test certain statements which are logical consequences of the assumption that it is really Jussi Bjoerling who is in my apartment. Thus I could call up Mr. Bing at the Metropolitan Opera and check if Jussi Bjoerling is performing in *Trovatore* as scheduled. If I am told that he is, this would indicate that I am the victim of an hallucination. If on the other hand I am told that Jussi Bjoerling had to be suddenly replaced, that he has lately gone in for skillful burglaries on the upper West Side in Manhattan and that he was last seen heading in the direction of my apartment, this would tend to confirm the veridical nature of my visual experience.

Are there any such tests in the case of religious experiences? The defenders of this argument maintain that there are at least analogous criteria. In the first place they point to the large quantity of reports and the relative agreement in their contents. This would correspond to calling in other observers in the case of sense-experiences. Secondly, they point to the high moral and intellectual caliber of at least some of those reporting religious experiences. This would correspond to the sanity and soberness of the observers. Finally, attention is drawn to the vast beneficial differences which religious experiences make to the lives of many who have them. This is compared by the defenders of the argument to affirmative tests of statements which logically follow from the assumption that a certain sense-experience is veridical. To do justice to the argument it is necessary to state each of these points at greater length.

It is argued that among people who have had religious experiences we must include not only mystics and saints who have perhaps had these experiences more intensely than others. We must also include countless modest and humble believers who experienced the presence of God in the course of prayers and meditations, and in moments of stress and crisis. These experiences furthermore are not confined to Christians and Jews but are equally or even more common in Eastern religions. "By the most conservative estimate," writes Professor Trueblood,

> . . . the number of persons who have reported religious experience, not in the sense of ecstatic trance, and not in the sense of mere inference from the order of nature, but with a deep assurance of the divine undergirding, is many millions . . .

It is true that religious experiences are not universal in the human race. But this proves nothing. No experience, not even sight, is universal. To have an experience, certain receptive powers are required. From the fact that there are blind people it does not follow that our visual experiences ar generally deceptive. Moreover, the testimony of those who fail to have an experience has no logical weight if they did not fulfil the conditions required for having the experience. "The religious opinions of the unreligious," to quote Trueblood, "are no more valuable than are the scientific opinions of the unscientific."

The mere quantity of reports of religious experiences would not provide much evidence if there were very great differences in their content. While they do vary greatly concerning details, depending on the age in which the person lived and the particular religious background from which he came, these reports are remarkably similar as regards their essential features. All or nearly all speak of contact with a Being immeasurably greater than the person himself which is in some sense the ultimate Reality and which provides love and assurance. "We could seldom guess," according to Dean Inge, "whether a paragraph describing the highest spiritual experiences was written in the Middle Ages or in modern times, in the north or south of Europe, by a Catholic or by a Protestant."

The "qualitative fitness" of the reporters is also important. The defenders of this argument would usually admit that those claiming religious experiences have included cranks, lunatics and plain frauds. A substantial number of them were, however, sincere beyond any question. It would be fantastic to suppose that men like Pascal, Newman, Fox, Gandhi, or Tolstoy were "engaged in a grand hoax." Nor can it be reasonably maintained that all these men were lacking in critical powers. There is, then, in Trueblood's words:

> . . . a substantial body of evidence coming from sensitive men, who are in command of their faculties, and properly qualified, on both moral and intellectual grounds, so that they inspire trust in that to which they bear testimony.

Finally, it is claimed that the beneficial consequences of religious experiences provide an indirect confirmation of their veridical character.

> In religion we cannot reasonably look for a mark on photographic plates, but we can reasonably look for a mark on human lives. If the experience of God is what men claim it is, we should expect to see a general change in their character; we should expect them to walk with a new step.

And that is precisely, according to Professor Trueblood and other defenders of the argument, what we find in abundance. Religious experience "suffuses entire lives with joy." It gives people "a new strength and a new tenderness." It "sensitizes their consciences to social wrong, such as that of slavery and poverty." It "makes weak men bold and proud men humble." It enables them to endure extreme sorrows and hardships and persecutions.

So much for the defense of this argument. Let us now look at the answers offered by those who reject it. Taking the last point first, many of them have questioned whether religious experiences really have such powerful effects for the good. It is true, they would argue, that some great mystics like St. Francis or William Blake, were persons of exceptional kindness and compassion; but it is very doubtful if this was due to their religious visions. There have after all been quite a few kindly unbelievers and perhaps St. Francis and Blake would have been kind and compassionate in the absence of religious experiences or even in the absence of any religious belief. Furthermore, if it is granted that religious experiences have sometimes had beneficial effects there seems equal evidence that some of the most dreadful persecutions were instigated by men who claimed to be fulfilling divine orders. Who has not heard of fanatics committing murders, arson, and all kinds of violent deeds in the conviction that they were thus carrying out the commands of the deity? If "marks on human lives" count, a critic would assert, it is not easy to see why these "negative marks" are to be ruled out. For there is no reason to suppose that the persecutors and the cranks were any less sincere in their reports than the gentle believers. If a defender of the argument condemns the experiences of fanatics as delusions on the ground that God is good (in his sense) and cannot therefore have given such hideous instructions he would be assuming the very thing he should prove.

In any case, however, a critic would maintain that beneficial results are no evidence that a belief is sound or an experience veridical. A heroic attitude has frequently been induced by beliefs which were illusory. Nazi spies and saboteurs willingly gave their lives in the service of the Führer whom they took to be noble, sane, and selfless. It is an understatement to say that he was none of these. Julius and Ethel Rosenberg showed great courage in going to their death, but their opinions about the nature of the Soviet system under Stalin were altogether mistaken as even Communists admit today. Nor is there any reason to suppose that hallucinations cannot have powerful effects on a person's life. In the case of paranoid individuals they do and the effects are not by any means always socially harmful. When the individual believes himself to be Christ or "the Ruler of the Universe" his delusions usually lead to kindly rather than to cruel deeds. The beneficial effects of religious experiences are hence not incompatible with the view that they are deceptive. They cannot properly be compared to the positive outcome of tests which prove a sense-experience to be veridical.

As for the "quality" of the reporters, a critic might well admit that quite a number of them were men of high moral and intellectual standing. But this, he would go on, can be considered evidence only for the claim that they were not lying when they reported their experiences. It cannot be considered evidence for the further claim that God was actually present on those occasions. It is certainly not impossible for a person of high moral and intellectual standing to become the victim of a delusion. There would be very general agreement that just this has happened in not a few cases. In earlier days, when the belief in demons was widespread, countless sincere and intelligent men reported struggles with the devil and his agents who were tempting them to commit immoral deeds. There is little doubt that these experiences were hallucinations. Again, William Blake had visions not only of the deity but also of Moses, David, Julius Caesar, Shakespeare, Dante, Voltaire, and King Edward III. He was a man of great gifts and matchless sincerity but it seems clear that these experiences were not veridical. William Gladstone, the great liberal Prime Minister of the Victorian era, habitually "consulted God" before making any major decision and God apparently always advised a course which was to the political and personal advantage of Mr. Gladstone. Even most devoutly religious people of that period, especially those favoring the Conservative Party, considered it very unlikely that God had really appeared to Mr. Gladstone in these "consultations." Men of intelligence and good moral reputation do not, in other words, seem to be immune from hallucinations. If the conditions which generally lead to delusions are present in such men, they are likely to produce the same result as in anybody else.

A critic would similarly contend that the quantity of the reports as well as their relative unanimity is not at all incompatible with the view that God is never actually present in any of these experiences. If religious experiences are due to certain ungratified needs in people who have been reared in a religious environment and if these unfulfilled needs ar widespread, then we would expect religious experiences to occur quite frequently even on the assumption that they are delusions. If the needs in question are similar and the religious backgrounds somewhat different we would expect the content of the experiences to be fairly similar as regards their basic features and to be rather different in peripheral details. And this, a critic would add, is precisely what we find.

All of this, even if sound, would not show that religious experiences are always delusive. It would merely show that their veridical nature had not been established. Some opponents of the argument would go a great deal further. They would offer a theory of the origin of religious experiences which in their opinion makes it extremely probable that all the alleged contacts with God are complete delusions. Since the days of the German philosopher Feuerbach (1804-1872) and more especially since the publication of the theories of Freud and certain of his disciples, many unbelievers have reasoned on this topic roughly along the following lines. People whose lives are devoid of certain forms of earthly love and warmth tend to escape into a world of dreams and make-believe. Not finding satisfaction for some of their deepest and most powerful longings in their physical and human environment, they seek consolation and substitute-gratification in a world of their own making which can be managed more easily than the hard and cold universe around them. People who have religious experiences and mystical longings, the critic would proceed, must be put into this class. Experience shows that every one of them has not found fulfilment of some very basic mundane yearning. It is only reasonable to infer that religious experiences are part and parcel of one of the systems of fantasy in which the person finds some semblance of the love and warmth that is denied to him in his earthly contacts. As confirmation of this theory the unbelievers would point to the fact or the alleged fact that those who have religious experiences most vividly and most frequently show a great many overt similarities to the insane, if they are not indeed generally so classified. The critics would also point to the observation of some eminent psychologists that a person's proneness to religious experiences and mystical feelings diminishes in almost exact proportion as he reestablishes contact with the terrestial world and finds satisfaction for his biological and social needs.

In the opinion of some writers it would not follow that religious experiences are always delusions even if a theory such as that outlined in the last paragraph were correct. Professor Broad offers the following rebuttal to the unbeliever's argument:

> Suppose, for the sake of argument, that there is an aspect of the world which remains altogether outside the ken of ordinary persons in their daily life. Then it seems very likely that some degree of mental and physical abnormality would be a necessary condition for getting sufficiently loosened from the objects of ordinary sense-perception to come into cognitive contact with this aspect of reality. Therefore the fact that those persons who claim to have this peculiar kind of cognition generally exhibit certain mental and physical abnormalities is rather what might be anticipated if their claims were true. One might need to be slightly "cracked" in order to have some peep-holes into the super-sensible world.

If this is a valid retort then Freudian theories of the genesis of religious experiences would not show them to be delusions. Perhaps such theories do nonetheless constitute a powerful challenge to the defenders of the appeal to religious experience. For it might be said that if we have a perfectly good explanation of a certain phenomenon in terms of natural causes it becomes superfluous to explain it in terms of some supernatural reality (see Feigl, Selection 41, pp. 535 ff.). There was a time when hysterical and other neurotic symptoms were explained as due to "possession" by evil spirits. For all we know such spirits do really inhabit the organisms of hysterics. But since we now have fairly plausible explanations of these symptoms in terms of such natural causes as repressed emotions or nervous lesions there is no need to resort to demons. Similarly, if the Freudian theory were true this would not show that the theological explanation is false, but it would make the latter redundant.

All this presupposes that such a naturalistic theory of the origin of religious experiences is sound. But is it? Not only apologists for religion but many others have expressed grave doubts about the adequacy of all theories of this kind which have so far been advanced. They assert that the psychologists who construct such theories are as a rule debarred from a full understanding of the phenomena they are trying to explain since they themselves have no first-hand experience of religion. Many of them, moreover, are very hostile to religious belief from the start. Their theories, to quote Broad, "wear too jaundiced a complexion to inspire complete confidence." "I should feel some hesitation" he goes on, "in accepting theories about the nature of music and its function in human life, excogitated by a tone-deaf psychologist whose wife had recently eloped with a musician."

P. E.

34

OF GOD—THAT HE EXISTS

Rene Descartes

The Idea of God and God's Objective Reality

. . . HENCE THERE REMAINS ALONE the idea of God, concerning which we must consider whether it is not something that is capable of proceeding from me myself. By the name God I understand a substance that is infinite (eternal, immutable), independent, all-knowing, all-powerful, and by which I myself and everything else, if anything else does exist, have been created. Now all these characteristics are such that the more diligently I attend to them, the less do they appear capable of proceeding from me alone; hence, from what has already been said, we must conclude that God necessarily exists.

For although the idea of substance is within me owing to the fact that I am substance, nevertheless I should not have the idea of an infinite substance—since I am finite—if it had not proceeded from some substance which was veritably infinite.

Nor should I imagine that I do not perceive the infinite by a true idea, but only by the negation of the finite, just as I perceive repose and darkness by the negation of movement and of light; for, on the contrary, I see that there is manifestly more reality in infinite substance than in finite, and therefore that in some way I have in me the notion of the infinite earlier than the finite—to wit, the notion of God before that of myself. For how would it be possible that I should know that I doubt and desire, that is to say, that something is lacking to me, and

---

[This selection comprises portions of the third and the fifth of Descartes' *Meditations,* a book first published in 1641. The first part of the selection gives Descartes' own argument, in which he infers the existence of an infinite Being from the mere fact that man can think of such a Being. The second part contains Descartes' defense of the ontological argument. The English translation of these passages is by Elizabeth S. Haldane and G. R. T. Ross and is reproduced with the kind permission of the Cambridge University Press.]

that I am not quite perfect, unless I had within me some idea of a Being more perfect than myself, in comparison with which I should recognise the deficiencies of my nature?

And we cannot say that this idea of God is perhaps materially false and that consequently I can derive it from nought (i.e., that possibly it exists in me because I am imperfect), as I have just said is the case with ideas of heat, cold and other such things; for, on the contrary, as this idea is very clear and distinct and contains within it more objective reality than any other, there can be none which is of itself more true, nor any in which there can be less suspicion of falsehood. The idea, I say, of this Being who is absolutely perfect and infinite, is entirely true; for although, perhaps, we can imagine that such a Being does not exist, we cannot nevertheless imagine that His idea represents nothing real to me, as I have said of the idea of cold. This idea is also very clear and distinct; since all that I conceive clearly and distinctly of the real and the true, and of what conveys some perfection, is in its entirety contained in this idea. And this does not cease to be true although I do not comprehend the infinite, or though in God there is an infinite of things which I cannot comprehend, nor possibly even reach in any way by thought; for it is of the nature of the infinite that my nature, which is finite and limited, should not comprehend it; and it is sufficient that I should understand this, and that I should judge that all things which I clearly perceive and in which I know that there is some perfection, and possibly likewise an infinitude of properties of which I am ignorant, are in God formally or eminently, so that the idea which I have of Him may become the most true, most clear, and most distinct of all the ideas that are in my mind.

But possibly I am something more than I suppose myself to be, and perhaps all those perfections which I attribute to God are in some way potentially in me, although they do not yet disclose themselves, or issue in action. As a matter of fact I am already sensible that my knowledge increases (and perfects itself) little by little, and I see nothing which can prevent it from increasing more and more into infinitude; nor do I see, after it has thus been increased (or perfected), anything to prevent my being able to acquire by its means all the other perfections of the Divine nature; nor finally why the power I have of acquiring these perfections, if it really exists in me, shall not suffice to produce the ideas of them.

At the same time I recognise that this cannot be. For, in the first place, although it were true that every day my knowledge acquired new degrees of perfection, and that there were in my nature many things potentially which are not yet there actually, nevertheless these excellences do not pertain to (or make the smallest approach to) the idea which I have of God in whom there is nothing merely potential (but in whom all is present really and actually); for it is an infallible token of imperfection in my knowledge that it increases little by little. And further, although my knowledge grows more and more, nevertheless I do not for that reason believe that it can ever be actually infinite, since it can never reach a point so high that it will be unable to attain to any greater increase. But I understand God to be actually infinite, so that He can add nothing to His supreme perfection. And finally I perceive that the objective being of an idea cannot be produced by a being that exists potentially only, which properly speaking is nothing, but only by a being which is formal or actual.

To speak the truth, I see nothing in all that I have just said which by the light of nature is not manifest to anyone who desires to think attentively on the subject; but when I slightly relax my attention, my mind, finding its vision somewhat obscured and so to speak blinded by the images of sensible objects, I do not easily recollect the reason why the idea that I possess of a being more perfect than I, must necessarily have been placed in me by a Being which is really more perfect; and this is why I wish here to go on to inquire whether I, who have this idea, can exist if no such being exists.

And I ask, from whom do I then derive my existence? Perhaps from myself or from my parents, or from some other source less perfect than God; for we can imagine nothing more perfect than God, or even as perfect as He is.

But (were I independent of every other and) were I myself the author of my being, I should doubt nothing and I should desire nothing, and finally no perfection would be lacking to me; for I should have bestowed on myself every perfection of which I possessed any idea and should thus be God. And it must not be imagined that those things that are lacking to me are perhaps more difficult of attainment than those which I already possess; for, on the contrary, it is quite evident that it was a matter of much greater difficulty to bring to pass that I, that is to say, a thing or a substance that thinks, should emerge out of nothing, than it would be to attain to the knowledge of many things of which I am ignorant, and which are only the accidents of this thinking substance. But it is clear that if I had of myself possessed this greater perfection of which I have just spoken (that is to say, if I had been the author of my own existence), I should not at least have denied myself the things which are the more easy to acquire (to wit, many branches of knowledge of which my nature is destitute); nor should I have deprived myself of the things contained in the idea which I form of God, because there are none of them which seem to me specially difficult to acquire: and if there were any that were more difficult to acquire, they would certainly appear to me to be such (supposing I myself were the origin of the other things which I possess) since I should discover in them that my powers were limited.

But though I assume that perhaps I have always existed just as I am at present, neither can I escape the force of this reasoning, and imagine that the conclusion to be drawn from this is, that I need not seek any author of my existence. For all the course of my life may be divided into an infinite number of parts, none of which is in any way dependent on the other; and thus from the fact that I was in existence a short time ago it does not follow that I must be in existence now, unless some cause at this instant, so to speak, produces me anew, that is to say conserves me. It is as a matter of fact perfectly clear and evident to all those who consider with attention the nature of time, that, in order to be conserved in each moment in which it endures, a substance has need of the same power and action as would be necessary to produce and create it anew, supposing it did not yet exist; so that the light of nature shows us clearly that the distinction between creation and conservation is solely a distinction of the reason.

All that I thus require here is that I should interrogate myself, if I wish to know whether I possess a power which is capable of bringing it to pass that I who now am shall still be in the future; for since I am nothing but a thinking thing, or at least since thus far it is only this portion of myself which is precisely in question at present, if such power did reside in me, I should certainly be conscious of it. But I am conscious of nothing of the kind, and by this I know clearly that I depend on some being different from myself.

Possibly, however, this being on which I depend is not that which I call God, and I am created either by my parents or by some other cause less perfect than God. This cannot be, because, as I have just said, it is perfectly evident that there must be at least as much reality in the cause as in the effect; and thus since I am a thinking thing, and possess an idea of God within me, whatever in the end be the cause assigned to my existence, it must bc allowed that it is likewise a thinking thing and it possesses in itself the idea of all the perfections which I attribute to God. We may again inquire whether this cause derives its origin from itself or from some other thing. For if from itself, it follows by the reasons before brought forward, that this cause must itself be God; for since it possesses the virtue of self-existence, it must also without doubt have the power of actually possessing all the perfections of which it has the idea, that is, all those which I conceive as existing in God. But if it derives its existence from some other cause than itself, we shall again ask, for the same reason, whether this second cause exists by itself or through another, until from one step to another, we finally arrive at an ultimate cause, which will be God.

And it is perfectly manifest that in this there can be no regression into infinity, since what is in question is not so much the cause which formerly created me, as that which conserves me at the present time.

Nor can we suppose that several causes may have concurred in my production, and that from one I have received the idea of one of the perfections which I attribute to God, and from another the idea of some other, so that all these perfections indeed exist somewhere in the universe, but not as complete in one unity which is God. On the contrary, the unity, the simplicity or the inseparability of all things which are in God is one of the principal perfections which I conceive to be in Him. And certainly the idea of this unity of all Divine perfections cannot have been placed in me by any cause from which I have not likewise received the ideas of all the other perfections; for this cause could not make me able to comprehend them as joined together in an inseparable unity without having at the same time caused me in some measure to know what they are (and in some way to recognise each one of them).

Finally, so far as my parents (from whom it appears I have sprung) are concerned, although all that I have ever been able to believe of them were true, that does not make it follow that it is they who conserve me, nor are they even the authors of my being in any sense, in so far as I am a thinking being; since what they did was merely to implant certain disposition in that matter in which the self—i.e. the mind, which alone I at present identify with myself—is by me deemed to exist. And thus there can be no difficulty in their regard, but we must of necessity conclude from the fact alone that I exist, or that the idea of a Being supremely perfect—that is of God—is in me, that the proof of God's existence is grounded on the highest evidence.

It only remains to me to examine into the manner in which I have acquired this idea from God; for I have not received it through the senses, and it is never presented to me unexpectedly, as is usual with the ideas of sensible things when these things present themselves, or seem to present themselves, to the external organs of my senses; nor is it likewise a fiction of my mind, for it is not in my power to take from or to add anything to it; and consequently the only alternative is that it is innate in me, just as the idea of myself is innate in me.

And one certainly ought not to find it strange that God, in creating me, placed this idea within me to be like the mark of the workman imprinted on his work; and it is likewise not essential that the mark shall be something different from the work itself. For from the sole fact that God created me it is most probably that in some way he has placed his image and similitude upon me, and that I perceive this similitude (in which the idea of God is contained) by means of the same faculty by which I perceive myself—that is to say, when I reflect on myself I not only know that I am something (imperfect), incomplete and dependent on another, which incessantly aspires after something which is better and greater than myself, but I also know that He on whom I depend possesses in Himself all the great things towards which I aspire (and the ideas of which I find within myself), and that not indefinitely or potentially alone, but really, actually and infinitely; and that thus He is God. And the whole strength of the argument which I have here made use of to prove the existence of God consists in this, that I recognise that it is not possible that my nature should be what it is, and indeed that I should have in myself the idea of a God, if God did not veritably exist—a God, I say, whose idea is in me, i.e. who possesses all those supreme perfections of which our mind may indeed have some idea but without understanding them all, who is liable to no errors or defect (and who has none of all those marks which denote imperfection). From this it is manifest that He cannot be a deceiver, since the light of nature teaches us that fraud and deception necessarily proceed from some defect.

But before I examine this matter with more care, and pass on to the consideration of other truths which may be derived from it, it seems to me right to pause for a while in order to contemplate God Himself, to ponder at leisure his marvellous attributes, to consider, and admire, and adore, the beauty of his light so resplendent, at least so far as the strength of my mind, which is in some measure dazzled by the sight, will allow me to do so. For just as faith teaches us that supreme felicity of the other life consists only in this contemplation of the Divine Majesty, so we continue to learn by experience that a similar meditation, though incomparably less perfect causes us to enjoy the greatest satisfaction of which we are capable in this life. . . .

The Ontological Argument

. . . Now, if just because I can draw the idea of something from my thought, it follows that all which I know clearly and distinctly as pertaining to this object does really belong to it, may I not derive from this an argument demonstrating the existence of God? It is certain that I no less find the idea of God, that is to say, the idea of a supremely perfect Being, in me, than that of any figure or number whatever it is; and I do not know any less clearly and distinctly that an (actual and) eternal existence pertains to this nature than I know that all that which I am able to demonstrate of some figure or number truly pertains to the nature of this figure or number, and therefore, although all that I concluded in the preceding Meditations were found to be false, the existence of God would pass with me as at least as certain as I have ever held the truths of mathematics (which concern only numbers and figures) to be.

This indeed is not at first manifest, since it would seem to present some appearance of being a sophism. For being accustomed in all other things to make a distinction between existence and essence, I easily persuade myself that the existence can be separated from the essence of God, and that we can thus conceive God as not actually existing. But, nevertheless, when I think of it with more attention, I clearly see that existence can no more be separated from the essence of God than can its having its three angles equal to two right angles be separated from the essence of a (rectilinear) triangle, or the idea of a mountain from the idea of a valley; and so there is not any less repugnance to our conceiving a God (that is, a Being supremely perfect) to whom existence is lacking (that is to say, to whom a certain perfection is lacking), than to conceive of a mountain which has no valley.

But although I cannot really conceive of a God without existence any more than a mountain without a valley, still from the fact that I conceive of a mountain with a valley, it does not follow that there is such a mountain in the world; similarly although I conceive of God as possessing existence, it would seem that it does not follow that there is a God which exists; for my thought does not impose any necessity upon things, and just as I may imagine a winged horse, although no horse with wings exists, so I could perhaps attribute existence to God, although no God existed.

But a sophism is concealed in this objection; for from the fact that I cannot conceive a mountain without a valley, it does not follow that there is any mountain or any valley in existence, but only that the mountain and the valley, whether they exist or do not exist, cannot in any way be separated one from the other. While from the fact that I cannot conceive God without existence, it follows that existence is inseparable from Him, and hence that He really exists; not that my thought can bring this to pass, or impose any necessity on things, but, on the contrary, because the necessity which lies in the thing itself, i.e. the necessity of the existence of God determines me to think in this way. For it is not within my power to think of God without existence (that is of a supremely perfect Being devoid of a supreme perfection) though it is in my power to imagine a horse either with wings or without wings.

And we must not here object that it is in truth necessary for me to assert that God exists after having presupposed that He possesses every sort of perfection, since existence is one of these, but that as a matter of fact my original supposition was not necessary, just as it is not necessary to consider that all quadrilateral figures can be inscribed in the circle; for supposing I thought this, I should be constrained to admit that the rhombus might be inscribed in the circle since it is a quadrilateral figure, which, however, is manifestly false. (We must not, I say, make any such allegations because) although it is not necessary that I should at any time entertain the notion of God, nevertheless whenever it happens that I think of a first and a sovereign Being, and, so to speak, derive the idea of Him from the storehouse of my mind, it is necessary that I should attribute to Him every sort of perfection, although I do not get so far as to enumerate them all, or to apply my mind to each one in particular. And this necessity suffices to make me conclude (after having recognised that existence is a perfection) that this first and sovereign Being really exists; just as though it is not necessary for me ever to imagine any triangle, yet, whenever I wish to consider a rectilinear figure composed only of three angles, it is absolutely essential that I should attribute to it all those properties which serve to bring about the conclusion that its three angles are not greater than two right angles, even although I may not then be considering this point in particular. But when I consider which figures are capable of being inscribed in the circle, it is in no wise necessary that I should think that all quadrilateral figures are of this number; on the contrary, I cannot even pretend that this is the case, so long as I do not desire to accept anything which I cannot conceive clearly and distinctly. And in consequence there is a great difference between the false suppositions such as this, and the true ideas born within me, the first and principal of which is that of God. For really I discern in many ways that this idea is not something factitious, and depending solely on my thought, but that it is the true image of a true and immutable nature; first of all, because I cannot conceive anything but God himself to whose essence existence (necessarily) pertains; in the second place because it is not possible for me to conceive two or more Gods in this same position; and, granted that there is one such God who now exists, I see clearly that it is necessary that He should have existed from all eternity, and that He must exist eternally; and finally, because I know an infinitude of other properties in God, none of which I can either diminish or change. . . .

. . . And as regards God, if my mind were not pre-occupied with prejudices, and if my thought did not find itself on all hands diverted by the continual pressure of sensible things, there would be nothing which I could know more immediately and more easily than Him. For is there anything more manifest than that there is a God, that is to say, a Supreme Being, to whose essence alone existence pertains?

35

THE FIVE WAYS

Thomas Aquinas

THE EXISTENCE OF GOD can be proved in five ways.

The first and more manifest way is the argument from motion. It is certain, and evident to our senses, that in the world some things are in motion. Now whatever is in motion is put in motion by another, for nothing can be in motion except it is in potentiality to that towards which it is in motion; whereas a thing moves inasmuch as it is in act. For motion is nothing else than the reduction of something from potentiality to actuality. But nothing can be reduced from potentiality to actuality, except by something in a state of actuality. Thus that which is actually hot, as fire, makes wood, which is potentially hot, to be actually hot, and thereby moves and changes it. Now it is not possible that the same thing should be at once in actuality and potentiality in the same respect, but only in different respects. For what is actually hot cannot simultaneously be potentially hot; but it is simultaneously potentially cold. It is therefore impossible that in the same respect and in the same way a thing should be both mover and moved, i.e., that it should move itself. Therefore, whatever is in motion must be put in motion by another. If that by which it is put in motion be itself put in motion, then this also must needs be put in motion by another, and that by another again. But this cannot go on to infinity, because then there would be no first mover, and, consequently, no other mover; seeing that subsequent movers move only inasmuch as they are put in motion by the first mover; as the staff moves only because it is put in motion by the hand. Therefore it is necessary to arrive at a first mover, put in motion by no other; and this everyone understands to be God.

[This selection is taken from the *Summa Theologica*, Part I, translated by the English Dominican Fathers. It is here reproduced with the kind permission of Benziger Brothers, New York, and Burns Oates Washbourne, Ltd., London.]

The second way is from the nature of the efficient cause. In the world of sense we find there is an order of efficient causes. There is no case known (neither is it, indeed, possible) in which a thing is found to be the efficient cause of itself; for so it would be prior to itself, which is impossible. Now in efficient causes it is not possible to go on to infinity, because in all efficient causes following in order, the first is the cause of the intermediate cause, and the intermediate is the cause of the ultimate cause, whether the intermediate cause be several or one only. Now to take away the cause is to take away the effect. Therefore, if there be no first cause among efficient causes, there will be no ultimate, nor any intermediate cause. But if in efficient causes it is possible to go on to infinity, there will be no first efficient cause, neither will there be an ultimate effect, nor any intermediate efficient causes; all of which is plainly false. Therefore it is necessary to admit a first efficient cause, to which everyone gives the name of God.

The third way is taken from possibility and necessity and runs thus. We find in nature things that are possible to be and not to be, since they are found to be generated, and to corrupt, and consequently, they are possible to be and not to be. But it is impossible for these always to exist, for that which is possible not to be at some time is not. Therefore, if everything is possible not to be, then at one time there could have been nothing in existence. Now if this were true, even now there would be nothing in existence, because that which does not exist only begins to exist by something already existing. Therefore, if at one time nothing was in existence, it would have been impossible for anything to have begun to exist; and thus even now nothing would be in existence—which is absurd. Therefore, not all beings are merely possible, but there must exist something the existence of which is necessary. But every necessary thing either has its necessity caused by another, or not. Now it is impossible to go on to infinity in necessary things which have their necessity caused by another, as has been already proved in regard to efficient causes. Therefore we cannot but postulate the existence of some being having of itself its own necessity, and not receiving it from another, but rather causing in others their necessity. This all men speak of as God.

The fourth way is taken from the gradation to be found in things. Among beings there are some more and some less good, true, noble, and the like. But "more" and "less" are predicated of different things, according as they resemble in their different ways something which is the maximum, as a thing is said to be hotter according as it more nearly resembles that which is hottest; so that there is something which is truest, something best, something noblest, and, consequently, something which is uttermost being; for those things that are greatest in truth are greatest in being, as it is written in *Metaph*. ii. Now the maximum in any genus is the cause of all in that genus; as fire, which is the maximum of heat, is the cause of all hot things. Therefore there must also be something which is to all beings the cause of their being, goodness, and every other perfection; and this we call God.

The fifth way is taken from the governance of the world. We see that things which lack intelligence, such as natural bodies, act for an end, and this is evident from their acting always, or nearly always, in the same way, so as to obtain the best result. Hence it is plain that not fortuitously, but designedly, do they achieve their end. Now whatever lacks intelligence cannot move towards an end, unless it be directed by some being endowed with knowledge and intelligence; as the arrow is shot to its mark by the archer. Therefore some intelligent being exists by whom all natural things are directed to their end; and this being we call God.

36

COMMENTARY ON
"THE FIVE WAYS" OF AQUINAS

F. C. Copleston

. . . AQUINAS DID NOT, of course, deny that people can come to know that God exists by other ways than by philosophic reflection. Nor did he ever assert that the belief of most people who accept the proposition that God exists is the result of their having elaborated metaphysical arguments for themselves or of their having thought through the metaphysical arguments developed by others. Nor did he confuse a purely intellectual assent to the conclusion of such a metaphysical argument with a living Christian faith in and love of God. But he did think that reflection on quite familiar features of the world affords ample evidence of God's existence. The reflection itself, sustained and developed at the metaphysical level, is difficult, and he explicitly recognized and acknowledged its difficulty: he certainly did not consider that everyone is capable of sustained metaphysical reflection. At the same time the empirical facts on which this reflection is based were for him quite familiar facts. In order to see the relation of finite things to the being on which they depend we are not required to pursue scientific research, discovering hitherto unknown empirical facts. Nor does the metaphysician discover God in a manner analogous to the explorer who suddenly comes upon a hitherto unknown island or flower. It is attention and reflection which are required rather than research or exploration.

What, then, are the familiar facts which for Aquinas imply the existence of God? Mention of them can be found in the famous "five ways" of proving God's existence, which are outlined in the *Summa*

[This selection is part of Chapter 3 of F. C. Copleston's *Aquinas*, published in the Pelican Philosophy Series in 1955. It is here reprinted with the kind permission of Father Copleston and Penguin Books, Ltd.]

theologica (Ia, 2, 3). In the first way Aquinas begins by saying that "it is certain, and it is clear from sense-experience, that some things in this world are moved." It must be remembered that he, like Aristotle, understands the term "motion" in the broad sense of change, reduction from a state of potentiality to one of act; he does not refer exclusively to local motion. In the second way he starts with the remark that "we find in material things an order of efficient causes." In other words, in our experience of things and of their relations to one another we are aware of efficient causality. Thus while in the first way he begins with the fact that some things are acted upon and changed by other things, the second way is based upon the fact that some things act upon other things, as efficient causes. In the third way he starts by stating that "we find among things some which are capable of existing or not existing, since we find that some things come into being and pass away." In other words, we perceive that some things are corruptible or perishable. In the fourth proof he observes that "we find in things that some are more or less good and true and noble and so on (than others)." Finally in the fifth way he says: "we see that some things which lack knowledge, namely natural bodies, act for an end, which is clear from the fact that they always or in most cases act in the same way, in order to attain what is best."

There is, I think, little difficulty in accepting as empirical facts the starting-points of the first three ways. For nobody really doubts that some things are acted upon and changed or 'moved', that some things act on others, and that some things are perishable. Each of us is aware, for example, that he is acted upon and changed, that he sometimes acts as an efficient cause, and that he is perishable. Even if anyone were to cavil at the assertion that he is aware that he himself was born and will die, he knows very well that some other people were born and have died. But the starting-points of the two final arguments may cause some difficulty. The proposition that there are different grades of perfections in things stands in need of a much more thorough analysis than Aquinas accords it in his brief outline of the fourth way. For the schematic outlining of the five proofs was designed, not to satisfy the critical minds of mature philosophers, but as introductory material for 'novices' in the study of theology. And in any case Aquinas could naturally take for granted in the thirteenth century ideas which were familiar to his contemporaries and which had not yet been subjected to the radical criticism to which they were later subjected. At the same time there is not very much difficulty in understanding the sort of thing which was meant. We are all accustomed to think and speak as though, for example, there were different degrees of intelligence and intellectual capacity. In order to estimate the different degrees we need, it is true, standards or fixed points of reference; but, given these points of reference, we are all accustomed to make statements which imply different grades of perfections.

And though these statements stand in need of close analysis, they refer to something which falls within ordinary experience and finds expression in ordinary language. As for the fifth way, the modern reader may find great difficulty in seeing what is meant if he confines his attention to the relevant passage in the *Summa theologica*. But if he looks at the *Summa contra Gentiles* (1, 13) he will find Aquinas saying that we see things of different natures co-operating in the production and maintenance of a relatively stable order or system. When Aquinas says that we see purely material things acting for an end, he does not mean to say that they act in a manner analogous to that in which human beings consciously act for definite purposes. Indeed, the point of the argument is that they do not do so. He means that different kinds of things, like fire and water, the behaviour of which is determined by their several "forms," co-operate, not consciously but as a matter of fact, in such a way that there is a relatively stable order or system. And here again, though much more would need to be said in a full discussion of the matter, the basic idea is nothing particularly extraordinary nor is it contrary to our ordinary experience and expectations.

It is to be noted also that Aquinas speaks with considerable restraint: he avoids sweeping generalizations. Thus in the first argument he does not say that all material things are "moved" but that we see that some things in this world are moved or changed. In the third argument he does not state that all finite things are contingent but that we are aware that some things come into being and pass away. And in the fifth argument he does not say that there is an invariable world-order or system but that we see natural bodies acting always or in most cases in the same ways. The difficulty, therefore, which may be experienced in regard to Aquinas' proofs of God's existence concerns not so much the empirical facts or alleged empirical facts with which he starts as in seeing that these facts imply God's existence.

Perhaps a word should be said at once about this idea of "implication." As a matter of fact Aquinas does not use the word when talking about the five ways: he speaks of "proof" and of "demonstration." And by "demonstration" he means in this context what he calls *demonstratio quia* (*S.T.*, Ia, 2, 2), namely a causal proof of God's existence, proceeding from the affirmation of some empirical fact, for example that there are things which change, to the affirmation of a transcendent cause. It is, indeed, his second proof which is strictly the causal argument, in the sense that it deals explicitly with the order of efficient causality; but in every proof the idea of ontological dependence on a transcendent cause appears in some form or other. Aquinas' conviction was that a full understanding of the empirical facts which are selected for consideration in the five ways involves seeing the dependence of these facts on a transcendent cause. The existence of things which change, for instance, is, in his opinion, not self-explanatory: it can be rendered intelligible only if seen as dependent on a transcendent cause, a cause, that is to say, which does not itself belong to the order of changing things.

This may suggest to the modern reader that Aquinas was concerned with causal explanation in the sense that he was concerned with framing an empirical hypothesis to explain certain facts. But he did not regard the proposition affirming God's existence as a causal hypothesis in the sense of being in principle revisable, as a hypothesis, that is to say, which might conceivably have to be revised in the light of fresh empirical data or which might be supplanted by a more economical hypothesis. This point can perhaps be seen most clearly in the case of his third argument, which is based on the fact that there are things which come into being and pass away. In Aquinas' opinion no fresh scientific knowledge about the physical constitution of such things could affect the validity of the argument. He did not look on a "demonstration" of God's existence as an empirical hypothesis in the sense in which the electronic theory, for example, is said to be an empirical hypothesis. It is, of course, open to anyone to say that in his own opinion cosmological arguments in favour of God's existence are in fact analogous to the empirical hypotheses of the sciences and that they have a predictive function; but it does not follow that this interpretation can legitimately be ascribed to Aquinas. We should not be misled by the illustrations which he sometimes offers from contemporary scientific theory. For these are mere illustrations to elucidate a point in terms easily understandable by his readers: they are not meant to indicate that the proofs of God's existence were for him empirical hypotheses in the modern sense of the term.

Does this mean, therefore, that Aquinas regarded the existence of God as being logically entailed by facts such as change or coming into being and passing away? He did not, of course, regard the proposition "there are things which come into being and pass away" as logically entailing the proposition "there is an absolutely necessary or independent being" in the sense that affirmation of the one proposition and denial of the other involves one in a verbal or formal linguistic contradiction. But he thought that metaphysical analysis of what it objectively means to be a thing which comes into being and passes away shows that such a thing must depend existentially on an absolutely necessary being. And he thought that metaphysical analysis of what it objectively means to be a changing thing shows that such a thing depends on a supreme unmoved mover. It follows that for Aquinas one is involved in a contradiction if one affirms the propositions "there are things which come into being and pass away" and "there are things which change" and at the same time denies the propositions "there is an absolutely necessary being" and "there is a supreme unmoved mover." But the contradiction can be made apparent only by means of metaphysical analysis. And the entailment in question is fundamentally an ontological or causal entailment. . . .

. . . After these general remarks I turn to Aquinas' five proofs of the existence of God. In the first proof he argues that "motion" or change means the reduction of a thing from a state of potentiality to one of act, and that a thing cannot be reduced from potentiality to act except under the influence of an agent already in act. In this sense "everything which is moved must be moved by another." He argues finally that in order to avoid an infinite regress in the chain of movers, the existence of a first unmoved mover must be admitted. "And all understand that this is God."

A statement like "all understand that this is God" or "all call this (being) God" occurs at the end of each proof, and I postpone consideration of it for the moment. As for the ruling out of an infinite regress, I shall explain what Aquinas means to reject after outlining the second proof, which is similar in structure to the first.

Whereas in the first proof Aquinas considers things as being acted upon, as being changed or "moved," in the second he considers them as active agents, as efficient causes. He argues that there is a hierarchy of efficient causes, a subordinate cause being dependent on the cause above it in the hierarchy. He then proceeds, after excluding the hypothesis of an infinite regress, to draw the conclusion that there must be a first efficient cause, "which all call God."

Now, it is obviously impossible to discuss these arguments profitably unless they are first understood. And misunderstanding of them is only too easy, since the terms and phrases used are either unfamiliar or liable to be taken in a sense other than the sense intended. In the first place it is essential to understand that in the first argument Aquinas supposes that movement or change is dependent on a "mover" acting here and now, and that in the second argument he supposes that there are efficient causes in the world which even in their causal activity are here and now dependent on the causal activity of other causes. That is why I have spoken of a "hierarchy" rather than of a "series." What he is thinking of can be illustrated in this way. A son is dependent on his father, in the sense that he would not have existed except for the causal activity of his father. But when the son acts for himself, he is not dependent here and now on his father. But he is dependent here and now on other factors. Without the activity of the air, for instance, he could not himself act, and the life-preserving activity of the air is itself dependent here and now on other factors, and they in turn on other factors. I do not say that this illustration is in all respects adequate for the purpose; but it at least illustrates the fact that when Aquinas talks about an "order" of efficient causes he is not thinking of a series stretching back into the past, but of a hierarchy of causes, in which a subordinate member is here and now dependent on the causal activity of a higher member. If I wind up my watch at night, it then proceeds to work without further interference on my part. But the activity of the pen tracing these words on the page is here and now dependent on the activity of my hand, which in turn is here and now dependent on other factors.

The meaning of the rejection of an infinite regress should now be clear. Aquinas is not rejecting the possibility of an infinite series as such. We have already seen that he did not think that anyone had ever succeeded in showing the impossibility of an infinite series of events stretching back into the past. Therefore he does not mean to rule out the possibility of an infinite series of causes and effects, in which a given member depended on the preceding member, say X on Y, but does not, once it exists, depend here and now on the present causal activity of the preceding member. We have to imagine, not a lineal or horizontal series, so to speak, but a vertical hierarchy, in which a lower member depends here and now on the present causal activity of the member above it. It is the latter type of series, if prolonged to infinity, which Aquinas rejects. And he rejects it on the ground that unless there is a "first" member, a mover which is not itself moved or a cause which does not itself depend on the causal activity of a higher cause, it is not possible to explain the 'motion' or the causal activity of the lowest member. His point of view is this. Suppress the first unmoved mover and there is no motion or change here and now. Suppress the first efficient cause and there is no causal activity here and now. If therefore we find that some things in the world are changed, there must be a first unmoved mover. And if there are efficient causes in the world, there must be a first efficient, and completely non-dependent cause. The word "first" does not mean first in the temporal order, but supreme or first in the ontological order.

A remark on the word "cause" is here in place. What precisely Aquinas would have said to the David Humes either of the fourteenth century or of the modern era it is obviously impossible to say. But it is clear that he believed in real causal efficacy and real causal relations. He was aware, of course, that causal efficacy is not the object of vision in the sense in which patches of colours are objects of vision; but the human being, he considered, is aware of real causal relations and if we understand "perception" as involving the co-operation of sense and intellect, we can be said to "perceive" causality. And presumably he would have said that the sufficiency of a phenomenalistic interpretation of causality for purposes of physical science proves nothing against the validity of a metaphysical notion of causality. It is obviously possible to dispute whether his analyses of change or 'motion' and of efficient causality are valid or invalid and whether there is such a thing as a hierarchy of causes. And our opinion about the validity or invalidity of his arguments for the existence of God will depend very largely on our answers to these questions. But mention of the mathematical infinite series is irrelevant to a discussion of his arguments. And it is this point which I have been trying to make clear.

In the third proof Aquinas starts from the fact that some things come into being and perish, and he concludes from this that it is possible for them to exist or not to exist: they do not exist "necessarily." He then argues that it is impossible for things which are of this kind to exist always; for "that which is capable of not existing, at some time does not exist." If all things were of this kind, at some time there would be nothing. Aquinas is clearly supposing for the sake of argument the hypothesis of infinite time, and his proof is designed to cover this hypothesis. He does not say that infinite time is impossible: what he says is that if time is infinite and if all things are capable of not existing, this potentiality would inevitably be fulfilled in infinite time. There would then be nothing. And if there had ever been nothing, nothing would now exist. For no thing can bring itself into existence. But it is clear as a matter of fact that there are things. Therefore it can never have been true to say that there was literally no thing. Therefore it is impossible that all things should be capable of existing or not existing. There must, then, be some necessary being. But perhaps it is necessary in the sense that it must exist if something else exists; that is to say, its necessity may be hypothetical. We cannot, however, proceed to infinity in the series or hierarchy of necessary beings. If we do so, we do not explain the presence here and now of beings capable of existing or not existing. Therefore we must affirm the existence of a being which is absolutely necessary (*per se necessarium*) and completely independent. "And all call this being *God*."

This argument may appear to be quite unnecessarily complicated and obscure. But it has to be seen in its historical context. As already mentioned, Aquinas designed his argument in such a way as to be independent of the question whether or not the world existed from eternity. He wanted to show that on either hypothesis there must be a necessary being. As for the introduction of hypothetical necessary beings, he wanted to show that even if there are such beings, perhaps within the universe, which are not corruptible in the sense in which a flower is corruptible, there must still be an absolutely independent being. Finally, in regard to terminology, Aquinas uses the common medieval expression "necessary being." He does not actually use the term "contingent being" in the argument and talks instead about "possible" beings; but it comes to the same thing. And though the words "contingent" and "necessary" are now applied to propositions rather than to beings, I have retained Aquinas' mode of speaking. Whether one accepts the argument or not, I do not think that there is any insuperable difficulty in understanding the line of thought.

The fourth argument is admittedly difficult to grasp. Aquinas argues that there are degrees of perfections in things. Different kinds of finite things possess different perfections in diverse limited degrees. He then argues not only that if there are different degrees of a perfection like goodness there is a supreme good to which other good things approximate but also that all limited degrees of goodness are caused by the supreme good. And since goodness is a convertible term with being, a thing being good in so far as it has being, the supreme good is the supreme being and the cause of being in all other things. "Therefore there is something which is the cause of the being and goodness and of every perfection in all other things; and this we call *God*."

Aquinas refers to some remarks of Aristotle in the *Metaphysics;* but this argument puts one in mind at once of Plato's *Symposium* and *Republic*. And the Platonic doctrine of participation seems to be involved. Aquinas was not immediately acquainted with either work, but the Platonic line of thought was familiar to him from other writers. And it has not disappeared from philosophy. Indeed, some of those theists who reject or doubt the validity of the "cosmological" arguments seem to feel a marked attraction for some variety of the fourth way, arguing that in the recognition of objective values we implicitly recognize God as the supreme value. But if the line of thought represented by the fourth way is to mean anything to the average modern reader, it has to be presented in a rather different manner from that in which it is expressed by Aquinas who was able to assume in his readers ideas and points of view which can no longer be presupposed.

Finally, the fifth proof, if we take its statement in the *Summa theologica* together with that in the *Summa contra Gentiles,* can be expressed more or less as follows. The activity and behaviour of each thing is determined by its form. But we observe material things of very different types co-operating in such a way as to produce and maintain a relatively stable world-order or system. They achieve an "end," the production and maintenance of a cosmic order. But non-intelligent material things certainly do not co-operate consciously in view of a purpose. If it is said that they co-operate in the realization of an end or purpose, this does not mean that they intend the realization of this order in a manner analogous to that in which a man can act consciously with a view to the achievement of a purpose. Nor, when Aquinas talks about operating "for an end" in this connexion, is he thinking of the utility of certain things to the human race. He is not saying, for example, that grass grows to feed the sheep and that sheep exist in order that human being should have food and clothing. It is of the unconscious co-operation of different kinds of material things in the production and maintenance of a relatively stable cosmic system that he is thinking, not of the benefits accruing to us from our use of certain objects. And his argument is that this co-operation on the part of heterogeneous material things clearly points to the existence of an extrinsic intelligent author of this co-operation, who operates with an end in view. If Aquinas had lived in the days of the evolutionary hypothesis, he would doubtless have argued that this hypothesis supports rather than invalidates the conclusion of the argument.

37

THE WATCH
AND THE HUMAN EYE

William Paley

A Watch Implies a Watchmaker

IN CROSSING A HEATH, suppose I pitched my foot against a *stone,* and were asked how the stone came to be there; I might possibly answer, that, for anything I knew to the contrary, it had lain there forever: nor would it perhaps be very easy to show the absurdity of this answer. But suppose I had found a *watch* upon the ground, and it should be inquired how the watch happened to be in that place: I should hardly think of the answer which I had before given, that, for anything I knew, the watch might have always been there. Yet why should not this answer serve for the watch as well as for the stone? Why is it not as admissible in the second case, as in the first? For this reason, and for no other, viz. that, when we come to inspect the watch, we perceive (what we could not discover in the stone) that its several parts are framed and put together for a purpose, e.g. that they are so formed and adjusted as to produce motion, and that motion so regulated, as to point out the hour of the day; that if the different parts had been differently shaped from what they are, of a different size from what they are, or placed after any other manner, or in any other order, that that in which they are placed, either no motion at all would have been carried on in the machine, or none which would have answered the use that is now served by it. . . . This mechanism being observed (it requires indeed an examination of the instrument, and perhaps some previous knowledge of the subject, to perceive and understand it; but being once, as we have said, observed

[This selection comprises part of Chapters I-VI of Paley's *Evidences of the Existence and Attributes of the Deity,* a book first published in 1802.]

483

and understood,) the inference, we think, is inevitable; that the watch must have had a maker; that there must have existed, at sometime, and at some place or other, an artificer or artificers, who formed it for the purpose which we find it actually to answer; who comprehended its construction, and designed its use.

Nor would it, I apprehend, weaken the conclusion, that we had never seen a watch made, that we had never known an artist capable of making one; that we were altogether incapable of executing such a piece of workmanship ourselves, or of understanding in what manner it was performed; all this being no more than what is true of some exquisite remains of ancient art, of some lost arts, and, to the generality of mankind, of the more curious productions of modern manufacture. Does one man in a million know how oval frames are turned? Ignorance of this kind exalts our opinion of the artist's skill, if he be unseen and unknown, but raises no doubt in our minds of the existence and agency of such an artist, at some former time, and in some place or other. Nor can I perceive that it varies at all the inference, whether the question arise concerning a human agent, or concerning an agent of a different species, or an agent possessing, in some respects, a different nature.

Neither, secondly, would it invalidate our conclusion, that the watch sometimes went wrong, or that it seldom went exactly right. The purpose of the machinery, the design and the designer, might be evident, and in the case supposed would be evident, in whatever way we accounted for the irregularity of the movement, or whether we could account for it or not. It is not necessary that a machine be perfect, in order to show with what design it was made: still less necessary, where the only question is, whether it were made with any design at all.

Nor, thirdly, would it bring any uncertainty into the argument, if there were a few parts of the watch, concerning which we could not discover, or had not yet discovered, in what manner they conduced to the general effect; or even some parts, concerning which we could not ascertain whether they conduced to that effect in any manner whatever. For, as to the first branch of the case; if by the loss, or disorder, or decay of the parts in question, the movement of the watch were found in fact to be stopped, or disturbed, or retarded, no doubt would remain in our minds as to the utility or intention of these parts, although we should be unable to investigate the manner according to which, or the connexion by which, the ultimate effect depended upon their action or assistance; and the more complex is the machine, the more likely is this obscurity to arise. Then, as to the second thing supposed, namely, that there were parts which might be spared, without prejudice to the movement of the watch, and that we had proved this by experiment—these superfluous parts, even if we were completely assured that they were such, would not vacate the reasoning which we had instituted concerning other parts.

The indication of contrivance remained, with respect to them, nearly as it was before.

Nor, fourthly, would any man in his senses think the existence of the watch, with its various machinery, accounted for, by being told that it was one out of possible combinations of material forms; that whatever he had found in the place where he found the watch, must have contained some internal configuration or other; and that this configuration might be the structure now exhibited, viz. of the works of a watch, as well as a different structure.

Nor, fifthly, would it yield to his inquiry more satisfaction to be answered, that there existed in things a principle of order, which had disposed the parts of the watch into their present form and situation. He never knew a watch made by the principle of order; nor can he even form to himself an idea of what is meant by a principle of order distinct from the intelligence of the watchmaker.

Sixthly, he would be surprised to hear that the mechanism of the watch was no proof of contrivance, only a motive to induce the mind to think so. . . .

Neither, lastly, would our observer be driven out of his conclusion, or from his confidence in its truth, by being told that he knew nothing at all about the matter. He knows enough for his argument. He knows the utility of the end: he knows the subserviency and adaptation of the means to the end. These points being known, his ignorance of other points, affect not the certainty of his reasoning. The consciousness of knowing little need not beget a distrust of that which he does know.

Even a "Self-Reproducing" Watch
Implies a Watchmaker

Suppose, in the next place, that the person who found the watch, should, after sometime, discover, that, in addition to all the properties which he had hitherto observed in it, it possessed the unexpected property of producing, in the course of its movement, another watch like itself (the thing is conceivable), that it contained within it a mechanism, a system of parts, a mould for instance, or a complex adjustment of lathes, files, and other tools, evidently and separately calculated for this purpose; let us inquire, what effect ought such a discovery to have upon his former conclusion.

The first effect would be to increase his admiration of the contrivance, and his conviction of the consummate skill of the contriver. Whether he regarded the object of the contrivance, the distinct apparatus, the intricate, yet in many parts intelligible mechanism, by which it was carried on, he would perceive in this new observation, nothing but an additional reason for doing what he had already done,—for referring the construction of the watch to design, and to supreme art. If that construction *without* this property, or which is the same thing, before this property had been noticed, proved intention and art to have been employed about it, still more strong would the proof appear, when he came to the knowledge of this farther property, the crown and perfection of all the rest.

He would reflect, that though the watch before him were, *in some sense,* the maker of the watch which was fabricated in the course of its movements, yet it was in a very different sense from that in which a carpenter, for instance, is the maker of a chair; the author of its contrivance, the cause of the relation of its parts to their use. With respect to these, the first watch was no cause at all to the second: in no such sense as this was it the author of the constitution and order, either of the parts which the new watch contained, or of the parts by the aid and instrumentality of which it was produced. We might possibly say, but with great latitude of expression, that a stream of water ground corn; but no latitude of expression would allow us to say, no stretch of conjecture could lead us to think, that the stream of water built the mill, though it were too ancient for us to know who the builder was. What the stream of water does in the affair, is neither more nor less than this; by the application of an unintelligent impulse to a mechanism previously arranged, arranged independently of it, and arranged by intelligence, an effect is produced, viz. the corn is ground. But the effect results from the arrangement. The force of the stream cannot be said to be the cause or author of the effect, still less of the arrangement. Understanding and plan in the formation of the mill were not the less necessary, for any share which the water has in grinding the corn; yet is this share the same as that which the watch would have contributed to the production of the new watch, upon the supposition assumed in the last section. Therefore:

Though it be now no longer probable, that the individual watch which our observer had found was made immediately by the hand of an artificer, yet doth not this alteration in anywise affect the inference, that an artificer had been originally employed and concerned in the production. The argument from design remains as it was. Marks of design and contrivance are no more accounted for now than they were before. In the same thing, we may ask for the cause of different properties. We may ask for the cause of the color of a body, of its hardness, of its heat; and these causes may be all different. We are now asking for the cause of that subserviency to a case, that relation to an end, which we have remarked in the watch before us. No answer is given to this question by telling us that a preceding watch produced it. There cannot be design without a designer; contrivance, without a contriver; order, without choice; arrangement, without anything capable of arranging; subserviency and relation to a purpose, without that which could intend a purpose; means suitable to an end, and executing their office in accomplishing that end, without the end ever having been contemplated, or the means accommodated to it. Arrangement, disposition of parts, subserviency of means to an end, relation of instruments to a use, imply the presence of intelligence and mind. No one, therefore, can rationally believe, that the insensible, inanimate watch, from which the watch before us issued, was the proper cause of the mechanism we so much admire in it;—could be truly said to have constructed the instrument, disposed its parts, assigned their office, determined their order, action, and mutual dependency, combined their several motions into one result, and that also a result connected with the utilities of other beings. All these properties, therefore, are as much unaccounted for as they were before.

Impossibility of an Infinite Regress

Nor is anything gained by running the difficulty farther back, i.e., by supposing the watch before us to have been produced from another watch, that from a former, and so on indefinitely. Our going back ever so far brings us no nearer to the least degree of satisfaction upon the subject. Contrivance is still unaccounted for. We still want a contriver. A designing mind is neither supplied by this supposition, nor dispensed with. If the difficulty were diminished the farther we went back, by going back indefinitely we might exhaust it. And this is the only case to which this sort of reasoning applies. Where there is a tendency, or, as we increase the number of terms, a continual approach towards a limit, *there,* by supposing the number of terms to be what is called infinite, we may conceive the limit to be attained: but where there is no such tendency, or approach, nothing is effected by lengthening the series. There is no difference, as to the point in question (whatever there may be as to many points), between one series and another; between a series which is finite, and a series which is infinite. A chain, composed of an infinite number of links, can no more support itself, than a chain composed of a finite number of links. And of this we are assured (though we never *can* have tried the experiment), because, by increasing the number of links, from ten, for instance, to a hundred, from a hundred to a thousand, etc. we make not the smallest approach, we observe not the smallest tendency, towards self-support. There is no difference in this respect (yet there may be a great difference in several respects) between a chain of a greater or less length, between one chain and another, between one that is finite and one that is infinite. This very much resembles the case before us. The machine which we are inspecting demonstrates, by its construction, contrivance and design. Contrivance must have had a contriver; design, a designer; whether the machine immediately proceeded from another machine or not. That circumstance alters not the case. That other machine may, in like manner, have proceeded from a former machine: nor does that alter the case; contrivance must have had a contriver. That former one from one preceding it: no alteration still; a contriver is still necessary. No tendency is perceived, no approach towards a diminution of this necessity. It is the same with any and every succession of these machines; a succession of ten, of a hundred, of a thousand; with one series as with another; a series which is finite, as with a series which is infinite. In whatever other respects they may differ, in this they do not. In all, equally, contrivance and design are unaccounted for.

The question is not simply, How came the first watch into existence? which question, it may be pretended, is done away by supposing the series of watches thus produced from one another to have been infinite, and consequently to have had no such *first,* for which it was necessary to provide a cause. This, perhaps, would have been nearly the state of the question, if nothing had been before us but an unorganized, unmechanized substance, without mark or indication of contrivance. It might be difficult to show that such substance could not have existed from eternity, either in succession (if it were possible, which I think it is not, for unorganized bodies to spring from one another) or by individual perpetuity. But that is not the question now. To suppose it to be so, is to suppose that it made no difference whether we had found a watch or a stone. As it is, the metaphysics of that question have no place; for, in the watch which we are examining, are seen contrivance, design; an end, a purpose; means for the end, adaptation to the purpose. And the question which irresistibly presses upon our thoughts, is, whence this contrivance and design? The thing required is the intending mind, the adapting hand, the intelligence by which the hand was directed. This question, this demand, is not shaken off, by increasing a number or succession of substances, destitute of these properties; nor the more, by increasing that number to infinity. If it be said, that upon the supposition of one watch being produced from another in the course of that other's movements, and by means of the mechanism within it, we have a cause for the watch in my hand, viz. the watch from which it proceeded: I deny, that for the design, the contrivance, the suitableness of means to an end, the adaptation of instruments to a use (all means which we discover in a watch), we have any cause whatever. It is in vain, therefore, to assign a series of such causes, or to allege that a series may be carried back to infinity; for I do not admit that we have yet any cause at all of the phenomena, still less any series of causes either finite or infinite. Here is contrivance, but no contriver: proofs of design, but no designer.

Our observer would farther also reflect, that the maker of the watch before him, was, in truth and reality, the maker of every watch produced from it; there being no difference (except that the latter manifests a more exquisite skill) between the making of another watch with his own hands, by the mediation of files, lathes, chisels, etc. and the disposing, fixing, and inserting of these instruments, or of others equivalent to them, in the body of the watch already made, in such a manner as to form a new watch in the course of the movements which he had given to the old one. It is only working by one set of tools instead of another.

The conclusion which the *first* examination of the watch, of its works, construction, and movement, suggested, was, that it must have had, for the cause and author of that construction, an artificer, who understood its mechanism, and designed its use. This conclusion is invincible. A *second* examination presents us with a new discovery. The watch is found, in the course of its movement, to produce another watch, similar to itself: and not only so, but we perceive in it a system or organization, separately calculated for that purpose. What effect would this discovery have or ought it to have, upon our former inference? What, as hath already been said, but to increase, beyond measure, our admiration of the skill which had been employed in the formation of such a machine! Or shall it, instead of this, all at once turn us round to an opposite conclusion viz. that no art or skill whatever has been concerned in the business, although all other evidences of art and skill remain as they were, and this last and supreme piece of art be now added to the rest? Can this be maintained without absurdity? Yet this is atheism.

This is atheism: for every indication of contrivance, every manifestation of design, which existed in the watch, exists in the works of nature; with the difference, on the side of nature, of being greater and more, and that in a degree which exceeds all computation. I mean, that the contrivances of nature surpass the contrivances of art, in the complexity, subtlety, and curiosity of the mechanism; and still more, if possible, do they go beyond them in number and variety: yet, in a multitude of cases, are not less evidently mechanical, not less evidently contrivances, not less evidently accommodated to their end, or suited to their office, than are the most perfect productions of human ingenuity.

The Eye and the Telescope

I know no better method of introducing so large a subject, than that of comparing a single thing with a single thing; an eye, for example, with a telescope. As far as the examination of the instrument goes, there is precisely the same proof that the eye was made for vision, as there is that the telescope was made for assisting it. They are made upon the same principles; both being adjusted to the laws by which the transmission and reflection of rays of light are regulated. I speak not of the origin of the laws themselves; but such laws being fixed, the construction in both cases, is adapted to them. For instance; these laws require, in order to produce the same effect, that the rays of light, in passing from water into the eye, should be refracted by a more convex surface than when it passes out of air into the eye. Accordingly we find, that the eye of a fish, in that part of it called the crystalline lens, is much rounder than the eye of terrestrial animals. What plainer manifestation of design can there be than this difference? What could a mathematical instrument-maker have done more, to show his knowledge, of his principle, his application of that knowledge, his suiting of his means to his end; I will not say to display the compass or excellence of his skill and art, for in these all comparison is indecorous, but to testify counsel, choice, consideration, purpose?

To some it may appear a difference sufficient to destroy all similitude between the eye and the telescope, that the one is a perceiving organ, the other an unperceiving instrument. The fact is, that they are both instruments. And as to the mechanism, at least as to mechanism being employed, and even as to the kind of it, this circumstance varies not the analogy at all. . . . The lenses of the telescope, and the humours of the eye, bear a complete resemblance to one another, in their figure, their position, and in their power over the rays of light, viz. in bringing each pencil to a point at the right distance from the lens; namely, in the eye, at the exact place where the membrane is spread to receive it. How is it possible, under circumstances of such close affinity, and under the operation of equal evidence, to exclude contrivance from the one, yet to acknowledge the proof of contrivance having been employed, as the plainest and clearest of all propositions, in the other?

The resemblance between the two cases is still more accurate, and obtains in more points than we have yet represented, or than we are, on the first view of the subject, aware of. In dioptric telescopes there is an imperfection of this nature. Pencils of light, in passing through glass lenses, are separated into different colors, thereby tinging the object, especially the edges of it, as if it were viewed through a prism. To correct this inconvenience had been long a desideratum in the art. At last it came into the mind of a sagacious optician, to inquire how this matter was managed in the eye; in which there was exactly the same difficulty to contend with as in the telescope. His observation taught him, that, in the eye, the evil was cured by combining lenses composed of different substances, i.e. of substances which possessed different refracting powers. Our artist borrowed thence his hint; and produced a correction of the

defect by imitating, in glasses made from different materials, the effects
of the different humours through which the rays of light pass before they
reach the bottom of the eye. Could this be in the eye without purpose,
which suggested to the optician the only effectual means of attaining that
purpose?

But farther; there are other points, not so much perhaps of strict
resemblance between the two, as of superiority of the eye over the telescope, which being found in the laws that regulate both, may furnish
topics of fair and just comparison. . . .

Further Evidence of Design in the Eye

In considering vision as achieved by the means of an image formed
at the bottom of the eye, we can never reflect without wonder upon the
smallness, yet correctness, of the picture, the subtility of the touch, the
fineness of the lines. A landscape of five or six square leagues is brought
into a space of half an inch diameter; yet the multitude of objects which
it contains, are all preserved; are all discriminated in their magnitudes,
positions, figures, colors. The prospect from Hampstead-hill is compressed into the compass of a sixpence, yet circumstantially represented.
A stage-coach, travelling at its ordinary speed for half an hour, passes,
in the eye, only over one-twelfth of an inch, yet is this change of place
in the image distinctly perceived throughout its whole progress; for it is
only by means of that perception that the motion of the coach itself is
made sensible to the eye. If anything can abate our admiration of the
smallness of the visual tablet compared with the extent of vision, it is a
reflection, which the view of nature leads us, every hour, to make, viz.
that in the hands of the Creator, great and little or nothing.

Sturmius held, that the examination of the eye was a cure for atheism.
Besides that conformity to optical principles which its internal constitution displays, and which alone amounts to a manifestation of intelligence
having been exerted in the structure; besides this, which forms no doubt,
the leading character of the organ, there is to be seen, in everything
belonging to it and about it, an extraordinary degree of care, and anxiety
for its preservation, due, if we may so speak, to its value and its tenderness. It is lodged in a strong, deep, bony socket, composed by the junction of seven different bones, hollowed out at their edges. In some few
species, as that of the coatimondi, the orbit is not bony throughout; but
whenever this is the case, the upper, which is the deficient part, is supplied by a cartilaginous ligament; a substitution which shows the same
care. Within this socket it is embedded in fat, of all animal substances
the best adapted both to its repose and motion. It is sheltered by the eye-

brows; an arch of hair, which like a thatched penthouse, prevents the sweat and moisture of the forehead from running down into it.

But it is still better protected by its lid. Of the superficial parts of the animal frame, I know none which, in its office and structure, is more deserving of attention than the eyelid. It defends the eye; it wipes it; it closes it in sleep. Are there, in any work of art whatever, purposes more evident than those which this organ fulfills? or an apparatus for executing those purposes more intelligible, more appropriate, or more mechanical? If it be overlooked by the observer of nature, it can only be because it is obvious and familiar. This is a tendency to be guarded against. We pass by the plainest instances, whilst we are exploring those which are rare and curious; by which conduct of the understanding, we sometimes neglect the strongest observations, being taken up with others, which though more recondite and scientific, are, as solid arguments, entitled to much less consideration.

In order to keep the eye moist and clean (which qualities are necessary to its brightness and its use), a wash is constantly supplied by a secretion for the purpose; and the superfluous brine is conveyed to the nose through a perforation in the bone as large as a goose-quill. When once the fluid has entered the nose, it spreads itself upon the inside of the nostril, and is evaporated by the current of warm air, which, in the course of respiration, is continually passing over it. Can any pipe or outlet for carrying off the waste liquor from a dye-house or a distillery, be more mechanical than this is? It is easily perceived, that the eye must want moisture: but could the want of the eye generate the gland which produces the tear, or bore the hole by which it is discharged, —a hole through a bone? . . . .

Some Objections Answered

Every observation which was made concerning the watch, may be repeated with strict propriety concerning the eye; concerning animals; concerning plants; concerning, indeed, all the organized parts of the works of nature:

1. Imperfections in the Mechanism

When we are inquiring simply after the existence of an intelligent Creator, imperfection, inaccuracy, liability to disorder, occasional irregularities, may subsist in a considerable degree, without inducing any doubt into the question; just as a watch may frequently go wrong, seldom perhaps exactly right, may be faulty in some parts, defective in some, without the smallest ground of suspicion from thence arising that it was not a watch; not made; or not made for the purpose ascribed to it. When faults are pointed out, and when a question is started concerning the skill of the artist, or the dexterity with which the work is executed, then, indeed, in order to defend these qualities from accusation, we must be able, either to expose some intractableness and imperfection in the materials, or point out some invincible difficulty in the execution, into which imperfection and difficulty the matter of complaint may be resolved; or if we cannot do this, we must adduce such specimens of consummate art and contrivance, proceeding from the same hand, as may convince the inquirer of the existence, in the case before him, of impediments like those which we have mentioned, although, what from the nature of the case is very likely to happen, they be unknown and unperceived by him. This we must do in order to vindicate the artist's skill, or, at least, the perfection of it; as we must also judge of his intention, and of the provision employed in fulfilling that intention, not from an instance in which they fail, but from the great plurality of instances in which they succeed. But, after all, these are different questions from the question of the artist's existence; or, which is the same, whether the thing before us be a work of art or not: and the question ought always to be kept separate in the mind. So likewise it is in the works of nature. Irregularities and imperfections are of little or no weight in the consideration, when that consideration relates simply to the existence of a Creator. When the argument respects his attributes, they are of weight; but are then to be taken in conjunction (the attention is not to rest upon them, but they are to be taken in conjunction) with the unexceptionable evidences which we possess, of skill, power, and benevolence, displayed in other instances; which evidences may, in strength, number; and variety, be such, and may so overpower apparent blemishes, as to induce us, upon the most reasonable ground, to believe, that these last ought to be referred to some cause, though we be ignorant of it, other than defect of knowledge or of benevolence in the author.

2. Apparently Useless Parts

There may be also parts of plants and animals, as there were supposed to be of the watch, of which, in some instances, the operation, in others, the use, is unknown. These form different causes; for the operation may be unknown, yet the use be certain. Thus it is with the lungs of animals. It does not, I think, appear, that we are acquainted with the action of the air upon the blood, or in what manner that action is communicated by the lungs; yet we find that a very short suspension of their office destroys the life of the animal. In this case, therefore, we may be said to know the use, nay we experience the necessity, of the organ, though we are ignorant of its operation. Nearly the same thing may be observed of what is called the lymphatic system. We suffer grievous inconveniences from its disorder, without being informed of the office which it sustains in the economy of our bodies. There may possibly also be some few examples of the second class, in which not only the operation is unknown, but in which experiments may seem to prove that the part is not necessary; or may leave a doubt, how far it is even useful to the plant or animal in which it is found. This is said to be the case with the spleen; which has been extracted from dogs, without any sensible injury to their vital function. Instances of the former kind, namely, in which we cannot explain the operation, may be numerous; for they will be so in proportion to our ignorance. They will be more or fewer to different persons, and in different stages of science. Every improvement of knowledge diminishes their number. There is hardly, perhaps, a year passes that does not, in the works of nature, bring some operation, or some mode of operation, to light, which was before undiscovered,— probably unsuspected. Instances of the second kind, namely, where the part appears to be totally useless, I believe to be extremely rare; compared with the number of those of which the use is evident, they are beneath any assignable proportion; and, perhaps, have never been submitted to a trial and examination sufficiently accurate, long enough continued, or often enough repeated. No accounts which I have seen are satisfactory. The mutilated animal may live and grow fat, (as was the case of the dog deprived of its spleen,) yet may be defective in some other of its functions; which, whether they can all, or in what degree of vigor and perfection, be performed, or how long preserved, without the extirpated organ, does not seem to be ascertained by experiment. But to this case, even were it fully made out, may be applied the consideration which we suggested concerning the watch, viz. that these superfluous parts do not negative the reasoning which we instituted concerning those parts which are useful, and of which we know the use. The indication of contrivance, with respect to them, remains as it was before.

3. The Possible Role of Chance

One atheistic way of replying to our observations upon the works of nature, and to the proofs of a Deity which we think that we perceive in them, is to tell us, that all which we see must necessarily have had some form, and that it might as well be its present form as any other. Let us now apply this answer to the eye, as we did before to the watch. Something or other must have occupied that place in the animal's head; must have filled up, we will say, that socket: we will say also, that it must have been of that sort of substance which we call animal substance, as flesh, bone, membrane, cartilage, etc. But that it should have been an eye, knowing as we do, what an eye comprehends—viz. that it should have consisted, first, of a series of transparent lenses (very different, by the by, even in their substance, from the opaque materials of which the rest of the body is, in general at least, composed; and with which the whole of its surface, this single portion of it excepted, is covered); secondly, of a black cloth or canvas (the only membrane of the body which is black) spread out behind these lenses, so as to receive the image formed by pencils of light transmitted through them; and placed at the precise geometrical distance at which, and at which alone, a distinct image could be formed, namely, at the concourse of the refracted rays; thirdly, of a large nerve communicating between this membrane and the brain; without which, the action of light upon the membrane; however modified by the organ, would be lost to the purposes of sensation: that this fortunate conformation of parts should have been the lot, not of one individual out of many thousand individuals, like the great prize in a lottery, or like some singularity in nature, but the happy chance of a whole species; nor of one species out of many thousand species, with which we are acquainted, but of by far the greatest number of all that exist; and that under varieties, not casual or capricious, but bearing marks of being suited to their respective exigencies—that all this should have taken place, merely because something must have occupied those points in every animal's forehead—or, that all this should be thought to be accounted for, by the short answer, "that whatever was there, must have had some form or other," is too absurd to be made more so by any augmentation. We are not contented with this answer; we find no satisfaction in it, by way of accounting for appearances of organization far short of those of the eye, such as we observe in fossil shells, petrified bones, or other substances which bear the vestiges of animal or vegetable recrements, but which, either in respect of utility, or of the situation in which they are discovered, may seem accidental enough. It is no way of accounting even for these things, to say that the stone, for instance, which is shown to us, (supposing the question to be concerning a petrification,) must have contained some internal conformation or other. Nor does it mend the answer to add, with respect to the singularity of the conformation, that, after the event, it is no longer to be computed what the chances were against it. This is always to be computed, when the question is, whether a useful or imitative conformation be the produce of chance, or not: I desire no greater certainty in reasoning, than that by which chance is excluded from the present disposition of the natural world. Universal experience is against it. What does chance ever do for us? In

the human body, for instance, chance, i.e., the operation of causes without design, may produce a wen, a wart, a mole, a pimple, but never an
eye. Amongst inanimate substances, a clod, a pebble, a liquid drop might
be; but never was a watch, a telescope an organized body of any kind;
answering a valuable purpose by a complicated mechanism, the effect
of chance. In no assignable instance hath such a thing existed without
intention somewhere.

4. The Theory of the Elimination of the Unfit

There is another answer, which has the same effect as the resolving
of things into chance; which answer would persuade us to believe,
that the eye, the animal to which it belongs, every other animal, every
plant, indeed every organized body which we see, are only so many out
of the possible varieties and combinations of being which the lapse of
infinite ages has brought into existence: that the present world is the
relic of that variety; millions of other bodily forms and other species
having perished, being by the defect of their constitutions incapable of
preservation, or of continuance by generation. Now there is no foundation whatever for this conjecture in anything which we observe in the
works of nature; no such experiments are going on at present; no such
energy operates, as that which is here supposed, and which should be
constantly pushing into existence new varieties of beings: Nor are there
any appearances to support an opinion, that every possible combination
of vegetable or animal structure has formerly been tried. Multitudes of
conformations, both of vegetables and animals, may be conceived capable of existence and succession, which yet do not exist. Perhaps almost
as many forms of plants might have been found in the fields, as figures
of plants can be delineated upon paper. A countless variety of animals
might have existed, which do not exist. Upon the supposition here stated,
we should see unicorns and mermaids, sylphs and centaurs, the fancies
of painters, and the fables of poets, realized by examples. Or, if it be
alleged that these may transgress the limits of possible life and propagation, we might, at least, have nations of human beings without nails
upon their fingers, with more or fewer fingers and toes than ten; some
with one eye, others with one ear, with one nostril, or without the sense
of smelling at all. All these, and a thousand other imaginable varieties,
might live and propagate. We may modify any one species many different
ways, all consistent with life, and with the actions necessary to preservation, although affording different degrees of conveniency and enjoyment
to the animal. And if we carry these modifications through the different
species which are known to subsist, their number would be incalculable.

No reason can be given why, if these deperdits ever existed, they have now disappeared. Yet, if all possible existences have been tried, they must have formed part of the catalogues.

But, moreover, the division of organized substances into animals and vegetables, and the distribution and sub-distribution of each into genera and species, which distribution is not an arbitrary act of the mind, but founded in the order which prevails in external nature, appear to me to contradict the supposition of the present world being the remains of an indefinite variety of existences; of a variety which rejects all plan. The hypothesis teaches, that every possible variety of being hath, at one time or other, found its way into existence (by what cause or in what manner is not said), and that those which were badly formed, perished; but how or why those which survived should be cast, as we see that plants and animals are cast, into regular classes, the hypothesis does not explain; or rather, the hypothesis is inconsistent with this phenomenon.

The hypothesis, indeed, is hardly deserving of the consideration which we have given to it. What should we think of a man who, because we had never ourselves seen watches, telescopes, stocking mills, steam engines, etc., made, knew not how they were made, or by whom,—would have us believe that these machines, instead of deriving their curious structures from the thought and design of their inventors and contrivers, in truth derive them from no other origin than this, viz. that a mass of metals and other materials having run when melted into all possible figures, and combined themselves in all possible forms and shapes, and proportions, these things which we see, are what were left from the accident, as best worth preserving: and, as such, are become the remaining stock of a magazine, which, at one time or other, has by this means, contained every mechanism, useful and useless, convenient and inconvenient, into which such like materials could be thrown? I cannot distinguish the hypothesis as applied to the works of nature, from this solution, which no one would accept as applied to a collection of machines. . . .

Our Ignorance of Many Points Need Not Suspend
Our Assurance of a Few

The confidence which we place in our observations upon the works of nature, in the marks which we discover of contrivance, choice, and design, and in our reasoning upon the proofs afforded us, ought not to be shaken, as it is sometimes attempted to be done, by bringing forward to our view our own ignorance, or rather the general imperfection of our knowledge of nature. Nor, in many cases, ought this consideration to affect us, even when it respects some parts of the subject immediately under our notice. True fortitude of understanding consists in not suffering what we know to be disturbed by what we do not know. If we perceive a useful end, and means adapted to that end, we perceive enough for our conclusion. If these things be clear, no matter what is obscure. The argument is finished. For instance; if the utility of vision to the animal which enjoys it, and the adaptation of the eye to this office, be evident and certain (and I can mention nothing which is more so), ought it to prejudice the inference which we draw from these premises, that we cannot explain the use of the spleen? Nay, more; if there be parts of the eye, viz. the cornea, the crystalline, the retina, in their substance, figure, and position, manifestly suited to the formation of an image by the refraction of rays of light, at least, as manifestly as the glasses and tubes of a dioptric telescope are suited to that purpose; it concerns not the proof which these afford of design, and of a designer, that there may perhaps be other parts, certain muscles, for instance, or nerves in the same eye, of the agency or effect of which we can give no account; any more than we should be inclined to doubt, or ought to doubt, about the construction of a telescope, viz. for what purpose it was constructed, or whether it were constructed at all, because there belonged to it certain screws and pins, the use or action of which we did not comprehend. I take it to be a general way of infusing doubts and scruples into the mind to recur to its own ignorance, its own imbecility; to tell us that upon these subjects we know little; that little imperfectly; or rather, that we know nothing properly about the matter. These suggestions so fall in with our consciousness, as sometimes to produce a general distrust of our faculties and our conclusions. But this is an unfounded jealousy. The uncertainty of one thing, does not necessarily affect the certainty of another thing. Our ignorance of many points need not suspend our assurance of a few. Before we yield, in any particular instance, to the skepticism which this sort of insinuation would induce, we ought accurately to ascertain, whether our ignorance or doubt concern those precise points upon which our conclusion rests. Other points are nothing. Our ignorance of other points may be of no consequence to these, though they be points, in various respects, of great importance. A just reasoner removes from his consideration, not only what he knows, but what he does not know, touching matters not strictly connected with his argument, i.e., not forming the very steps of his deduction; beyond these, his knowledge and his ignorance are alike relative.

Were there no example in the world of contrivance except that of the eye, it would be alone sufficient to suppose the conclusion which we draw from it, as to the necessity of an intelligent Creator. It could never be got rid of because it could not be accounted for by any other supposition, which did not contradict all the principles we possess of knowledge:

the principles, according to which things do, as often as they can be brought to the test of experience, turn out to be true or false. . . . If other parts of nature were inaccessible to our inquiries, or even if other parts of nature presented nothing to our examination but disorder and confusion, the validity of this example would remain the same. If there were but one watch in the world, it would not be less certain that it had a maker. If we had never in our lives seen any but one single kind of hydraulic machine, yet, if of that one kind we understood the mechanism and use, we should be as perfectly assured that it proceeded from the hand, and thought, and skill of a workman, as if we visited a museum of the arts, and saw collected there twenty different kinds of machines for drawing water, or a thousand different kinds for other purposes. Of this point, each machine is a proof, independently of all the rest. So it is with the evidences of a divine agency. The proof is not a conclusion which lies at the end of a chain of reasoning, of which chain each instance of contrivance is only a link, and of which, if one link fail, the whole fails; but is an argument separately supplied by every separate example. An error in stating an example affects only that example. The argument is cumulative, in the fullest sense of that term. The eye proves it without the ear; the ear without the eye. The proof in each example is complete; for when the design of the part, and the conduciveness of its structure to that design is shown, the mind may set itself at rest; no future consideration can detract anything from the force of the example.

38

THE EXISTENCE OF GOD

J. C. C. Smart

THIS LECTURE IS NOT TO DISCUSS whether God exists. It is to discuss reasons which philosophers have given for saying that God exists. That is, to discuss certain arguments.

First of all it may be as well to say what we may hope to get out of this. Of course, if we found that any of the traditional arguments for the existence of God were sound, we should get out of our one hour this Sunday afternoon something of inestimable value, such as one never got out of any hour's work in our lives before. For we should have got out of one hour's work the answer to that question about which, above all, we want to know the answer. This is assuming for the moment that the question "Does God exist?" is a proper question. The fact that a question is all right as far as the rules of ordinary grammar are concerned does not ensure that it has a sense. For example, "Does virtue run faster than length?" is certainly all right as far as ordinary grammar is concerned, but it is obviously not a meaningful question. Again, "How fast does time flow?" is all right as far as ordinary grammar is concerned, but it has no clear meaning. Now some philosophers would ask whether the question "Does God exist?" is a proper question. The greatest danger to theism at the present moment does not come from people who deny the validity of the arguments for the existence of God, for many Christian theologians do not believe that the existence of God can be proved, and certainly nowhere in the Old or New Testaments do we find any evidence of people's religion having a metaphysical basis. The main danger to theism today comes from people who want to say that "God exists" and "God does not exist" arc equally absurd. The concept of God, they would say, is a nonsensical one. . . .

[This selection was delivered as a public lecture at the University of Adelaide in 1951. It is here reprinted, with some omissions, by the kind permission of the author and the editor of the *Church Quarterly Review*, where it was first published.]

However, let us assume for the moment that the question "Does God exist?" is a proper question. We now ask: Can a study of the traditional proofs of the existence of God enable us to give an affirmative answer to this question? I contend that it cannot. I shall point out what seem to me to be fallacies in the main traditional arguments for the existence of God. Does proving that the arguments are invalid prove that God does not exist? Not at all. For to say that an argument is invalid is by no means the same thing as to say that its conclusion is false. Still, if we do find that the arguments we consider are all fallacious, what do we *gain* out of our investigation? Well, one thing we gain is a juster (if more austere) view of what philosophical argument can do for us. But, more important, we get a deeper insight into the logical nature of certain concepts, in particular, of course, the concepts of deity and existence. Furthermore we shall get some hints as to whether philosophy can be of any service to theologians, and if it can be of service, some hints as to how it can be of service. I think that it can be, but I must warn you that many, indeed perhaps the majority, of philosophers today would not entirely agree with me here.

One very noteworthy feature which must strike anyone who first looks at the usual arguments for the existence of God is the extreme brevity of these arguments. They range from a few lines to a few pages. St. Thomas Aquinas presents five arguments in three pages! Would it not be rather extraordinary if such a great conclusion should be got so easily? . . . It is my belief that in the case of any metaphysical argument it will be found that if the premises are uncontroversial the argument is unfortunately not valid, and that if the argument is valid the premises will unfortunately be just as doubtful as the conclusion they are meant to support.

Let us proceed to the discussion of the three most famous arguments for the existence of God. These are:

(1) The Ontological Argument.
(2) The Cosmological Argument.
(3) The Teleological Argument.

The first argument—the ontological argument—really has no premises at all. It tries to show that there would be a contradiction in denying that God exists. It was first formulated by St. Anselm and was later used by Descartes. It is not a convincing argument to modern ears, and St. Thomas Aquinas gave essentially the right reasons for rejecting it. However, it is important to discuss it, as an understanding of what is wrong with it is necessary for evaluating the second argument, that is, the cosmological argument. This argument does have a premise, but not at all a controversial one. It is that something exists. We should all, I think, agree to that. The teleological argument is less austere in manner than the other two. It tries to argue to the existence of God not purely *a priori* and not from the mere fact of *something* existing, but from the actual features we observe in nature, namely those which seem to be evidence of design or purpose.

We shall discuss these three arguments in order. I do not say that they are the only arguments which have been propounded for the existence of God, but they are, I think, the most important ones. For example, of St. Thomas Aquinas' celebrated "Five Ways" the first three are variants of the cosmological argument, and the fifth is a form of the teleological argument.

The Ontological Argument

This as I remarked, contains no factual premise. It is a *reductio-ad-absurdum* of the supposition that God does not exist. Now *reductio-ad-absurdum* proofs are to be suspected whenever there is doubt as to whether the statement to be proved is *significant*. For example, it is quite easy, as anyone who is familiar with the so-called Logical Paradoxes will know, to produce a not *obviously* nonsensical statement, such that both it *and* its denial imply a contradiction. So unless we are sure of the significance of a statement we cannot regard a *reductio-ad-absurdum* of its contradictory as proving its truth. This point of view is well known to those versed in the philosophy of mathematics; there is a well-known school of mathematicians, led by Brouwer, who in certain circumstances refuse to employ *reductio-ad-absurdum* proofs. However, I shall not press this criticism of the ontological argument, for this criticism is somewhat abstruse (though it has been fore-shadowed by Catholic philosophers, who object to the ontological argument by saying that it does not first show that the concept of an infinitely perfect being is a *possible one*). We are at present assuming that "Does God exist?" is a proper question, and if it is a proper question there is no objection so far to answering it by means of a *reductio-ad-absurdum* proof. We shall content ourselves with the more usual criticisms of the ontological argument.

The ontological argument was made famous by Descartes. It is to be found at the beginning of his Fifth Meditation. As I remarked earlier it was originally put forward by Anselm, though I am sorry to say that to read Descartes you would never suspect that fact! Descartes points out that in mathematics we can deduce various things purely *a priori*, "as for example," he says, "when I imagine a triangle, although there is not and perhaps never was in any place . . . one such figure, it remains true nevertheless that this figure possesses a certain determinate nature, form, or essence, which is . . . not framed by me, nor in any degree dependent on my thought; as appears from the circumstance, that diverse properties of the triangle may be demonstrated, for example that its three angles are equal to two right, that its greatest side is subtended by its greatest angle, and the like." Descartes now goes on to suggest that just as having the sum of its angles equal to two right angles is involved in the idea of a triangle, so *existence* is involved in the very idea of an infinitely perfect being, and that it would therefore be as much of a contradiction to assert that an infinitely perfect being does not exist as it is to assert that the three angles of a triangle do not add up to two right angles or that two of its sides are not together greater than the third side. We may then, says Descartes, assert that an infinitely perfect being *necessarily* exists, just as we may say that two sides of a triangle are together *necessarily* greater than the third side.

This argument is highly fallacious. To say that a so-and-so exists is not in the least like saying that a so-and-so has such-and-such a property. It is not to amplify a concept but to say that a concept applies to something, and whether or not a concept applies to something can not be seen from an examination of the concept itself. Existence is not a property. "Growling" is a property of tigers, and to say that "tame tigers growl" is to say something about tame tigers, but to say "tame tigers exist" is not to say something about tame tigers but to say that there are tame tigers. Prof. G. E. Moore once brought out the difference between existence and a property such as that of being tame, or being a tiger, or being a growler, by reminding us that though the sentence "some tame tigers do not *growl*" makes perfect sense, the sentence "some tame tigers do not *exist*" has no clear meaning. The fundamental mistake in the ontological argument, then, is that it treats "exists" in "an infinitely perfect being exists" as if it ascribed a property existence to an infinitely perfect being, just as "is loving" in "an infinitely perfect being is loving" ascribes a property, or as "growl" in "tame tigers growl" ascribes a property: the verb "to exist" in "an infinitely perfect being exists" does not ascribe a property to something already conceived of as existing, but says that the concept of an infinitely perfect being applies to something. The verb "to exist" here takes us right out of the purely conceptual world. This being so, there can never be any *logical contradiction* in denying that God exists. It is worth mentioning that we are less likely to make the sort of mistake that the ontological argument makes if we use the expression "there is a so-and-so" instead of the more misleading form of words "a so-and-so exists."

I should like to mention another interesting, though less crucial, objection to Descartes' argument. He talks as though you can deduce further properties of, say, a triangle, by considering its definition. It is worth pointing out that from the definition of a triangle as a figure bounded by three straight lines you can only deduce trivialities, such as that it is bounded by more than one straight line, for example. It is not at all a contradiction to say that the two sides of a triangle are together not greater than the third side, or that its angles do not add up to two right angles. To get a contradiction you have to bring in the specific axioms of Euclidean geometry. Remember school geometry, how you used to prove that the angles of a triangle add up to two right angles. Through the vertex C of the triangle ABC you drew a line parallel to BA, and so you assumed the axiom of parallels for a start. Definitions, by themselves, are not deductively potent. Descartes, though a very great mathematician himself, was profoundly mistaken as to the nature of mathematics. However, we can interpret him as saying that from the definition of a triangle, *together with the axioms of Euclidean geometry,* you can deduce various things, such as that the angles of a triangle add up to two right angles. But this just shows how pure mathematics is a sort of game with symbols; you start with a set of axioms, and operate on them in accordance with certain rules of inference. All the mathematician requires is that the axiom set should be *consistent.* Whether or not it has application to reality lies outside pure mathematics. Geometry is no fit model for a proof of real existence.

The Cosmological Argument

This argument does at least seem more promising than the ontological argument. It does start with a factual premise, namely that something exists. The premise that something exists is indeed a very abstract one, but nevertheless it *is* factual, it does give us a foothold in the real world of things, it does go beyond the consideration of mere concepts. The argument has been put forward in various forms, but for present purposes it may be put as follows:

Everything in the world around us is *contingent.* That is, with regard to any particular thing, it is quite conceivable that it might not have existed. For example, if you were asked why you existed, you could say that it was because of your parents, and if asked why they existed you could go still further back, but however far you go back you have not, so it is argued, made the fact of your existence really intelligible. For however far back you go in such a series you only get back to something which itself might not have existed. For a really satisfying explanation of why anything contingent (such as you or me or this table) exists you must eventually begin with something which is not itself contingent, that is, with something of which we cannot say that it might not have existed, that is we must begin with a necessary being. So the first part of the argument boils down to this. *If anything exists an absolutely necessary being must exist. Something exists. Therefore an absolutely necessary being must exist.* The second part of the argument is to prove that a necessarily existing being must be an infinitely perfect being, that is, God. . . .

The cosmological argument is radically unsound. The trouble comes much earlier than where Kant locates it. The trouble comes in the *first* stage of the argument. For the first stage of the argument purports to argue to the existence of a necessary being. And by "a necessary being" the cosmological argument means "a *logically* necessary being," i.e., "a being whose non-existence is inconceivable in the sort of way that a triangle's having four sides in inconceivable." The trouble is, however, that the concept of a logically necessary being is a self-contradictory concept, like the concept of a round square. For in the first place "necessary" is a predicate of *propositions,* not of things. That is, we can contrast *necessary* propositions such as "3 + 2 = 5," "a thing cannot be red and green all over," "either it is raining or it is not raining," with *contingent* propositions, such as "Mr. Menzies is Prime Minister of Australia," "the earth is slightly flattened at the poles," and "sugar is soluble in water." The propositions in the first class are guaranteed solely by the rules for the use of the symbols they contain. In the case of the propositions of the second class a genuine possibility of agreeing or not agreeing with reality is left open; whether they are true or false depends not on the conventions of our language but on reality. (Compare the contrast between "the equator is 90 degrees from the pole," which tells us nothing about geography but only about our map-making conventions, and "Adelaide is 55 degrees from the pole," which does tell us a geographical fact.) So no informative proposition can be logically necessary. Now since "necessary" is a word which applies primarily to propositions, we shall have to interpret "God is a necessary being" as "The proposition 'God exists' is logically necessary." But this *is* the principle of the ontological argument, and there is no way of getting round it this time in the way that we got out of Kant's criticism. No existential proposition can be logically necessary, for we saw that the truth of a logically necessary proposition depends only on our symbolism, or to put the same thing in another way, on the relationship of concepts. We saw, however, in discussing the ontological argument, that an existential proposition does not say that one concept is involved in another, but that a concept applies to something. An existential proposition must be very different from any logically necessary one, such as a mathematical one, for example, for the conventions of our symbolism clearly leave it open for us either to affirm or deny an existential proposition; it is not our symbolism but reality which decides whether or not we must affirm it or deny it.

The demand that the existence of God should be *logically* necessary is thus a self-contradictory one. When we see this and go back to look at the first stage of the cosmological argument it no longer seems compelling, indeed it now seems to contain an absurdity. If we cast our minds back, we recall that the argument was as follows: that if we explain why something exists and is what it is, we must explain it by reference to something else, and we must explain that thing's being what it is by reference to yet another thing, and so on, back and back. It is then suggested that unless we can go back to a logically necessary first cause we shall remain intellectually unsatisfied. We should otherwise only get back to something which might have been otherwise, and with reference to which the same questions can again be asked. This is the argument, but we now see that in asking for a logically necessary first cause we are doing something worse than asking for the moon. It is only *physically* impossible for us to get the moon; if I were a few million times bigger I could reach out for it and give it to you. That is, I know what it would be *like* to give you the moon, though I cannot in *fact* do it. A logically necessary first cause, however, is not impossible in the way that giving you the moon is impossible; no, it is *logically* impossible. "Logically necessary being" is a self-contradictory expression like "round square." It is not any good saying that we would only be intellectually satisfied with a logically necessary cause, that nothing else would do. We can easily have an absurd wish. We should all like to be able to eat our cake and have it, but that does not alter the fact that our wish is an absurd and self-contradictory one. We reject the cosmological argument, then, because it rests on a thorough absurdity.

The Teleological Argument

The cosmological argument, we saw, failed because it made use of the absurd conception of a *logically* necessary being. We now pass to the third argument which I propose to consider. This is the *Teleological Argument*. It is also called "the Argument from Design." It would be better called the argument *to* design, as Kemp Smith does call it, for clearly that the universe has been designed by a great architect is to assume a great part of the conclusion to be proved. Or we could call it "the argument from apparent design." The argument is very fully discussed in Hume's *Dialogues concerning Natural Religion,* to which I should like to draw your attention. In these dialogues the argument is presented as follows: "Look round the world: Contemplate the whole and every part of it: You will find it to be nothing but one great machine, subdivided into an infinite number of lesser machines. . . . The curious adapting of means to ends, throughout all nature, resembles exactly, though it much exceeds, the productions of human contrivance. . . . Since therefore the effects resemble each other, we are led to infer, by all the rules of analogy, that the causes also resemble; and that the Author of nature is somewhat similar to the mind of man; though possessed of much larger faculties, proportioned to the grandeur of the work which he has executed."

This argument may at once be criticized in two ways: (1) We may question whether the analogy between the universe and artificial things like houses, ships, furniture, and machines (which admittedly are designed) is very close. Now in any ordinary sense of language, it is true to say that plants and animals have *not* been designed. If we press the analogy of the universe to a plant, instead of to a machine, we get to a very different conclusion. And why should the one analogy be regarded as any better or worse than the other? (2) Even if the analogy were close, it would only go to suggest that the universe was designed by a *very great* (not infinite) architect, and note, an *architect,* not a *creator.* For if we take the analogy seriously we must notice that we do not create the materials from which we make houses, machines and so on, but only *arrange* the materials.

This, in bare outline, is the general objection to the argument from design, and will apply to any form of it. In the form in which the argument was put forward by such theologians as Paley, the argument is, of course, still more open to objection. For Paley laid special stress on such things as the eye of an animal, which he thought must have been contrived by a wise Creator for the special benefit of the animal. It seemed to him inconceivable how otherwise such a complex organ, so well suited to the needs of the animal, should have arisen. Or listen to Henry More: "For why have we three joints in our legs and arms, as also in our fingers, but that it was much better than having two or four? And why are our fore-teeth sharp like chisels to cut, but our inward teeth broad to grind, [instead of] the fore-teeth broad and the other sharp? But we might have made a hard shift to have lived through in that worser condition. Again, why are the teeth so luckily placed, or rather, why are there not teeth in other bones as well as in the jaw-bones? For they might have been as capable as these. But the reason is, nothing is done foolishly or in vain; that is, there is a divine Providence that orders all things." This type of argument has lost its persuasiveness, for the theory of Evolution explains why our teeth are so luckily placed in our jaw-bones, why we have the most convenient number of joints in our fingers, and so on. Species which did not possess advantageous features would not survive in competition with those which did.

The sort of argument Paley and Henry More used is thus quite unconvincing. Let us return to the broader conception, that of the universe as a whole, which seems to show the mark of a benevolent and intelligent Designer. Bacon expressed this belief forcibly: "I had rather beleave all the Fables in the Legend and the Talmud and the Alcoran than that this Universal Frame is without a Minde." So, in some moods, does the universe strike us. But sometimes, when we are in other moods, we see it very differently. To quote Hume's dialogues again: "Look around this Universe. What an immense profusion of beings, animated and organized, sensible and active! You admire this prodigious variety and fecundity. But inspect a little more narrowly these living existences, the only beings worth regarding. How hostile and destructive to each other! How insufficient all of them for their own happiness! . . . the whole presents nothing but the idea of a blind Nature, impregnated by a great vivifying principle, and pouring forth from her lap, without discernment or parental care, her maimed and abortive children!"* There is indeed a great deal of suffering, some part of which is no doubt attributable to the moral choices of men, and to save us from which would conflict with what many people would regard as the greater good of moral freedom, but there is still an immense residue of apparently needless suffering, that is, needless in the sense that it could be prevented by an omnipotent being. The difficulty is that of reconciling the presence of evil and suffering with the assertion that God is both omnipotent and benevolent. If we *already* believe in an omnipotent and benevolent God, then some attempt may be made to solve the problem of evil by arguing that the values in the world form a sort of organic unity, and that making any *part* of the world better would perhaps nevertheless reduce the value of the whole. Paradoxical though this thesis may appear at first sight, it is perhaps not theoretically absurd. If, however, evil presents a *difficulty* to the believing mind, it presents an *insuperable* difficulty to one who wishes to argue rationally from the world as we find it to the existence of an omnipotent and benevolent God. As Hume puts it: "Is the world considered in general, and as it appears to us in this life, different from what a man . . . would *beforehand* expect from a very powerful, wise and benevolent Deity? It must be a strange prejudice to assert the contrary. And from thence I conclude, that, however consistent the world may be, allowing certain suppositions and conjectures, with the idea of such a Deity, it can never afford us an inference concerning his existence."†

The teleological argument is thus extremely shaky, and in any case, even if it were sound, it would only go to prove the existence of a very great architect, not of an omnipotent and benevolent Creator.

Nevertheless, the argument has a fascination for us that reason can not easily dispel. Hume, in his twelfth dialogue, and after pulling the argument from design to pieces in the previous eleven dialogues, nevertheless speaks as follows: "A purpose, an intention, a design strikes everywhere the most careless, the most stupid thinker; and no man can

---

* See below, Selection 40, p. 531.
† See below, p. 525.

be so hardened in absurd systems as at all times to reject it . . . all the sciences almost lead us insensibly to acknowledge a first Author." Similarly Kant, before going on to exhibit the fallaciousness of the argument, nevertheless says of it: "This proof always deserves to be mentioned with respect. It is the oldest, the clearest and the most accordant with the common reason of mankind. It enlivens the study of nature, just as it itself derives its existence and gains ever new vigour from that source. It suggests ends and purposes, where our observation would not have detected them by itself, and extends our knowledge of nature by means of the guiding-concept of a special unity, the principle of which is outside nature. This knowledge . . . so strengthens the belief in a supreme Author of nature that the belief acquires the force of an irresistible conviction." It is somewhat of a paradox that an invalid argument should command so much respect even from those who have demonstrated its invalidity. The solution of the paradox is perhaps somewhat as follows: The argument from design is no good as an argument. But in those who have the seeds of a genuinely religious attitude already within them the facts to which the argument from design draws attention, facts showing the grandeur and majesty of the universe, facts that are evident to anyone who looks upwards on a starry night, and which are enormously multiplied for us by the advance of theoretical science, these facts have a powerful effect. But they only have this effect on the already religious mind, on the mind which has the capability of feeling the religious type of awe. That is, the argument from design is in reality no argument, or if it is regarded as an argument it is feeble, but it is a potent instrument in heightening religious emotions. . . .

39

THE DELUSION OF
DESIGN AND PURPOSE

Clarence Darrow

SELDOM DO THE BELIEVERS in mysticism fail to talk about the evidence of purpose and design shown in the universe itself. This idea runs back at least one hundred and five years, to Paley's "Natural Theology." There was a time when this book was a part of the regular course in all schools of higher learning, which then included theology; but the book is now more likely to be found in museums.

Paley points out that if a man travelling over the heath should find a watch and commence examining it he would soon discover in the watch itself abundant evidence of purpose and design. He would observe the wheels that fit into each other and turn the hour hand and the minute hand, the crystal made to fit over the face, etc., etc.

What the hypothetical man would observe and conclude would depend on the man. Most men that we know would think that the watch showed a design to accomplish a certain purpose, and therefore must have had a maker. They would reach that conclusion because they are familiar with tools and their use by man. But, suppose the watch had been picked up by a bushman or some other savage or an ape? None of them would draw an inference, for the article would be new to them. Supposing, instead of a man, a coyote or wolf came upon the watch, turned it over and examined it, would the animal read or sense any design? Most assuredly not. Suppose the civilized man should pick up an unfamiliar object, a stone, or a piece of quartz; he might view it and examine it, but it would never enter his head that it was designed, and yet on close inspection and careful study the stone or quartz is just as marvellous as the watch.

[This selection is the whole of Chapter 44 of Darrow's book, *The Story of My Life*, published in 1932. It is reproduced with the kind permission of Charles Scribner's Sons, New York and London.]

Paley passes from the watch to the human structure and shows how the mouth and teeth are adjusted to prepare the food for man's digestion, and how his stomach is formed to digest it; how the eye and ear were made to carry sensations to the brain, etc. Many of the clergy say the same thing to-day, in spite of the fact that the organs of man were never made for any such purpose. In fact, man never was made. He was evolved from the lowest form of life. His ancestors in the sea slowly threw its jellylike structure around something that nourished it and absorbed it. Slowly through ages of continued development and change and mutations the present man was evolved, and with him the more perfect and adaptable and specialized structure, with which he sees and hears and takes his food, and digests it and assimilates it to his structure. The stomach was not made first, and then food created for its use. The food came first, and certain forms of life slowly developed, an organ that would absorb food to be utilized in the process of growth. By degrees, through the survival of the construction most fitted for life, the stomach and digestive apparatus for men and other animals gradually grew and unfolded in endless time.

To discover that certain forms and formations are adjusted for certain action has nothing to do with design. None of these developments are perfect, or anywhere near so. All of them, including the eye, are botchwork that any good mechanic would be ashamed to make. All of them need constant readjustment, are always out of order, and are entirely too complicated for dependable work. They are not made for any purpose; they simply grew out of needs and adaptations; in other words, they happened. Just as God must have happened, if he exists at all.

Turning from Paley and his wornout watch to the universe and the physical world in general, is there any more evidence here? First, the "design and order" sharks ought to tell what they mean by their terms, and how they find out what they think they understand. To say that a certain scheme or process shows order or system, one must have some norm or pattern, and that is the universe itself, from which we fashion our ideas. We have observed this universe and its operation and we call it order. To say that the universe is patterned on order is to say that the universe is patterned on the universe. It can mean nothing else.

The earth revolves around the sun in a long curve not far from a circle. Does that show order? Let us suppose that instead of going in a circle it formed a rectangle. Would this not have been accepted as order? Suppose it were a triangle, or any other figure. Suppose it took a tooth-like course, would that, then be considered order? As a matter of fact, the earth does not go regularly in the same path around the sun; it is drawn out into the universe with the whole solar system, and never travels the same course twice. The solar system really has an isolated place in space. The sun furnishes light and heat to nine different planets, of which the earth is one of the smallest and most insignificant. The earth has one satellite, the moon. Saturn and Jupiter have eight moons each, and, besides that, Saturn has a ring that looks very beautiful from here, running all around the planet. We do know that all the planets of the solar system, and the sun as well, are made of the same stuff. It is most likely that every moving thing in the universe has the same constituents as the earth. What is the plan that gave Jupiter eight moons, while only one was lavished upon the earth, supposed to be the special masterpiece of the Almighty, and for whose benefit all the hosts of the heavens were made? Jupiter is three hundred and seventeen times the weight of the earth, and it takes four years for it to go around the sun. Perhaps the universe was made for inhabitants that will one day live on Jupiter.

It is senseless to talk about order and system and design in the universe. Sir James Jeans' book, published in 1931, *The Stars in Their Course,* tells us his theory of the origin of our solar system, which is of more interest to us than the Milky Way. The theory of Jeans, and most of the other astronomers, is that there was a time when all the planets of the solar system were a part of the sun, and that some wandering star in its course across the heavens entered the sphere of the sun and dragged after it the planets and the moons that make up the solar system by the power of gravitation. This is the planetismal theory, postulated by Professors Chamberlain and Moulton, of the University of Chicago. These mighty chunks of matter were drawn from the sun rushed on through space at a terrific speed, and each was caught by gravitation and revolved around the sun. Their distance from the sun depended largely upon their size before gravitation held them in its grasp.

There is nothing in the solar system that could be called design and order. It came from a catastrophe of whose immensity no one could even dream. Religionists have pointed to the ability of an astronomer to fix the time of an eclipse as evidence of system. There are only a few heavenly bodies involved in an eclipse of the sun or moon, from the standpoint of the earth. The motions and positions of all these bodies are well known, and from this the passage of another heavenly planet or the moon between the earth and the sun can be easily determined. It matters not whether the date of an eclipse is far-off or near-by, the method is the same. To an astronomer the computation is as simple as the question propounded to the first grade pupil: "If John had three apples and James gave him two more, how many apples would John then have?"

We know that gravitation caught the various planets at a certain point as they sped across space, and that these accidents of colliding bodies are very rare; the reason is that regardless of what seems to be the distance between the stars, they are so far apart that it is almost impossible for them ever to meeet. To quote from Jeans: "For the most part, each voyage is in splendid isolation, like a ship on the ocean. In a scale model on which the stars are ships, the average ship will be well over a million miles from its neighbor."

Still, catastrophes have occurred and do occur. Our solar system was probably born from one. The moon was thrown from the earth by some pull of gravitation. The heavens are replete with dark planets, and parts of planets, and meteors hurrying through space. Now and then one drops onto the earth, and is preserved in some park or museum; so that in various parts of the world numerous specimens exist. If there was any purpose in the creation of the universe, or any part of it, what was it? Would any mortal dare to guess?

Our solar system is one of the smallest of the endless systems of which we have any knowledge. Our earth is eight thousand miles in diameter. The star, Betelgeuse, is so large that it would fill all space occupied in the heavens in the whole orbit made by the earth going around the sun. There are many stars known to be much larger than Betelgeuse. The diameter of this sun is thirty-seven thousand times that of our little earth, for which all the universe is supposed to have been made, and whose inhabitants are endowed with everlasting life.

When the telescope is turned toward the heavens we learn another story. Leaving the sparsely settled section of eternity in which we live forever, and going out into the real main universe, we find worlds on worlds, systems upon systems, and nebula after nebula. No one can possibly imagine the dimensions of endless space. The great Nebula M.31 in Andromeda is so far away from the earth that it takes light nine hundred thousand millions of years to reach our planet. The nebula itself is so vast that it takes fifty thousand years for light to cross it. To make it still more simple I have taken the pains to figure the distance of this nebula from our important planet, called the earth, which boasts of a diameter of eight thousand miles. This nebula is 5,279,126,-400,000,000,000 miles away from us, if my computations are right. I would not positively guarantee the correctness of the answer, but I think it is all right, although I did it by hand. I have gone over the figures three times, and got a different result each time, so I think the answer can be pretty well depended upon. I cannot help feeling sorry for the residents of Nebula M.31 in Andromeda, when I think what a great deprivation they must suffer through living so far away from our glorious planet, which Mark Twain named "the wart," but which theology has placed at the centre of the universe and as the sole concern of gods and men.

What lies beyond Andromeda? No one can answer that question.

And still there is every reason to believe that other worlds and systems and nebulae reach out into stellar space, without end. It is obvious that no one can form a conception of the extent of space or the infinite number of suns and planets with which the limitless sky is strewn. No one can vision a beginning or an end. If it were possible for any fertile mind to imagine a conception of the end of space, then we should wonder what lies beyond that limit. We cannot attain the slightest comprehension of the extent of our pigmy solar system, much less any of the greater ones. The planet which is the farthest from our sun is Pluto, one of the smallest in our system. The diameter of Pluto's orbit around the sun is only about 7,360,000,000 miles. This may be taken as the extent of our solar system. This can be compared with the distance to the nebula in Andromeda, which I hesitate to record again, showing the trifling importance of our whole solar system in so much of the universe as we can scan.

When the new telescope is completed and mounted on the top of Mount Wilson, it is hoped that we can produce figures of distance that are real figures.

Among the endless number of stars that whirl in the fastnesses of illimitable space, how many millions of billions of planets are likely to be in existence? How many of these may possibly have as much special and historical importance as the tiny globe to which we so frantically cling? To find that number, go and count the grains of sand on all the coasts of all the waters of the earth, and then think of the catastrophe that would result to the coasts if one grain were shattered or lost.

In spite of the countless numbers of bodies moving about in limitless space, and the distances between them so great that they seldom clash, still they do sometimes clash. What is our solar system in comparison with the great nebula out there in the beginning, or end, or middle stretch of real space? Compared with that part of the heavens the density of the stellar population of our solar system is like the prairies of Kansas compared with the city of New York. Can anything be inferred about the origin or arrangement of all this, so far as man can tell, except that it is the outcome of the merest, wildest chance?

But let us try to clear the cobwebs from our brains, and the dizziness from our stomachs, and come back to earth, as it were. Let us talk of something where we can deal with what at least approaches facts. Does the earth show design, and order, and system, and purpose? Again, it would be well for the designers to tell what the scheme really is. If the plan is so clear as to justify the belief in a master designer, then it must be plain that the believers should be able to give the world some idea of the purpose of it all. Knowing winks and Delphic utterances and cryptic insinuations are not enough. Was the earth ever designed for the home of man? Sir James Jeans, in his admirable book on astronomy, shows us in no uncertain way that it evidently was not; that the human race has made the most of a bad environment and a most unfortunate habitation. Strange that the high-priests of superstition should so convulsively clutch Jeans and Eddington; neither one believes in the God of the theologians; neither believes in a special revelation, although Jeans does manage to say that Venus is the planet that the religionists thought was the star that led the camels over the desert to the stable where Jesus was born. Is this science or religion?—this bit of hearsay.

Even had this planet been meant for life, it plainly was not meant for human life. Three-fourths of the surface is covered with water, which would show that if it was ever designed for life it was designed for fishes and not for men. But what about the dry land? Two-thirds of this is not fitted for human beings. Both the polar zones are too cold for the abode of man. The equatorial regions are too hot. Vast deserts are spread out in various sections, and impassable and invincible mountain ranges make human habitation and the production of food impossible over immense areas. The earth is small enough, to begin with; the great seas, the wide useless stretches of land and the hostile climates have shrunk the livable portion almost to the vanishing point, and it is continually shrinking day by day. The human race is here because it is here, and it clings to the soil because there is nowhere else to go.

Even a human being of very limited capacity could think of countless ways in which the earth could be improved as the home of man, and from the earliest time the race has been using all sorts of efforts and resources to make it more suitable for its abode. Admitting that the earth is a fit place for life, and certainly every place in the universe where life exists is fitted for life, then what sort of life was this planet designed to support? There are some millions of different species of animals on this earth, and one-half of these are insects. In numbers, and perhaps in other ways, man is in a great minority. If the land of the earth was made for life, it seems as if it was intended for insect life, which can exist almost anywhere. If no other available place can be found they can live by the million on man, and inside of him. They generally succeed in destroying his life, and, if they have a chance, wind up by eating his body.

Aside from the insects, all sorts of life infest the earth and sea and air. In large portions of the earth man can make no headway against the rank growths of jungles and the teeming millions of animals that are seeking his death. He may escape the larger and most important of these only to be imperilled and probably eaten by the microbes, which seem instinctively to have their own idea of the worth and purpose of man's existence. If it were of any importance, we might view man from the standpoint of the microbe and consider his utility as the microbe's "meal-ticket." Can any one find any reason for claiming that the earth was meant for man, any more than for any other form of life that is spawned from land and sea and air?

But, how well is the earth itself adapted to human life? Even in the best parts of this world, speaking from the standpoint of man, one-fourth of the time it is too cold and another fourth of the seasons it is too hot, leaving little time for the comfort and pleasure of the worthiest product of the universe, or, that small fraction of it that we have some limited knowledge about.

Passing up the manifold difficulties that confront man and his brief life and career upon this mundane sphere, let us look at the world itself. It is a very wobbly place. Every year, upon the surface of this globe, and in the seas that cover such a major part of it, there are ten thousand earthquakes, ranging from light shocks to the total destruction of large areas of territory and annihilation of great numbers of human lives. Were these, too, designed? Then, there is no such meaning as is usually applied to the word "design." What "design" was there in the earthquake that destroyed Lisbon in 1755? The entire city was blotted out, together with the destruction of thirty thousand to forty thousand human beings. This earthquake occurred on a Sunday which was also a saint's day, and a large number were killed in a cathedral, which was also destroyed. And yet people talk about design and purpose and order and system as though they knew the meaning of the words.

Let us look at the earth as it exists to-day. It is not the same earth that came into some sort of separate existence millions of years ago. It has not only experienced vast and comparatively sudden changes, like the throwing up of mountain ranges in the cooling and contracting processes, but other changes not so sudden and acute have worked their way through ages of time, and changes are still going on all the time all over the earth. New lands keep rising, others sinking away. Volcanoes are sending out millions of tons of matter each year, new islands are rising above the surface of the sea, while other islands are lowered beneath the waves. Continents are divided by internal forces and the ruthless powers of the sea.

Great Britain was cut off from the mainland not so very long ago, according to geological time. The shores of America and Africa were once connected, as seems evident from looking at the maps, and countless other geological shiftings have happened all over the surface and inside the earth, so that the world was no more made as it is now than was man created as we find him to-day. The destruction of the island of Martinique, and the Mont Pelée disaster, the earthquake of San Francisco, are all within the memory of many now living. Active volcanoes are continuously pouring solid matter into the waters and slowly or rapidly building up new land where once was only sea.

The various archipelagoes are instances of this formation of fairly recent times. The Allegheny Mountains were once thirty thousand feet high. The crevices of their rocks have been penetrated by rain, split by frost and ice, pulverized by friction, and every minute are moving off toward the Gulf of Mexico. This range of mountains, which once reached an altitude of thirty thousand feet at the highest point, now has its highest peak but six thousand feet above the sea. These mountains have been worn down day after day, and the Ohio and Tennessee and Mississippi Rivers, carrying off the sediment, are building up the delta on the Louisiana coast. The earth and its seas were never made; they are in constant flux, moved by cold and heat and rain, and with no design or purpose that can be fathomed by the wit of man.

The delta of the Nile has through the long ages been carried down in mud and sand and silt from two thousand miles away and deposited in the open sea; and this is also called design by those who look for things they wish to find.

Nature brings hordes of insects that settle over the land and destroy the farmers' crops. Who are the objects of the glorious design: the farmers who so patiently and laboriously raise the crops or the grasshoppers that devour them? It must be the insects, because the farmers hold prayer meetings and implore their God to kill the bugs, but the pests go on with their deadly work unmolested. Man prates glibly about design, but Nature furnishes not a single example or fact as proof. Perhaps the microbe who bores a hole into the vitals of man and brings him down to his death may believe in a Providence and a design. How else could he live so royally on the vitals of one of the lords of creation?

All that we know is that we were born on this little grain of sand we call the earth. We know that it is one of the smallest bits of matter that floats in the great shoreless sea of space, and we have every reason to believe that it is as inconsequential in every other respect. On board the same craft, sailing the same seas, are all sorts of living things, fighting each other, and us, that each may survive. Most of these specimens are living on the carcasses of the dead. The strongest instinct of most of our crew is to stay here and live. The strongest in intellect and prowess live the longest. Nature, in all her manifestations, is at war with life, and sooner or later will doubtless have her way. No one can give a reason for any or all of the manifestations which we call life. We are like a body of shipwrecked sailors clutching to a raft and desperately engaged in holding on.

Men have built faith from hopes. They have struggled and fought in despair. They have frantically clung to life because of the will to live. The best that we can do is to be kindly and helpful toward our friends and fellow passengers who are clinging to the same speck of dirt while we are drifting side by side to our common doom.

40

EVIL AND THE ARGUMENT
FROM DESIGN

David Hume

The Whole Earth Is Cursed and Polluted

. . . THE WHOLE EARTH, believe me, Philo, is cursed and polluted. A
perpetual war is kindled amongst all living creatures. Necessity, hunger,
want stimulate the strong and courageous; fear, anxiety, terror agitate
the weak and infirm. The first entrance into life gives anguish to the
new-born infant and to its wretched parent; weakness, impotence, distress attend each stage of that life, and it is, at last, finished in agony and
horror.

Observe, too, says Philo, the curious artifices of nature in order to
embitter the life of every living being. The stronger prey upon the weaker
and keep them in perpetual terror and anxiety. The weaker, too, in their
turn, often prey upon the stronger, and vex and molest them without
relaxation. Consider that innumerable race of insects, which either are
bred on the body of each animal or, flying about, infix their stings in
him. These insects have others still less than themselves which torment
them. And thus on each hand, before and behind, above and below,
every animal is surrounded with enemies which incessantly seek his misery
and destruction.

Man alone, said Demea, seems to be, in part, an exception to this

---

[This selection comprises most of Parts X and XI of Hume's *Dialogues Concerning
Natural Religion,* a book published after Hume's death, in 1779. The parties in the dialogues
are Demea, who represents rationalist theology; Cleanthes, who tries to combine belief in
God with empiricism; and Philo, who is an unbeliever. Throughout the dialogues, Cleanthes
has been arguing that the existence of God can be inferred from the traces of design which
are observable in the world around us. Demea, who allows only *a priori* arguments for the
existence of God, and Philo, have been arguing against the possibility of such an inference.
It is generally agreed among contemporary scholars that Philo is the spokesman for Hume's
own views. Demea is speaking as our selection begins.]

rule. For by combination in society he can easily master lions, tigers, and bears, whose greater strength and agility naturally enable them to prey upon him.

On the contrary, it is here chiefly, cried Philo, that the uniform and equal maxims of nature are most apparent. Man, it is true, can, by combination, surmount all his *real* enemies and become master of the whole animal creation; but does he not immediately raise up to himself *imaginary* enemies, the demons of his fancy, who haunt him with superstitious terrors and blast every enjoyment of life? His pleasure, as he imagines, becomes in their eyes a crime; his food and repose give them umbrage and offence; his very sleep and dreams furnish new materials to anxious fear; and even death, his refuge from every other ill, presents only the dread of endless and innumerable woes. Nor does the wolf molest more the timid flock than superstition does the anxious breast of wretched mortals.

Besides, consider, Demea: This very society by which we surmount those wild beasts, our natural enemies, what new enemies does it not raise to us? What woe and misery does it not occasion? Man is the greatest enemy of man. Oppression, injustice, contempt, contumely, violence, sedition, war, calumny, treachery, fraud—by these they mutually torment each other, and they would soon dissolve that society which they had formed were it not for the dread of still greater ills which must attend their separation.

But though these external insults, said Demea, from animals, from men, from all the elements, which assault us form a frightful catalogue of woes, they are nothing in comparison of those which arise within ourselves, from the distempered condition of our mind and body. How many lie under the lingering torment of diseases? Hear the pathetic enumeration of the great poet.

> Intestine stone and ulcer, colic-pangs,
> Demoniac frenzy, moping melancholy,
> And moon-struck madness, pining atrophy,
> Marasmus, and wide-wasting pestilence.
> Dire was the tossing, deep the groans: *Despair*
> Tended the sick, busiest from couch to couch.
> And over them triumphant *Death* his dart
> Shook: but delay'd to strike, though oft invok'd
> With vows, as their chief good and final hope.[1]

The disorders of the mind, continued Demea, though more secret, are not perhaps less dismal and vexatious. Remorse, shame, anguish, rage, disappointment, anxiety, fear, dejection, despair—who has ever passed through life without cruel inroads from these tormentors? How many have scarcely ever felt any better sensations? Labour and poverty,

---

1. Milton: *Paradise Lost*, Bk. XI.

so abhorred by everyone, are the certain lot of the far greater number; and those few privileged persons who enjoy ease and opulence never reach contentment or true felicity. All the goods of life united would not make a very happy man, but all the ills united would make a wretch indeed; and any one of them almost (and who can be free from every one?), nay, often the absence of one good (and who can possess all?) is sufficient to render life ineligible.

Were a stranger to drop on a sudden into this world, I would show him, as a specimen of its ills, an hospital full of diseases, a prison crowded with malefactors and debtors, a field of battle strewed with carcases, a fleet foundering in the ocean, a nation languishing under tyranny, famine, or pestilence. To turn the gay side of life to him and give him a notion of its pleasures—whether should I conduct him? To a ball, to an opera, to court? He might justly think that I was only showing him a diversity of distress and sorrow.

There is no evading such striking instances, said Philo, but by apologies which still further aggravate the charge. Why have all men, I ask, in all ages, complained incessantly of the miseries of life? . . . They have no just reason, says one: these complaints proceed only from their discontented, repining, anxious disposition. . . . And can there possibly, I reply, be a more certain foundation of misery than such a wretched temper?

But if they were really as unhappy as they pretend, says my antagonist, why do they remain in life? . . .

Not satisfied with life, afraid of death—

this is the secret chain, say I, that holds us. We are terrified, not bribed to the continuance of our existence.

It is only a false delicacy, he may insist, which a few refined spirits indulge, and which has spread these complaints among the whole race of mankind. . . . And what is this delicacy, I ask, which you blame? Is it anything but a greater sensibility to all the pleasures and pains of life? And if the man of a delicate, refined temper, by being so much more alive than the rest of the world, is only so much more unhappy, what judgment must we form in general of human life?

Let men remain at rest, says our adversary, and they will be easy. They are willing artificers of their own misery. . . . No! reply I: an anxious languor follows their repose: disappointment, vexation, trouble, their activity and ambition.

I can observe something like what you mention in some others, replied Cleanthes, but I confess I feel little or nothing of it in myself, and hope that it is not so common as you represent it.

If you feel not human misery yourself, cried Demea, I congratulate you on so happy a singularity. Others, seemingly the most prosperous, have not been ashamed to vent their complaints in the most melancholy strains. Let us attend to the great, the fortunate emperor, Charles V, when, tired with human grandeur, he resigned all his extensive dominions into the hands of his son. In the last harangue which he made on that memorable occasion, he publicly avowed *that the greatest prosperities which he had ever enjoyed had been mixed with so many adversities that he might truly say he had never enjoyed any satisfaction or contentment.* But did the retired life in which he sought for shelter afford him any greater happiness? If we may credit his son's account, his repentance commenced the very day of his resignation.

Cicero's fortune, from small beginnings, rose to the greatest lustre and renown; yet what pathetic complaints of the ills of life do his familiar letters, as well as philosophical discourses, contain? And suitably to his own experience, he introduces Cato, the great, the fortunate Cato protesting in his old age that had he a new life in his offer he would reject the present.

Ask yourself, ask any of your acquaintance, whether they would live over again the last ten or twenty years of their life. No! but the next twenty, they say, will be better:

> And from the dregs of life, hope to receive
> What the first sprightly running could not give.[2]

Thus, at last, they find (such is the greatness of human misery, it reconciles even contradictions) that they complain at once of the shortness of life and of its vanity and sorrow.

And is it possible, Cleanthes, said Philo, that after all these reflections, and infinitely more which might be suggested, you can still persevere in your anthropomorphism, and assert the moral attributes of the Deity, his justice, benevolence, mercy, and rectitude, to be of the same nature with these virtues in human creatures? His power, we allow, is infinite; whatever he wills is executed; but neither man nor any other animal is happy; therefore, he does not will their happiness. His wisdom is infinite; he is never mistaken in choosing the means to any end; but the course of nature tends not to human or animal felicity; therefore, it is not established for that purpose. Through the whole compass of human knowledge there are no inferences more certain and infallible than these. In what respect, then, do his benevolence and mercy resemble the benevolence and mercy of men?

Epicurus' old questions are yet unanswered.

Is he willing to prevent evil, but not able? then is he impotent. Is he able, but not willing? then is he malevolent. Is he both able and willing? whence then is evil?

You ascribe, Cleanthes, (and I believe justly) a purpose and inten-

---

2. John Dryden, *Aureng-Zebe,* Act IV, sc. 1.

tion to nature. But what, I beseech you, is the object of that curious artifice and machinery which she has displayed in all animals—the preservation alone of individuals, and propagation of the species? It seems enough for her purpose, if such a rank be barely upheld in the universe, without any care or concern for the happiness of the members that compose it. No resource for this purpose: no machinery in order merely to give pleasure or ease; no fund of pure joy and contentment; no indulgence without some want or necessity accompanying it. At least, the few phenomena of this nature are overbalanced by opposite phenomena of still greater importance.

Our sense of music, harmony, and indeed beauty of all kinds, gives satisfaction, without being absolutely necessary to the preservation and propagation of the species. But what racking pains, on the other hand, arise from gouts, gravels, megrims, toothaches, rheumatisms, where the injury to the animal machinery is either small or incurable? Mirth, laughter, play, frolic seem gratuitous satisfactions which have no further tendency; spleen, melancholy, discontent, superstition are pains of the same nature. How then does the Divine benevolence display itself, in the sense of you anthropomorphites? None but we mystics, as you were pleased to call us, can account for this strange mixture of phenomena, by deriving it from attributes infinitely perfect but incomprehensible.

And have you, at last, said Cleanthes smiling, betrayed your intentions, Philo? Your long agreement with Demea did indeed a little surprise me, but I find you were all the while erecting a concealed battery against me. And I must confess that you have now fallen upon a subject worthy of your noble spirit of opposition and controversy. If you can make out the present point, and prove mankind to be unhappy or corrupted, there is an end at once of all religion. For to what purpose establish the natural attributes of the Deity, while the moral are still doubtful and uncertain?

You take umbrage very easily, replied Demea, at opinions the most innocent and the most generally received, even amongst the religious and devout themselves; and nothing can be more surprising than to find a topic like this—concerning the wickedness and misery of man—charged with no less than atheism and profaneness. Have not all pious divines and preachers who have indulged their rhetoric on so fertile a subject, have they not easily, I say, given a solution of any difficulties which may attend it? This world is but a point in comparison of the universe; this life but a moment in comparison of eternity. The present evil phenomena, therefore, are rectified in other regions, and in some future period of existence. And the eyes of men, being then opened to larger views of things, see the whole connection of general laws, and trace, with adoration, the benevolence and rectitude of the Deity through all the mazes and intricacies of his providence.

The Only Method of Supporting Divine Benevolence

No! replied Cleanthes, no! These arbitrary suppositions can never be admitted, contrary to matter of fact, visible and uncontroverted. Whence can any cause be known but from its known effects? Whence can any hypothesis be proved but from the apparent phenomena? To establish one hypothesis upon another is building entirely in the air; and the utmost we ever attain by these conjectures and fictions is to ascertain the bare possibility of our opinion, but never can we, upon such terms, establish its reality.

The only method of supporting Divine benevolence—and it is what I willingly embrace—is to deny absolutely the misery and wickedness of man. Your representations are exaggerated; your melancholy views mostly fictitious; your inferences contrary to fact and experience. Health is more common than sickness; pleasure than pain; happiness than misery. And for one vexation which we meet with, we attain, upon computation, a hundred enjoyments.

Admitting your position, replied Philo, which yet is extremely doubtful, you must at the same time allow that, if pain be less frequent than pleasure, it is infinitely more violent and durable. One hour of it is often able to outweigh a day, a week, a month of our common insipid enjoyments; and how many days, weeks, and months are passed by several in the most acute torments? Pleasure, scarcely in one instance, is ever able to reach ecstasy and rapture; and in no one instance can it continue for any time at its highest pitch and altitude. The spirits evaporate, the nerves relax, the fabric is disordered, and the enjoyment quickly degenerates into fatigue and uneasiness. But pain often, good God, how often! rises to torture and agony; and the longer it continues, it becomes still more genuine agony and torture. Patience is exhausted, courage languishes, melancholy seizes us, and nothing terminates our misery but the removal of its cause or another event which is the sole cure of all evil, but which, from our natural folly, we regard with still greater horror and consternation.

But not to insist upon these topics, continued Philo, though most obvious, certain, and important, I must use the freedom to admonish you, Cleanthes, that you have put the controversy upon a most dangerous issue, and are unawares introducing a total scepticism into the most essential articles of natural and revealed theology. What! no method of fixing a just foundation for religion unless we allow the happiness of human life, and maintain a continued existence even in this world, with all our present pains, infirmities, vexations, and follies, to be eligible and desirable! But this is contrary to everyone's feeling and experience; it is contrary to an authority so established as nothing can subvert. No decisive proofs can ever be produced against this authority; nor is it possible for you to compute, estimate, and compare all the pains and all the pleasures in the lives of all men and of all animals; and thus, by your resting the whole system of religion on a point which, from its very nature, must for ever be uncertain, you tacitly confess that that system is equally uncertain.

Why Is There any Misery at all in the World?

But allowing you what never will be believed, at least, what you never possibly can prove, that animal or, at least, human happiness in this life exceeds its misery, you have yet done nothing; for this is not, by any means, what we expect from infinite power, infinite wisdom, and infinite goodness. Why is there any misery at all in the world? Not by chance, surely. From some cause then. Is it from the intention of the Deity? But he is perfectly benevolent. Is it contrary to his intention? But he is almighty. Nothing can shake the solidity of this reasoning, so short, so clear, so decisive, except we assert that these subjects exceed all human capacity, and that our common measures of truth and falsehood are not applicable to them—a topic which I have all along insisted on, but which you have, from the beginning, rejected with scorn and indignation.

But I will be contented to retire still from this intrenchment, for I deny that you can ever force me in it. I will allow that pain or misery in man is *compatible* with infinite power and goodness in the Deity, even in your sense of these attributes: what are you advanced by all these concessions? A mere possible compatibility is not sufficient. You must *prove* these pure, unmixt, and uncontrollable attributes from the present mixed and confused phenomena, and from these alone. A hopeful undertaking! Were the phenomena ever so pure and unmixed, yet, being finite, they would be insufficient for that purpose. How much more, where they are also so jarring and discordant!

Here, Cleanthes, I find myself at ease in my argument. Here I triumph. Formerly, when we argued concerning the natural attributes of intelligence and design, I needed all my sceptical and metaphysical subtilty to elude your grasp. In many views of the universe and of its parts, particularly the latter, the beauty and fitness of final causes strike us with such irresistible force that all objections appear (what I believe they really are) mere cavils and sophisms; nor can we then imagine how it was ever possible for us to repose any weight on them. But there is no view of human life or of the condition of mankind from which, without the greatest violence, we can infer the moral attributes or learn that infinite benevolence, conjoined with infinite power and infinite wisdom, which we must discover by the eyes of faith alone. It is your turn now to tug the labouring oar, and to support your philosophical subtilties against the dictates of plain reason and experience.

I scruple not to allow, said Cleanthes, that I have been apt to suspect the frequent repetition of the word *infinite,* which we meet with in all theological writers, to savour more of panegyric than of philosophy, and that any purposes of reasoning, and even of religion, would be better served were we to rest contented with more accurate and more moderate expressions. The terms *admirable, excellent, superlatively great, wise,* and *holy*—these sufficiently fill the imaginations of men, and anything beyond, besides that it leads into absurdities, has no influence on the affections or sentiments. Thus, in the present subject, if we abandon all human analogy, as seems your intention, Demea, I am afraid we abandon all religion and retain no conception of the great object of our adoration. If we preserve human analogy, we must forever find it impossible to reconcile any mixture of evil in the universe with infinite attributes; much less can we ever prove the latter from the former. But supposing the Author of nature to be finitely perfect, though far exceeding mankind, a satisfactory account may then be given of natural and moral evil, and every untoward phenomenon be explained and adjusted. A less evil may then be chosen in order to avoid a greater; inconveniences be submitted to in order to reach a desirable end; and, in a word, benevolence, regulated by wisdom and limited by necessity, may produce just such a world as the present. You, Philo, who are so prompt at starting views and reflections and analogies, I would gladly hear, at length, without interruption, your opinion of this new theory; and if it deserve our attention, we may afterwards at more leisure, reduce it into form.

My sentiments, replied Philo, are not worth being made a mystery of; and, therefore, without any ceremony, I shall deliver what occurs to me with regard to the present subject. It must, I think, be allowed that, if a very limited intelligence whom we shall suppose utterly unacquainted with the universe were assured that it were the production of a very good, wise, and powerful Being, however finite, he would, from his conjectures, form *beforehand* a different notion of it from what we find it to be by experience; nor would he ever imagine, merely from these attributes of the cause of which he is informed, that the effect could be so full of vice and misery and disorder, as it appears in this life. Supposing now that this person were brought into the world, still assured that it was the workmanship of such a sublime and benevolent Being, he might, perhaps, be surprised at the disappointment, but would never retract his former belief if founded on any very solid argument, since such a limited intelligence must be sensible of his own blindness and ignorance, and must allow that there may be many solutions of those phenomena which will for ever escape his comprehension. But supposing, which is the real case with regard to man, that this creature is not antecedently convinced of a supreme intelligence, benevolent, and powerful, but is left to gather such a belief from the appearances of things—this entirely alters the case, nor will he ever find any reason for such a conclusion. He may be fully convinced of the narrow limits of his understanding, but this will not help him in forming an inference concerning the goodness of superior powers, since he must form that inference from what he knows, not from what he is ignorant of. The more you exaggerate his weakness and ignorance, the more diffident you render him, and give him the greater suspicion that such subjects are beyond the reach of his faculties. You are obliged, therefore, to reason with him merely from the known phenomena, and to drop every arbitrary supposition or conjecture.

Did I show you a house or palace where there was not one apartment convenient or agreeable, where the windows, doors, fires, passages, stairs, and the whole economy of the building were the source of noise, confusion, fatigue, darkness, and the extremes of heat and cold, you would certainly blame the contrivance, without any further examination. The architect would in vain display his subtilty, and prove to you that, if this door or that window were altered, greater ills would ensue. What he says may be strictly true: the alteration of one particular, while the other parts of the building remain, may only augment the inconveniences. But still you would assert in general that, if the architect had had skill and good intentions, he might have formed such a plan of the whole, and might have adjusted the parts in such a manner as would have remedied all or most of these inconveniences. His ignorance, or even your own ignorance of such a plan, will never convince you of the impossibility of it. If you find any inconveniences and deformities in the building, you will always, without entering into any details, condemn the architect.

In short, I repeat the question: Is the world, considered in general and as it appears to us in this life, different from what a man or such a limited being would, *beforehand,* expect from a very powerful, wise, and benevolent Deity? It must be strange prejudice to assert the contrary. And from thence I conclude that, however consistent the world may be, allowing certain suppositions and conjectures with the idea of such a Deity, it can never afford us an inference concerning his existence. The consistency is not absolutely denied, only the inference. Conjectures, especially where infinity is excluded from the Divine attributes, may perhaps be sufficient to prove a consistency, but can never be foundations for any inference.

The Four Causes of Avoidable Evil

There seem to be *four* circumstances on which depend all or the greatest part of the ills that molest sensible creatures; and it is not impossible but all these circumstances may be necessary and unavoidable. We know so little beyond common life, or even of common life, that, with regard to the economy of a universe, there is no conjecture, however wild, which may not be just, nor any one, however plausible, which may not be erroneous. All that belongs to human understanding, in this deep ignorance and obscurity, is to be sceptical or at least cautious, and not to admit of any hypothesis whatever, much less of any which is supported by no appearance of probability. Now this I assert to be the case with regard to all the causes of evil and the circumstances on which it depends. None of them appear to human reason in the least degree necessary or unavoidable, nor can we suppose them such, without the utmost license of imagination.

The *first* circumstance which introduces evil is that contrivance or economy of the animal creation by which pains, as well as pleasures, are employed to excite all creatures to action, and make them vigilant in the great work of self-preservation. Now pleasure alone, in its various degrees, seems to human understanding sufficient for this purpose. All animals might be constantly in a state of enjoyment; but when urged by any of the necessities of nature, such as thirst, hunger, weariness, instead of pain, they might feel a diminution of pleasure by which they might be prompted to seek that object which is necessary to their subsistence. Men pursue pleasure as eagerly as they avoid pain; at least, they might have been so constituted. It seems, therefore, plainly possible to carry on the business of life without any pain. Why then is any animal ever rendered susceptible of such a sensation? If animals can be free from it an hour, they might enjoy a perpetual exemption from it, and it required as particular a contrivance of their organs to produce that feeling as to endow them with sight, hearing, or any of the senses. Shall we conjecture that such a contrivance was necessary, without any appearance of reason, and shall we build on that conjecture as on the most certain truth?

But a capacity of pain would not alone produce pain were it not for the *second* circumstance, viz., the conducting of the world by general laws; and this seems nowise necessary to a very perfect Being. It is true, if everything were conducted by particular volitions, the course of nature would be perpetually broken, and no man could employ his reason in the conduct of life. But might not other particular volitions remedy this inconvenience? In short, might not the Deity exterminate all ill, wherever it were to be found, and produce all good, without any preparation or long progress of causes and effects?

Besides, we must consider that, according to the present economy of the world, the course of nature, though supposed exactly regular, yet to us appears not so, and many events are uncertain, and many disappoint our expectations. Health and sickness, calm and tempest, with an infinite number of other accidents whose causes are unknown and variable, have a great influence both on the fortunes of particular persons and on the prosperity of public societies; and indeed all human life, in a manner, depends on such accidents. A being, therefore, who knows the secret springs of the universe might easily, by particular volitions, turn all these accidents to the good of mankind and render the whole world happy, without discovering himself in any operation. A fleet whose purposes were salutary to society might always meet with a fair wind. Good princes enjoy sound health and long life. Persons born to power and authority be framed with good tempers and virtuous dispositions. A few such events as these, regularly and wisely conducted, would change the face of the world, and yet would no more seem to disturb the course of nature or confound human conduct than the present economy of things where the causes are secret and variable and compounded. Some small touches given to Caligula's brain in his infancy might have converted him into a Trajan. One wave, a little higher than the rest, by burying Caesar and his fortune in the bottom of the ocean, might have restored liberty to a considerable part of mankind. There may, for aught we know, be good reasons why Providence interposes not in this manner, but they are unknown to us; and, though the mere supposition that such reasons exist may be sufficient to *save* the conclusion concerning the Divine attributes, yet surely it can never be sufficient to *establish* that conclusion.

If everything in the universe be conducted by general laws, and if animals be rendered susceptible of pain, it scarcely seems possible but some ill must arise in the various shocks of matter and the various concurrence and opposition of general laws; but this ill would be very rare were it not for the *third* circumstance which I proposed to mention, viz., the great frugality with which all powers and faculties are distributed to every particular being. So well adjusted are the organs and capacities of all animals, and so well fitted to their preservation, that, as far as history or tradition reaches, there appears not to be any single species which has yet been extinguished in the universe. Every animal has the requisite endowments, but these endowments are bestowed with so scrupulous an economy that any considerable diminution must entirely destroy the creature. Wherever one power is increased, there is a proportional abatement in the others. Animals which excel in swiftness are commonly defective in force. Those which possess both are either imperfect in some of their senses or are oppressed with the most craving wants. The human species, whose chief excellence is reason and sagacity, is of all others the most necessitous, and the most deficient in bodily advantages, without clothes, without arms, without food, without lodging, without any convenience of life, except what they owe to their own skill and industry. In short, nature seems to have formed an exact calculation of the necessities of her creatures, and, like a *rigid master,* has afforded them little more powers or endowments than what are strictly sufficient to supply those necessities. An *indulgent parent* would have bestowed a large stock in order to guard against accidents, and secure the happiness and welfare of the creature in the most unfortunate concurrence of circumstances. Every course of life would not have been so surrounded with precipices that the least departure from the true path, by mistake or necessity, must involve us in misery and ruin. Some reserve, some fund, would have been provided to ensure happiness, nor would the powers and the necessities have been adjusted with so rigid an economy. The Author of nature is inconceivably powerful; his force is supposed great, if not altogether inexhaustible, nor is there any reason, as far as we can judge, to make him observe this strict frugality in his dealings with his creatures. It would have been better, were his power extremely limited, to have created fewer animals, and to have endowed these with more faculties for their happiness and preservation. A builder is never esteemed prudent who undertakes a plan beyond what his stock will enable him to finish.

In order to cure most of the ills of human life, I require not that man should have the wings of the eagle, the swiftness of the stag, the force of the ox, the arms of the lion, the scales of the crocodile or rhinoceros; much less do I demand the sagacity of an angel or cherubim. I am contented to take an increase in one single power or faculty of his soul. Let him be endowed with a greater propensity to industry and labour, a more vigorous spring and activity of mind, a more constant bent to business and application. Let the whole species possess naturally an equal diligence with that which many individuals are able to attain by habit and reflection, and the most beneficial consequences, without any allay of ill, is the immediate and necessary result of this endowment. Almost all the moral as well as natural evils of human life arise from idleness; and were our species, by the original constitution of their frame, exempt from this vice or infirmity, the perfect cultivation of land, the improvement of arts and manufactures, the exact execution of every office and duty, immediately follow; and men at once may fully reach that state of society which is so imperfectly attained by the best regulated government. But as industry is a power, and the most valuable of any, nature seems determined, suitably to her usual maxims, to bestow it on men with a very sparing hand, and rather to punish him severely for his deficiency in it than to reward him for his attainments. She has so contrived his frame that nothing but the most violent necessity can oblige him to labour; and she employs all his other wants to overcome, at least in part, the want of diligence, and to endow him with some share of a faculty of which she has thought fit naturally to bereave him. Here our demands may be allowed very humble, and therefore the more reasonable. If we required the endowments of superior penetration and judgment, of a more delicate taste of beauty, of a nicer sensibility to benevolence and friendship, we might be told that we impiously pretend to break the order of nature, that we want to exalt ourselves into a higher rank of being, that the presents which we require, not being suitable to our state and condition, would only be pernicious to us. But it is hard, I dare to repeat it, it is hard that, being placed in a world so full of wants and necessities, where almost every being and element is either our foe or refuses its assistance . . . we should also have our own temper to struggle with, and should be deprived of that faculty which can alone fence against these multiplied evils.

The *fourth* circumstance whence arises the misery and ill of the universe is the inaccurate workmanship of all the springs and principles of the great machine of nature. It must be acknowledged that there are few parts of the universe which seem not to serve some purpose, and whose removal would not produce a visible defect and disorder in the whole. The parts hang all together, nor can one be touched without affecting the rest, in a greater or less degree. But at the same time, it must be observed that none of these parts or principles, however useful, are so accurately adjusted as to keep precisely within those bounds in which their utility consists; but they are, all of them, apt, on every occasion, to run into the one extreme or the other. One would imagine that this grand production had not received the last hand of the maker—so little finished is every part, and so coarse are the strokes with which it is executed. Thus the winds are requisite to convey the vapours along the surface of the globe, and to assist men in navigation; but how often, rising up to tempests and hurricanes, do they become pernicious? Rains are necessary to nourish all the plants and animals of the earth; but how often are they defective? how often excessive? Heat is requisite to all life and vegetation, but is not always found in the due proportion. On the mixture and secretion of the humours and juices of the body depend the health and prosperity of the animal; but the parts perform not regularly their proper function. What more useful than all the passions of the mind, ambition, vanity, love, anger? But how often do they break their bounds and cause the greatest convulsions in society? There is nothing so advantageous in the universe but what frequently becomes pernicious, by its excess or defect; nor has nature guarded, with the requisite accuracy, against all disorder or confusion. The irregularity is never perhaps so great as to destroy any species, but is often sufficient to involve the individuals in ruin and misery.

On the concurrence, then, of these *four* circumstances does all or the greatest part of natural evil depend. Were all living creatures incapable of pain, or were the world administered by particular volitions, evil never could have found access into the universe; and were animals endowed with a large stock of powers and faculties, beyond what strict necessity requires, or were the several springs and principles of the universe so accurately framed as to preserve always the just temperament and medium, there must have been very little ill in comparison of what we feel at present. What then shall we pronounce on this occasion? Shall we say that these circumstances are not necessary, and that they might easily have been altered in the contrivance of the universe? This decision seems too presumptuous for creatures so blind and ignorant. Let us be more modest in our conclusions. Let us allow that, if the goodness of the Deity (I mean a goodness like the human) could be established on any tolerable reasons *a priori,* these phenomena, however untoward, would not be sufficient to subvert that principle, but might easily, in some unknown manner, be reconcilable to it. But let us still assert that, as this goodness is not antecedently established but must be inferred from the phenomena, there can be no grounds for such an inference while there are so many ills in the universe, and while these ills might so easily have been remedied, as far as human understanding can be allowed to judge on such a subject. I am sceptic enough to allow that the bad appearances, notwithstanding all my reasonings, may be compatible with such attributes as you suppose, but surely they can never prove these attributes. Such a conclusion cannot result from scepticism, but must arise from the phenomena, and from our confidence in the reasonings which we deduce from these phenomena.

The First Causes Have Neither Goodness nor Malice

Look round this universe. What an immense profusion of beings, animated and organized, sensible and active! You admire this prodigious variety and fecundity. But inspect a little more narrowly these living existences, the only beings worth regarding. How hostile and destructive to each other! How insufficient all of them for their own happiness! How contemptible or odious to the spectator! The whole presents nothing but the idea of a blind nature, impregnated by a great vivifying principle, and pouring forth from her lap, without discernment or parental care, her maimed and abortive children!

Here the Manichaean system occurs as a proper hypothesis to solve the difficulty; and, no doubt, in some respects it is very specious and has more probability than the common hypothesis, by giving a plausible account of the strange mixture of good and ill which appears in life. But if we consider, on the other hand, the perfect uniformity and agreement of the parts of the universe, we shall not discover in it any marks of the combat of a malevolent with a benevolent being. There is indeed an opposition of pains and pleasures in the feelings of sensible creatures; but are not all the operations of nature carried on by an opposition of principles, of hot and cold, moist and dry, light and heavy? The true conclusion is that the original Source of all things is entirely indifferent to all these principles, and has no more regard to good above ill than to heat above cold, or to drought above moisture, or to light above heavy.

There may *four* hypotheses be framed concerning the first causes of the universe: that they are endowed with perfect goodness; that they have perfect malice; that they are opposite and have both goodness and malice; that they have neither goodness nor malice. Mixed phenomena can never prove the two former unmixed principles; and the uniformity and steadiness of general laws seem to oppose the third. The fourth, therefore, seems by far the most probable.

What I have said concerning natural evil will apply to moral with little or no variation; and we have no more reason to infer that the rectitude of the Supreme Being resembles human rectitude than that his benevolence resembles the human. Nay, it will be thought that we have still greater cause to exclude from him moral sentiments, such as we feel them, since moral evil, in the opinion of many, is much more predominant above moral good than natural evil above natural good.

But even though this should not be allowed, and though the virtue which is in mankind should be acknowledged much superior to the vice, yet, so long as there is any vice at all in the universe, it will very much puzzle you anthropomorphites how to account for it.

. . . Hold! hold! cried Demea: Whither does your imagination hurry you? I joined in alliance with you in order to prove the incomprehensible nature of the Divine Being, and refute the principles of Cleanthes, who would measure everything by human rule and standard. But I now find you running into all the topics of the greatest libertines and infidels, and betraying that holy cause which you seemingly espoused. Are you secretly, then, a more dangerous enemy than Cleanthes himself?

And are you so late in perceiving it? replied Cleanthes. Believe me, Demea, your friend Philo, from the beginning, has been amusing himself at both our expense. . . .

41

EMPIRICISM VERSUS THEOLOGY

Herbert Feigl

B: Although I must admit that I have little confidence in the traditional (ontological, cosmological and teleological) proofs for the existence of God, I do think that there is an empirical or inductive argument that cannot be so easily dismissed. I am referring to the facts of religious experience. There have been and there still are, millions of sincere believers in the existence of a personal God. At all times, in all climes, in the most varied cultures; there have been people who have experienced the reality of God in the moments of prayer, worship or occasionally of mystical ecstasy.

A: You mean to say, millions of people can't be wrong?

B: Precisely. At least it's extremely unlikely that they are completely mistaken.

A: They could all be deluded, couldn't they?

B: You wouldn't say that we might all be deluded in believing in the existence of the sun, would you?

A: I admit it as a logical possibility. But since we have an enormous amount of evidence regarding the sun, it is overwhelmingly probable that it does objectively exist. We can see the sun, we feel its warmth, we notice the countless and varied effects of its radiation. Our senses certainly bear ample testimony in this case.

B: You trust your outer senses with little hesitation. Why don't you equally trust the inner sense? Immediate experience includes not only sense data but also thoughts, feelings, emotions and sentiments. And just as sense data confirm the existence of the sun, and assertions about physical reality quite generally, data of religious experience confirm the existence of a personal God or some spiritual reality.

[This dialogue is used here with the kind permission of Professor Feigl. It has not previously been published.]

A: Frankly, my inner sense (I use your phrase reluctantly) indicates nothing of the sort.

B: Some people are blind. And even some who can see fail to apprehend the beauty of some works of art. You must grant that this is a personal limitation. The existence of the sun could be confirmed even if the whole human race were without eyesight.

A: Yes, but all the sensory evidence that confirms the existence of the sun cannot plausibly be explained in any other way but by the assumption of the existence of the sun (i.e. that astronomical body at a distance from the earth of eight light minutes, of about 6000° surface temperature, etc.). The data of religious experience, however, can quite satisfactorily be explained within a naturalistic view of the world. Laplace maintained that we don't need the theistic or deistic hypothesis in order to account for cosmological facts. Similarly modern psychology and social science can account for religious experience without resorting to transcendent hypotheses. Let me just mention a few points in this regard. The facts of belief in a higher being can be explained on the basis of infantile experience. The relatively helpless young child is surrounded by comparatively all-powerful adults. The child depends on them, first for his physical comfort and security, later for moral education and guidance. All the encouragements and discouragements received from parents or elders in the long and slow process of upbringing establish a very basic and enduring pattern. It is perfectly natural that in moments of stress or despair later in life we should tend to turn to some super-father or super-mother; and that quite generally we should tend to cling to some form of authority in whichever form the given culture facilitates such projection. Since every child grows up surrounded by adults there can be little surprise over the wide range in which belief occurs. Furthermore, the tenacity of religious tradition is a cultural phenomenon which may be explained by various political and economic conditions. One important factor, among many others, is the advantage to those who are benefiting by the exploitation of others to console those others with promises of compensation in a hereafter. And on the whole, to bribe with the hope of heaven and to blackmail with the threat of hell is still one of the more powerful ways of motivating moral conduct.

B: Aren't you committing a genetic fallacy? You are attempting to refute the truth-claim of a belief by explaining its origin. I could turn the tables on you and discredit your disbelief by showing that it arose from your particular training and experience, possibly from a powerful Oedipus complex that was set up in your childhood or adolescence.

A: You misunderstood my argument. The point at issue in our discussion was this: Are the facts of religious experience valid evidence for the theistic (or, if you prefer, deistic) hypothesis? I have suggested that they are evidence for something else instead. I should be quite willing to have my own psychological attitude of disbelief explained by hypotheses of the very same scientific type as those which I used in order to explain religious experience and belief.

B: Even if you could account for all the facts of religious experience in this naturalistic way (and I reserve serious doubts) your very presuppositions dogmatically exclude any alternative ways of explanation. I shall refrain from accusing you of materialism for I don't believe in name-calling. But I must say, you take the scientific, naturalistic point of view too much for granted. It is your frame of justification. Whatever does not fit this frame is ruled out.

A: Let me remind you that you yourself commenced our discussion within this frame. You proposed an empirical or inductive argument. You quoted evidence. If I show you that the very principles of empirical, inductive (scientific) method demand this psycho-sociological interpretation of the facts on hand, there may be room for argument as to detail, but all essential disagreement would be removed.

B: Essential disagreement *within your* frame of reference (of scientific method!) will disappear, perhaps. But I maintain that our disagreement is more fundamental than that. It concerns the frames of reference themselves. Yours is that of science; mine that of theology.

A: You are now shifting to a very different position. Perhaps I can show you what you are driving at by an *ad hoc* simile: Suppose you had the (fantastic) notion that mirrors were "really" windows through which we can look into a (genuinely *spatial*) fourth dimension of space. If you assume furthermore that everything and everybody has an exact double in the fourth dimension, you would be able with the help of a few more hypotheses to give a rather complete explanation of the mirror phenomena. But suppose you learn optics and find that the mirror phenomena are merely evidence for the processes of light reflection; in other words, that the laws of optics yield a satisfactory, qualitatively and quantitatively adequate explanation of the observed mirror images. Anyone adhering to the principles of scientific method would thereupon abandon the first hypothesis as superfluous. Just remember the principle of parsimony already formulated in Occam's razor: *Entia non sunt multiplicanda praeter necessitatem* or in Newton's first *regula philosophandi*.

B: The principle of parsimony is a rule of scientific method. Your metaphysician might say: The optical hypothesis is quite adequate for the purposes of natural science. But there are truths that cannot be verified and cannot be refuted by the scientific procedures of observation and test. Such truths are of a higher order. You prevent yourself from apprehending them because of your preoccupation with science. You admit only the kind of truth that is verifiable by measurement and experiment.

A: I subscribe to no such narrow-minded point of view. Measurement and experiment are certainly welcome devices for enhancing the precision and the reliability of knowledge. But there is a good deal of perfectly legitimate knowledge that is based on qualitative observation. And, I agree, observation includes introspection in addition to (external) perception.

B: I still maintain that you deliberately disregard the higher truths that are accessible only through our more intimate experiences.

A: The word "truth" derives its prestige precisely from the ordinary meaning that it has in common life and in science. To know the truth about matters of fact is eminently important in all practical concerns. You use the honorific emotive appeal of the word "truth" but you do not retain its ordinary meaning. You engage in a persuasive re-definition of the term. This is the besetting evil of all metaphysics: the systematic misuse of a terminology that originally served a different (and better, because clearer) purpose.

B: I use the word "truth" in exactly the same sense as you do. I say that an assertion or statement is true if what it asserts is the case; if the state of affairs described by the statements exists, or actually corresponds to the description. You and I diverge only in that I admit ways of ascertaining truth which you do not admit.

A: Very well. But what sort of statements is it that you countenance beyond those whose truth is ascertainable by observation and test? Obviously you do not wish to attribute merely logical meaning (as we find it, for example in the truths of arithmetic) to metaphysical or theological assertions. You do maintain that they have factual reference. I fear that the strong pictorial and emotional appeals of certain words and phrases mislead you here. I can't admit that sentences which are in principle incapable of empirical confirmation are factually meaningful. If between the assertion and the denial of a sentence there is no difference that makes a difference as regards the deducible facts of experience, then the sentence may have logical meaning and/or emotive appeal, but it is devoid of factual reference.

B: Is your last statement factually meaningful? I don't see how it could be.

A: The formulation of the criterion of factual meaningfulness is a definition, a proposal—not a statement of fact.

B: Well, I don't accept your proposal. It rules out as meaningless a great deal that is profoundly meaningful to me.

A: I have already suggested that you mistake emotive appeals for factual meaning.

B: This very distinction merely expresses your scientific point of view. You keep begging the question at issue.

A: I fear we have reached the limits of rational argument. All I can say is, that acceptance of my meaning-criterion helps in avoiding pseudo-problems and has generally a most clarifying effect.

B: To me it seems utterly dogmatic. You use your criterion as a weapon in the defence of your world view.

A: You are very unjust. I am not proposing any world view at all. Let the advancing knowledge of the sciences build and rebuild world views to the extent that the evidence on hand warrants such syntheses. I am merely trying to find out what sort of meaning our words and sentences have; and I am suggesting to use language in such a way that it will not lead us into confusions.

But I will gladly put my cards on the table. The reason why I consider the proposed meaning criterion helpful is that it eliminates (as pseudo-problems) questions that would otherwise needlessly torment us. Such questions are in principle, guaranteed 100% insoluble. Traditional theology and metaphysics are replete with them. Through the very manner in which they are formulated they preclude altogether any sort of responsible answer. And if we have no consistently statable criterion that would enable us to recognize an answer when we see one, then surely we don't know what the corresponding question means. This repudiation of unsolvable riddles does of course not imply any conceit to the effect that we shall actually be able to answer all questions. I grant the practical and natural limitations of our powers. But a question which is so conceived that confirmation of any kind of answer is *logically* impossible (i.e., that any attempt of deciding it would be inconsistent with the presuppositions of the question) is nothing but a perplexity arising out of linguistic confusion.

B: I appreciate your candor. But now that you have revealed your reasons it must be obvious to you that you yourself have employed persuasive definitions. "Meaningful" and "meaningless" are terms with strong emotive appeals. You use these terms and their appeals and delimit their reference by definitions that fulfill your purposes. If I find that my purposes are not thus served, I need not accept your definitions.

A: I am not legislating for you. You are free to try it all in your own way. Do let me know when you have a set of definitions of your own. Permit me in the meantime to remain sceptical as to the success of your enterprise.

B: *Success* as judged by whom?

A: It's no use. We can't start all over again.

SELECTED BIBLIOGRAPHY

(ITEMS PROVIDED WITH ASTERISK ARE MORE ADVANCED)

Saint Anselm's *Proslogium* (LaSalle, Illinois: Open Court, 1938, ed. S. Deane) contains the first formulation of the ontological argument. In this valuable book the reader will also find some early criticisms of the argument as well as discussions of it by later philosophers. The other traditional arguments for the existence of God are defended in elaborate detail in G. H. Joyce, *The Principles of Natural Theology* (London and New York: Longmans, Green, and Co., 1951), R. P. Phillips, *Modern Thomistic Philosophy*, Vol. II (Westminster, Maryland: The Newman Bookshop, 1935), and R. Garrigou-Lagrange, *God, His Existence and His Nature** (English translation in two volumes, St. Louis: Herter Book Co., 1934 and 1936). All these are written from a Catholic standpoint. Discussions by Protestant writers are contained in G. Dawes Hicks, *The Philosophical Bases of Theism** (London: Allen and Unwin, 1937), in Chapter XI of A. C. Ewing, *The Fundamental Questions of Philosophy* (London: Routledge and Kegan Paul, 1951), and in D. E. Trueblood, *The Logic of Belief* (New York: Harper and Brothers, 1942). The last two books include detailed expositions of the argument from religious experience. The moral argument which was not covered in our selections is defended in the three Catholic works mentioned above, also in Kant's *Critique of Practical Reason,** in Chapter III of Hastings Rashdall, *Philosophy and Religion* (London: Duckworth, 1909) and in Chapter 13 of W. R. Sorley, *Moral Values and the Idea of God* (New York: Cambridge University Press, 1919). The deistic position is presented in Thomas Paine's famous book, *The Age of Reason* and in several articles of Voltaire's *Philosophical Dictionary* (complete English edition in six volumes, London 1824). The belief in a finite deity is supported by John Stuart Mill, *Three Essays on Religion* (New York: Henry Holt and Co., 1874). Mill based his conclusion on the design argument after rejecting all others. An unorthodox pro-theological position is also advocated by William James in his *The Will to Believe* (New York: Longmans, Green, and Co., 1897) and *The Varieties of Religious Experience* (New York: Longmans, Green, and Co., 1902).

The most famous critique of the design argument is found in Hume's *Dialogues Concerning Natural Religion* and in Section XI of his *Inquiry Concerning Human Understanding*. The former of these books also contains, in Section IX, an examination of the cosmological argument. Kant's attack on the traditional arguments occurs toward the end of the *Critique of Pure Reason,* in the chapter entitled "The Ideal of Pure Reason." Contemporary works in which arguments for the existence of God are critically examined are John Hospers, *An Introduction to Philosophical Analysis* (New York: Prentice-Hall, 1953), John Laird, *Theism and Cosmology** (London: Allen and Unwin, 1940), the same author's *Mind and Deity** (London: Allen and Unwin, 1941), C. J. Ducasse, *A Philosophical Scrutiny of Religion* (New York:

The Ronald Press Co., 1953), and C. D. Broad, *Religion, Philosophy and Psychical Research* (New York: Harcourt, Brace and Co., 1953). Broad, though critical of all other arguments, has some sympathy for the appeal to religious experience. There are discussions of the concept of explanation which have a close bearing on the validity of one main form of the cosmological argument in Chapter I of Ernest Nagel, *Sovereign Reason* (Glencoe, Illinois: Free Press, 1954) and in John Hospers' "What is Explanation?" The latter is reprinted in A. Flew (ed.), *Essays in Conceptual Analysis* (London: Macmillan, 1956). Bertrand Russell's objections to the different defenses of theology may be found in his *A Critical Exposition of the Philosophy of Leibniz** (London: Allen and Unwin, second edition, 1937), in *Religion and Science* (London: Oxford University Press, 1935), and in *Why I am not a Christian and Other Essays* (London: Allen and Unwin, New York: Simon and Schuster, 1957). The English edition of the last-mentioned book contains Russell's debate with Father Copleston to which reference was made in the editorial introduction to this section. A. J. Ayer's objections to the design and first cause arguments are formulated in "The Fallacies of Deism," *Polemic*, No. 1. There is an interesting discussion of the ontological argument by Gilbert Ryle in "Mr. Collingwood and the Ontological Argument," *Mind*, 1935. The topic of "chance" and "design" is treated in Chapter 9 of Arthur Pap, *Elements of Analytic Philosophy* (New York: Macmillan, 1949), and in Chapter VIII of Phillip Frank, *Das Kausalgesetz und seine Grenzen* (Vienna: Julius Springer, 1932). Frank's book which is one of the classics of logical positivism is unfortunately not available in English.

The argument from evil against the belief in a deity which is claimed to be both all-good and all-powerful is strikingly presented by Mill in his essay "Nature" which forms part of his *Three Essays on Religion, op. cit.* It is also forcibly stated in J. M. E. McTaggart, *Some Dogmas of Religion* (London: Edward Arnold, 1906), C. H. Whitely, *An Introduction to Metaphysics* (London: Methuen and Co., 1950), and in a more technical form by John Wisdom in "God and Evil,"* *Mind*, 1935, and John Mackie in "Evil and Omnipotence,"* *Mind*, 1955. Replies to the argument on the part of believers may be found in D. J. B. Hawkins, *The Essentials of Theism* (London and New York: Sheed and Ward, 1949), Josiah Royce, *The Religious Aspect of Philosophy* (New York: Houghton Mifflin and Co., 1887), F. R. Tennant, *Philosophical Theology,** Vol. II (Cambridge: University Press, 1930), and in the three Catholic works listed earlier. Paul Siwek, *The Philosophy of Evil** (New York: The Ronald Press Co., 1956) is a full-length treatment of this problem by a distinguished Catholic philosopher. There are also answers to Mackie's article in subsequent issues of *Mind*.

The classical formulations of agnosticism are Chapter I of Sir Leslie Stephen, *An Agnostic's Apology* (New York: G. P. Putnam, 1903) and T. H. Huxley's essay "Agnosticism," reprinted in his book, *Science and the Christian Tradition* (New York: Appleton and Co., 1894). The atheist's position is given in Charles Bradlaugh's lecture "A Plea for Atheism" which is reprinted in the Centenary Volume, *Charles Bradlaugh—Champion of Liberty* (London: Watts and Co., 1933). Atheism is also defended in Volume II of Holbach's *System of Nature* (English translation, Boston, 1853) and in his shorter work, *Good Sense* (New York: 1856). Robert Ingersoll called himself an "agnostic," but most of his arguments are really arguments for atheism. His main arguments are found in Volume IV, pp. 497 ff. of his *Works* (New York: Dresden Publishing Co., 1902). Although he retains the word "god," John Dewey can also be regarded as an atheist in the most customary sense of the term. His views are expressed in "A God or the God?" *The Christian Century*, 1933, and in the book, *A Common Faith* (New Haven: Yale University Press, 1934). The standpoint of the logical positivists is explained in Chapter VI of A. J. Ayer, *Language, Truth, and Logic* (London: Victor Gollancz, New York: Dover Publications, second edition 1946). John Wisdon's essay "Gods" which is reprinted in A. Flew (ed.), *Essays in Logic and Language*, First Series (Oxford: Basil Blackwell, 1951), has had a great deal of influence on contemporary British philosophers. The volume, *New Essays in Philosophical Theology*, edited by A. Flew and A. MacIntyre (New York: Macmillan, 1955) contains a number of contributions by British philosophers who have in one way or another been influenced by logical positivism and the so-called "linguistic movement" in philosophy.

There has been much controversy as to whether recent findings in physics and other sciences lend support to the belief in God. Sir James Jeans in *The Mysterious Universe* (New York: Macmillan, 1930) took the affirmative side in this dispute. Sir Arthur Eddington endorsed similar conclusions, though with some reservations. His views are expressed in *The Nature of the Physical World* (New York: Macmillan, 1928) and in *Science and the Unseen World* (New York: Macmillan, 1929). Lecomte du Noüy, in his best-selling book, *Human Destiny* (New York: Longmans, Green, and Co., 1947), defends the position that certain facts of biology imply the existence of God. The view that science and religion are perfectly compatible is also defended by the mathematician Warren Weaver in "Can a Scientist Believe in God?" which is reprinted in L. Rosten (ed.), *A Guide to the Religions of America* (New York: Simon and Schuster, 1955). The views of Jeans and Eddington are critically examined in Bertrand Russell, *The Scientific Outlook* (Glencoe, Illinois: Free Press, 1948), L. Susan Stebbing, *Philosophy and the Physicists* (London: Methuen and Co., 1937), and W. R. Inge, *God and the Astronomers* (London: Longmans, Green, and Co., 1933). Du Noüy's book is criticized in Chapter 19 of Ernest Nagel, *Logic Without Metaphysics* (Glencoe, Illinois: Free Press, 1957). Einstein's views on this subject are found in *The World as I See It* (London: Watts and Co., 1935) and *Out of My Later Years* (New York: Philosophical Library, 1950).

The mystic's approach is explained in Evelyn Underhill, *Mysticism* (London: Macmillan, 1930), W. R. Inge, *Mysticism in Religion* (Chicago: University of Chicago Press, 1948), E. Herman, *The Meaning and Value of Mysticism* (New York: G. H. Doran Co., 1915), and Rufus M. Jones, *Pathways to the Reality of God* (New York: Macmillan, 1931). Sympathetic but also critical is W. T. Stace, *Time and Eternity* (Princeton: Princeton University Press, 1952). Critical of mysticism is J. H. Leuba, *The Psychology of Religious Mysticism* (New York: Harcourt, Brace and Co., 1925) and the same author's *God and Man* (New York: Henry Holt and Co., 1933). Interesting logical issues are raised in Paul Henle's article "Mysticism and Semantics,"* *Philosophy and Phenomenological Research*, 1949. Some similar problems are also discussed in F. C. Copleston's "The Philosophical Relevance of Religious Experience," *Philosophy*, 1956.

Approaches to the Philosophy of Religion, edited by D. J. Bronstein and H. M. Schulweis (New York: Prentice-Hall, 1954) and *Philosophers Speak of God*, edited by C. Hartshorne and W. L. Rease (Chicago: University of Chicago Press, 1953) are valuable anthologies in which conflicting viewpoints are fairly represented. Two unusually interesting books are Arnold Lunn and J. B. S. Haldane, *Science and the Supernatural* (London: Eyre and Spottiswoode, 1935), and Arnold Lunn and C. E. M. Joad, *Christianity—Is It True?*

(London: Eyre and Spottiswoode, 1933). Both consist of exchanges of letters between a believer and well-known unbelievers. A. E. Taylor's article "Theism" in *Hastings Encyclopedia of Religion and Ethics* (New York: Charles Scribner's Sons, 1928) is a particularly useful historical survey of the entire subject of rational arguments concerning the existence of God. Readers should be warned, however, that some of Taylor's historical interpretations, especially his reading of Hume, are not shared by most other scholars.

VIII

Meaning, Verification and Metaphysics

INTRODUCTION

There has been repeated reference, both in the editorial introductions and in selected readings, to *logical positivism*. The rise of logical positivism after the first world war is undoubtedly one of the most significant revolutions in the history of philosophy. We have already seen that in its radical rejection of all claims to *a priori* knowledge of synthetic propositions, logical positivism denies the very possibility of metaphysics in the Kantian sense; for as Kant defined "metaphysics," metaphysics is a discipline that pretends to offer *a priori* proofs of important synthetic propositions, like "there is a God," "the soul is immortal," "the material universe has a beginning in time." This attack on metaphysics from the platform "all necessary propositions (i.e., propositions that can be known *a priori*) are analytic" must, however, be distinguished from the attitude of the agnostic who says: "Perhaps such metaphysical propositions are true, perhaps they are false, but we shall never know whether they are true or whether they are false—at least not during this life. For they cannot be empirically verified, by sense-perception and inference from perceived facts, nor is human reason strong enough to discover *a priori* whether they are true or false. Therefore the metaphysician is just wasting his, and his audience's time." The logical positivists also maintain that the metaphysician is wasting his time, but for the very different reason that his statements are devoid of cognitive meaning. For the logical positivists maintain that all cognitively significant statements are either analytic—in which case they elucidate the meanings of words but convey no information about the world—or else empirical—in which case they make assertions about the world, but can be determined as true or false only by experience, not *a priori;* hence it follows that sentences which allegedly express metaphysical propositions in the above sense of "metaphysical" do not express propositions at all.

We are thus led to the positivist theory of meaning, the so-called *verifiability theory of meaning*. It is the most trenchant weapon with which metaphysics, in the sense in which Kant used the word when he inquired into the possibility of metaphysics as a science, has ever been fought. If a sentence by which a speaker purports to state a fact, to make an assertion, is not empirically verifiable, says our theory, then nothing is asserted by it at all; it is neither true nor false, just the way "he eats quadratic equations for breakfast" or "time walks faster than space" would ordinarily be said to be neither true nor false but just meaningless. If, for example, the statement "there is an infinite spirit which is omniscient, omnipotent, and good, and this spirit is the creator of the universe" is not empirically verifiable in the sense that observations can be described that would, if they were made, confirm or disconfirm it, then nothing that is either true or false is asserted by it. There is only a cognitively meaningless sentence which seems to many people to be meaningful because it is grammatically similar to unquestionably meaningful sentences, and because *emotions* of a religious kind, as well as mental pictures, are associated with it. The sentence is cognitively meaningless, according to the positivist, in the sense that no conceivable state of affairs is described by it, just the way the sentence "he eats quadratic equations for breakfast" and "time walks faster than space" do not describe conceivable states of affairs if the constituent words are used in their customary senses.

The logical positivists' attack on metaphysics might be succinctly stated by the following syllogism: all metaphysical statements are empirically unverifiable; all empirically unverifiable statements are (cognitively) meaningless; therefore all metaphysical statements are (cognitively) meaningless. The second premise of the argument is the verifiability theory of meaning, in negative form; the equivalent positive form is, of course, "all (cognitively) meaningful statements are empirically verifiable." We shall presently examine the relevant concept of empirical verifiability, but let us first focus attention on the minor premise. Obviously even a philosopher who accepts the verifiability theory of meaning need not accept the conclusion of the syllogism, for he may hold that some metaphysical statements are empirically verifiable. Clearly, whether such a position is tenable depends on the meaning of "metaphysical." Now a logical positivist would contend that empirical unverifiability is a common characteristic of many statements that have been subjects of perennial controversy in the history of philosophy and that have been called "metaphysical" by philosophers. For example, he maintains that no conceivable observations could settle the dispute as to whether the essence of reality is spiritual or material; that no conceivable observations could settle the dispute between Platonists and Aristotelians as to whether there exist universals apart from particulars (see Introduction to Section I, p. 10), or between Aristotelians and Nominalists as to whether there are universals identically present in many particulars at the same time or whether, as the Nominalists contend, there exist only particulars that resemble each other in varying degrees. We shall consider further examples of such metaphysical disputes later on, but in the meantime it should be conceded that not all statements that have been called "metaphysical" by various philosophers confirm the positivists' minor premise. Some philosophers, for example, would say that the law of universal causation, or the law of the uniformity of nature, are metaphysical propositions even if, as maintained by Mill, they should themselves be generalizations from experience which are confirmed, though not conclusively verified, by experience. It is, however, far more likely that a philosopher who refers to these propositions as metaphysical thereby means to say that their validity is to be discovered *a priori*. Again, the assertion by materialists that all consciousness is causally conditioned by material processes, or that consciousness has a merely "epiphenomenal" existence (see Introduction to Section IV), may be called "metaphysical" by some philosophers though they would not deny that empirical evidence is relevant to the question of the truth of materialism, or of epiphenomenalism.

Very likely, "metaphysical proposition" in this usage means "a very general, fundamental proposition about reality."

If, then, we interpret the positivists' minor premise as a generalization about all statements that have ever been called "metaphysical" in the history of philosophy, it is probably false. If, on the other hand, it is intended by the positivist as analytic, as a *definition* of "metaphysical statement," then we must keep in mind that even if the major premise is granted, the argument does not prove that metaphysical statements in some other sense of "metaphysical," e.g., the vague sense specified and illustrated above, are (cognitively) meaningless. But from the question whether the verifiability theory of meaning entails the (cognitive) meaninglessness of all metaphysics in every conventional sense of the word "metaphysics," we must distinguish the question whether that theory itself is valid. And the latter question obviously cannot be decided until the *meaning* of that very theory of meaning is clarified. To this task we must now turn.

An important ancestor of the positivist view that statements which are claimed to express profound insight into the nature of the universe, though they are neither analytic (and thus subject to the judgment of logic and mathematics) nor empirical (and thus subject to the judgment of the empirical sciences), are cognitively meaningless, is the empiricism of Locke, Berkeley, and Hume. Locke attempted to show in detail, in the second book of his great *Essay Concerning Human Understanding,* how all simple ideas come into the mind through the channels of sensation or reflexion (by "reflexion" he meant what is nowadays called "introspection"; thus the ideas of pain and pleasure are acquired by introspective awareness of felt pain and pleasure). Hume formulated the principle "no (simple) idea without corresponding, antecedent impression," using the term "impression" to cover both perceptions and introspectable feelings. This principle implies that if an alleged idea does not correspond to any impression nor is resolvable into simpler ideas that do correspond to impressions, then it is not a genuine idea at all. To illustrate the principle: it led Hume to the conclusion that the allegedly innate idea of "substance" is no idea at all, that "substance" is just a meaningless word. He was more consistent than Berkeley on this point, for he rejected the alleged idea of mental substance ("soul," "self," "mind") just as decidedly as Berkeley had rejected the alleged idea of material susbtance: when I introspect, said Hume, I come upon a succession of perceptions and feelings, but I do not discover an alleged "self." In modern semantical terminology, Hume's principle reads as follows: if a term allegedly refers to something which is in principle unobservable then it does not refer to anything, i.e., it has no *descriptive meaning.* Of course, a term may have a perfectly clear descriptive meaning although nothing *exists* to which it applies; we know what we are talking about when we talk about dragons, mermaids, giants, golden mountains, etc. But in that case we understand the term because it is defined by means of terms that do apply to items of experience: fire, breathing, serpent, fish, woman, higher than ten feet, gold, mountain.

Now, says the positivist, take an expression like "infinite spirit." I am not rejecting it as meaningless on the ground that an infinite spirit is not directly observable; after all, if I rejected metaphysics because it talks about things that are not directly observable, I would have to reject theoretical physics too, for surely electrons and fields of force are not directly observable either. However, there is this difference between the sentences of theoretical physics and the sentences of metaphysics: the former are indirectly testable in experience, i.e., the physicists are prepared to tell me what sort of observations would confirm (though not perhaps verify conclusively) and what sort of observations would disconfirm their hypotheses. If two physicists offer conflicting hypotheses in order to explain the observed facts, empirical tests can be described for deciding which hypothesis is true, or probably true. For example, the wave theory and the particle theory of light imply incompatible consequence as regards the ratio of the velocity of light in water to the velocity of light in air. But suppose that one metaphysician, to pick a random example, asserts that the observable qualities of an apple inhere in a substance, call it "the apple-in-itself," and another metaphysician denies this, maintaining that qualities can exist without being supported by a substance. Are there any conceivable observations that are relevant for deciding the question who is right? No. It follows, says the positivist, that neither metaphysician has asserted anything at all; though he may think that he has made an assertion because he fails to distinguish metaphorical meaning from literal meaning. The statement that there exists an infinite spirit is in this respect just like the statement that all observable qualities are attached to unobservable substances ("substrata") : no conceivable observations can be described that have a clear bearing on the truth or falsehood of the theistic hypothesis, the way the outcome of measurements of the velocity of light in water had a bearing on the question whether the wave theory of light is true. There is no agreement among theologians, for example, what amount of suffering in the world is compatible with the assertion that the world is the creation of a spirit which is both omnipotent and good. It follows that the theologian is not saying anything about the world when he utters the sentence "the world was created by an infinite spirit."

The positivist does not mean to say that a sentence which is not analytic is cognitively meaningful only if it is *actually possible* to find out whether it is true or false. That there exists on Mars a rock exactly like the rock of Gibraltar is a factual proposition, he would admit, though it is at present *practically* impossible to verify it. All that the positivist requires of a man who utters a sentence in order to assert something is that he be able to describe the sort of observations, whether perceptual or introspective, which would confirm or disconfirm his statement *if* they were actually made. Take the physician's assertion, satirized by Molière, that opium tends to put those who consume it asleep because it has a sleep-inducing power. If the physician cannot specify what sort of observations would confirm or disconfirm his statement about the sleep-inducing power ("it is something hidden"), then, according to the positivist, he has not made a genuine assertion at all, he has just bluffed knowledge by means of pompous language. If, on the other hand, he replies that the empirical evidence for his assertion is that usually people fall asleep after consumption of opium, then *this* is what the statement about the sleep-inducing power really means, and it is absurd to bring it forth as an explanation of the observed fact.

This simple, and well-worn, illustration brings out that the verifiability theory of meaning in its original formulation consists really of two claims: that no factual (i.e., not analytic, not tautological) proposition is expressed by a sentence unless relevant empirical evidence can be described; and that the empirical evidence which would make the sentence true *is* the meaning of the sentence, the factual proposition it expresses. Thus, devout Christians often speak of the ways in which God manifests Himself in human experience; they profess to feel certain indescribable emotions during worship which cannot but be manifestations of God. If only, they would say to a positivist, you will accept as "empirical evidence" modes of experience other than sense-perception, such as religious emotions, then undeniably there is empirical evidence for the existence of God. Here is the positivist's reply: I understand what "manifestation" means in such sentences as "smoke is a manifestation of fire," "ice is a manifestation of low temperature," "screams are manifestations of pain." For here that which is said to manifest itself is itself observable *apart from its manifestation.* But since, as you admit, God is not observable apart from His manifestations, it follows that in asserting His existence you assert nothing else than the existence of the "manifestations." Why not just report the psychological fact, then, that during worship you feel unique emotions; why produce obfuscation by a pseudo-explanation in terms of a transcendent spirit which is logically in the same boat as the explanation ridiculed by Molière (see Ayer in Selection 46, pp. 612 ff.)?

The critics of logical positivism have fired back many arguments, some relevant, some irrelevant. The most important and serious of their counter-arguments are well presented by Stace and Ewing (see Selections 44 and 45). The verifiability theory of meaning has proved most vulnerable in its second claim, the identification of the meaning of a statement with the evidence in terms of which it would be verified if it were true. Statements about past events beyond the reach of the speaker's and his contemporaries' memory can only be verified in terms of *present* evidence, like carefully preserved historical documents; but is a statement about the past then really a statement about the present? To this criticism some positivists reply by distinguishing between *direct* and *indirect* evidence. The meaning of a statement is to be identified only with the direct evidence for it. To assert that Caesar crossed the Rubicon at such and such a time is not to assert that it says so in such and such documents; it is to say that anyone alive at that time would have observed such and such if he had been suitably placed (cf. the discussion of phenomenalism, pp. 153 ff.!), for this alone would constitute direct evidence. This line of defense, however, seems to break down as we turn to statements about other minds, like "he sees blue," "she has warm feelings for me," "he feels a pain in his left foot," "he believes what he is saying now." Since such statements can be verified by their speakers only indirectly, by observing behavior (including speech behavior), facial expressions, states of the cerebro-neural system, etc., the identification of meaning and direct evidence seems to lead in this case to the preposterous conclusion that the speakers of such statements are not asserting anything at all. If, on the other hand, it is maintained that such statements are about observable behavior and physiological processes, that they must be rendered significant by a *behavioristic* interpretation, then a curious consequence seems to follow: when I say about you "you feel pain in your left foot" and you reply "yes, I feel pain in my left foot," we are not asserting the same fact at all; for surely you can truly say, with closed eyes, that you feel pain without having the faintest idea how you behave, what your face looks like, and what is happening in your brain.

Some have attempted to refute the verifiability theory of meaning by showing that it refutes itself (see Selection 45, pp. 576 ff.) : if the theory were true, they argue, it would itself be meaningless. For it is not a tautology; and if it were an empirical proposition, then it would be conceivable that there are meaningful statements which are not empirically verifiable, just as it is conceivable that there should be crows which are not black. But this is just what the positivists deny. And if the theory is neither a tautology nor an empirical proposition, then it is either meaningless or else synthetic *a priori*. But it cannot be the latter on positivist principles, therefore it condemns itself as meaningless! What a formidable indictment of positivism! But perhaps one possibility has been overlooked: perhaps the verifiability theory of meaning is put forth as an *analysis* of an important sense of the word "meaningful." An analysis is not a tautology. In saying "a circle is a closed line all of whose points have the same distance from a given point enclosed by it," we are not giving an arbitrary definition of the word "circle" (if it were arbitrary, why not define a circle as a husband with an annual income of 5000 dollars?), nor are we just saying "a circle is a circle." And any positivist who is worth his salt would admit that some definitions are not arbitrary stipulations but analyses of more or less vague meanings.

The controversy about the justification of metaphysics in the light of criteria of cognitively significant language, i.e., language capable of expressing and communicating knowledge, which was belligerently started by the "Vienna Circle," has not ended yet. Howsoever the verifiability theory of meaning may have fared during the two decades of attack and counterattack after the publication of A. J. Ayer's manifesto of logical positivism, *Language, Truth, and Logic,* in 1936, one thing must be admitted by all advocates of *clear* philosophical writing and speaking: the positivist preoccupation with meaningful language has forced philosophers to be more self-critical about the language they use than they have ever been before, and quite apart from the intrinsic fascination of the problems of the philosophy of language, such criticism is good discipline. Nowhere is the temptation to talk nonsense parading as profundity as great as in philosophy. Further, in forcing philosophers' attention upon language, the positivists are continuing a tendency that is characteristic of the philosophy of Kant: to examine the tools of knowledge in order to discover the limits of possible knowledge. A wise fisherman will make sure that there are not too many holes in his net before he starts out fishing. A wise philosopher, said Kant, will inquire into the powers of human reason before exerting, perhaps wasting, his intellect to unfold the secrets of the universe. A wise philosopher, says the logical positivist, knows that only what can be expressed in meaningful statements deserves to be called "knowledge." Therefore he must try to discover the limits of meaningful language, to formulate a general criterion of significant statements.

A good many eminent contemporary philosophers join the critics of logical positivism in feeling that the formulation of a general criterion of distinction between sense and nonsense is a hopeless enterprise, or that at any rate the line of demarcation cannot be drawn in terms of the notion of empirical verification. Yet, these same philosophers are congenial to logical positivism, perhaps more so than they like to admit, in recognizing that analysis, or clarification of meanings, is the distinctive job of philosophers. Since our readings abound in original examples of specific analyses, it will not be necessary to give an abstract (probably obscure) definition of "analysis." What is the meaning of good, right, free will, mental, physical, necessity, certainty, truth, rational belief, cause, probability? In a sense we all know, but in a sense we don't. We know vaguely, not clearly. One of the tasks of philosophy is to produce a clearer understanding of such fundamental concepts. Whether this is *the* task of philosophy, or at least the only goal of philosophy that could not be better achieved by empirical science or formal logic, is a continuing dispute among professional philosophers—a more fundamental dispute than the one about the merits or demerits of the verifiability theory of meaning.

A. P.

42

OF THE ORIGIN OF IDEAS

David Hume

EVERYONE WILL readily allow that there is a considerable difference between the perceptions of the mind when a man feels the pain of excessive heat or the pleasure of moderate warmth, and when he afterwards recalls to his memory this sensation or anticipates it by his imagination. These faculties may mimic or copy the perceptions of the senses, but they never can entirely reach the force and vivacity of the original sentiment. The utmost we say of them, even when they operate with greatest vigor, is that they represent their object in so lively a manner that we could *almost* say we feel or see it. But, except the mind be disordered by disease or madness, they never can arrive at such a pitch of vivacity as to render these perceptions altogether undistinguishable. All the colors of poetry, however splendid, can never paint natural objects in such a manner as to make the description be taken for a real landscape. The most lively thought is still inferior to the dullest sensation.

We may observe a like distinction to run through all the other perceptions of the mind. A man in a fit of anger is actuated in a very different manner from one who only thinks of that emotion. If you tell me that any person is in love, I easily understand your meaning and form a just conception of his situation, but never can mistake that conception for the real disorders and agitations of the passion. When we reflect on our past sentiments and affections, our thought is a faithful mirror and copies its objects truly, but the colors which it employs are faint and dull in comparison of those in which our original perceptions were clothed. It requires no nice discernment or metaphysical head to mark the distinction between them.

Here, therefore, we may divide all the perceptions of the mind into

[This selection is Section II of Hume's *An Inquiry Concerning Human Understanding*, a book first published in 1748.]

two classes or species, which are distinguished by their different degrees of force and vivacity. The less forcible and lively are commonly denominated "thoughts" or "ideas." The other species want a name in our language, and in most others; I suppose, because it was not requisite for any but philosophical purposes to rank them under a general term or appellation. Let us, therefore, use a little freedom and call them "impressions," employing that word in a sense somewhat different from the usual. By the term "impression," then, I mean all our more lively perceptions, when we hear, or see, or feel, or love, or hate, or desire, or will. And impressions are distinguished from ideas, which are the less lively perceptions of which we are conscious when we reflect on any of those sensations or movements above mentioned.

Nothing, at first view, may seem more unbounded than the thought of man, which not only escapes all human power and authority, but is not even restrained within the limits of nature and reality. To form monsters and join incongruous shapes and appearances costs the imagination no more trouble than to conceive the most natural and familiar objects. And while the body is confined to one planet, along which it creeps with pain and difficulty, the thought can in an instant transport us into the most distant regions of the universe, or even beyond the universe into the unbounded chaos where nature is supposed to lie in total confusion. What never was seen or heard of, may yet be conceived, nor is anything beyond the power of thought except what implies an absolute contradiction.

But though our thought seems to possess this unbounded liberty, we shall find upon a nearer examination that it is really confined within very narrow limits, and that all this creative power of the mind amounts to no more than the faculty of compounding, transposing, augmenting, or diminishing the materials afforded us by the senses and experience. When we think of a golden mountain, we only join two consistent ideas, "gold" and "mountain," with which we were formerly acquainted. A virtuous horse we can conceive, because, from our own feeling, we can conceive virtue; and this we may unite to the figure and shape of a horse, which is an animal familiar to us. In short, all the materials of thinking are derived either from our outward or inward sentiment; the mixture and composition of these belongs alone to the mind and will, or, to express myself in philosophical language, all our ideas or more feeble perceptions are copies of our impressions or more lively ones.

To prove this, the two following arguments will, I hope, be sufficient. *First,* when we analyze our thoughts or ideas, however compounded or sublime, we always find that they resolve themselves into such simple ideas as were copied from a precedent feeling or sentiment. Even those ideas which at first view seem the most wide of this origin are found, upon a nearer scrutiny, to be derived from it. The idea of God, as meaning an infinitely intelligent, wise, and good Being, arises from reflecting on the operations of our own mind and augmenting, without limit, those qualities of goodness and wisdom. We may prosecute this inquiry to what length we please; where we shall always find that every idea which we examine is copied from a similar impression. Those who would assert that this position is not universally true, nor without exception, have only one, and that an easy, method of refuting it by producing that idea which, in their opinion, is not derived from this source. It will then be incumbent on us, if we would maintain our doctrine, to produce the impression or lively perception which corresponds to it.

Secondly, if it happen, from a defect of the organ, that a man is not susceptible of any species of sensation, we always find that he is as little susceptible of the correspondent idea. A blind man can form no notion of colors, a deaf man of sounds. Restore either of them that sense in which he is deficient by opening this new inlet for his sensations, you also open an inlet for the ideas, and he finds no difficulty in conceiving these objects. The case is the same if the object proper for exciting any sensation has never been applied to the organ. A Laplander or Negro has no notion of the relish of wine. And though there are few or no instances of a like deficiency in the mind where a person has never felt or is wholly incapable of a sentiment or passion that belongs to his species, yet we find the same observation to take place in a less degree. A man of mild manners can form no idea of inveterate revenge or cruelty, nor can a selfish heart easily conceive the heights of friendship and generosity. It is readily allowed that other beings may possess many senses of which we can have no conception, because the ideas of them have never been introduced to us in the only manner by which an idea can have access to the mind, to wit, by the actual feeling and sensation.

There is, however, one contradictory phenomenon which may prove that it is not absolutely impossible for ideas to arise independent of their correspondent impressions. I believe it will readily be allowed that the several distinct ideas of color, which enter by the eye, or those of sound, which are conveyed by the ear, are really different from each other, though at the same time resembling. Now, if this be true of different colors, it must be no less so of the different shades of the same color; and each shade produces a distinct idea, independent of the rest. For if this should be denied, it is possible, by the continual graduation of shades, to run a color insensibly into what is most remote from it; and if you will not allow any of the means to be different, you cannot, without absurdity, deny the extremes to be the same. Suppose, therefore, a person to have enjoyed his sight for thirty years and to have become perfectly acquainted with colors of all kinds, except one particular shade of blue, for instance, which it never has been his fortune to meet with; let all the different shades of that color, except that single one, be placed before him, descending gradually from the deepest to the lightest, it is plain that he will perceive a blank where that shade is wanting, and will be sensible that there is a greater distance in that place between the contiguous colors than in any other. Now I ask whether it be possible for him, from his own imagination, to supply this deficiency and raise up to himself the idea of that particular shade, though it had never been conveyed to him by his senses? I believe there are few but will be of opinion that he can; and this may serve as a proof that the simple ideas are not always, in every instance, derived from the correspondent impressions, though this instance is so singular that it is scarcely worth our observing, and does not merit that for it alone we should alter our general maxim.

Here, therefore, is a proposition which not only seems in itself simple and intelligible, but, if a proper use were made of it, might render every dispute equally intelligible, and banish all that jargon which has so long taken possession of metaphysical reasonings and drawn disgrace upon them. All ideas, especially abstract ones, are naturally faint and obscure. The mind has but a slender hold of them. They are apt to be confounded with other resembling ideas; and when we have often employed any term, though without a distinct meaning, we are apt to imagine it has a determinate idea annexed to it. On the contrary, all impressions, that is, all sensations either outward or inward, are strong and vivid. The limits between them are more exactly determined, nor is it easy to fall into any error or mistake with regard to them. When we entertain, therefore, any suspicion that a philosophical term is employed without any meaning or idea (as is but too frequent), we need but inquire, *from what impression is that supposed idea derived?* And if it be impossible to assign any, this will serve to confirm our suspicion. By bringing ideas in so clear a light, we may reasonably hope to remove all dispute which may arise concerning their nature and reality.

43

DEMONSTRATION OF
THE IMPOSSIBILITY OF METAPHYSICS

A. J. Ayer

Foreword

THE VIEWS EXPRESSED in this paper are not original. The work of Wittgenstein inspired it. The arguments which it contains are for the most part such as have been used by writers in *Erkenntnis,* notably by Moritz Schlick in his "Positivismus und Realismus" and Rudolf Carnap in his "Überwindung der Metaphysik durch logische Analyse der Sprache." But some may find my presentation of them the clearer. And I hope to convince others by whom the work of Wittgenstein and the Viennese school has so far been ignored or misunderstood.

Definition of Metaphysics

My purpose is to prove that any attempt to describe the nature or even to assert the existence of something lying beyond the reach of empirical observation must consist in the enunciation of pseudo-propositions, a pseudo-proposition being a series of words that may seem to have the structure of a sentence but is in fact meaningless. I call this a

[This article originally appeared in *Mind,* 1934. It is here reprinted with the kind permission of the author and the editor of *Mind.* In fairness to Professor Ayer it should be mentioned that he later modified his views on certain of the topics he discussed in this early piece. He treated the same subject in Chapter I of *Language, Truth and Logic* (1936) and again in the preface to the second edition of the same work (1946). His most recent views on the subject may be found in his debate with Father Copleston (see Selection 46, below) and in his introduction to *Logical Positivism* (The Free Press, Glencoe, Illinois, 1957). The last mentioned book which is edited by Professor Ayer also contains English translations of the two papers mentioned in the first paragraph of this article.]

demonstration of the impossibility of metaphysics because I define a metaphysical enquiry as an enquiry into the nature of the reality underlying or transcending the phenomena which the special sciences are content to study. Accordingly if I succeed in showing that even to ask whether there is a reality underlying the world of phenomena is to formulate a bogus question, so that any assertion about the existence or nature of such a reality is a piece of nonsense, I shall have demonstrated the impossibility of metaphysics in the sense in which I am using the term. If anyone considers this an arbitrary definition, let him refer to any work which he would call metaphysical, and consider how it differs from an enquiry in one of the special sciences. He will find, not that the authors are merely using different means to derive from the same empirical premises the same sort of knowledge, but that they are seeking totally different types of knowledge. The metaphysician is concerned with a reality transcending the phenomena about which the scientist makes his generalizations. The metaphysician rejects the methods of the scientist, not because he believes them to be unfruitful in the field in which the scientist operates, but because he believes that by his own metaphysical methods he will be able to obtain knowledge in his own metaphysical field. It will be shown in this paper not that the metaphysician ought to use scientific methods to attain his end, but that the end itself is vain. Whatever form of reasoning he employs, he succeeds in saying nothing.

Comparisons with Kant's Procedure

That the speculative reason falls into self-contradiction when it ventures out beyond the limits of experience is a proposition maintained by Kant. But by his formulation of the matter he is committed to a view different from that which will here be maintained. For he implies that there is a transcendent reality, but the constitution of our speculative reason is such that we cannot hope to gain knowledge of it: he should therefore find no absurdity in imagining that some other being, say a god, had knowledge of it, even though the existence of such a being could not be proved. Whereas on our view to say that there is or that there is not a transcendent reality is to utter a pseudo-proposition, a word-series empty of logical content: and no supposition about the knowledge of a higher reality possessed by a higher being is for us even a significant hypothesis. The difference between the two views is best expressed by saying that while the speculative reason was in virtue of its own nature incapable of solving, our aim is to show that these are not genuine problems.

No criticism of Kant's transcendental philosophy will be undertaken in this paper. But the method by which we demonstrate the impossibility of metaphysics, in the sense in which Kant too held it to be impossible, serves also to show that no knowledge is both synthetic and *a priori*. And this is enough to prove the impossibility of metaphysics, in the special sense which Kant reserved for the term, though it in no way discredits the excellent pieces of philosophical analysis which the *Critique of Pure Reason* contains.

Formulation of a Criterion of Significance

The method of achieving these results lies in the provision of a criterion by which the genuineness of all *prima facie* propositions may be tested. Having laid down the conditions which must be fulfilled by whatever is to be a significant proposition, we shall find that the propositions of metaphysics fail to satisfy the conditions and are therefore meaningless.

What is it, then, that we are asking when we ask what is the meaning of a proposition? I say "ask the meaning of a proposition" rather than "ask the meaning of a concept," because questions about the meaning of concepts reduce themselves to questions about the meanings of propositions. To discover the meaning of a concept we form its corresponding primary proposition, *i.e.* the simplest proposition in which it can significantly occur, and attempt to analyse this. I repeat "what is it that we are asking when we ask what is the meaning of a proposition?" There are various ways in which the correct answer can be formulated. One is to say that we are asking what are the propositions to which the proposition in question is reducible. For instance, if "being an amphisbæna" means "being a serpent with a head at both ends," then the proposition "X is an amphisbæna" is reducible to (or derivable from) the propositions "X is a serpent" and "X has a head at either end of its body." These propositions are in turn reducible to others until we reach the elementary propositions which are not descriptive at all but ostensive. When the analysis reaches its furthest point the meaning of the proposition can no longer be defined in terms of other propositions but only pointed to or shown. It is to this process that those philosophers refer who say that philosophy is an activity and not a doctrine.

Alternatively the procedure of definition may be described by saying that to give the meaning of a proposition is to give the conditions under which it would be true and those under which it would be false. I understand a proposition if I know what observations I must make in order to establish its truth or falsity. This may be more succinctly expressed by saying that I understand a proposition when I know what facts would verify it. To indicate the situation which verifies a proposition is to indicate what the proposition means.

Application of the Criterion

Let us assume that some one says of my cat that it is corylous. I fail to understand him and enquire what circumstances would make it true to say that the cat was corylous. He replies "its having blue eyes." I conclude that in the sense in which he uses the word corylous "X is corylous" means "X has blue eyes." If he says that, although the fact that my cat has blue eyes and no other fact makes it true to say that it is corylous, nevertheless he means by "corylous" something more than "blue-eyed," we may infer that the use of the word "corylous" has for him a certain emotional value which is absent when he merely says "blue-eyed." But so long as its having blue eyes is all that is necessary to establish the truth of the proposition that something is corylous, and its having eyes of another colour all that is necessary to establish its falsehood, then "having blue eyes" is all that "being corylous" means.

In the case when something is called corylous and no description or indication can be given of the situation which verifies the proposition, we must conclude that the assertion is meaningless. If the speaker protests that he does mean something, but nothing that mere observation can establish, we allow that he has certain feelings which are in some way connected with the emission of the sound "corylous": and it may be a matter of interest to us that he should express these feelings. But he does not thereby make any assertion about the world. He utters a succession of words, but they do not form a genuine proposition. His sentence may provide good evidence of his feelings. In itself it has no sense.

So in every case where we have a series of words which seems to be a good grammatical sentence, and we wish to discover whether it really makes sense—i.e., whether it expresses a genuine proposition—we must consider what are the circumstances in which the proposition apparently expressed would be called true or false: what difference in the world its truth or falsity would entail. And if those who have uttered it or profess to understand it are unable to describe what in the world would be different if it were true or false, or in any way to show how it could be verified, then we must conclude that nothing has been asserted. The series of words in question does not express a genuine proposition at all, but is as much a piece of nonsense as "the moon is the square root of three" or "Lenin or coffee how." The difference is merely that in some cases where a very slight transformation of the phrase, say the alteration of a single word, would turn it into a propositional sign, its senselessness is harder to detect.

Meaninglessness of Every Metaphysical Assertion

In this way it can quickly be shown that any metaphysical assertion is nonsensical. It is not necessary to take a list of metaphysical terms such as the Absolute, the Unconditioned, the Ego, and so forth, and prove each of them to be meaningless: for it follows from the task metaphysics sets itself that all its assertions must be nonsense. For it is the aim of metaphysics to describe a reality lying beyond experience, and therefore any proposition which would be verified by empirical observation is *ipso facto* not metaphysical. But what no observation could verify is not a proposition.The fundamental postulate of metaphysics "There is a super- (or hinter-) phenomenal reality" is itself not a proposition. For there is no observation or series of observations we could conceivably make by which its truth or falsehood would be determined. It may seem to be a proposition, having the sensible form of a proposition. But nothing is asserted by it.

An example may make this clearer. The old conflict between Idealism and Realism is a fine instance of an illusory problem. Let us assume that a picture is unearthed, and that the finder suggests that it was painted by Goya. There are definite means of settling this question. The critics examine the picture and consider what points of resemblance it has to other works of Goya. They see if there is any contemporary or subsequent reference to the existence of such a work—and so on. Suppose now that two of the experts have also read philosophy and raise a further point of dispute. One says that the picture is a collection of ideas (his own or God's): the other that its colours are objectively real. What possible means have they of settling the question? Can either of them indicate any circumstances in which to the question "are those colours a collection of ideas?" or to the question "are those colours objective sensibilia?" the answer "yes" or "no" could be given? If they cannot then no such questions arise. And plainly they cannot. If it is raining now outside my window my observations are different from what they would be if it were fine. I assert that it rains and my proposition is verifiable. I can indicate the situation by which its truth or falsity is established. But if I ask "is the rain real or ideal?" this is a question which no observations enable me to answer. It is accordingly not a genuine question at all.

It is advisable here to remove a possible source of misunderstanding. I am not maintaining that if we wish to discover whether in a *prima facie* proposition anything is really being asserted, we must consider whether what seems to be asserted is practically verifiable. As Professor Schlick has pointed out, it makes perfectly good sense to say "there is a mountain

10,000 feet high on the other side of the moon," although his is a proposition which through practical disabilities we are not and may never be in a position to verify. But it is in principle verifiable. We know what sort of observations would verify or falsify it. If we got to the other side of the moon we should know how to settle the question. But the assertions of metaphysics are in principle unverifiable. We may take up any position in space and time that our imagination allows us to occupy, no observation that we can make therefrom makes it even probable in the least degree that any answer to a metaphysical question is correct. And therefore we conclude that there are no such questions.

Metaphysical Assertions Not Hypotheses

So the conclusion is not that metaphysical assertions are uncertain or arbitrary or even false, but that they are nonsensical. They are not hypotheses, in the sense in which general propositions of law are hypotheses. It is true that assertions of such general propositions are not assertions of fact in the way that assertions of singular propositions are assertions of fact. To that extent they are in no better case than metaphysical assertions. But variable hypotheticals (general propositions of law) make sense in a way in which metaphysical assertions do not. For a hypothesis has grounds. A certain sequence of events occurs and a hypothesis is formulated to account for it—*i.e.,* on the strength of the hypothesis, when we make one such observation, we assume that we shall be able to make the others. It is the essence of a hypothesis that it admits of being used. In fact, the meaning of such general propositions is defined by reference to the situations in which they serve as rules for prediction, just as their truth is defined by reference to the accuracy of the predictions to which believing them gives rise. A so-called hypothesis which is not relevant to any situation is not a hypothesis at all. As a general proposition it is senseless. Now there is no situation in which belief in a metaphysical proposition bridges past and potential observations, in the way in which my belief in the poisonousness of arsenic connects my observation of a man's swallowing it with my expectation that he will shortly die. Therefore metaphysical propositions are not hypotheses. For they account for nothing.

How Metaphysics Has Arisen. Defence against
the Objection from Piety

There may be some who find no flaw in our reasoning and yet hesitate to accept the conclusion that all metaphysical assertions are nonsensical. For such hesitation there appear to remain three grounds. First, a failure to understand how, if they are unintentionally nonsensical, such assertions ever come to be made. Secondly, a doubt whether metaphysical assertions, if nonsensical, could be made so often. Thirdly, a reluctance to admit that so many men of great intellect could have made a number of what they considered to be true and important statements, which are in fact not statements at all. I proceed to answer these objections in the order in which they have been stated.

(1) The fact that sentences may appear grammatically on a level and yet have quite different logical forms makes it easy for philosophers to formulate bogus questions. For example, "he suffers from an imaginary illness" is grammatically on a par with "he suffers from a severe illness." And philosophers are in consequence misled into asking what sort of being imaginary objects have, on the ground that they must have some sort of being in order to be imaginary, since what has no being can have no property. But in fact, as a minority of distinguished philosophers have seen, being imaginary is not a property like being severe; and "his illness is imaginary" means "he is not ill although he thinks he is." When the proposition is so formulated, the bogus question "what is the ontological status of an imaginary illness?" does not even seem to arise. The sentence "his illness is imaginary" is of a type calculated to lead philosophers astray; but it is translatable into a sentence wherein no such danger lies. The question "what type of object is an imaginary object?" and the answer sometimes given to it that "it is a subsistent entity" are both pieces of sheer nonsense.

The case of the word "subsist" illustrates how words which have meaning in a certain context are used by philosophers in a context where they are meaningless. The sentence "he subsists on a small income" makes perfectly good sense. "Subsists" here means "manages to exist," "keeps himself alive." Philosophers, falling into the trap mentioned above, wish to assert that imaginary and illusory objects have some sort of being. It seems a self-contradiction to say that they exist. But somehow or other they "manage to keep alive." Therefore it is said that they subsist. But in this usage the word "subsist" is nonsense. It is a mere symbol of confusion.

There is a further class of words which are coined as a direct outcome of logical mistakes and possess no meaning from the outset. Such is the word "being" used as a substantive. This error originated with the Greeks. Because where X is an incomplete symbol it makes sense in some cases to say "X exists" ($\dot{\epsilon}\sigma\tau\iota\nu$) and existence is wrongly assumed to be a property, it seems legitimate to talk about the being ($o\dot{v}\sigma\iota a$) of X, just as one may talk about the cleverness of X where it makes sense to say that X is clever. Once it is seen that "X exists" means not that a something X has a certain property "being" but merely that something is X—is or is an X, the temptation to ask questions about "being" disappears.

(2) One reason for which men have persistently succumbed to the

temptation to assert something metaphysical is that they are not content to make observations and generalisations and predictions but desire also to express their feelings about the world. Literature and the arts afford the most satisfactory medium for such expression. Metaphysics results when men attempt to extrapolate their emotions: they wish to present them not as feelings of their own, but somehow objectively as facts; therefore they express them in the form of argument and theory. But nothing is thereby asserted. All that has happened is that the form of a rational enquiry has been used for the expression of emotions which more commonly find their outlet in a work of literature or art.

Another motive for the construction of metaphysical systems arises from a man's desire to unify his knowledge. In the natural sciences one is not content with the discovery of some uniform sequence of events: one seeks also to explain it, that is, to show its occurrence to have been predictable from knowledge of some more general principle. The metaphysician feels this impulse. But, lacking either the patience or the ability to understand the propositions of natural science, being ignorant of the grounds on which the scientist's hypotheses are based and the uses which they serve, he postulates a new and superior kind of knowledge, obtainable by his own ready method of intellectual intuition. And succeeds in knowing nothing.

(3) We need not go to the length of saying that all the great men who have written books of metaphysics are poets who have chosen what seems to us an unsuitable medium of expression. For, in many cases, once the work has been made to shed its metaphysical coating, pieces of genuine philosophizing remain. For instance, Berkeley may be regarded not as one who denied the existence of matter, but as one who attempted to analyse the concept of a physical object. His merit is to have shown that when we make a proposition about a physical object we are giving some more complicated statement than the description of a single sensedatum. Similarly Locke, as Mr. Ryle has pointed out, deserves our gratitude for distinguishing our different types of inquiry, Leibniz for maintaining that what is meant by a body's having a certain position in space is that it lies in certain spatial relations to other bodies, and so forth. Whereby it appears that the discovery that all metaphysical assertions are nonsensical is consistent with piety towards the great philosophers of the past.

Justification of Our Procedure

In sum, as metaphysical propositions are by definition such as no possible experience could verify, and as the theoretical possibility of verification has been taken as our criterion of significance, there is no difficulty in concluding that metaphysical propositions are meaningless. There is no escape from this conclusion, provided that we can show that our criterion is correct. Can we do this?

If we assert that the meaning of a proposition consists in its method of verification, the proposition which this sentence would naturally be taken to assert would be a proposition about the meaning of the concept of meaning. So interpreted it would be an assertion about what was meant by the word "meaning" in one of its common uses; and as such a significant empirical proposition. Observation of the linguistic habits of the class of people whose use of the "meaning" the proposition was about would show it to be true or false: and whatever their linguistic habits were, they might logically have been otherwise. But this is not the proposition which formulating our criterion we intended to assert. In our criterion we have something that is presupposed in any enquiry into the meaning of meaning, or any other philosophical enquiry, and therefore cannot appear as the conclusion of such an enquiry. For the business of philosophy is to give definitions. And in setting out to define meaning or any other concept we must adopt some rule according to which we conduct our enquiry, and by reference to which we determine whether its conclusions are correct. In formulating our criterion we are attempting to show what this rule should be. We cannot do more.

It may be doubted by some whether we can even do as much. They would say that the *prima facie* proposition in which we formulated our criterion was itself nonsensical, and that it only seemed to be significant because we expressed it in sentences which; like the one given just above, would naturally be understood in a way other than we intended them to be. What we really mean was something that cannot be significantly said. To adopt this standpoint is to follow the example of Wittgenstein, who at the end of his *Tractatus Logico-Philosophicus* asserts that the propositions contained in it are nonsensical. They are a means for enabling the sympathetic reader to "see the world rightly." Having profited by them he must discard them. He must throw away the ladder after he has climbed up on it. But it is not a secure standpoint. Having said something which on your own showing no one can say, you attempt to save your face by pretending you really have not said it. But if you admit that your propositions are nonsensical, what ground have you given anybody for accepting the conclusions that you deduce from them? If we admit that the proposition in which we attempt to formulate our criterion of significance is nonsensical, does not our whole demonstration of the impossibility of metaphysics collapse? We may be able to *see* that metaphysical propositions are nonsensical and by making a special set of nonsensical utterances we may induce others to see it also: but for the rest we must do as Wittgenstein recommends: wait until some one says something metaphysical and then show him that he has used certain symbols to which no meaning can be attached; and this would only prove that one more attempt to assert a significant metaphysical proposition had been a failure, not that no attempt could ever be a success.

Fortunately we can assert all that we need without entering the realm of the unsayable. The proposition "the way to discover whether a *prima facie* proposition has meaning, and what its meaning is, is to consider what experience would verify it" is a significant empirical proposition. It asserts that certain discoveries, in fact those discoveries about the meaning of concepts which it is the business of philosophy to make, may be made and checked by using a certain criterion. We test the validity of the criterion by seeing if the results obtained by means of it are accurate. The difficulty is that in all doubtful cases, which means in very nearly all cases, we have recourse to the criterion to decide whether some suggested definition is correct. This procedure is obviously circular. What saves it from being wholly vicious is the possibility of determining psychologically in certain cases that a proposition is significant without it being necessary to apply the criterion. There are some *prima facie* propositions which by universal agreement are given as significant and some expressions which are agreed to be meaningless. Trusting our criterion if it accepts the former class and rejects the latter, we apply it to such doubtful cases as that of the propositions of metaphysics, and if they fail to satisfy it we pronounce them nonsensical. If we were to take as our criterion of significance the possibility of influencing action we should allow metaphysical propositions to be significant, but we should lose faith in our criterion when we found that it also admitted the significance of expressions which were universally agreed to be meaningless: since there is practically no limit to what can influence action.

If therefore a philosopher maintains that our criterion is too narrow and that metaphysical propositions are significant, it is for him to put forward a more liberal criterion: one that allows the significance of metaphysical propositions yet is not so liberal as to allow the significance of expressions such as "jealousy pronoun live" or "siffle hip brim" which are agreed by all parties to be meaningless. Until he can do this, he has no right to object to our procedure and no means of escaping our conclusions.

44

METAPHYSICS AND MEANING

W. T. Stace

The Positivist Attack on Metaphysics

IN THE ISSUE OF MIND for July, 1934, Mr. A. J. Ayer published an article entitled "A Demonstration of the Impossibility of Metaphysics"* in which he outlined the contention of the logical positivists that all metaphysical propositions are meaningless; that they are, in fact, merely pseudo-propositions, that is, sets of words which, although arranged in propositional form, do not actually assert or deny anything, and so are not properly propositions at all. The word "metaphysical" may, of course, be variously defined, but in this context what is meant by it is evidently any type of thought which depends upon the distinction between an outer appearance and an inner reality, and which asserts that there is a reality lying behind appearances, which never itself appears. If any proposition which purports to assert a reality of this kind is meaningless, then presumably the central tenets of many of the most famous philosophers of the world, such as Spinoza, Kant, Hegel, Schopenhauer, Bradley, and the Hindu Vedantists, must fall under this condemnation. For all these philosophers maintained that reality is somehow quite different from anything which ever appears, though they differed among themselves as to its nature. Spinoza called it Substance, Kant the thing-in-itself, Bradley the Absolute, and so on. And by these different *words* these philosophers purported to convey different *meanings*. But according to the contention of the Viennese circle and their followers, none of these philosophical creeds possesses any meaning at all.

It is admitted, of course, that metaphysical propositions evoke within

[This article originally appeared in *Mind*, 1935. It is here reprinted, with omissions, by the kind permission of the author and the editor of *Mind*.]

* See Selection 43, above.

us streams of images and emotions, and for this reason they may often possess a value analogous to the value of the products of the fine arts. But they do not possess intelligible meaning, because they do not give any information, true or false, about the universe. They do not *say* anything. The logical positivists make a point of the contentions that the contradictory of a meaningless (pseudo-) proposition it iself meaningless, that only meaningful propositions can be false, and that the denial of any metaphysical statement is just as much without meaning as is its assertion. In either case what you have is simply a senseless conglomeration of words, a jumble of noises.

This attack upon metaphysics is based upon the now famous "principle of verifiability," which asserts that "the meaning of a statement is the method of its verification." This definition of meaning yields a criterion for distinguishing the meaningful from the meaningless. I shall call it the verificational theory of meaning. As applied to metaphysics, the argument is, briefly, that what never appears can never be experienced or verified. And if verifiability is the essence of meaning, it follows that the assertion of a reality which never appears has no meaning.

The principle of verifiability is also supposed by its adherents to render meaningless, not only all metaphysical propositions in the sense defined, but most other problems hitherto agitated by philosophers. To give a few examples. The question whether moral and other values are objective or subjective is said to be destitute of meaning. For verification is possible only of what *is,* never of what *ought* to be. And if such a statement be made as "murder is wrong," the only meaning which can be attached to it would be that certain people experience certain feelings, such as those of disapproval or disgust, towards murder; or, more properly, that certain people behave in certain ways in regard to murder. For these feelings (interpreted as behaviour) are capable of verification. But the supposed objective property of the "wrongness" of an action is in principle incapable of verification.

The problem of the existence of other minds is also declared to be meaningless. All that can be verified in regard to another person's "mind" is his behaviour. This behaviour, therefore, must be what I *mean* when I speak of his mind. His so-called inner "consciousness" is in principle incapable of being experienced by me, and therefore it is not only meaningless to say, in this sense, that he has a consciousness, but it is equally meaningless to say that he has not. Thus the logical positivists are led to embrace some kind of behaviourism.

It is, of course, quite senseless to ask whether one person's sensations bear any resemblance to the corresponding sensations of another person, whether, for example, what I call "red" is anything like what you call "red." For it is in principle impossible for me or anyone else to compare my red with your red or to verify whether the object of consciousness exists during intervals of unconsciousness.

Thus the new theory of meaning threatens violent revolution over the whole domain of philosophy. For if the theory be accepted, a great deal of the philosophy of the past is simply blown up. Philosophers have always been accustomed to hear from their opponents that their conceptions were false, their arguments fallacious. But they have retained at least the right to defend themselves, to retort on their opponents, if they could. But now they are to have no right to open their mouths at all. For whatever they say, whatever opinions they believe themselves to be advocating, they are to be told that they are merely uttering nonsensical noises. In these circumstances linguistic analysis may remain, and this may be called philosophy if you like. But any other kind of philosophy must simply disappear. Thus the new theory constitutes perhaps the gravest challenge which philosophy has ever had to face.

The contemporary philosophical world seems to be largely divided into those who blindly and uncritically swallow whole the verificational theory of meaning as the latest gospel from heaven, and those who complacently ignore it, oblivious apparently to the seriousness of their position. The former lack judgment; the latter are asleep. But a few contemporary writers, such as Prof. Stebbing and Prof. C. I. Lewis, are making valiant efforts to sift the wheat from the chaff, to ascertain *what* is the element of truth which lies behind the extravagances of the new doctrine. They feel, I think, that it probably contains within itself some very genuine and very important insight, but that its advocates express this in a form which renders it unacceptable. The present essay is intended as a contribution to these efforts. And to both of the above-named writers I am heavily indebted.[1]

The Strength of the New Theory of Meaning

I will begin by stating in my own way what I believe to be the real grounds upon which the new theory of meaning rests, so as to exhibit it first in its strength. It will be found that this strength is very great, and cannot be ignored. The arguments which I shall put forward may or may not be those on which the logical positivists themselves would rely. They may or may not approve of them, or of my way of stating them. This is not intended, however, as an exposition of logical positivism, but rather as an attempt to exhibit the truth which, in the present writer's opinion, lies behind it.

---

1. Especially to Prof. Lewis's paper "Experience and Meaning," in the *Philosophical Review,* 1934, and Prof. Stebbing's "Communication and Verification" in *Proceedings of the Aristotelian Society,* Supplementary Vol. XIII (1934).

The first of these arguments is that the meaning of any statement which a man makes about the world, or about part of it, has to be interpreted, in the long run, in terms of possible experiences. If it has meaning, it must be analysable into statements each of which sets forth a possible or actual experience. Any part of it which is not so analysable cannot be said to have meaning. Thus if I say, "This is a wooden table," this statement means that I am now seeing a certain oblong coloured patch, that if I touch it I shall receive a tactile feeling of resistance in my fingers, that if I tap it it will emit a sound, that if I cut it open I shall receive certain visual sensations characteristic of unvarnished wood, that if I walk across the room I shall see the other side of it, and so on. The statement probably means also that other people will, in similar circumstances, have experiences which they will describe in similar language. Thus the meaning of the statement consists in certain possible experiences.[2] But these very same experiences would also constitute its verification. For how should I verify the fact that this object before me is a wooden table except by observing whether it resists pressure, emits sound when tapped, is of such and such a shape, looks like wood when scratched, and so forth? Hence the verification of the statement would consist in bringing to actuality the very same experiences the assertion of whose possibility constitutes its meaning. From whence it may be concluded that "the meaning of a statement is identical with the method of its verification."

Now suppose I were to say "this table is cotilaginous," and you were to ask me what I mean by this new word. If I were able to describe some possible experience which in some possible circumstances might be received from the table, and were to say that the character of yielding that experience in those circumstances was what I meant by "being cotilaginous," you would then understand me, and I should have succeeded in communicating to you a meaning for my word. But if I were unable to specify any experiencible character of the table which I meant to convey by the word "cotilaginous," if I were unable to tell you what would be the difference in experience between a table which is cotilaginous and one which is not, would you not conclude that the word was in fact nothing but a meaningless noise?

The same conclusions may be supported by a second argument which is, perhaps, even stronger. All meaning is clearly conceptual. Hence the problem is to find a criterion by which one can differentiate between a concept which has meaning and one which has not. (Strictly speaking this is inaccurate, because meaning is not an accompaniment of the concept, but is identical with it, so that a meaningless concept is really a contradiction in terms; one should speak rather of a meaningless word. But I think no confusion will be caused by this manner of speaking, which

2. All this has been expressed, with singular clarity, in Prof. Lewis' *Mind and the World-Order*.

is in accordance with common usage.) Thus if it be said that the world, or any part of it, is X, the term X must be supposed to represent some concept. Now there may be two opinions about the genesis of concepts. According to the empiricist view all concepts are derived by abstraction from experience. According to a rationalistic view, such as that of Kant, some concepts at least are an original part of the structure of the mind which goes to meet experience, and so in some sense exist in it before any experience accrues to it. The point I want to make here is that, whichever view we take, a concept is meaningless unless it has application in experience.

If, as the empiricists assert, all concepts have been abstracted from experience, then every concept must at least apply to the experience from which it has been abstracted. If the concept "horse" means the common elements abstracted from many observed individual horses, then when I return to these horses I must be able to experience these common elements in them. A concept which had no application in experience at all would therefore be meaningless. Strictly speaking there could, on the empiricist view, *be* no such concept. This is the same as saying that, if there is a word which purports to stand for something nowhere found in experience, then there is not really any concept attached to this word; it has, in fact, no meaning. Therefore if I say that the world, or some part of it, is X, this X must assert some experiencible characteristic of the world. It must assert something in principle verifiable in experience. If not, it is simply an empty sound.

A Priori *Concepts*

Suppose, however, that we take the Kantian view. What has just been said will still be true of all those concepts which Kant called empirical. They, having been derived from experience, must have application in experience. But what about the so-called *a priori* concepts? Even here we shall have to admit, I think, that such concepts, although they were not derived *from* experience, would be empty and meaningless unless they had application *in* experience. For example, the category of causality might be, as Kant supposed, a primordial part of the structure of our minds. But it could only attain meaning for us when we come into contact with actual causes and effects. If the mind were emptied of experience, the Kantian categories would themselves disappear. They cannot be thought of except as potential or dormant forms which only spring into living actuality when the mind makes contact with empirical reality. They are the structure of experience. But structure cannot exist by itself. It must be the structure *of* something. And the categories cannot come to be, cannot come to consciousness of themselves, until they have become embodied in actual perception. On all this Kant has himself insisted in the famous words "concepts without percepts are empty." This phrase might very well be taken by the logical positivists as their motto, disgusted though they might be to find that their essential insight comes from such a source as Kant. At any rate these words of Kant express in the clearest fashion the truth that a concept without application in experience is meaningless; and this truth has to be admitted, therefore, whether we take an empiricist or a rationalistic view of the genesis of concepts. But if so, does it not follow that to have meaning a concept must be empirically verifiable, or in other words that "the meaning of a statement is the method of its verification?"

Objections to the Verificational Theory

Now that we have seen the main grounds upon which the verificational theory of meaning may be urged—and have seen, I hope, how strong they are—let us turn to the other side of the picture. It is no part of my purpose completely to catalogue all the objections which may be, or have been, raised against it. Most of them turn upon the consideration that the verificational theory is so narrow that it excludes as meaningless, not only those wordy disputes of philosophers and those poetical effusions of mystics which we are all glad to see belaboured, but also many sober propositions which the most hardheaded men of common-sense everywhere in the world have always believed to be plain statements of everyday fact. We all know that philosophers have been accustomed to make statements which are so vague that we cannot find out what they mean and wonder if they have any meaning at all. We have long suspected that the alleged opinions of those who disagree with us in philosophy are in fact senseless. We know that words may be substituted for thoughts, and that mere emotional edification may be purveyed to us as philosophy. And we are delighted with a definition of meaning which promises at last to catch out the delinquents, and to yield us a definite technique by which the meaningful may be separated from the meaningless. But it is another matter when the proposed definition of meaning places in the category of nonsense half of those ordinary everyday statements about tables and chairs, the meaning of which everyone clearly understands. After all, any definition of anything must in the end be derived by induction from observation of admitted members of the class to be defined.[3] And a definition of meaning must be

---

3. Except those arbitrary definitions which do not necessarily refer to anything in the real world.

abstracted from propositions previously admitted to be meaningful. For example, how did we above attempt to show the plausibility of the verificational theory of meaning except by taking the admittedly meaningful statement "this is a wooden table," and revealing that its meaning seemed to consist in its method of verification. And it will be found that logical positivists themselves do the same thing, as for example when Mr. Ayer analyses the meaning of a statement about the color of his cat's eyes. There would necessarily be something wrong with a definition of "horse" which should exclude from that class most of the animals in the world which are by common consent called horses. And there *must* be something wrong with a definition of meaning which rules out as meaningless statements which everyone in the world, except logical positivists, *know* to possess meaning and clearly understand. Such a theory lays itself open to accusation of attempting to dictate *a priori* to the facts instead of following and explaining them. In other words, the function of a theory of meaning is to find the common element or concept of what we already *know* to be meaningful, and if it cannot do this it is a bad theory.

I believe this is really the trouble with the verificational theory. Numerous instances might be given, but I shall only emphasize one which seems to me to be decisive. I should like to urge that a belief in the consciousness of other persons possesses a meaning (other than behaviouristic) to everyone not wholly debauched by the study of philosophy, and that a theory of meaning which is forced to deny this *must* be wrong. But I am afraid that this particular example would not carry much weight with some philosophers, so I shall select another example which seems to me to constitute a decisive and complete *reductio ad absurdum* of the verificational theory.

Propositions about the Past

As has been pointed out by many before me,[4] all statements about the past are, on the principle of verifiability, meaningless. If I say, "I ate bacon and eggs for breakfast this morning," this statement can have no meaning. For it is just as much in principle impossible to go back in time and verify what happened in the past as it is to get inside another person's mind to see—whether his sensation of red is like mine. But no one outside a lunatic asylum will accept the view that all statements about the past are meaningless, and therefore this conclusion seems to me to show conclusively that the principle of verifiability is untrue.

Prof. Lewis's philosophical position is certainly not to be identified

---

4. See, for example, Prof. Stebbing, *op. cit.*

with that of the logical positivists. But he is in close sympathy with their attitude. And there is a passage in his *Mind and the World-Order* which expresses very well the answer which the logical positivists make to the objection. Knowledge of the past, he tells us, is verifiable. "At any date after the happening of an event," he says, "there is always something, which at least is conceivably possible of experience, by means of which it can be known. Let us call these items its effects. The totality of such effects quite obviously constitute all of the object which is knowable. . . . The event is spread throughout all after-time."[5] The contention here is that the past is verifiable in its present effects. Thus that Brutus killed Caesar is verifiable now because, among other reasons, it is found so written in history books, which fact is one of the present effects of the murder. But I must deny that to know the present effects of a past event is the same as knowing the past event itself. If this were so, then to know that the murder is described in a history book would (if that happened to be the only extant effect) be the same thing as knowing that the murder took place. The proposition "Brutus killed Caesar" would have the same *meaning* as the proposition "It is stated in a book that Brutus killed Caesar." But this is obviously not the case, since the latter proposition might be true, and yet the former false. A false proposition cannot have the same meaning as a true one. And there would, on this account of the matter, be no way of distinguishing a truth about the past from a fairly tale. In order to know that Brutus really did kill Caesar I must not only know that it is written in a book, but also that this sentence in the book *is* one of the remote effects of a murder which actually happened, and that it is not, as it well might be, a sentence in a fairy tale. And I cannot know that a present event had a certain cause in the past unless I have a knowledge of the past which, though the present may have been the clue which led me to it, is a logically distinct piece of knowledge from my knowledge of the present. That I cannot know the past except by a causal inference from the present is quite irrelevant. From rain in the night I may infer clouds which, because of the dark, I cannot see. But knowing that it is raining is not the same thing as knowing that there are clouds. Knowing B (an effect) is not the *same thing* as knowing A (its cause). For in the one case what I know about is B, while in the other case what I know about is A. It is impossible to get away from the fact that if knowing the past is simply identical with knowing the present, then the past is itself simply identical with knowing the present, then the past is itself simply identical with the present. A proposition about the past has for its subject a thing or event which no longer now exists. A proposition about the present effect of something past has for its subject a thing or event which exists now. Therefore, since these two propositions

5. See *Mind and the World-Order*, p. 151.

have different subjects, they cannot be the same proposition, and the knowledge conveyed by the one is not the same as the knowledge conveyed by the other. I therefore think that the past is absolutely unverifiable and that this constitutes a *reductio ad absurdum* of the principle of verifiability.

What, then, are we to do? We seem to be in the dilemma that there are at once strong grounds for accepting the verificational theory and also at least one *fatal* objection to it. This position of affairs probably indicates that there is some genuine truth at the bottom of it, but that it has been wrongly seized, distorted, stated in an incorrect form. Our duty will be to try to seize this truth aright.

The Empirical Theory of Meaning

If we look back at the fundamental grounds on which, as it seemed to us, the theory must in the last analysis rest, we shall see pretty clearly, I think, that they do not really imply the principle of verifiability, but another, slightly different principle. That the statement "this is a wooden table" means (among other things) that when scratched it will look whitish, does not imply that anyone must now, or in the future, be able actually to verify this. If the table were annihilated at this instant, so that any kind of verification would be in principle impossible, the statement would not thereby become meaningless. In order to give it meaning it is quite sufficient that there should have been, at any time during its existence, the possibility of experiencing the whitish interior. And it begins to emerge that what is necessary for meaning is simply that what is asserted in the statement should be something of a kind which is in general an *experiencible character* of the world. This will become clearer, and the meaning of it can be more clearly stated, if we revert to the second fundamental ground of the theory, namely, that which is summed up in Kant's averment that "concepts without percepts are empty." This means simply that *a concept, to be meaningful, must have application in experience*. We may therefore formulate the correct principle by saying; either that *any statement, to have meaning, must symbolize experiencible characters of the world;* or, what is the same thing, that *every concept employed in it must have empirical application*. I shall call this the empirical theory of meaning in order to distinguish it from the verificational theory.

I do not suppose that the exact point of difference between the two theories will as yet be absolutely clear. This is partly because it still requires further specification and analysis. The most difficult question which arises in its interpretation is one which I have not yet touched. If the criterion of meaning is experiencible character, *whose* experience is to form the criterion? I shall consider this problem shortly. But even without answering that question it is already possible to give examples which will clarify the empirical theory, and will show that many of the common-sense statements which are ruled out as meaningless by the verificational theory possess meaning on the empirical theory.

First let us consider statements about the past. The proposition "Caesar's hat was red" is meaningless on the verificational theory, because its redness cannot now be verified. But on the empirical theory it is meaningful because redness is in general an experiencible character of things—as is proved by the fact that it is often experienced. Or, to express the matter otherwise, "redness" is a concept which has application in experience, and this is all that is required for meaningfulness. The same would be true of all the other concepts which are employed, or implied, in this proposition, such as "hat," "existence," etc.

Again, the existence of other minds is, on our theory, meaningful. I cannot verify your consciousness, and therefore, on the verificational view, my statement that you are conscious is without meaning. But "consciousness" is a concept which has application in experience. I experience *my own* consciousness. Therefore it has meaning to attribute this same experiencible character of myself to you. The fact that it is impossible for me to experience your particular consciousness is just as irrelevant as the fact that it is impossible for me to experience the particular redness of Caesar's hat. In other words, the essential difference between the two theories is this. On the verificational view, in order to give meaning to my assertion that a certain entity has a certain character I must be in a position actually to experience (if I want to) that very instance of the character in its very entity. I must be able to experience every particular example of the concept which I want to assert. That is what is meant by verifiability. But on the empirical theory, all that is necessary is that I should have had experience of *some* instance or instances of the concept. The concept then has application in experience and can be extended by me to other cases far beyond the horizon of my own limited experience. That I have seen a few red pillar boxes and geraniums is sufficient to render it possible for me to know the meaning of "Caesar's hat was red." That I have experienced consciousness in a single case, my own, is sufficient to render meaningful my assertion that you are conscious. Of course, if anyone says that a man cannot even experience his own consciousness,—on some such ground as that there cannot be an awareness of an awareness—he is raising quite another question, and one which it is outside the scope of this article to discuss. I am here assuming that a man can *in some sense* experience his own inner consciousness, and I believe this to be self-evident, notwithstanding that the difficulties which philosophers have discovered in the *analysis* of this experience may be very great, and may be as yet unsolved.

The question whether the sensations of one mind are qualitatively similar to the corresponding sensations of another mind, which is of course dismissed as senseless by the logical positivists, also now turns out to have meaning. It is true that the likeness or unlikeness of A's green to B's green is in principle unverifiable. This shows that we can never *discover* whether they are alike or not. But it has no bearing on the question of meaning. If A makes the statement "B's green is similar to my green," the statement is meaningful since both "green" and "similarity" are concepts which have application in experience (in A's experience, and in B's experience, and in that of other people). Therefore the question is not meaningless, though the answer to it may be impossible to discover.

In order to make still clearer the way in which the empirical theory of meaning is to be applied, I will now give one or two examples of concepts (or rather words) which it discovers to be meaningless. My first example is Aristotle's concept of "potentiality." To assert that something is potentially X, but not actually X, is, I think, perfectly meaningless, for the simple reason that it is impossible to experience anything which is not actual. Suppose it is said that the oak is potentially present in the acorn. What does this mean? Of course it is an experiencible fact that acorns in the course of time turn into oaks. And if this is all that is intended when it is said that the oak is potentially present in the acorn, then in this sense "potentiality" is a meaningful concept. But undoubtedly something more than this was intended by Aristotle, by the scholastics, and by others who have used this terminology. For they have supposed that the potential presence of the oak in the acorn is something which explains the observed facts of growth. And they cannot have intended to explain the facts by the facts themselves. It was undoubtedly supposed, not merely that the oak would in the future grow out of the acorn, but that the oak was even *now* in some way present in the acorn, not actually, but potentially. It is this conception which is totally meaningless. For the potential presence of the oak in the acorn is something which could never be experienced by any mind, human or non-human. If it were so experienced, it would be actually existent. In other words "potentiality" is not an experiencible character of anything. It is a concept without any application in any conceivable experience. And it therefore has no meaning. In the gracious language of the logical positivists it is nothing but a senseless noise.

The concept of gravitational "force" can probably be pronounced meaningless on the same principle. That the earth attracts a stone can really mean only to assert such experiencible facts as that the stone, if unsupported, falls to the ground; that if it is supported by the hand, a sensation of pressure is felt; and so forth. Any supposition of an occult "force" which cannot be analysed in terms of any conceivably possible experience must necessarily be without meaning. . . .

45

MEANINGLESSNESS

A. C. Ewing

IN THIS ARTICLE I intend to examine the conditions under which a sentence may be said to be meaningless. I have been stimulated to do so by a belief that present-day thinkers are often far too ready to dismiss a philosophical statement as meaningless, and particularly by my opposition to the theory that the meaning of all statements is to be analysed solely in terms of verification by sense-experience. (Note that only sentences can be properly said to have meaning, not propositions. A proposition is what certain sorts of sentences mean and cannot again itself have meaning except in a quite different sense of the word, such as that in which the "meaning" of something is equivalent to its implications. A meaningful sentence is a sentence which expresses a proposition, a meaningless sentence is a sentence which expresses no proposition. "Statement," on the other hand, is used both to stand for a proposition and for a sentence expressing a proposition. I shall use it in the latter sense. I am not hereby intending to imply that propositions are separate subsistent entities; this is not a theory which I hold, but I have no time to discuss the question here). In this article I shall use the term *positivist* for short to mean simply "upholder of any of the verification theories which I shall consider." I shall use "meaning" in the same sense in which it would be used, say, in the *Strand Magazine*.

The Verification Theory of Meaning Is not Verifiable

I shall first take the extremer form of the theory, according to which a statement is said to be verifiable, and therefore to have meaning, if and only if its truth could be conclusively established by sense-experience.

[This article originally appeared in *Mind*, 1937. It is here reprinted, with omissions, by the kind permission of the author and the editor of *Mind*.]

"Sense-experience" is used to include (a) sense-perception, (b) introspection of images and emotions. Positivists would not usually admit that the occurrence of "mental acts" could be verified by experience, and would presumably have either to regard these as logical constructions out of sense-data and images, or deny their existence altogether. Still less would the term cover apprehension of "non-natural" properties or relations. Now I should have thought the first duty of any advocate of a verification theory of meaning would be to inquire how his theory itself was to be verified, and I propose to be a good positivist in this one case at least and put the question to myself. How could we verify the statement that all meaningful statements are verifiable?

The first difficulty is that it is a universal proposition and therefore can never be conclusively established merely by experience; but we shall relax the condition, as probably most positivists themselves would, so far as to allow of progressive and incomplete verification, and count the verification theory of meaning as verified for all practical purposes if an adequate number of samples of all the different kinds of meaningful statements we can think of are found on examination to be verifiable and we are unable to think of any which are not verifiable. I doubt the consistency of this but I will be as charitable as possible and let it pass. How could the theory then be verified in this sense? It would not doubt be verified if we could take examples of all the different kinds of statements which have ever been made, find by direct inspection what was meant by them, and then discover that they were all verifiable. But I do not think the positivist would or could admit that we can always detect the meanings of statements by direct inspection. If we always can, why all the difficulties about analysis? And it is not by any means sufficient for the purpose that we should *sometimes* be able to do so, for what has to be verified is a proposition about all, not about some, meaningful statements. I doubt in fact whether the positivist would even admit that meaning is the sort of thing that could ever be detected by direct inspection. Further, if we relied on the meaning that statements seem to have when we try to inspect their meaning directly, I do not see how we could ever become positivists. It is surely not by direct inspection of the propositions in question that a positivist learns that propositions about other people's toothache are really propositions about his own sense-data, or that so-called propositions about the past are merely rules for the prediction of those experiences in the future which would verify them. Surely they only come to such conclusions because they first assume the general principle that all meaningful statements are verifiable and then deduce that, since statements about other people can be verifiable only if they are analysed as statements about one's own sense-data, they must be thus analysed. No doubt they can find examples of meaningful statements which are directly verifiable. Perhaps even all meaningful statements on certain kinds of topics are thus verifiable, *e.g.,* all singular propositions about one's present sense-data; but to argue that, because this is true of all of one kind of propositions, it is true of other kinds is as dangerous as to argue that because cats always live on the land, and cats and whales are both mammals, whales must also live on the land. Finally, I do not see how the positivists could establish the truth of their view even in a single case merely by sense-experience. For how can we ever know by sense-experience that there is not a part of the meaning of a statement that we cannot verify? The fact that we do not have any sense-experience of such a part proves nothing, since the point at issue is whether there is something in what we mean beyond sense-experience; and how can we know by sense-experience that there is not?

It therefore seems impossible that the verification theory could be verified in the way suggested, and I cannot conceive what other way there could be of verifying it. For according to the fundamental principles of those who hold the theory it could not be established by any sort of *a priori* argument, and therefore it must presumably be established, if at all, by the empirical examination of particular cases. Now, not merely is it the case that it has not in fact been verified in that way; we have just seen that it is logically impossible that it could be so verified. The statement that all meaningful statements are verifiable is therefore not itself verifiable. It follows that if it is true it is meaningless. But a sentence cannot possibly be both true and meaningless. Therefore the sentence in question cannot be true, but must be either meaningless or false. According to my view it is the latter.

Perhaps it will be said that, although the verification theory is nonsense, it is important and useful nonsense, while the kind of nonsense I talk is unimportant and useless nonsense. But if the statement that it is important and useful nonsense is to be accepted this statement in turn ought to be verified by sense-experience, and how that could possibly be done puzzles me. It migth be held that it is useful because it helps to solve philosophical problems; but how can we tell by sense-experience whether a philosophical problem is solved or not? The mere fact that we do not feel an emotion of puzzlement does not prove that we have reached a solution. Otherwise unlettered peasants would have solved all philosophical problems far better than philosophers, and persistent neglect to think would be the golden method for attaining success in philosophy. Also the method prescribed might easily remove the emotion of puzzlement in some men but not in others, and be useful for some philosophical problems but misleading for others.

The Verification Theory of Meaning
Is not Susceptible of A Priori *Proof*

It might be suggested that the statement of the verification theory should be regarded as a tautology and therefore as meaningless only in the comparatively innocuous sense in which all correct *a priori* statements are meaningless according to the theory. But, if this line were taken, it would be necessary to show that some formal contradiction was committed by denying the theory; and this is not claimed. The only *a priori* propositions that the theory admits are analytic tautologies, if these indeed can be called propositions, but the statement of the theory itself is essentially synthetic. It gives new information, and information not capable of formal proof. The theory therefore cannot, if it is true, be known *a priori*. No *a priori* arguments for it are possible on its own showing since it is synthetic, and it therefore cannot be meaningful even in the modified sense in which a positivist might admit analytic *a priori* statements to be so. It can be meaningful only in the sense in which synthetic statements are supposed to be, i.e., in the sense of being verifiable by sense-experience, and this I claim to have shown it can never be. It is true that it might be deduced analytically from some definition of meaning, but the definition itself must, like all definitions, be synthetic. A proposition giving an analysis must be distinguished from an analytic proposition, or, to put the same thing in different language, a proposition true by definition is not the same as a definition. There can be no self-contradiction in denying a given analysis of the meaning of a term unless some definition is already presupposed, thus begging the question; for there certainly is no analytic logically necessary connection between a word and the analysis of its meaning, and this undoubtedly applies to the word, meaning, itself. That certain marks or noises express propositions and others do not is surely a synthetic proposition if any is. No doubt a positivist can decide to use "meaning" in any way he chooses, but then he will not be giving an analysis of the ordinary sense of "meaning," but inventing an arbitrary usage of his own. However this can hardly be what he is doing, for he certainly claims that those who use meaning in a sense in which unverifiable statements are meaningful are committing an error, attributing to certain statements a property they do not possess.

The positivist is thus debarred from giving *a priori* reasons for his theory because it is synthetic, and also from giving empirical reasons because it cannot be based on an empirical inspection of meaning. His only refuge is to make his theory a purely arbitrary convention which therefore requires no justification. But, if this is allowed, a philosopher may assert anything whatever he pleases. The positivist is excused from having to prove his theory, but only at the expense of admitting that there is no more ground for accepting it than there is for accepting any theory whatever. Even such an argument as that it is simpler than other accounts or more useful for establishing deductive systems would be an appeal to a criterion conformity with which certainly cannot be discovered by sense-experience. And it remains true that his theory could mean nothing on its own showing, being neither an *a priori* analytic proposition nor one verifiable by sense-experience.

Now if a theory means nothing I really cannot be expected to refute it. Perhaps it is a very good lyrical expression of the positivist's emotions, but while not wishing to show any lack of sympathy towards his emotions I cannot see that this of itself could make it a useful contribution to philosophy. I add the autobiographical detail that I have never had any emotion myself of which it seemed to me at all a suitable expression. Or perhaps it is a command to treat only those propositions as meaningful which are verifiable; but with all due respect to the positivists I do not see why I should obey their commands unless they can show me that I (or the world) will gain by my doing so.

Is Experience Really Irrelevant to Metaphysical Statements?

Let us now turn to the milder form of the theory which was sponsored by Mr. Ayer in *Language, Truth and Logic*. According to this a statement is meaningful if and only if it is logically possible that observations might be made which would be relevant to its truth or falsehood, i.e., make its truth more or less probable (He does not use the word probable here, but since he thinks no conclusive verification of anything is possible this must be what he means). Now this formulation of the theory does not give Mr. Ayer nearly as much as he wants. For, with the possible exception of the ontological proof, which I do not wish to defend, it is doubtful whether any philosophers have ever asserted a proposition to the truth of which they did not think some experience or other was relevant. What I mean may be made clear by taking a few examples from among the most abstract of metaphysical arguments. The cosmological proof, for instance, starts with the premise that something or other exists, this being regarded as given in experience; the argument for an Absolute Mind including all human minds professes to start from the incomplete and incoherent character of our experience, which is held therefore to point to a more complete experience, and to be supported by citing the empirical facts of co-operation and love; the realist view of physical objects claims to be based on the experience of perception either as in itself a proof of their existence (the direct theory of perception) or as a premise from which causal inferences can be made showing that they probably exist. No doubt in some of the cases I have mentioned the metaphysician may be wrong in thinking that experience renders his conclusion probable, but we can only decide whether this is so after we have examined and refuted his argument. Since he claims that experience is relevant we cannot dismiss his theory as meaningless without examination, as the positivist would like to do, merely on the ground that its probability cannot be affected by any experience. Most metaphysical arguments may be hopelessly wrong, but I do not see how we can tell whether they are except by examining them separately on their own merits, to see whether they can really be supported by experience. We cannot nonsuit all of them *en masse* by the positivist criterion without begging the whole question.

The statement that the world of sense-experience is altogether unreal, which is taken by Mr. Ayer as a good example of a nonsensical utterance, is certainly a statement to the truth or falsity of which experience is relevant, and it should therefore by his criterion have a meaning. For it is contradicted by all our sense-experience and therefore ought to be rejected as false (not meaningless), unless the man who makes it is speaking in metaphors. And, even if he is speaking in metaphors and does not mean "altogether unreal," but e.g., "incoherent when taken by itself" or "relatively unimportant," his statement certainly claims to be based on the alleged self-contradictory or otherwise defective character of our sense-experience, and therefore the specific empirical character of our sense-experience is certainly relevant to it. Again take the statement that the whole universe was created by a morally perfect God. This would be held by Mr. Ayer to be meaningless, and would be generally admitted to be a metaphysical doctrine if anything is. Yet it is quite clear that empirical facts regarding the amount and distribution of suffering in the world will affect its probability. If we came to the conclusion that there was much more suffering in the word than we had thought and that there were hardly any empirical cases of suffering producing any good result, it would obviously make the truth of the belief in some degree less probable. Further the truth of the belief would increase the probability of some propositions about the future being true. For it would certainly at least increase the probability of the proposition that I shall survive bodily death being true. Now the latter is a proposition which clearly could be verified and presumably will in fact be verified, if it is true. For if it is true I shall verify it by having experiences after bodily death. The metaphysical proposition about God is therefore one which is relevant to experiential propositions and to which experiential propositions are relevant.

Incidentally the question of survival seems to create a first-class puzzle for the positivists. That I shall survive bodily death is a proposition capable of future verification, if it is true, through my having experiences after death, but the contradictory proposition that I shall not survive bodily death could never by any possible chance be verified because I cannot experience myself as having no experiences. It seems then the positivist ought to conclude that the proposition that I shall survive death is logically necessary because the only alternative is meaningless. But that such a proposition should be logically necessary is obviously inconsistent with his theories; it is clearly synthetic. Therefore I fear he will not be as grateful to me as he ought to be for having shown that his theory has proved that we can never die.

Mr. Ayer has, therefore, not succeeded in giving a criterion which rules out metaphysics any more or less than the proposition he wishes to admit. Further in its second, as in its first, form it remains highly doubtful whether the verification theory can itself be verified. For we could only verify it by examining all the different kinds of meaningful statements and seeing whether sense-experience was relevant to their truth, i.e., whether they could be proved or refuted by sense-experience or rendered more or less probable. But once a positivist has admitted, as Mr. Ayer has now done, that a statement may have meaning, even if it asserts something which cannot be directly experienced, provided only there could be experiences from which we might make legitimate inferences to the effect that its probability is increased or diminished, he is open to the objection that we cannot possibly learn from sense-experience alone whether an inference is legitimate or not. That B follows from A is not anything that can be sensed, and mere sense-experience cannot justify us even in thinking it probable that it will follow from A unless the sense-experience is accompanied by some principles of probable inference which are not themselves objects of the senses.

If I am right the verification theory is completely suicidal, because, if it succeeds, it shows itself to be meaningless, and therefore not true. But, even if you are not willing to go as far as this with me, you must remember that philosophers have no right to assert a theory without reasons, at least unless they seem to themselves to see quite clearly that it is self-evident; and this cannot be so in the present case, for the positivist would certainly reject self-evidence as a criterion of truth and therefore cannot use it in defense of his own doctrine. Further you must remember that, unless a theory is proved with complete certainty, part of its criterion lies in the consequences which can be deduced from it, and if these are very unplausible they will cast doubt on the theory itself.

To refuse to reconsider a theory of yours because it leads to absurd consequences is, unless the theory has been proved with certainty, not to deserve praise for being logical but to deserve blame for being prejudiced. . . .

An Alternative Criterion of Meaninglessness

Having rejected the verification theory of meaning, it is perhaps incumbent on me to give some account of the conditions under which verbal expressions could be said to be meaningless. This I shall now proceed to do. It seems clear that the following classes of expressions, at least, are meaningless.

1. There are sentences which express exclamations, wishes, commands, exhortations. These do not assert propositions, and therefore there is a sense in which they have no meaning, though no doubt in another sense they have a meaning since they can certainly be understood (or misunderstood). It is possible that a philosopher might confuse such a sentence with a sentence expressing a proposition and so utter a sentence which had no meaning, thinking it had a meaning, though I doubt whether this occurs at all frequently.

2. There are expressions such as "the table is beside" or "Cambridge is between York" which are meaningless because incomplete, i.e., the form of the expression is such as to require an additional term to give it meaning and the additional term is absent. In the first example there is a dyadic relation with only one term, in the second a triadic relation with only two terms. There are, I think, cases where philosophers have thought that probability was a quality, so that you could say A was probable significantly without either asserting or understanding any data to which the probability of A was relative, while probability is really a relative term (The statement, A is probable, made in ordinary conversation is not meaningless, because another term, i.e., one's present data, to which the probability is relative, is understood if not expressed).

3. An expression may be said to be meaningless if it includes some word or words which do not stand for anything. If the meaning of the word in question is complex, it might be said to be meaningless on the ground that it was self-contradictory, in which case it will come under a later heading; but apart from this we might conceivably have a sentence containing indefinable or undefined words which stood, not for something self-contradictory, but for absolutely nothing at all. I do not mean merely "for nothing existent" but for nothing of which we have any idea at all. I do not know any clear instances of sentences containing such words in any philosopher except Lewis Carroll, but it would no doubt

be alleged by some philosophers that, e.g., "subsist" as opposed to exist or "good" as used in *Principia Ethica* are examples.

4. An expression (we should hardly call it a sentence) might consist of words all of which had a meaning and yet be itself meaningless because the words were combined in a way contrary to the rules of syntax, e.g., are of fond not dogs cats. The term "syntax" is used here in its strictly grammatical sense, not in the extended sense in which "grammar" is used by certain positivists. I do not know whether there are instances of such expressions in philosophical works excepting those due to momentary slips or misprints.

There no doubt are these four classes of meaningless expressions, but I come now to two other alleged classes of meaningless sentences, about which I feel a good deal of doubt. In fact I shall contend against most philosophers that they are not meaningless at all.

5. It is usually held that a sentence which ascribes to something a relatively determinate value of a determinable which does not qualify it is meaningless, whether the determinate value is asserted or denied of it. The most usual example of this cited lately at Cambridge is—Quadratic equations go to race-meeting, the example in my days at Oxford was— Virtue is a fire-shovel. It is generally held that such statements are not false but meaningless. It is further held that their contradictories,— Quadratic equations do not go to race-meetings—and Virtue is not a fire-shovel,—are not true, but likewise meaningless. This, however, I am prepared to dispute. For after all—quadratic equations do not go to race-meetings—is entailed by—quadratic equations do not move in space, and entails—quadratic equations do not watch the Newmarket horse-races; but, if it is capable of entailing and being entailed, surely it must be a proposition and not a mere meaningless set of words. Again, surely you do really know that quadratic equations do not go to race-meetings? But how could you possibly know it if the words did not express a proposition, did not mean anything? There would be nothing to know.

No doubt if I frequently made assertions such as—Virtue is not a fireshovel—or—Quadratic equations do not go to race-meetings, I should be in danger of being consigned to an asylum, and it may be asked why I should be regarded as a lunatic because I say what is true. The answer is that to qualify as a lunatic it is not necessary to say what is false or meaningless; it is sufficient persistently to say what is true in an unsuitable context. The proposition—2 + 2 = 4—is impeccably and indisputably true, but if I frequently asserted this proposition in unsuitable contexts, e.g., whenever anybody asked me a question about something totally different, I should soon be regarded as a lunatic. Now the proposition that quadratic equations do not go to race-meetings is a proposition of such a kind that there is hardly any context in which its assertion is suitable. It is, I hope, suitable in this article, but this is certainly the first occasion in my life on which I have found it suitable to assert it, and most people go through their whole lives without finding such an occasion at all. Consequently the assertion of it outside philosophical gatherings would generally be regarded as a mark of insanity. The reason why the context is never suitable is because the proposition is so obviously true that it can never enter into anybody's mind to think of questioning it, and because, unlike $2 + 2 = 4$, it also happens to be of such a kind that it can never, as far as I know, be used as a means of making inferences that are practically or theoretically useful.

The proposition that quadratic equations do not go to race-meetings belongs to a large class of propositions that may best be characterised as true but misleading. I shall give you another proposition that belongs to this class. The proposition is this—I did not commit more than six murders last week. This proposition, I assert, is true. I did not commit any murders last week, and therefore I did not commit more than six. But it is misleading because nobody would in fact ask whether I had committed more than six murders unless he assumed that I had probably committed some. Similarly, nobody would ask whether quadratic equations went to race-meetings unless he assumed that quadratic equations were at any rate the sort of things that could move in space. Other instances of true but misleading propositions are—I worked an hour yesterday (when I really worked eight), he has not stopped beating his wife (when he never started). No doubt there is an important difference between a proposition such as—Quadratic equations do not attend race-meetings—and the other examples I have mentioned in that it is logically impossible that quadratic equations should attend race-meetings while it is not logically impossible that, e.g., I should have committed six murders last week. All I am suggesting is that the propositions are similar in being both true and misleading, not that they are similar in other respects. . . .*

---

* The sixth class of allegedly meaningless sentences, whose discussion is here omitted, consists of self-contradictory sentences. (Eds.)

46

LOGICAL POSITIVISM—A DEBATE

A. J. Ayer and F. C. Copleston

Metaphysics, Analytic Philosophy and Science

AYER: Well, Father Copleston, you've asked me to summarize Logical Positivism for you and it's not very easy. For one thing, as I understand it, Logical Positivism is not a system of philosophy. It consists rather in a certain technique—a certain kind of attitude towards philosophic problems. Thus, one thing which those of us who are called logical positivists tend to have in common is that we deny the possibility of philosophy as a speculative discipline. We should say that if philosophy was to be a branch of knowledge, as distinct from the sciences, it would have to consist in logic or in some form of analysis, and our reason for this would be somewhat as follows. We maintain that you can divide propositions into two classes, formal and empirical. Formal propositions, like those of logic and mathematics, depend for their validity on the conventions of a symbol system. Empirical propositions, on the other hand, are statements of actual or possible observation, or hypotheses, from which such statements can be logically derived; and it is they that constitute science in so far as science isn't purely mathematical. Now our contention is that this exhausts the field of what may be called speculative knowledge. Consequently we reject metaphysics, if this be understood, as I think it commonly has been, as an attempt to gain knowledge about the world by non-scientific means. In as much as metaphysical statements are not testable by observation, we hold they are not descriptive of anything. And from this we should conclude that if philosophy is to be a cognitive activity it must be purely critical. It would take the

[This debate took place on the Third Program of the British Broadcasting Corporation on June 13, 1949. It is here published for the first time with the kind permission of Professor Ayer and Father Copleston.]

form of trying to elucidate the concepts that were used in science or mathematics or in everyday language.

COPLESTON: Well, Professor Ayer, I can quite understand, of course, philosophers confining themselves to logical analysis if they wish to do so, and I shouldn't dream of denying or of belittling in any way its utility: I think it's obviously an extremely useful thing to do to analyse and clarify the concepts used in science. In everyday life, too, there are many terms used that practically have taken on an emotional connotation—"progressive" or "reactionary" or "freedom" or "the modern mind":—to make clear to people what's meant or what they mean by those terms, or the various possible meanings, is a very useful thing. But if the Logical Positivist means that logical analysis is the *only* function of philosophy—that's the point at which I should disagree with him. And so would many other philosophers disagree—especially on the continent. Don't you think that by saying what philosophy is, one presupposes a philosophy, or takes up a position as a philosopher? For example, if one divides significant propositions into two classes, namely purely formal propositions and statements of observation, one is adopting a philosophical position: one is claiming that there are no necessary propositions which are not purely formal. Moreover, to claim that metaphysical propositions, to be significant, should be verifiable as scientific hypotheses are verifiable is to claim that metaphysics, to be significant, should not be metaphysics.

AYER: Yes, I agree that my position is philosophical, but not that it is metaphysical, as I hope to show later. To say what philosophy is, is certainly a philosophical act, but by this I mean that it is itself a question of philosophical analysis. We have to decide, among other things, what it is that we are going to call "philosophy" and I have given you my answer. It is not, perhaps, an obvious answer but it at least has the merit that it rescues philosophical statements from becoming either meaningless or trivial. But I don't suppose that we want to quarrel about how we're going to use a word, so much as to discuss the points underlying what you've just said. You would hold, I gather, that in the account I gave of the possible fields of knowledge something was left out.

COPLESTON: Yes.

AYER: And that which is left out is what people called philosophers might well be expected to study?

COPLESTON: Yes, I should hold that philosophy, at any rate metaphysical philosophy, begins, in a sense, where science leaves off. In my personal opinion, one of the chief functions of metaphysics is to open the mind to the Transcendent—to remove the ceiling of the room, as it were, the room being the world as amenable to scientific handling and investigation. But this is not to say that the metaphysician is simply concerned with the Transcendent. Phenomena themselves (objects of what you would probably call "experience") can be considered from the metaphysical angle. The problem of universals, for instance, is a metaphysical problem. I say that metaphysical philosophy begins, *in a sense,* where science leaves off, because I do not mean to imply that the metaphysician cannot begin until science has finished its work. If this were so, the metaphysician would be quite unable to start. I mean that he asks other questions than those asked by the scientist and pursues a different method.

AYER: To say that philosophy begins where science leaves off is perfectly all right if you mean that the philosopher takes the results of the scientist, analyses them, shows the logical connection of one proposition with another, and so on. But if you say that it leaps into a quite different realm—the realm which you describe as the "transcendent"—then I think I cease to follow you. And I think I can explain why I cease to follow you. I hold a principle, known as the principle of verification, according to which a statement intended to be a statement of fact is meaningful only if it's either formally valid, or some kind of observation is relevant to its truth or falsehood. My difficulty with your so-called transcendent statements is that their truth or falsehood doesn't, it seems to me, make the slightest difference to anything that any one experiences.

COPLESTON: I don't care for the phrase "transcendent statement." I think myself that some positive descriptive statements about the Transcendent are possible; but, leaving that out of account, I think that one of the possible functions of the philosopher (a function which you presumably exclude) is to reveal the limits of science as a complete and exhaustive description and analysis of reality.

AYER: Limits of science? You see I can quite well understand your saying that science is limited if you mean only that many more things may be discovered. You may say, for example, that the physics of the seventeenth century was limited in so far as physicists of the eighteenth, nineteenth and twentieth centuries have gone very much further.

COPLESTON: No, I didn't mean that at all. Perhaps I can illustrate what I mean in reference to anthropology. The biochemist can describe Man within his own terms of reference and up to a certain extent. But, although biochemistry may doubtless continue to advance, I see no reason to suppose that the biochemist will be able to give an exhaustive analysis of Man. The psychologist certainly would not think so. Now, one of the possible functions of a philosopher is to show how all these sceintific analyses of man—the analyses of the biochemist, the empirical psychologist and so on—are unable to achieve the exhaustive analysis of the individual human being. Karl Jaspers, for example, would maintain that Man as free, i.e. precisely as free, cannot be adequately handled by any scientist who presupposes the applicability of the principle of deterministic causality and conducts his investigations with that presupposition in mind. I am not a follower of Karl Jaspers; but I think that to call attention to what he calls *Existenz* is a legitimate philosophical procedure.

Metaphysical and Scientific Explanation

AYER: I do not see that you can know *a priori* that human behaviour is inexplicable. The most you can say is that our present stock of psychological hypotheses isn't adequate to explain certain features of it: and you may very well be right. But what more is required is better psychological investigation. We need to form new theories and test the theories by further observation, which is again the method of science. It seems to me that all you've said, when you've talked of the limits of science, is simply that a given science may not explain things, or explain as much as you would like to see explained. But that, which to me seems to be perfectly acceptable, is only a historical statement about a point which science has reached at a given stage. It doesn't show that there's room for a quite different kind of discipline, and you haven't made clear to me what that different kind of discipline which you reserve for the philosopher is supposed to be.

COPLESTON: Well, I think that one of the possible functions of the philosopher is to consider what is sometimes called the non-empirical or intelligible self. There is an obvious objection, from your point of view, against the phrase "non-empirical self;" but I would like to turn to metaphysics in general. The scientists can describe various particular aspects of things, and all the sciences together can give, it is true, a very general description of reality. But the scientist, precisely as scientist, does not raise, for example, the question why anything is there at all. To raise this question is, in my opinion, one of the functions of the philosopher. You may say that the question cannot be answered. I think that it can; but, even if it could not be answered, I consider that it is one of the functions of the philosopher to show that there is such a problem. Some philosophers would say that metaphysics consists in raising problems rather than in answering them definitively; and, though I do not myself agree with the sheerly agnostic position, I think that there is value in raising the metaphysical problems, quite apart from the question whether one can or cannot answer them definitively. That is why I said earlier on that one of the functions of the philosopher is to open the mind to the Transcendent, to take the ceiling off the room—to use again a rather crude metaphor.

AYER: Yes, but there's a peculiarity about these "why" questions. Supposing someone asks you "Why did the light go out?" You may tell him the light went out because there was a fuse. And he then says "Why does the light go out when it is fused?" Then perhaps you tell him a story about electrical connections, wires, and so on. That is the "how" story. Then, if he's not satisfied with that, you may give him the general theory of electricity which is again a "how" story. And then if he's not satisfied with that, you give him the general theory of electromagnetics, which is again a "how" story. You tell him that things function in this way at this level, and then your "why" answers are deductions from that. So that in the ordinary sense of a "why" question, putting a "why" question is asking for a "how" answer at a higher logical level—a more general "how" answer. Well now if you raise this question with regard to the world as a whole, you're asking for what? The most general possible theory?

COPLESTON: No, the metaphysical question I have in mind is a different sort of question. If I ask, for example, how the earth comes to be in its present condition, I expect an answer which refers to empirical causes and conditions. There I quite agree with you. I go to the astronomer for an answer. And if one persists in asking such questions, I dare say one could, in theory, go back indefinitely. At least, I am prepared to admit the possibility. But if I ask why there are phenomena at all, why there is something rather than nothing, I am not asking for an answer in terms of empirical causes and conditions. Even if the series of phenomena did go back indefinitely, without beginning, I could still raise the question as to why the infinite series of phenomena exists, how it comes to be there. Whether such a question can be answered or not is obviously another matter. But if I ask whether anything lies behind phenomena, whether anything is responsible for the series, finite or infinite, of phenomena, the answer—supposing that there is an answer—must, in my opinion, refer to a reality beyond or behind phenomena. But in any case to ask why any finite phenomena exist, why there is something rather than nothing, is to ask a different sort of question from the question why water tends to flow downhill rather than uphill.

AYER: But my objection is that your very notion of an explanation of all phenomena is self-contradictory.

COPLESTON: What is the contradiction?

AYER: The contradiction is, I think, that if you accept my interpretation of what "why" questions are, then asking a "why" question is always asking for a more general description; and asking for the "why" of that is asking for a more general description still. And then you say, "Give me an answer to a 'why' which doesn't take the form of a description," and that's a contradiction. It's like saying "Give me a description more general than any description, which itself is not a description." And clearly nobody can do that.

COPLESTON: That is not the question I am asking. There would be a contradiction if I did not distinguish between a scientific question and a metaphysical question, but a metaphysical question concerns the intelligible structure of reality in so far as it is *not* amenable to the investigation by the methods of empirical science. It seems to me that when I propose a metaphysical question you ask me to re-state the question as though it were a scientific question. But, if I could do that, the question would not be a metaphysical question, would it?

AYER: Well, what form would your metaphysical question take?

COPLESTON: Well, in my opinion, the existence of phenomena in general requires some explanation, and I should say explanation in terms of a transcendent reality. I maintain that this is a possible philosophical question. Whatever the answer may be, it obviously cannot consist in a further description of phenomena. Aristotle asserted that philosophy begins with wonder. If someone feels no wonder at the existence of the physical world, he is unlikely to ask any questions about its existence as such.

AYER: If you say anything of that kind, it still means that you're treating your transcendent reality, or rather the statements about your transcendent reality, in the same way as a scientific hypothesis. It becomes a very, very general scientific hypothesis. Only you want to say it's not like a scientific hypothesis. Why not? I suppose it's because you can't test it in any way. But if you can't test it in any way, then you've not got an explanation and you haven't answered my question.

COPLESTON: Well, at this point I should like to remark that you're presupposing that one must be able to test every hypothesis in a certain way. I do not mean to allow that every metaphysical statement is a hypothesis; but even if it were, it would not be scientifically testable without ceasing to be a metaphysical statement. You seem to me to reject from the beginning the reflective work of the intellect on which rational metaphysics depends. Neither Spinoza nor Fichte nor Hegel nor St. Thomas Aquinas supposed that one could investigate scientifically what they respectively believed to be the metaphenomenal reality. But each of them thought that intellectual reflection can lead the mind to postulate that reality.

AYER: Well in one sense of the words, of course it can. You can penetrate disguises. If something's heavily camouflaged you can understand that it's there even if you can't see it. That's because you know what it would be like to see it independently of seeing it in disguise. Now your kind of penetration is a very queer one, because you say you can discern thinks lying behind other things with simply no experience of stripping off the disguise and coming across the thing undisguised.

COPLESTON: It's not exactly a question of a disguise. I can strip off camouflage and see the camouflaged thing with my eyes. But no metaphysician would pretend that one could see a metaphenomenal reality with the eyes: it can be apprehended only by an intellectual activity, though that activity must, of necessity, begin with the objects of sense-experience and introspection. After all, you yourself *reflect on* the data of experience: your philosophy does not consist in stating atomic experiences.

AYER: No indeed it doesn't. Since I hold that philosophy consists in logical analysis, it isn't in my view a matter of stating experiences at all: if by stating experiences you mean just describing them.

COPLESTON: It seems to me that we are discussing my particular brand of metaphysics rather than Logical Positivism. However, I should maintain that the very ability to raise the question of the existence of the world (or of the series of phenomena, if you like) implies a dim awareness of the non-self-sufficiency of the world. When this awareness becomes articulate and finds expression, it may lead to a metaphysical speculation, to a conscious thinking of contingent existence *as such*. And I should maintain that an intellectual apprehension of the nature of what I call contingent being as such involves an apprehension of its relatedness to self-grounded Being. Some philosophers (Hegel among them, I think) would hold that one cannot think finite being *as such* without implicitly thinking the Infinite. The words "as such" are, I should say, important. I can perfectly well think of a cow, for example, without thinking of any metaphysical reality; but if I abstract from its characteristics as a cow and think of it merely as contingent being, I pass into the sphere of metaphysics.

AYER: But it's precisely questions like this question about the world as a whole that I think we should rule out. Supposing you asked a question like "Where do all things come from?" Now that's a perfectly meaningful question as regards any given event. Asking where it came from is asking for a description of some event prior to it. But if you generalize that question, it becomes meaningless. You're then asking what event is prior to all events. Clearly no event can be prior to all events, because if it's a member of the class of all events it must be included in it and therefore can't be prior to it. Let me give another instance which illustrates the same point. One can say of any one perception that it's a hallucination, meaning by this that it isn't corroborated by one's own further perceptions or by those of other people, and that makes sense. Now, some people, and philosophers too, I'm afraid, want to generalize this and say with a profound air: "Perhaps all our experiences are hallucinatory." Well, that of course becomes meaningless. In exactly the same way I should say that this question of where does it all come from isn't meaningful.

COPLESTON: It isn't meaningful if the only meaningful questions are those which can be answered by the methods of empirical science, as you presuppose. In my opinion, you are unduly limiting "meaningfulness" to a certain restricted kind of meaningfulness. Now, the possibility of raising the question of the Absolute seems to depend largely on the nature of relations. If one denies that one can discern any implication or internal relation in the existing phenomena considered as such, then a metaphysic of the absolute becomes an impossible thing. If the mind can discern such a relation, then I think a metaphysic of the Absolute is possible.

AYER: Metaphysic of the Absolute? I am afraid my problem still is, What questions are being asked? Now supposing one were to ask, Is the world dependent on something outside itself? Would you regard that as a possible question?

COPLESTON: Yes I think it's a possible question.

AYER: Well then you're using a very queer sense of causation aren't you? Because in the normal sense in which you talk of one event being dependent or consequent on another, you'd be meaning that they had some kind of temporal relation to each other. In fact, normally if one uses the word causation one is saying that the later event is dependent on the earlier, in the sense that all cases of the earlier are also cases of the later. But now you can't be meaning that, because if you were you'd be putting your cause in the world.

COPLESTON: Well now, aren't you presupposing the validity of a certain philosophical interpretation of causality? It may be true or false; but it is a philosophical view, and it is not one which I accept.

AYER: But surely on any view of causality, the causal relation holds between things that happen, and presumably anything that happens is in the world. I don't know what you mean by your other-worldly reality, but if you make it a cause you automatically bring this supposed reality into the world.

COPLESTON: It would bring the world into relation with the reality; and personally I should not dream of adopting any metaphysic which did not start with experience of this world. But the relating of the world to a Being outside the world would not bring that Being into the world. Incidentally, I have just used the word "outside." This illustrates admirably the inadequacy of language for expressing metaphysical ideas. "Outside" suggests distance in space, "independent" would be better. But I should like to make some remarks about this use of the word "cause." I am very glad you brought the question up. First of all, as far as I understand the use of the term by scientists, causal laws would mean for them, I suppose, statistical generalizations from observed phenomena. At least this would be one of the meanings, I think.

AYER: That makes it rather more genetic than it need be. I mean the question is not really where these scientific expressions have come from, but what use they're put to. Let us say that they are generalizations which refer to observable events or phenomena, if you will.

COPLESTON: I agree, of course, that one cannot use the principle of causality, if understood in a sense which involves references to phenomena exclusively, in order to transcend phenomena. Supposing, for example, that I understood by the principle of causality the proposition that the initial state of every phenomena is determined by a preceding phenomenon or by preceding phenomena, quite apart from the fact that it may not apply even to all phenomena. But what I understand by the philosophic principle of causality is the general proposition that every being which has not in itself its reason of existence depends for its existence on an extrinsic reality which I call, in this connection, cause. This principle says nothing as to the character of the cause. It may be free or not free. Therefore it cannot be refuted by infra-atomic indeterminism, if there is such a thing, any more than it is refuted by the free acts of men. Some philosophers would probably say that this principle has only subjective necessity; but I don't hold this view myself, nor do I see any very cogent reason for holding it. Moreover, though the principle is, in a sense, presupposed by the scientist when he traces the connection between a phenomenal effect and a phenomenal cause, the principle mentions not phenomenal causes, but an extrinsic reality. If one is speaking of all beings which have not in themselves the reason for their existence, the extrinsic reality in question must transcend them. To my way of thinking the philosophic principle of causality is simply an implication of the intelligibility of phenomena, if these are regarded as contingent events.

AYER: Well then, again I think I should accuse you of the fallacy of misplaced generalization. You see, what is the intelligibility of phenomena? You can understand sentences; you can understand an argument; they can be intelligible or not. But what is the understanding of phenomena? Even a particular one, let alone all phenomena? Well I think you could give a sense to understanding a particular phenomenon. You would recognize some description of it as an accurate description, and then understanding the phenomenon would be a matter of explaining this description, that is, of deducing it from some theory. Now, you say, are all phenomena intelligible? Does that mean that you are looking for a single theory from which every true proposition can be deduced? I doubt if you could find one, but even if you did, you'd want that theory again, wouldn't you, to be explained in its turn, which gives you an infinite regress? You see, phenomena just happen, don't they? Is there a question of their being intelligible or not intelligible?

COPLESTON: No, phenomena don't "just happen." I didn't "just happen." If I did, my existence would be unintelligible. And I'm not prepared to acquiesce in the idea that the series of phenomena, even if infinite, just happens, unless you can give me a good reason for doing so. I think you can legitimately raise the question why there is finite existence as such. Whether it's answerable or not is another pair of shoes.

AYER: Well, I quite agree that many metaphysicians have supposed themselves to be asking and answering questions of this kind. But I still want to say that I don't regard these as genuine questions, nor do I regard the answers as intelligible. For example, let us take the case of someone who says that the answer is that Reality is the Absolute expressing itself. I say such an answer explains nothing because I can do nothing with it, and I don't know what it would be like for such a proposition to be true. I should say the same about all statements of this kind.

COPLESTON: And why should it be necessary to do anything with a proposition?

AYER: Because you put this up as a hypothesis, and a hypothesis is supposed to explain.

COPLESTON: An explanation is meant to explain, certainly. What I meant was that there is no reason why we should be able to deduce "practical" consequences from it.

AYER: Well, if you don't get practical answers what kind of answers do you get?

COPLESTON: Theoretical answers, of course. I should have thought, as a simpleminded historian of philosophy, that one has been given a good many metaphysical answers. They cannot all be true; but the answers are forthcoming all the same.

AYER: Yes, but the trouble still is that these answers are given not as explanations of any particular event, but of all events. And I wonder if this notion of an explanation of all events isn't itself faulty. When I explain something by telling you that *this* is the way it works, I thereby exclude other possibilities. So that any genuine explanation is compatible with one course of events, and incompatible with another. That, of course, is what distinguishes one explanation from another. But something which purported to explain all events, not merely all events that did occur, but any event that could occur, would be empty as an explanation because nothing would disagree with it. You might explain all events as they do occur, provided you allowed the possibility that if they occurred differently your explanation would be falsified. But the trouble with these so-called metaphysical explanations is that they don't merely purport to explain what does happen, but to serve equally for anything that could conceivably happen. However you changed your data, the same explanation would still hold, but that makes it as an explanation absolutely vacuous.

COPLESTON: I think that what you are demanding is that any explanation of the existence of phenomena should be a scientific hypothesis. Otherwise you will not recognize it as an explanation. This is to say, "All explanations of facts are of the type of scientific hypotheses or they are not explanations at all." But the explanation of all finite beings cannot be a scientific explanation, i.e. in the technical use of the word "scientific." But it can be a rational explanation all the same. "Rational" and "scientific" are not equivalent terms, and it is a prejudice to think that they are equivalent.

AYER: But does a non-scientific explanation explain anything? Let me take an example. Suppose someone said that the explanation for things happening as they did was that it answered the purposes of the deity. Now I should say that would only be meaningful if you could show that events going this way rather than that way answered his purpose. But if you're going to say that whatever happens is going to answer his purpose, then it becomes useless as an explanation. In fact it's not an explanation at all. It becomes empty of significance because it's consistent with everything.

COPLESTON: If I seek the explanation of the world, I am considering an ontological question, and what I am looking for is an ontological explanation and not simply a logical explanation.

Necessary and Contingent Propositions

AYER: Now I think I get more of what you're saying. But aren't you asking for something contradictory? You see, so long as an explanation is contingent, that is something that might be otherwise logically, you're going to say it's not a sufficient explanation. So that you want for your proposition something that is logically necessary. But of course once your proposition becomes logically necessary it is a purely formal one, and so doesn't explain anything. So what you want is to have a proposition that is both contingent and necessary, contingent in so far as it's got to describe the world, necessary in so far as it's not just something happening to be, but something that must be. But that's a contradiction in terms.

COPLESTON: There is a contradiction only if one grants an assumption of yours which I deny. A proposition which is applicable to a contingent thing or event is not necessarily a contingent proposition. Nor is the proposition that it is contingent an analytic or self-evident proposition. In any case I'm not seeking the ontological explanation of the world in a proposition.

AYER: But shouldn't you be?

COPLESTON: Why should one be?

AYER: Well, what is explanation except a matter of deriving one proposition from another? But perhaps you prefer to call your ontological principle a fact. Then what you're asking for is a fact that is at one and the same time contingent and necessary, and you can't have it.

COPLESTON: Why should it at one and the same time be contingent and necessary?

AYER: It's got to be contingent in order to do for an explanation. It's got to be necessary because you're not satisfied with anything contingent.

COPLESTON: I shouldn't admit that it's got to be contingent in order to do its work of explanation. I'd say that it didn't do its work of explanation if it was contingent.

AYER: But how possibly could you derive anything empirical from a necessary proposition?

COPLESTON: I am not attempting to derive an empirical thing from a necessary proposition. I do attempt, however, to render empirical things intelligible by reference to an absolute or necessary being.

AYER: But surely a necessary being can only be one concerning which the proposition that it exists is necessary?

COPLESTON: The proposition would be necessary, yes. But it doesn't follow that one can discern its necessity. I'm not holding, for instance, the ontological argument for the existence of God, though I do believe that God's existence is the ultimate ontological explanation of phenomena.

AYER: Well now, ultimate in what sense? In the sense that you can't find a more general proposition from which it can be deduced?

COPLESTON: An ultimate principle or proposition is obviously not deducible—if you must speak of propositions instead of beings.

AYER: Well, it is better so.

COPLESTON: The world doesn't consist of contingent propositions, though things may be expressed in contingent propositions. Nor should I say that a necessary being consists of necessary propositions.

AYER: No, of course I shouldn't say that the world consists of propositions: it's very bad grammar, bad logical grammar. But the words necessary and contingent, which you introduced, do apply to propositions in their ordinary logical acceptance.

COPLESTON: Yes, they do apply to propositions, but I do not accept the position that all necessary or certain propositions are tautologies. I think that there are necessary or certain propositions which also apply to things.

AYER: Yes, but not in any different sense. A statement to the effect that a being is necessary could be translated into a statement that a proposition referring to that being was necessary. Now you've got into the difficulty that from a logically necessary proposition, which I should say meant a *formally* valid proposition, and therefore a materially empty proposition, you want to derive a proposition with material content. You do want to have it both ways, you want to have statements, facts if you like, which are both contingent and necessary, and that, of course, you can't have. And a metaphysician can't have it either.

COPLESTON: But, you see, I do not believe that all certain propositions are only formally valid, in the sense of being tautologies. I am not saying that there are propositions which are both necessary and contingent: what I am saying is that there are, in my opinion, propositions which are certain and which are yet applicable to reality. If the reality in question happens to be contingent, that doesn't make the proposition contingent, if by contingent you mean an uncertain empirical hypothesis.

AYER: Well the I must protest I *don't* understand your use of the word "necessary." You see, it seems to me we've got a fairly clear meaning for "logically necessary:" propositions that are formally valid, I should call logically necessary; and I can understand "causally necessary." I should say that events are linked by causal necessity when there is some hypothesis, not itself logically necessary, from which their connection is deducible. Now you want to introduce a third sense of necessity, which is the crucial sense for you, which isn't either of those, but is—what?

The Nature of Logical Necessity

COPLESTON: By a necessary proposition I mean a *certain* proposition. You may say that there are no certain propositions which are applicable to reality; but that is another matter. Earlier in our discussion I distinguished at least two senses of the principle of causality. I regard the philosophic version as certain. In other words, besides purely logical propositions and what you would, I think, call empirical hypotheses, I believe that there are metaphysical propositions which are certain. Now take the principle of contradiction. I think that there is a metaphysical version of the principle which is not simply what is sometimes called "a law of thought," but is rather imposed on the mind by its experience of being, or, better, by its reflection on its experience of being. But I presume that you would say that the principle is only formal. Well, it seems to me that if it's purely formal, then I ought to admit there's a possibility of this piece of paper being white and not white at the same time. I can't think it, but I ought, I think, on your assumption, to admit the abstract possibility of it. But I can't think it, I can't admit its abstract possibility.

AYER: Well, if you tell me that the paper is both white and not-white, of course you don't tell me anything about fact, do you?

COPLESTON: Well, no, I should say that is because one can't admit the possibility of its being both white and not-white at the same time.

AYER: You can't admit that possibility, given existing conventions, about the use of the word "not," but of course you could perfectly well introduce a convention by which it would be meaningful. Supposing you chose, when the paper was grey, to say it was white and not-white. Then you would have altered your logic. But given that you're using a logic in which you exclude "p and not-p," then of course you exclude the paper's being white and not-white.

COPLESTON: A logic in which you don't exclude "p and not-p" may have uses; but I do not see that any significant statement can be made about this piece of paper in such a logic. It seems to me that if the principle of contradiction is purely formal and tautological, that I ought to admit the possibility of its being white—what I *call* white—of its being white and not-white at the same time; but I can't think that.

AYER: No, of course you can't. You shouldn't be expected to, because to think that would be to use symbols in a way not in accordance with the conventions under which that particular group of symbols are to be used. But of course you could describe the same experience in a different sort of logic; you could introduce a different grammar of color-classification which allowed you to say that the paper was and was not a certain color, for example in the case where the color is changing. Certain Hegelians want to do that, and we have no call to stop them. There's no particular advantage in doing it, because you can equally well describe that phenomenon in the Aristotelian logic; but if, in the case where it's changing its color you like to say that it's both white and not-white, that's all right, so long as it's understood how your terms are being used.

COPLESTON: It seems to me that it would be the nature of the thing itself that forced me to speak in a certain way. If I have before me Smith and Jackson, I can't think of Smith being Smith-and-Jackson at the same time. I should say that it's not merely a law of thought or an analytic tautology that forces me to say that, but the nature of the things themselves.

AYER: I agree that such conventions are based on empirical facts, the nature of your experiences, and adapted to meet them; but you can again quite easily imagine circumstances in which you would be inclined to change your logic in that respect. Certain neurotic phenomena might very well incline one to say that Smith had acquired some of Jackson's personality, and then if such things were very common, you might get a new usage of "person," according to which you could have two different persons inhabiting one body, or one person inhabiting different bodies.

COPLESTON: Well, I can agree to speak about things using any terms I like, I suppose: I can agree to call this paper red, when I know that it's white, but that in no way alters the nature of the paper.

AYER: No. No one is claiming that it does. The fact is that the paper looks as it does. If you have a symbol system which you use to describe those facts, then that symbol system will itself have certain conventions, governing the use of certain symbols in it. Now I think in any given symbol system I could separate what I call the logical expressions, and the descriptive expressions. Words like "not," I should say, were logical expressions.

COPLESTON: Supposing one had another logical system. Is there any rule of speaking within that system? And suppose now you are using a three-valued logic. You could perfectly well use that to describe what you now describe, could you?

AYER: Yes, the difference would be that you couldn't make certain inferences that you now make. Thus, from the fact that the paper was *not* not-white you couldn't then infer that it was white: you could only infer that it was either white or the intermediate state, which you would choose to describe, not by a separate word, which brings you back to your two-valued system, but by saying both white and not-white.

COPLESTON: My point is that there are, in my opinion, certain propositions which are founded on an experience of reality and which are not, therefore, simply formal propositions or tautologies. If one wishes to keep within the sphere of purely formal logic one can, on this understanding, employ a three-valued logic. But purely formal propositions are not likely to help one in metaphysics. No doubt you would say "Hear, hear." But I admit, and you do not, propositions which are certain and yet not purely formal. Some people would call such propositions "synthetic *a priori* propositions," but I do not care for the phrase myself, on account of its association with the philosophy of Kant. However, the issue between us is in any case whether or not there are propositions which are certain and which yet apply to reality; and I do not think that the introduction of the three-valued logic really affects the point. I have no wish to deny that there may be propositions which *are* purely formal. But I am convinced of the existence of valid metaphysical propositions. However, I should like to raise another question, in order to get your views on it. Perhaps you would help me to attain clarity in the matter. My question is this. Within a three-valued system of logic is there any rule of consistency at all?

AYER: Yes. Otherwise it wouldn't be a system of logic.

COPLESTON: Then does it not seem that there is at least one proto-proposition which governs all possible systems of logic?

AYER: No, that doesn't follow.

COPLESTON: Well, supposing in a system without the principle of contradiction one simply disregarded the principles of consistency within the system. Would you say then that one was contradicting oneself?

AYER: No, because in that sense the notion of contradiction as you understand it wouldn't apply.

COPLESTON: Well, would you say one was at variance with the rules of the game?

AYER: Yes, you wouldn't be playing that game.

COPLESTON: Then there *are* some laws, if one likes to speak in that way, that govern all games?

AYER: No, there are no laws that govern all games, but each game has a certain set of laws governing it.

COPLESTON: Well, consistency, or observation of law, within a game, whatever these laws may be, is itself, it seems to me, a kind of proto-principle.

AYER: What's common to all of them is that if the game is conducted in accordance with certain rules, then if you don't observe those rules, you're not playing that game, though possibly some other.

COPLESTON: And are you producing unintelligible statements?

AYER: Whether the statements were intelligible or not, of course, would depend on whether they could be interpreted as counters in some other game.

COPLESTON: Ah, but within the game itself . . .

AYER: No, they would not be.

COPLESTON: Well then, it does seem to me that there is, at any rate, a principle of consistency, which seems to me to be a kind of proto-proposition governing all reasoning.

AYER: Well, take it this way. Take it in the case of chess, or bridge. Now you might play bridge, and revoke.

COPLESTON: Yes.

AYER: And if it's done once, occasionally, that's considered to be a slip, and you haven't stopped playing bridge. But supposing now you make revoking a general habit, and nobody worries, you're allowed to revoke when you please, then you're playing some different game. Now possibly you might be able to determine the rules of that game too.

COPLESTON: Yes.

AYER: Well now, exactly the same with logic, you see: in an ordinary, say Aristotelian, logic, certain moves are allowed.

COPLESTON: Necessitated, I should say. Yes.

AYER: And certain moves, including not admitting contradictories, are disallowcd.

COPLESTON: Well?

AYER: Now supposing you have a game which breaks those rules, then you have a different game.

COPLESTON: Granted. But I don't admit that all logics are games, in the sense that no logic applies to reality or that all possible logics apply equally well. I see no *reason* to say this. If one did say it, the statement would be a philosophical, even a metaphysical, statement, and therefore, I suppose, according to your view, technically meaningless. However, supposing that they are games, there is a certain architectonic governing the playing of those games.

AYER: No. All you can say is, not that there's any given rule that must be observed in every game, because there isn't, but that in any game there must be some rule. And it is an empirical question which logic is the most useful. Compare the case of alternative geometries.

COPLESTON: Observance of consistency seems to me to mean something more than "Unless you observe the rules of the game you do not observe the rules of the game." It means, "If you contradict yourself, that is, if you contradict your premises and definitions, you do not reason significantly." That is not an arbitrary or conventional principle, I should suggest.

AYER: But surely all that you are saying is that in a language, namely the one we are now using, where one of the principles of correct reasoning is the observance of the law of non-contradicition, anyone who violates this law isn't reasoning correctly. That is certainly a valid statement, but it *is* conventional.

The Relation of Language to Philosophy

COPLESTON: I should like to know what you, as a logical positivist, think about the relation of language to philosophy. Would you say that philosophy depends on language, in the sense that philosophical ideas depend on grammatical and syntactical structure?

AYER: Not quite in that sense, but I think that philosophy can be said to be about language.

COPLESTON: And you think that to some extent it depends on the language you use to do it in?

AYER: What you can imagine to be possible depends very much upon what kind of symbol system you're using. Yes.

COPLESTON: Can you give me an illustration of the way in which philosophy depends on language?

AYER: Well, I should say, for example, that the belief of Western philosophers in substance was very much bound up with the subject-predicate form of most sentences in Western languages.

COPLESTON: In that case it's a question of empirical investigation, isn't it? I mean as to whether that is the case or not. And we should find, if the theory is true, that if the grammatical and syntactical structure of different languages is different, philosophical problems raised in those languages are different. Surely you can translate the western philosophical problems into some quite primitive non-European languages. And where difficulty in doing so arises, this is not owing to the grammatical and syntactical structure of the language in question, but owing to the absence of the abstract expression which will correspond to the western idea. It seems to me that the ideas come before the expression. To say that the expression governs the ideas and the formation of the ideas, is to put the cart before the horse.

AYER: The idea comes before the expression? As an image, or something of that sort?

COPLESTON: Sometimes, of course, it will be an image, but I'm a little doubtful whether all ideas are accompanied by images. But let us take your concrete example, substance. Presumably the Greeks got the idea of substance before they applied the word "ousia" to it. Let's take a test case. Aristotle wrote in Greek, Avicenna and Averroes in Arabic, and Maimonides, partly at least, in Hebrew. Well, if the theory of the dependence of philosophy on language is true, it ought, I think, to be empirically provable that the difference between the philosophies of Aristotle, Avicenna, Averroes and Maimonides were due to differences in the grammatical and syntactical structures of the languages they respectively employed. As far as I know that's never been shown. It seems to me that the differences are due to quite other causes, partly theological.

AYER: Maybe. But I still maintain that philosophers have been influenced by language. Of course the interesting thing now is not to find out why they said what they did, but evaluate what it was they were saying, and how far it was significant or true. Now I do think it rather queer that people have been so inclined to believe in substance with no empirical evidence about it whatsoever. I think the grammatical distinction of subject and predicate may be one cause, but I admit that I haven't made the empirical investigation. This is only a conjecture. Similarly I should expect people with ideographic languages to be less concerned about the problem of universals, for example, not being easily able to isolate abstract words.

COPLESTON: Yes, in some cases I should think it would be due not to deficiency of language so much as to direction of interest.

AYER: And then you get things like the tendency to treat all words as names.

COPLESTON: Yes, I know. I mean, I'm not trying to adopt an extreme position. I should question any such extreme position, which I understand you don't hold, as that philosophical problems are simply due to the form of the language which the philosophers who raised those problems used. But I don't wish to deny that some philosophers have been misled by language. For example, if one supposes that to every word there is a corresponding thing, that to redness, for example, there corresponds a redness which is different from the redness of a rose, or any particular red thing; then I should say that the philosopher was misled by language. What I would emphasize would be that this question of the influence of language on philosophy is simply a question of empirical investigation in any given case. The dogmatic *a priori* statement concerning the influence of language on philosophy should be studiously avoided.

AYER: I agree that it's an empirical question how our own philosophical problems have grown up. But that doesn't affect my contention that the method of solving these problems is that of linguistic analysis.

The Principle of Verifiability

COPLESTON: Well, perhaps we'd better attend to your principle of verifiability. You mentioned the principle of verification earlier. I thought possibly you'd state it, Professor, would you?

AYER: Yes. I'll state it in a fairly loose form, namely that to be significant a statement must be either, on the one hand, a formal statement, one that I should call analytic, or on the other hand empirically testable, and I should try to derive this principle from an analysis of understanding. I should say that understanding a statement meant knowing what would be the case if it were true. Knowing what would be the case if it were true means knowing what observations would verify it, and that in turn means being disposed to accept certain situations as warranting the acceptance or rejection of the statement in question. From which there are two corollaries: one, which we've been talking about to some extent, that statements to which no situations are relevant one way or the other are ruled out as non-factual; and, secondly, that the content of the statement, the cash value, to use James's term, consists of a range of situations, experiences, that would substantiate or refute it.

COPLESTON: Thank you. Now I don't want to misinterpret your position, but it does seem to me that you are presupposing a certain philosophical position. What I mean is this. If you say that any factual statement, in order to be meaningful, must be verifiable, and if you mean by "verifiable" verifiable by sense-experience, then surely you are presupposing that all reality is given in sense-experience. If you are presupposing this, you are presupposing that there can be no such thing as a metaphysical reality. And if you presuppose this, you are presupposing a philosophical position which cannot be demonstrated by the principle of verification. It seems to me that logical positivism claims to be what I might call a "neutral" technique, whereas in reality it presupposes the truth of positivism. Please pardon my saying so, but it looks to me as though the principle of verifiability were excogitated partly *in order to* exclude metaphysical propositions from the range of meaningful propositions.

AYER: Even if that were so, it doesn't prove it invalid. But, to go back, I certainly should not make any statement about *all* reality. That is precisely the kind of statement that I use my principle in order not to make. Nor do I wish to restrict experience to sense experience: I should not at all mind counting what might be called introspectible experiences, or feelings, mystical experiences if you like. It would be true, then, that people who haven't had certain experiences won't understand propositions which refer to them; but that I don't mind either. I can quite well believe that you have experiences different from mine. Let us assume (which after all is an empirical assumption) that you have even a sense different from mine. I should be in the position of the blind man, and then I should admit that statements which are unintelligible to me might be meaningful for you. But I should then go on to say that the factual content of your statements *was* determined by the experiences which counted as their verifiers or falsifiers.

COPLESTON: Yes, you include introspection, just as Hume did. But my point is that you assume that a factually informative statement is significant only if it is verifiable, at least in principle, by direct observation. Now obviously the existence of a metaphysical reality is not verifiable by direct observation, unless you are willing to recognize a purely intellectual intuition as observation. I am not keen on appealing to intuition, though I see no compelling reason to rule it out from the beginning. However, if you mean by "verifiable" verifiable by direct sense-observation and/or introspection, you seem to me to be ruling out metaphysics from the start. In other words, I suggest that acceptance of the principle of verifiability, as you appear to understand it, implies the acceptance of philosophical positivism. I should probably be prepared to accept the principle if it were understood in a very wide sense, that is, if "verifiable by experience" is understood as including intellectual intuition and also as meaning simply that some experience, actual or conceivable, is relevant to the truth or falsity of the proposition concerned. What I object to is any statement of the principle of verifiability which tacitly assumes the validity of a definite philosophical position.

Now, you'd make a distinction, I think, between analytic statements on the one hand, and empirical statements, and metaphysical and ethical statements on the other. Or at any rate metaphysical statements; leave ethical out of it. You'd call the first group cognitive, and the second emotive. Is that so?

AYER: I think the use of the word emotive is not very happy, although I have used it in the past, because it suggests that they're made with emotion, which isn't necessarily the case; but I accept what you say, if you mean by "emotive" simply "non-cognitive."

COPLESTON: Very well. I accept, of course, your substitution of "non-cognitive" for "emotive." But my objection still remains. By cognitive statements I presume that you mean statements which satisfy the criterion of meaning, that is to say, the principle of verifiability: and by non-cognitive statements I presume you mean statements which do not satisfy that criterion. If this is so, it seems to me that when you say that metaphysical statements are non-cognitive you are not saying much more than that statements which do not satisfy the principle of verifiability do not satisfy the principle of verifiability. In this case, however, no conclusion follows as to the significance or non-significance of metaphysical propositions. Unless, indeed, one has previously accepted your philosophical position; that is to say, unless one has first assumed that they are non-significant.

AYER: No, it's not as simple as that. My procedure is this: I should claim that the account I've given you of what understanding a statement is, is the account that does apply to ordinary common-sense statements, and to scientific statements, and then I would give a different account of how mathematical statements functioned, and a different account again of value-judgments.

COPLESTON: Yes.

AYER: I then say that statements which don't satisfy these conditions are not significant, not to be understood; and I think you can quite correctly object that by putting my definitions together, all I come down to saying is that statements that are not scientific or common sense statements are not scientific or common sense statements. But then I want to go further and say that I totally fail to understand—again, I'm afraid, using my own use of understanding: what else can I do?—I fail to understand what these other non-scientific statements and non-common sense statements, which don't satisfy these criteria, are supposed to be. Someone may say he understands them, in some sense of understanding other than the one I've defined. I reply, It's not clear to me what this sense of understanding is, nor, *a fortiori* of course, what it is he understands, nor how these statements function. But of course you may say that in making it a question of how these statements function, I'm presupposing my own criterion.

COPLESTON: Well, then, in your treatment of metaphysical propositions you are either applying the criterion of verifiability or you are not. If you are, then the significance of metaphysical propositions is ruled out of court *a priori,* since the truth of the principle of verifiability, as it seems to be understood by you, inevitably involves the non-significance of such propositions. In this case the application of the criterion to concrete metaphysical propositions constitutes a proof neither of the non-significance of these propositions nor of the truth of the principle. All that is shown, it seems to me, is that metaphysical propositions do not satisfy a definite assumed criterion of meaning. But it does not follow that one must accept that criterion of meaning. You may legitimately say, if you like, "I will accept as significant factual statements only those statements which satisfy these particular demands"; but it does not follow that I, or anyone else, has to make those particular demands before we are prepared to accept a statement as meaningful.

AYER: What I do is to give a definition of certain related terms: understanding, meaningful, and so on. I can't force you to accept them, but I can perhaps make you unhappy about the consequences of not accepting them. What I should do is this. I should take any given proposition, and show how it functioned. In the case of a scientific hypothesis, I would show that it had a certain function, namely that, with other premises, you could deduce certain observational consequences from it. I should then say, This is how this proposition works, this is what it does, this is what it amounts to. I then take a mathematical proposition and play a slightly different game with that, and show that it functions in a certain way, in a calculus, in a symbolic system. You then present me with these other statements, and I then say: On the one hand, they have no observational consequences; on the other hand, they aren't statements of logic. All right. So you understand them. I have given a definition of understanding according to which they're not, in my usage of the term, capable of being understood. Nevertheless you reject my definition. You're perfectly entitled to, because you can give understanding a different meaning if you like. I can't stop you. But now I say, Tell me more about them. In what sense are they understood? They're not understood in my sense. They aren't parts of a symbolic system. You can't do anything with them, in the sense of deriving any observational consequences from them. What *do* you want to say about them? Well, you may just want to say, "They're facts," or something of that sort. Then again I press you on your use of the word "facts."

COPLESTON: You seem to me to be demanding that in order for a factual statement to be significant one must be able to deduce observational consequences from it. But I do not see why this should be so. If you mean directly observable consequences, you appear to me to be demanding too much. In any case are there not some propositions which are not verifiable, even in principle, but which would yet be considered by most people to have meaning and to be either true or false? Let me give an example. I don't want to assume the mantle of a prophet, and I hope that the statement is false; but it is this: "Atomic warfare will take place, and it will blot out the entire human race." Now, most people would think that this statement has meaning; it means what it says. But how could it possibly be verified empirically? Supposing it were fulfilled, the last man could not say with his last breath, "Copleston's prediction has been verified," because he would not be entitled to say this until he was dead, that is, until he was no longer in a position to verify the statement.

AYER: It's certainly practically unverifiable. You can't be man, surviving all men. On the other hand, there's no doubt it describes a possible situation. Putting the observer outside the story, one knows quite well what it would be like to observe devastation, and fail to observe any men. Now it wouldn't necessarily be the case that, in order to do that, one had to observe oneself. Just as, to take the case of the past, there were dinosaurs before there were men. Clearly, no man saw that, and clearly I, if I am the speaker, can't myself verify it: but one knows what it would be like to have observed animals and not to have observed men.

COPLESTON: The two cases are different. In regard to the past we have empirical evidence. For example, we have fossils of dinosaurs. But in the case of the prediction I mentioned there would be nobody to observe the evidence and so to verify the proposition.

AYER: In terms of the evidence, of course, it becomes very much easier for me. That would be too easy a way of getting out of our difficulty, because there is also evidence for the atomic thing.

COPLESTON: Yes, but there would be no evidence for the prediction that it will blot out the human race, even if one can imagine the state of affairs that would verify it. Thus by imagining it, one's imagining oneself into the picture.

AYER: No, no.

COPLESTON: Yes, yes. One can imagine the evidence and one can imagine oneself verifying it; but, in point of fact, if the prediction were fulfilled there would be no one there to verify. By importing yourself imaginatively into the picture, you are cancelling out the condition of the fulfilment of the prediction. But let us drop the prediction. You have mentioned imagination. Now, what I should prefer to regard as the criterion of the truth or falsity of an existential proposition is simply the presence or absence of the asserted fact or facts, quite irrespective of whether I can know whether there are corresponding facts or not. If I can at last imagine or conceive the facts, the existence of which would verify the proposition, the proposition has significance for me. Whether I can or cannot know that the facts correspond is another matter.

AYER: I don't at all object to your use of the word "facts" so long as you allow them to be observable facts. But take the contrary case. Suppose I say "There's a 'drogulus' over there," and you say 'What?' and I say "drogulus," and you say "What's a drogulus?" Well I say "I can't describe what a drogulus is, because it's not the sort of thing you can see or touch, it has no physical effects of any kind, but it's a disembodied being." And you say, "Well how am I to tell if it's there or not?" and I say "There's no way of telling. Everything's just the same if it's there or it's not there. But the fact is it's there. There's a drogulus there standing just behind you, spiritually behind you." Does that make sense?

COPLESTON: It seems to me to do so. I should say that to state that there is a drogulus in the room or not is true or false, provided that you can—that you, at any rate, have some idea of what is meant by a drogulus; and if you can say to me it's a disembodied spirit, then I should say that the proposition is either true or false whether one can verify it or not. If you said to me "By drogulus I merely mean the word 'drogulus,' and I attach no other significance to it whatsoever," then I should say that it isn't a proposition any more than if I said "piffle" was in the room.

AYER: That's right. But what is "having some idea" of something? I want to say that having an idea of something is a matter of knowing how to recognize it. And you want to say that you can have ideas of things even though there's no possible situation in which you could recognize them, because nothing would count as finding them. I would say that I understand the words "angel," "table," "cloth," "drogulus," if I'm disposed to accept certain situations as verifying the presence or absence of what the word is supposed to stand for. But you want to admit these words without any reference to experience. Whether the thing they are supposed to stand for exists or not, everything is to go on just the same.

COPLESTON: No. I should say that you can have an idea of something if there's some experience that's relevant to the formation of the idea, not so much to its verification. I should say that I can form the idea of a drogulus or a disembodied spirit from the idea of body and the idea of mind. You may say that there's no mind and there's no spirit, but at any rate there are, as you'll admit, certain internal experiences of thinking and so on which at any rate account for the formation of the idea. Therefore I can say I have an idea of a drogulus or whatever it is, even though I'm quite unable to know whether such a thing actually exists or not.

AYER: You would certainly not have to know that it exists, but you would have to know what would count as its existing.

COPLESTON: Yes. Well, if you mean by "count as its existing" that there must be some experience relevant to the formation of the idea, then I should agree.

AYER: Not to the formation of the idea, but to the truth or falsity of the propositions in which it is contained.

Are Statements About God Meaningful?

COPLESTON: The word "metaphysics" and the phrase "metaphysical reality" can have more than one meaning: but when I refer to a metaphysical reality in our present discussion, I mean a being which in principle, and not merely in fact, transcends the sphere of what can be sensibly experienced. Thus God is a metaphysical reality. Since God is *ex hypothesi* immaterial, He cannot *in principle* be apprehended by the senses. May I add two remarks? My first remark is that I do not mean to imply that no sense-experience is in any way relevant to establishing or discovering the existence of a metaphysical reality. I certainly do believe that metaphysics must be based on experiences of some sort. But metaphysics involves intellectual reflection on experience: no amount of immediate sense-experience will disclose the existence of a metaphysical reality. In other words, there is a half-way house between admitting only the immediate data of experience and on the other hand leaping to the affirmation of a metaphysical reality without any reference to experience at all. You yourself reflect on the data of experience. The metaphysician carries that reflection a stage further. My second remark is this. Because one cannot have a sense-experience of a metaphysical reality, it does not follow that one could not have another type of experience of it. And if anyone has such an experience, it does not mean that the metaphysical reality is deprived, as it were, of its metaphysical character and becomes non-metaphysical. I think that this is an important point.

AYER: Yes, but asking are these metaphysical realities isn't like asking are there still wolves in Asia, is it? It looks as if you've got a clear usage for metaphysical reality, and are then asking "Does it occur or not? Does it exist or not?" and as if I'm arbitrarily denying that it exists. My difficulty is not in answering the question "Are there, or are there not, metaphysical realities?" but in understanding what usage is being given to the expression "metaphysical reality." When am I to count a reality as metaphysical? What would it be like to come upon a metaphysical reality? That's my problem. It isn't that I arbitrarily say there can't be such things, already admitting the use of the term, but that I'm puzzled about the use of the term. I don't know what people who say there are metaphysical realities *mean* by it.

COPLESTON: Well, that brings us back to the beginning, to the function of philosophy. I should say that one can't simply raise in the abstract the question "Are there metaphysical realities?" Rather one asks, "Is the character of observable reality of such a kind that it leads one to postulate a metaphysical reality, a reality beyond the physical sphere?" If one grants that it is, even then one can only speak about that metaphysical reality within the framework of human language. And language is after all primarily developed to express our immediate experience of surrounding things, and therefore there's bound to be a radical inadequacy in any statements about a metaphysical reality.

AYER: But you're trying to have it both ways, you see. If it's something that you say doesn't have a meaning in my language, then I don't understand it. It's no good saying "Oh well, of course it really has a meaning," because what meaning could it have except in the language in which it's used?

COPLESTON: Let's take a concrete example. If I say, for example, "God is intelligent," well, you may very well say to me "What meaning can you give to the word 'intelligent,' because the only intelligence you have experienced is the human intelligence, and are you attributing that to God?" And I should have to say no, because I'm not. Therefore, if we agreed to use the word intelligent simply to mean human intelligence, I should have to say "God is not intelligent;" but when I said that a stone is not intelligent, I should mean that a stone was, speaking qualitatively, less than intelligent. And when I said that God was intelligent, I should mean that God was more than intelligent, even though I could give no adequate account of what that intelligence was in itself.

AYER: Do you mean simply that he knows more than any given man knows? But to what are you ascribing this property? You haven't begun to make that clear.

COPLESTON: I quite see your point, of course. But what you are inviting me to do is to describe God in terms which will be as clear to you as the terms in which one might describe a familiar object of experience, or an unfamiliar object which is yet so like to familiar objects that it can be adequately described in terms of things which are already familiar to you. But God is *ex hypothesi* unique; and it is quite impossible to describe Him adequately by using concepts which normally apply to ordinary objects of experience. If it were possible, He would not be God. So you are really asking me to describe God in a manner which would be possible only if He were not God. I not only freely admit that human ideas of God are inadequate, but also affirm that this must be so, owing to the finitude of the human intellect and to the fact that we can come to a philosophical knowledge of God only through reflection on the things we experience. But it does not follow that we can have *no* knowledge of God, though it does follow that our philosophical knowledge of God cannot be more than analogical.

AYER: Yes, but in the case of an ordinary analogy, when you say that something is like something else you understand what both things are. But in this case if you say something is analogical, I say "analogical of what?" And then you don't tell me of what. You merely repeat the first term of analogy. Well I *got* no analogy. It's like saying that something is "taller than," and I say "taller than?" and you repeat the first thing you say. Then I understand it's taller than itself, which is nonsense.

COPLESTON: I think that one must distinguish physical analogy and metaphysical analogy. If I say that God is intelligent, I do not say so simply because I want to call God intelligent, but either because I think that the world is such that it must be ascribed in certain aspects at least to a Being which can be described in human terms only as intelligent, or because I am satisfied by some argument that there exists an Absolute Being and then deduce that that Being must be described as intelligent. I am perfectly aware that I have no adequate idea of what that intelligence is in itself. I am ascribing to God an attribute which, translated into human terms, must be called intelligence. After all, if you speak of your dog as intelligent, you are using the word in an analogous sense, and it has some meaning for you, even though you do not observe the dog's psychical operations. Mathematicians who speak of multidimensional space have never observed such a space; but presumably they attach some meaning to the term. When we speak of "extra-sensory perception" we are using the word "perception" analogously.

AYER: Yes, but mathematical physicists do test their statements by observation, and I know what counts as a case of extra-sensory perception. But in the case of your statements I don't know what counts. Of course you *might* give them an empirical meaning, you might say that by "God is intelligent" you meant that the world had certain features. Then we'd inspect it to see if it had these features or not.

COPLESTON: Well of course I should prefer to start from the features of the world before going to God. I shouldn't wish to argue from God to the features of the world. But to keep within your terms of reference of empiricism, well then I'd say that if God is personal, then He's capable, for example, of entering into relationship with human beings. And it's possible to find human beings who claim to have a personal intercourse with God.

AYER: Then you've given your statement a perfectly good empirical meaning. But it would then be like a scientific theory, and you would be using this in exactly the same way as you might use a concept like electron to account for, explain, predict, a certain range of human experience, namely, that certain people did have these experiences which they described as "entering into communion with God." Then one would try to analyse it scientifically, find out in what conditions these things happened, and then you might put it up as a theory. What you'd have done would be psychology.

COPLESTON: Well, as I said, I was entering into your terms of reference. I wouldn't admit that when I say God is personal I merely mean that God can enter into intercourse with human beings. I should be prepared to say that He was personal even if I had no reason for supposing that He entered into intercourse with human beings.

AYER: No, but it's only in that case that one has anything one can control. The facts are that these human beings have these experiences. They describe these experiences in a way which implies more than that they're having these experiences. But if one asks what more, then what answer does one get? Only, I'm afraid, a repetition of the statement that was questioned in the first place.

COPLESTON: Let's come back to this religious experience. However you subsequently interpret the religious experience, you'd admit that it was relevant to the truth or falsity of the proposition that, say, God existed.

AYER: Relevant in so far as the proposition that God existed is taken as a description or prediction of the occurrence of these experiences. But not, of course, relevant to any inference you might want to draw, such as that the world was created, or anything of that kind.

COPLESTON: No, we'll leave that out. All I'm trying to get at is that you'd admit that the proposition "God exists" could be a meaningful form of metaphysical proposition.

AYER: No, it wouldn't then be a metaphysical proposition. It'd be a perfectly good empirical proposition like the proposition that the unconscious mind exists.

COPLESTON: The proposition that people have religious experiences would be an empirical proposition; and the proposition that God exists would also be an empirical proposition, provided that all I meant by saying that God exists was that some people have a certain type of experience. But it is *not* all I mean by it. All I originally said was that if God is personal, then one of the consequences would be that He could enter into communication with human beings. If He does so, that does not make God an empirical reality, in the sense of not being a metaphysical reality. God can perfectly well be a metaphysical reality, that is, independent of *physis* or nature, even if intelligent creatures have a non-sensible experience of Him. However, if you wish to call metaphysical propositions empirical propositions, by all means do so. It then becomes a question of terminology.

AYER: No. I suggest that you're trying to have it both ways. You see, you allow me to give these words, these shapes or noises, an empirical meaning. You allow me to say that the test whereby what you call God exists or not is to be that certain people have experiences, just as the test for whether the table exists or not is that certain people have experiences, only the experiences are of a different sort. Having got that admission you then shift the meaning of the words "God exists." You no longer make them refer simply to the possibility of having these experiences, and so argue that I have admitted a metaphysical proposition, but of course I haven't. All I've admitted is an empirical proposition, which you've chosen to express in the same words as you also want to use to express your metaphysical proposition.

COPLESTON: Pardon me, but I did not say that the test whereby what I call God exists or not is that certain people have certain experiences. I said that if God exists, one consequence would be that people could have certain experiences. However, even if I accept your requirements, it follows that in one case at least you are prepared to recognize the word "God" as meaningful.

AYER: Of course I recognize it as meaningful if you give it an empirical meaning, but it doesn't follow there's any empirical evidence for the truth of your metaphysical proposition.

Again: Are There Metaphysical Explanations?

COPLESTON: But then I don't claim that metaphysical propositions are not in some way founded on reflection on experience. In a certain sense I should call myself an empiricist, but I think that your empiricism is too narrow. Another point. You will not allow a factual statement to be significant unless it is verifiable. Now, suppose I say that we both have immortal souls. If we have, then the proposition will be empirically verified in due course. Are you then prepared to admit that my statement that we both have immortal souls is a significant statement? If you are not prepared, is this because you demand a particular kind of verification and reject any other type? Such an attitude would not seem to me to be warranted. And I don't see that thereby any statement about reality to which one concludes via the experience is deprived of its metaphysical character, and introduced into the empirical sphere.

AYER: Oh, surely. Let us take a case of a common sense proposition, such as that there is a glass of water in front of us. The evidence of that is my seeing it, touching it. But of course the meaning of that proposition, the factual content of that proposition, isn't exhausted by any one particular piece of evidence of that sort. I may be having a hallucination. What my proposition predicts is more evidence of the same kind. It isn't that my seeing what I do is evidence for the existence of something totally unobservable. I go beyond the immediate evidence only in so far as I take this experience to be one of an indefinite series of experiences of seeing, touching it, etc., which my statement covers. Equally in the case of your statement I should want to say that if you want to treat it empirically, you must then treat it as predicting, in exactly the same way, in certain conditions, religious experiences. What it will mean will be the possibility of further religious experiences.

COPLESTON: It's this predicting that I don't like, because it doesn't seem to me that even a scientific proposition necessarily consists in a prediction. Surely it's explicative, and also can be simply explicative, not necessarily a prediction.

AYER: But isn't it explicative in the sense that it links up with a particular phenomenon, or with lots and lots of other ones that either will occur, have occurred, or would occur in certain circumstances? Take the case of physics. Do you want a world of electrons somehow behind the perceptual world? Is that what you're after?

COPLESTON: No. We'll take the electronic theory. I should have thought that its function was to explain certain phenomena; that it originated in an endeavour to explain certain phenomena or, more generally, that it is part of the attempt to discover the constitution of matter. I should not describe it as an attempt to predict events, except secondarily perhaps.

AYER: Oh, I don't want to make the prediction a practical question, but I do want to say that understanding phenomena is a matter of lining them, of grouping them, and that the test of an explanation is that it applies to the hitherto unobserved cases. Suppose I am describing the path of a body and I draw a graph. Then the test of my having explained the observations is that hitherto unobserved points fall on the line I draw.

COPLESTON: Then my idea of metaphysics would be that of explaining, as I said at the beginning, the series of phenomena, so that the reasoning would rise out of the phenomena themselves, or out of things themselves. In that sense it would be based on experience, even though the term of the reasoning might not itself be an object of experience. I can understand your ruling out all that reflective enquiry and reasoning that constitutes metaphysics, but if you rule it out it would seem to me to be in virtue of a presupposed philosophy.

AYER: No, I want to say that I rule out nothing as an explanation so long as it explains. I make no statements about what is real and what is not real. That seems to me again an empirical question. My objection to the kind of statements that we've agreed to call metaphysical is that they don't explain.

COPLESTON: That's a matter for detailed argument and detailed discussion of some particular argument. It's distinct, it seems to me, from the question of meaning. I can quite imagine somebody saying, "Your argument for, say, the existence of God is false. Your principles on which you're arguing are quite false." And if so, there's a conclusion.

AYER: No, I don't want to say it isn't an accurate explanation. What I want to say is that it isn't an explanation at all. That's to say it doesn't even purport to do the work that an explanation does, simply because any given observation or situation is compatible with it. Now if you want to say that you are using the word in some peculiar sense, of course I can't stop you, but equally I should say that (a) it isn't the ordinary sense, and (b) that this peculiar sense hasn't been made clear to me.

COPLESTON: But you see I consider that the existence of what we call the world not only is compatible with God's existence, but demands the conclusion that God exists. I may have misunderstood you: but you seem to me to be saying that if the proposition that God exists means anything, one should be able to deduce some observation-statement from it. If you mean by deducing an observation-statement deducing a thing, I certainly do not think that one can do this. I believe that the existence of God can be inferred from the existence of the world, but I do not think that the world can be deduced from God. Spinoza might think otherwise, of course. If you are demanding that I should deduce the world from God, if I am to make the proposition "God exists" significant, you are demanding that I should adopt a particular idea of God and of creation. For, if one could deduce the world from God, creation would be necessary, and God would create necessarily. If I say that I cannot deduce observation-statements from the existence of God, it is not because I have no idea of God, but because my idea of God will not permit me to say this.

AYER: You said that the existence of the world demands the conclusion that God exists. Do you mean that this conclusion follows logically, or follows causally?

COPLESTON: I should say causally. I'm certainly not going to say that God exists means that a world exists, if by that you mean that the world follows necessarily from God, but given the world then I should say that there is a necessary relationship.

AYER: Logical or causal?

COPLESTON: Causal.

AYER: Well then we're back on the point we've already been over, aren't we? This difficulty of a notion of causation that isn't the ordinary notion of causation, a notion that's still totally unexplained.

COPLESTON: On the contrary. I mentioned earlier on that what I mean by the principle of causality is that anything which comes into existence owes that existence to an extrinsic reality, which I term "cause." Incidentally, this notion of causality is much more like the ordinary notion of causation than the phenomenalistic notion which you would regard as the scientific notion. However, I agree that we are back where we were, namely at the question whether there are any principles which can be called certain metaphysical principles. That seems to me one of the chief issues between logical positivist and the metaphysician.

Summary of the Major Disagreements

AYER: It seems to me, indeed, that this has been my quarrel with you all along, that you fail to supply any rules for the use of your expressions. I am not asking for explicit definitions. All that I require is that some indication be given of the way in which the expression relates to some possible experience. It is only when a statement fails to refer, even indirectly, to anything observable that I wish to dismiss it as metaphysical. It is not necessary that the observations should actually be made. There are cases, as you have pointed out, where for practical, or even for theoletical reasons, the observations could not in fact be made. But one knows what it would be like to make them. The statements which refer to them may be said to be verifiable in principle, if not in fact. To put the point more simply, I understand a statement of fact if I know what to look for on the supposition that it is true. And my knowing what to look for is itself a matter of my being able to interpret the statement as referring at least to some possible experience.

Now, you may say, indeed you have said, that this is all entirely arbitrary. The principle of verifiability is not itself a descriptive statement. Its status is that of a persuasive definition. I am persuaded by it, but why should you be? Can I prove it? Yes, on the basis of other definitions. I have, in fact, tried to show you how it can be derived from an analysis of understanding. But if you are really obstinate, you will reject these other definitions too. So it looks as if we reach a deadlock. But let us then see in what positions we are left. I claim for my method that it does yield valuable results in the way of analysis, and with this you seem disposed to agree. You do not deny the importance of the analytic method in philosophy, nor do you reject all the uses to which I put it. Thus you accept in the main the account that I give of empirical propositions. You have indeed objected to my treatment of the propositions of logic, but there I think that I am in the right. At least I am able to account for their validity: whereas on your view it is utterly mysterious. The main difference between us is that you want to leave room for metaphysics. But now look at the results you get. You put forward your metaphysical statements as ultimate explanations of fact, but you admit that they are not explanations, in any accepted sense of the term, and you cannot say in what sense they are explanations. You cannot show me how they are to be tested, and you seem to have no criterion for deciding whether they are true or false. This being so, I say they are unintelligible. You say, No, you understand them; but for all the good they do you (I mean cognitively, not emotionally) you might just as well abandon them. This is my case against your metaphysical statements. You may decline to be persuaded by it, but what sort of a case can you make for them? I leave the last word to you.

COPLESTON: I have enjoyed our discussion very much. I have contended that a metaphsyical idea has meaning if some experience is relevant to the formation of that idea, and that a rational metaphysic is possible if there are, as I think there are, principles which express an intellectual apprehension of the nature of being. I think that one *can* have an intellectual experience—or intuition if you like—of being. A metaphysical proposition is testable by rational discussion, but not by purely empirical means. When you say that metaphysical propositions are meaningless because they are unverifiable in your sense, I do not think that this amounts to more than saying that metaphysics are not the same thing as empirical science. In short, I consider that logical positivism, apart from its theory of analytic propositions, simply embodies the notion of nineteenth century positivism that the terms "rational" and "scientific" have the same extension. This notion may correspond to a popular prejudice, but I see no adequate reason for accepting it.

I still find it difficult to understand the status of the principle of verification. It is either a proposition or no proposition. If it is, it must be, on your premises, either a tautology or an empirical hypothesis. If the former, no conclusion follows as to metaphysics. If the latter, the principle itself would require verification. But the principle of verification cannot itself be verified. If, however, the principle is not a proposition, it must, on your premises, be meaningless. In any case, if the meaning of an existential proposition consists, according to the principle, in its verifiability, it is impossible, I think, to escape an infinite regress, since the verification will itself need verification, and so on indefinitely. If this is so, then all propositions, including scientific ones, are meaningless.

SELECTED BIBLIOGRAPHY

(ITEMS PROVIDED WITH ASTERISK ARE MORE ADVANCED)

The history of the "Vienna Circle" and of its doctrines is covered in V. Kraft, *The Vienna Circle*, (New York: Philosophical Library, 1952) and in J. Joergenson, *The Development of Logical Empiricism* (Chicago: University of Chicago Press, 1951). The following are systematic and sympathetic expositions of logical positivism: A. J. Ayer, *Language, Truth and Logic* (the second edition contains a substantial introduction in which some of the theses are more accurately stated and some criticisms are answered), R. von Mises, *Positivism, a Study in Human Understanding*, (Cambridge: Harvard University Press, 1951), and H. Reichenbach, *The Rise of Scientific Philosophy*, (Berkeley and Los Angeles: University of California Press, 1951). R. Carnap, *Philosophy and Logical Syntax*, (London: Kegan Paul, 1935) is a concise and elementary exposition of the logical positivists' conception of philosophy as logical analysis of language (this part is somewhat out of date) and of their rejection of metaphysics. A. Pap, *Elements of Analytic Philosophy*, (New York: Macmillan, 1949) contains a sympathetic, but partly critical, exposition, with reference to both the teachings of the Vienna Circle and those of the Cambridge analysts (Russell, Moore). An impartial, though sympathetic discussion of logical positivism may be found in J. Hospers, *An Introduction to Philosophical Analysis*, (New York: Prentice-Hall, 1953). A. J. Ayer's volume *Logical Positivism* (Glencoe, Illinois: Free Press, 1957), is a collection of papers by leading logical positivists. Most of these were originally published in German in *Erkenntnis*, the organ of the Vienna Circle, and are here available in English for the first time. Critical discussions of logical positivism are to be found in W. F. H. Barnes, *The Philosophic Predicament*, (London: A. and C. Black, 1950), C. E. M. Joad, *A Critique of Logical Positivism*, (Chicago: University of Chicago Press, 1950), J. Weinberg, *A Critical Examination of Logical Positivism*, (London: Kegan Paul, 1936), and F. C. Copleston, *Contemporary Philosophy*, (London: Burns and Oates, 1956). The last-mentioned of these works is written from a Catholic standpoint.

Charles Peirce's "How to Make Our Ideas Clear," in J. Buchler (ed.), *The Philosophy of Peirce*, (New York: Harcourt, Brace and Co., 1940), is a classical statement of an empiricist theory of meaning by the founder of American pragmatism. M. Schlick's "Meaning and Verification" in H. Feigl and W. Sellars (eds.), *Readings in Philosophical Analysis*, (New York: Appleton-Century-Crofts, 1949), is a classic defense of the verifiability theory of meaning, against C. I. Lewis' "Experience and Meaning" which is reprinted in the same volume. Written from the same viewpoint is R. Carnap's *"The Elimination of Metaphysics through Logical Analysis of Language,"* in A. J. Ayer (ed.), *Logical Positivism, op. cit.* The same author's "Testability and Meaning,"* *Philosophy of Science*, 1936/37 (sold as monograph by Whitlock's Inc., Yale University), is the most precise formulation of the logical positivist theory of meaning. It presupposes some knowledge of symbolic logic. "The Methodological Character of Theoretical Concepts,"* in H. Feigl and M. Scriven (eds.), *Minnesota Studies in Philosophy of Science,* Vol. I. (Minneapolis: University of Minnesota Press, 1956) contains Carnap's most recent views on the empiricist criterion of cognitive significance, with special reference to "theoretical" languages, like the language of theoretical physics. H. Feigl's "Logical Empiricism," reprinted in Feigl and Sellars, *op. cit.,* gives a good introductory exposition of the major tenets of the school. In "Problems and Changes in the Empiricist Criterion of Meaning," reprinted in A. J. Ayer (ed.), *Logical Positivism, op. cit.,* C. G. Hempel surveys the history of the criterion, and closes with a formulation that is closely patterned after Carnap's "Testability and Meaning." In "The Criterion of Cognitive Significance: a Reconsideration,"* in *Proc. of the American Academy of Arts and Sciences,* vol. 80, no. 1, the same author doubts whether a sharp distinction between the cognitively meaningful and the cognitively meaningless can be made. For a critique of the attempt of the early logical positivists to formulate a general criterion of cognitive significance, see P. Marhenke's "The Criterion of Significance,"* reprinted in L. Linsky (ed.) *Semantics and the Philosophy of Language* (Urbana: University of Illinois Press, 1952). A. J. Ayer's "The Principle of Verifiability," *Mind,* 1936, is a reply to the 1935 paper by Stace which is (with omissions) printed as Selection 44 of our book. Another of Ayer's discussions is "The Genesis of Metaphysics," in M. Macdonald (ed.), *Philosophy and Analysis* (Oxford, Basil Blackwell, 1954). A discussion of the Ayer-Stace controversy may be found in J. Wisdom's "Metaphysics and Verification,"* *Mind,* 1938. (This author should not be confused with J. O. Wisdom.) A new criticism by Stace of the verifiability theory of meaning is given in "Positivism," *Mind,* 1944. Among other things Stace argues that the theory is not entailed by the principle of (concept-) empiricism.

Further discussions of the verifiability principle may be found in C. J. Ducasse's "Verification, Verifiability and Meaningfulness," *Journal of Philosophy,* 1936; M. Lazerowitz' "Strong and Weak Verification," in two parts, which refers to Ayer's formulation of the verifiability theory, and the same author's "The Positivist's Use of Nonsense" (All the Lazerowitz articles may be found in his book *The Structure of Metaphysics,* London: Routledge and Kegan Paul, 1955); D. J. O'Connor's "Some Consequences of Prof. Ayer's Verification Principle," *Analysis,* 1950; R. Brown and J. Watling's "Amending the Verification Principle," *Mind,* 1951, which is a critique of O'Connor, J. L. Evan's "On Meaning and Verification," *Mind,* 1953, which is critical of the verifiability theory; and F. Waismann's "Verifiability,"* in A. Flew (ed.), *Essays in Logic and Language,* First Series, (Oxford: Basil Blackwell, 1951). For the views of Bertrand Russell, who is critical of the verifiability theory, see his "Logical Positivism," *Polemic,* No. 1, and "Logical Positivism," which is reprinted in his book, *Logic and Knowledge,* (London: Allen and Unwin, 1956). Other critical articles are A. D. Ritchie's "The Errors of Logical Positivism," *Philosophy,* 1937, and P. Henle's "The Problem of Meaning," in *Proc. and Addresses of the American Philos. Association,* vol. 27, 1956. An early evaluation is C. A. Maces's "Representation and Expression," which is reprinted in M. Macdonald (ed.), *Philosophy and Analysis, op. cit.* For a comprehensive discussion of logical positivism as it was twenty years ago see E. Nagel's "Impressions and Appraisals of Analytic Philosophy in Europe," *Journal of Philosophy,* 1936, reprinted in E. Nagel, *Logic Without Metaphysics,* (Glencoe, Illinois: Free Press, 1957). The following two papers both argue that a physicalistic interpretation of statements about other minds is not an inevitable consequence of the principle of verifiability: A. J. Ayer, "Our Knowledge About Other Minds," reprinted in A. J. Ayer, *Philosophical Essays,* (London: Macmillan, 1954) and A. Pap, "Other Minds and the Principle of Verifiability," *Revue Int. de Philosophie,* 1951. C. H. Whiteley's "On Meaning and Verifiability," *Analysis,* 1939 and the same author's "On Understanding," *Mind,* 1949, are two valuable discussions of problems concerning the nature of meaningful discourse by a writer who is sympathetic to the verifiability theory without wholly subscribing to it.

BIOGRAPHICAL NOTES

THOMAS AQUINAS (c. 1226-1274). St. Thomas is generally acknowledged as the greatest of the medieval philosophers. He produced an imposing intellectual system which is really a synthesis of Christian theology and Aristotle's metaphysics. While many contemporary philosophers are not sympathetic either to his conclusions or his method, the sharpness and power of his mind are universally admired. The two main works of Aquinas are the *Summa theologica* and the *Summa contra Gentiles*. The latter of these is addressed to a reader who is assumed not to be a Christian already. In his attempts to refute anti-Christian doctrines, Aquinas took great care to state these theories with full force and fairness—something which is unfortunately not true of all great philosophers.

Aquinas was of noble descent. When quite young he joined the Dominican order which he selflessly served for the rest of his life. He was asked to fill numerous important posts in the Church, including that of Archbishop of Naples, but declined all such offers. In 1323 he was canonized by Pope John XXII. In 1879 Pope Leo XIII, in an Encyclical, directed the Catholic clergy to make the teachings of Aquinas the basis of their theological outlook. Although his ideas became before long a conservative force, Aquinas was in his own day quite a bold innovator and on occasions he was denounced for his unorthodox positions.

A. J. AYER, born 1910, Grote Professor of Philosophy of Mind and Logic in the University of London. Ayer is the leading exponent of logical positivism in Great Britain and his *Language, Truth and Logic* (1936) is regarded as a kind of textbook of this school. Few philosophical works in any age have been more widely discussed. His other works are *The Foundations of Empirical Knowledge* (1940), *Philosophical Essays* (1954), and *The Problem of Knowledge* (1956). Ayer is the editor of the Pelican series of philosophy books and co-editor (with Raymond Winch) of *British Empirical Philosophers* (1952). He is also editor of *Logical Positivism* (1957), the second volume in "The Library of Philosophical Movements." Ayer is a Fellow of the British Academy.

GEORGE BERKELEY (1685-1753). Born in Kilkenny County, Ireland, Berkeley studied at Trinity College, Dublin, and there became first a tutor and later a lecturer in Greek and Theology. Berkeley wrote his three most important works very early in life. These are *An Essay Toward a New Theory of Vision* (1709), *The Principles of Human Knowledge* (1710) and *Three Dialogue Between Hylas and Philonous* (1713). A volume on ethics was never published. Berkeley lost the manuscript while travelling in Italy and did not return to the subject. Like Locke and Hume, Berkeley was a critic of the abstractions dominant in scholastic philosophy, but he was equally critical of the mathematical abstractions, especially infinitesimals, that helped Newtonian physics to such spectacular success. His epistemological idealism ("esse est percipi") was motivated partly by his dissatisfaction with Locke's theory of knowledge and partly by the desire to find a new justification for belief in God. He considerably influenced the German tradition of idealistic metaphysics, but his manner of philosophizing was much more akin to contemporary British analysis.

One of Berkeley's pet ideas was the foundation of a college in the Bermudas which would train missionaries and clergymen for the American colonies. This project brought him to America where he spent three years at Newport, Rhode Island. The House of Commons, however, failed to carry out its promise of a substantial subsidy and the scheme was never carried into practice. Berkeley, who was a model of theological orthodoxy, eventually became a Bishop in the Church of England and in his later years he was more occupied with his ecclesiastical duties than with philosophy.

BRAND BLANSHARD, born 1892, Professor of Philosophy at Yale University since 1945. Blanshard is one of the most distinguished contemporary American philosophers. His main work is *The Nature of Thought*, published in two volumes in 1939, which contains a detailed defense and restatement of idealistic theories while fully taking into account the work of recent opponents of idealism. Unlike many of the other great figures in his tradition, Blanshard is a master of lucid English prose. He is a past president of the American Philosophical Association and the American Theological Society. In 1952 and 1953 he delivered the Gifford Lectures at St. Andrews in Scotland.

C. D. BROAD, born 1887, Knightsbridge Professor of Philosophy in the University of Cambridge since 1933. He is also President of the Society for Psychical Research. Broad has had a great influence on contemporary philosophers both in Britain and in the United States, perhaps second only to that of Moore, Russell and Wittgenstein. He is the author of the following works: *Perception, Physics and Reality* (1913), *Scientific Thought* (1923), *The Mind and its Place in Nature* (1925), *Five Types of Ethical Theory* (1930), *An Examination of McTaggart's Philosophy* (1933 and 1938), *Ethics and the History of Philosophy* (1952), and *Religion, Philosophy, and Psychical Research* (1953).

C. A. CAMPBELL, born 1897, Professor of Logic and Rhetoric in the University of Glasgow since 1938. He is the author of *Sceptism and Construction* (1931), and numerous articles in philosophical periodicals. In 1954 and 1955 he delivered the Gifford Lectures in the University of St. Andrews. Campbell is a Fellow of the British Academy.

F. C. COPLESTON, born 1907, Professor of Metaphysics at the Pontifical

Gregorian University, Rome, and of the History of Philosophy at Heythrop College, Oxford. Father Copleston has been a member of the Society of Jesus since 1930 and is widely considered the leading Catholic philosopher in the Anglo-Saxon world. His books include *Friedrich Nietzsche* (1942), *Arthur Schopenhauer* (1946), *A History of Philosophy* (Vols. I-III, 1946-1953), *Medieval Philosophy* (1952), *Aquinas* (1955), *Contemporary Philosophy* (1956). The last-mentioned book contains a number of papers on logical positivism. Further volumes of Father Copleston's *History of Philosophy* are scheduled for the near future.

CLARENCE DARROW (1857-1938). For nearly fifty years Darrow was one of the most colorful figures on the American scene. He appeared as counsel for the defense in many classic cases, especially those involving the activities of political radicals and pioneer union organizers. Believing that no human being is ever morally responsible for his actions, Darrow constantly worked for a more humane attitude towards criminals and was a leader in the movement to abolish capital punishment. In the sensational trial of the "Nietzschean" murderers Loeb and Leopold, his moving plea saved the accused boys from an otherwise certain death-sentence. Darrow was one of the very few men in American public life to speak out openly against religion and in 1925 he defended the biology teacher, John T. Scopes, in the notorious "monkey trial" in Dayton, Tennessee. His best known books are *Resist Not Evil* (1904), *Farmington* (1905), *Crime, Its Cause and Treatment* (1925), *Infidels and Heretics* (1927, with Walter Rice), and *The Story of My Life* (1932).

RENE DECARTES (1596-1650). Descartes is usually referred to as the founder of modern Western philosophy. In raising fundamental questions about the nature of the human mind and the extent to which our claims to knowledge can be trusted he was a forerunner of Kant's critique of dogmatic metaphysics. By his insistence that whatever we immediately know must be a content of our minds he greatly influenced the idealist movement. Although Descartes had much contempt for the scholastics he shared their view that the existence of God can be logically demonstrated. He endorsed some of the medieval arguments and to these he added one of his own. Descartes believed that animals were feelingless and unthinking automata all of whose actions could be completely explained in mechanical terms. Human beings, however, had souls in addition to bodies and Descartes worked out a detailed theory of body-mind interaction. The automaton theory was extended by subsequent philosophers to human beings and greatly influenced the materialists of the 18th and 19th centuries. Some of Descartes' immediate successors accepted his conception of the body and the mind as radically different substances, but could not see how interaction was possible between them. They became the founders of "parallelism."

Descartes was also intensely interested in science and mathematics. He is the inventor of analytic geometry and was one of the first to note the significance of the work of Galileo and Harvey. He did not dare to publish his great work *Le Monde* during his life-time since it contained the heretical doctrines of the earth's rotation and the infinity of the universe. Lamettrie and other later unbelievers were convinced that Descartes was merely diplomatic when he professed to be a champion of religion but most historians today agree that his professions of piety were sincere. His most important philosophical works are *The Discourse on Method* (1637), *The Meditations* (1641), *The Principles of Philosophy* (1644), and the *Passions of the Soul* (1650). Some of his most interesting observations are contained in his letters to Princess Elizabeth of Holland and in his answers to various critics.

CURT J. DUCASSE, born 1881 in France, Professor Philosophy at Brown University since 1929. Ducasse is one of the most influential philosophers teaching in the United States and is the author of several important books including *The Philosophy of Art* (1930), *Philosophy as a Science* (1941), *Nature, Mind and Death* (1951), and *A Philosophical Scrutiny of Religion* (1953). He is a past president of the American Philosophical Association.

A. C. EWING, born 1899, Reader in Moral Science in the University of Cambridge. Ewing is one of the leading contemporary defenders of Rationalism. He has written numerous articles in philosophical journals including several which criticize the key-doctrines of logical positivism. He is the author of *The Morality of Punishment* (1929), *Idealism: A Critical Survey* (1934), *The Individual, The State and World Government* (1947), *The Definition of Good* (1947), and *The Fundamental Questions of Philosophy* (1951). He is also the editor of *The Idealist Tradition—From Berkeley to Blanshard*, the first volume in "The Library of Philosophical Movements." Ewing is a Fellow of the British Academy.

HERBERT FEIGL, born 1902, Professor of Philosophy at the University of Minnesota and Director of the Minnesota Center for the Philosophy of Science. Feigl was one of the early members of the "Vienna Circle" and has done a great deal to introduce the theories of logical positivism in the United States. He is editor (with Wilfred Sellers) of the journal "Philosophical Studies." He has written numerous articles, chiefly on topics in the philosophy of science, and is the editor of several important anthologies: *Readings in Philosophical Analysis* (1949, with Wilfrid Sellars), *Readings in the Philosophy of Science* (1953, with May Brodbeck), and *Minnesota Studies in the Philosophy of Science* (Vol. I, 1956, with Michael Scriven).

PAUL H. D. HOLBACH (1723-1789). Baron Holbach was one of the great figures of the French Enlightenment. He was probably the most radical unbeliever among the encyclopedists and one of the first writers in Western Europe who openly advocated atheism and materialism. According to him, religion and priestcraft were the source of most man-made evil. In ethics he was a thoroughgoing utilitarian. His main works are *Christianisme Dévoilé* (1767), *The System of Nature* (1770) and *Good Sense* (1772). The last two are available in English translations. *The System of Nature* produced a great stir when it first appeared and elicited answers from Voltaire, Frederick the Great and other illustrious men. Goethe regarded it as the most repulsive book ever written. The virtuous atheist Wolmar in Rousseau's *New Heloise* is generally taken to be a portrait of Holbach whose generosity and integrity were praised by all who knew him.

JOHN HAYNES HOLMES was born in 1879 and is Minister Emeritus of the Community Church of New York. He is a graduate of the Harvard Divinity School and holds numerous honorary degrees. Dr. Holmes has been a leader in many reform movements and humanitarian causes. He was among the founders of the American Civil Liberties Union and the National Association for the Advancement of Colored People.

DAVID HUME (1711-1776). Hume is by general agreement one of the most important philosophers who ever lived. The two major elements in his philosophy are a scepticism about our ability to draw inferences beyond what has actually been experienced and an empiricist account of various troublesome concepts like those of causation, the self, good and bad, universals, space and time, and freedom. According to Kant's own report, Hume wakened him out of his "dogmatic slumber" and stimulated the development of his "critical philosophy." The empiricist element in Hume's philosophy anticipates to a considerable extent the main doctrines of logical positivism. Hume's greatest philosophical work is the *Treatise of Human Nature* (1739). *An Inquiry Concerning Human Understanding* (1748) and *An Inquiry Concerning the Principles of Morals* (1751) are more popular restatements of many of the theories contained in the *Treatise*. These books are more polished, but less profound and thorough than the early work. In his own day and in the 19th century Hume was equally noted as a historian and his huge *History of England,* published in 1755 and succeeding years, is one of the classics of its kind.

Hume was very hostile to religion. He thought religious belief not only logically indefensible but also morally harmful. Several of his antireligious writings such as the essays on immortality and on suicide and the *Dialogues Concerning Natural Religion* were published after his death. Hume was bitterly denounced for his lack of religious belief and could never attain an academic appointment. By his many friends, however, he was loved for his exquisite sense of humor and his great kindness. He was known as "le bon David" among the French encyclopedists. "I have always considered him," wrote Adam Smith, the economist, in a tribute to Hume's character, "both in his lifetime and since his death, as approaching as nearly to the ideal of a perfectly wise and virtuous man, as perhaps the nature of human frailty will permit."

T. H. HUXLEY (1825-1895). Huxley is probably best known as the man who fought the battle for the recognition of Darwin's theories against the attacks of certain ecclesiastic authorities and conservative scientists. He frequently called himself "Darwin's bulldog." Huxley was, however, a great biologist in his own right who made numerous important discoveries, especially in anatomy and physiology. He was secretary and president of the Royal Society. Huxley was also intensely interested in philosophy. He wrote a book on Hume and some important papers on the body-mind problem and other philosophical topics. It was Huxley who coined the term "agnosticism," though there were quite a few people holding this position before his day. His most important books are *Man's Place in Nature* (1863), the *Physical Basis of Life* (1868) and *Evolution and Ethics* (1893).

WILLIAM JAMES (1842-1910). James is by general consent one of the most original thinkers America has so far produced. He taught physiology and psychology for a number of years before becoming Professor of Philosophy at Harvard in 1880. His *Principles of Psychology,* which was published in two volumes in 1890, is one of the great classics of that subject. James had an intense interest in psychopathology and was one of the first to recognize the importance of Freud's theories. In philosophy his main ambition was to reconcile the fundamental tenets of religion with an empiricist theory of knowledge. He thought that the "pragmatic" theory of truth could be employed as a means to such a synthesis. James was always suspicious of stuffy traditions and, even when he supported conservative conclusions, the reasons he gave were novel and frequently quite shocking. His most important philosophical works are *The Will to Believe and Other Essays* (1897), *The Varieties of Religious Experience* (1902), *Pragmatism* (1907), *A Pluralistic Universe* (1909), and *The Meaning of Truth* (1909).

IMMANUEL KANT (1726-1806). Kant is widely regarded as one of the greatest philosophers of modern times and his *Critique of Pure Reason* (1781) as one of the most profound systematic books ever written by a philosopher. Kant believed that by his theory of knowledge he had effected a kind of "Copernican revolution." Just as Copernicus showed that the sun and not the earth is the central body of the planetary system, so Kant thought he had shown that a great deal of what we take to be features of objective reality—e.g., space and time and causality—are really in some sense manufactured by the human mind. In ethics Kant was an extreme rationalist maintaining that moral principles are objectively valid commands of the *apriori* reason. An action, according to him, has moral worth only if it is done from a sense of duty and never because it has been inspired by utilitarian considerations. In religion and politics Kant was a liberal. He favored the American Revolution and also the French Revolution in its earlier, less violent stages. He was one of the very first advocates of international government as a means of preventing wars. He had some difficulties with the Prussian King over his lack of religious orthodoxy. In his early days Kant was preoccupied with physics and in his *A General Natural History and Theory of the Heavens* (1755) he anticipated the nebular hypothesis of the origin of planetary systems. Aside from the *Critique of Pure Reason* his main works are *The Prolegomena to All Future Metaphysics* (1783), *The Foundations of the Metaphysics of Morals* (1785), *The Critique of Practical Reason* (1788),

The Critique of Judgment (1790), *Religion within the Limits of Pure Reason* (1793) and *Perpetual Peace* (1795).

JOHN LOCKE (1632-1706). Locke's *Essay Concerning Human Understanding* (1690) is the first comprehensive treatise on the origin, analysis and extent of human knowledge. His view that the direct objects of knowledge are ideas and that we have but an indirect knowledge of physical objects (epistemological dualism) has been very influential in modern discussions of the problem of perception. In his criticism of the verbal abstractions which thrived in scholastic philosophy Locke's work resembles that of contemporary analytic philosophers. Like most of the other major figures in British philosophy, Locke contributed both to the theory of knowledge and to social and political thought. His *Treatises on Government* (1685) contain one of the first statements of the principles of democratic government. His *Letters on Toleration,* published in 1689 and succeeding years, advocated complete religious freedom for all groups except Roman Catholics and atheists. Locke's political ideas had an enormous influence on Jefferson and the other founding fathers of the American Republic and they also dominated the thought of the French Encyclopedists.

JOHN STUART MILL (1806-1873). Mill is one of the greatest figures in the history of empiricism. Like Locke before and Bertrand Russell after him, he was also actively engaged in practical affairs. In politics he carried on the radical reform ideas of Jeremy Bentham and his father James Mill. He was also one of the earliest advocates of birth-control. For a short time Mill was a member of the House of Commons where he set an almost unparalleled example for honesty and integrity. When Mill appeared at election meetings he made it a point to tell his voters, most of whom were pious believers, that he did not accept the Christian religion.

His most important philosophical work is the *System of Logic* (1843) which is really a comprehensive philosophy of science from the standpoint of empiricism. It is comparable in scope to Kant's *Critique of Pure Reason,* but immeasurably more lucid than Kant's great work. In the *System of Logic* Mill presents his theories on many philosophical topics not usually discussed in books on logic. A fuller statement of his philosophical views is contained in *An Examination of Sir William Hamilton's Philosophy* (1865). His other important works include *The Principles of Political Economy* (1848), *On Liberty* (1859), *Utilitarianism* (1863), *Autobiography* (1873), and *Three Essays On Religion* (1874). It is not generally known that Mill was Bertrand Russell's godfather.

G. E. MOORE, born 1873, Professor of Philosophy in the University of Cambridge 1925-1939, now retired; editor of *Mind* 1921-1947. In many circles Moore is regarded as one of the greatest living philosophers. He is equally renowned for his work in moral philosophy and his defences of "commonsense" against "philosophical paradoxes." His most important works are *Principia Ethica* (1903), *Ethics* (1911), *Philosophical Studies*

(1922), "A Defence of Common Sense" (in *Contemporary British Philosophy*, Second Series, 1925), and *Some Main Problems of Philosophy* (1953). Moore's classical essay "The Refutation of Idealism" is included in *Philosophical Studies*. The valuable book *The Philosophy of G. E. Moore* (1942, edited by P. A. Schilpp) contains an autobiographical sketch by Moore, and numerous critical articles as well as Moore's rejoinder. Moore is a Fellow of the British Academy and holds the Order of Merit.

WILLIAM PALEY (1743-1805). Before becoming a minister in The Church of England, Paley was a teacher of philosophy at Cambridge. He wrote an influential book on ethics, *The Principles of Moral and Political Philosophy* (1785), in which he advocated a kind of utilitarianism. Most of his other writings were defenses of Christian theology. Of these the most important is his *Natural Theology, or Evidence of the Existence and Attributes of the Deity Collected from the Appearance of Nature* (1802). Paley was a liberal both in politics and in religion. He strenuously worked for the abolition of the slave trade. His liberal religious views prevented him from reaching the highest positions in the Church.

PLATO (427-347 B.C.). Plato was an Athenian aristocrat who early in life came under the influence of Socrates. When Plato was twenty-eight, Socrates was tried by the democratic rulers of Athens on the charge of undermining the morals of the young and sentenced to death. This event was decisive in Plato's life. He retired from Athens to Megara where he began to write his dialogues. Their main character is always Socrates, though only the early dialogues, if even these, seem to be accounts of actual episodes in which Socrates participated. Mostly Socrates functions simply as the transmitter of Plato's ideas. At the age of forty Plato returned to Athens, founding his Academy which was really the first university in Europe. The subjects taught were philosophy, mathematics and political science. At the same time he went on writing his dialogues. Plato's metaphysical theories and also his political ideas, as set forth in these works, have been of tremendous influence on Western thought. His best known writings are the *Apology, Crito, Protagoras, Meno, Gorgias, Symposium, Phaedo, Republic, Phaedrus, Theatetus, Parmenides, Sophist, Politicus, Philebus, Timaeus,* and the *Laws*. Plato was a consummate literary artist and even those who do not admire his theories usually find the dialogues delightful reading. Plato hoped to put some of his political theories into practice when he became adviser to Dionysius II of Syracuse. Through no fault of Plato's the experiment did not turn out well and brought him nothing but grief.

BERTRAND RUSSELL, born 1872. Russell is widely regarded as the greatest living philosopher. He has made important contributions to logic and the foundations of mathematics, the theory of knowledge, the philosophy of science, and almost every other department of philosophy. He is also renowned for the graceful and witty style in which he expresses his ideas. His philosophical works include *An Essay on the Foundations of Geometry*

(1897), *The Principles of Mathematics* (1903), *Philosophical Essays* (1910), *Principia Mathematica* (3 volumes, 1910-1913, with A. N. Whitehead), *The Problems of Philosophy* (1912), *Our Knowledge of the External World* (1914), *Mysticism and Logic* (1918), *Introduction to Mathematical Philosophy* (1919), *The Analysis of Mind* (1921), *The Analysis of Matter* (1927), *An Outline of Philosophy* (1927), *An Inquiry into Meaning and Truth* (1940), *A History of Western Philosophy* (1946), *Human Knowledge* (1948), *Human Society in Ethics and Politics* (1955), and *Why I Am Not a Christian and Other Essays* (1957). *The Philosophy of Bertrand Russell* (1944, ed. P. A. Schilpp) is a valuable work containing an autobiographical sketch by Russell, numerous critical articles on his philosophy, and Russell's reply to the critics.

Philosophy has not by any means been the only interest in Russell's life. He is the author of important books on education, partly based on his own experimental school which he founded in 1927. His book *Marriage and Morals* (1929) created a great stir by its advocacy of a sexual moral code very much opposed to that officially sanctioned in our society. For his radical views in politics and morals and his outspoken criticisms of religion Russell has been bitterly denounced and persecuted. During the First World War he was an ardent pacifist. He was dismissed from his positions at Trinity College, Cambridge, and sentenced to six months in prison. In 1940 he was invited to become Professor of Philosophy at City College, New York. This appointment was judicially annulled on the ground that Russell was likely to undermine the "health and morals" of his students. Elsewhere, however, Russell's work has received due recognition. He is a Fellow of the Royal Society and holds numerous distinguished awards including the Order of Merit and the Nobel Prize for Literature.

MORITZ SCHLICK (1882-1936). Schlick was Professor Philosophy at the University of Vienna until his death at the hands of a paranoid student. He was the founder of the Vienna Circle and one of the most important figures in the development of logical positivism. His books include *Space and Time in Modern Physics* (1920), *Allgemeine Erkenntnislehre* (1925), *The Problems of Ethics* (1931) and *Gesammelte Aufsaetze* (1938). Schlick wrote with great ease in English and French as well as in German and several of the papers in the last-mentioned book are in English. There are English translations of some of his most famous essays in *Logical Positivism,* edited by A. J. Ayer.

J. C. C. SMART, born 1920, Professor of Philosophy in the University of Adelaide, Australia. Smart is one of the most distinguished of the younger British philosophers. His main field is the philosophy of science.

W. T. STACE, born 1886, Professor of Philosophy at Princeton University, 1932-1955, now retired. Stace calls himself an empiricist, but is not otherwise affiliated with any particular school of thought. In recent years he has been particularly interested in Eastern religions. His numerous important books include *The Meaning of Beauty* (1930), *The Theory of*

Knowledge and Existence (1932), *The Concept of Morals* (1936), *The Nature of the World* (1946), *Time and Eternity* (1952), and *The Gate of Silence* (1952).

C. L. STEVENSON, born 1908, Professor of Philosophy at the University of Michigan since 1946. Stevenson is the leading exponent of the emotive theory of moral judgments in the United States. He is the author of the two extremely influential articles "The Emotive Meaning of Ethical Terms" (*Mind*, 1937) and "Persuasive Definitions" (*Mind*, 1938) and the equally influential books, *Ethics and Language* (1943).

C. H. WHITELEY, born 1911, Lecturer in Philosophy in the University of Birmingham. Whiteley is the author of *An Introduction to Metaphysics* (1950) and is a frequent contributor to British philosophical periodicals.

F. L. WILL, born 1909, Professor of Philosophy at the University of Illinois. Will is a distinguished representative of contemporary American analytic philosophy who has specialized in the problem of induction and probability.

INDEX OF NAMES

KEY: auth.—author; biog.—biographical sketch; fn.—footnote; ment.—mentioned; ref.—reference, bibliographical, in text or footnote. Where a subject is listed in connection with a name, it refers to a discussion or mention of the author's views *by another writer;* e.g., Aristotle; philosophy, 591, refers to a discussion of Aristotle's views on philosophy by Prof. Ayer and Father Copleston in their debate.

INDEX OF SUBJECTS

Absolute, the, 565, 580, 593
Abstract ideas, 150, 185 f.; *see also* Universals
Abstract of a Treatise of Human Nature (Hume), 131
Accidents, 158
Actuality, and possibility, 329 ff., 523; and potentiality, 472 ff.
Agnosticism, 446 f.
Algebra, 14 f., 47 ff., 106
Alternatives, 368; and determinism, 312, 330; *see also* Choice
Ampliative judgment, 30 ff.; *see also* Synthetic judgments
Analogy, physical and metaphysical, 611 f.
Analysis of Mind (Russell), 202 fn.
Analytic propositions, 10, 30 ff., 65 ff., 78 ff., 85, 579 f., 604 f.
Analytical philosophy, *see* Philosophy as analysis
Ancestral memory, 53 f.
Animal spirits, 243
Animals, and soul, 243-56 passim
Animism, *see* Anthropomorphism
Anthropology, 588
Anthropomorphism, 220, 315, 521, 532
Appearance, and reality, 213-23 passim, 565
A posteriori knowledge, 26
A priori knowledge, 8, 25-36 passim, 61-73 passim, 92, 502, 544, 569 f.; and axioms, 41 f., 47; and causality, 107, 109; and certainty, 9; defined by Kant, 26; and ethics, 391, 434 f.; evidence for, 38; and existence of God, 525; and intuition, 29; and matters of fact, 131; and "principle of induction," 95; and reason, 113; synthetic (*see* Synthetic *a priori*); of universal principles, 4, 93
Approval, *see* Subjectivism
Aquinas (Copleston), 475 fn.
Argument, and ethics, 402; and inference, 112; nature of, 56 ff.
Aristotelians, 545
Arithmetic, 47 ff., 50, 72, 106; and certainty, 102; laws of, 12; logical foundations of, 13
Arithmetic (Segner), 32
Association of ideas, 44 ff., 53 ff.
Astronomy, 102
Atheism, 447, 489, 510-38 passim
Atomic theory, 92
Atoms, 92; and perception, 149; *see also* Insensible particles
Aureng-Zebe (Dryden) 521 fn.
Automaton theory, 243-56; *see also* Epiphenomenalism

Behaviorism, 257, 548; and body-mind problem, 234, 242
Belief, cause of, 127; ground of, 95, 117; and induction, 130; justification of, 4, 42, 46, 125; and rationality, 61 f.
Benevolence, divine, 523 ff.; *see also* God
Body(ies), and mind, 4, 230-303 passim; mutual action of, 42; ownership of, 101, 296 f.
Brain, and consciousness, 245; and extrasensory perception, 296; and mind, 239 ff., 253; and motor nerves, 248; and sensation, 286; and volition, 318

Categories, Kantian, 569 f.
Causality, 4, 34, 109, 111, 113, 262, 298, 300, 310 ff., 324 ff., 328, 341, 349, 363, 369, 373, 449 ff., 452 ff., 466 ff., 472 f., 476, 479 f., 486, 488, 506, 531 ff., 545, 572, 581, 588 ff.; *a priori* knowledge of, 27, 31, 107; and belief, 127; and body-mind relation, 237 f., 254, 269; and compulsion, 314; and conjunction, 107; and connection, 109; and experience, 108, 126; and explanation, 455 ff.; and freedom, 314, 317-26 passim, 341-56 passim; and generalization, 94; and God, 616; and idealism, 203; and induction, 122 ff.; and interactionism, 233, 286, 292, 296; as Kantian category, 9, 569; law of universal causation, 93; and matters of fact, 107; and motivation, 323; multiple, 468; and